征服108新課綱

學測英文
五大關鍵題型

綜合測驗、文意選填、篇章結構
閱讀測驗、混合題

增修版

詳解本

Mastering Reading
Comprehension Tests

CONTENTS 目錄

簡答表 2

Unit 01
綜合測驗 6
文意選填 9
篇章結構 12
閱讀測驗 15
混合題 17

Unit 02
綜合測驗 22
文意選填 25
篇章結構 28
閱讀測驗 31
混合題 33

Unit 03
綜合測驗 36
文意選填 39
篇章結構 42
閱讀測驗 45
混合題 47

Unit 04
綜合測驗 50
文意選填 53
篇章結構 56
閱讀測驗 58
混合題 60

Unit 05
綜合測驗 66
文意選填 69
篇章結構 72
閱讀測驗 75
混合題 77

Unit 06
綜合測驗 80
文意選填 83
篇章結構 86
閱讀測驗 89
混合題 91

Unit 07
綜合測驗 94
文意選填 97
篇章結構 100
閱讀測驗 103
混合題 105

Unit 08
綜合測驗 108
文意選填 111
篇章結構 115
閱讀測驗 117
混合題 119

Unit 09
綜合測驗 124
文意選填 127
篇章結構 131
閱讀測驗 133
混合題 136

Unit 10
綜合測驗 140
文意選填 143
篇章結構 146
閱讀測驗 149
混合題 151

Unit 11
綜合測驗	154
文意選填	157
篇章結構	161
閱讀測驗	163
混合題	165

Unit 12
綜合測驗	168
文意選填	171
篇章結構	174
閱讀測驗	176
混合題	178

Unit 13
綜合測驗	182
文意選填	185
篇章結構	188
閱讀測驗	191
混合題	193

Unit 14
綜合測驗	196
文意選填	198
篇章結構	202
閱讀測驗	204
混合題	207

Unit 15
綜合測驗	210
文意選填	213
篇章結構	217
閱讀測驗	219
混合題	221

Unit 16
綜合測驗	226
文意選填	228
篇章結構	231
閱讀測驗	233
混合題	236

Unit 17
綜合測驗	240
文意選填	243
篇章結構	246
閱讀測驗	249
混合題	251

Unit 18
綜合測驗	256
文意選填	259
篇章結構	262
閱讀測驗	264
混合題	266

Unit 19
綜合測驗	270
文意選填	273
篇章結構	276
閱讀測驗	279
混合題	281

Unit 20
綜合測驗	284
文意選填	287
篇章結構	290
閱讀測驗	293
混合題	295

簡答表

Unit 01

1. C 2. D 3. B 4. A 5. C
6. J 7. D 8. F 9. B 10. C
11. I 12. G 13. E 14. H 15. A
16. A 17. C 18. D 19. B
20. D 21. B 22. D 23. C
24. (1) D (2) C (3) A (4) G
25. Brigit, Hilda
26. deepfake
27. (D)

Unit 02

1. B 2. D 3. A 4. C 5. D
6. B 7. G 8. D 9. A 10. C
11. I 12. E 13. J 14. H 15. F
16. A 17. C 18. E 19. D
20. A 21. B 22. C 23. C
24. contribute
25. education
26. captivity
27. Manon: (A)、(E)
    Camille: (B)、(D)
    Gabriel: (C)、(G)
    Lucas: (F)、(H)

Unit 03

1. C 2. A 3. B 4. B 5. D
6. G 7. H 8. F 9. B 10. C
11. A 12. D 13. I 14. E 15. J
16. D 17. A 18. E 19. B
20. D 21. B 22. A 23. C
24. educated / trained
25. accept
26. myth
27. (C), (E)

Unit 04

1. B 2. C 3. A 4. B 5. D
6. A 7. G 8. D 9. H 10. B
11. F 12. I 13. C 14. J 15. E
16. C 17. A 18. B 19. E
20. B 21. C 22. B 23. D
24. For a ban: Chloe, Deepak, Felix, Giselle
    Against a ban: Anna, Boris, Elena, Hiroshi
25. Boris, Deepak
26. (B)

Unit 05

1. B 2. D 3. C 4. C 5. A
6. I 7. H 8. C 9. D 10. F
11. J 12. A 13. E 14. B 15. G
16. E 17. D 18. C 19. B
20. D 21. B 22. C 23. C
24. motivation
25. confident
26. entitlement
27. Paula: (A)
    Viola: (D)
    James: (C)
    Franklin: (B)

Unit 06

① D ② A ③ D ④ B ⑤ C
⑥ E ⑦ G ⑧ J ⑨ A ⑩ B
⑪ D ⑫ I ⑬ F ⑭ C ⑮ H
⑯ E ⑰ A ⑱ C ⑲ B
⑳ D ㉑ B ㉒ B ㉓ C
㉔ collision
㉕ destruction / damage
㉖ imitate
㉗ (C)

Unit 07

① C ② D ③ A ④ B ⑤ A
⑥ F ⑦ B ⑧ E ⑨ D ⑩ I
⑪ C ⑫ A ⑬ G ⑭ J ⑮ H
⑯ B ⑰ D ⑱ E ⑲ A
⑳ C ㉑ D ㉒ D ㉓ C
㉔ failure
㉕ windy
㉖ (the) perfect storm
㉗ (A) Kaimana
　 (B) Ariel
　 (C) Nalu
　 (D) Malia

Unit 08

① B ② D ③ D ④ A ⑤ B
⑥ J ⑦ A ⑧ H ⑨ I ⑩ C
⑪ F ⑫ E ⑬ D ⑭ G ⑮ B
⑯ C ⑰ E ⑱ B ⑲ D
⑳ D ㉑ C ㉒ B ㉓ C
㉔ (1) False (2) False (3) True (4) False
㉕ optimal
㉖ (C)

Unit 09

① B ② C ③ D ④ A ⑤ C
⑥ I ⑦ G ⑧ A ⑨ F ⑩ E
⑪ B ⑫ J ⑬ D ⑭ H ⑮ C
⑯ B ⑰ E ⑱ A ⑲ D
⑳ C ㉑ D ㉒ C ㉓ A
㉔ waste
㉕ stress
㉖ diversion
㉗ 1. (D) 2. (A) 3. (B)

Unit 10

① A ② C ③ D ④ B ⑤ A
⑥ I ⑦ E ⑧ B ⑨ D ⑩ F
⑪ H ⑫ A ⑬ C ⑭ G ⑮ J
⑯ D ⑰ C ⑱ B ⑲ A
⑳ D ㉑ D ㉒ C ㉓ C
㉔ survive
㉕ threatens
㉖ animated
㉗ Prediction: [3]
　 Finding:　　[4]
　 Drawback: [5]

簡答表

Unit 11

1. C 2. D 3. A 4. B 5. A
6. C 7. J 8. F 9. A 10. E
11. I 12. H 13. D 14. B 15. G
16. E 17. D 18. C 19. B
20. B 21. A 22. C 23. B
24. preference
25. complications / difficulties
26. distant
27. lobby
28. (C)

Unit 12

1. A 2. A 3. D 4. C 5. D
6. H 7. B 8. E 9. G 10. F
11. J 12. A 13. I 14. C 15. D
16. A 17. D 18. E 19. B
20. B 21. B 22. C 23. D
24. Beverley > Freya > Delilah
25. Christof
26. Alfonso, Enrique
27. focused

Unit 13

1. B 2. D 3. A 4. D 5. C
6. G 7. A 8. D 9. H 10. B
11. C 12. I 13. J 14. F 15. E
16. E 17. C 18. A 19. D
20. B 21. C 22. D 23. C
24. protection
25. reduction
26. hot potato
27. (C), (D)

Unit 14

1. A 2. D 3. C 4. C 5. A
6. H 7. I 8. D 9. F 10. E
11. B 12. J 13. C 14. G 15. B
16. B 17. E 18. D 19. C
20. A 21. D 22. C 23. C
24. neutralize cancer-causing free radicals in the body
25. complete proteins
26. 5
27. include superfoods / them in your diet
28. (B)

Unit 15

1. D 2. A 3. D 4. B 5. B
6. F 7. B 8. J 9. C 10. A
11. H 12. I 13. D 14. G 15. E
16. B 17. D 18. A 19. C
20. D 21. C 22. A 23. D
24. construction
25. completion
26. Paragraph 1: (D)
    Paragraph 2: (C)
    Paragraph 3: (A)
27. (C)

Unit 16

1. A
2. D
3. B
4. B
5. D
6. I
7. H
8. J
9. E
10. B
11. C
12. D
13. G
14. A
15. F
16. E
17. C
18. A
19. D
20. D
21. C
22. B
23. C
24. contamination
25. concern / concerns
26. (D)
27. (A), (D), (E)

Unit 17

1. B
2. D
3. B
4. A
5. D
6. J
7. E
8. B
9. A
10. G
11. H
12. D
13. F
14. I
15. C
16. C
17. E
18. A
19. B
20. B
21. D
22. C
23. B
24. (D), (I)
25. Crystal, Georgina, Julius
26. menace
27. (C)

Unit 18

1. A
2. C
3. C
4. B
5. A
6. C
7. D
8. E
9. A
10. B
11. H
12. F
13. J
14. I
15. G
16. C
17. D
18. A
19. B
20. C
21. C
22. B
23. D
24. challenges
25. determination
26. Fatima's and her parents'
27. (B), (D)

Unit 19

1. D
2. A
3. B
4. D
5. B
6. I
7. C
8. J
9. A
10. E
11. G
12. F
13. H
14. D
15. B
16. D
17. A
18. C
19. B
20. B
21. B
22. D
23. C
24. participation
25. difficult
26. Michelle
27. Jake
28. chase up

Unit 20

1. C
2. A
3. B
4. D
5. B
6. B
7. J
8. H
9. D
10. C
11. E
12. G
13. F
14. A
15. I
16. D
17. A
18. E
19. C
20. D
21. C
22. C
23. B
24. conversion
25. adjustment
26. set people back
27. (A), (E)

Unit 01

一 綜合測驗

　　1974 年，貝蒂和裘克・萊斯里・麥菲兒買了一間距離肯亞首都奈洛比二十英里的老宅邸。這對夫婦花了好幾個月的時間以及一大筆錢來修繕這棟房子。

　　身為非洲瀕臨絕種野生動物基金會創辦人，貝蒂知道羅氏長頸鹿面臨的挑戰。目前野外尚存的羅氏長頸鹿只有幾百隻，牠們正面臨絕種的危機。因此，當這對夫婦搬進他們夢寐以求的房子後，他們也把一對羅氏長頸鹿遷移到他們房屋周圍一百二十畝的自然森林環境中。這個行動要拯救的不只是長頸鹿，還有將被用來蓋房屋和工廠的土地。1984 年，裘克・萊斯里・麥菲兒去世，貝蒂決定將她那擁有十間房間的屋子改作為飯店。她稱這間飯店為長頸鹿莊園。

　　每個早晨，莊園裡的幾隻羅氏長頸鹿會前往飯店和客人一起吃早餐。這些長頸鹿溫柔地把頭穿過飯店窗戶，讓客人有機會用手拿食物餵食牠們。這個特別的近距離親密接觸提供旅客一個千載難逢的經驗，也為大自然裡其中一種最迷人的動物資助了一處保育區。

__C__ 1. 理由

  a. (A) **repeat** [rɪˋpit] *vt.* 重複

  例 Could you please repeat the question?
  請你再把問題重複一遍好嗎？

  (B) **rely** [rɪˋlaɪ] *vi.* 依賴；信賴
  rely on / upon...　　依賴……；信賴……

  例 I trust Steve very much. I knew he is a man I can always rely on.
  我很信任史提夫。我知道他是個我永遠可以信賴的人。

  (C) **repair** [rɪˋpɛr] *vt. & n.* 修理

  例 It took me almost a week to repair the machine.
  我花了將近一星期才修好這臺機器。

  (D) **receive** [rɪˋsiv] *vt.* 收到

  例 Molly received a bouquet of roses from her fiancé on her birthday.
  茉莉生日那天收到她未婚夫送給她的一束玫瑰花。

  b. 根據語意，(C) 項應為正選。

__D__ 2. 理由

  a. (A) **mansion** [ˋmænʃən] *n.* 宅邸，豪宅

  例 There have been strange noises coming from this mansion at night recently.
  這棟豪宅最近晚上常傳出怪聲。

(B) prison [ˈprɪzn̩] *n.* 監獄
　例 That prison has about 200 prisoners.
　　那所監獄裡有大約二百名囚犯。
(C) silence [ˈsaɪləns] *n.* 安靜，寂靜
　例 The silence in the room made me very nervous.
　　房間裡鴉雀無聲，讓我很緊張。
(D) challenge [ˈtʃælɪndʒ] *n.* 挑戰
　face the challenge　　面對挑戰
　meet the challenge　　迎接挑戰
　例 This job is not easy, but I think I'm ready to meet the challenge.
　　這份工作不容易，不過我想我已準備好迎接挑戰了。
b. 根據語意，(D) 項應為正選。

B **3.** **理由**
a. (A) memorial [məˈmɔrɪəl] *a.* 紀念的
　例 There's a memorial statue of this historical hero in front of the park.
　　公園前有一座紀念這位歷史英雄的雕像。
(B) natural [ˈnætʃərəl] *a.* 自然的
　例 This drink is all natural and is good for your body.
　　這飲料全都是天然成分，對你的身體很好。
(C) loyal [ˈlɔɪəl] *a.* 忠實的
　be loyal to sb　　對某人忠實
　例 The couple were loyal to each other throughout their lives.
　　這對夫妻一生都對彼此忠誠。
(D) mineral [ˈmɪnərəl] *a.* 礦物的 & *n.* 礦物質
　例 This brand of mineral water contains many minerals that are good for our health.
　　這種牌子的礦泉水含有很多對我們健康有益的礦物質。
b. 根據語意，(B) 項應為正選。

A **4.** **理由**
a. 本題測驗下列固定用法：
　not only... but (also)...　　不僅……而且……
　例 A good leader is not only communicative but also willing to listen.
　　好的領導人不只要善於溝通也要願意傾聽。
b. 根據語意及上述用法，(A) 項應為正選。

Unit 01

__C__ 5. 理由

a. (A) **state-of-the-art technology**　先進的技術
state-of-the-art [ˌstetəvðɚˈɑrt] *a.* 先進的
　例 This hospital has state-of-the-art medical equipment and technology.
　這家醫院擁有最先進的醫療設備和技術。

(B) **run-of-the-mill trip**　普通的旅行
run-of-the-mill [ˌrʌnəvðəˈmɪl] *a.* 普通的；平淡無奇的；乏味的
　例 The restaurant serves run-of-the-mill food—nothing special.
　這家餐廳的食物普通，沒什麼特別。

(C) **once-in-a-lifetime experience**　千載難逢的經驗
once-in-a-lifetime [ˌwʌnsɪnəˈlaɪftaɪm] *a.* 千載難逢的，機會難得的
　例 Seeing the Northern Lights was a once-in-a-lifetime experience for me.
　觀賞極光對我來說是一次難忘的體驗。

(D) **out-of-the-question plan**　不可能的計畫
out-of-the-question [ˌaʊtəvðəˈkwɛstʃən] *a.* 不可能的
　例 Traveling abroad this year is out-of-the-question due to costs.
　由於費用問題，今年是不可能出國旅遊了。

b. 根據語意，可知 (C) 項應為正選。

重要單字與片語

1. **capital** [ˈkæpət!] *n.* 首都
2. **considerable** [kənˈsɪdərəb!] *a.* 相當大的
3. **property** [ˈprɑpɚtɪ] *n.* 財產，資產（不可數）；莊園，房屋（可數）
4. **be aware of...**　知道……；察覺到……
　例 Mary was aware of Tom's bad intentions, so she refused to go out with him.
　瑪麗察覺湯姆不懷好意，所以拒絕和他約會。
5. **extinction** [ɪkˈstɪŋkʃən] *n.* 絕種（不可數）
6. **surround** [səˈraʊnd] *vt.* 環繞
　例 I live in a small village surrounded by lush hills.
　我住在一座青山環繞的小村莊裡。

7. **make one's way to + 地點**　前進……，出發前往……
　例 I made my way to Grandma's house after breakfast.
　早餐後我出發前往奶奶家。
8. **provide sb with sth**　提供某物給某人
　= provide sth for sb
　例 I'll provide you with the right tools.
　= I'll provide the right tools for you.
　我會提供正確的工具給你。
9. **fund** [fʌnd] *vt.* 提供資金
　例 The research was primarily funded by the government.
　這項研究計畫主要是由政府資助。
10. **sanctuary** [ˈsæŋktʃʊˌɛrɪ] *n.* 保育區
11. **appealing** [əˈpilɪŋ] *a.* 有吸引力的

二 文意選填

　　憂鬱症是最常見的醫學疾病之一。事實上，百分之十的人至少會經歷一次憂鬱症。患有憂鬱症的人會感受到強烈的憂傷、焦慮和負面情緒。某些人生經驗例如摯愛的人死亡可能會導致憂鬱症。然而，憂鬱症也可能在沒有明顯原因的情況下發生。

　　許多憂鬱症患者會看醫生接受治療。不幸的是，有些患者感到強烈的罪惡感且羞愧，以致於他們完全不和家人討論這個問題，更別說是和醫生討論。這可能是極度危險的，因為重度憂鬱症最終可能導致自殺。

　　2003 年，一名十八歲女孩的父親因憂鬱症未經治療而自殺。失去父親使她也罹患憂鬱症並開始酗酒來消除痛苦。幸運的是，她接受了醫師的治療並康復了。

　　之後她創立了「分號計畫」，這是一個提供憂鬱症患者希望的機構。分號計畫藉由請人們在身上刺上分號的刺青圖案來吸引大眾關注憂鬱症。分號是用來繼續創造句子，否則句子便會結束。不想擁有永久刺青的人可以用筆在身體某處畫上一個暫時的分號。

__J__ 6. 理由
　　a. 空格前有關係代名詞 who 引導形容詞子句並作該子句的主詞，得知空格應置形容詞子句的動詞。
　　b. 空格後為介詞 from，得知空格應置不及物動詞 suffer，以形成下列固定用法：
　　　suffer from...　飽受（疾病）之苦，罹患（疾病）
　　　例 My father suffers from diabetes.
　　　　我爸爸患有糖尿病。
　　c. 根據上述，(J) 項應為正選。

__D__ 7. 理由
　　a. 空格前有副詞 no，空格後有名詞 reason（原因），得知空格應置形容詞來修飾該名詞。
　　b. 選項中可作形容詞的有 (A) temporary（暫時的）、(D) apparent（明顯的）及 (F) dangerous（危險的），惟根據語意，(D) 項應為正選。
　　c. **apparent** [əˋpærənt] *a.* 明顯的；表面的

__F__ 8. 理由
　　a. 空格前有 be 動詞 be 及副詞 extremely（極度地），得知空格應置形容詞以作主詞補語並可被副詞修飾。
　　b. 剩餘選項中 (A) temporary（暫時的）及 (F) dangerous（危險的）為形容詞，惟根據語意，(F) 項應為正選。
　　c. **dangerous** [ˋdendʒərəs] *a.* 危險的

Unit 01

__B__ 9. 理由

    a. 空格前為本句主詞 an 18-year-old girl's father（一位十八歲女孩的爸爸），得知空格應置本句動詞。此外，由 In 2003 得知本句時態為過去式，因此空格應置過去式動詞。

    b. 空格後為名詞 suicide（自殺行為），得知空格應置及物動詞。剩餘選項中 (B) committed（做、犯）及 (I) recovered（恢復）為過去式及物動詞，惟根據語意，(B) 項應為正選。

    c. **commit** [kəˋmɪt] *vt.* 做（錯事等）；犯（罪）

        commit suicide　　自殺

        例 The bomber committed suicide after being caught.
            那名炸彈客被抓之後就自殺了。

__C__ 10. 理由

    a. 空格前有引導不定詞的 to，空格後為受詞 her pain（她的痛苦），得知空格應置原形及物動詞。

    b. 剩餘選項中 (C) remove（消除）及 (H) continue（繼續）為原形及物動詞，惟根據語意，(C) 項應為正選。

    c. **remove** [rɪˋmuv] *vt.* 移除；搬移

        例 Use some soap to remove the stains from your clothes.
            用點肥皂去除你衣服上的汙漬。

__I__ 11. 理由

    a. 由空格前的對等連接詞 and 得知空格應置另一過去式動詞以與前面的動詞 received（接受）形成對等。

    b. 剩餘選項中僅剩 (I) recovered（恢復）為過去式動詞，且置入空格後符合語意，故為正選。

    c. **recover** [rɪˋkʌvɚ] *vi.* 恢復（與介詞 from 並用）& *vt.* 找回；恢復

        例 Tony has completely recovered from his illness.
            東尼的病完全痊癒了。

__G__ 12. 理由

    a. 空格前為冠詞 an，空格後為關係代名詞 that，得知空格應置一單數名詞作為 that 的先行詞，且該名詞應以母音起首，以與 an 並用。

    b. 剩餘選項中 (E) attention（注意力）及 (G) organization（組織）為母音起首的單數名詞，惟根據語意，(G) 項應為正選。

    c. **organization** [ˌɔrgənaɪˋzeʃən] *n.* 組織；籌辦

__E__ 13. 理由

    a. 空格前為及物動詞 draw（吸引），得知空格應置名詞作 draw 的受詞。

    b. 剩餘選項中僅剩 (E) attention（注意力）為名詞，且置入空格後符合語意，故為正選。

    c. **attention** [əˋtɛnʃən] *n.* 注意力；注意
    pay attention to...　　注意……

H **14.** 理由
    a. 空格前有引導不定詞的 to，空格後為動名詞 making，得知空格應置原形及物動詞，以接 making 作其受詞。
    b. 剩餘選項中僅剩 (H) continue（繼續）為原形及物動詞，且置入空格後符合語意，故為正選。
    c. **continue** [kənˋtɪnju] *vt.* 繼續
       例 If we continue to abuse the environment, more animals will become extinct.
       如果我們繼續破壞環境，會有更多的動物瀕臨絕種。

A **15.** 理由
    a. 空格前為冠詞 a，空格後為名詞 semicolon（分號），得知空格應置形容詞以修飾 semicolon。
    b. 剩餘選項 (A) temporary（暫時的）為形容詞，且置入空格後與前面的形容詞 permanent（永久的）語意對應，故為正選。
    c. **temporary** [ˋtɛmpəˏrɛrɪ] *a.* 暫時的

重要單字與片語

1. **depression** [dɪˋprɛʃən] *n.* 沮喪；憂鬱症
2. **medical** [ˋmɛdɪkḷ] *a.* 醫療的
3. **condition** [kənˋdɪʃən] *n.* 狀況；疾病
4. **experience** [ɪkˋspɪrɪəns] *vt.* 經歷
   例 John experienced a lot of setbacks before becoming what he is today.
   約翰經歷了許多挫敗才有今天的成就。
5. **intense** [ɪnˋtɛns] *a.* 強烈的
6. **anxiety** [æŋˋzaɪətɪ] *n.* 焦慮
7. **negative** [ˋnɛɡətɪv] *a.* 否定的，負面的
   positive [ˋpɑzətɪv] *a.* 肯定的，正面的
8. **treatment** [ˋtritmənt] *n.* 治療
9. **severe** [səˋvɪr] *a.* 嚴重的
10. **lead to...**　　導致……
   例 Stress can lead to illness.
   壓力會讓人生病。
11. **abuse** [əˋbjuz] *vt.* 濫用
   例 Charles abused his position as manager to steal money from the company.
   查爾斯濫用經理的職位從公司竊取錢財。
12. **establish** [ɪˋstæblɪʃ] *vt.* 建立
   例 The company was established in 1988.
   這家公司於 1988 年創立。
13. **semicolon** [ˋsɛmɪˏkolən] *n.* 分號
14. **tattoo** [tæˋtu] *n.* 刺青
15. **otherwise** [ˋʌðəˏwaɪz] *adv.* 否則，要不然的話

Unit 01

Unit 01

篇章結構

　　你走進一間擁擠的教室。大家好像都在盯著你看。你聽到角落裡一群學生的嬉笑聲。他們是在嘲笑你嗎？你的心跳立即加速，你恨不得躲起來。你的手心開始冒汗，整個身體變得僵硬緊繃。

　　如果你對上述經驗感到很熟悉，你可能患了社交焦慮症。社交焦慮症又稱為社交恐懼症，是一種與他人互動時會產生焦慮的病症。患有這種症狀的人幾乎不可能愉快地與他人交談、和朋友相聚或甚至無法到公共場合。甚至會覺得像點餐或打電話這樣的日常任務都讓人感到難以承受。

　　社交恐懼症有很多種形式，從害怕在眾人面前發表言論，到身處人群中會感到不自在，都屬於社交恐懼症。此種病症會引發生理不適的症狀，像是流汗、臉紅、呼吸困難以及感到噁心想吐。人們為何會有社交恐懼症的原因有幾種解釋。有可能是父母經由基因遺傳給下一代。如果患者曾在眾人面前嚴重出糗也可能得到此症。而此經驗也許會讓患者極度懼怕再度落入類似的情況中。過去被欺負或遭受批評等負面經驗也可能造成這種恐懼感。

　　幸好對那些有社交恐懼症的人來說，此症狀是有辦法醫治的。首先，有藥物可幫助控制這些症狀。冥想和放鬆運動也有助於治療。最重要的是，還有一些技術性療法有助於完全治癒此症狀。其中最常見的一種方法是在心理學家的協助下，一點一點地體驗那些令人感到不自在的社交場合。這種方法經證實能幫助患有社交焦慮症的人面對及了解他們的恐懼。隨著時間的推移，這些小小的成功經驗能夠建立信心，讓社交互動變得更輕鬆。

　　對某些人來說，社交恐懼症阻礙他們獲得多數人視之為理所當然的樂趣。不過，藉由正確的治療，社交活動對每個人來說都可以是有趣又愉快的。

__A__ 16. 理由
　　a. 空格前句提到如果你對上述經驗感到很熟悉，你可能患了 social anxiety disorder（社交焦慮症），因此空格內容應會解釋何謂社交焦慮症，此即如 (A) 所述「社交焦慮症又稱為社交恐懼症，是一種與他人互動時會產生焦慮的病症。」
　　b. 根據上述，(A) 項應為正選。

__C__ 17. 理由
　　a. 第三段第三句之後提到會有社交恐懼症的原因有幾種解釋，第一種原因是如同空格前句所提：是父母遺傳的，因此可推知空格應提到第二種原因，即如選項 (C) 所述「如果患者曾在眾人面前嚴重出糗也可能得到此症。」
　　b. 根據上述，(C) 項應為正選。

__D__ 18. 理由

a. 第四段第一句提到社交恐懼症是有辦法醫治的，第三至五句皆是提到如何治療的方法：如冥想和放鬆運動，或是在心理學家的協助下，慢慢地體驗那些令人感到不自在的社交場合，因此可推知空格內容也是提到如何治療社交恐懼症的方法，此即如選項 (D) 所述「首先，有藥物可幫助控制這些症狀。」

b. 根據上述，(D) 項應為正選。

__B__ 19. 理由

a. 第四段整段在講述治療社交恐懼症的方法，又空格前句提到 One of the most common methods（其中最常見的一種方法）是在心理學家的協助下，一點一點地體驗那些令人感到不自在的社交場合，因此可推知這方法基本上是有效的，此正如選項 (B) 所述「這種方法經證實能幫助患有社交焦慮症的人面對及了解他們的恐懼。」

b. 根據上述，(B) 項應為正選。

(E) 選項翻譯　你意識到學生們其實是在嘲笑其中一個人上傳到 YouTube 的影片。

重要單字與片語

1. **stare at...**　　盯著……

2. **in the corner**　　在（室內的）角落裡
   on the corner　　在（室外的）轉角處

3. **instantly** [ˋɪnstəntlɪ] *adv.* 立即，馬上
   = **immediately** [ɪˋmidɪətlɪ]
   例 The company is famous for its product that instantly relieves headaches.
   該公司以其能立即消除頭痛的產品而聞名。

4. **pound** [paʊnd] *vi.*（心臟）劇烈跳動

5. **desperately** [ˋdɛspərətlɪ] *adv.* 極度地，拼命地
   例 The spider's prey was trying desperately to escape the web.
   這隻蜘蛛的獵物拼命想逃離蜘蛛網。

6. **sth is familiar to sb**　　某人熟悉某物
   = **sb is familiar with sth**
   例 Is this picture familiar to you?
   = Are you familiar with this picture?
   你對這幅圖畫熟悉嗎？

7. **anxiety** [æŋˋzaɪətɪ] *n.* 焦慮，緊張
   anxious [ˋæŋkʃəs] *a.* 焦慮的

8. **disorder** [dɪsˋɔrdɚ] *n.* 失調

9. **phobia** [ˋfobɪə] *n.* 恐懼症
   social phobia　社交恐懼症

10. **individual** [͵ɪndəˋvɪdʒʊəl] *n.* 個人

11. **interact** [͵ɪntɚˋækt] *vi.* 互動
    interact with...　　與……互動
    例 Sociologists study how people interact with one another.
    社會學家研究人與人之間如何互動。

12. **in public**　公開地；當眾
    in private　私底下

13. **overwhelming** [͵ovɚˋ(h)wɛlmɪŋ] *a.* 難以抵抗的；巨大的

14. **uncomfortable** [ʌnˋkʌmfɚtəbl̩] *a.* 不自在的

15. **unpleasant** [ʌnˋplɛzn̩t] *a.* 不愉快的

16. **symptom** [ˋsɪmptəm] *n.* 症狀

Unit 01

17. **blush** [blʌʃ] *vi.* （因害羞、尷尬而）臉紅
    例 I always blush when I speak in public.
    我在眾人面前演說時總是會臉紅。

18. **as to...** 關於……，至於……

19. **pass... down** 使……世代相傳
    例 The design of this lace was passed down from early French settlers.
    這種蕾絲設計是法國早期移民流傳下來的。

20. **genetically** [dʒəˋnɛtɪkəlɪ] *adv.* 基因方面

21. **embarrassed** [ɪmˋbærəst] *a.* 感到尷尬／困窘的
    embarrassing [ɪmˋbærəsɪŋ] *a.* 令人難為情的
    例 Jane was embarrassed by her friend's rudeness at the party.
    珍對她朋友在派對上的粗魯行為感到很難為情。
    My most embarrassing experience was forgetting my lines on stage.
    我最尷尬的經驗是在臺上忘了臺詞。

22. **end up + 介詞片語／V-ing** 到頭來／最後……
    例 The thief ended up in prison.
    那個小偷最後進了監獄。
    The gambler ended up losing everything.
    那個賭徒到頭來輸得一乾二淨。

23. **bullying** [ˋbʊlɪɪŋ] *n.* 欺負，霸凌

24. **treatable** [ˋtritəbḷ] *a.* 可治療的

25. **for one thing** （用以引出兩個以上的理由之一）首先；其一
    例 I never eat fish. For one thing, I can't stand the smell.
    我從來不吃魚，原因之一是我受不了魚腥味。

26. **meditation** [ˏmɛdəˋteʃən] *n.* 冥想；打坐

27. **technique** [tɛkˋnik] *n.* 技巧，技法

28. **altogether** [ˏɔltəˋgɛðɚ] *adv.* 完全地（= completely）；一共（= in total）
    例 This new car is altogether different from the old one.
    這輛新車和那輛舊的完全不同。
    There are 300 people altogether in the stadium.
    體育場裡總共有三百個人。

29. **at a time** 一次

30. **psychologist** [saɪˋkɑlədʒɪst] *n.* 心理學家

31. **confront** [kənˋfrʌnt] *vt.* 對抗，克服
    例 The rookie fireman confronted his fears and entered the burning building.
    那個新手消防員克服自己的恐懼，進入著火的建築物裡。

32. **stand in the way (of...)** 妨礙（……），阻擋（……）
    例 Nothing can stand in the way of Kevin's dreams.
    任何東西都無法阻擋凱文追求夢想。

33. **enjoyment** [ɪnˋdʒɔɪmənt] *n.* 樂趣
    enjoyable [ɪnˋdʒɔɪəbḷ] *a.* 有樂趣的

34. **take... for granted** 將……視為理所當然
    例 Don't take your good health for granted. Be thankful for it.
    別把你健康的身體視為理所當然，要心存感激。

四 閱讀測驗

　　直到二十世紀中葉，大多數媽媽們在處理嬰幼兒的個人衛生需求時，都還沒有什麼選擇。她們得使用布尿布，又難綁、清洗又費時，而且容易外漏。瑪麗恩・唐納文就是每天都得處理這情況的媽媽之一。把唐納文帶大的父親是工程師，培養了她探究的精神和發明的渴望。因此她正是想出尿布問題解方的最佳人選。

　　一開始，唐納文拿了一條浴簾剪成小片，用來做防水的尿布兜。然後，她開始換成用透氣的降落傘布來做尿布兜。這些尿布兜可以清洗並重複使用。她也導入了撳扣，這麼一來就可以調整尿布的尺寸。最後她加上一塊具有吸收力的尿布內襯墊，在其中塞入衛生紙，用後可拋棄。唐納文認為她的發明像一條船，因此將它命名為「小船」。

　　然而，在 1940 年代主導製造業的男人們，剛開始一點都不喜歡。她後來回憶說：「他們說：我們不要這東西。沒有女人跟我們要求過這類產品。」唐納文選擇自己來製造尿布，1949 年她在一家連鎖百貨公司裡找到一個經銷商。兩年後，她得到尿布兜的專利，之後賣給了 Keko 公司，價值相當於現在的一千萬美元。又過了十年，幫寶適開始大規模生產自己版本的全拋棄式尿布，但瑪麗恩・唐納文的歷史地位早已經穩固了。

D　**20.** 關於瑪麗恩・唐納文，我們得知什麼？
　　(A) 她是兩個孩子的單親媽媽。
　　(B) 她努力訓練想成為工程師。
　　(C) 她也發明了大型帆船。
　　(D) 她深受父親影響。

理由
根據本文第一段倒數第二句，可知 (D) 項應為正選。

B　**21.** 第二段的主要目的為何？
　　(A) 概述拋棄式尿布的問題。
　　(B) 詳細介紹唐納文不同階段的設計。
　　(C) 提及對傳統布尿布的不滿。
　　(D) 深入探究唐納文在發明之前的人生。

理由
第二段提及唐納文一開始使用浴簾做防水的尿布兜，後來使用降落傘布。之後採用可以調整尿布尺寸的撳扣，最後加上具有吸收力的尿布內襯墊，可知此段在介紹唐納文不同階段的設計，故 (B) 項應為正選。

Unit 01

__D__ 22. 關於瑪麗恩・唐納文的發明，下列何者正確？
(A) 它的專利以數百萬元賣給了幫寶適。
(B) 它在形狀、尺寸及舒適度上有一些限制。
(C) 它的內外層主要由厚衛生紙製成。
(D) 它有一些部分可重複使用，有一些則是拋棄式的。

理由
根據第二段第三句及倒數第二句，可知 (D) 項應為正選。

__C__ 23. 為何本文要引用「我們不要這東西。沒有女人跟我們要求過這類產品」？
(A) 證明女性是嬰幼兒的主要照顧者。
(B) 顯示全拋棄式尿布比預期更不受歡迎。
(C) 闡明唐納文必須克服的障礙。
(D) 解釋唐納文為何放棄了她的第一個設計。

理由
根據本文第三段提及因為當時男性對唐納文的發明不買單，她只好選擇自己來製造尿布，可知 (C) 項應為正選。

重要單字與片語

1. **toddler** [ˋtɑdlɚ] *n.*（處於學步期或剛學會走路的）幼童
2. **toiletry** [ˋtɔɪlɪtrɪ] *n.* 個人衛生用品
3. **diaper** [ˋdaɪ(ə)pɚ] *n.* 尿布
4. **fasten** [ˋfæsn̩] *vt.* 繫緊
   例 For your safety, always fasten your seatbelt while driving.
   為了安全起見，開車上路一定要繫安全帶。
5. **cultivate** [ˋkʌltə͵vet] *vt.* 培養；建立（關係、友誼等）；耕種
   例 Cindy cultivates her knowledge of art by reading magazines.
   辛蒂藉由閱讀雜誌增進她的藝術知識。
6. **invention** [ɪnˋvɛnʃən] *n.* 發明（不可數）；發明物（可數）
7. **solution** [səˋluʃən] *n.* 解決辦法；答案
8. **parachute** [ˋpærə͵ʃut] *n.* 降落傘
9. **adjust** [əˋdʒʌst] *vt.* 調整，調節
   例 Before the interview, the candidate spent several minutes adjusting his tie.
   面試前，這位應徵者花了幾分鐘調整他的領帶。
10. **stuff** [stʌf] *vt.* 塞滿 & *n.* 東西（不可數）
    be stuffed with sth　塞滿了某物
    例 This closet is stuffed with clothes I don't wear anymore.
    這個衣櫥塞滿我再也不穿的衣服。
11. **resemble** [rɪˋzɛmbl̩] *vt.* 和……相似
    例 Kelly closely resembles her mother.
    凱莉長得很像她媽媽。
12. **dominate** [ˋdɑmə͵net] *vt.* 統治，支配
    例 The strong animal dominated the weak animal.
    這隻強壯的動物支配那隻弱小的動物。

13. **patent** [ˈpætn̩t] *n.* 專利（權）& *vt.* 取得專利 & *a.* 專利的
14. **disposable** [dɪˈspozəbḷ] *a.* 用完即丟棄的
    a disposable diaper　紙尿布
15. **vessel** [ˈvɛsḷ] *n.* 船艦；容器；血管
16. **outline** [ˈaʊtˌlaɪn] *vt.* 重點說明 & *n.* 大綱；輪廓
    例 At the interview, Nancy outlined the requirements for the position.
    面試的時候，南西大致說了一下這個職位的需求。
17. **probe** [prob] *vi.* & *n.* 調查
    probe into...　調查……
    例 The FBI has been called in to probe into the case.
    聯邦調查局被召來調查這樁案子。
18. **restriction** [rɪˈstrɪkʃən] *n.* 限制，約束
19. **illustrate** [ˈɪləstret] *vt.* 說明；為……畫插圖
    例 The graphs illustrate the growth of our business.
    這些圖表說明了我們事業的成長幅度。
20. **obstacle** [ˈɑbstəkḷ] *n.* 障礙
21. **overcome** [ˌovɚˈkʌm] *vt.* 克服（三態為：overcome, overcame [ˌovɚˈkem], overcome）
    例 I could not overcome the difficulty of learning French, so I changed my major.
    我無法克服學法文的困難，因此我換了主修科系。
22. **abandon** [əˈbændən] *vt.* 放棄
    例 The manager abandoned the plan to set up a new factory in Mexico.
    經理放棄在墨西哥建立新廠的計畫。

Unit 01

五 混合題

人工智慧是個發燒議題，許多人對於它對社會的影響是正面抑或負面，都有著強烈的看法。我們訪問了一些人，聽取他們的意見。

(A) 艾伯特
訓練和運行 AI 系統需要大量能源，這勢必會導致碳排放量的增加。我擔心這會加速破壞環境，所以我投入大量時間參與活動，反對這種技術以及容納 AI 系統的龐大資料中心。

(B) 布麗姬
AI 是相對新穎的科技，但它已經改變了我的工作方式。從分析病歷到協助診斷疾病，AI 系統已經徹底改變了我的工作樣貌。我每天都要用到它，並且非常期待它未來的發展。

(C) 賽德瑞克
我多年來都在寫有關人工智慧的主題。我寫的書大部分都圍繞著一個假想的未來：AI 發展失控，統治世界，導致人類滅亡。我希望這不會在現實中發生，但我真怕它會。

Unit 01

(D) 達莉亞

我的觀點很單純：AI 威脅到我們的工作保障。我的工作是顧好我們產業工人的權益，但管理階級用 AI 系統取代人力，讓我的工作越來越艱難。穩定就業很快就會成為歷史。

(E) 埃利亞斯

AI 的能力與發展性讓我相當鼓舞。我看過報導說它可以提升效率、將枯燥單調的工作予以自動化、並且加速研發工作的進展。如果有強大的全球性管制機制，我堅信 AI 將有助於解決全球性難題，例如飢餓和氣候變遷等等。

(F) 法蒂瑪

人工智慧的潛在經濟效益太大了！我們不應該為了某些產業喪失工作機會而裹足不前，相反地，我們應該專注發展 AI 提升生產力、推動創新，以及在難以想像的新產業中創造新就業機會的能力。

(G) 古斯塔夫

我最廣為人知的歌都是花了許多個月譜曲填詞，好不容易才完成的，但顯然 AI 在幾秒鐘內就能生成歌曲。先不論那些旋律到底好不好，更急迫而令人憂心的是：這現象對藝術的可信度和人類創意的前景有著何種意義？

(H) 希爾達

我承認我常用 ChatGPT 幫忙我寫報告，但這種助益帶來的快樂，遠不及我對 AI 遭到濫用的恐懼。例如，它能製作深偽影片，操控人們相信假消息。

24. 這些人之中誰最符合以下描述？在下方寫出對應的英文字母。

(1) 工會領袖：   __(D)__
(2) 科幻小說作家：   __(C)__
(3) 環保社運人士：   __(A)__
(4) 知名音樂人：   __(G)__

理由

(1) 根據 (D) Dalia（達莉亞）的回應第二句 "My role is to look after the rights of the workers in my industry..."（我的工作是保障我們產業工人的權益……），保障工人權益應是工會領袖的職責，故 (D) Dalia（達莉亞）應為正解。

(2) 根據 (C) Cedric（賽德瑞克）的回應第一至二句 "I've been writing about artificial intelligence for years. Most of my books..."（關於人工智慧的主題我已經寫了很多年。

我寫的書大部分……），可推知他是作家，且後面提到的書的內容多為與 AI 相關的假想未來，故 (C) Cedric（賽德瑞克）應為正解。

(3) 根據 (A) Albert（艾伯特）的回應第二至三句 "I worry that this will hasten environmental damage. ... I spend a great deal of time campaigning against this technology and the enormous data centers that house AI systems."（我擔心這會加速破壞環境。……我花很多時間參與反對這項技術以及容納 AI 系統的龐大資料中心的活動。），可推知他可能是積極型的環保人士，故 (A) Albert（艾伯特）應為正解。

(4) 根據 (G) Gustav（古斯塔夫）的回應第一句 "I spent months writing the music and lyrics to my most well-known songs..."（我花了好幾個月為我最知名的幾首歌曲填詞譜曲……），可推知他可能是詞曲作家，故 (G) Gustav（古斯塔夫）應為正解。

25. 誰在回應中提到自己實際使用過 AI 系統？

<u>Brigit（布麗姬）、Hilda（希爾達）</u>

理由

根據 (B) Brigit（布麗姬）的回應第二句 "From analyzing patient records to providing assistance in diagnosing diseases, AI systems have revolutionized my job."（從分析病歷到協助診斷疾病，AI 系統讓我的工作發生了大幅改變。）及 (H) Hilda（希爾達）的回應第一句 "I admit that I often use ChatGPT to help me write papers..."（我承認我經常使用 ChatGPT 協助我寫報告……），可推知兩人都實際使用過 AI 系統，故 Brigit（布麗姬）和 Hilda（希爾達）應為正解。

26. 回應中哪一個字最有可能表示「一種換掉某人的臉或聲音，看起來很真實的錄製影音」？

<u>deepfake（深偽（影音））</u>

理由

根據 (H) Hilda（希爾達）的回應第二句 "... it can create deepfake videos which manipulate people into believing things that aren't true."（……它能製作深偽影片，引導人們去相信假訊息。），可推知 deepfake 應指以 AI 技術製作的假影像或音訊，故 deepfake（深偽（影音））應為正解。

D **27.** 根據各人的回應，下列哪一項敘述是正確的？
    (A) 法蒂瑪和希爾達對關於 AI 的那些驚悚故事無動於衷。
    (B) 賽德瑞克對 AI 的未來感到害怕，而埃利亞斯也同樣憂心。
    (C) 艾伯特和布麗姬都對 AI 技術的影響感到擔憂。
    (D) 埃利亞斯和法蒂瑪都對 AI 可能的益處十分憧憬。

理由

(1) Elias（埃利亞斯）表示對 AI 的發展充滿希望，認為它能解決飢餓和氣候變遷等全球性問題，而 Fatima（法蒂瑪）強調人們應該把注意力放在 AI 能提升生產力、推動創新、甚至創造新的工作機會等能力上，足見兩人都積極看待 AI 的潛力，故 (D) 項敘述正確。

Unit 01

Unit 01

(2) Hilda（希爾達）提到 deepfake 的危害，顯示她被「AI 的可怕故事」所困擾，而 Fatima（法蒂瑪）主張應著眼於 AI 的長期經濟價值，並未受「恐慌式報導」影響，故 (A) 項敘述錯誤。

(3) Cedric（賽德瑞克）表示他不希望 AI 有一天會掌控全世界甚至導致人類滅亡，但是擔心這可能會發生，而 Elias（埃利亞斯）認為 AI 未來能解決全球性問題，樂觀看待 AI 的發展，故 (B) 項敘述錯誤。

(4) Albert（艾伯特）擔心 AI 會加速對環境的破壞，例如碳排放量增加，也反對龐大的 AI 資料中心，而 Brigit（布麗姬）表示 AI 已改善她的醫療工作方式，並期待它未來的發展，故 (C) 項敘述錯誤。

重要單字與片語

1. **artificial intelligence** 人工智慧（簡稱 AI）
2. **hot-button** [ˈhɑtˌbʌtn̩] *a.* 重要而敏感的
3. **a range of...** 許多 / 各種 / 一系列的……
   例 The store offers a range of organic vegetables for health-conscious customers.
   這家商店提供多種有機蔬菜給注重健康的顧客。
4. **inevitably** [ɪnˈɛvətəblɪ] *adv.* 不可避免地
5. **hasten** [ˈhesn̩] *vt.* 加速；催促 & *vi.* 急忙，趕快
   例 Stress and poor sleep can hasten the aging process.
   壓力和睡眠不足會加速老化。
6. **analyze** [ˈænəˌlaɪz] *vt.* 分析，解析
   例 The professor carefully analyzed the poem's structure and meaning.
   教授仔細分析這首詩的結構與意涵。
7. **spiral** [ˈspaɪrl] *vi.* 急速成長 / 上升 & *n.* 螺旋形
8. **downfall** [ˈdaʊnˌfɔl] *n.* 衰敗；垮臺
9. **humanity** [hjuˈmænətɪ] *n.* 人類（總稱，不可數）；人性；仁愛，慈悲
10. **efficiency** [ɪˈfɪʃənsɪ] *n.* 效率
11. **boost** [bust] *vt.* 增加，提升 & *n.* 促進，推動
    例 The company planned to boost sales through online advertising.
    該公司計畫透過線上廣告來提升銷售額。
12. **productivity** [ˌprodʌkˈtɪvətɪ] *n.* 生產力
13. **innovation** [ˌɪnəˈveʃən] *n.* 創新（不可數）
14. **leave aside sth / leave sth aside** 將（話題等）擱置，不考慮某事物
    例 The manager left aside his personal feelings to make a fair decision.
    經理把個人情感放一邊，以做出公正的決定。
15. **integrity** [ɪnˈtɛgrətɪ] *n.* 誠實，正直；完整
16. **outweigh** [aʊtˈwe] *vt.* 比……重要，大於……
17. **deepfake** [ˈdipˌfek] *n.* 深偽（影音）

18. **manipulate sb into + N/V-ing**
    巧妙操控某人做某事
    - 例 The salesman manipulated customers into buying unnecessary products.
      那名業務員誘導顧客購買不必要的產品。

19. **activist** [ˈæktəvɪst] *n.* 社運人士

Unit 02

一、綜合測驗

　　吉姆‧湯普森以建築學位從大學畢業後，便準備度過一個寧靜、平凡的人生。但這只維持到戰爭爆發前。第二次世界大戰爆發時，他隨即自願加入美國陸軍。身兼軍人與間諜，他曾在義大利以及法國作戰，然後便被派往泰國的曼谷駐防。當他駐防泰國首都之際，戰爭結束了。

　　湯普森愛上了泰國及泰國文化，尤其喜愛傳統泰絲。他發現現代合成織品正在破壞弱小的絲綢產業。為了拯救這個產業，他決定運用商業技巧建立泰絲公司。他的公司出產的絲綢迅速聞名全球。了不起的是，這間公司僱用了數千名泰國女性，讓她們在家工作而不是在工廠工作。這種安排意味著她們可以一邊賺錢謀生，一邊照顧孩子。

　　1967 年，湯普森在馬來西亞度假時到叢林裡散步，之後卻神祕地失蹤了，一去毫無影蹤。至今尚未發現他的遺體。

B 1. 理由

　　a. (A) **break up**　　分手
　　　　例 Nina just broke up with her boyfriend.
　　　　　妮娜剛和男友分手。
　　　(B) **break out**　　（疾病、戰爭）爆發
　　　　例 War broke out two days ago.
　　　　　兩天前戰爭爆發了。
　　　(C) **break off...**　　斷絕……（某種關係）
　　　　例 We may break off relations with that country.
　　　　　我們可能和那個國家斷交。
　　　(D) **break down**　　（車輛）故障
　　　　例 My car broke down again.
　　　　　我的車子又壞了。
　　b. 根據語意與用法，(B) 項應為正選。

D 2. 理由

　　a. (A) **organic foods**　　有機食品
　　　　例 Consuming organic foods can reduce exposure to pesticides.
　　　　　食用有機食品可以減少接觸農藥。
　　　(B) **natural resources**　　天然資源
　　　　例 We must protect our natural resources from overuse.
　　　　　我們必須保護天然資源以免過度使用。

(C) **medical supplies** 醫療用品
　例 The volunteers delivered medical supplies to the disaster areas.
　　志工將醫療用品送往災區。

(D) **synthetic fabrics** 合成布料
　synthetic [sɪnˋθɛtɪk] *a.* 合成的
　fabric [ˋfæbrɪk] *n.* 布料，織物；結構
　例 Many sportswear brands use synthetic fabrics for durability.
　　許多運動服飾品牌使用合成布料來增加耐用性。

b. 根據語意，可知 (D) 項應為正選。

A　3. 理由

a. (A) **establish** [ɪˋstæblɪʃ] *vt.* 建立，創立
　例 The company was established in 1980.
　　這家公司於 1980 年創立。

(B) **threaten** [ˋθrɛtn̩] *vt.* 威脅
　threaten sb with sth　以某事威脅某人
　例 Todd threatened his wife with divorce.
　　陶德以離婚威脅他老婆。

(C) **endure** [ɪnˋdjʊr] *vt.* 忍耐
　例 We must try to endure any pain in our quest for success.
　　在追求成功的過程中，我們必須設法忍受任何痛苦。

(D) **isolate** [ˋaɪslˏet] *vt.* 使隔離，使孤立
　isolate A from B　將 A 與 B 隔離
　例 John has isolated himself from everyone since quitting his job.
　　辭職後約翰便過著與世隔絕的生活。

b. 根據語意，(A) 項應為正選。

C　4. 理由

a. (A) **less than...** 少於……（經常與數字連用）
　例 In less than three years, Johnny has grown into a tall teenager.
　　不到三年的時間，強尼已經長成高個子的青少年了。

(B) **more than...** 多於……（經常與數字連用）
　例 David travels a lot and has been to more than 100 cities around the world.
　　大衛常旅行，世界各地他去過的城市已超過一百座了。

(C) **rather than...** 而非……
　例 Rather than chicken, I'd like to have fish for dinner.
　　我晚餐不想吃雞肉而想吃魚肉。

Unit 02

(D) **other than...** 除了……（= except...）
例 Nobody is in the classroom other than Tom.
教室裡除了湯姆沒有別人。

b. 根據語意，(C) 項應為正選。

D 5. 理由

a. (A) **trap** [træp] *n.* 陷阱
例 The lion was caught in a trap.
那頭獅子困在陷阱裡。

(B) **concept** [ˈkɑnsɛpt] *n.* 觀念，想法
例 It is difficult to grasp some of the concepts of Buddhism.
有些佛學觀念很難理解。

(C) **breeze** [briz] *n.* 微風
例 The trees are swaying in the breeze.
樹木在微風中搖曳。

(D) **trace** [tres] *n.* 蹤跡
disappear without a trace　消失得無影無蹤
例 The bank robber disappeared without a trace.
那名銀行大盜消失得無影無蹤。

b. 根據語意與用法，(D) 項應為正選。

重要單字與片語

1. **architecture** [ˈɑrkəˌtɛktʃɚ] *n.* 建築學（不可數）
2. **degree** [dɪˈgri] *n.* 學位
3. **ordinary** [ˈɔrdəˌnɛrɪ] *a.* 平常的，普通的
4. **volunteer** [ˌvɑlənˈtɪr] *vi.* 自告奮勇
volunteer to V　自願從事……
例 The taxi driver volunteered to help.
這位計程車司機自告奮勇要幫忙。
5. **spy** [spaɪ] *n.* 間諜
6. **station** [ˈsteʃən] *vt.* 使駐紮（常用被動）
例 While he was stationed in Germany, Smith met his future wife.
史密斯駐紮德國時遇見了他未來的妻子。
7. **capital** [ˈkæpətl̩] *n.* 首都（可數）
8. **destroy** [dɪˈstrɔɪ] *vt.* 破壞
9. **rescue** [ˈrɛskju] *vt.* 拯救
例 The fireman rescued a child from the blaze.
那位消防員從火場裡拯救一名孩童出來。
10. **industry** [ˈɪndəstrɪ] *n.* 產業；工業
11. **remarkably** [rɪˈmɑrkəblɪ] *adv.* 了不起地，非凡地
12. **employ** [ɪmˈplɔɪ] *vt.* 僱用
例 Are you presently employed?
你目前有工作嗎？
13. **arrangement** [əˈrendʒmənt] *n.* 安排

14. **look after...** 照顧……
    = take care of...
    例 You should always look after your younger brothers and sisters.
    你始終都要照顧好弟弟妹妹。

15. **make a living** 賺錢謀生
    = earn a living
    例 Joseph makes a living teaching English.
    喬瑟夫以教英文為生。

16. **vacation** [veˈkeʃən] *vi.* 度假

    例 I learned how to surf while vacationing in Hawaii.
    我在夏威夷度假時學會衝浪。

17. **mysteriously** [mɪsˈtɪrɪəslɪ] *adv.* 神祕地

18. **disappear** [ˌdɪsəˈpɪr] *vi.* 消失
    例 The necklace seemed to have magically disappeared from the safe.
    那條項鍊似乎神奇地從保險箱中消失了。

二 文意選填

　　1975 年與 1979 年之間，殘暴的獨裁者波布統治柬埔寨。他殘忍的政黨名為赤棉，他們關閉了學校、醫院和工廠。所有的城市被遷移到鄉間，在那裡所有人被迫用原始的工具從事農務勞動。

　　波布命令赤棉殺害任何反對政府政策的人、受過教育的知識分子或是有某些種族基因的人，估計有三百萬名柬埔寨人死亡。1980 年，鄰國越南在俄國的協助下入侵並統治了這個國家，波布失去政權。

　　因為國家形同廢墟，新政府尋找方法讓這裡的文化起死回生。其中一個辦法是創立柬埔寨國家馬戲團學校 —— 這是一個教導學生表演柬埔寨馬戲團技藝的創新計畫，這項技藝在柬埔寨受大眾歡迎已超過千年之久。

　　一開始報名的學生大部分是孤兒，他們的雙親被赤棉殺害。許多孩子撿拾街頭的回收垃圾維生。他們賺的錢幾乎不夠提供每日一餐的溫飽。這所學校提供這群學生相較過去來得好很多的生活。

　　該校最早期的老師是越南籍及俄籍。他們傳授雜技，有十名優秀學生在俄國接受專家指導的進階訓練。後來，該校也在中國、越南和法國訓練學生。現今，柬埔寨國家馬戲團學校每天都有表演，是柬埔寨最成功的事業之一。

B　6. 理由
　　a. 空格前有所有格形容詞 His，後有名詞詞組 political party（政黨），得知空格應置形容詞來修飾該名詞詞組。

Unit 02

  b. 選項中可作形容詞的有 (B) brutal（殘酷的）、(G) forced（強迫的）及 (I) popular（受歡迎的），惟根據語意，(B) 項應為正選。

  c. **brutal** [ˋbrutḷ] *a.* 殘酷的

G **7. 理由**

  a. 空格位於關係副詞 where 引導的形容詞子句，空格前有主詞 people（人們）和過去式 be 動詞 were，空格後為不定詞 to labor，得知空格應置過去分詞 forced，以形成下列固定用法：

  be forced to V 　　被迫從事……

  例 I don't like to be forced to do anything I don't want to do.
  　　我不喜歡被強迫做任何我不想做的事。

  b. 根據上述，(G) 項應為正選。

D **8. 理由**

  a. 原句實為：

  ... anybody who / that opposed his government's policies, ...

  上句中的限定形容詞子句 who / that opposed his government's policies 可簡化為分詞詞組，即省略作主詞的關係代名詞 who / that，再將過去式動詞 opposed 改為現在分詞 opposing。

  b. 根據上述，可知 (D) 項應為正選。

  c. **oppose** [əˋpoz] *vt.* 反對；反抗
    oppose + N/V-ing　　反對……
  = be opposed to + N/V-ing（此處 opposed 是形容詞，表「反對的」）
  = object to + N/V-ing

  例 The two opposition parties teamed up to oppose the ruling party.
  　　那兩個反對黨團結起來反對執政黨。

A **9. 理由**

  a. 本句前有主要子句 Pol Pot lost power（波布失去政權），而空格位於連接詞 after 引導的副詞子句中，此副詞子句的主詞為 neighboring Vietnam（鄰國越南），with help from Russia（在俄國的協助下）為插入語作為補充說明，得知空格應置副詞子句之動詞，此處須用過去式動詞以與 and 之後的 took control of（控制）對等，共有受詞 the country。

  b. 選項中僅剩 (A) invaded（侵略）為過去式及物動詞，且置入空格後符合語意，故為正選。

  c. **invade** [ɪnˋved] *vt.* 侵入，侵略

  例 The enemy invaded the town while everyone was sound asleep.
  　　敵軍趁大家熟睡時入侵這個城鎮。

C **10.** 理由
   a. 空格前有介詞 in，得知空格應置名詞作其受詞。
   b. 剩餘選項中 (C) ruins（廢墟）與 (F) undertakings（工作）為名詞，惟根據語意，(C) 項應為正選。
   c. **ruin** [ˋruɪn] *n.* 廢墟 & *vt.* 毀滅
      be in ruins　　成為廢墟

I **11.** 理由
   a. 空格所在的非限定形容詞子句主詞為關係代名詞 which，指涉前面的先行詞 Cambodian circus art（柬埔寨馬戲團技藝），而空格前有 has been，得知空格應置名詞或形容詞以作主詞補語。
   b. 剩餘選項中 (F) undertakings（工作）為名詞、(I) popular（受歡迎的）為形容詞，惟根據語意，(I) 項應為正選。
   c. **popular** [ˋpɑpjəlɚ] *a.* 流行的；受歡迎的

E **12.** 理由
   a. 空格所在的限定形容詞子句主詞為關係代名詞 that，指涉前面的先行詞 students（學生），而空格位於主詞與片語動詞 enrolled at（報名）之間，得知空格應置副詞，以修飾後面的動詞詞組。
   b. 剩餘選項中 (E) initially（最初）及 (H) barely（幾乎不）為副詞，惟根據語意，(E) 項應為正選。
   c. **initially** [ɪˋnɪʃəlɪ] *adv.* 開始時，最初

J **13.** 理由
   a. 空格前有介詞 by，空格後有名詞詞組 recyclable trash，得知空格應置名詞或動名詞作為 by 的受詞。
   b. 剩餘選項中僅剩 (J) gathering（蒐集）為動名詞，且置入空格後符合語意，故為正選。
   c. **gather** [ˋɡæðɚ] *vt.* 蒐集；召集 & *vi.* 聚集
      例 The president gathered a group of experts to find a solution to the crisis.
      總統召集了一群專家來尋找解決這個危機的辦法。

H **14.** 理由
   a. 空格前有主詞 They（他們）和過去進行式動詞 were earning（正在賺錢），空格後有受詞 enough money（足夠的錢），已是一完整句子，得知空格應置副詞，以修飾後方形容詞 enough。
   b. 剩餘選項中僅剩 (H) barely（幾乎不）為副詞，且置入空格後符合語意，故為正選。
   c. **barely** [ˋbɛrlɪ] *adv.* 勉強，幾乎不

F 15. 理由
  a. 空格前有最高級形容詞 most successful（最成功的），得知空格內應置名詞以被該形容詞修飾。
  b. 剩餘選項 (F) undertakings（工作）為名詞，且置入空格後符合語意，故為正選。
  c. **undertaking** [ˌʌndɚˋtekɪŋ] *n.* 工作；任務；事業

重要單字與片語

1. **murderous** [ˋmɝdərəs] *a.* 殘忍的
2. **dictator** [ˋdɪkˌtetɚ] *n.* 獨裁者
3. **political** [pəˋlɪtɪk!] *a.* 政治的
4. **relocate** [ˌriˋloket] *vi.* 重新安置；搬遷
   例 The couple relocated to Chicago.
   這對夫妻搬家到芝加哥。
5. **primitive** [ˋprɪmətɪv] *a.* 原始的
6. **an estimated** + 數字　估計有若干……
   例 An estimated 100 people were killed in the earthquake.
   = It was estimated that 100 people were killed in the earthquake.
   這次地震估計有一百人喪生。
7. **instruct** [ɪnˋstrʌkt] *vt.* 命令；教導；吩咐
   例 I'll find a good trainer to instruct me.
   我要找一位一流的訓練員來指導我。
8. **rouge** [ruʒ] *n.* 胭脂（不可數）
9. **intellectual** [ˌɪntəˋlɛktʃʊəl] *n.* 知識分子
10. **ethnic** [ˋɛθnɪk] *a.* 種族的
11. **gene** [dʒin] *n.* 基因
12. **neighboring** [ˋnebərɪŋ] *a.* 鄰近的
13. **bring sth back to life**　使某事物起死回生
    例 It is impossible to bring dead people back to life.
    讓死去的人起死回生是不可能的。
14. **circus** [ˋsɝkəs] *n.* 馬戲團
15. **innovative** [ˋɪnəˌvetɪv] *a.* 創新的
16. **enroll** [ɪnˋrol] *vi.* 註冊（與介詞 in 並用）
    例 About 100 students enrolled in Professor Johnson's writing course this semester.
    這學期約有一百名學生報名參加強森教授的寫作課程。
17. **recyclable** [riˋsaɪkləb!] *a.* 可回收利用的
18. **otherwise** [ˋʌðɚˌwaɪz] *adv.* 以相反的方式
19. **acrobatics** [ˌækrəˋbætɪks] *n.* 雜技
20. **eventually** [ɪˋvɛntʃʊəlɪ] *adv.* 終究，到頭來

篇章結構

　　生孩子是女性經歷中最能改變人生的事情之一。對於母親來說，養育出生後頭幾個月的嬰兒非常具挑戰性。如果寶寶是母親的第一胎，這種情況尤為明顯。不規律睡眠、哺乳和大筆待繳帳單導致身心俱疲。許多新手媽媽還要面對情緒上的變化，例如產後憂鬱症與焦慮感。

孩子出生後的前幾週最為關鍵，因為這個觀念，許多國家會對雙親和新生兒提供協助。其中一個如此貼心的國家便是芬蘭了。

　　芬蘭是一個面積廣大、經濟富庶的斯堪地那維亞國家。<u>因此，它有足夠的財力來支持發展其社會福利計畫。</u>芬蘭政府提供多達三百二十個工作日的有薪育嬰假。<u>還有，雙親會收到所謂的芬蘭寶寶箱。</u>八十多年前創立的芬蘭寶寶箱計畫提供父母尿布、圍兜、食物、衣服、玩具、床墊以及毛毯。這些物品確保新生兒能夠擁有安全舒適的成長起點。寶寶箱裡的物品目前價值一百四十歐元。這項計畫被認為是芬蘭以其擁有世界最低的嬰兒死亡率為傲的原因之一。此外，該計畫還鼓勵父母接受健康檢查，因為要領取寶寶箱，家長必須先登記醫療服務。

　　一名美國居民丹妮兒・塞拉西聽聞芬蘭的這個計畫後，決定在美國她家鄉所在的州創立類似的計畫。該計畫名為「寶寶要箱子」，就像芬蘭寶寶箱一樣提供必要的物品。然而，該計畫並無足夠的資金。<u>所以只有貧窮的單親媽媽（而非所有的媽媽）才會收到這個箱子。</u>儘管有這樣的限制，該計畫已經幫助了數百位陷入困境的母親。塞拉西女士的非營利組織所帶來的非凡成就也許會推廣到其它州去。如果資金充足，這項計畫將能夠幫助更多有需要的家庭。

Unit 02

__A__ **16. 理由**
  a. 空格前句提到養育才剛生出來幾個月的嬰兒是 extremely challenging for a mother（對於一個母親來說非常具有挑戰性），又空格後句提到會讓母親 fatigue（勞累）的原因，皆呼應選項 (A) 所述「如果寶寶是母親的第一胎，這種情況尤為明顯。」
  b. 根據上述，(A) 項應為正選。

__C__ **17. 理由**
  a. 空格前句提到芬蘭是一個 wealthy（富庶的）國家，與選項 (C) 中的 has adequate financial support（有足夠的財力來支持）形成關聯。又空格後句提及芬蘭政府提供給準媽媽和準爸爸產後放假的福利，呼應選項 (C) 中的 develop its social welfare programs（來發展其社會福利計畫）。
  b. 根據上述，(C) 項應為正選。

__E__ **18. 理由**
  a. 空格前句提到芬蘭政府提供給準媽媽和準爸爸產後放假的福利，又空格後句提到 the Finnish Baby Box program（芬蘭寶寶箱計畫）之創立時間和箱子裡裝有何物，因此空格應是開始提及 the Finnish Baby Box（芬蘭寶寶箱）。
  b. 根據上述，(E) 項應為正選。

Unit 02

D 19. 理由

    a. 空格前句提到美國一女性在美國所建立的類似寶寶箱計畫 doesn't have sufficient funds（無足夠的資金），可知如此的原因會造成選項 (D) 所述的結果：所以只有貧窮的單親媽媽（而非所有的媽媽）才會收到這個箱子。

    b. 根據上述，(D) 項應為正選。

(B) 選項翻譯 塞拉西女士將她女兒的性命得救歸功於芬蘭寶寶箱計畫。

重要單字與片語

1. **give birth (to a baby)** 生小孩
   例 Yesterday Mrs. Smith gave birth to a six-pound baby boy.
   昨天史密斯太太產下了一個六磅重的男嬰。

2. **extremely** [ɪkˋstrimlɪ] *adv.* 極度地

3. **fatigue** [fəˋtig] *n.* 疲勞

4. **irregular** [ɪˋrɛgjələ] *a.* 不規則的

5. **pattern** [ˋpætən] *n.* 模式

6. **breastfeeding** [ˋbrɛstˌfidɪŋ] *n.* 哺乳（不可數）

7. **a mountain of...** 大量的……
   例 Tom was not happy because he had a mountain of homework to do.
   湯姆不開心，因為他有大量的作業要做。

8. **postpartum** [ˌpostˋpɑrtəm] *a.* 產後的
   postpartum depression 產後憂鬱症

9. **assistance** [əˋsɪstəns] *n.* 幫助（不可數）

10. **adequate** [ˋædəkwət] *a.* 足夠的

11. **financial** [faɪˋnænʃəl] *a.* 財務的；財政的；金融的

12. **social welfare** 社會福利

13. **parental** [pəˋrɛntḷ] *a.* 父母的
    parental leave 育嬰假

14. **be known as** + 身分 以做為……著名
    例 Lions are known as the King of the Jungle.
    獅子被稱為叢林之王。

15. **establish** [ɪˋstæblɪʃ] *vt.* 建立，創立

16. **bib** [bɪb] *n.*（小孩的）圍兜

17. **mattress** [ˋmætrɪs] *n.* 床墊

18. **currently** [ˋkɝəntlɪ] *adv.* 目前

19. **credit** [ˋkrɛdɪt] *vt.* 信任，相信
    be credited with... 被認為擁有……；歸功於……

20. **boast** [bost] *vt.*（某國、某城市、某地區）擁有……而自豪
    比較
    boast of / about...（某人）自吹自擂……
    = brag of / about...

21. **mortality** [mɔrˋtælətɪ] *n.* 必死性；死亡數字
    the mortality rate 死亡率

22. **checkup** [ˋtʃɛkˌʌp] *n.* 健康檢查

23. **register for...** 登記 / 報名……
    = sign up for...
    例 If you're interested in the summer camp, you should register for it by next Monday.
    如果你對夏令營有興趣，要在下禮拜一前報名。

24. **resident** [ˋrɛzədənt] *n.* 居民

25. **essential** [ɪˋsɛnʃəl] *a.* 必要的，必不可少的
26. **phenomenal** [fəˋnɑmənḷ] *a.* 了不起的
27. **expand** [ɪkˋspænd] *vt.* 擴大，拓展

例 We've expanded our business by opening two more restaurants lately.
我們最近擴大營業，新開了兩家餐廳。

四 閱讀測驗

在 1997 那一年，麥可‧庫茲就如同許多住在夏威夷的青少年一樣。十七歲活力充沛的他一有機會就會去海邊衝浪玩上好幾個鐘頭。然而他並不知道他最喜愛的休閒活動有一天會改變他的人生。

某天早晨，庫茲和一個朋友決定在他們最喜歡的海灘逐浪，此時悲劇發生了。他們倆離岸邊才幾百公尺時，就注意到一條很大的虎鯊正在快速接近。他們二人開始瘋狂地快速划水，想逃離這個危險的掠食者。很不幸對他們其中一人來說，這努力是不夠的。那條殺手魚將剃刀般鋒利的牙齒深深咬住庫茲的右腿。庫茲用盡全力不斷地打著這條食人鯊魚，直到牠最後鬆口游開。劇烈的疼痛讓他陷入休克，在朋友的幫忙下回到陸地上。

庫茲失血量已達危險程度，數度昏厥又甦醒，所以圍觀者把他放在一臺舊卡車的後面，迅速將他送到最近的醫院。醫生救回了他的性命，但令人心碎的小腿截肢決定是無可避免的了。手術後庫茲恢復了意識，向所有救他的人表達感謝，並勇敢而優雅地接受了自己的命運。

當庫茲做完幾個月痛苦的復健，並學會使用義肢走路後，他回到自己被那海中猛獸奪去右腿的海灘，再度開始衝浪。他也開始遊說夏威夷政治人物保護當時經常遭漁民獵殺取魚翅的鯊魚。麥可‧庫茲的遊說活動最終成功了，夏威夷政府禁止了販賣與持有鯊魚魚翅。麥可‧庫茲將他的個人悲劇轉化成為公眾的勝利。

A **20.** 本文主旨為何？
(A) 一名少年如何雍容地處理個人的不幸。
(B) 保護虎鯊為何很重要。
(C) 夏威夷衝浪者所面臨的問題為何增加。
(D) 大眾如何合作可以救人一命。

理由
本文描述一名少年衝浪發生悲劇意外後他所面對的方式，可知 (A) 項應為正選。

Unit 02

__B__ **21.** 第二段中的 this 的指涉為何？
(A) 逐浪的渴望。
(B) 逃離鯊魚所做的努力。
(C) 呼救的適當時機。
(D) 為止血所做的努力。

理由
此處 this 所指的是前一句 "They both frantically began to paddle as fast as they could to escape the dangerous predator." 中表達為逃離鯊魚所做的努力，可知 (B) 項應為正選。

__C__ **22.** 哪些字被本文拿來形容攻擊麥可·庫茲的鯊魚？
(A) 悲劇、殺手魚、勝利
(B) 危險的掠食者、食人鯊魚、命運
(C) 危險的掠食者、殺手魚、海中猛獸
(D) 食人鯊魚、命運、下顎

理由
根據本文第二段第三、五句及第四段第一句，可知 (C) 項應為正選。

__C__ **23.** 根據本文，下列哪一項關於麥可·庫茲的敘述正確？
(A) 他在這場悲劇後遭受心理創傷。
(B) 他鼓吹讓夏威夷的海灘更安全。
(C) 他在海中受到兇殘攻擊後失去了某段肢體。
(D) 他還沒完成復健療程。

理由
根據本文第三段第二句，可知 (C) 項應為正選。

重要單字與片語

1. **course** [kɔrs] *n.* 路線；過程
2. **approach** [əˋprotʃ] *vt. & vi.* 接近 & *n.* 方法
   例 The dogcatchers approached the dangerous dog with caution.
   捕犬員小心翼翼地接近那隻危險的狗。
3. **rapidly** [ˋræpɪdlɪ] *adv.* 迅速地
4. **frantically** [ˋfræntɪklɪ] *adv.* 發狂似地
   frantic [ˋfræntɪk] *a.* 發狂似的
5. **paddle** [ˋpædl̩] *vi. & vt.* 划水 & *n.* 槳
   例 Tom and Jerry paddled as hard as they could in order not to fall over the waterfall.
   湯姆與傑瑞盡全力划船，以免掉到瀑布下面去。

6. **escape** [əˋskep] *vi.* & *vt.* 逃脫；躲過 & *n.* 逃脫
   例 According to the news, a notorious drug dealer escaped from prison.
   據新聞報導，一名惡名昭彰的毒販越獄了。

7. **sink** [sɪŋk] *vi.* 沉；把……插入；挖（三態為：sink, sank [sæŋk], sunk [sʌŋk]）
   例 Two boats sank off the coast of the island during the storm.
   暴風雨中，兩艘船在島嶼的外海沉沒。
   John sank the ax into the log.
   約翰把斧頭劈入木頭。

8. **consciousness** [ˋkɑnʃəsnɪs] *n.* 知覺，意識

9. **bystander** [ˋbaɪˏstændɚ] *n.* 旁觀者

10. **amputate** [ˋæmpjəˏtet] *vt.* 截肢
    例 The patient's toes were amputated because of frostbite.
    病人的腳趾因凍瘡而遭截肢。
    ＊frostbite [ˋfrɔstˏbaɪt] *n.* 凍傷；凍瘡

11. **calf** [kæf] *n.* 小腿（複數為 calves [kævz]）

12. **gratitude** [ˋgrætəˏtjud] *n.* 感激（不可數）

13. **rehabilitation** [ˏrihəˏbɪləˋteʃən] *n.* 復健（常簡寫為 rehab [ˋriˏhæb]）（不可數） a rehab center　復健中心；菸毒勒戒所

14. **prosthetic** [prɑsˋθɛtɪk] *a.* 義肢的

15. **limb** [lɪm] *n.* 四肢之一

Unit 02

五 混合題

我們向四個人詢問他們對於動物園的看法。以下是他們的回答。

瑪儂
我從本身經驗的了解是，管理得當的動物園會是非常有教育意義的地方。透過導覽和資訊豐富的展示方式，我們已經幫助提高人們對世界各地各種動物的認識。近距離觀察像老虎、貓熊和長頸鹿這些特別的動物是種極好的經驗。如果我們這樣優質動物園的遊客從幼年就開始認識這些動物，他們的成長過程將是尊重動物並想要保護動物的。

卡米爾
我直接說重點：動物園是殘酷的。無論多少年來做了多少改善，動物園仍然是把動物隔離在一點也不自然的環境當中。我是動物權益組織的成員，正在努力提醒全世界一個事實，那就是動物園的動物身心兩方面都受到折磨。我呼籲那些看到被關籠子、被迫圈養的不快樂動物的民眾，大家來拍照並貼到社群媒體上。這可以讓我們的重要使命被更清楚看到。

Unit 02

> **加百列**
> 動物園對其內和其外廣大世界的動物們的福祉做了很大的貢獻。例如我所投資的一家動物園參與了以保護瀕危物種——例如大猩猩、大貓熊、獵豹和野馬——為目標的繁殖計畫。等動物園在圈養環境裡安全繁育這些動物後，會將其中一部分野放。我們大家都來提供資金援助，協助動物園改進並擴大這些計畫，這是很重要的。從工作中我也了解到，動物園在許多領域如動物行為與疾病防控等進行重要的研究，大大增加了人類對動物世界的了解。

> **盧卡斯**
> 人們總說動物園幫助兒童認識動物，但在我心中這是錯誤的論點。可憐的動物並沒有生活在牠們的天然環境裡，所以並未展現正常的行為。因此孩童去參觀動物園時並不能看到動物真實的一面。所以我不會帶學童們去動物園校外教學，而是給他們看實際在野外拍攝的紀錄片。我希望現在的小孩，包括我自己的，能得到與世間這麼多美麗動物相關的正確教育，但坦白說，這在動物園中是無法得到的。

24. 加百列對動物園持正面態度，表示動物園透過繁育計畫和重要研究來為動物福祉做出<u>貢獻</u>。

理由
空格前為代名詞 they，空格後為介詞 to，可得知空格應置動詞。根據加百列看法的第一句 "Zoos make great contributions to animal welfare, ..."（動物園對……動物們的福祉做了很大的貢獻。）得知，空格應置與 contributions 相關的動詞 contribute。

25. 與瑪儂不同，盧卡斯認為對孩童來說動物園不是獲得關於世間各種動物的<u>教育</u>的好方式。

理由
空格前為不定冠詞 an，空格後為介詞 about，可得知空格應置名詞。根據盧卡斯看法的最後一句 "..., to be properly educated about all the wonderful creatures on this planet, but quite frankly, they can't get that from a zoo."（……，能得到與世間這麼多美麗動物相關的正確教育，但坦白說，這在動物園中是無法得到的。）得知，空格應置與 educated 相關的名詞 education。

26. 卡米爾和加百列的回答中，哪個字表示「將動物或人關在某處且不允許離開的情況」？

captivity（囚禁）

理由
根據卡米爾看法的倒數第二句 "... unhappy animals locked in cages and forced to stay in captivity to take pictures and post them on social media."（……被關籠子、被迫圈

養的不快樂動物的民眾，大家來拍照並貼到社群媒體上。）及加百列看法的第三句 "Once the zoo has safely bred these animals in captivity, ..."（等動物園在圈養環境裡安全繁育這些動物後，⋯⋯）可推測 captivity（囚禁）應為正解。

27. 以下哪些角色最適合這些回答者？請為每位回答者選擇兩個角色。每個角色只能使用一次。

| (A) 動物園老闆 | (B) 民眾 | (C) 投資者 | (D) 抗議者 |
| (E) 動物園管理員 | (F) 老師 | (G) 研究人員 | (H) 家長 |

瑪儂：<u>(A)</u>、<u>(E)</u>
卡米爾：<u>(B)</u>、<u>(D)</u>
加百列：<u>(C)</u>、<u>(G)</u>
盧卡斯：<u>(F)</u>、<u>(H)</u>

理由
根據瑪儂看法的第一、二句得知，(A)、(E) 應為正選。卡米爾看法的第二至四句得知，(B)、(D) 應為正選。加百列看法的第二及最後一句得知，(C)、(G) 應為正選。盧卡斯看法的倒數第一、二句得知 (F)、(H) 應為正選。

重要單字與片語

1. **psychological** [ˌsaɪkəˈlɑdʒɪkl̩] *a.* 心理的，心理學的
2. **captivity** [kæpˈtɪvətɪ] *n.* 囚禁（不可數）
3. **undertake** [ˌʌndɚˈtek] *vt.* 進行，承接
   （三態為：undertake, undertook [ˌʌndɚˈtʊk], undertaken [ˌʌndɚˈtekən]）
   例 Prof. Smith undertook a project of writing a book on zoology.
   史密斯教授接下了撰寫動物學專書的計畫。

4. **exhibit** [ɪgˈzɪbɪt] *vt.* 顯示，現出；展示 & *vi.* 展示 & *n.* 展覽會
   例 The patient exhibited some early signs of the disease.
   該名病患出現了這種疾病的若干早期症狀。
5. **documentary** [ˌdɑkjəˈmɛntərɪ] *n.* 紀錄片 & *a.* 文件的；紀錄的
6. **assessment** [əˈsɛsmənt] *n.* 評估

Unit 03

一 綜合測驗

　　居酒屋已經存在很久了。它們源自日本江戶時期，在十七世紀到十九世紀之間的某個時間。它們的起源城市無法確定；有人說是東京，也有人說居酒屋起源於大阪。這些簡約的營業場所可以輕易地從戶外高掛的紅色紙燈籠來辨識。起初居酒屋的常客是下班後想喝杯清酒的領薪上班族，以男性為主。而後加上了簡單的餐點讓顧客能保持好心情又能持續喝酒。隨著時間的推移，居酒屋不再只是單純的飲酒場所，而是發展成社區聚會的中心，人們可以在這裡放鬆身心，並透過美食建立情誼。

　　現在無論男女都喜歡在居酒屋會面和社交，它們已成為現代日本美食的一大特點。顧客通常會先點杯啤酒來喝，邊喝邊決定餐點。具代表性的食物選項有雞肉串（烤肉串上的燒烤雞肉）、唐揚（小塊的炸雞）以及各式各樣的豆腐料理。餐點會擺放在小盤子上讓大家一同享用。居酒屋近期已紅到國外，尤其是在美國。因此，許多海外的居酒屋開始調整菜單，融入當地風味，同時保留其傳統特色與魅力。

__C__ 1. 理由

a. (A) **adapt** [əˋdæpt] *vi.* & *vt.*（使）適應（與介詞 to 並用）

例 Paul adapted to his new job very well.
　保羅在新工作上適應得非常好。

(B) **concentrate** [ˋkɑnsn͵tret] *vi.* & *vt.* 專注，集中
concentrate on...　　專注於……

例 During the class, Anna concentrated on the professor's lecture.
　上課期間，安娜專注聆聽教授講課。

(C) **originate** [əˋrɪdʒə͵net] *vi.* 源自
originate in + 地方　　源自某地

例 Many Christmas traditions are thought to have originated in Germany.
　許多聖誕節的傳統被認為是起源於德國。

(D) **cooperate** [koˋɑpə͵ret] *vi.* 合作（與介詞 with 並用）
cooperate with...　　與……合作

例 I was upset when Jane refused to cooperate with us.
　珍拒絕與我們合作時，我很難過。

b. 根據語意，(C) 項應為正選。

A 2. 理由
   a. (A) **salaried workers**　領薪上班族
      salaried [ˈsælərɪd] *a.* 領薪水的
      例 Some salaried workers prefer flexible hours rather than a fixed nine-to-five schedule.
      有些領薪上班族更喜歡彈性工時，而非固定的朝九晚五。

   (B) **dismissed employees**　被解僱的員工
      dismissed [dɪsˈmɪst] *a.* 被解僱的
      例 Many dismissed employees struggle to find new jobs in a competitive market.
      許多被解僱的員工在競爭激烈的市場中難以找到新工作。

   (C) **adopted children**　收養的子女
      例 The couple treated their adopted children with love and care, just like biological parents would.
      這對夫妻像親生父母一樣愛護他們收養的小孩。

   (D) **retired teachers**　退休教師
      例 The school invited retired teachers to speak at the graduation ceremony.
      學校邀請退休教師在畢業典禮上致詞。

   b. 根據語意，可知 (A) 項應為正選。

B 3. 理由
   a. (A) **reminder** [rɪˈmaɪndɚ] *n.* 提醒用的物品
      例 I wrote my girlfriend's birthday down on a sticky note as a reminder.
      我把女友的生日寫在一張便利貼上作為提醒。

   (B) **gender** [ˈdʒɛndɚ] *n.* 所有的男性和女性；性別
      例 Both genders should pursue their dreams fearlessly.
      無論男女都應無所畏懼地追逐自己的夢想。

   (C) **disorder** [dɪsˈɔrdɚ] *n.* 無秩序；失調
      例 Panic disorder can be a very horrible experience.
      恐慌症會是個很可怕的經驗。

   (D) **border** [ˈbɔrdɚ] *n.* 國界；邊緣
      例 My aunt and uncle live on the border of Germany and France.
      我的嬸嬸和叔叔住在德法交界處。

   b. 根據語意，(B) 項應為正選。

Unit 03

[B] **4.** 理由

　　a. 原句實為：
　　Patrons usually start with a beer while they decide on the food.
　　對等連接詞 while 連接兩個完整句構的子句，且兩個子句主詞相同，皆為 patrons（顧客），故可將 while 引導的副詞子句之主詞省略，並將動詞 decide（決定）改為現在分詞 deciding。

　　b. 根據上述，(B) 項應為正選。

[D] **5.** 理由

　　a. (A) **historical** [hɪˋstɔrɪkḷ] *a.* 與歷史有關的
　　　　比較
　　　　historic [hɪˋstɔrɪk] *a.* 有歷史性的；歷史上著名的
　　　　例 I don't enjoy historical novels; I like modern short stories instead.
　　　　我不喜歡歷史小說，我倒喜歡現代短篇小說。
　　　　This invention is of historic significance.
　　　　這項發明具有歷史性的意義。

　　　(B) **critical** [ˋkrɪtɪkḷ] *a.* 重要的，關鍵的；批評的
　　　　be critical to...　　對……很重要
　　　　be critical of...　　批評……
　　　　例 Your dedication is critical to the success of our company.
　　　　你的奉獻對本公司的成功來說極為重要。
　　　　Environmentalists are critical of building a dam in that area.
　　　　環保人士批評在那個地區建造水壩一事。

　　　(C) **vertical** [ˋvɝtɪkḷ] *a.* 垂直的
　　　　horizontal [ˏhɔrəˋzɑntḷ] *a.* 水平的
　　　　例 There are several blue vertical lines on Lisa's skirt.
　　　　莉莎的裙子上有幾條藍色的垂直線條。

　　　(D) **typical** [ˋtɪpɪkḷ] *a.* 典型的，有代表性的
　　　　例 It was a typical summer morning.
　　　　那是個典型的夏日早晨。

　　b. 根據語意，(D) 項應為正選。

重要單字與片語

1. **sometime** [ˋsʌmˏtaɪm] *adv.*（在過去或未來的）某個時候
　　sometime yesterday　　昨天某時
　　sometime next week　　下星期某時

2. **uncertainty** [ʌnˋsɝtṇtɪ] *n.* 不確定性（不可數）；不確定的事（常用複數）

3. **origin** [ˋɔrədʒɪn] *n.* 起源

4. **establishment** [ɪˋstæblɪʃmənt] *n.*（企業、商店）機構、單位

5. **frequent** [ˈfrɪkwɛnt] *vt.* 常去（某地）
   例 Sophie and her friends frequent the Italian restaurant around the corner on weekends.
   蘇菲和她的朋友週末經常光顧轉角那間義大利餐廳。
6. **hub** [hʌb] *n.* 中心，樞紐
7. **socialize** [ˈsoʃəˌlaɪz] *vi.* 交際
   例 Jane enjoys socializing with people from different fields.
   珍喜歡與來自不同領域的人交流。
8. **staple** [ˈstepḷ] *n.* 主食
9. **patron** [ˈpetrən] *n.* 顧客
10. **grilled** [grɪld] *a.* 燒烤的
11. **skewer** [ˈskjuɚ] *n.* 串肉籤
12. **adjust** [əˈdʒʌst] *vt.* 調整，調節
    例 Megan adjusted the chair to make it more comfortable.
    梅根調整椅子讓它更舒適。

二 文意選填

一般相信咖啡起源於非洲，最初以享用黑咖啡為主，不添加任何東西。幾百年前，歐洲人開始將牛奶加入咖啡中。之後這項作法開始傳開，最後成了喝咖啡最常見的方式。然而，一直到八〇年代中期，咖啡拉花的熱潮才開始盛行。拉花一詞意指咖啡店中浮在供應的咖啡表面美麗又精巧的設計圖形。紐約一位名為大衛・史蓋摩的咖啡師是帶動這個風潮的領頭者。他的文章出現在咖啡雜誌上，他也撰寫了第一本以咖啡拉花為主題的書。在此同時，義大利一位名為路易吉・路比的咖啡師也正在創作咖啡拉花。

創作拉花不是件容易的事。過程中要很細心且嚴苛謹慎，並得堅持不懈才能精通。除此之外，還需要一種特別的牛奶，稱為奶泡。製作奶泡要將蒸氣加進一般的牛奶中，快速地加熱。下個步驟是最難的部分，就是將熱牛奶倒入濃縮咖啡中。把奶泡倒進去時要先倒出牛奶。最後，咖啡師再將泡沫淋在表層，創作出精美的圖案。

飲用咖啡多年來在臺灣受到喜愛。喝咖啡的人隨處可見，臺灣甚至生產自己的咖啡。世界咖啡大師賽是國際間首屈一指的咖啡比賽，臺灣的咖啡在比賽中創下佳績，也獲得國際的尊崇。每年有來自五十多個國家的咖啡師在這項比賽中亮相。他們泡的咖啡達到嚴苛的標準，以表演的方式展現，最後再以口感、創意、專業技巧及呈現方式來評比。參與世界咖啡大師賽會是個一窺新穎拉花藝術的好方式。

G 6. 理由
   a. 空格前有及物動詞 began（開始），其後可接不定詞或動名詞作受詞，空格前無引導不定詞的 to，得知空格應置動名詞。
   b. 選項中為動名詞的有 (D) creating（創作）及 (G) adding（加入），惟根據語意，(G) 項應為正選。

Unit 03

c. **add** [æd] *vt.* 添加

例 This dish will taste better if you add some vinegar.
如果你加點醋的話，這道菜會更好吃。

H **7.** 理由

a. 空格前為本句主詞 The practice（這項作法），空格後為對等連接詞 and、副詞 eventually 及其所修飾的過去式動詞 became（變成），得知空格應置另一過去式動詞以與 became 形成對等。

b. 選項中為過去式動詞的有 (A) heated（加熱）、(B) credited（歸功於）、(H) spread（傳開）及 (J) judged（評判），惟根據語意，(H) 項應為正選。

c. **spread** [sprɛd] *vi. & n.* 蔓延，散播 & *vt.* 攤開；伸展；塗抹（三態同形）

例 The disease was spreading more rapidly than expected.
這疾病蔓延的速度比預料中快。

F **8.** 理由

a. 空格前為本句主詞 The term latte art（拉花一詞），空格後為 to those beautiful, artistic designs...，得知空格應置本句動詞，且依語意應為現在式。

b. 剩餘選項中 (E) produces（生產）及 (F) refers（談及，與介詞 to 並用）為現在式動詞，惟根據語意及用法，(F) 項應為正選。

c. **refer** [rɪˋfɝ] *vi.* 言及，提到；查（字典）（皆與介詞 to 並用）

refer to...　　談到……；提及……

B **9.** 理由

a. 空格前有 be 動詞 is，空格後有介詞詞組 with starting this trend（帶動這個風潮），得知空格應置及物動詞的過去分詞，以與 is 形成被動語態。

b. 剩餘選項中為及物動詞的過去分詞的有 (B) credited（歸功於）及 (J) judged（評判），惟根據語意及用法，(B) 項應為正選。

c. **credit** [ˋkrɛdɪt] *vt.* 歸功

sb is credited with sth　　某事要歸功於某人
= sth is credited to sb

例 Mr. Wang is credited with the success of this project.
= The success of this project is credited to Mr. Wang.
這項計畫的成功是王先生的功勞。

C **10.** 理由

a. 空格前有關係代名詞 that（= which）和及物動詞 takes（需要），空格後有不定詞 to master（精通）作形容詞，得知空格應置名詞，以被不定詞修飾。

b. 剩餘選項中為名詞的有 (C) perseverance（毅力）及 (I) favor（喜愛），惟根據語意，(C) 項應為正選。

c. **perseverance** [ˌpɝsəˋvɪrəns] *n.* 毅力，堅持不懈

<u>A</u> 11. 理由

   a. 空格位於關係代名詞 which 引導的形容詞子句中，且空格前有 be 動詞 is，得知空格應置及物動詞的過去分詞，以與 is 形成被動語態。

   b. 剩餘選項中為及物動詞的過去分詞的有 (A) heated（加熱）及 (J) judged（評判），惟根據後句中之 hot 得知 (A) 項應為正選。

   c. **heat** [hit] *vt.* 加熱 & *n.* 熱（不可數）

   例 Stacy heated the leftovers in the microwave before she sat down to eat.
   史黛西用微波爐把剩菜加熱，然後坐下來吃。

<u>D</u> 12. 理由

   a. 原句實為：
   Finally, the barista pours the foam on top and creates those exquisite patterns.
   上句中主詞為 the barista（咖啡師），對等連接詞 and 連接兩個動詞 pours（倒）及 creates（創作），此時可省略 and，再將第二個動詞 creates 改為現在分詞 creating，形成分詞構句。

   b. 根據上述，可知 (D) 項應為正選。

   c. **create** [krɪˋet] *vt.* 創造；創作

   例 Mellow music and dim lighting created a cozy atmosphere at this high-class restaurant.
   柔和的音樂和微暗的照明為這家高檔餐廳創造出舒適的氛圍。

Unit 03

<u>I</u> 13. 理由

   a. 空格前有片語動詞 come into（變得），得知空格應置名詞，以作為該片語動詞的受詞。

   b. 剩餘選項中僅 (I) favor（喜愛）為名詞，且置入空格後符合語意，故為正選。

   c. **favor** [ˋfevɚ] *n.* 喜愛；歡迎

   come into favor　受到喜愛

<u>E</u> 14. 理由

   a. 空格前有本句主詞 Taiwan 及副詞 even（甚至），空格後有名詞 its own coffees（自己的咖啡），得知空格應置及物動詞，以接受詞 its own coffees。

   b. 剩餘選項中僅 (E) produces（生產）為及物動詞，且置入空格後符合語意，故為正選。

   c. **produce** [prəˋdjus] *vt.* 生產；製造

   例 The factory promised to cut down the amount of waste it produces.
   這間工廠承諾要減少廢料的製造量。

<u>J</u> 15. 理由

   a. 本句主詞為 Their coffees（他們的咖啡），其後動詞為被動語態 are prepared（準備）及另一動詞 presented（呈現），可知 presented 為過去分詞，與 prepared

Unit 03

對等，由此得知對等連接詞 and 之後的空格應置動詞的過去分詞，以與 prepared 及 presented 形成對等。

b. 剩餘選項 (J) judged（評判）為動詞 judge 的過去式及過去分詞，且置入空格後符合語意，故為正選。

c. **judge** [dʒʌdʒ] vt. 裁判，評判
例 Is Edward going to judge the singing contest again?
愛德華將再次擔任這次歌唱比賽的評審嗎？

重要單字與片語

1. **practice** [ˈpræktɪs] n. 作法
2. **consume** [kənˈsum] vt. 吃；喝；消費
   例 Visitors are not allowed to consume any food in the museum.
   遊客禁止於博物館內飲食。
3. **beverage** [ˈbɛvrɪdʒ] n. 飲料
4. **latte art** 拉花
5. **craze** [krez] n. 熱潮，狂潮
6. **take hold** 開始盛行
   例 A new type of music is now taking hold in that country.
   該國現正流行一種新型態的音樂。
7. **artistic** [ɑrˈtɪstɪk] a. 精巧的；藝術的
8. **float** [flot] vi. 漂浮
9. **barista** [bəˈristə] n. 咖啡師
10. **trend** [trɛnd] n. 潮流
11. **meticulous** [məˈtɪkjələs] a. 注意細節的，小心的
12. **exacting** [ɪgˈzæktɪŋ] a. 嚴格的，嚴苛的
13. **pour** [pɔr] vt. 倒（液體）& vi.（大量液體或氣體）湧出；下大雨
    例 Ellen poured boiling water into a bowl to make instant noodles.
    愛倫把沸騰的水倒進碗裡泡速食麵。
14. **foam** [fom] n. 泡沫（不可數）
15. **exquisite** [ɪkˈskwɪzɪt] a. 精美的
16. **premier** [prɪˈmɪr] a. 最好的；首要的
17. **technical** [ˈtɛknɪkḷ] a. 專門的；技術的
18. **cutting-edge** [ˌkʌtɪŋˈɛdʒ] a. 最新的；走在尖端的

篇章結構

沒人想在荒野裡迷路或受困。雖然對多數人而言，困在山邊或在森林中迷路的機率不高，但學點困境求生的技能也不是件壞事。擁有這些知識，你的生或死便有很大的差別。

如果你在荒野中迷了路，第一件事就是先找個能遮風避雨的庇護之地。<u>洞穴、樹洞，甚至大石頭，都能用來暫時擋風</u>。天氣冷的時候，一定要保持身體乾燥。溼衣服加上寒風，就可能成為荒野中的致命死因。溼透的身體末梢如手指或腳趾，只要幾分鐘就能造成凍傷。在天氣較熱的情況下，也存在著另一種危險：<u>受到太陽直接曝晒，人很有可能中暑或脫水。</u>

由於相較於沒有水喝，人沒有食物還可以多撐一陣子，所以儘快找到可飲用的水是非常重要的。如果你人在河邊或湖邊，在離岸邊幾英尺以外的地面挖個洞，這樣就能在喝水前先行過濾。另一個取得水的方法，就是在地上放一塊塑膠，並放一整個晚上。隔日早上收集到的露水就能飲用。

　　如果你受困野外的時間比意料中來得長，那麼就必須尋找食物來源。找堅果類或莓類來吃有時是最好的選擇。但重要的是要自己熟悉的東西才能吃。亂吃不認識的野莓或植物都不是好主意，因為可能會中毒。

　　當然，在荒野中最好的求生法則就是未雨綢繆。如果知道有迷路的危險，就確保你的朋友或家人知道你的計畫。只要把自己的去向和行動告訴別人，就可以避免可能發生的不幸。

Unit 03

D **16. 理由**
   a. 空格前句提到若你在荒野中迷了路，首先就是找個能遮風避雨的地方，依語意空格內容應提到有哪些地方是可以遮風避雨的，此即如選項 (D) 所述「洞穴、樹洞，甚至大石頭，都能用來暫時擋風。」
   b. 根據上述，(D) 項應為正選。

A **17. 理由**
   a. 空格前句提到在天氣較熱的情況下，也存在著另一種危險，因此空格內容應是提到在溫度較高的情況下在野外會遇到的危險，此即如選項 (A) 所述「受到太陽直接曝曬，人很有可能中暑或脫水。」
   b. 根據上述，(A) 項應為正選。

E **18. 理由**
   a. 第三段第一句提到相較於沒有水喝，人沒有食物還可以多撐一陣子，所以儘快找到可飲用的水是非常重要的；第二至三句提到找到乾淨水源的第一個方法：在離河邊或湖邊幾英尺以外的地面挖個洞；又空格後提到隔日早上收集到的露水就能飲用；因此可推知空格內文為介紹另一個找到乾淨水源的方法，正如選項 (E) 所述「另一個取得水的方法，就是在地上放一塊塑膠，並放一整個晚上。」
   b. 根據上述，(E) 項應為正選。

B **19. 理由**
   a. 空格前兩句提到在荒野中最好的求生法則就是 be prepared beforehand（未雨綢繆），如果知道有迷路的危險，就確保你的朋友或家人知道你的計畫，因此空格內文應為如此做的結果，即如選項 (B) 所述「只要把自己的去向和行動告訴別人，就可以避免可能發生的不幸。」
   b. 根據上述，(B) 項應為正選。

(C) 選項翻譯 以這種方式生火會引起任何山區救援隊的注意。

Unit 03

重要單字與片語

1. **strand** [strænd] *vt.* 使困住（常用被動語態）
   - 例 After our car broke down, we were stranded in the mountain for a whole week.
   汽車拋錨後，我們在山中受困了一整個禮拜。
2. **in the wild** 在野生環境中
3. **stuck** [stʌk] *a.* 被困住的
4. **get lost** 迷路
5. **survive** [sɚˋvaɪv] *vi.* 生存
6. **shelter** [ˋʃɛltɚ] *n.* 掩蔽（處）；遮蔽（處）
   find / take shelter 躲避
7. **protection** [prəˋtɛkʃən] *n.* 保護
8. **the elements** （通常指惡劣）天氣（恆用複數）
9. **hollowed-out** [ˋhɑlodˏaʊt] *a.* 中空的
10. **a layer of...** 一層的……
11. **be combined with...** 與……結合
    - 例 In this movie, action is combined with comedy.
    這部電影結合了動作與喜劇。
12. **chill** [tʃɪl] *n.* 寒冷
13. **deadly** [ˋdɛdlɪ] *a.* 致命的
14. **extremities** [ɪkˋstrɛmətɪz] *n.* 手足四肢的末端
15. **frostbitten** [ˋfrɔstˏbɪtn] *a.* 凍傷的
16. **in a matter of minutes** 幾分鐘的光景，在幾分鐘之內
17. **exist** [ɪgˋzɪst] *vi.* 存在
18. **exposure** [ɪkˋspoʒɚ] *n.* 暴露
    exposure to... 面臨……；遭受……
19. **heatstroke** [ˋhitˏstrok] *n.* 中暑（不可數）
20. **dehydration** [ˏdihaɪˋdreʃən] *n.* 脫水（不可數）
21. **It is essential to + V** 做……是必須的
22. **drinkable** [ˋdrɪŋkəb!] *a.* 可以喝的 (= potable [ˋpotəb!])
23. **filter** [ˋfɪltɚ] *vt.* 過濾
24. **overnight** [ˏovɚˋnaɪt] *adv.* 一夜間的；在夜間的，在晚上的
25. **dew** [du] *n.* 露水（不可數）
26. **Should + S1 + V1 + ..., S2 + V2 + ...** 萬一／要是……，……
    = If + S1 + should + V1 + ..., S2 + V2 + ...
    - 例 Should Mitch call me while I'm out, ask him to leave a message.
    萬一米契在我外出時打電話找我，請他留言。
27. **forage** [ˋfɔrɪdʒ] *vi.* 搜尋
    forage for... 尋找……
28. **option** [ˋɑpʃən] *n.* 選擇
29. **beforehand** [bɪˋforˏhænd] *adv.* 預先 (= in advance)
    - 例 Don't pay Jack for the computer; I paid him beforehand.
    別付給傑克電腦的錢；我已經事先付給他了。
30. **potential** [pəˋtɛnʃəl] *a.* 潛在的，可能的

四 閱讀測驗

孟德斯鳩是法國的律師、哲學家和作家，生於 1689 年，卒於 1755 年。他最著名的作品是《法意》，出版於 1748 年。在這本一千多頁的書中，孟德斯鳩探討了人類法律、社會制度和政治體系，將後者分為共和制、君主制與專制。這分類在當時聲名大噪，因為它與典型的政體形式分類迥異。孟德斯鳩主張某類型的政體更適合某類型的社會，而氣候和地理條件也可能會對此產生影響。

孟德斯鳩的足跡遍布歐洲各處，對英國的政治體系尤其印象深刻，他在《法意》中也強烈主張分權制度，亦即將政治權力劃分為立法、司法和行政三個不同體系。他認為這種分權制對促進自由有利並可防止濫權。孟德斯鳩在這個領域的論點有如此強大的說服力，以至於它後來啟發了美國憲法。因此，《法意》在孟德斯鳩的生前及死後都受到高度重視且深具影響力，但也少不了爭議。

他另一部著名作品是《波斯人信札》。雖然在 1721 年是以匿名出版，但書的真實作者是個公開的祕密，並讓孟德斯鳩初嘗成名的滋味。這本書由兩個虛構的波斯（現今的伊朗地區）旅人所寫的一系列評論法國文化和社會的信札組成。這種手法讓孟德斯鳩能以幽默的方式表達自己的觀點，批判從宗教到君主制再到階級制度的一切，由於既有趣又挑戰威權，在當時得到極佳的評價，而且讓孟德斯鳩站上啟蒙時代重要哲學家之一的地位。

__D__ **20.** 本文按何種邏輯安排？
  (A) 按時間日期。
  (B) 按孟德斯鳩的旅行。
  (C) 按出版地點。
  (D) 按孟德斯鳩的成就。

  理由
  根據本文第一、二段提及孟德斯鳩的著作《法意》，啟發了美國憲法，並在他的生前及死後都深具影響力。第三段則提到另一部作品《波斯人信札》，使他成為啟蒙時代重要的哲學家之一，可知 (D) 項應為正選。

__B__ **21.** 關於《法意》，下列何者敘述正確？
  (A) 它引用了美國憲法的內容。
  (B) 它對政體的分類方式在當時是很獨特的。
  (C) 它討論了英國政治體系的重大瑕疵。
  (D) 它主張權力的分立是過時的概念。

  理由
  根據本文第一段第三至四句，可知 (B) 項應為正選。

Unit 03

A **22.** 關於《波斯人信札》，我們得知什麼？
(A) 它代表了孟德斯鳩自己的想法與意見。
(B) 它大肆批評波斯的文化和社會。
(C) 孟德斯鳩在這本書出版後名聲下降。
(D) 和孟德斯鳩同時代的人不知道這本書是他寫的。

理由
根據本文第三段第四句，可知 (A) 項應為正選。

C **23.** 哪些字被本文拿來形容孟德斯鳩的作品？
(A) 著名的、強烈地、具影響力的、極佳的
(B) 典型的、有說服力的、幽默的、有挑戰性的
(C) 聲名大噪的、有說服力的、爭議的、有趣的
(D) 著名的、印象深刻的、高度重視的、匿名地

理由
根據本文第一段第四句、第二段第四、五句及第三段最後一句，得知 (C) 項應為正選。

重要單字與片語

1. **philosopher** [fəˋlɑsəfɚ] *n.* 哲學家
2. **categorize** [ˋkætəgə͵raɪz] *vt.* 將……分類
   categorization [͵kætəgəraɪˋzeʃən] *n.* 分類
   例 The author's latest work was categorized as an autobiography.
   該作家最近的一部作品被歸類為自傳。
3. **classify** [ˋklæsə͵faɪ] *vt.* 分類；歸類
   例 Non-fiction books in the library are classified according to subject matter.
   圖書館內非小說類的書籍是依主題內容來分類。
4. **liberty** [ˋlɪbɚtɪ] *n.* 自由（不可數）
5. **persuasive** [pɚˋswesɪv] *a.* 有說服力的
6. **forceful** [ˋfɔrsfəl] *a.* 強有力的；有說服力的

7. **influential** [͵ɪnfluˋɛnʃəl] *a.* 有影響力的
8. **controversial** [͵kɑntrəˋvɝʃəl] *a.* 有爭議的
9. **anonymously** [əˋnɑnəməslɪ] *adv.* 匿名地
10. **fame** [fem] *n.* 名氣，名聲（不可數）
11. **fictional** [ˋfɪkʃənḷ] *a.* 虛構的
12. **device** [dɪˋvaɪs] *n.* 裝置；設計；方法，手段
13. **entertaining** [͵ɛntɚˋtenɪŋ] *a.* 有趣的；使人愉快的
14. **challenging** [ˋtʃæləndʒɪŋ] *a.* 具有挑戰性的
15. **chronological** [͵krɑnəˋlɑdʒɪkḷ] *a.* 按事件時間順序排列的
16. **outdated** [͵aʊtˋdetɪd] *a.* 過時的
17. **contemporary** [kənˋtɛmpə͵rɛrɪ] *n.* 同時期的人 & *a.* 當代的；同時期的

五、混合題

世界各地都有盜伐行為，從非洲和亞洲到歐洲和南美洲皆然。我們訪談了兩個人，詢問他們對這種非法活動的看法。

路易斯

我不想美化事實：我就是一個盜伐工人。但這對我來說已經不是合不合法的問題，而是要不要活命的問題。我砍樹然後把木材賣給出價最高的人，所取得的收入讓我和家人能活下去，這收入是非常重要的。我住在亞馬遜雨林的邊緣地帶，這裡幾乎沒有就業機會，所以我得自己創造機會。在我心目中，那些買賣木材的人才是更大的罪犯 —— 就是將木材賣給有錢西方人而藉此賺取大把鈔票的人，因為有錢的西方人會想要那些稀有、珍貴樹木製成的精緻家具。但冒所有風險的人卻是我。我得尋覓目標樹種、砍下來、運送穿越危險地形，還要跟那些收購木材的惡棍打交道。或許說政府若更關注改善我們這裡的教育系統，或者給我這種人提供就業培訓，我就不用做這些事啦。但說難聽點，他們才懶得管呢。

茱莉安娜

盜伐對環境造成嚴重的後果。無節制的砍伐樹木導致無數生物的主要棲息地遭到摧毀，可能會造成許多動植物的滅絕。也會對氣候變遷造成重大的負面影響，因為濫伐森林會釋放大量的二氧化碳到大氣當中。盜伐者聲稱他們別無選擇，只能從事犯罪活動。然而合法伐木工的存在 —— 那些花時間精力取得正式許可證的人 —— 駁倒了這錯誤的觀念，揭露真正的事實。為了阻止盜伐者，我們需要一往無前地聚焦於永續伐木業，令其成為唯一被接受的作法。我們也需要提升消費者對其所購買木料、紙張或家具的實際來源的關注。如果人們知道某些產品是經由盜伐管道所生產，並理解這種作法會造成重大破壞，就比較不會去購買那些產品。沒有需求就不會有供應，盜伐將會成為歷史。

24. 路易斯聲稱如果像他這樣的人能被適當地教育／培訓，他們就不必從事盜伐。

理由

空格前為過去式 be 動詞 were，空格後為副詞 properly，可得知空格應置過去分詞。根據路易斯看法的倒數第二句 "Perhaps if the government were more interested in improving the education system around here or providing job training for people like me, ..."（或許說政府若更關注改善我們這裡的教育系統，或者給我這種人提供就業培訓，……）得知，空格應置與 education 相關的過去分詞 educated 或與 training 相關的過去分詞 trained。

Unit 03

Unit 03

25. 茉莉安娜認為我們應該聚焦於永續伐木產業，並確保這是人們唯一接受的伐木方式。

理由

空格前為助動詞 will，可得知空格應置原形動詞。根據茉莉安娜看法的第六句 "...we need to focus relentlessly on sustainable logging and make this the only acceptable practice." （……我們需要一往無前地聚焦於永續伐木業，令其成為唯一被接受的作法。）得知，空格應置與 acceptable 相關的原形動詞 accept。

26. 茉莉安娜回答中的哪個字表示「一個被普遍相信但是錯誤的觀念」？

myth（錯誤的想法，迷思）

理由

根據茉莉安娜看法的第五句 "...the existence of legal loggers—those who have taken the time and effort to get the proper permits—disproves this myth and exposes the real truth."（……合法伐木工的存在 —— 那些花時間精力取得正式許可證的人 —— 駁倒了這錯誤的觀念，揭露真正的事實。）可推測 myth（錯誤的想法，迷思）應為正解。

CE 27. 下列對於盜伐的諸多看法，哪些並未在這兩則回應中提到？

(A) 盜伐對人類與動物造成影響。
(B) 教導人們關於盜伐的常識可以將其終結。
(C) 暴風雨過後撿取漂流木的行為應該在各地都列為非法。
(D) 參與盜伐幫助某些人得以存活。
(E) 對盜伐的刑罰不夠嚴重。
(F) 販售木材的人比伐木工罪孽更重。

理由

根據路易斯看法的第三、五句及倒數第二句，以及茉莉安娜看法的第二句，可得知 (C) 與 (E) 項並未在本文中提及，故應為正選。

重要單字與片語

1. **logging** [ˈlɔgɪŋ] *n.* 伐木（不可數）
2. **sugarcoat** [ˈʃugɚˌkot] *vt.* 美化；給……裹一層糖衣
3. **virtually** [ˈvɝtʃuəlɪ] *adv.* 幾乎
4. **peddle** [ˈpɛdl] *vt.* 兜售；散播
   例 The man was caught peddling drugs on the street.
   該男子在街上兜售毒品時被逮。
5. **terrain** [təˈren] *n.* 地勢，地形（不可數）
6. **unsavory** [ʌnˈsevrɪ] *a.* 不道德的；令人討厭的
7. **bluntly** [ˈblʌntlɪ] *adv.* 直言不諱地
   To put it bluntly, ...　直接了當地說……

8. **deforestation** [diˌfɔrəsˋteʃən] *n.* 砍伐森林（不可數）
9. **alternative** [ɔlˋtɝnətɪv] *n.* 選擇，替代方案 & *a.* 替代的
10. **myth** [mɪθ] *n.* 錯誤的想法，迷思；神話
11. **relentlessly** [rɪˋlɛntləslɪ] *adv.* 持續地，不間斷地
12. **devastation** [ˌdɛvəsˋteʃən] *n.* 毀滅，極大的破壞（不可數）
13. **retrieve** [rɪˋtriv] *vt.* 取回；重新找回
    例 Many people wonder if the police chief will retrieve the billionaire's money that was stolen.
    許多人懷疑警察局局長是否能找回那億萬富翁失竊的錢。

Unit 03

Unit 04

一、綜合測驗

　　三千多年前，放風箏活動首次在亞洲出現，長久以來已成為全球許多文化的一部分。這個活動的其它型態如鬥風箏和追風箏在印度次大陸和中東及南美都廣受歡迎。萊特兄弟對於風箏飛行的觀察幫助他們發明了第一架飛機。風箏有許多實際用途，例如救援任務、科學實驗及風能發電。如今，放風箏依然是全球各年齡層喜愛的熱門休閒活動，各地還舉辦風箏節來慶祝其多彩多姿的歷史。

　　雷尼爾・赫夫曼是世界上首屈一指的風箏製作家，他已經設計了三百多架翱翔天際的壯麗風箏，一路走來已贏得了好幾次德國的風箏製作冠軍。他的航空動力作品中有一件曾於德國科技博物館展出。這位天賦異稟的藝術家兼工匠在柏林應用科技大學教授精美風箏的製作藝術，分享他的熱情。赫夫曼一年只設計一個風箏，但是讓熱愛風箏人士開心的是，他的作品中最引人注目的其中二十件已被德國諸多玩具公司量產。他的作品持續啟發新一代的風箏愛好者，讓這項工藝的傳統得以延續發展。

B 1. 理由
  a. 無 (A) 項與 (D) 項的用法。
  b. (B) **well-liked** [ˌwɛlˈlaɪkt] *a.* 深受喜愛的
    例 Peter is well-liked and respected by his colleagues.
    彼得受到同事喜愛和尊敬。
  (C) **good-looking** [ˌɡʊdˈlʊkɪŋ] *a.* 相貌好看的
    例 John is a tall, good-looking man who stands out in any crowd.
    約翰個頭高大又長得帥，在任何人群中都很突出。
  c. 根據語意，(B) 項應為正選。

C 2. 理由
  a. (A) **prevention** [prɪˈvɛnʃən] *n.* 阻止
    例 They organized an association for the prevention of child abuse.
    他們組織了一個防止虐童的協會。
  (B) **accusation** [ˌækjəˈzeʃən] *n.* 指控
    例 Alice reacted calmly to the plaintiff's accusation.
    愛麗絲對原告的指控反應冷靜。
    *plaintiff [ˈplentɪf] *n.* 原告
  (C) **observation** [ˌɑbzɚˈveʃən] *n.* 觀察
    例 Raymond is a man of keen observation but of few words.
    雷蒙是個觀察敏銳但話不多的人。

(D) **corruption** [kəˈrʌpʃən] *n.* 貪汙
   例 The politician's corruption was exposed by the press.
   該名政客的貪汙行為被新聞界披露出來。

b. 根據語意，(C) 項應為正選。

A 3. 理由
   a. (A) **practical** [ˈpræktɪkl̩] *a.* 實際的；務實的
      例 This job calls for at least five years of practical experience.
      這份工作需要至少五年的實際經驗。
   (B) **medical** [ˈmɛdɪkl̩] *a.* 醫療的
      例 You need a medical checkup before the surgery.
      手術前你需要做一次醫療檢查。
   (C) **physical** [ˈfɪzɪkl̩] *a.* 身體的，生理的
      例 Laura has been suffering from constant physical pain.
      蘿拉飽受持續不斷的身體病痛。
   (D) **tropical** [ˈtrɑpɪkl̩] *a.* 熱帶的
      例 The Amazon River basin contains the world's largest tropical rainforest.
      亞馬遜河流域有全世界最大片的熱帶雨林。

   b. 根據語意，(A) 項應為正選。

B 4. 理由
   a. (A) **disdain** [dɪsˈden] *vt.* 蔑視（= look down upon...）
      例 The man tends to disdain the poor.
      那人往往會瞧不起窮人。
   (B) **display** [dɪˈsple] *vt.* 展示
      例 The toys displayed in the window attracted the attention of every child that passed by.
      櫥窗內展示的玩具吸引了每個路過小朋友的目光。
   (C) **dismiss** [dɪsˈmɪs] *vt.* 解散；解僱
      例 Rachel was dismissed from her job for incompetence.
      瑞秋因不適任而遭解僱。
      *incompetence [ɪnˈkɑmpətəns] *n.* 不適任，無能力
   (D) **disassemble** [ˌdɪsəˈsɛmbl̩] *vt.* 分解
      例 Tom disassembled the computer, but he couldn't assemble its parts back.
      湯姆拆解了電腦，但他無法將零件組裝回來。

   b. 根據語意，(B) 項應為正選。

Unit 04

Unit 04

D 5. 理由

a. (A) **clarify the point**　　闡明觀點

例 A good introduction should clarify the point of the essay.
一篇好的引言應該闡明文章的重點。

(B) **express the opinions**　　表達意見

例 A great leader must express the opinions of the whole team.
優秀的領導者必須表達整個團隊的意見。

(C) **discover the techniques**　　發現技巧

例 The artist studied for years to discover the techniques of oil painting.
這位藝術家研究多年來發現油畫的技法。

(D) **teach the art**　　教授藝術

例 The academy offers courses that teach the art of filmmaking.
這所學院提供教授電影製作藝術的課程。

b. 根據語意，可知 (D) 項應為正選。

重要單字與片語

1. **variant** [ˈvɛrɪənt] n. 變體；不同版本
2. **subcontinent** [sʌbˈkɑntənənt] n. 次大陸
3. **rescue** [ˈrɛskju] n. 拯救，營救
   come to sb's rescue　　營救某人
   例 We came to John's rescue when we learned he was in financial trouble.
   我們獲知約翰陷入財務困境時便前去援助他。
4. **generation** [ˌdʒɛnəˈreʃən] n.（能源的）產生；世代
5. **pastime** [ˈpæsˌtaɪm] n. 消遣
6. **soaring** [ˈsɔrɪŋ] a. 翱翔的
7. **spectacular** [spɛkˈtækjələ˞] a. 壯麗的
8. **aerodynamic** [ˌɛrodaɪˈnæmɪk] a. 空氣動力學的
9. **gifted** [ˈɡɪftɪd] a. 有天賦的
   be gifted in...　　有……的天賦
   = be talented in...
   例 Believing that his son is gifted in painting, John has decided to send him to art school.
   約翰相信他兒子有繪畫天賦，決定送他到藝術學校唸書。
10. **craftsman** [ˈkræftsmən] n. 工匠
11. **exquisite** [ˈɛkskwɪzɪt / ɪkˈskwɪzɪt] a. 精美的
12. **delight** [dɪˈlaɪt] n. 欣喜
    To sb's delight, ...　　令某人高興的是，……
    = To sb's joy, ...
13. **enthusiast** [ɪnˈθjuzɪˌæst] n. 熱衷者
14. **eye-catching** [ˈaɪˌkætʃɪŋ] a. 引人注目的

二 文意選填

我們身處資訊的時代。資訊，也可說是知識，被認為和黃金一樣珍貴。我們所重視的資訊是由某些人發現、創造或是以其它方式產生，而所謂的智慧財產權法存在的目的即是保障這些人的權利，只要資訊的持有者抽空將他們的版權註冊即可。這包含了各式各樣的書本、歌曲、電影、軟體、藝術以及發明和科技。幾乎沒有東西可以豁免。版權一詞用來形容某人販賣或製造上述商品的專利權。版權在特定期間內是有效力的。一旦版權過期，這項產品可能會變成公共領域的一部分。也就是說任何人皆可合法使用它。在音樂版權有效的這段期間，歌手或音樂家公開演奏該音樂必須付給版權所有人一筆費用。

《生日快樂歌》無疑是英語中最為大眾所熟知的歌曲。這首歌是一百三十多年前由米爾翠德和派蒂‧席爾所編，它簡單、琅琅上口的曲調被全世界幾十億人傳唱，同時跨越了各大洲之間與語言的藩籬。後來席氏姊妹賣出了她們的歌曲，這首歌轉售了數次，最後被娛樂界巨擘華納音樂集團買下。歌曲版權過期的時間無法確定。有些消息來源說是 1921 年，有些則主張有效期到 1963 年為止。無論如何，華納音樂集團宣稱每次電視、電臺或是影片播放《生日快樂歌》時，他們都應收到一筆費用。他們認為這些都是利用此首歌曲進行公開表演，因此把這件事告上了法庭。令許多人安心的是，法官判定該公司的版權聲明沒有法律依據，所以駁回此案。現在我們都可以放心地唱《生日快樂歌》了。

Unit 04

A 6. 理由
  a. 空格前後兩句皆為完整句子，得知空格應置連接詞連接兩句。
  b. 選項中可作連接詞的僅有 (A) provided（假如；只要），需注意的是，provided 亦為動詞 provide 的過去式或過去分詞，表「提供」。
  c. **provided / providing (that)...**　　如果……；只要……
    例 Ed said I could borrow his car provided that I fill up the tank before returning it.
    艾德說如果我能在還車時把汽油加滿，他就把車子借給我。

G 7. 理由
  a. 空格前有所有格 someone's（某人的），空格後有名詞 right（權利），得知空格應置形容詞以修飾該名詞，形成一名詞詞組。
  b. 選項 (B) best-known（最廣為人知的）、(D) valid（有效的）及 (G) exclusive（專有的）均為形容詞，惟根據語意，(G) 項應為正選。
  c. **exclusive** [ɪkˋsklusɪv] *a.* 獨家的，專用的

Unit 04

__D__ 8. 理由

  a. 空格前為 be 動詞 are，空格後為介詞詞組 for a specified period of time，得知空格應置名詞或形容詞作主詞補語。

  b. 剩餘選項中為名詞或形容詞的有 (B) best-known（最廣為人知的）、(D) valid（有效的）、(E) relief（放心）、(F) entertainment（娛樂界）、(I) uncertainty（不確定性）、(J) court（法庭），惟根據語意，(D) 項應為正選。

  c. **valid** [ˈvælɪd] *a.* 有效力的；令人信服的

__H__ 9. 理由

  a. 空格前有 be 動詞 are，空格後為不定詞 to pay（支付），得知空格應置及物動詞的過去分詞，以與 are 形成被動語態。

  b. 剩餘選項中只有 (H) required（要求）為及物動詞的過去分詞，故為正選。

  c. **require** [rɪˈkwaɪr] *vt.* 要求；需要

   例 It requires a lot of patience to be an editor.
   當編輯需要很大的耐心。

__B__ 10. 理由

  a. 空格前有定冠詞 the，空格後有名詞 song（歌曲），得知空格應置形容詞以修飾該名詞。

  b. 剩餘選項中僅剩 (B) best-known（最廣為人知的）為形容詞，且置入空格後符合語意，故為正選。

  c. **best-known** [ˌbɛstˈnon] *a.* 最廣為人知的（為 well-known 的最高級）

__F__ 11. 理由

  a. 空格前有介詞 of，空格後有名詞 giant（巨人；偉人），得知空格應置形容詞以修飾該名詞。

  b. 剩餘選項中無形容詞，惟名詞 (F) entertainment（娛樂界）可作形容詞，且置入空格後符合語意，故為正選。

  c. **entertainment** [ˌɛntɚˈtenmənt] *n.* 娛樂，樂趣（不可數）；娛樂節目（可數）

__I__ 12. 理由

  a. 空格前有形容詞 some，空格後為介詞詞組 about when the copyright expired，得知空格應置名詞，作為 some 及介詞詞組所修飾的對象。

  b. 剩餘選項中為名詞的有 (E) relief（放心）、(I) uncertainty（不確定性）及 (J) court（法庭），惟根據語意，(I) 項應為正選。

  c. **uncertainty** [ʌnˈsɝtn̩tɪ] *n.* 不確定性（不可數）

__C__ 13. 理由

  a. 連接詞 while 引導副詞子句 others claim (that)...，而空格位於 that 所引導的名詞子句內，空格前有名詞子句的主詞 the copyright（版權），空格後為形容詞 valid（有效的）作主詞補語，得知空格應置連綴動詞以連接該形容詞。

b. 剩餘選項中僅 (C) remained（仍是）為連綴動詞，故為正選。

　　c. **remain** [rɪˋmen] *vi.* 仍是；保持（之後接名詞或形容詞作補語）
　　　例 Wendy has decided to remain single for the rest of her life.
　　　溫蒂已經決定後半輩子單身。

J　14. 理由
　　a. 空格前有 took the matter to，得知空格應置 court（法庭），以形成下列用法：
　　take sb/sth to court　　將某人/事告進法院
　　　例 I'll take you to court if you do not issue a public apology.
　　　如果你不公開道歉，我會上法院告你。

　　b. 根據上述，(J) 項應為正選。

E　15. 理由
　　a. 空格前有定冠詞 the，得知空格應置名詞。
　　b. 剩餘選項 (E) relief（寬心）為名詞，且置入空格後符合語意，故為正選。
　　c. **relief** [rɪˋlif] *n.* 寬心
　　To sb's relief,...　　讓某人寬心的是，……
　　　例 To our relief, Jeff came back safe and sound.
　　　讓我們安心的是，傑夫安然無恙地回來了。

重要單字與片語

1. **consider** [kənˋsɪdɚ] *vt.* 把……視為
   consider A (to be) + N/Adj.　　將 A 視為……
   例 We don't consider him (to be) a friend of ours.
   我們不把他當作是我們的朋友。

2. **intellectual** [ˏɪntəˋlɛktʃuəl] *a.* 智力的
   intellectual property　　智慧財產

3. **holder** [ˋholdɚ] *n.* 持有人

4. **register** [ˋrɛdʒɪstɚ] *vt.* 登記，註冊
   例 The Coca-cola company registered its trademark to prevent it from being copied by the competition.
   可口可樂公司註冊該商標以防止同行仿冒。

5. **copyright** [ˋkɑpɪˏraɪt] *n.* 版權，著作權

6. **virtually** [ˋvɝtʃuəlɪ] *adv.* 幾乎（＝ almost）

7. **expire** [ɪkˋspaɪr] *vi.* 期滿，過期
   例 My passport is going to expire in another two weeks.
   我的護照再兩個禮拜就過期了。

8. **domain** [doˋmen] *n.* 領域，範圍

9. **legally** [ˋligəlɪ] *adv.* 合法地

10. **compose** [kəmˋpoz] *vt.* 作（詩、文、曲）
    例 Beethoven composed nine symphonies.
    貝多芬作了九首交響樂。

Unit 04

Unit 04

11. **catchy** [ˈkætʃɪ] *a.*（曲調等）動聽而易記的
12. **tune** [tjun] *n.* 曲調
13. **conquer** [ˈkɑŋkɚ] *vt.* 征服
    例 When was England conquered by the Normans?
    英格蘭是在何時被諾曼人征服的？
14. **barrier** [ˈbærɪɚ] *n.* 障礙
15. **end up + in +** 地方　　最後處於某地
16. **claim** [klem] *vt. & n.* 主張；宣稱
17. **reason** [ˈrizn̩] *vt. & vi.* 思考，推斷
    例 I reasoned that Paul wouldn't accept the idea.
    我推斷保羅不會接受這個主意。
18. **ground** [ɡraʊnd] *n.* 根據，理由
    on legal grounds　以法律為基礎
19. **dismiss** [dɪsˈmɪs] *vt.* 駁回，不受理（法律用語）
    例 The judge dismissed the case for lack of evidence.
    法官因缺乏證據而駁回該案件。

篇章結構

　　雖然入監服刑被視為一種懲罰犯罪，卻很難能改造犯人，使其成為對社會有生產力的一員。一個令人難過的事實是，太多被釋放的犯人都會因為再犯其他罪行而再度入獄。這就是為什麼紐約州發起了巴德監獄計畫，為的就是要反轉這個趨勢。這個很有挑戰性又篩選嚴格的計畫提供囚犯一個機會入學取得大學學位。這項計畫背後的用意是讓受過教育的更生人有更好的機會來擺脫犯罪的人生。並非所有申請的人都能錄取，這自然是有原因的。參與該計畫就是對毅力和決心的一種考驗。這三百位剛參與計畫的囚犯不能使用網路。沒有獄警的允許，他們也不能使用教科書甚至是圖書館的書籍。即使面臨這些難題，這個創新的計畫非常成功。只有百分之三參加過巴德監獄計畫的畢業生二度入獄。這和該州監獄總體人數形成很大的對比，有百分之四十的受刑人在三年內會再度入獄。

　　最近在一場公開辯論賽中，巴德監獄計畫的辯論隊對抗哈佛大學辯論隊的三位學生，而巴德監獄計畫的辯論隊獲勝了。監獄隊必須主張他們不允許非美國公民的孩童上學受教，而這想法和該隊伍真正的理念恰恰相反。即使辯論的內容有違他們自己的意願，他們充足的準備和獨到的論證徹底擊敗了補助較多、限制較少又受過更好教育的哈佛大學參賽者。這場勝利是監獄隊和該計畫非常榮耀的時刻。該計畫的成功顯示了只要給予機會，人是可以克服龐大的障礙而改過自新的。

C　16. 理由
　　a. 空格前句提到入監服刑被視為對犯罪的一種懲罰，但這其實卻 rarely rehabilitates a criminal（很難能改造犯人），又空格後句提到為了要反轉這個趨勢，紐約州發起了巴德監獄計畫，因此空格應填紐約州發起這計畫的原因，即如選項 (C) 所述「一個令人難過的事實是，太多被釋放的犯人都會因為再犯其他罪行而再度入獄。」
　　b. 根據上述，(C) 項應為正選。

A 17. 理由
　　a. 空格前兩句提到參與巴德監獄計畫非常考驗受刑人的毅力和決心，例如他們 are not allowed access to the internet（不能使用網路），與選項 (A) 所述「沒有獄警的允許，他們也不能使用教科書甚至是圖書館的書籍」形成關聯。
　　b. 根據上述，(A) 項應為正選。

B 18. 理由
　　a. 空格前兩句提到巴德監獄計畫 highly successful（非常成功），只有百分之三參加過巴德監獄計畫的畢業生二度入獄，因此空格應是和沒有參加過此計畫的人來做對比，即如選項 (B) 所述「這和該州監獄總體人數形成很大的對比，有百分之四十的受刑人在三年內會再度入獄。」
　　b. 根據上述，(B) 項應為正選。

E 19. 理由
　　a. 第二段第一句至空格前句提到在一場辯論賽中，巴德監獄計畫的辯論隊打敗哈佛大學辯論隊，此呼應選項 (E) 所述「這場勝利是監獄隊和該計畫非常榮耀的時刻。」
　　b. 根據上述，(E) 項應為正選。

(D) 選項翻譯　在兩週內，該囚犯又犯下新罪行並被送回監獄。

重要單字與片語

1. **punishment** [ˈpʌnɪʃmənt] *n.* 處罰
2. **commit** [kəˈmɪt] *vt.* 犯（罪、錯誤）
3. **rehabilitate** [ˌrihəˈbɪləˌtet] *vt.* （出獄或康復後）開始新生活
　例 The aim of this program is to rehabilitate the prisoners so that they can make a fresh start after they are released.
　本計畫的目的是要讓受刑人重新做人，以便出獄後能展開新的生活。
4. **criminal** [ˈkrɪmənl] *n.* 罪犯
5. **initiative** [ɪˈnɪʃətɪv] *n.* 倡議；新措施
6. **reverse** [rɪˈvɜs] *vt.* 反轉
　例 The manager reversed his own decision the next day.
　經理第二天就推翻了自己的決定。
7. **selective** [səˈlɛktɪv] *a.* 有選擇性的；嚴格篩選的

8. **inmate** [ˈɪnmet] *n.* 囚犯（= prisoner）
9. **enroll** [ɪnˈrol] *vi.* 註冊；（使）加入；招（生）
　enroll in + 課程　　報名參加某課程
　例 I enrolled in the class in the hope that it would sharpen my writing ability.
　我報名這堂課是想要加強我的寫作能力。
10. **enrollment** [ɪnˈrolmənt] *n.* 註冊
11. **perseverance** [ˌpɜsəˈvɪrəns] *n.* 毅力（不可數）
12. **access** [ˈæksɛs] *n.* 接近、使用（人、地、物）的權利、門徑（不可數）
　have access to sb/sth　　接觸到某人/利用某物
　例 Students in this school have easy access to the lab.
　該校的學生可隨時使用實驗室。

13. **permission** [pəˈmɪʃən] *n.* 同意，許可（不可數）
14. **face off** 對決，競爭（與介詞 **against** 並用）
    例 The Japanese team will face off against the France team in the first round.
    日本隊將在第一輪對戰法國隊。
15. **obstacle** [ˈɑbstəkl̩] *n.* 障礙
16. **turn over a new leaf** 翻開新的一頁；改過自新
    例 I'm going to give the boy a chance to turn over a new leaf.
    我要給男孩一個改過自新的機會。

四 閱讀測驗

　　捕蠅草是一種奇特的植物，主要生長在美國北卡羅萊納州和南卡羅萊納州。它們生長在沼澤和溼地等地區，這些地區的土壤酸度高但養分低，因此捕蠅草演化出一種獲取養分的獨特方式，也就是透過捕食昆蟲和其他小型動物的肉來獲取養分。

　　捕蠅草的外型特徵使它們能夠完成這項食肉任務。例如它們有凹陷的葉子，兩片中間有鉸鏈般的連結軸，讓葉子能在不到一秒時間內閉合並將未能覺察的獵物包住。葉子表面有小小的觸感絨毛，當被快速碰觸兩次時，就會告知葉子進行閉合。根據《史密森尼》雜誌的報導，這特色意味捕蠅草可以聰明地區分「甲蟲爬過時碰到或是雨滴打在上面」之間的差別。等葉子閉合後，酵素會幫捕蠅草在平均約十天的時間內消化昆蟲並吸收牠們的養分。每片捕蟲葉 —— 其邊緣還長了一排齒狀刺毛，並且很像打開的蚌殼 —— 可以執行約三次捕蟲任務，然後就會從植物體脫落。此外，捕蠅草在春天時會開由昆蟲授粉的小白花。

　　可惜的是捕蠅草現被視為易危物種。在南卡羅萊納州，新建住宅快速侵占它的天然棲地。在北卡羅萊納州，雖然它們生長在保護區，但常成為偷兒們的目標，利用捕蠅草淺根與簇生的特性輕鬆盜採。全球對它的需求也過高，因為人們被它們獨特的外觀和行為所吸引。保育工作正努力進行，希望能為未來的子孫保護捕蠅草。

__B__ 20. 關於捕蠅草，我們知道什麼事？
(A) 它們生長在不怎麼潮溼或酸性的地區。
(B) 它們擁有被碰觸兩次就會閉合的葉子。
(C) 它們的花上有許多細毛和齒狀物。
(D) 它們無法區別昆蟲和雨滴的不同。

理由
根據本文第二段第三句，可知 (B) 項應為正選。

__C__ **21.** 第二段的 carnivorous 最有可能是什麼意思？
  (A) 噴灑殺蟲劑
  (B) 葉子生長
  (C) 食肉
  (D) 種植蔬菜

  理由
  根據第一段最後一句 "... through the consumption of insects and the meat of other small creatures."可推知承接此句的 carnivorous task 為「食肉任務」，故 (C) 項應為正選。

__B__ **22.** 哪一項對捕蠅草的威脅並未在本文中提及？
  (A) 無視規定並偷盜它們的盜採者。
  (B) 氣候變化影響它們的生長能力。
  (C) 太多人因為它們的獨特性而想要它們。
  (D) 在它們一般生長的地方蓋房子。

  理由
  根據本文第三段第二至四句，可知 (B) 項應為正選。

__D__ **23.** 哪一張圖最有可能是捕蠅草？
  (A)   (B) 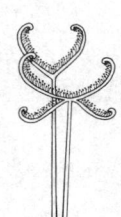
  (C)    (D)

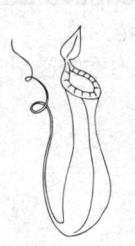

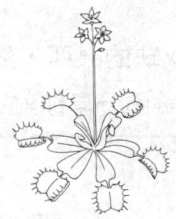

  理由
  根據本文第二段倒數第一至二句，可知 (D) 項應為正選。

Unit 04

重要單字與片語

1. **bog** [bɑg] *n.* 沼澤；泥塘
2. **accomplish** [əˋkɑmplɪʃ] *vt.* 完成（任務）；達到（目標）
   - 例 Through teamwork, we finally accomplished our mission.
     透過團隊合作，我們終於完成任務。
3. **carnivorous** [kɑrˋnɪvərəs] *a.* 食肉的
4. **hinged** [hɪndʒd] *a.* 有鉸鏈的
5. **trigger** [ˋtrɪgɚ] *n.* 引發物；扳機 & *vt.* 引發
6. **plop** [plɑp] *n.* （物體落水的）撲通聲
7. **enzyme** [ˋɛnzaɪm] *n.* 酵素；酶
8. **digest** [daɪˋdʒɛst] *vt.* 消化
   - 例 They say it takes eight hours to digest the food you've eaten.
     據說食物要花八個小時才能消化完畢。
9. **absorb** [əbˋsɔrb] *vt.* 吸收；理解
   - 例 Sponges are used to absorb liquids.
     海綿可用來吸收液體。
10. **edge** [ɛdʒ] *n.* 邊緣；刀鋒
11. **pollinate** [ˋpɑləˏnet] *vt.* 給……傳授花粉
12. **vulnerable** [ˋvʌlnərəb!] *a.* 脆弱的；（生理或心理）易受傷的
13. **encroach** [ɪnˋkrotʃ] *vi.* 侵占，侵入
    encroach on / upon sth 侵犯／蝕某物
    - 例 New development is now encroaching upon the fields where I played as a child.
      新土地的開發已入侵至我兒時遊玩的田野地帶。
14. **poacher** [ˋpotʃɚ] *n.* 盜獵者
15. **cluster** [ˋklʌstɚ] *n.* 群；串；束
16. **captivate** [ˋkæptəˏvet] *vt.* 吸引；使著迷
    - 例 Lily is captivated by the fragrance of roses.
      玫瑰花的香味讓莉莉著迷。

五 混合題

智慧手機是現代生活中是不可或缺的東西，然而對於是否該禁止學生在校園裡使用手機，人們一直爭論不休。請在這個討論區分享你對這個議題的看法。

(A) 安娜
我認為能在學校用手機是比較好的。這麼一來，如果發生緊急狀況，或是因為社團要留校比較晚，或是要跟朋友出去，都可以跟父母聯絡上。

(B) 鮑里斯
與其禁止手機，不如好好想想怎樣把它們融入到課程裡面。我發現當我把科技整合到講課內容裡面時，學生的興致就會高很多。每個人都有手機，就讓他們用嘛！

(C) 克蘿伊
我兒子曾是網路霸凌的受害者，這讓他對上學感到焦慮，因此我支持任何能減少孩子接觸手機的措施。當然，他們放學後還是可以用手機，但至少能夠遠離手機幾個小時。

(D) 迪帕克
一般來說，我不會主張禁止某樣東西，但手機確實對上課造成嚴重的干擾。儘管我要求學生不要用手機，他們還是會在桌子底下偷看。有個禁令會讓管理變得比較容易。

(E) 艾琳娜
禁用手機並不會讓我們這些學生在課堂上變得更專心。我們只會找其他方法來消磨時間，像是聊天或傳紙條。而且，我有時候會用手機查資料，這對我的學習很有幫助。

(F) 菲利克斯
首先別誤會：我是愛用手機的。但如果真的禁用手機，或許我們在下課時就會互相聊天，而不是一直盯著手機螢幕。而且有些人會用手機來霸凌同學，如果禁用手機，就可以阻止這種情況發生。

(G) 吉賽兒
我有些當老師的朋友經常抱怨學生在學校的手機行為問題。我是科班出身的心理學家，知道手機的危險性。過度使用智慧手機，和行為問題、睡眠障礙、溝通技巧缺失以及焦慮等都有關聯。

(H) 廣志
科技已經成為生活的一部分，試圖改變它是沒有意義的。相反的，學校應該鼓勵孩子以負責任的態度使用手機。此外，如果發生緊急情況，我會希望我的女兒能夠馬上聯絡我。

24. 根據以上各人的說法判斷他們支持或反對手機禁令，並將人名填入下表。

支持禁令	反對禁令
Chloe（克蘿伊）	Anna（安娜）
Deepak（迪帕克）	Boris（鮑里斯）
Felix（菲利克斯）	Elena（艾琳娜）
Giselle（吉賽兒）	Hiroshi（廣志）

Unit 04

理由

(1) 根據 (C) Chloe（克蘿伊）的回應第二句 "... I support any measure that reduces kids' access to phones."（……我支持任何能減少孩子接觸手機的措施。）、(D) Deepak（迪帕克）的回應第一及第三句 "... phones are a major distraction during lessons. ... A ban would be much easier to police."（……手機確實對上課造成嚴重的干擾。……有個禁令會讓管理變得比較容易。）、(F) Felix（菲利克斯）的回應第二至三句 "... if there were a ban, maybe we would talk to each other during breaks rather than just stare at our screens. Plus, some kids use their phones to bully other kids, so a ban would put a stop to that."（……如果真的禁用手機，或許我們在下課時就會互相聊天，而不是一直盯著手機螢幕。而且有些人會用手機來霸凌同學，如果禁用手機，就可以阻止這種情況發生。）、及 (G) Giselle（吉賽兒）的回應第二至三句 "As a trained psychologist, I know how dangerous phones can be. Excessive smartphone use is linked to behavioral problems, sleep disturbances, weak communication skills, and anxiety."（我是科班出身的心理學家，知道手機的危險性。過度使用智慧手機，和行為問題、睡眠障礙、溝通技巧缺失以及焦慮等都有關聯。），得知此四人支持禁令，即 Chloe（克蘿伊）、Deepak（迪帕克）、Felix（菲利克斯）及 Giselle（吉賽兒）。

(2) 根據 (A) Anna（安娜）的回應 "I think it's better that we have access to our phones during school hours. That way, we can contact our parents if there's an emergency, or tell them we're staying late for a club or going out with friends."（我認為能在學校用手機是比較好的。這麼一來，如果發生緊急狀況，或是因為社團要留校比較晚，或是要跟朋友出去，都可以跟父母聯絡上。）、(B) Boris（鮑里斯）的回應第一及第三句 "Rather than ban phones, we should focus on integrating them into the curriculum. ... Everyone has a phone, so we should let them use it!"（與其禁止手機，不如好好想想怎樣把它們融入到課程裡面。……每個人都有手機，就讓他們用嘛！）、(E) Elena（艾琳娜）的回應第一及第三句 "Banning phones would not stop us students being distracted during class. ... I sometimes use my phone to look up information that can help me in my studies."（禁用手機並不會讓我們這些學生在課堂上變得更專心。……我有時候會用手機查資料，這對我的學習很有幫助。）、及 (H) Hiroshi（廣志）的回應第二至三句 "... schools should encourage children to use their phones responsibly. Besides, I want my daughter to be able to contact me immediately if there's an emergency."（……學校應該鼓勵孩子以負責任的態度使用手機。此外，如果發生緊急情況，我會希望我的女兒能夠馬上聯絡我。），得知此四人反對禁令，即 Anna（安娜）、Boris（鮑里斯）、Elena（艾琳娜）及 Hiroshi（廣志）。

25. 這些人之中哪幾位最有可能是教師？在下方寫下他們的名字。

<u>Boris（鮑里斯），Deepak（迪帕克）</u>

理由

根據 (B) Boris（鮑里斯）的回應第二句 "I've noticed that my students are much more engaged when I incorporate technology into my lessons."（我發現當我把科技整合到

講課內容裡面時，學生的興致就會高很多。）及 (D) Deepak（迪帕克）的回應第二句 "Even when I ask my class not to use their phones, they sneak a look at them under their desks."（儘管我要求學生不要用手機，他們還是會在桌子底下偷看。），可推知兩人的職業應是教師，故 Boris（鮑里斯）及 Deepak（迪帕克）應為正解。

B **26.** 以下哪一句最能總結吉賽兒的觀點？
(A) 教師應採取行動來防止學生使用智慧手機而不光是抱怨。
(B) 過度使用手機與好幾種壞影響都有關聯。
(C) 心理學家正觀察到各個年齡層都有人手機成癮。
(D) 晚上使用智慧手機的時間過長，會導致學生在課堂上愛打瞌睡。

理由
根據 (G) Giselle（吉賽兒）的回應第三句 "Excessive smartphone use is linked to behavioral problems, sleep disturbances, weak communication skills, and anxiety."（過度使用智慧手機，和行為問題、睡眠障礙、溝通技巧缺失以及焦慮等都有關聯。），可知吉賽兒認為過度使用手機會產生多種壞影響，故 (B) 項應為正選。

Unit 04

重要單字與片語

1. **raging** [ˈredʒɪŋ] *a.* 猛烈的；極端的
2. **ban** [bæn] *vt.* 下令禁止（三態為：ban, banned [bænd], banned）& *n.* 禁令
   例 Many countries ban smoking in public places now.
   現在許多國家禁止在公共場所吸菸。
3. **forum** [ˈforəm] *n.* 論壇，討論會
4. **contribute** sth to + N/V-ing　將某物貢獻／奉獻／捐獻給……
   例 Linda contributed a lot of time to helping local children in that town.
   琳達奉獻許多時間來幫助該城鎮的在地孩童。
5. **curriculum** [kəˈrɪkjələm] *n.* 課程
   （複數形為：curricula [kəˈrɪkjələ] 或 curriculums）

6. **cyberbullying** [ˈsaɪbɚˌbʊlɪɪŋ] *n.* 網路霸凌
   bully [ˈbʊlɪ] *vt.* 欺負，霸凌（三態為：bully, bullied [ˈbʊlɪd], bullied）& *n.* 霸凌者（複數形為：bullies [ˈbʊlɪz]）
   例 Some students bully others to feel powerful.
   有些學生會欺負別人來滿足自己的權力慾。
7. **distraction** [dɪˈstrækʃən] *n.* 分散注意力的事物
   distract [dɪˈstrækt] *vt.* 使分心
   distract sb from sth　使某人在某事上分心
   例 The noise from the construction upstairs distracted me from doing my homework.
   樓上工程的噪音讓我無法專心寫作業。

8. **sneak** [snik] *vt.* 偷拿 & *vi.* 偷偷地走
（三態為：sneak, sneaked / snuck [snʌk], snuck）
sneak a look / glance at...　　快速偷看……一眼
   - 例 Mandy sneaked a look at Jeff before telling us the truth.
   曼蒂偷瞄了傑夫一眼才對我們說出實情。

9. **look up sth / look sth up**　　查閱
（字典、資訊）
   - 例 You can easily look up train times online.
   你可以輕鬆地在網路上查到火車時刻。

10. **Don't get me wrong.**　　別誤會我。

11. **excessive** [ɪkˋsɛsɪv] *a.* 過多的
excessive drinking / eating　　暴飲／食

12. **behavioral** [bɪˋhevjərəl] *a.* 行為的

13. **disturbance** [dɪsˋtɝbəns] *n.* 干擾

14. **summarize** [ˋsʌməˌraɪz] *vt.* & *vi.* 概述，摘錄大意
   - 例 Gloria summarized the story for those who hadn't heard it.
   葛蘿莉亞為沒聽到這個故事的人講了個概要。

15. **outcome** [ˋaʊtˌkʌm] *n.* 結果

16. **be / become addicted to + N/V-ing**
對……上癮
   - 例 Terence is addicted to watching drama series every night.
   泰倫斯每天晚上都沉迷於追劇。

Unit 05

一 綜合測驗

　　水果蝙蝠是全世界約一千種蝙蝠品種中的一種。牠們不同於其它多數的蝙蝠，因為大部分的物種以昆蟲為食，而水果蝙蝠的飲食則由水果組成，就如牠們的名字所暗示。這種蝙蝠也會食用花朵，代表牠們能幫許多種類的植物傳播花粉。另一個可以區分水果蝙蝠與其它蝙蝠的特點是牠們依賴氣味，而不是依賴一種被稱為回聲定位的雷達。這種敏銳的嗅覺幫助牠們找到成熟的果實與芳香的花朵，指引牠們前往下一頓美食。

　　對於棲息在澳洲北部熱帶雨林的水果蝙蝠而言很不幸的是，一種從南美洲傳入的壁蝨正使牠們大量死亡。澳洲的托加蝙蝠醫院對於這項危機已做出回應並投入救援。他們集合了一群無私奉獻的生物學家及動物愛好者定期進入雨林檢查是否有年幼的蝙蝠從樹上落下。這種事可能在蝙蝠媽媽死於壁蝨病後發生。工作人員在醫院中會幫忙養育年幼的蝙蝠，藉由照顧牠們與餵食牛奶讓牠們恢復健康。托加蝙蝠醫院以這樣的方式救了數百隻蝙蝠，確實是水果蝙蝠的好朋友。

__B__ 1. 理由
　　a. (A) **impose** [ɪmˋpoz] *vt.* 強加於
　　　　　impose sth on sb　　將某事強加於某人身上
　　　　　例 The government imposed strict hygiene regulations on all restaurants.
　　　　　政府對所有餐廳強制執行嚴格的衛生規定。
　　　(B) **imply** [ɪmˋplaɪ] *vt.* 暗示，暗指
　　　　　例 The lawyer's statement implied his client was guilty.
　　　　　那名律師的陳述暗指他的當事人有罪。
　　　(C) **imagine** [ɪˋmædʒɪn] *vt.* 想像
　　　　　例 My five-year-old sister likes to imagine herself as a princess.
　　　　　我五歲的妹妹喜歡想像自己是一位公主。
　　　(D) **imitate** [ˋɪməˏtet] *vt.* 模仿，仿效
　　　　　例 Peter is good at imitating different English accents.
　　　　　彼得很會模仿英語中不同的口音。
　　b. 根據語意，(B) 項應為正選。

__D__ 2. 理由
　　a. (A) **focus on sound**　　專注於聲音
　　　　　focus on...　　專注於……
　　　　　例 The professor focused on environmental issues during the seminar.
　　　　　那位教授在研討會上專注於環境問題。

(B) **adjust to light**　　適應光線
adjust to + N　　適應……
例 It took Miley a while to adjust to the cold weather in that country.
米莉花了一些時間才適應那個國家寒冷的天氣。

(C) **react to touch**　　對觸摸有反應
react to + N　　對……有反應
例 The body reacts to allergens by producing antibodies.
身體對過敏原的反應是產生抗體。

(D) **rely on scent**　　依賴氣味
rely on...　　依賴……
scent [sɛnt] n. 氣味
例 Nowadays, students often rely on the internet for research.
現在的學生經常依賴網路來進行研究。

b. 根據語意，可知 (D) 項應為正選。

C 3. 理由

a. (A) **in contrast to...**　　與……形成對比
例 The puppy appears small in contrast to its mother.
這隻小狗的體型和狗媽媽比起來小多了。

(B) **in favor of...**　　贊同……
例 The manager was in favor of the proposal.
經理贊同這提案。

(C) **in response to...**　　對……做出回應
例 Sara gave a chuckle in response to the tricky question.
莎拉以輕聲一笑來回應這個弔詭的問題。

(D) **by means of...**　　藉由……
例 Thoughts are usually expressed by means of language.
思想通常經由語言表達。

b. 根據語意，(C) 項應為正選。

C 4. 理由

a. (A) **frustrated** [ˈfrʌstretɪd] a. 感到沮喪的
例 Louis was frustrated with the outcome of the presidential election.
路易士對總統大選的結果感到沮喪。

(B) **introverted** [ˈɪntrəˌvɝtɪd] a. 內向的
extroverted [ˈɛkstrəˌvɝtɪd] a. 外向的
例 Ruby is very introverted, and she always talks in a small voice.
露比十分內向，她說話的聲音總是很小。

(C) **dedicated** [ˈdɛdəˌketɪd] *a.* 盡心盡力的；盡職的
　例 The company awarded ten dedicated staff members this year.
　　該公司今年授獎給十位盡職的員工。
(D) **intimidated** [ɪnˈtɪməˌdetɪd] *a.* 膽怯的
　例 George feels intimidated whenever he is on stage.
　　每當在臺上時，喬治就會感到膽怯。
b. 根據語意，(C) 項應為正選。

A 5. 理由
a. (A) **die of...** 死於……（多指疾病）
　比較
　die from... 死於……（多指外傷、事故）
　例 The poor young man died of lung cancer.
　　這個可憐的年輕人死於肺癌。
　　The girl died from head injuries.
　　這名女孩死於頭部創傷。
(B) **talk of...** 談到……
　例 Kevin and Kate are talking of their love story.
　　凱文與凱特正談到他們的戀愛故事。
(C) **look for...** 尋找……；期盼……
　例 My lipstick is missing. Could you help me look for it?
　　我的口紅不見了。你可以幫我找找看嗎？
(D) **die for...** 為……而死
　例 I would rather die for my belief than go against it.
　　我寧願為信念而死，也不願違背它。
b. 根據語意及用法，(A) 項應為正選。

重要單字與片語

1. **roughly** [ˈrʌflɪ] *adv.* 大約
2. **species** [ˈspiʃiz] *n.* 物種（單複數同形）
　a species of...　一種……
　two species of...　兩種……
3. **feed on sth**　（動物）以……為食
　例 Pandas feed on bamboo.
　　熊貓以竹子為食。
4. **pollinate** [ˈpɑləˌnet] *vt.* 授粉
5. **fragrant** [ˈfregrənt] *a.* 芬芳的
6. **import** [ɪmˈpɔrt] *vt.* & [ˈɪmpɔrt] *n.* 進口；引入
7. **kill off...**　使……大量死亡；使……滅絕
　例 Global warming is killing off polar bears.
　　全球暖化使得北極熊大量死亡。

8. **leap into action** 開始行動，馬上做
   leap [lip] *vi.* 跳躍（三態為：leap, leaped / leapt [lɛpt], leaped / leapt [lɛpt]）

   例 Upon hearing the fire alarm, all the staff members leapt into action and left the building.
   一聽到火警聲響，所有員工都馬上離開那棟建築。

9. **nurse** [nɝs] *vt.* 看護，照顧

二 文意選填

　　白頭捲尾猴的自然棲息地在中美洲及南美洲的北部，牠們會以約二十隻的群體成群行動。即使你從未去過那些地方，你也很有可能看過這群有著長尾巴、大部分為黑色毛髮的身體、粉色的臉蛋以及在脖子和肩膀周圍有白色毛髮的生物。牠們與黑猩猩是電影中最常見的靈長類動物。《博物館驚魂夜》三部曲主打一隻名叫水晶的白頭捲尾猴。那隻猴子似乎是天生的喜劇女演員，也曾出演《森林泰山》及《美國派》系列電影。

　　除了讓白頭捲尾猴躍上大銀幕，人類也為這群極其聰穎的動物找到另一項有意義的用處。我們發現牠們具有幫助行動不便人士的潛能。一個名為「伸出猿手：身障人士的猴子好幫手」的非營利組織於 1979 年創立，該組織訓練捲尾猴也教導人們與猴子互動的最佳方式。猴子有諸多優點勝過其它傳統上作為服務性動物的生物，譬如導盲犬或是陪伴老年人的貓咪。其一，牠們的雙手有手指，使牠們可以執行各類普通且有用的任務。身體功能受損的人士因此得以獲得協助。這些任務包括將書本翻頁、按電子設備的按鈕、將吸管插入瓶子裡，以及撿拾掉落的物品。此外，白頭捲尾猴身上長的是毛髮而不是軟毛，因此人們比較不會對這些非人類幫手產生過敏。另一項好處是牠們的壽命通常超過三十年，這讓牠們成為良好又長久的夥伴。讓我們一起舉杯，或至少吃根香蕉，來向白頭捲尾猴致敬吧！

I　6. 理由
　　a. 空格前有定冠詞 the，空格後有介詞詞組 with their... shoulders，得知空格應置名詞，作為介詞詞組所修飾的對象。
　　b. 選項中為名詞的有 (D) disabilities（障礙）、(G) partners（夥伴）、(H) feature（特色）、(I) creatures（生物）及 (J) advantages（優點），惟根據語意，(I) 項應為正選。
　　c. **creature** [ˈkritʃɚ] *n.* 生物

H　7. 理由
　　a. 空格前有主詞 All three *Night at the Museum* movies（《博物館驚魂夜》三部曲），空格後有名詞 a white-headed capuchin（一隻白頭捲尾猴），得知空格應置及物動詞。

b. 選項中 (A) enable（使能夠）及 (H) feature（主打）為及物動詞，惟根據語意，(H) 項應為正選。

c. **feature** [ˈfitʃɚ] *vt.* 主打；以……為特色

例 This teen magazine features street fashion.
這本青少年雜誌的主要特色為街頭流行。

C **8.** 理由

a. 空格前有指示代名詞 these 及副詞 highly（非常），空格後有名詞 animals（動物），得知空格應置形容詞，以被 highly 修飾，並能修飾 animals。

b. 選項中 (C) intelligent（聰明的）及 (E) impaired（受損的）為形容詞，惟根據語意，(C) 項應為正選。

c. **intelligent** [ɪnˈtɛlədʒənt] *a.* 聰穎的，聰明的

D **9.** 理由

a. 空格前有名詞 mobility（活動性），得知空格應置另一名詞以與 mobility 形成名詞詞組，並與介詞 with 形成介詞詞組修飾前面的名詞 people（人）。

b. 剩餘選項中為名詞的有 (D) disabilities（障礙）、(G) partners（夥伴）及 (J) advantages（優點），惟根據語意，(D) 項應為正選。

c. **disability** [ˌdɪsəˈbɪlətɪ] *n.* 障礙

F **10.** 理由

a. 原句實為：

A non-profit organization called Helping Hands: Monkey Helpers for the Disabled was set up in 1979, <u>and it</u> <u>trains</u> the capuchins and also <u>teaches</u> people how best to interact with the monkeys.

上句中對等連接詞 and 連接兩個主詞相同的子句，可省略 and 及第二個子句的主詞 it，再將動詞 trains 及 teaches 分別改為現在分詞 training 及 teaching，形成分詞構句。

b. 根據上述，(F) 項應為正選。

c. **train** [tren] *vt.* 訓練；培養

J **11.** 理由

a. 空格前有修飾複數可數名詞的數量形容詞 several（數個的），得知空格應置複數可數名詞，以被 several 修飾。

b. 剩餘選項中 (G) partners（夥伴）及 (J) advantages（優點）均為複數可數名詞，惟根據語意，(J) 項應為正選。

c. **advantage** [ədˈvæntɪdʒ] *n.* 優點；優勢；益處
   disadvantage [ˌdɪsədˈvæntɪdʒ] *n.* 缺點；劣勢

A 12. 理由
    a. 空格前有關係代名詞 that 作形容詞子句的主詞，指涉前面的先行詞 fingers（手指），空格後有代名詞 them（牠們），得知空格應置及物動詞，以接 them 作其受詞。
    b. 剩餘選項中僅 (A) enable（使能夠）為及物動詞，且置入空格後符合語意，故為正選。
    c. **enable** [ɪnˋeb!̣] *vt.* 使能夠
       enable sb to V　　使某人能夠……
       例 Todd's mastery of Spanish enabled him to get the job.
          陶德精通西班牙文，所以得到了那份工作。

E 13. 理由
    a. 空格前有介詞 with，其後方應接名詞或名詞詞組，空格後有名詞詞組 physical functions（身體功能），得知空格應置形容詞，以修飾 physical functions，此處 with 引導的介詞詞組修飾前面的名詞 people（人）。
    b. 剩餘選項中僅 (E) impaired（受損的）為形容詞，且置入空格後符合語意，故為正選。
    c. **impaired** [ɪmˋpɛrd] *a.* 受損的

B 14. 理由
    a. 本句動詞為及物動詞 include（包括），其後接兩個動名詞詞組 turning the pages of books（將書本翻頁）及 pressing buttons on electronic devices（按電子設備的按鈕）作受詞，而空格後有對等連接詞 and 連接另一個動名詞詞組 picking up dropped objects（撿拾掉落的物品），得知空格應置動名詞，以與上述三個動名詞形成對等。
    b. 剩餘選項中僅 (B) inserting（插入）為動名詞，且置入空格後符合語意，故為正選。
    c. **insert** [ɪnˋsɝt] *vt.* 投入，插入
       例 Insert coins into the machine and press the button.
          將錢幣投入機器，再按下按鈕。

G 15. 理由
    a. 空格前有形容詞 good（良好的）及 long-term（長久的），得知空格應置名詞以被此兩個形容詞修飾。
    b. 剩餘選項 (G) partners（夥伴）為名詞，且置入空格後符合語意，故為正選。
    c. **partner** [ˋpɑrtnɚ] *n.* 夥伴；搭檔；合夥人；配偶

重要單字與片語

1. **habitat** [ˋhæbə͵tæt] *n.* （動物）棲息地
2. **troop** [trup] *n.* 一群（人或動物等）；軍隊（恆用複數）
   a troop of elephants　　一群大象
3. **along with...** 與……一起
= together with...
   例 Pat along with his colleagues took part in the meeting.
      派特與他的同事們一起參加該場會議。

4. **chimpanzee** [ˌtʃɪmpænˈzi] *n.* 黑猩猩
（可簡寫成：chimp [tʃɪmp]）

5. **primate** [ˈpraɪmet] *n.* 靈長類動物

6. **comic** [ˈkɑmɪk] *a.* 喜劇的；滑稽的，好笑的
a comic actor / actress　男 / 女諧星
a comic strip　　連環漫畫
a comic book　　漫畫書

7. **mobility** [moˈbɪlətɪ] *n.* 活動性，靈活性（不可數）

8. **set up...**　建立……
= establish...
    例 Lilly decided to set up a design studio of her own.
    莉莉決定成立自己的設計工作室。

9. **interact** [ˌɪntɚˈækt] *vi.* 互動
interact with...　與……互動
    例 At the end of her performance, Helen interacted with the audience.
    在表演的最後，海倫與觀眾互動。

10. **a seeing-eye dog**　導盲犬
= a guide dog

11. **companion** [kəmˈpænjən] *n.* 伴侶，同伴（可數）

companionship [kəmˈpænjənˌʃɪp] *n.* 友誼（不可數）
比較
company [ˈkʌmpənɪ] *n.* 伴侶，同伴，作伴（集合名詞，不可數）

12. **assist** [əˈsɪst] *vt.* & *vi.* 幫助
assist sb in + V-ing　幫助某人做……
    例 Could you assist me in installing the new software?
    你能不能協助我安裝這套新軟體？

13. **electronic** [ɪˌlɛkˈtrɑnɪk] *a.* 電子的

14. **straw** [strɔ] *n.* 吸管（可數）；稻草（不可數）

15. **allergy** [ˈælədʒɪ] *n.* 過敏

16. **make a toast to sb**　向某人敬酒
toast [tost] *n.* 敬酒，乾杯 & *vt.* 向……敬酒

17. **in honor of...**　向……致敬；以紀念……
    例 In Rita's retirement party, everybody toasted her in honor of her dedication to the job.
    在莉塔的退休派對上，大家舉杯向她對工作的奉獻致敬。

三 篇章結構

阿米爾・罕出生於 1965 年，是名電影製作人的兒子。他是印度寶萊塢影壇中最知名和成功的人物之一。多年來，他以挑選多樣化且饒富意義的角色聞名，這些角色往往挑戰社會常規。在投入一個角色後，罕會專注地融入其中，儘可能使該角色更具說服力。他對角色和其他企畫盡心盡力的職業道德感很強烈，因而獲得了一個綽號：完美先生。他的敬業精神體現在為角色進行的身體改造與深入研究每個角色之中。截至目前四十多年的職業生涯中，他的努力為他贏得了無數的獎項。

然而，罕還有另外一面。他很熱衷於政治、人道主義和環境議題。這些興趣促使他在演藝界以外的地方帶來更大的影響。聯合國兒童基金會曾任命他為南亞地區的親善大使。透由

這樣的身分，他積極倡導和兒童權利、教育及健康相關的新措施。2013 年，《時代雜誌》將他列入全球百大影響力人物之中。

　　罕透過他所製作的談話節目《真相訪談》而對印度社會的影響甚鉅。<u>他藉由該節目來處理印度普遍存在的社會問題。</u>節目中涵蓋性別不平等、童工問題和貪腐等議題，並引發全國性的討論。然而，他的觀點有時被認為具有爭議性。他的想法、提議和理念在印度這樣保守的國家並非總是受到支持。<u>儘管如此，罕仍持續為社會正義奮鬥，試圖改變這個世界讓它更美好。</u>即使面對批評，他依舊堅持利用自身的影響力推動有意義的改變。他期許自己的努力能不斷地帶出那些社會中被多數人忽略的難題。

__E__ **16.** 理由
  a. 空格前句提到阿米爾・罕的個人基本資料，如出生年分及是名製作人的小孩，而選項 **(E)** 也提及罕個人的相關資訊，即「他是印度寶萊塢影壇中最知名和成功的人物之一。」
  b. 根據上述，**(E)** 項應為正選。

__D__ **17.** 理由
  a. 空格前句提到罕對政治、人道主義和環境議題 is passionately interested（很熱衷），又空格後三句提到聯合國兒童基金會曾任命他為南亞地區的親善大使，他也積極倡導和兒童權利、教育及健康相關的新措施，且《時代雜誌》曾將他列入全球百大影響力人物之中，這些皆與選項 **(D)** 中的 these interests（這些興趣）和 even greater influence outside the entertainment world（在演藝界以外的地方帶來更大的影響）形成關聯。
  b. 根據上述，**(D)** 項應為正選。

__C__ **18.** 理由
  a. 空格前句提到罕透過他製作的談話節目而對印度社會的影響甚鉅，又空格後句提到節目中涵蓋性別不平等、童工問題和貪腐等議題，因此可推知罕應是如同選項 **(C)** 所述「他藉由該節目來處理遍布印度的社會問題。」
  b. 根據上述，**(C)** 項應為正選。

__B__ **19.** 理由
  a. 空格前兩句提到罕的觀點和想法等被認為 controversial（具有爭議性）且 have not always been popular（並非總是受到支持），又空格後兩句提到罕仍努力推動有意義的改變並不斷地帶出那些社會中被多數人忽略的難題，此呼應選項 **(B)** 所述「儘管如此，罕仍持續為社會正義奮鬥，試圖改變這個世界讓它更美好。」
  b. 根據上述，**(B)** 項應為正選。

(A) 選項翻譯 在這部電影中，罕飾演一名業餘摔角手，並訓練他的女兒從事這項運動。

Unit 05

重要單字與片語

1. **prominent** [ˈprɑmənənt] *a.* 重要的；顯著的，醒目的
2. **societal** [səˈsaɪətḷ] *a.* 與社會相關的
   a societal norm　社會規範
3. **commit** [kəˈmɪt] *vt.* 投入；承諾；（使）忠於；（使）致力於
   commit to + N/V-ing　承諾（做）……
   commit oneself to + N/V-ing
   某人致力於……
   例 You can think it over; you don't have to commit to anything right now.
   您可以考慮一下；您現在不必承諾任何事情。
   Mr. White has committed himself to teaching over the past twenty years.
   懷特先生過去二十年來都獻身於教育。
4. **intently** [ɪnˈtɛntlɪ] *adv.* 專心地，專注地
5. **so as to + V**　為了……
   = in order to + V
   例 Karen got up early so as to see the sunrise.
   凱倫早起以便觀看日出。
6. **convincing** [kənˈvɪnsɪŋ] *a.* 令人信服的
7. **ethic** [ˈɛθɪk] *n.* 道德準則（常用複數）
   work ethic　職業道德；敬業心
   a code of ethics　道德規範
8. **acquire** [əˈkwaɪr] *vt.* 獲得
9. **perfectionist** [pɚˈfɛkʃənɪst] *n.* 完美主義者
10. **dedication** [ˌdɛdəˈkeʃən] *n.* 奉獻（不可數）（與介詞 to 並用）
11. **span** [spæn] *vt.* （時間）持續；橫跨
    （三態為：span, spanned [spænd], spanned）
12. **ambassador** [æmˈbæsədɚ] *n.* 大使

13. **initiative** [ɪˈnɪʃətɪv] *n.* 新措施，倡議；自發性，進取心（不可數）
14. **influential** [ˌɪnfluˈɛnʃəl] *a.* 有影響力的
15. **prevail** [prɪˈvel] *vi.* 勝過（與介詞 over 並用）；流行
    prevail over sb/sth　勝過某人／某事
    例 I believe that right will prevail over wrong in the end.
    我相信正義終將戰勝不公。
    Those kinds of superstitions still prevail in certain areas.
    那種迷信在某些地區還是很普遍。
16. **tackle** [ˈtækḷ] *vt.* 處理（問題）
    例 The government is determined to take immediate measures to tackle inflation.
    政府決心立即採取行動來處理通貨膨脹的問題。
17. **inequality** [ˌɪnɪˈkwɑlətɪ] *n.* 不平等，不均等
18. **controversial** [ˌkɑntrəˈvɝʃəl] *a.* 有爭議性的
19. **recommendation** [ˌrɛkəmɛnˈdeʃən] *n.* 建議
20. **cause** [kɔz] *n.* 理想，大業，抱負
21. **conservative** [kənˈsɝvətɪv] *a.* 保守的
22. **advocate** [ˈædvəˌket] *vi. & vt.* 主張，提倡 & [ˈædvəkət] *n.* 支持者，擁護者
    advocate for...　主張／提倡……
    例 Worried about deforestation, the group advocates for stricter laws to protect forests.
    擔心森林砍伐，該團體主張制定更嚴格的法律來保護森林。
23. **amateur** [ˈæməˌtʃɚ] *a.* 業餘的 & *n.* 業餘人士
24. **wrestler** [ˈrɛslɚ] *n.* 摔角手

四 閱讀測驗

　　鎧甲在整個人類歷史上被用來保護戰士、騎士和士兵免受敵方武器的傷害。鎧甲所使用的材料反映當時的科技發展以及所需要抵禦的武器類型。遠古文明可能已經使用了某些形式的鎧甲。例如有證據顯示西元前十一世紀的中國戰士披掛著多層犀牛皮製成的鎧甲。

　　不過現在許多人聽到「鎧甲」一詞時，可能想到的是中世紀，在這一千年的期間，確實有兩種主要的防護衣。第一種是鎖子甲，通常由串在一起的小鐵環製成，實際上自羅馬帝國時代以來一直都在使用，但由於對矛、劍和箭提供不錯的保護，讓它在中世紀變得更加普遍。而板甲是在此時期的後段發展出來的。板甲通常由鋼製成，複雜程度逐漸遞增，到了能讓穿戴者幾乎能活動自如的地步。甚至連手指的每個關節都會被小小的金屬板覆蓋。由於強度較佳以及有讓致命武器偏斜出去的能力，板甲在中世紀接近尾聲時幾乎已經取代了鎖子甲。

　　現代鎧甲堅固且輕量。例子之一是合成材料克維拉纖維，由波蘭裔的美國化學家史蒂芬妮‧克沃勒克於 1960 年代研發，通常用於製造防彈背心。士兵們常穿著結合克維拉纖維和陶瓷板的護甲。這種護板嵌入防彈背心的夾層中，增加對高速發射的步槍子彈多一層的防護。

　D　**20.** 下列鎧甲種類出現的順序為何？
　　a. 鋼板
　　b. 獸皮
　　c. 鐵環
　　d. 人造材質

　(A) d > a > b > c
　(B) a > d > c > b
　(C) c > b > d > a
　(D) b > c > a > d

理由
本文第一段先提及遠古時代的戰士穿以犀牛皮製成的鎧甲，第二段提到中世紀時出現由串在一起的小鐵環製成的鎖子甲，之後則出現用鋼製的板甲，第三段提及現代鎧甲是由合成材料克維拉纖維製成。可知 (D) 項應為正選。

　B　**21.** 本文為何提及羅馬帝國？
　(A) 因為羅馬人穿戴讓他們移動不費力的鎧甲。
　(B) 因為那個時期使用了某特別類型的鎧甲。
　(C) 因為羅馬士兵用了和中國戰士相同的材料。
　(D) 因為那遠古時代的鎧甲尚未被超越。

理由
根據本文第二段第二句，可知 (B) 項應為正選。

Unit 05

__D__ 22. 第二段的 **deflect** 最有可能是哪個意思？
(A) 使某物感覺疼痛。
(B) 讓某物輕易進入。
(C) 防止某物變得堅固。
(D) 使某物改變方向。

> 理由
> 根據本文第二段最後一句 "With its superior strength and ability to deflect lethal weapons so that they changed course, ..."（由於強度較佳以及有讓致命武器偏斜出去的能力，……）可知，(D) 項應為正選。

__C__ 23. 作者如何總結本文？
(A) 藉由詳細介紹一位知名化學家的背景。
(B) 藉由提及古代和現代鎧甲的相似處。
(C) 藉由提供現代鎧甲的例子。
(D) 藉由討論槍枝和子彈的歷史。

> 理由
> 根據本文最後一段提及現代鎧甲的材質作為例子，可知 (C) 項應為正選。

重要單字與片語

1. **reflective** [rɪˋflɛktɪv] *a.* 反映／表現……的；反光的
2. **repel** [rɪˋpɛl] *vt.* 抵禦；擊退
   例 The soldiers managed to repel the invading army and maintain control of the area.
   士兵終能擊退來犯的敵軍，並維持對該地區的掌控。
3. **primitive** [ˋprɪmətɪv] *a.* 原始的，遠古的
4. **rhinoceros** [raɪˋnɑsərəs] *n.* 犀牛
5. **chain mail** 鎖子甲（古代用於保護士兵的鎧甲）
6. **commonplace** [ˋkɑmən͵ples] *a.* 普遍的；普通的
7. **sophistication** [sə͵fɪstəˋkeʃən] *n.* 精密化；老練（不可數）
8. **joint** [dʒɔɪnt] *n.* 關節
9. **deflect** [dɪˋflɛkt] *vt.* & *vi.* （使）轉向；（使）偏斜
   例 The police used their shields to deflect the bottles thrown by the rioters.
   警察用他們的防護盾將暴民丟過來的瓶子擋開。
10. **lethal** [ˋliθəl] *a.* 致命的
11. **synthetic** [sɪnˋθɛtɪk] *a.* 合成的 & *n.* 合成物／纖維（常用複數）
12. **ceramic** [səˋræmɪk] *a.* 陶瓷的 & *n.* 陶瓷作品（常用複數）
13. **round** [raʊnd] *n.* （子彈的）一發

五 混合題

父母是否應該給孩子零用錢是一個眾說紛紜的話題。我們向兩名父母和兩名孩子詢問了他們對此事的看法。

寶拉
我之前會每週給女兒零用錢。我認為這能教她經濟獨立和花錢的責任感。我希望她能明白有些東西是必買的，有些則是想買的，我們沒法總是兩者兼得。但她根本沒有安排支出的優先順序。零用錢也讓她覺得是天經地義的事：她理所當然認為應該得到這筆錢，甚至為了金額跟我爭論。因此我堅不讓步，乾脆取消了她的零用錢。

維歐拉
有零用錢真好！對自己的金錢有更多的掌控權，讓我自覺像是個負責的大人了，而且因為我的零用錢取決於我完成多少家事，這讓我在幫忙做家事更有動力。我甚至自願打掃廁所和通排水管，這可真是世界上最噁爛的家事了！不過週末拿到錢時，所有的辛苦工作都變得值得，我覺得我的努力實實在在地得到了回報。

詹姆士
毫無疑問，給我兒子零用錢幫助他成為獨立的年輕人。他現在處理金錢時更自信，零用錢讓他明白金錢的價值。如果他想買某樣東西，他會看價錢並計算需要多久才能有足夠的錢。然後他每週都會存錢直到存夠所需的金額。這些重要的能力對他成年後會有幫助。基於我們的經驗，我會鼓勵所有父母給孩子零用錢。

富蘭克林
我喜歡拿零用錢！和朋友出去玩時能花自己的錢是很棒的感覺。不過零用錢不只是有錢拿來犒賞自己而已。我很喜歡幫助別人和回饋社區，所以我已經開始小額捐款給本地慈善機構。我認為有能力的人幫助社會上的弱勢群體是很重要的。我打算一直把我的部分零用錢用於這個目的，並希望能激勵我的朋友也來效法。

24. 維歐拉的零用錢和她完成多少家事有關，這讓她有<u>動力</u>幫忙做更多家事。

理由
空格前為定冠詞 the，空格後為不定詞 to，可得知空格應置名詞。根據維歐拉看法的第二句 "..., **I have been motivated to help out around the house more.**"（……，這讓我在幫忙做家事更有動力。）得知，空格應置與 **motivated** 相關的名詞 **motivation**。

Unit 05

25. 詹姆士確信給他兒子零用錢讓他在處理金錢上更有信心。

> 理由

空格前為副詞 more，可得知空格應置形容詞。根據詹姆士看法的第二句 "He now has much more confidence when dealing with money, ..."（他現在處理金錢時更自信，……）得知，空格應置與 confidence 相關的形容詞 confident。

26. 這些回應中的哪個字表示「你相信你應得到某種特權或特別待遇」？

entitlement（應得的權利）

> 理由

根據寶拉看法的倒數第二句 "Her allowance also gave her a sense of entitlement: ..."（零用錢也讓她覺得是天經地義的事：……）可推測 entitlement（應得的權利）應為正解。

27. 下列哪些金錢觀念是受訪者聚焦的所在？在正確的名字旁寫下對應的字母。

(A) 區別需要和想要
(B) 做對社會負責的決定
(C) 理解預算和儲蓄
(D) 感恩勞動所得到的回報

寶拉：　(A)
維歐拉：　(D)
詹姆士：　(C)
富蘭克林：(B)

> 理由

根據寶拉看法的第三句，得知 (A) 項應為正選。維歐拉看法的最後一句，得知 (D) 項應為正選。詹姆士看法的第三、四句，得知 (C) 項應為正選。富蘭克林看法的最後一句，得知 (B) 項應為正選。

重要單字與片語

1. **allowance** [əˋlaʊəns] *n.* 零用錢〔美〕
   （= pocket money〔英〕）

2. **prioritize** [praɪˋɔrəˌtaɪz] *vt.* & *vi.* 確定優先順序

3. **entitlement** [ɪnˋtaɪt!mənt] *n.* 應得的權利

4. **take sth for granted** 視某事物為理所當然
   例 Those who are not grateful tend to take everything they have for granted.
   不懂得感恩的人往往視所擁有的一切為理所當然。

5. **put my foot down** 堅決制止
6. **chore** [tʃɔr] *n.* 雜務
7. **unclog** [ʌnˋklɑg] *vt.* 使暢通
8. **without (a) doubt** 無疑地
   例 Phil is without a doubt a man you can trust.
   毫無疑問菲爾是一個你可以信任的人。
9. **set... aside** 留出（金錢 / 時間）
   例 Sarah sets aside some time for exercising every day.
   莎拉每天都會留點時間做運動。
10. **means** [minz] *n.* 金錢；財富（恆為複數），方法（單複數同形）
11. **privilege** [ˋprɪvəlɪdʒ] *n.* 特權
12. **differentiate** [͵dɪfəˋrɛnʃɪ͵et] *vt. & vi.* 區別
    differentiate A from B 區別 A 和 B 的不同
    例 I can't differentiate the genuine designer bag from the fake one because they look so much alike.
    我分不清真的名牌包跟仿冒品，因為它們看起來太像了。
13. **labor** [ˋlebɚ] *n.* 勞動，勞力

Unit 05

Unit 06

一 綜合測驗

　　在餐廳用餐除了是一種飲食經驗，也是一種社交活動。因此有些人認為獨自吃飯這件事是孤單的人在不情願的情形下採取的方式。這真是大錯特錯。事實上，許多人偏好單獨用餐，原因可多了。

　　首先，一整天工作下來，沉浸在有品質的「個人時間」是很棒的放鬆方式。放鬆的方式可能包含邊吃邊閱讀，或是邊觀賞最喜歡的線上電視劇。但是如果有個同伴堅持要小聊一下，或需要你在他們近期處理的個人危機上提供建議，這些活動便無法進行。此外，獨自用餐提供了安靜思考的機會，讓人能夠在沒有外界干擾的情況下沉澱心情。

　　另一個小確幸是想吃什麼就能吃什麼。舉例來說，和素食者一起用餐會大幅減少自己擁有的餐點選擇。但若單獨用餐則沒有這些限制，能夠盡情享受自己最愛的食物而無需妥協。最後，單獨用餐讓人不被其他人打擾，能盡情享受餐點的香氣和美味。在不需談話的情況下，人們能夠完全沉浸在食物的風味之中。

D **1.** 理由

　　a. (A) **as a result**　因此
　　　　例 Charles didn't study hard. As a result, he failed the test.
　　　　　　查爾斯沒有用功唸書。因此，他考試不及格。
　　(B) **in addition**　此外
　　　　例 John has a heart of gold. In addition, he is hard-working.
　　　　　　約翰有一副仁慈的心腸。此外，他也很認真。
　　(C) **as usual**　如往常一樣
　　　　例 As usual, Blake was late for work again this morning.
　　　　　　和往常一樣，布萊克今天早上上班又遲到了。
　　(D) **in fact**　事實上
　　　　例 Tommy looks like a regular guy, but in fact, he is a billionaire.
　　　　　　湯米看起來像普通人，但事實上他是個億萬富翁。

　　b. 根據語意，(D) 項應為正選。

A **2.** 理由

　　a. (A) **unwind** [ʌnˋwaɪnd] *vi.* 放鬆（三態為：unwind, unwound [ʌnˋwaʊnd], unwound）
　　　　例 Listening to music can help me unwind.
　　　　　　聽音樂可以幫助我放鬆。

(B) **depart** [dɪˋpɑrt] *vi.* 出發
depart for + 地點　　出發前往某地
例 Bobby departed for New York last Sunday.
巴比上星期天動身前往紐約。

(C) **unpack** [ʌnˋpæk] *vi. & vt.* 打開（行李、包裹）
例 I have been so busy that I haven't had time to unpack since returning from my trip.
我忙到連旅行回來後都沒時間打開行李整理。

(D) **delay** [dɪˋle] *vt.* 延誤
例 Don't delay paying the bill.
不要延誤繳納帳單的時間。

b. 根據語意，(A) 項應為正選。

D　3. 理由
a. (A) **coincide with...**　　與……同時發生
例 My business trip to New York coincided with Thanksgiving, so I indulged myself with a big turkey dinner there.
我去紐約出差剛好遇上感恩節，所以我在那兒縱情享用一頓火雞大餐。

(B) **consult with sb**　　與某人商量
例 If you want more advice, you can consult with Richard.
如果你要更多的建議，可以跟理查討論。

(C) **suffer from...**　　飽受……之苦
例 My father suffers from diabetes.
我爸爸患有糖尿病。

(D) **deal with...**　　處理……
例 This problem is hard to deal with.
這個問題很難處理。

b. 根據語意及用法，(D) 項應為正選。

B　4. 理由
a. (A) **improbable** [ɪmˋprɑbəbḷ] *a.* 不大可能的
= unlikely
例 It seems improbable the rain will stop within the next hour.
雨似乎不大可能在一小時內就停。

(B) **available** [əˋveləbḷ] *a.* 可使用的
例 We still have three rooms available.
我們還有三間空房。

Unit 06

Unit 06

  (C) **dependable** [dɪˋpɛndəbl̩] *a*. 可靠的

  例 You can count on Jeff because he is always very dependable.
  你可以信賴傑夫，因為他向來很可靠。

  (D) **incapable** [ɪnˋkepəbl̩] *a*. 無能的
  be incapable of V-ing　無能力從事……
  = be unable to V
  be capable of V-ing　有能力從事……
  = be able to V

  例 The firm was incapable of handling such a large order.
  那家公司沒有能力處理如此龐大的訂單。

  b. 根據語意，(B) 項應為正選。

C 5. 理由

  a. (A) **color and shape of a dish**　菜餚的顏色和外形

  (B) **weight and texture of a plate**　盤子的重量和質地
  texture [ˋtɛkstʃɚ] *n*.（紡織物等的）質地，觸感；（食物、飲品的）口感

  (C) **aroma and taste of a meal**　餐點的香氣和味道
  aroma [əˋromə] *n*. 香味，芬芳

  (D) **sound and content of a chat**　聊天的聲音和內容

  b. 後句敘述「在沒有對話的情況下，人們能夠完全沉浸於食物的風味之中」，選項中惟 (C) 項所述「餐點的香氣和味道」呼應「食物的風味」，故應為正選。

重要單字與片語

1. **undertake** [ˌʌndɚˋtek] *vt*. 從事
（三態為：undertake, undertook [ˌʌndɚˋtʊk], undertaken [ˌʌndɚˋtekən]）
   例 We undertook a trip to Europe.
   我們去歐洲旅行。

2. **Nothing could be further from the truth.**　事實完全不是如此。

3. **numerous** [ˋnjumərəs] *a*. 為數眾多的

4. **indulge** [ɪnˋdʌldʒ] *vt*. & *vi*.（使）沉迷；縱容
   indulge (oneself) in...　（某人）沉迷於……
   例 Shortly after he got fired, Tom began to indulge in drinking.
   湯姆被炒魷魚後不久便開始酗酒。

5. **me time**　個人時間，享受單獨一個人的時光

6. **companion** [kəmˋpænjən] *n*. 同伴，朋友

7. **distraction** [dɪˋstrækʃən] *n*. 分散注意力的事物
   distract [dɪˋstrækt] *vt*. 使分心
   distract sb from sth　使某人自某事分心
   例 Noise from the street distracted the writer from his work.
   街上的吵雜聲讓這位作家無法專心工作。

8. **dramatically** [drəˋmætɪklɪ] *adv*. 大幅度地

9. **constraint** [kənˈstrent] *n.* 限制，約束
10. **solo** [ˈsolo] *a.* & *adv.* 獨自的／地，單獨的／地
11. **compromise** [ˈkɑmprəˌmaɪz] *n.* & *vi.* 妥協 & *vt.* 危害（名譽、原則）

12. **in the absence of...** 沒有……的情況下
例 In the absence of fresh ingredients, the chef had to modify the original recipe.
在沒有新鮮食材的情況下，主廚只得修改原本的食譜。

二 文意選填

　　個人衛生對於個人健康以及群體的福祉來說至關重要。不論是餐後刷牙還是每天更換衣服，衛生都非常重要。尤其是在大眾聚集處如大眾運輸中心裡，上百甚至上千人被迫同處於密閉空間中，更顯衛生的重要性。僅僅是接觸手扶梯的扶手或是售票櫃檯的桌面，大量潛在有害病菌立即在人群中散播。這裡面可能包含從感冒或流感病毒到腸胃炎或致命的肝炎病毒株等各種病菌。唯一有效避免這類疾病傳播的方式是每個人一天至少徹底洗手三到四次。

　　斯里蘭卡的大眾運輸既狹小又擁擠是出了名的，一間名為阿西里醫療集團的保健公司與一家成功的大型廣告商聯手合作，除了喚起大眾運輸上的衛生意識，也提供一個實用的解決方法 ── 肥皂公車票。肥皂公車票是由浸泡於芳香肥皂裡的紙張所製成，這種肥皂也是強力消毒劑。當乘客抵達目的地時，他們不會把車票丟入垃圾桶，反而用它來洗手。除了肥皂公車票，另外也依策略把海報張貼在公車站和公共廁所 ── 這些地方幾乎無法取得肥皂 ── 以提倡合宜衛生習慣的好處。這種環保的車票也解決了全國每日丟棄幾百萬張廢棄車票的問題。無庸置疑的是，當大家談起防止疾病傳播，這項親身經驗的宣傳活動正符合所需。

E　6. 理由
　　a. 空格前為 be 動詞 is，得知空格應置名詞或形容詞作主詞補語。
　　b. 選項中為名詞或形容詞的有 (C) proper（適合的）、(D) awareness（意識）、(E) crucial（重要的）、(F) destination（目的地）及 (H) address（地址），惟根據語意，(E) 項應為正選。
　　c. **crucial** [ˈkruʃəl] *a.* 決定性的，重要的

G　7. 理由
　　a. 空格前有表地方的名詞詞組 public transportation hubs（大眾運輸中心），空格後為一完整句子，得知空格應置關係副詞 where (= in which)，引導形容詞子句修飾前面的名詞詞組。
　　b. 根據上述，(G) 項應為正選。

Unit 06

Unit 06

J 8. 理由

a. 空格前有不定數量詞 billions of（大量的），其後通常接複數名詞，空格後有形容詞 dangerous（危險的）及其修飾的名詞 germs（細菌），得知空格應置副詞以修飾該形容詞。

b. 剩餘選項中 (B) thoroughly（徹底地）及 (J) potentially（潛在地）為副詞，惟根據語意，(J) 項應為正選。

c. **potentially** [pəˈtɛnʃəlɪ] *adv.* 潛在地

A 9. 理由

a. 空格前有主詞 These germs（這些細菌）及助動詞 may（可能），空格後有名詞 anything（任何東西），得知空格應置原形及物動詞，以接後面的名詞作其受詞。

b. 剩餘選項中 (A) include（包含）及 (H) address（解決）為原形及物動詞，惟根據語意，(A) 項應為正選。

c. **include** [ɪnˈklud] *vt.* 包含

　例 Does the price include room and board?
　　這個價錢包含膳宿在內嗎？

B 10. 理由

a. 空格前有動詞 wash（洗）及其受詞 their hands（他們的手），得知空格應置副詞以修飾該動詞。

b. 剩餘選項中僅剩 (B) thoroughly（徹底地）為副詞，且置入空格後合乎語意，故為正選。

c. **thoroughly** [ˈθɜolɪ] *adv.* 徹底地

D 11. 理由

a. 空格前有及物動詞 raise（喚起），空格後為介詞詞組 of hygiene on public transport（大眾運輸上的衛生），得知空格應置名詞 awareness（意識）以形成以下固定用法：

　raise awareness of / about...　喚起關於……的意識

　例 The government is trying to raise public awareness about environmental protection.
　　政府正設法提高民眾的環保意識。

b. 根據上述，(D) 項應為正選。

I 12. 理由

a. 空格前為一完整句子 The Soap Bus Ticket is made from paper infused with a piece of pleasantly fragrant soap（肥皂公車票是由浸泡於芳香肥皂裡的紙張所製成），空格後有 be 動詞 is、副詞 also（也）與名詞詞組 a powerful disinfectant（強力消毒劑），得知空格應置關係代名詞 which，以引導非限定形容

詞子句修飾先行詞 pleasantly fragrant soap（芳香肥皂）。which 亦作形容詞子句的主詞，而 a powerful disinfectant 為主詞補語。
b. 根據上述，(I) 項應為正選。

F 13. 理由
a. 空格前有代名詞所有格 his or her，得知空格應置名詞。
b. 剩餘選項中 (F) destination（目的地）及 (H) address（地址）為名詞，惟根據語意，(F) 項應為正選。
c. **destination** [ˌdɛstəˈneʃən] *n.* 目的地

C 14. 理由
a. 空格前有介詞 of，空格後有名詞 hygiene（衛生），得知空格應置形容詞以修飾該名詞。
b. 剩餘選項中僅剩 (C) proper（適合的）為形容詞，且置入空格後符合語意，故為正選。
c. **proper** [ˈprɑpɚ] *a.* 適合的

H 15. 理由
a. 空格前有本句主詞 The environmentally friendly tickets（這種環保的車票）及副詞 also，得知空格應置本句的動詞。
b. 剩餘選項 (H) address（解決）可為動詞，且置入空格後符合語意，故為正選。
c. **address** [əˈdrɛs] *vt.* 解決；對……發表演說 & [ˈædrɛs / əˈdrɛs] *n.* 地址；演說
例 The school addressed the issue of bullying by installing cameras in the hallways.
校方藉由在走廊安裝監視器來解決霸凌問題。

重要單字與片語

1. **hygiene** [ˈhaɪdʒin] *n.* 衛生（不可數）
2. **essential** [ɪˈsɛnʃəl] *a.* 必要的
3. **individual** [ˌɪndəˈvɪdʒuəl] *n.* 個人
4. **well-being** [ˌwɛlˈbiɪŋ] *n.* 福祉（不可數）
5. **community** [kəˈmjunətɪ] *n.* 群體；社區
6. **brush** [brʌʃ] *vt.* 刷；梳
7. **particularly** [pɚˈtɪkjəlɚlɪ] *adv.* 特別地（= in particular）
8. **confined** [kənˈfaɪnd] *a.* 狹窄的；受限制的
9. **handrail** [ˈhændˌrel] *n.* 扶手
10. **gastroenteritis** [ˌgæstroˌɛntəˈraɪtɪs] *n.* 腸胃炎（不可數）
11. **deadly** [ˈdɛdlɪ] *a.* 致命的
12. **strain** [stren] *n.* 品種
13. **hepatitis** [ˌhɛpəˈtaɪtɪs] *n.* 肝炎（不可數）
hepatitis A / B / C　　A / B / C 型肝炎

Unit 06

Unit 06

14. **transport** [ˈtrænspɔrt] *n.* & [trænsˈpɔrt] *vt.* 運送，運輸
15. **notoriously** [noˈtɔrɪəslɪ] *adv.* 惡名昭彰地
16. **cramped** [kræmpt] *a.* 狹小的
17. **infuse** [ɪnˈfjuz] *vt.* 浸漬
    infuse A with B　　將 A 浸漬在 B 中
    例 The pastry chef infused different kinds of fruit with rum.
    這位甜點師將各種水果浸漬在萊姆酒中。
18. **fragrant** [ˈfregrənt] *a.* 芬芳的
19. **disinfectant** [ˌdɪsɪnˈfɛktənt] *n.* 消毒劑
20. **dispose** [dɪˈspoz] *vi.* 處置（與介詞 of 並用）
    dispose of...　處理掉⋯⋯
    例 Most countries have difficulty disposing of nuclear waste.
    大部分的國家都面臨處理核廢料的困境。
21. **strategically** [strəˈtidʒɪkəlɪ] *adv.* 策略性地
22. **environmentally friendly**　環保的；對生態環境無害的
23. **no doubt**　無庸置疑地
    例 Teaching is no doubt a painstaking job.
    教書無疑是一份很辛苦的工作。
24. **hands-on** [ˌhændzˈɑn] *a.* 實際動手做的；親身實踐的
25. **be just the ticket**　正是所需要的東西

三 篇章結構

安吉・塔葛洛生下了她兒子布萊恩時，這不是她期待中的歡樂時刻：她的兒子生下來就沒有雙臂。布萊恩出生後的第一年，安吉每天哭泣。<u>一想到她的殘障兒子將來要面對的巨大挑戰和艱難的生活，就讓她非常難受</u>。但是，她認為她的悲傷會對兒子造成負面影響。因此，安吉振作了起來，並開始鼓勵她兒子嘗試越多事物越好。她堅信，培養布萊恩的正向思維是幫助他建立自信和獨立的關鍵。

令安吉高興的是，布萊恩在她的鼓勵下克服了他的殘疾。而讓人難以置信的是，他學會了用雙腿和雙腳來當作手臂和手。隨著時間流逝，他幾乎學會了所有其他同齡男孩能做的事，例如打電動和開車。他也培養了身為藝術家應具備的技能。<u>這些成就使布萊恩確信他可完成任何他決心要做的事</u>。他的毅力與堅持感動了身邊的人，證明了身體上的限制並不能決定一個人的潛能。

布萊恩在藝術的興趣激勵他追求成為一名刺青藝術家，而若干年前他成功地接受訓練當上一名合格認證的刺青師。<u>然而，獲得認證證實比被僱用還來得容易</u>。他不斷找工作，不幸的是，沒有聲譽良好的刺青店願意僱用他。儘管他的才華有目共睹，但許多僱主仍有疑慮，擔心他無法達到顧客的期望。

在過了好幾年收到拒絕信和沒有收到電話通知的日子後，布萊恩決定在亞歷桑納州土桑市，即他成長的地方，自己開一間名為「用腳刺青」的刺青店。<u>令他大吃一驚的是，他的生意蒸蒸日上，吸引當地和來自世界各地的顧客。</u>他非凡的技藝與獨特的故事使他的刺青店成為刺青愛好者的必訪之地。這個成功的故事也因而引起了新聞媒體和網路的極大關注。透過社群媒體與新聞報導，他的作品廣獲讚譽，並激勵了世界各地無數民眾。

E 16. 理由
　　a. 空格前兩句提到安吉・塔葛洛在生下了她兒子布萊恩時的頭一年，她 cried daily（每天都在哭泣），因為她兒子 was born without arms（生來無雙臂），可知如此的原因會造成選項 (E) 所述的結果：一想到她的殘障兒子將來要面對的巨大挑戰和艱難的生活，就讓她非常難受。
　　b. 根據上述，(E) 項應為正選。

A 17. 理由
　　a. 空格前兩句提到布萊恩漸漸學會了幾乎所有其他同齡男孩能做的事，他也培養了身為藝術家所應具備的技能，這些皆與選項 (A) 中的 these accomplishments（這些成就）和 could do anything that he set his mind on（可完成任何他決心要做的事）形成關聯。
　　b. 根據上述，(A) 項應為正選。

C 18. 理由
　　a. 空格前句提到布萊恩想當一名刺青藝術家，且後來也成功地取得了相關證照，又空格後句提到布萊恩不斷地找工作，但都沒有下文，空格前後語意相反，因此空格應填有語意轉折之語句，而選項 (C) 所述「然而，獲得認證證實比被僱用還來得容易」與此點相符。
　　b. 根據上述，(C) 項應為正選。

B 19. 理由
　　a. 空格前句提到布萊恩求職到處碰壁後，他決定自己創業 —— 在家鄉開一間刺青店，又空格後句提到他非凡的技藝與獨特的故事使他的刺青店成為刺青愛好者的必訪之地，因此可知空格應是關於布萊恩自己開的店很成功之類的敘述，此與選項 (B) 所述「令他大吃一驚的是，他的生意蒸蒸日上，吸引當地和來自世界各地的顧客」相符。
　　b. 根據上述，(B) 項應為正選。

(D) 選項翻譯　看到他令人驚嘆的設計後，這家公司立刻提供工作機會給布萊恩。

Unit 06

重要單字與片語

1. **anticipate** [æn'tɪsəˌpet] *vt.* 預期
   anticipate + V-ing　預期……
   例 The law firm anticipates having dozens of applicants for the job.
   那家律師事務所預計將有很多人應徵這個工作。

2. **immense** [ɪ'mɛns] *a.* 巨大的

3. **ahead** [ə'hɛd] *adv.* 在前面
   例 He stared straight ahead as if something bad was about to happen.
   他直直瞪著前方，彷彿有不祥的事情即將發生。

4. **disabled** [dɪs'ebld] *a.* 殘廢的
   the disabled　殘疾人士，殘障者

5. **foster** ['fɔstɚ] *vt.* 培養；養育；培育
   例 Reading books from different cultures can foster a deeper understanding of global diversity.
   閱讀不同文化的書籍可以培養對全球多樣性更深的理解。

6. **mindset** ['maɪndˌsɛt] *n.* 心態

7. **encouragement** [ɪn'kɝɪdʒmənt] *n.* 鼓勵（不可數）

8. **disability** [ˌdɪsə'bɪlətɪ] *n.* （身心方面的）殘疾

9. **accomplishment** [ə'kʌmplɪʃmənt] *n.* 成就

10. **confirm** [kən'fɝm] *vt.* 確認
    例 I would like to confirm my dinner reservation.
    我想要確認晚餐的訂位資料。

11. **set one's mind on sth**　決心做某事
    例 I know I can do one thing if I set my mind on it.
    我知道只要我決心做好一件事，我一定能做好。

12. **perseverance** [ˌpɝsə'vɪrəns] *n.* 堅持不懈

13. **certify** ['sɝtəˌfaɪ] *vt.* 證明，確定（本文為過去分詞當形容詞）
    例 This diploma certifies that you have finished high school.
    這份文憑證明你已完成高中學業。

14. **certification** [ˌsɝtɪfə'keʃən] *n.* 證書

15. **employment** [ɪm'plɔɪmənt] *n.* 受僱；就業

16. **unfortunately** [ən'fɔrtʃənɪtlɪ] *adv.* 不幸地

17. **established** [ɪ'stæblɪʃt] *a.* 被認可的，（因長期存在而）已確立的；被承認的

18. **parlor** ['pɑrlɚ] *n.* 店舖

19. **raise** [rez] *vt.* 撫養（= bring sb up）
    例 Irene was raised by her grandfather.
    艾琳是由她爺爺撫養長大的。

20. **in turn**　因此，因而；依序，輪流
    例 Interest rates were cut and, in turn, share prices rose.
    利率降低了，接著股價便上漲了。
    Each student made a brief speech in turn.
    每位學生依序發表簡短演講。

21. **generate** ['dʒɛnəˌret] *vt.* 造成，引起
    例 Tourism generates more income for the seaside resort.
    旅遊業為濱海勝地帶來更多的收入。

22. **outlet** ['aʊtlɛt] *n.* 經銷點，零售店
    a media outlet　新聞媒體

四 閱讀測驗

儘管咖哩源自印度，它卻是日本最受喜愛的料理之一。事實上，咖哩在日本普遍到許多人都覺得它是日本的國民料理。

咖哩傳到日本的時間，與十九世紀大英帝國的擴張屬於同一時期。英國人自創的咖哩料理，基本上就是他們在印度吃到的各種咖哩的簡易版本。雖然英國沒有殖民日本，但在明治時期設立了許多以日本為總部的商行，目的是跟英國殖民地如印度、現在的巴基斯坦與孟加拉等地進行商品貿易賺錢。咖哩就是在這期間引進至日本的眾多商品之一。日本與咖哩的第一次接觸，據說是因為運送咖哩粉的英國水手遭遇船難，被日本漁船救援所致。雖然我們不知道這是否史實，但我們能確定日本人立刻愛上了這美味料理的辣味。

自從咖哩引進至日本後，咖哩的味道就演變到比較不辣而是偏甜的口味。這與印度式的咖哩形成強烈的對比。大體來說，日本人發展出三種不同的咖哩料理：咖哩飯、咖哩麵條與咖哩麵點。日式咖哩通常會加入豬肉、雞肉以及蔬菜，但全國四十七縣當中有許多都擁有因為展現地方食材而被在地人稱為在地限定的咖哩料理。例如廣島就以其牡蠣咖哩而聞名。相對於較繁複的日本傳統料理而言，咖哩食譜烹調起來快速而且輕鬆。這是學校與部隊常會有咖哩料理，以及咖哩如此受到忙碌日本家庭愛戴的原因之一。

D 20. 有關日式咖哩，本文沒有提及下列哪一方面？
    (A) 咖哩裡面通常有什麼。
    (B) 咖哩來自哪裡。
    (C) 誰吃得特別多。
    (D) 咖哩通常如何製作。

    理由
    根據本文第三段第四句、第二段第五句、第三段最後一句，可知 (D) 項應為正選。

B 21. 根據本文，英國人對印度咖哩做了什麼？
    (A) 把日式的味道添加進去。
    (B) 把咖哩變成英式的。
    (C) 尋求販賣咖哩的許可。
    (D) 增加咖哩中香料的種類。

    理由
    根據本文第二段第二句，可知 (B) 項應為正選。

Unit 06

__B__ **22.** 下列哪一項有標記號碼的句子是推測而非事實？

(A) ❶

(B) ❷

(C) ❸

(D) ❹

理由

根據本文標記號碼二號的句子表示 It is said that...（據說……），可知 (B) 項應為正選。

__C__ **23.** 下列哪一項最接近第三段中 reflects 的意思？

(A) 丟回去。

(B) 思考。

(C) 展現。

(D) 呈現影像。

理由

根據本文第三段第四、五句，可推知 (C) 項應為正選。

重要單字與片語

1. **originate** [əˋrɪdʒə͵net] *vi.* 源於
   originate in + 地方　起源／源自於某地
   例 The Olympics originated in Greece over 2,000 years ago.
   奧運起源於兩千多年前的希臘。

2. **prevalent** [ˋprɛvələnt] *a.* 普遍的，流行的

3. **coincide** [͵koɪnˋsaɪd] *vi.* 巧合
   coincide with...　與……同時發生／一致
   例 My birthday coincides with Chinese New Year this year.
   我今年生日和農曆新年同一天。

4. **encounter** [ɪnˋkaʊntɚ] *vt.* 遇到；面臨
   例 We may encounter many setbacks in the process of learning.
   我們在學習過程中有可能會遇到許多挫折。

5. **colonize** [ˋkɑlə͵naɪz] *vt.* 將……開拓為殖民地
   例 By that time, only a small part of the world had not been colonized.
   到了那個時期，世界上只有一小部分的地區尚未被殖民。

6. **era** [ˋɪrə] *n.* 時代，年代

7. **capitalize** [ˋkæpət!͵aɪz] *vi.* 利用（與介詞 on 並用）
   capitalize on...　利用……（獲利）
   例 Mr. Smith capitalized on the opportunity to invest in a profitable real estate venture.
   史密斯先生利用這個機會投資很好賺錢的不動產事業。

8. **It is said that...**　據說……
   例 It is said that dogs are more loyal than cats.
   據說狗狗比貓咪更忠心。

9. **shipwreck** [ˈʃɪpˌrɛk] vt. 使遭受海難（本文為過去分詞作形容詞）& n. 海難
10. **evolve** [ɪˈvɑlv] vi. 演變，發展為……
    例 Through months of teamwork, our idea finally evolved into a feasible plan.
    經過數個月的團隊合作，我們的想法終於化為可行的計畫。
11. **prefecture** [ˈprifɛktʃɚ] n.（日本的）縣
12. **elaborate** [ɪˈlæbərət] a. 繁複的
13. **permission** [pɚˈmɪʃən] n. 允許，許可
    without (one's) permission 未經（某人的）允許
    例 Matt used my computer without my permission, which made me angry.
    馬特未經我允許就使用我的電腦，這讓我很生氣。
14. **assumption** [əˈsʌmpʃən] n. 臆測，假定

五 混合題

　　虎鯨又稱殺人鯨，是巨大、黑白花色的海洋哺乳動物。牠們分布於世界各地的海洋，以高智商和複雜的溝通技能聞名。在 2020 年代初期，出現了許多虎鯨在西班牙和葡萄牙沿海地區疑似攻擊漁船的報導。牠們通常會瞄準並衝撞小船的舵的部位，使得船體受損，在極少數案例中甚至造成船隻沉沒。水手和漁民們說虎鯨群的雌性領袖會率先攻擊船，然後年幼的虎鯨會模仿她的行為。科學家和研究人員提出兩種主要的理論來解釋這種情況發生的原因。

第一種理論是，雌虎鯨可能有過痛苦的經歷，像是與船隻相撞或被非法魚網纏住等。這事導致她開始對船隻表現出攻擊性，同時有意無意地教會了群體中的年輕成員做出相同的行為。葡萄牙生物學家阿爾弗雷多‧羅培茲‧費南德茲認為這是最有可能的理論。他告訴 Live Science 網站「是那頭受創的虎鯨帶頭去實體碰觸船隻的。」不過他提到，大部分虎鯨和航行船隻的接觸並沒有造成船或船員的傷害，而且這種行為對虎鯨來說是相當危險的，它們可能會因為衝撞船舵而受傷。

第二種理論是，這並不是攻擊，而是嬉鬧事件。這理論基於以下信念：有鑑於虎鯨的體型和力量，如果牠們真的想摧毀船隻或傷害船上的人類，將是輕而易舉的。雖然未知其真正的動機，但丹麥的永續學家大衛‧盧索向《新聞週刊》提出他的推斷：這些動機可能包含「遊戲、社交行為、靈活度練習、樂趣」或多種其他原因，而非出於經歷創傷後的報復行為。虎鯨天生好奇愛玩，牠們可能只是在找樂子。無論牠們的實際意圖為何，值得深思的是：漁船才是進入虎鯨天然環境中的那一個，而不是反過來的情況。正如西班牙環保志工努利亞‧里拉對英國廣播公司所述：「我們必須記住，海洋是牠們的家，我們才是入侵者。」

Unit 06

24. 關於虎鯨為什麼開始衝撞漁船的一項理論是，雌虎鯨有痛苦的經歷，例如曾與船隻碰撞，然後就開始對其他船隻表現出攻擊行為。

理由

空格前為不定冠詞 a，空格後為介詞 with，可得知空格應置可數單數名詞。根據表格左欄第一句 "The first theory was that a female orca had been through a traumatic experience, such as colliding with a boat or..."（第一種理論是，雌虎鯨可能有過痛苦的經歷，像是與船隻相撞或……）得知，空格應置與 colliding 相關的名詞 collision。

25. 另一個理論是，這些虎鯨如果認真起來，是可以對人們造成巨大傷害或破壞／損害船隻的，但牠們只是在玩鬧而已，而不是在尋求報復。

理由

空格前為對等連接詞 or，可推測空格應置與 harm 對等的名詞。根據表格右欄第二句 "... if they had truly wanted to destroy a boat or harm the humans inside, they would very easily have been able to do so."（……如果牠們真的想摧毀船隻或傷害船上的人類，將是輕而易舉的。）得知，空格應置與 destroy 相關的名詞 destruction 或相似詞 damage。

26. 引文中的哪個字與下面句子引號內的字意思相同？
瑪麗安去唱卡拉 OK 時，總是要「模仿」她偶像的唱歌方式。

imitate（模仿）

理由

根據本文第一段倒數第二句 "..., and then the younger orcas would imitate her behavior."（……，然後年幼的虎鯨會模仿她的行為。），可推測 imitate（模仿）應為正解。

C　**27.** 我們並未被告知這些攻擊事件的哪一項資訊？
　　(A) 攻擊事件的大致地點。
　　(B) 虎鯨專門攻擊的船隻部位。
　　(C) 這些攻擊事件的總數。
　　(D) 少數此類事件的最終結果。

理由

根據引文提及虎鯨在西班牙和葡萄牙沿海地區疑似襲擊漁船，並說明牠們會瞄準並衝撞小船的舵，以及在極少數案例中甚至造成船隻沉沒。並未提及這些攻擊事件的總數，故 (C) 項應為正選。

重要單字與片語

1. **orca** [ˈɔrkə] *n.* 虎鯨
2. **sophisticated** [səˈfɪstəˌketɪd] *a.* 複雜的，精密的；世故的
3. **ram** [ræm] *vi.* & *vt.* 猛撞
4. **rudder** [ˈrʌdɚ] *n.* 舵
5. **vessel** [ˈvɛsḷ] *n.* 船艦；容器；血管
6. **pod** [pɑd] *n.* 海洋哺乳類動物群
7. **imitate** [ˈɪməˌtet] *vt.* 模仿，仿效
   例 The comedian is good at imitating famous people.
   這名喜劇演員很擅長模仿名人。
8. **traumatic** [trɔˈmætɪk] *a.* (經歷) 痛苦難忘的
   traumatized [ˈtrɔməˌtaɪzd] *a.* 有心理創傷的
   trauma [ˈtrɔmə] *n.* (情感的) 創傷；外傷
9. **entangle** [ɪnˈtæŋgḷ] *vt.* 纏住 (常用被動)
10. **speculate** [ˈspɛkjəˌlet] *vi.* & *vt.* 推測；猜測
    例 The political analyst refused to speculate about why the finance minister stepped down.
    這位政治分析師拒絕臆測財政部長下臺的原因。
11. **revenge** [rɪˈvɛndʒ] *n.* 報復 & *vt.* 為……報仇
    例 That young man took revenge on the bad guy for his father's death.
    那年輕人為父親的死亡向該壞蛋報仇。
12. **inquisitive** [ɪnˈkwɪzətɪv] *a.* 好奇的
13. **intruder** [ɪnˈtrudɚ] *n.* 入侵者
14. **vengeance** [ˈvɛndʒəns] *n.* 報仇 (不可數)

Unit 06

Unit 07

一 綜合測驗

　　蘿倫・辛格是紐約大學畢業生，主修環境研究。她堅信自己可以過著趨近零垃圾的生活。她把所有無法避免或無法回收的垃圾都收集在一個十六盎司的罐子裡。罐子裡包含黏貼在新鮮水果和蔬菜上的貼紙，以及辛格建議我們購買的二手衣物上繫有標價的塑膠標籤。這些小東西凸顯了徹底消除垃圾的困難，但辛格的決心證明了經過深思熟慮而做選擇，便有可能減少垃圾。

　　辛格在她的網站 Trash is for Tossers（只有丟垃圾的人才會製造垃圾）上提供好用的建議給那些同樣想減少垃圾製造量的人。她分享了在日常生活中減少垃圾的實用策略。除了像是購物時攜帶環保袋及可重複使用的容器這些明確的建議外，辛格也說明了如何製作零包裝環保牙膏以及自製美味沙拉醬。這些替代方案有助於減少塑膠垃圾。她也鼓勵造訪其網站的訪客接受健康的飲食習慣。想知道更多有關蘿倫・辛格的事，到 trashisfortossers.com 這個網站看看吧。

C　**1.** 理由

　　a. (A) **evenly** [ˈivənlɪ] *adv.* 平均地

　　　　例 The waiter spread the butter evenly over the toast.
　　　　服務生將奶油均勻地塗在吐司上。

　　(B) **namely** [ˈnemlɪ] *adv.* 換言之

　　　　例 We have only two days left. Namely, we are hard pressed for time to do the job.
　　　　我們只剩兩天。換言之，我們完成這件工作的時間非常緊迫。

　　(C) **firmly** [ˈfɝmlɪ] *adv.* 堅定地

　　　　例 I'm firmly convinced that David is innocent.
　　　　我堅信大衛是無辜的。

　　(D) **widely** [ˈwaɪdlɪ] *adv.* 廣泛地

　　　　例 The president was widely criticized for failing to keep his promises.
　　　　那位總統因未能遵守承諾而遭受各方批評。

　　b. 根據語意，(C) 項應為正選。

D　**2.** 理由

　　a. (A) **convict** [kənˈvɪkt] *vt.* 使定罪
　　　　be convicted of...　　被判有……的罪

　　　　例 The man was convicted of theft and sentenced to two years in prison.
　　　　這名男子被判竊盜罪，處以兩年有期徒刑。

- (B) **collide** [kəˋlaɪd] *vi.* 碰撞
  collide with sth　　與某物碰撞
  - 例 The bus ran a red light and collided with a truck.
    這輛巴士闖紅燈，和一臺卡車相撞。
- (C) **concede** [kənˋsid] *vi.* 讓步
  concede to...　　對……讓步
  = yield to...
  = surrender to...
  - 例 By no means will I concede to Peter's demands.
    我絕對不會對彼得的要求讓步。
- (D) **collect** [kəˋlɛkt] *vt.* 收集
  - 例 Bill has been collecting stamps for more than thirty years.
    比爾集郵已有三十多年之久。

b. 根據語意，(D) 項應為正選。

__A__ 3. 理由

a. (A) **plastic tags**　　塑膠標籤
  - 例 Henry removed the plastic tags from his new backpack before using it.
    亨利使用新背包前取下了上面的塑膠標籤。
- (B) **wooden pegs**　　木製掛夾
  peg [pɛg] *n.* 掛（衣）勾，掛物釘
  - 例 Irene used wooden pegs to hang the wet clothes on the clothesline.
    艾琳用木製掛夾把溼衣服吊在曬衣繩上。
- (C) **printed receipts**　　紙本收據／發票
  - 例 Many stores now offer digital instead of printed receipts.
    許多商店現在提供電子發票，而非紙本發票。
- (D) **rubber bands**　　橡皮筋
  - 例 Overstretching rubber bands can cause them to snap suddenly.
    過度拉伸橡皮筋可能會導致它們突然斷裂。

b. 根據語意，可知 (A) 項應為正選。

__B__ 4. 理由

a. (A) **on account of...**　　因為……
  = because of...
  = due to...
  = owing to...
  - 例 Many farms and rice fields were flooded on account of the typhoon.
    許多農場和稻田都因為颱風而淹水。

Unit 07

(B) **as well as...**　　（除了……外，）還有……

　　例 John owns five restaurants as well as a movie theater.
　　約翰擁有五間餐廳還有一家戲院。

(C) **on behalf of...**　　代表……

　　例 On behalf of our company, I would like to make a toast to the newlyweds.
　　本人謹代表公司向這對新人敬酒。

(D) **as far as...**　　達到……的程度（常用於下列結構）
　　As far as sb knows, ...　　就某人所知，……
= To sb's understanding, ...
= To sb's knowledge, ...

　　例 As far as I know, Karen will move to Canada.
　　據我所知，凱倫將搬到加拿大。

b. 根據語意，(B) 項應為正選。

A 5. 理由

a. (A) **embrace** [ɪmˋbres] *vt.* 欣然接受（建議等）；擁抱

　　例 Linda embraces every opportunity to learn new skills.
　　琳達敞開雙手接受每次學新技能的機會。

(B) **displace** [dɪsˋples] *vt.* 迫使離開（原來的地方）

　　例 War and famine have displaced hundreds of thousands of this country's citizens.
　　戰爭和飢荒迫使該國數十萬的人民流離失所。

(C) **preface** [ˋprɛfɪs] *vt.* 作為……的序言

　　例 The book is prefaced by a quotation from the former president.
　　本書引用前總統所說的話作為序言。

(D) **replace** [rɪˋples] *vt.* 取代
　　replace A with B　　以 B 取代 A，把 A 換成 B

　　例 I'm considering replacing my old PC with a notebook.
　　我正考慮把舊的個人電腦換成一臺筆記型電腦。

b. 根據語意，(A) 項應為正選。

重要單字與片語

1. **major** [ˋmedʒɚ] *vi.* 主修（與介詞 in 並用）& *n.* 主修科目
　　major in...　　主修……

　　例 I majored in accounting in college.
　　我大學主修會計。

2. **environmental** [ɪnˌvaɪrənˋmɛntḷ] *a.* 環境的
   例 We cannot lay too much emphasis on the importance of environmental protection.
   環保的重要性我們再怎麼強調都不為過。

3. **highlight** [ˋhaɪˌlaɪt] *vt.* 凸顯，強調 & *n.* 最精彩的部分
   例 The teacher highlighted the key points of the lesson on the whiteboard.
   老師在白板上強調了這堂課的重點。

4. **eliminate** [ɪˋlɪməˌnet] *vt.* 消除，殲滅；剔除，淘汰
   例 Regular exercise can help eliminate stress and improve mental health.
   規律運動可以幫助消除壓力並改善心理健康。

5. **commitment** [kəˋmɪtmənt] *n.* 承諾；奉獻（不可數）

6. **hint** [hɪnt] *n.* 暗示；建議

7. **lessen** [ˋlɛsn̩] *vt.* 減少
   例 A low-sodium and low-fat diet can lessen the risk of high blood pressure.
   低鈉與低脂的飲食可以減少罹患高血壓的風險。

8. **reusable** [riˋjuzəbḷ] *a.* 可再度使用的

9. **container** [kənˋtenɚ] *n.* 容器

10. **packaging** [ˋpækɪdʒɪŋ] *n.* 包裝；包裝材料（不可數）

11. **homemade** [ˌhomˋmed] *a.* 自製的

12. **minimize** [ˋmɪnəˌmaɪz] *vt.* 使降到最低；輕描淡寫
    例 Wearing sunscreen helps minimize skin damage from the sun.
    塗抹防曬霜有助於減少陽光對皮膚的傷害。

二 文意選填

義大利迄今已推出數種席捲全球的代表性美食和飲品。披薩、義大利麵和義式濃縮咖啡是當中最著名的。提拉米蘇則是一種美味的夾層蛋糕，同樣迅速揚名四海。

提拉米蘇由一系列特殊的食材混合而成，包含手指餅乾、奶油乳酪、蛋黃、咖啡、糖以及可可粉。這個食譜有不少變化型式，包含加入紅酒或白蘭地以及卡士達醬。端出時有時會搭配打發的鮮奶油、水果或莓果，用圓形玻璃杯裝盛以展現蛋糕的層次，或是切成方形。

提拉米蘇的起源並不確定；然而，大部分的烹飪學者一致認為它最早是在六〇年代晚期出現於義大利北部。也有較不具公信力的報告聲稱提拉米蘇是為了向一位十七世紀時造訪托斯卡尼的公爵致敬而製作的。這個說法的可能性很低，因為在六〇年代晚期之前，沒有一本烹飪書提過提拉米蘇的食譜。此外，提拉米蘇一詞直到八〇年代才出現在字典中。

羅伯托・菱格諾托是特雷維索市一間餐廳的老闆，餐廳名為 Le Beccherie，他和他的學徒法蘭西絲卡・法洛力宣稱是他們創造出這款蛋糕。他們的聲明是有些說服力的，因為法洛

Unit 07

力的娘家姓氏就是提拉米蘇。然而，同一座小鎮裡的一名糕點師傅也宣稱他創造了這個食譜。他說他花了兩年的時間讓他的食譜臻於完美，並堅稱是他提供這種甜點給菱格諾托的餐廳。

還有另一個傳說，描述了二戰時期一名義大利軍官的太太如何為即將前往前線作戰的丈夫準備這種甜點。當時食物匱乏，所以這名女子將一些剩下的食物湊合在一起做成甜點。無論你相信哪一個故事，大家都同意提拉米蘇很美味。

F 6. 理由
   a. 空格前有不定數量詞 a collection of（大量的），得知空格應置複數可數名詞。
   b. 選項中為複數可數名詞的有 (B) variations（變化型）、(D) origins（起源）及 (F) ingredients（原料），惟根據語意，(F) 項應為正選。
   c. **ingredient** [ɪnˋɡridɪənt] *n.* 食材，原料

B 7. 理由
   a. 空格前有形容詞 numerous（許多的），得知空格應置複數可數名詞。
   b. 剩餘選項中為複數可數名詞的有 (B) variations（變化型）與 (D) origins（起源），惟根據語意，(B) 項應為正選。
   c. **variation** [ˌvɛrɪˋeʃən] *n.* 變化（的種類）

E 8. 理由
   a. 空格前有本句主詞 It 及 be 動詞 is，空格後有介詞詞組 with whipped cream, fruit or berries（搭配打發的鮮奶油、水果或莓果），得知空格應置及物動詞的過去分詞，以與 is 形成被動語態。
   b. 剩餘選項中為及物動詞的過去分詞有 (A) supplied（供應）與 (E) served（上餐），惟根據語意，(E) 項應為正選。
   c. **serve** [sɝv] *vt.* 供應（餐點）；服務
      例 Lunch is served from 11:00 a.m. to 2:00 p.m.
         午餐供應的時間為上午十一點到下午兩點。

D 9. 理由
   a. 空格前有定冠詞 The，空格後有介詞詞組 of tiramisu（提拉米蘇的）及本句動詞 are，得知空格應置複數可數名詞。
   b. 剩餘選項中僅剩 (D) origins（起源）為複數可數名詞，且置入空格後符合語意，故為正選。
   c. **origin** [ˋɔrədʒɪn] *n.* 起源；出身

I 10. 理由
   a. 空格前有本句主詞 This、be 動詞 is 及副詞 highly，得知空格應置形容詞，以作主詞補語，並被前面的副詞修飾。

b. 剩餘選項中為形容詞的有 (C) convincing（使人信服的）、(H) scarce（稀少的）、(I) unlikely（不太可能的）及 (J) front（前面的），惟根據語意，(I) 項應為正選。

c. **unlikely** [ʌnˈlaɪklɪ] *a.* 不太可能的

C 11. 理由

a. 空格前有本句主詞 Their claim（他們的聲明）、be 動詞 is 及副詞 somewhat（有點），得知空格應置形容詞，以作主詞補語，並被前面的副詞修飾。somewhat 後面通常置其修飾的形容詞或副詞。

b. 剩餘選項中 (C) convincing（使人信服的）、(H) scarce（稀少的）及 (J) front（前面的）為形容詞，惟根據語意，(C) 項應為正選。

c. **convincing** [kənˈvɪnsɪŋ] *a.* 使人信服的

A 12. 理由

a. 空格位於作 insists（堅稱）受詞之 that 名詞子句中，空格前有該子句的主詞 he，後有名詞 Roberto Linguanotto's restaurant，得知空格應置子句的動詞，且為及物動詞。

b. 剩餘選項中僅剩 (A) supplied（供應）為及物動詞，且置入空格後符合語意，故為正選。

c. **supply** [səˈplaɪ] *vt.* 供應 & *n.* 補給品（恆用複數）；供給

    supply sb with sth   供應某物給某人
= supply sth to sb

例 The power plant supplies the city with electricity.
這座發電廠供電給整個城市。

G 13. 理由

a. 空格前有形容詞 another，得知空格應置單數名詞。

b. 剩餘選項中 (G) myth（傳說）及 (J) front（前面）可作單數名詞，惟根據語意，(G) 項應為正選。

c. **myth** [mɪθ] *n.* 傳說；神話

J 14. 理由

a. 空格前有定冠詞 the，空格後有名詞 line（線），得知空格應置形容詞以修飾後方的名詞。

b. 剩餘選項中 (H) scarce（稀少的）及 (J) front（前面的）可作形容詞，惟根據語意，(J) 項應為正選。

c. **front** [frʌnt] *a.* 前面的 & *n.* 前面
    the front line   前線

Unit 07

Unit 07

__H__ 15. 理由

a. 空格前有本句主詞 Food（食物）與 be 動詞 was，得知空格應置名詞或形容詞以作主詞補語。

b. 剩餘選項 (H) scarce（稀少的）為形容詞，且置入空格後符合語意，故為正選。

c. scarce [skɛrs] *a.* 稀少的；缺乏的

重要單字與片語

1. **take the world / country / city by storm** （像風暴一樣）席捲整個世界 / 國家 / 城市

   例 The opera took New York by storm.
   這齣歌劇轟動全紐約。

2. **layered** [ˋleəd] *a.* 有夾層的；分層的

3. **custard** [ˋkʌstəd] *n.* 卡士達醬

4. **whip** [(h)wɪp] *vt.* 攪打（蛋，奶油）
   （三態為：whip, whipped, whipped）
   （本文為過去分詞做形容詞用）

   例 I whipped the egg white until it got light and fluffy.
   我打發蛋白直到它變輕柔且蓬鬆。

5. **culinary** [ˋkʌləˏnɛrɪ] *a.* 烹飪的

6. **concoct** [kənˋkakt] *vt.* 調製，烹製

   例 The chef concocted the amazing dish from all sorts of leftover food.
   主廚使用各類剩餘食物來烹製出這道驚喜的料理。

7. **reputable** [ˋrɛpjətəbļ] *a.* 聲譽好的

8. **apprentice** [əˋprɛntɪs] *n.* 學徒 & *vt.* 使當學徒（常與介詞 to 並用）

9. **maiden name** 娘家姓氏

10. **perfect** [pəˋfɛkt] *vt.* 使完美；改良 & [ˋpɝfɪkt] *a.* 完美的

    例 Vera hoped to perfect her dancing technique.
    薇拉希望她的舞技能臻於完美。

11. **scrape** [skrep] *vt.* （艱難地）湊集，積攢
    scrape sth up / together 湊集某物

    例 The couple have scraped together enough money to buy a car.
    這對情侶已湊足了買一輛汽車的錢。

篇章結構

　　一名男子坐在舞臺上，大腿上放著一個大型的木偶娃娃。當男子開口對它說話時，這隻木偶，或「人偶」，用自己的聲音回應他。觀眾知道回答的其實是這名男子，而不是那個人偶，但腹語師的表演讓觀眾嘖嘖稱奇，因為他完全沒有動嘴唇，沒有人能看出他有正在說話的跡象。觀眾常常會疑惑，腹語師是如何如此熟練地控制自己的聲音。這名男子和人偶對話，互相開起玩笑並對罵。這是場機智對戰，製造出不少笑料。這就是典型的現代腹語術表演。

　　在腹語術尚未加入人偶和玩笑等元素之前，腹語師的角色帶有宗教的色彩。他們不用動嘴唇就能說話，看起來像是種奇怪的魔法。這些聲音像是直接從他們的腹部發出來的。古代文化認為這些奇異的聲音是超自然的訊息。當時普遍相信從腹語師腹部所發出的聲音是鬼魂所為，而人們認為這些鬼魂能夠預測未來。

隨著時間演變，腹語師的絕技被視為一種單純的娛樂表演，而非宗教方面的信息。腹語術的表演形式在十九世紀末時有所改變，一名叫做佛瑞德・羅素的喜劇演員是第一位與人偶一起表演腹語術的人。這些表演大多是羅素在展現用他的聲音「配腹語」的能力，或是人偶對觀眾說話的同時他在喝水。後來的幾位腹語師和他們的人偶都成為家喻戶曉的人物。布法洛・鮑伯・史密斯和他的人偶哈迪・杜迪或許是全美知名度最高的，成為一九〇〇年代中期廣播和電視的巨星。另一個知名的木偶叫做小羊排，也相當受到小朋友的歡迎。

現在人們可以看到各種形式的腹語表演，從 YouTube 網站上經典的兒童節目，到喜劇演員說著難登大雅之堂的笑話都有。儘管時代變遷，腹語表演依舊能為觀眾帶來樂趣。這種奇怪又有趣的才能如今變成了一種老少咸宜的娛樂方式。

- B **16.** 理由
  - a. 空格前句提到一名男子坐在舞臺上，大腿上放著一個大型的木偶娃娃，又空格後句提到觀眾知道回答的其實是這名男子，而不是那個人偶，但令觀眾嘖嘖稱奇的是這男子完全沒有動嘴唇，所以沒有人能看出他有正在說話的跡象，因此空格內容應是在描述男子在舞臺上和他腿上的木偶娃娃有何互動，此即選項 (B) 所述「當男子開口對它說話時，這隻木偶，或「人偶」，用自己的聲音回應他。」
  - b. 根據上述，(B) 項應為正選。

- D **17.** 理由
  - a. 第二段第一句至空格前句提到很久以前，腹語師的角色帶有 spiritual（宗教的；精神的，心靈的）色彩。他們不用動嘴唇就能說話，看起來像是魔法，且這些聲音像是直接從他們的腹部發出來的，而古代文化認為這些聲音是超自然的訊息，因此可推知空格內容應與宗教色彩有關，此即如選項 (D) 所述「當時普遍相信從腹語師腹部所發出的聲音是鬼魂所為，而人們認為這些鬼魂能夠預測未來。」
  - b. 根據上述，(D) 項應為正選。

- E **18.** 理由
  - a. 空格前句首度提到 Fred Russell（佛瑞德・羅素）這個喜劇演員，他是最早用人偶表演腹語術的人，又選項 (E) 也提到 Russell（羅素），並說明他表演的情況。
  - b. 根據上述，(E) 項應為正選。

- A **19.** 理由
  - a. 空格前兩句提到在羅素之後出現的幾位腹語師及其人偶都成為家喻戶曉的人物，如一九〇〇年代中期的布法洛・鮑伯・史密斯與其人偶哈迪・杜迪，因此可推知空格內容可再另外列舉另一知名的腹語師或其人偶，此即如選項 (A) 所述「另一個知名的木偶叫做小羊排，也相當受到小朋友的歡迎。」
  - b. 根據上述，(A) 項應為正選。

- (C) 選項翻譯 可惜的是，腹語表演近年來已經不再流行了。

Unit 07

重要單字與片語

1. **puppet** [ˈpʌpɪt] *n.* 木偶
2. **lap** [læp] *n.* 大腿，膝部
   on sb's lap 在某人的大腿上
3. **dummy** [ˈdʌmɪ] *n.* 人體模型，假人
4. **respond to...** 回應……
   例 Peter didn't respond to my question, which made me angry.
   彼得沒有回答我的問題，令我很生氣。
5. **ventriloquist** [vɛnˈtrɪləkwɪst] *n.* 腹語表演者，腹語師
   ventriloquism [vɛnˈtrɪləkwɪzəm] *n.* 腹語（術）（不可數）
6. **amaze** [əˈmez] *vt.* 使驚奇，使驚愕
   be amazed at / by... 對……感到驚訝
   例 They were all amazed at the little boy's ability to play the piano.
   他們都對那小男孩彈鋼琴的能力感到很驚訝。
7. **lip** [lɪp] *n.* 嘴唇（因有兩片嘴唇，故常用複數）
8. **trade** [tred] *vt.* 交換
   trade insults 對罵
9. **wits** [wɪts] *n.* 機智（恆用複數）
   be at one's wits' end （某人）黔驢技窮，（某人因非常擔憂或生氣等而）不知道下一步該怎麼辦
   例 I'm at my wits' end. I can't come up with any idea to solve this problem.
   我已黔驢技窮了。我想不出任何方法來解決這個問題。
10. **make for...** 造成……，促成……
    例 Candlelight, champagne, and music can make for a romantic evening.
    燭光、香檳和音樂可以營造出一個浪漫的夜晚。

11. **hilarious** [hɪˈlɛrɪəs] *a.* 極好笑的，引人發笑的
12. **belly** [ˈbɛlɪ] *n.* 腹部
13. **predict** [prɪˈdɪkt] *vt.* 預言，預測
    例 The fortune-teller predicted that Terry would become rich.
    算命師預言泰瑞會發大財。
14. **stunt** [stʌnt] *n.* 絕技；特技
15. **entertainment** [ˌɛntɚˈtenmənt] *n.* 娛樂，消遣
16. **message** [ˈmɛsɪdʒ] *n.* 訊息
17. **comedian** [kəˈmidɪən] *n.* 喜劇演員
18. **involve** [ɪnˈvɑlv] *vt.* 包含；需要；牽涉
    例 Mountain climbing involves strength and concentration.
    登山需要體力和專注力。
19. **household** [ˈhaʊsˌhold] *n.* 家庭
    a household name 家喻戶曉的人／物
    例 This brand name has become a household name all over the world.
    這品牌名稱已成為全球家喻戶曉的名字。
20. **hit** [hɪt] *n.* 非常受歡迎的人（或事）；非常成功的人（或事）
    a big / huge / smash hit 熱門／受歡迎的事物
    例 The new movie about aliens is sure to be a huge hit.
    這部有關外星人的新電影絕對會大受歡迎。
21. **classic** [ˈklæsɪk] *a.* 典型的；經典的

22. **turn out to be...** 最終成為……；最終發現……
   例 The footsteps I heard turned out to be my grandfather's.
   我聽到的腳步聲原來是我爺爺傳來的。

23. **fall out of fashion** 不再流行
   例 Writing letters by hand has fallen out of fashion due to the rise of digital communication.
   由於數位通訊的興起，手寫信件已經變得不流行了。

四 閱讀測驗

　　由於太空旅行的特殊狀況和環境，當太空人是會傷身的。例如太空船內的極微弱重力會導致骨質流失和肌肉無力。根據美國國家航空暨太空總署（NASA）指出，在太空飛行期間，骨骼每個月最多會流失 1.5% 的骨質密度，而肌肉量流失的速度也比在地球時快。原因是缺乏明顯的重力意味太空人的骨骼和肌肉基本上沒有被用來支撐和移動他們的身體。為了應對這個問題，太空總署鼓勵太空人進行專為太空船所設計的特殊運動。

　　太空旅行也會影響免疫系統、累壞身體、讓太空人容易感冒和感染其他病毒。同時細菌也很容易在太空船這種封閉環境中傳播。根據《國家地理》報導，在國際太空站（ISS）上的太空人曾罹患呼吸道感染和皮膚疹。該雜誌所報導的研究指出，國際太空站的組員「在抵達太空站後的幾天內免疫功能就會下降」。雖然對此現象原因的研究仍在進行，但太空總署正在採集太空人的唾液和血液樣本，以監測其免疫系統的變化。

　　太空旅行的影響不僅是生理上的，也可能是心理上的。就算太空人在進入軌道繞行前經過密集的訓練，但被關在一個相對狹小的太空站中連續好幾個月，對人的身心也是一種衝擊。太空人可能會感覺與地球上的家人斷了聯繫，因日夜週期的紊亂感到疲憊，以及對受限的環境感到枯燥無味。這些都會導致心理健康問題。為了對付這個問題，太空總署正在研究虛擬實境是否可以用來為太空人創造放鬆的環境並提升他們的心情。

C 20. 關於太空人的肌肉和骨質，我們得知什麼？
   (A) 由於缺乏運動，它們完全消耗殆盡。
   (B) 在特殊的太空環境中難免被使用更多。
   (C) 它們比太空人在地球上時弱。
   (D) 它們受到太空人所穿著的太空衣種類而影響。

   理由
   根據本文第一段第三句，可知 (C) 項應為正選。

Unit 07

Unit 07

D 21. 《國家地理》引用的研究說明什麼？
(A) 呼吸道感染在國際太空站上的傳播只要幾小時，用不著幾天。
(B) 皮膚疹在國際太空站上比在地球上明顯較輕。
(C) 太空人在太空中變得較無法清楚思考。
(D) 國際太空站的太空人免疫力幾乎是立即下降。

理由
根據本文第二段倒數第二句，可知 (D) 項應為正選。

D 22. 本文未提及哪一項太空旅行的潛在心理影響？
(A) 感到無聊。
(B) 因為睡不好而疲憊。
(C) 感覺和親人分離。
(D) 由於強烈的壓力而焦慮。

理由
根據本文第三段第三句，可知唯有 (D) 項並未提及，故為正選。

C 23. 下列哪一項可從本文中推斷？
(A) 國際太空站增加太空人須完成的訓練量。
(B) 國際太空站上的細菌和病毒比其他太空站更活躍。
(C) 太空總署持續努力減少太空人所面臨的問題。
(D) 在太空中服用藥物的效果明顯降低。

理由
根據本文第一段最後一句提及太空總署鼓勵太空人進行為太空船所設計的訓練。第二段最後一句提及太空總署正採集太空人的唾液和血液樣本來監測其免疫系統的變化。第三段最後一句則提及太空總署在研究利用虛擬實境來處理太空人心理層面的問題。以上可推知，(C) 項應為正選。

重要單字與片語

1. **astronaut** [ˋæstrəˌnɔt] *n.* 太空人
2. **toll** [tol] *n.* 傷亡（不可數）
   take its toll　　造成損失
3. **gravity** [ˋgrævətɪ] *n.* 重力，地心引力（皆不可數）
4. **density** [ˋdɛnsətɪ] *n.* 密度；密集度
5. **combat** [ˋkɑmbæt] *vt.* 打擊；對付

例 To combat the sun's harmful rays, Tim used sunscreen.
為了抵擋陽光中的有害輻射，提姆擦防晒乳液。

6. **immune** [ɪˋmjun] *a.* 免疫的
   the immune system　　免疫系統
7. **saliva** [səˋlaɪvə] *n.* 唾液，口水（不可數）

8. **orbit** [ˈɔrbɪt] *n.* （天體繞行的）軌道
9. **confine** [kənˈfaɪn] *vt.* 監禁；限制
   例 That man was confined in prison for many years.
   那名男子被關在牢裡很多年了。
10. **a shock to the system** 對身心系統的衝擊
11. **fatigued** [fəˈtigd] *a.* 疲勞的
12. **counteract** [ˌkaʊntəˈækt] *vt.* 對抗
    例 This antidote should counteract the effects of the poison.
    這個解藥應該可以解這種毒。
13. **waste away** 逐漸消瘦
14. **medication** [ˌmɛdɪˈkeʃən] *n.* 藥物

五 混合題

2023 年 8 月，夏威夷茂宜島的野火帶來死亡和毀滅。以下是四位親身經歷這場災難的人的故事。

瑪麗亞

一切都發生得如此突然。我聞到煙味時，整個社區就已經陷入火海。好在我鄰居有車，他帶著我和其他幾個人到達安全地帶。我不是很確定，但恐怕我美麗的家園已經完全被摧毀了。近日的強風和乾燥條件相結合，為野火蔓延創造了完美的環境。但我腦中一直縈繞著一個問題：為什麼應該提醒我們緊急情況的警報器沒有響？這個系統為什麼失靈了？

凱馬納

我知道天候狀況不佳。所以當我們接到憂心市民打來電話，告知我們倒塌的電線桿引發火災時，我就擔心會發生最糟的狀況。我立刻派員警前往最高風險的地區，盡可能幫助該地居民。但悲哀的是，面對如此強大的大自然敵人，我們也只能做到這樣。我也必須考量我部下的安全，他們是冒著生命危險在進行搶救的。

艾莉兒

我熱愛衝浪還有熱情友好的夏威夷當地人，所以我年年來茂宜島，已經很多年了。我一直以為他們有完善的緊急警報系統，但我想這次是失靈了。有關當局好像毫無準備。在野火發生前的極乾燥天氣以及強風應該讓人有所警覺了吧。我和飯店裡的其他客人得跳進海裡躲避大火。真是太可怕了，感謝老天我們有獲救。

Unit 07

Unit 07

> **納魯**
>
> 在這樣的悲劇中，人們自然會向我這個政府當局之中的高階公務員究責。記者和民眾質問我為什麼緊急警報沒有響，稱其為致命的錯誤。但這套警報系統通常用於海嘯警報，因而需要配備完全不同的緊急反應偵測系統。我反倒認為應該調查為何在這樣危險的天氣狀況下，倒塌的電線桿還繼續通電。假以時日，官方調查將會找出這場災難的真正原因。

以上內容是根據真實事件改編。

這些回應指出茂宜島野火的幾個可能原因，以及為何導致如此大的破壞：緊急警報系統明顯 **24.** 失靈；倒塌的電線桿；以及野火發生前乾燥又 **25.** 颳風的天氣狀況。

理由

第一題空格前為形容詞 apparent，空格後為介詞 of，可得知空格應置名詞。根據瑪麗亞故事的最後一句 "Why did the system fail?"（這個系統為什麼失靈了？），艾莉兒與納魯也皆提及緊急警報系統失靈，得知，空格應置與 fail 相關的名詞 failure。

第二題空格前為形容詞 dry + 對等連接詞 and，空格後為名詞 conditions，可得知空格應置與 dry 對等的形容詞。根據瑪麗亞故事的第五句 "The strong winds and dry conditions of recent days..."（近日的強風和乾燥條件相結合……），艾莉兒與納魯也皆提及強風和危險的天氣狀況，得知，空格應置與 winds 相關的形容詞 windy。

26. 瑪麗亞回應中的哪個片語表示「一個由好幾種負面狀況結合而成的極惡劣狀況」？

(the) perfect storm（完美風暴；惡劣條件的集大成）

理由

根據瑪麗亞回應的倒數第三句 "The strong winds and dry conditions of recent days combined to create the perfect storm for these wildfires."（近日的強風和乾燥條件相結合，為野火蔓延創造了完美的環境。）可推測 (the) perfect storm（完美風暴；惡劣條件的集大成）應為正解。

27. 提供回應的人是誰？請將他們的名字填在以下正確位置。

(A) 警察局長：Kaimana（凱馬納）
(B) 遊客：Ariel（艾莉兒）
(C) 市長：Nalu（納魯）
(D) 當地人：Malia（瑪麗亞）

理由

根據瑪麗亞故事的第四句，可得知她是當地人。根據凱馬納故事的第二至三句及最後一句，可得知他是警察局長。根據艾莉兒故事的倒數第二句，可得知她是遊客。根據納魯故事的第一句，可得知他是市長。

重要單字與片語

1. **engulf** [ɪnˋgʌlf] *vt.* 吞沒；淹沒；包圍
   例 The apartment was engulfed in flames.
   那間公寓被火焰吞噬。

2. **perfect storm**　　完美風暴；惡劣條件的集大成

3. **dwell** [dwɛl] *vi.* 居住（三態為：dwell, dwelt [dwɛlt] / dwelled, dwelt / dwelled）
   dwell on...　　老想著……
   例 Stop dwelling on the past and feeling sorry for yourself! You must move on.
   別再老想著過去在那裡自怨自艾了！你該往前看。

4. **siren** [ˋsaɪrən] *n.* 警報器

5. **foe** [fo] *n.* 敵人

6. **robust** [roˋbʌst] *a.* 健全的；強健的

7. **in place**　　就緒，就位
   例 Over 100 policemen are in place to deal with any violence.
   超過一百名員警已經就位以應付任何暴力行為。

8. **set alarm bells ringing**　　敲警鐘；發出危險信號

9. **civic** [ˋsɪvɪk] *a.* 市民的

10. **confront** [kənˋfrʌnt] *vt.* 對質；使面對
    例 This was the first time John confronted an armed robber.
    這是約翰第一次與武裝搶匪對峙。

11. **necessitate** [nɪˋsɛsəˌtet] *vt.* 需要，使成為必要
    例 The success of this project necessitates your backup.
    本計畫的成功需要你的支持。

Unit 07

Unit 08

一 綜合測驗

　　亞歷山大‧漢密爾頓是一位才華洋溢的政治人物、具影響力的律師以及備受尊崇的財金專家。身為美國開國元勳之一，他也曾為美國獨立而奮鬥。他的貢獻在塑造國家早期的金融體系方面發揮了至關重要的作用。

　　2015 年，一齣名為《漢密爾頓》的百老匯音樂劇讓漢密爾頓的人生故事流傳千古。這齣戲劇是以 2004 年出版的漢密爾頓的傳記為藍本，深獲評論家與觀眾好評。音樂劇以創新的敘事方式和多元化的演員陣容贏得了廣泛的關注，使其達到前所未有的票房佳績。

　　劇中，男主角漢密爾頓的童年以及婚姻故事在革命活動前展開。他在喬治‧華盛頓執政時期掌權並力抗敵手。這些衝突凸顯了早期美國政治激烈的競爭。整場演出在漢密爾頓與一名失意的政治候選人亞倫‧伯爾對決而不幸身亡時達到最高潮。

　　這場演出和其它歷史音樂劇大相逕庭，因為它的配樂使用了當代嘻哈音樂伴隨饒舌對話和歌詞。這種歷史與當代音樂的獨特結合使《漢密爾頓》成為一場令人難忘的戲劇體驗。

B 1. 理由
- a. (A) **correspondence** [ˌkɔrəˈspandəns] *n.* 書信（集合名詞，不可數）
  be in correspondence with sb　　與某人通信聯繫
  例 I have been in correspondence with my cousin for years.
  我和我表妹通信聯繫已經有好幾年了。
  (B) **independence** [ˌɪndɪˈpɛndəns] *n.* 獨立
  例 That country went through many stages before it achieved independence.
  那個國家經過很多階段才獲得獨立。
  (C) **persistence** [pɚˈsɪstəns] *n.* 堅持（與介詞 in 並用）
  sb's persistence in + N/V-ing　　某人對……的堅持
  例 The manager's persistence in carrying out the project finally paid off.
  經理對執行該企畫的堅持總算開花結果。
  (D) **adolescence** [ˌædəˈlɛsn̩s] *n.* 青春期
  in / during one's adolescence　　在某人青春期的時候
  例 I left home during my adolescence.
  我在青少年時期就離開家自己生活了。
- b. 根據語意，(B) 項應為正選。

__D__ **2.** 理由

    a. (A) **peril** [ˈpɛrəl] *n.* 危險

        例 Tom put himself in peril to rescue his dog from the fire.
          湯姆不顧自身危險進入火場救他的狗。

      (B) **pursuit** [pəˈsut] *n.* 追求
         in pursuit of...　　追求……

        例 She spent her entire life in pursuit of her career goals and never got married.
          她終其一生追求事業目標而從未結婚。

      (C) **offense** [əˈfɛns] *n.* 冒犯;犯罪;攻擊

        例 Prosecution for minor offenses rarely leads to imprisonment.
          因輕微的犯罪而被起訴很少會被關。

      (D) **acclaim** [əˈklem] *n.* 稱讚

        例 Jack receives great acclaim as one of the best pitchers ever.
          傑克被大力讚揚為有史以來最棒的投手之一。

    b. 根據語意,(D) 項應為正選。

__D__ **3.** 理由

    a. (A) **unpredictable** [ˌʌnprɪˈdɪktəbl̩] *a.* 不可預料的

        例 Sally's mood is as unpredictable as the weather.
          莎莉的心情就像天氣一樣捉摸不定。

      (B) **unemployed** [ˌʌnɪmˈplɔɪd] *a.* 失業的

        例 Edward has been unemployed for more than a year.
          愛德華已經失業超過一年了。

      (C) **unconditional** [ˌʌnkənˈdɪʃən!] *a.* 無條件的

        例 It is needless to say that true love is unconditional.
          真愛無條件是無庸置疑的。

      (D) **unprecedented** [ʌnˈprɛsəˌdɛntɪd] *a.* 史無前例的

        例 The mayor was elected for an unprecedented fourth term.
          這位市長史無前例地於第四屆連任選舉中獲勝。

    b. 根據語意,(D) 項應為正選。

__A__ **4.** 理由

    a. (A) **take place**　　發生

        例 Where did the accident take place?
          這場意外是在哪裡發生的呢?

Unit 08

(B) **take action** 採取行動

例 Let's take action before it is too late.
咱們採取行動以免太遲。

(C) **take turns** 輪流（之後接現在分詞詞組）

例 My roommates and I take turns cleaning the room.
我的室友和我輪流打掃房間。

(D) **take sides (with sb)** 偏袒（某人）

例 I didn't take sides during their fight. I tried to remain neutral.
他們爭吵時我沒偏袒任何一方。我試著保持中立。

b. 根據語意和用法，(A) 項應為正選。

B 5. 理由

a. (A) **close friendships** 親密的友誼

例 Close friendships are built on trust, communication, and mutual support.
親密的友誼建立在信任、溝通和相互支持之上。

(B) **intense rivalries** 激烈的競爭
rivalry [ˈraɪvl̩rɪ] *n.* 競爭

例 The two schools have had intense rivalries in sports for decades.
這兩所學校在體育方面相互激烈較勁已有數十年了。

(C) **peaceful alliances** 和平的結盟
alliance [əˈlaɪəns] *n.* 結盟，聯盟

例 Throughout history, peaceful alliances have strengthened diplomatic relations.
在歷史上，和平聯盟加強了外交關係。

(D) **economic strategies** 經濟策略

例 The government introduced new economic strategies to boost employment rates.
政府推出新的經濟策略來提高就業率。

b. 根據語意，可知 (B) 項應為正選。

重要單字與片語

1. **influential** [ˌɪnfluˈɛnʃəl] *a.* 有影響力的
be influential in + N/V-ing 在……很有影響力

例 The non-profit organization is very influential in forming public opinion.
這個非營利組織對輿論的形成很有影響力。

2. **financier** [ˌfɪnənˈsɪr] *n.* 金融家，財金專家

3. **crucial** [ˈkruʃəl] *a.* 重要的，決定性的

4. **immortalize** [ɪˋmɔrtə͵laɪz] *vt.* 使永恆，使不朽
   例 The actress was immortalized through her role in this movie.
   這位女演員因為在這部電影裡演出的角色而揚名後世。

5. **musical** [ˋmjuzɪkḷ] *n.* 音樂劇

6. **innovative** [ˋɪnəˏvetɪv] *a.* 創新的

7. **widespread** [ˋwaɪdˏsprɛd] *a.* 廣泛的；普遍的

8. **box office** 票房

9. **protagonist** [proˋtægənɪst] *n.* 重要人物；主角

10. **unfold** [ʌnˋfold] *vi.* (隨時間或故事) 展開 & *vt.* & *vi.* 攤開，打開
    例 As the historical drama unfolds, viewers witness the rise and fall of an ancient empire.
    隨著這部歷史劇展開，觀眾見證了一個古老帝國的興衰。

11. **revolutionary** [͵rɛvəˋluʃənˏɛrɪ] *a.* 革命性的

12. **rise to power** 掌權

13. **administration** [ədˏmɪnəˋstreʃən] *n.* (某人執政時期的) 政府
    the Trump Administration 川普政府
    比較
    the US Government 美國政府

14. **struggle** [ˋstrʌgḷ] *n.* 努力

15. **hostile** [ˋhɑstḷ] *a.* 有敵意的
    be hostile to / towards sb 對某人有敵意
    例 Adolescents are often hostile to their parents.
    青少年常對父母抱持敵意。

16. **opponent** [əˋponənt] *n.* 對手

17. **performance** [pɚˋfɔrməns] *n.* 表現；表演，演出

18. **untimely** [ʌnˋtaɪmlɪ] *a.* 過早的

19. **climax** [ˋklaɪmæks] *n.* 高潮

20. **historical** [hɪsˋtɔrɪkḷ] *a.* 與歷史有關的

21. **lyrics** [ˋlɪrɪks] *n.* 歌詞（恆用複數）

二 文意選填

美國奧克拉荷馬州塔爾薩大學教授華倫・布斯近期所從事的一項研究有了驚人的發現——一小部分的雌性野生蛇類無需雄性也能夠繁殖下一代。

研究者怎麼會有這項令人讚嘆的發現呢？這是將懷孕的銅頭蛇和棉口蝮移離自然環境後發現的。這些蛇當中有兩隻與牠們產下的小蛇擁有一模一樣的基因組合。這項 DNA 證據證實了繁殖過程中沒有雄性蛇介入。這項研究總結出在野外產下的小蛇中有 2.5% 到 5% 可能源自無性生殖。

單性生殖在像是螞蟻和蜜蜂之類的無脊椎動物中十分常見。然而，在脊椎動物中卻很少見。事實上，為人所知的案例只有那些被飼養、與雄性分離的樣本。起初，科學家認為荷爾蒙或病毒會促使飼養的動物產生單性生殖，某些黃蜂就有這樣的情形。另一項理論則表示多餘的無性生殖功能對於不易找到雄性配偶的史前時期是必要的，在沒有雄性的環境中，該功

Unit 08

Unit 08

能會再度啟動。因此單性生殖在繁衍後代上可能具有備用的功能，提供物種長久生存的機會。布斯教授與他的研究團隊所做的發現已使這些理論受到質疑，因為他們的研究是關於在沒有雄性參與的情況下──即使牠們在場──而懷孕的蛇。然而，美國堪薩斯大學醫療中心的彼得‧包曼認為如果無性生殖在繁衍後代上真的具有備用功能，那麼當野生物種整體數量減少時，單性生殖發生的數量理當會上升才對。

__J__ 6. 理由

    a. 空格前有定冠詞 the，空格後有名詞 discovery（發現），得知空格應置形容詞以修飾該名詞。

    b. 選項中 (C) rare（稀有的）及 (J) fascinating（迷人的）為形容詞，惟根據語意，(J) 項應為正選。

    c. **fascinating** [ˈfæsəˌnetɪŋ] *a.* 迷人的

__A__ 7. 理由

    a. 空格前有代名詞所有格 their（牠們的），得知空格應置名詞。

    b. 剩餘選項中 (A) offspring（子孫）、(B) increase（增加）、(D) chance（機會）、(G) question（問題）、(I) result（結果）均為名詞，惟根據語意，(A) 項應為正選。

    c. **offspring** [ˈɔfˌsprɪŋ] *n.* 子孫（單複數同形）

__H__ 8. 理由

    a. 空格前有 be 動詞的過去完成式 had been，空格後有介詞 in，得知空格應置 involved（涉入），以形成下列固定用法：

    be involved in...   涉入……

    例 The evidence shows that Freddy was involved in that murder.
        證據顯示弗萊迪涉入那起謀殺案。

    b. 根據上述，(H) 項應為正選。

__I__ 9. 理由

    a. 空格位於 that 所引導的名詞子句中，子句的主詞為 between 2.5 and 5 percent of wild snake litters（在野外產下的小蛇中有 2.5% 到 5% 的比例），其後有助動詞 could 及副詞 potentially（可能），而空格後有介詞 from，得知空格應置原形動詞 result（產生），以形成下列固定用法：

    result from...   起因於……

    例 Tom's failure resulted from laziness.
    = Laziness resulted in Tom's failure.
        湯姆的失敗起因於懶惰。

    b. 根據上述，(I) 項應為正選。

__C__ 10. 理由
  a. 空格前有主詞 they（單性生殖）和 be 動詞 are，得知空格應置形容詞或名詞以作主詞補語。
  b. 剩餘選項中僅 (C) rare（稀有的）為形容詞，且置入空格後符合語意，故為正選。
  c. **rare** [rɛr] *a.* 稀有的

__F__ 11. 理由
  a. 空格位於動詞 thought 所接的 that 名詞子句中，而 that 於本文中省略，子句的主詞為 hormones or a virus（荷爾蒙或病毒），as is the case with some wasps（某些黃蜂就有這樣的情形）作插入補充用，空格後為名詞 virgin births（單性生殖），得知空格應置 that 子句的動詞，且為過去式及物動詞，以接後面的名詞作受詞。
  b. 剩餘選項中 (E) suggested（表示，顯示）與 (F) triggered（促成）為過去式及物動詞，惟根據語意，(F) 項應為正選。
  c. **trigger** [ˈtrɪɡɚ] *vt.* 引發 & *n.* 扳機
      例 The celebrity's comments triggered many debates among the public.
      這位名人的評論引發了大眾之間許多口水戰。

__E__ 12. 理由
  a. 空格前有主詞 Another theory（另一項理論），空格後有 that 引導的名詞子句，得知空格應置過去式及物動詞，以接 that 子句作受詞。
  b. 剩餘選項中僅剩 (E) suggested（表示，顯示）為過去式及物動詞，且置入空格後符合語意，故為正選。
  c. **suggest** [sə(ɡ)ˈdʒɛst] *vt.* 顯示；暗示（之後 that 子句採一般時態）；提議，建議（之後 that 子句應使用助動詞 should 接原形動詞，should 往往予以省略）
      例 The way John talked to me suggested that he was getting angry.
      約翰跟我說話的態度顯示他在生氣了。
      Tina suggested that I wear a white dress to the wedding.
      提娜建議我穿白色洋裝去參加婚禮。

__D__ 13. 理由
  a. 空格前有不定冠詞 a 及形容詞 greater，得知空格應置單數可數名詞。
  b. 剩餘選項中 (B) increase（增加）、(D) chance（機會）及 (G) question（問題）均為名詞，惟根據語意，(D) 項應為正選。
  c. **chance** [tʃæns] *n.* 機會，可能性
      have a good chance of...　……有很高的可能性

Unit 08

__G__ 14. 理由

a. 空格前有 brought these theories into...（使這些理論……），得知本句使用了下列句型：

bring sth into question　　使某事物受到質疑

例 Tom's misbehavior brought his integrity into question.
湯姆行為不端使他的誠信受到質疑。

b. 根據上述，(G) 項應為正選。

__B__ 15. 理由

a. 空格前有助動詞 may，得知空格應置原形動詞。

b. 剩餘選項 (B) increase（增加）為原形動詞，且置入空格後符合語意，故為正選。

c. **increase** [ɪnˈkris] *vi.* & *vt.* & [ˈɪnkris] *n.* 增加，增大，增強

例 The number of tourists has increased greatly.
遊客的人數已大量增加了。

重要單字與片語

1. **undertake** [ˌʌndɚˈtek] *vt.* 從事
（三態為：undertake, undertook [ˌʌndɚˈtʊk], undertaken [ˌʌndɚˈtekən]）

   例 Prof. Smith undertook a project of writing a book on psychology.
   史密斯教授從事一項撰寫心理學專書的計畫。

2. **sensational** [sɛnˈseʃənəl] *a.* 轟動的

3. **female** [ˈfimel] *a.* 女性的；雌性的 & *n.* 女性；雌性
   male [mel] *a.* 男性的；雄性的 & *n.* 男性；雄性

4. **reproduce** [ˌriprəˈd(j)us] *vi.* 生殖，繁殖

   例 Rabbits are known to reproduce at an extraordinary rate.
   兔子以繁殖迅速著稱。

5. **pregnant** [ˈprɛgnənt] *a.* 懷孕的

6. **copperhead** [ˈkɑpɚˌhɛd] *n.* 銅頭蛇

7. **cottonmouth snake**　　棉口蝮

8. **identical** [aɪˈdɛntɪkl] *a.* 相同的
   A is identical to B　　A 與 B 完全相同

9. **genetic** [dʒəˈnɛtɪk] *a.* 基因的，遺傳（學）的

10. **evidence** [ˈɛvədəns] *n.* 證據，證明（集合名詞，不可數）
    an evidence（✗）
    a piece of evidence（○）一項證據
    a lot of evidence（○）許多證據

11. **confirm** [kənˈfɝm] *vt.* 確認

    例 I would like to confirm my dinner reservation.
    我想要確認晚餐的訂位資料。

12. **litter** [ˈlɪtɚ] *n.* 一窩幼崽
    a litter of puppies　　一窩小狗

13. **asexual** [eˈsɛkʃʊəl] *a.* 無性生殖的；無性別的

14. **virgin** [ˈvɝdʒɪn] *a.* 處女的 & *n.* 處女

15. **invertebrate** [ɪnˈvɝtəbrət] *n.* 無脊椎動物

16. **vertebrate** [ˈvɝtəbrət] *n.* 脊椎動物
17. **specimen** [ˈspɛsəmən] *n.* 樣本
18. **captivity** [kæpˈtɪvətɪ] *n.* 囚禁（不可數）
    be in captivity　　被囚禁起來
19. **hormone** [ˈhɔrmon] *n.* 荷爾蒙
20. **virus** [ˈvaɪrəs] *n.* 病毒，濾過性病毒
21. **redundant** [rɪˈdʌndənt] *a.* 多餘的
22. **prehistoric** [ˌprihɪsˈtɔrɪk] *a.* 史前的
23. **backup** [ˈbækˌʌp] *n.* 備用；備用品
24. **dwindle** [ˈdwɪndl̩] *vi.* 漸漸減少
    例 The number of wild rhinos all over the world has dwindled drastically.
    全球野生犀牛的數目已劇烈減少。

篇章結構

　　回聲定位是一種藉由聲波和回聲所產生的知覺型態。蝙蝠正是具備這項能力的動物中最為人熟知的。蝙蝠在黑暗中獵食之際，牠們會發送高頻而急促的聲納訊號。訊號從蝙蝠身上散發出去，當這些訊號碰到物體，例如樹、鳥或者更棒的是一隻鮮美可口的昆蟲，這些訊號會反彈回蝙蝠身上。蝙蝠跟著反彈到身上的訊號來源，就能鎖定牠們獵物的位置，並從半空中將之攫取入口。換句話說，蝙蝠利用牠們製造的聲音所發出的回聲來尋找鎖定的目標；這就是我們所謂的回聲定位。

　　其他動物也會使用回聲定位。海豚就是很好的例子之一。不過你大概會很驚訝地知另一種使用回聲定位的生物：人類。並非所有人類都有此能力，但少數人已將之發展為一種技能，以彌補其生理上的限制。其中一位這樣的人就是名叫班‧安德伍德的美國人。班雙眼全盲，大腦無法感應任何一道光線。然而，他卻以一種神奇的方式來適應失明。當他移動的時候，他發出「卡嗒」聲來獲取周遭環境的資訊。科學家對班的能力進行研究後發現，他的大腦能夠處理這些「卡嗒」聲的回音，就如同視力正常的人處理視覺資訊一樣。

　　有趣的是，雖然已失去視覺的人由於眼睛沒法正常運作而無法獲取周遭環境視覺方面的訊息，但大腦中的視覺皮層卻不會失去其功能。例如，對班而言，回聲定位取代了雙眼，幫助他在大腦中形成「視覺」影像。就像班說的：「我可以聽見你身後的那道牆。我可以聽見就在那裡 —— 那裡有收音機和電風扇。」他的故事激勵了許多視障人士學習回聲定位，將其作為提升獨立性的工具。透過回聲定位，班和其他視障者能和世界溝通，而世界能回應他們的呼喚。

Unit 08

C 16. 理由
　　a. 空格前句提到回聲定位是一種藉由聲波和回聲所產生的知覺型態，又空格後句到第一段最後一句皆以 bats（蝙蝠）來解釋何謂「回聲定位」，因此空格內容應是要先提到「蝙蝠」，而較能讓語意連貫的為選項 (C) 所述「蝙蝠正是具備這項能力的動物中最為人熟知的。」
　　b. 根據上述，(C) 項應為正選。

Unit 08

E **17.** 理由

a. 空格後句提到：換句話說，蝙蝠利用牠們製造的聲音所發出的回聲來尋找鎖定的目標。由關鍵字 that is（換句話說），可知空格內容應與空格後句相似，此即如選項 (E) 所述「蝙蝠跟著反彈到身上的訊號來源，就能鎖定牠們獵物的位置，並從半空中將之攫取入口。」

b. 根據上述，(E) 項應為正選。

B **18.** 理由

a. 空格前句提到班雙眼全盲，大腦無法感應任何一道光線，又空格後兩句提到：當班移動的時候，他發出「卡嗒」聲來獲取周遭環境的資訊，而他的大腦能夠處理這些「卡嗒」聲的回音，就如同視力正常的人處理視覺資訊一樣，因此空格前後語意相反，空格內容應有轉折語，此正如選項 (B) 所述「然而，他卻以一種神奇的方式來適應失明。」

b. 根據上述，(B) 項應為正選。

D **19.** 理由

a. 空格前句提到：有趣的是，雖然已失去視覺的人由於眼睛沒法正常運作而無法獲取周遭環境視覺方面的訊息，但大腦中的視覺皮層卻不會失去其功能，又空格後句提到班是可「聽到」某些東西在哪裡，且本段最後一句提到：透過 echolocation（回聲定位），班和其他視障者能和世界溝通，而世界能回應他們的呼喚；因此空格內容應為 echolocation（回聲定位）是如何幫助班的，此即如選項 (D) 所述「例如，對班而言，回聲定位取代了雙眼，幫助他在大腦中形成『視覺』影像。」

b. 根據上述，(D) 項應為正選。

(A) 選項翻譯 班研究這些飛行生物多年後，才將他的理論付諸實踐。

重要單字與片語

1. **echolocation** [ˌɛkoloˈkeʃən] n. 回聲定位（不可數）
2. **perception** [pɚˈsɛpʃən] n. 感應，知覺；感知
3. **by means of...** 用……；藉由……的方法
   例 Tom communicated with his French friend by means of email.
   湯姆透過電子郵件與他的法國朋友溝通交流。
4. **emit** [ɪˈmɪt] vt. 發出
5. **sonar** [ˈsonɑr] n. 聲納（不可數）
6. **burst** [bɝst] n.（尤指短期的）突然增加，迸發；爆裂 & vi. 爆開（三態同形）
7. **preferably** [ˈprɛfərəblɪ] adv. 更好地，更可取地；可能的話
   例 Let's meet here—preferably as soon as possible.
   咱們在這裡見面 —— 最好是越快越好。
8. **snatch** [snætʃ] vt. 奪走，搶走
9. **midair** [ˌmɪdˈɛr] n.（半）空中
   in midair   在半空中

10. **learn of...** 獲知……，得知……
    例 I came over as soon as I learned of your accident.
    我一接獲你出意外的消息便立即趕過來。
11. **trace** [tres] *n.* 痕跡
12. **adapt to...** 適應……
    例 It took me years to adapt to city life.
    我花了好多年的時間才適應都市生活。
13. **no longer...** 不再……
14. **visual** [ˈvɪʒuəl] *a.* 視力的
15. **cortex** [ˈkɔrtɛks] *n.* 腦皮層
    visual cortex 視覺皮層
16. **for instance** 例如（= for example）
17. **replace** [rɪˈples] *vt.* 取代
    replace A with B 用 B 取代 A

例 Many employees in the factory were replaced with temporary workers.
這家工廠的許多員工都被臨時僱員取代了。

18. **as sb puts it** 正如某人所說
    例 The movie was "absurd," as Jack put it.
    正如傑克說的，這部電影「荒謬至極」。
19. **communicate with...** 和……溝通
20. **respond to...** 回應……
    例 How did Tim respond to the news that his wife is pregnant?
    提姆對他太太懷孕的消息有何回應？
21. **put... into practice** 將……付諸實行
    例 The company put the new safety measures into practice last month.
    這家公司上個月將新的安全措施付諸實踐。

四 閱讀測驗

1787 年 5 月 13 日，由亞瑟·菲利普船長統率的十一艘船隻從英國的朴茨茅斯啟航。這些船隻被稱為第一艦隊，它們的目的地是澳洲。在這支艦隊共有超過一千四百人，其中約一半是因犯罪而被判處「流放」到遙遠監獄作為懲罰的犯人。另一半由水手、海軍、政府官員以及早期移民組成，他們希望在由英國規劃的澳洲波特尼灣殖民地建立新生活。這支艦隊花了約八個月航行 24,000 公里（途經巴西和南非停靠補給站）才抵達目的地。不可思議的是，儘管當時的天候不佳和疾病傳播，絕大部分旅客都在這趟旅程中存活下來。

然而菲利普和船員一抵達波特尼灣就大失所望。當初選擇這個特定地點，部分是因為早先的探險家詹姆士·庫克船長對此地讚譽有加。然而事實上此地的海灣太淺，土質太貧瘠，淡水來源太少，無法撐起新殖民地的建設。好在菲利普找到一處更有潛力的海灣，既可遮風蔽雨又土地肥沃，而且就在北邊不遠。他以英國的顯貴政治人物雪梨男爵之名，將此地命名為雪梨灣，這支艦隊於 1788 年 1 月 26 日在那裡落腳。

這處澳洲首個英國殖民地的建立，對其產生了深遠的影響。它為人口暴增和經濟繁榮奠定了基礎，更多英國及其他地方的移民登上這片大陸。導入英國法律體系以及英語的傳播，永久性地改變了當地的社會和文化。然而，第一艦隊的到來也最終導致原住民社區被強迫連根拔起，並且無可避免地讓天花之類的疾病傳入，對原住民人口造成毀滅性的破壞。

Unit 08

__D__ 20. 關於第一艦隊，我們得知何事？
(A) 它最初目的是作為罪犯的流動監獄。
(B) 它的船長是個探險家，也是一名政府官員。
(C) 它完全由罪犯組成。
(D) 它並沒有從英國直航到澳洲。

理由
根據第一段倒數第二句，可知 (D) 項應為正選。

__C__ 21. 第二段以「這個特定地點……」開頭的句子暗指什麼？
(A) 庫克船長對波特尼灣沒有好感。
(B) 波特尼灣並非定居的首選。
(C) 詹姆士・庫克比亞瑟・菲利普先造訪澳洲。
(D) 早期的探險家製作了不準確的澳洲地圖。

理由
根據第二段第二句提及因為庫克船長先前對此地讚譽有加，所以他們才選擇這裡，可推知庫克船長先造訪此地，故 (C) 項應為正選。

__B__ 22. 菲利普船長為何更改第一個英國殖民地的地點？
(A) 由於天氣惡劣，他找不到最初選擇的地點。
(B) 他發現雪梨灣有更有利的條件。
(C) 他未能與當地人就波特尼灣達成協議。
(D) 一位重要的英國政治家建議他改變路線。

理由
根據本文第二段第四句，可知 (B) 項應為正選。

__C__ 23. 最後一段的主旨為何？
(A) 殖民者和當地人之間的衝突變得暴力。
(B) 1788 年之後，澳洲人口成長緩慢。
(C) 移民者的到來產生了正面和負面的影響。
(D) 澳洲不再使用英國的法律體系。

理由
根據本文最後一段提及英國殖民地的建立對澳洲人口和經濟繁榮奠定了基礎。但也導致原住民社區被強迫連根拔起，以及疾病的傳入。可得知 (C) 項應為正選。

重要單字與片語

1. **fleet** [flit] *n.* 艦隊
2. **convict** [ˋkɑnvɪkt] *n.* 囚犯 & [ˌkənˋvɪkt] *vt. & vi.* （使）定罪
3. **sentence** [ˋsɛntn̩s] *vt.* 判刑 & *n.* 句子；判刑
   - 例 The robber was sentenced to ten years in prison.
     該搶匪被判十年有期徒刑。
4. **punishment** [ˋpʌnɪʃmənt] *n.* 懲罰
5. **bay** [be] *n.* 海灣
6. **given** [ˋɡɪvən] *prep.* 由於，考慮到
7. **account** [əˋkaʊnt] *n.* 描述，報導；帳戶 & *vi.* 說明，解釋
8. **shallow** [ˋʃælo] *a.* 淺的；膚淺的
9. **scarce** [skɛrs] *a.* 稀少的
10. **prominent** [ˋprɑmənənt] *a.* 重要的；顯著的，突出的
11. **profound** [prəˋfaʊnd] *a.* 深遠的；很有深度的
12. **boom** [bum] *n. & vi.* 突趨繁榮，迅速增長
13. **continent** [ˋkɑntənənt] *n.* 大陸；洲
14. **indigenous** [ɪnˋdɪdʒənəs] *a.* 本地的，土生土長的；當地的
15. **inaccurate** [ɪnˋækjərɪt] *a.* 不精準的
16. **conflict** [ˋkɑnflɪkt] *n.* 衝突 & [kənˋflɪkt] *vi.* 衝突，相抵觸

五 混合題

大家都知道充足睡眠對身心健康是有多麼地重要，但說得容易，做起來難。我們訪問了幾位民眾對此話題發表看法並分享其個人經驗。

(A) 亞瑟
我在廣告公司擔任高階管理職，經常需要加班，因此睡滿八小時對我來說是遙不可及的夢想。我通常只有睡五到六個小時，雖然不夠，但至少不常被打斷。

(B) 貝拉
我以前有睡眠障礙，但自從開始養成在睡前兩小時內不碰電子產品的習慣後，就都睡得很好了。現在我每天起床時都是神清氣爽。我建議大家：在睡前蠻早的時間就該放下手機和平板。

(C) 克里特斯
我忙於社交生活，又得早起上班，所以週間絕對是睡不夠的。不過週末我一定會睡到很晚才起來。如果偶爾睡不著，我會吃褪黑激素。

Unit 08

Unit 08

(D) 朵莉絲
我的新生兒寶寶晚上會醒來好幾次，一直打斷我的睡眠。我會在她白天睡覺時小睡片刻，想說多少補點眠，但我對這種生活方式頗為認命 —— 至少還得要好幾個月吧。

(E) 爾尼
我每晚都睡十小時而且睡得很沉。我能這樣是因為我讓臥室保持涼爽且黑暗，還要遵守固定的睡眠作息：我十點一定上床，早上八點左右就起床。

(F) 芬恩
我每晚盡量睡滿七個小時，而且通常都能做到。我有固定的睡前習慣，包括喝一杯洋甘菊茶以及洗個放鬆身心的熱水澡。一夜好眠比什麼都重要！

(G) 基頓
我臥室的床墊太軟了，影響了睡眠品質。我得去弄張新的。我不確定自己每晚睡了多久，但確知不如理想。也許我該買支智慧手錶來監測睡眠。

(H) 海蒂
我年輕時不太在意睡眠是否充足，寧可犧牲睡眠時間來社交。現在年紀稍長，我知道睡眠的重要了，因此每晚都要睡八小時。睡前看書能幫助我更快入睡。

24. 下面關於各段訪談的說法是正確還是錯誤的？

(1) 朵莉絲認為固定的夜晚作息和每天小憩能幫助她睡得安穩。	False	錯誤
(2) 基頓利用穿戴裝置來確認自己持續擁有深度且消除疲勞的睡眠品質。	False	錯誤
(3) 貝拉決定在睡前不使用電子設備，睡眠品質因而大幅改善。	True	正確
(4) 克里特斯每晚都要靠處方安眠藥來幫助自己入睡。	False	錯誤

理由

(1) 根據 (D) Doris（朵莉絲）的回應 "My new baby wakes up several times during the night, so my sleep is constantly interrupted. I nap during the day when she's sleeping in a vain attempt to catch up..."（我的新生兒寶寶晚上會醒來好幾次，一直打斷我的睡眠。我會在她白天睡覺時小睡片刻，想說多少補點眠……），得知她的睡眠經常被中斷，並沒有固定的夜晚作息，也未提及白天小睡能幫助她睡得安穩，故本句敘述錯誤（False）。

(2) 根據 (G) Gideon（基頓）的回應 "The mattress in my bedroom is too soft, which impacts my sleep quality. I need to get a new one. ... Maybe I should get a smartwatch to monitor it."（我臥室的床墊太軟了，影響了睡眠品質。我得去弄張新的。……也許我該買支智慧手錶來監測睡眠。），僅提到他需要買新的床墊，並考慮或許可以買智慧手錶來監測睡眠，並未提及他已經在使用穿戴裝置來確認擁有深度且消除疲勞的睡眠品質，故本句敘述錯誤（False）。

(3) 根據 (B) Bella（貝拉）的回應第一至二句 "I used to have trouble sleeping, but ever since I started avoiding screens for two hours before bedtime, I've slept like a baby. Now, I wake up feeling refreshed."（我以前有睡眠障礙，但自從開始養成在睡前兩小時內不碰電子產品的習慣後，就都睡得很好了。現在我每天起床時都是神清氣爽。），得知她因為決定在睡前兩小時不使用電子設備，睡眠品質大幅改善，故本句敘述正確（True）。

(4) 根據 (C) Cleetus（克里特斯）的回應第二句 "... if occasionally I have trouble sleeping, I take a melatonin supplement."（……如果偶爾睡不著，我會吃褪黑激素。），得知他偶爾會服用褪黑激素，但並沒有提到自己「每晚都要靠處方安眠藥來幫助自己入睡」，故本句敘述錯誤（False）。

25. 在所有回應中，哪個單字的意思是「最理想的、最令人滿意的或最適合的」？

optimal（最佳的，最優的）

理由

根據 (G) Gideon（基頓）在回應中提及他臥室的床墊太軟因而影響睡眠品質，應該換張新床墊，而第三至四句說 "I'm not sure how much sleep I get each night, but I know it's not optimal."（我不確定自己每晚睡了多久，但確知不如理想。），並考慮買智慧手錶來監測睡眠，可推知他認為自己的睡眠長度並不理想（optimal），故 optimal（最佳的，最優的）應為正解。

C **26.** 從睡眠時間最長到最短，以下哪個選項的排序正確？

(C) 爾尼 > 海蒂 > 芬恩 > 亞瑟

理由

根據 (A) Arthur（亞瑟）的回應第二句 "I usually get five or six hours."（我通常只有睡五到六個小時。）、(E) Ernie（爾尼）的回應第一句 "I sleep like a log for around ten hours a night."（我每晚都睡十小時而且睡得很沉。）、(F) Fern（芬恩）的回應第一句 "I try to get seven hours of sleep a night..."（我每晚盡量睡滿七個小時……）及 (H) Heidi（海蒂）的回應第二句 "I... get eight hours a night."（我……每晚都要睡八小時。），得知四人的睡眠時間由長到短排列為：爾尼（十小時）> 海蒂（八小時）> 芬恩（七小時）> 亞瑟（六小時），故 (C) 項應為正選。

Unit 08

重要單字與片語

1. **be easier said than done** 說來容易做來難
2. **comment on...** 評論……，對……發表意見
   = make a comment on...
   > 例 The teacher asked the students to comment on the article they had just read.
   > 老師請學生評論他們剛剛讀過的文章。
3. **a pipe dream** 白日夢，幻想
4. **refreshed** [rɪˋfrɛʃt] *a.* 已恢復精神的
5. **put away sth / put sth away** 把某物收拾好
   > 例 After dinner, they put away the dishes and cleaned the table.
   > 晚餐後，他們收拾了碗盤並清理了桌面。
6. **definitely** [ˋdɛfənətlɪ] *adv.* 絕對，非常
7. **sleep in** 睡懶覺
8. **occasionally** [əˋkeʒənlɪ] *adv.* 偶爾
9. **supplement** [ˋsʌpləmənt] *n.* 補充物；（雜誌 / 報紙的）副刊（皆為可數）& [ˋsʌpləmɛnt] *vt.* 補充
10. **vain** [ven] *a.* 空虛的，徒勞的；愛慕虛榮的，自負的
    in vain 徒勞地，枉然地
11. **resign oneself to + N/V-ing** 不得不接受……
    > 例 After failing the exam, Dale resigned himself to taking the course again.
    > 考試不及格後，戴爾不得不接受得重修這門課的事實。
12. **optimal** [ˋɑptəml] *a.* 最理想的，最佳的
13. **sacrifice** [ˋsækrəˏfaɪs] *vt. & n.* 犧牲
    > 例 Rita sacrificed her weekend plans to help her friend move.
    > 莉塔犧牲原本週末的安排，去幫朋友搬家。
14. **drop off** 入睡
15. **ensure** [ɪnˋʃur] *vt.* 確認
    > 例 Please ensure that all the windows are closed before leaving the house.
    > 請確認離開房子前所有窗戶都已關好。
16. **restorative** [rɪˋstorətɪv] *a.* 使恢復精力的

Unit 09

一、綜合測驗

　　2006 年，簡彥豪在他的頭上裝了一臺網路攝影機，開始在網路上直播他的生活。Justin.tv 因此誕生。這個點子迅速引起了大眾的注意，吸引了許多好奇的觀眾。過了大約一年，簡彥豪停播了他的生活，而將 Justin.tv 改建成一個任何人都可以開設頻道並使用行動裝置或電腦做直播的網站。這個網站隨著時間擴增，包含許多電視節目、教學課程以及遊戲實況，使其成為內容創作者的多功能平臺。

　　到了 2011 年，Justin.tv 的遊戲類別廣受歡迎，因而獲得了自己的網址 —— Twitch.tv。玩家有一個設備齊全的社群平臺，提供他們直播遊戲過程與觀看其他玩家直播時所需的所有工具。這個網站的受歡迎程度一飛衝天，很快就成為網路流量前四大的網站，僅次於網飛、谷歌以及蘋果。當 Twitch 公開出售時，科技巨頭谷歌公司錯過了收購它的機會。之後在 2014 年八月，亞馬遜公司以將近十億美金收購了 Twitch。這項收購進一步鞏固了 Twitch 作為直播平臺的成功地位。

__B__　1. 理由
　　　a. (A) **build a network**　　建立網路
　　　　　例 The engineers worked hard to build a network that ensured fast communication.
　　　　　　工程師們努力建立一個確保快速通訊的網路。
　　　　(B) **launch a channel**　　開設頻道
　　　　　例 The singer launched a channel focused on travel and adventure content.
　　　　　　那位歌手開設了一個內容聚焦在旅行與冒險的頻道。
　　　　(C) **purchase a server**　　購買伺服器
　　　　　purchase [ˈpɝtʃəs] *vt.* & *n.* 購買
　　　　　server [ˈsɝvɚ] *n.* 伺服器；服務生
　　　　　例 William plans to purchase a server for his growing online business.
　　　　　　威廉計劃買一臺伺服器來因應他日益成長的線上業務。
　　　　(D) **gain some support**　　獲得支持
　　　　　例 The politician tried to gain some support before the election.
　　　　　　這位政治人物試圖在選舉前獲得支持。
　　　b. 根據語意，可知 (B) 項應為正選。

__C__ 2. 理由

    a. (A) **not more than** + 數字　　最多不超過……
        = at most + 數字
        例 I hope it takes me not more than two hours to finish my homework.
        我希望花最多不超過兩小時來完成功課。
      (B) **not a little**　　非常，極其（= quite / very）
        例 Tom is not a little excited about his trip to France.
        湯姆非常期待他的法國之旅。
      (C) **a good many** + 複數名詞　　很多的……
        例 Sophie has a good many things to do tonight.
        蘇菲今晚有很多的事要做。
      (D) **a far cry from...**　　與……大不相同
        例 Taipei is a far cry from my hometown in Alaska.
        臺北與我的故鄉阿拉斯加大相逕庭。
    b. 根據語意，(C) 項應為正選。

__D__ 3. 理由

    a. (A) **province** [ˋprɑvɪns] *n.* 省
        例 The province of Alberta, Canada is magnificent.
        加拿大的亞伯達省景色很美。
      (B) **myth** [mɪθ] *n.* 迷思；神話；虛構的人事物
        例 The story in the newspaper is just a myth. It is not true at all.
        這篇報紙上的故事不過是虛構的，根本不是真的。
      (C) **gender** [ˋdʒɛndɚ] *n.* 性別
        例 To the young couple, the gender of their baby is not that important.
        對這對年輕夫妻來說，小寶寶的性別並不是那麼重要。
      (D) **category** [ˋkætəˏgɔrɪ] *n.* 種類，類別
        例 In this game show, players have to answer questions from seven different categories.
        在這個遊戲節目中，玩家必須回答七個不同類別的問題。
    b. 根據語意，(D) 項應為正選。

__A__ 4. 理由

    a. (A) **sophisticated** [səˋfɪstɪˏketɪd] *a.* （機器、系統）精密的；世故的
        例 This machine is very sophisticated. Therefore, it should only be run by professionals.
        這臺機器很精密。所以應該由專業人士來操作。

Unit 09

(B) **redundant** [rɪˈdʌndənt] *a.* 多餘的
  例 These three sentences are redundant. Your composition would be better without them.
  這三個句子是多餘的。把它們刪除你的文章會更好。

(C) **sacred** [ˈsekrɪd] *a.* 神聖的
  例 Cows are considered to be sacred animals in India.
  牛在印度被視為是神聖的動物。

(D) **tedious** [ˈtidɪəs] *a.* 枯燥乏味的，沉悶無聊的
  例 The movie was so tedious that I didn't finish watching it.
  這部電影太過沉悶，所以我沒把它看完。

b. 根據語意，(A) 項應為正選。

C 5. 理由

a. (A) **plunge** [plʌndʒ] *vi.* 跳入
    plunge into...   跳入……
  = jump into...
  例 The lifeguard plunged into the river and saved the drowning boy.
  救生員跳入河中，救起差點溺斃的男孩。

(B) **split** [splɪt] *vi.* 分開，分割 & *vt.* 分裂（三態同形）
   split sth in two / in half   將某物分成兩塊
   split sth into...   將某物分成……
  例 The cake was split into two parts.
  蛋糕被切成兩塊。

(C) **skyrocket** [ˈskaɪˌrɑkɪt] *vi.* 猛升，劇增
  例 The company's share price has skyrocketed to a record high.
  該公司的股價飆升到創新高的紀錄。

(D) **freeze** [friz] *vi.* 結冰，凝固（三態為：freeze, froze [froz], frozen [ˈfrozn̩]）
  例 The water froze on the road, making it dangerous to drive.
  水在馬路上結成冰，因此在上面開車很危險。

b. 根據語意，(C) 項應為正選。

重要單字與片語

1. **attach** [əˈtætʃ] *vt.* 附上；繫住；連接
   attach A to B   將 A 附著於 B 上
  例 Please attach a reference letter to your resume.
  請在你的履歷表上附一封推薦信。

2. **cease** [sis] *vt.* & *vi.* 停止
   cease + V-ing　　停止做……；不做……
   = cease to V
   > 例 Since her son died, she has never ceased regretting her neglect of him.
   = Since her son died, she has never ceased to regret her neglect of him.
   自從她的兒子死後，她一直不斷懊悔對他的疏忽。

3. **stream** [strim] *vt.* 線上收聽或收看

4. **tutorial** [tuˋtɔrɪəl] *n.* 個別指導

5. **versatile** [ˋvɝsətḷ] *a.* 多用途的；多才多藝的

6. **popularity** [ˏpɑpjəˋlærətɪ] *n.* 聲望，名氣（不可數）

7. **pass sth up**　　錯過某事物；放棄某事物

> 例 Hans likes to eat, so he never passes up a free meal.
漢斯很愛吃，所以他從不錯過免費的餐點。

8. **purchase** [ˋpɝtʃəs] *vt.* 購買
> 例 Many computer components can be purchased online at a low price.
許多電腦零件可以在網路上以低價購得。

9. **acquisition** [ˏækwəˋzɪʃən] *n.* 收購；獲得（不可數）；添購的物品

10. **solidify** [səˋlɪdəˏfaɪ] *vt.* & *vi.* （使）鞏固，（使）穩固；（液體或氣體）固化
> 例 The new policy will solidify our commitment to environmental protection.
新政策將鞏固我們對環境保護的承諾。

二 文意選填

平均來說，消費者每一天每分鐘在美容產品上花費一百萬美元。這使得美容產業的年度經濟成長產生超過四千二百六十億美元的收入。

美妝產業所銷售的產品包含使眼睛看起來更大更明亮的眼影、眼線筆和睫毛膏，還有口紅和唇蜜創造出魅力四射的雙唇，而粉底和腮紅則隱藏了肌膚的瑕疵，讓肌膚看起來像絲綢般滑順細緻。另外，還有好幾千種不同色彩的化妝品和幾百種化妝品塗抹用品。此外，如果我們不希望化完妝後變得像個馬戲團小丑，知道正確的化妝品使用技巧和適當的使用量也非常重要。

美妝影音部落客蜜雪兒‧潘已成了 YouTube 網紅明星。潘小姐是美妝產品達人。她提供青少女和輕齡女子有趣又實用的美妝教學課程，也提供美妝上的訣竅和其他好用的建議。此外，她傳遞了無形特質的重要性，例如自信、態度以及獲得更美好體態的技巧。

潘小姐來自波士頓，她是越南籍移民的女兒。她在 2008 年開啟了她的 YouTube 頻道，現在有三百多支影片和超過八百萬名訂閱者。她的頻道有十三億觀看人次，相當驚人，讓潘小姐年收入超過一百萬美金。她也運用她龐大的關注量獲得了法國美妝產品公司巴黎蘭蔻的資金贊助合約，創造了名為 Ipsy 的實體商店，富比士估計有五億市值。

Unit 09

__I__ 6. **理由**
 a. 空格前有本句主詞 That、動詞 makes 及其受詞 the beauty industry（美容產業），根據 make 的用法得知空格可置名詞形成 make + A + B（讓 A 變成 B）的固定用法，或置形容詞形成 make sb/sth + adj.（讓某人或某物變得……）的固定用法。
 b. 選項中為名詞或形容詞的有 (B) tips（訣竅）、(D) subscribers（訂閱者）、(F) essential（重要的）、(I) responsible（負有責任的）、(J) qualities（特質），惟根據語意，(I) 項應為正選。
 c. **responsible** [rɪˋspɑnsəb!] *a.* 應負責的；負責任的
  be responsible for...　　為……負責
  例 The airline company is legally responsible for the safety of all its passengers.
   航空公司依法必須為所有乘客的安全負責。

__G__ 7. **理由**
 a. 空格前為本句主詞 Products（產品）及其修飾語 sold by the cosmetic industry（美妝產業所銷售的），得知空格應置本句動詞，且為複數動詞。上述修飾語為形容詞子句 which / that are sold by the cosmetic industry 省略關係代名詞 which / that 及 be 動詞 are 而來。
 b. 選項中為複數動詞的有 (A) apply（塗抹）、(C) receive（收到）及 (G) include（包括），惟根據語意，(G) 項應為正選。
 c. **include** [ɪnˋklud] *vt.* 包括
  例 The assistant's job included running errands for the busy photographer.
   那位助理的工作包含替忙碌的攝影師跑腿。

__A__ 8. **理由**
 a. 原句實為：
  ...applicators which / that are used to...
  上句可省略關係代名詞 which / that 及 be 動詞 are，而 used 後面有引導不定詞的 to，且空格後有名詞 cosmetics（化妝品），得知空格應置原形及物動詞，以形成下列固定用法：
  be used to V　　被用來……
  例 The beautiful painting is used to decorate my room.
   這幅美麗的畫作是用來裝飾我的房間。
  比較
   sb is used to + N/V-ing　　某人習慣……
  = sb is accustomed to + N/V-ing
  例 John is used to having sandwiches as his breakfast.
   約翰已習慣早餐吃三明治。

b. 剩餘選項中為原形及物動詞的有 (A) apply（塗抹）及 (C) receive（收到），惟根據語意及用法，(A) 項應為正選。

　　c. **apply** [ə`plaɪ] *vt.* 塗抹
　　　　例 You can apply sunscreen to avoid sunburn.
　　　　　你可以塗抹防曬乳以免曬傷。

F　9. 理由

　　a. 空格前有動名詞詞組 knowing the correct application techniques（知道正確的化妝品使用技巧）及 using just the right amount of makeup（適當的使用量）作本句主詞及 be 動詞 are，得知空格應置名詞或形容詞以作主詞補語。

　　b. 剩餘選項中為名詞或形容詞的有 (B) tips（訣竅）、(D) subscribers（訂閱者）、(F) essential（重要的）及 (J) qualities（特質），惟根據語意，(F) 項應為正選。

　　c. **essential** [ɪ`sɛnʃəl] *a.* 重要的，不可或缺的

E　10. 理由

　　a. 空格前有第三人稱單數主詞 Ms. Phan（潘小姐），且空格後有介詞 in，得知空格應置 specializes（專精），以形成下列固定用法：
　　　　specialize in...　　專精於從事……
　　　　例 That musician specializes in playing the violin.
　　　　　那位音樂家專精於演奏小提琴。

　　b. 根據上述，(E) 項應為正選。

B　11. 理由

　　a. 空格前有介詞片語 along with（以及……），此片語後方應置名詞或名詞詞組，得知空格應置名詞，以與名詞 beauty（美）形成名詞詞組。

　　b. 剩餘選項中 (B) tips（訣竅）、(D) subscribers（訂閱者）及 (J) qualities（特質）均為名詞，惟根據語意，(B) 項應為正選。

　　c. **tip** [tɪp] *n.* 訣竅；小費

J　12. 理由

　　a. 空格前有形容詞 intangible（無形的），得知空格應置名詞以被該形容詞修飾。

　　b. 剩餘選項中 (D) subscribers（訂閱者）及 (J) qualities（特質）均為名詞，惟根據語意，(J) 項應為正選。

　　c. **quality** [`kwɑlətɪ] *n.* 品質；特質

D　13. 理由

　　a. 空格前有數量詞 eight million（八百萬），得知空格應置複數名詞。

　　b. 剩餘選項中僅 (D) subscribers（訂閱者）為複數名詞，且置入空格後符合語意，故為正選。

　　c. **subscriber** [səb`skraɪbɚ] *n.* 訂閱者

Unit 09

Unit 09

__H__ 14. 理由

a. 空格前有關係代名詞 that 引導形容詞子句，修飾前面的名詞詞組即其先行詞 an annual income（年收入），空格後有名詞詞組 US$1 million（一百萬美金），得知空格應置第三人稱單數及物動詞作形容詞子句的動詞，並接後面的名詞詞組作受詞。

b. 剩餘選項中僅 (H) exceeds（超過）為第三人稱單數及物動詞，且置入空格後符合語意，故為正選。

c. **exceed** [ɪkˋsid] *vt.* 超過
  例 Don't exceed the speed limit when driving.
  開車時千萬不要超速。

__C__ 15. 理由

a. 空格前有本句動詞 used（利用）及其受詞 her massive following（她龐大的關注量），得知空格應置原形動詞，以與前面的 to 形成不定詞片語，表示目的，以修飾整句。

b. 剩餘選項中僅剩 (C) receive（收到）為原形動詞，且置入空格後符合語意及用法，故為正選。

c. **receive** [rɪˋsiv] *vt.* 收到；接待
  例 The general received the Medal of Honor for his service in World War II.
  那位將軍因在二次大戰裡的表現而獲得榮譽勳章。

重要單字與片語

1. **on average** 平均來說
2. **consumer** [kənˋsumɚ] *n.* 消費者
3. **industry** [ˋɪndəstrɪ] *n.* 工業；產業
4. **generation** [ˌdʒɛnəˋreʃən] *n.* 產生；世代
5. **economic** [ˌikəˋnɑmɪk] *a.* 與經濟有關的
6. **annually** [ˋænjʊəlɪ] *adv.* 每一年（= every year 或 yearly）
7. **cosmetic** [kɑzˋmɛtɪk] *n.* 化妝品（常用複數形 cosmetics）& *a.* 化妝的
   比較
   makeup [ˋmekˌʌp] *n.* 彩妝（不可數）
   注意
   化妝品包括睫毛膏、口紅、眼影等等，因此 cosmetic 常用複數形 cosmetics。許多人常將 makeup（彩妝）與 cosmetics（化妝品）混為一體，makeup 指的是塗在臉上的彩妝。
   例 The doctor suggested I use oil-free cosmetics because I have acne problems.
   醫師建議我使用不含油的化妝品因為我有青春痘的問題。
   Mary didn't wear any makeup today, but she looks beautiful just the same.
   瑪麗今天沒有上妝，但還是一樣漂亮。
   Mary didn't wear any cosmetics today.（✗，無此用法）
8. **mascara** [mæsˋkærə] *n.* 睫毛膏（不可數）
9. **lip gloss** [glɑs] 唇蜜

10. **foundation** [faʊnˋdeʃən] *n.* 粉底
11. **blush** [blʌʃ] *n.* 腮紅
12. **blemish** [ˋblɛmɪʃ] *n.* （皮膚上的）疤痕；汙點
13. **variation** [ˏvɛrɪˋeʃən] *n.* 變化
14. **intangible** [ɪnˋtændʒəbḷ] *a.* （具價值但）無形的
15. **obtain** [əbˋten] *vt.* 獲得
16. **immigrant** [ˋɪməgrənt] *n.* 移民者（由外移入）

比較
emigrant [ˋɛməgrənt] *n.* 移民者（由內移出）

17. **staggering** [ˋstægərɪŋ] *a.* 驚人的
18. **lucrative** [ˋlukrətɪv] *a.* 高獲利的
    例 Nowadays, the computer industry is a lucrative market.
    現今，電腦產業是個高獲利的市場。
19. **sponsorship** [ˋspɑnsɚˏʃɪp] *n.* 贊助金
20. **bricks-and-mortar** [ˋbrɪksəndˏmɔrtɚ] *a.* 實體的；具體的
    a bricks-and-mortar store　　實體店面

三 篇章結構

　　馬卡龍是一種來自於法國小巧又美味的甜點，似乎到處都很流行。從巴黎最好的烘焙坊到德國及日本的糕點小舖，以及美國的咖啡店，這種以蛋白酥為基底的甜點正風靡全世界。萬一你不知道的話，蛋白酥是蛋白及糖粉的混合物，常被作為派和蛋糕的配料。當談到馬卡龍時，蛋白酥總是關注的焦點。

　　普遍認為是義大利麥第奇家族的皇家糕點師傅於 1533 年將馬卡龍帶入法國，為了當時麥第奇家族的凱薩琳與法國國王亨利二世的婚禮。根據另一說法，馬卡龍是 1791 年法國一間修道院製作出來的。不論真相為何，馬卡龍漸漸地受到越來越多的關注。

　　二十世紀初迎來現代版馬卡龍：一種迷你糕點三明治，由兩塊餅乾之間填滿奶油、果醬或名為甘納許的一種甜甜的巧克力鮮奶油混合物。這種較新的馬卡龍原本被稱作吉伯特馬卡龍或巴黎馬卡龍。然而，這些可口的甜點並不侷限處於法國的糕點小舖中。

　　馬卡龍的超高人氣可以從網路或電影、電視節目、雜誌文章以及像是日本糕點師傅所撰寫的《我愛馬卡龍》這種書籍中看到。這些當今似乎無所不在的甜點，在各式各樣的商家和食物零售商都有販售。馬卡龍的食用量是前所未有地高，且不斷出現新型態。在法國亞眠市，馬卡龍會以杏仁醬、蜂蜜及水果製成。日式烘焙坊則會用花生粉取代杏仁粉。在日本和南韓，綠茶粉或茶葉被用來製作成亞洲風味的馬卡龍。在南韓首爾的弘大一帶甚至還有店家販賣馬卡龍雪糕夾心三明治。

　　此外，三月二十日為世界馬卡龍日。當天參加活動的商店不僅提供免費的馬卡龍，還捐款給當地的慈善機構。不要錯過這個可免費享用很多馬卡龍的難得機會。

Unit 09

Unit 09

__B__ 16. 理由
  a. 空格前兩句提到馬卡龍,即 these meringue-based treats（這種以蛋白酥為基底的甜點）正風靡全世界,又空格後句提到當談到馬卡龍時,meringue always takes center stage（蛋白酥總是關注的焦點）,因此空格應是詳加解釋何謂 meringue（蛋白酥）,此即選項 (B) 所述「萬一你不知道的話,蛋白酥是蛋白及糖粉的混合物,常被作為派和蛋糕的配料。」
  b. 根據上述,(B) 項應為正選。

__E__ 17. 理由
  a. 第二段第一至二句提到有關馬卡龍的起源有不同的說法,與選項 (E) 中的 whatever the truth（不論真相為何）形成關聯。
  b. 根據上述,(E) 項應為正選。

__A__ 18. 理由
  a. 第二段在講述馬卡龍的起源,又空格前一句提到二十世紀初 the modern macaron（現代版馬卡龍）的特色,與選項 (A) 中的 this newer creation（這種較新的馬卡龍）形成關聯。
  b. 根據上述,(A) 項應為正選。

__D__ 19. 理由
  a. 第四段第三句後半提到馬卡龍不斷出現新型態,接著第四至五句提到法國亞眠市、日本和南韓等都依自己的特色或創意來變化馬卡龍,因此空格應是再提及另一個創意馬卡龍的例子,即如選項 (D) 所述「在南韓首爾的弘大一帶甚至還有店家販賣馬卡龍雪糕夾心三明治。」
  b. 根據上述,(D) 項應為正選。

(C) 選項翻譯 這種馬卡龍口味被認為是過去亨利二世和他新任妻子的獨寵。

重要單字與片語

1. **treat** [trit] *n.* 美味的東西；特別的款待
2. **catch on**　　變得流行；變得受歡迎
   例 This song has caught on and now almost everybody can sing or at least hum it.
   這首歌很流行,現在幾乎每個人都會唱或至少哼這首歌。
3. **Parisian** [pəˋrɪʒən] *a.* 巴黎的；巴黎人的；和巴黎有關的 & *n.* 巴黎人
4. **pastry** [ˋpestrɪ] *n.* 油酥糕點；油酥點心
5. **meringue** [məˋræŋ] *n.* 蛋白酥
6. **captivate** [ˋkæptə͵vet] *vt.* 使著迷
   例 Lisa is captivated by the fragrance of roses.
   玫瑰花的香味使麗莎著迷。
7. **when it comes to + N/V-ing**　　一談到……時
   例 When it comes to movies, Tom is fond of fantasy.
   說到電影,肯尼喜歡奇幻電影。

8. **take center stage**　成為關注的焦點
   例 Among all the singers in the concert, Laura's voice took center stage.
   在演唱會的所有歌手中，蘿拉的歌聲成為了焦點。

9. **convent** [ˈkɑnvɛnt] *n.* 女修道院

10. **consist** [kənˈsɪst] *vi.* 由……組成
    consist of...　由……所組成
    = be made up of...
    = be composed of...
    注意 consist of... 無被動形式
    例 This class consists of twenty boys and five girls.
    這個班級是由二十位男孩和五位女孩所組成的。

11. **delectable** [dɪˈlɛktəbḷ] *a.* 美味的

12. **popularity** [ˌpɑpjəˈlærətɪ] *n.* 流行；聲望（不可數）

13. **consumption** [kənˈsʌmpʃən] *n.* 消耗（量）；消費（量）（不可數）

14. **substitute** [ˈsʌbstəˌtut] *vt.* 代替，取代
    substitute A for B　以 A 取代 B
    例 You can substitute apple sauce for oil when baking a cake.
    烤蛋糕時，你可以使用蘋果醬替代油。

15. **a large number of** + 可數複數名詞
    很多……
    a small number of + 可數複數名詞
    少數……
    例 A large number of students are against the new project.
    很多學生反對這新計畫。
    比較
    a large amount of + 不可數名詞
    很多……
    a small amount of + 不可數名詞
    少數……
    例 A large amount of money was stolen from the private bank.
    那間私人銀行有一大筆錢遭竊。

四 閱讀測驗

　　大多數人想到蝴蝶，腦中的畫面會是美麗、脆弱的昆蟲，在花園或公園裡翩翩飛舞，而不會想成一種長途旅行的有毒動物，在較溫暖的地帶過冬後，能夠不可思議地找到回家的路。大家通常不會這樣看待蝴蝶，是因為只有一個蝴蝶品種符合這種描述：帝王斑蝶。

　　帝王斑蝶有毒這件事有助於保護牠們不被掠食者吃掉。牠會擁有這個特點，是因為牠們在還未蛻變為蝴蝶的毛毛蟲時期會以乳草為食。帝王斑蝶也因此被稱為乳草斑蝶。牠們的翅膀也很獨特，上面有像是血管分布般的獨特紋路，而翅膀的邊緣則布滿斑點。而其他蝴蝶的翅緣是素色或是只有些許斑點，有些則會有幾個看似眼睛的斑點。關於牠們的遷徙習慣，必須指出並非所有帝王斑蝶都會有此表現。事實上，只有當年最後一代出生的斑蝶會遵循雙向的遷徙模式。這是因為在春夏兩季出生的斑蝶，大多數只能存活最多五週，因此沒必要為了過冬而長途飛行到氣候宜人的地方。

Unit 09

　　在北美洲，從九月、十月開始，就有大量帝王斑蝶從加拿大與美國遷徙至墨西哥中部，飛行抵達目的地的距離最多可達五千公里。從三月起牠們會開始北返，沿途雌蝶會產下下一代的卵。科學家長久以來都著迷於帝王斑蝶找路回家的本領，這種驚人的方向感被認為與太陽的方位及地球的磁場引力有關。這些特質讓帝王斑蝶絕不是你想像中的普通蝴蝶。

C　20. 根據本文，是什麼讓帝王斑蝶具有毒性？
(A) 牠們獨特的交配習慣。
(B) 牠們翅膀上的特殊物質。
(C) 牠們還是毛毛蟲時的食物。
(D) 一種代代相傳的基因。

理由
根據本文第二段第二句，可知 (C) 項應為正選。

D　21. 下列何者為帝王斑蝶？
(A)　　(B)
(C)　　(D)

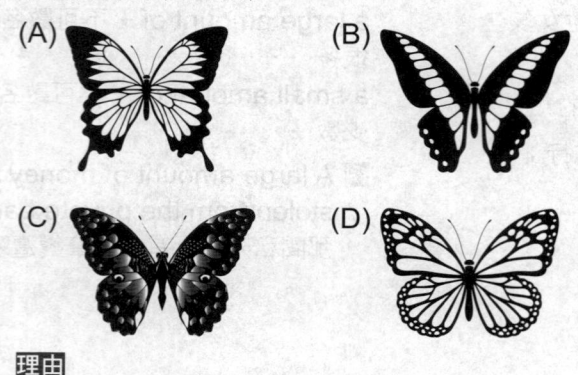

理由
根據本文第二段第四句，可知 (D) 項應為正選。

C　22. 第三段中的 they 所指為何？
(A) 目的地。
(B) 下一代。
(C) 帝王斑蝶。
(D) 科學家。

理由
此處 they 所指的是前一句 "...large populations of monarch butterflies travel from Canada and the United States to central Mexico, ..." 中大量的帝王斑蝶，可知 (C) 項應為正選。

A 23. 有關帝王斑蝶,下列哪一項敘述不正確?
(A) 帝王斑蝶的每一代都會南遷過冬。
(B) 帝王斑蝶的遷徙在秋季從北美洲出發。
(C) 有些帝王斑蝶的壽命只比一個月多一點。
(D) 帝王斑蝶的能力與地球引力有關。

理由
根據本文第二段第六至八句,可知 (A) 項應為正選。

重要單字與片語

1. **delicate** [ˋdɛləkət] *a.* 脆弱的;精緻的
   例 This ancient book is very delicate and should be handled with care.
   這本古書很脆弱,必須小心拿。
2. **poisonous** [ˋpɔɪznəs] *a.* 有毒的
3. **routinely** [ruˋtinlɪ] *adv.* 例行地
4. **species** [ˋspiʃiz] *n.* 品種(單複數同形)
5. **monarch** [ˋmɑnɚk] *n.* 君主,帝王
6. **predator** [ˋprɛdətɚ] *n.* 掠食者
7. **attribute** [əˋtrɪbjut] *n.* 特質
8. **caterpillar** [ˋkætɚˏpɪlɚ] *n.* 毛毛蟲
9. **distinctive** [dɪˋstɪŋktɪv] *a.* 特殊的,獨特的
   例 Each country has its distinctive culture.
   每個國家有自身獨特的文化。
10. **pattern** [ˋpætɚn] *n.* 型態,模式;圖案,花紋
11. **migratory** [ˋmaɪgrəˏtɔrɪ] *a.* 遷徙的
    migratory birds 候鳥
12. **moderate** [ˋmɑdərɪt] *a.* 適度的
13. **population** [ˏpɑpjəˋleʃən] *n.* 人口,動物總數
14. **northward** [ˋnɔrθwɚd] *adv.* 向北方地(也作 northwards)
    southward [ˋsaʊθwɚd] *adv.* 向南方地(也作 sourthwards)
15. **fascinate** [ˋfæsnˏet] *vt.* 使著迷(通常用過去分詞當形容詞用)
    be fascinated by / with... 對……著迷
    例 Jane was fascinated with the man who was playing the guitar.
    珍對那位彈吉他的男子著迷不已。
16. **magnetic** [mægˋnɛtɪk] *a.* 磁性的
17. **mating** [ˋmetɪŋ] *n.* 交配(不可數)

Unit 09

Unit 09

五 混合題

抖音是個廣受歡迎的社群媒體平臺，用戶可以創作與分享短片。以下四人對於這個應用程式表達出他們的意見。

(A) 柔依
我每次想要逃避考試或家庭作業時，都會去看抖音。看點有創意又爆笑的影片著實可以幫助我放鬆，然後感覺壓力沒那麼大。我會限制自己只看個幾分鐘，通常也都能做到。不過有時候我的確會失控。然而抖音不僅是有趣的消遣而已，它也是可以幫助課業的教學工具。如果在某個特定主題上，我能在抖音找到一些簡短、精闢而資訊量豐富的影片，那麼我的理解以及記住細節就更容易。

(B) 戴爾
我女兒永遠都掛在抖音上，在她房間裡、在車子裡，甚至在餐桌上都在看，她辯稱抖音讓她放鬆、感覺紓壓。但我覺得她就是在浪費時間。她就坐在那手機滑來滑去沒停過，滑一滑就停下來看些無腦的動物、小嬰兒以及跳舞的人的影片。她說那些影片很好玩，我則覺得它們是極度讓人心智麻木的東西。我也很擔心她可能會不小心看到不合宜的影片內容。

(C) 艾莉西亞
你可能以為身為高中老師的我會排斥抖音。你可能認為我視抖音為浪費時間、干擾工作或學習等更重要事情的東西。但它能讓我的學生投入，讓他們對之前斥為無聊的主題產生興趣，這點讓我相當驚喜。我甚至曾把使用抖音當作學生家庭作業的一部分。所以我認為，只要偶爾使用並在對的情況下使用，這個應用程式可以成為很方便的教學工具。

(D) 泰勒
我曾經是抖音的愛用者。我會花上許多小時在這程式裡滑來滑去，看食物跟運動的影片。但我後來意識到我根本什麼正事都沒幹。事實上我根本是在做完全相反的事：我不管家庭作業、忘記家族活動、忽略了朋友。現在我已經完全禁止自己使用抖音。每當我看到有人無腦地在手機上看廢片時，我都會暗地嘲笑他們。在他們浪費生命看著螢幕的同時，我正在做實際而有建設性的事情。

各個回應主要都圍繞在抖音被視為 **24.** 浪費時間，其教學工具的用途，以及幫助使用者減輕 **25.** 壓力三個點上。

理由
第一格空格前有不定冠詞 a，空格後有介詞 of，得知空格應置名詞。根據戴爾意見的第二句 "However, I think she's just wasting her time."（但我覺得她就是在浪費時間。）、艾莉西亞意見的第二句 "... I would consider it a time-wasting diversion from..."（……我視抖音為浪費時間、干擾……）及泰勒意見的最後一句 "They're wasting their lives looking at a screen..."（在他們浪費生命看著螢幕的同時，……）得知，空格應置與 wasting 相關的名詞 waste。第二格空格前為及物動詞 relieve，得知空格應置名詞做受詞。根據柔依與戴爾皆提及 "feel less stressed"（感覺紓壓）得知，空格應置與 stressed 相關的名詞 stress。

26. 艾莉西亞回應裡的哪個字表示「使你從其他事分心的事物」？

diversion（分心的事物）

理由
根據艾莉西亞意見的第二句 "... I would consider it a time-wasting diversion from more important tasks like work or study."（……我視抖音為浪費時間、干擾工作或學習等更重要事情的東西。），可推知 diversion（分心的事物）應為正解。

27. 請根據當事人或他們描述的目前情況，將他們抖音成癮的程度從最低排到最高。

1. (D) < (C) < 2. (A) < 3. (B)

理由
根據泰勒意見的第五句 "These days, I have banned myself from using it entirely."（現在我已經完全禁止自己使用抖音。）得知，第一格空格應選 (D)。根據柔依意見的第三、四句 "I try to restrict myself to watching them for only a few minutes, and I usually succeed. But sometimes I do get carried away."（我會限制自己只看個幾分鐘，通常也都能做到。不過有時候我的確會失控。）得知，第二格空格應選 (A)。據戴爾意見的第一句 "My daughter uses TikTok all the time—in her bedroom, in the car, even at the dinner table..."（我女兒永遠都掛在抖音上，在她房間裡、在車子裡，甚至在餐桌上都在看，……）得知，第三格空格應選 (B)。

重要單字與片語

1. **hilarious** [həˋlɛrɪəs] *a.* 極好笑的，引人發笑的
2. **be / get carried away** 失去控制，忘乎所以

例 We must be careful and not be carried away by our achievements. 我們得當心不要被自己的成就給沖昏頭。

3. **snappy** [ˋsnæpɪ] *a.* 精闢的

Unit 09

Unit 09

4. **unwind** [ʌnˈwaɪnd] *vi.* 放鬆（三態為：unwind, unwound [ʌnˈwaʊnd], unwound）
   - 例 The soldiers often go out to the club to unwind after a long week of being on duty.
     士兵們經過一星期漫長的執勤後通常會到俱樂部放鬆一下。

5. **scroll** [skrɔl] *vi.* 上下滾動（文件、電腦頁面）

6. **contend** [kənˈtɛnd] *vt.* 聲稱
   - 例 The lawyer contended that his client was not at the scene when the crime was committed.
     這名律師聲稱案發當時他的當事人並沒有在現場。

7. **numbing** [ˈnʌmɪŋ] *a.* 麻木的
   numb [nʌm] *vt.* 使麻木 & *a.* 失去感覺的，麻痺的

8. **stumble across...**　偶然發現 / 碰見……
   = come across...
   - 例 This morning, Becky stumbled across a purse with NT$10,000 in it.
     貝琪今早撿到一個錢包，裡頭有新臺幣一萬元。

9. **diversion** [daɪˈvɝʒən / dɪˈvɝʒən] *n.* 分散注意力的事物；消遣，娛樂

10. **dismiss** [dɪsˈmɪs] *vt.* 不理會，駁回
    - 例 Roy dismissed the reports as ridiculous.
      羅伊將這些報導斥為無稽之談。

11. **circumstance** [ˈsɝkəmˌstæns] *n.* 情況，環境（常用複數）
    - 例 Under no circumstances should you lie to me.
      你絕不可以對我說謊。

12. **laugh at...**　看不起……；嘲笑……

13. **productive** [prəˈdʌktɪv] *a.* 多產的；富有成效的

Unit 10

一 綜合測驗

　　美國俄亥俄州的特溫斯堡這個名字取得很好，因為它舉辦了世界最大型的雙胞胎聚會：雙胞胎節。這個特別的節日從 1976 年開始每年夏季都會舉行，慶祝同卵雙胞胎、異卵雙胞胎、三胞胎、四胞胎及其他多胞胎的誕生，該節日吸引了來自北美洲、歐洲、非洲及亞洲不同城市的人。然而因為這場年度盛會是在美國舉辦，因此參與人士大部分為美國人並不足以為奇。雖然任何人參加這項活動須付小額費用 ── 無論是否為雙胞胎，但事先預約的多胞胎及特溫斯堡的住戶可以免費參加。

　　對參加雙胞胎節的人而言，裡頭可是有一堆樂子，包括舉辦烤香腸活動來歡迎大家、各項競賽及通常由雙胞胎所帶來的音樂演奏。有一個潛規則保證可以拍出美照的機會，那就是所有的雙胞胎必須穿著相像的打扮。無論參與的人是否為雙胞胎，雙胞胎節絕對是個令人難忘的慶典，帶來許多歡笑及快樂時光。你甚至可以說雙胞胎節比其他的節慶多了一倍的趣味。

A 1. **理由**
　　a. 本句主詞為單數主詞 This special festival（這個特別的節日），且此句所描述為一事實，故動詞應使用第三人稱單數現在式。
　　b. 根據上述，(A) 項應為正選。

C 2. **理由**
　　a. (A) **surface** [ˈsɝfɪs] *n.* 表面
　　　　on / beneath the surface　　在表面上 / 下
　　　　例 On the surface of my desk is a bouquet of roses.
　　　　　在我的書桌上有一束玫瑰花。
　　　(B) **surgery** [ˈsɝdʒərɪ] *n.* 外科手術（不可數）
　　　　perform surgery on...　　對……動手術
　　　= perform an operation on...
　　　　例 A team of doctors were performing surgery on Gary's tumor.
　　　　　一組醫生團隊正在對蓋瑞的腫瘤進行手術。
　　　(C) **surprise** [səˈpraɪz] *n.* 驚訝
　　　　It comes as no surprise that...　　……並不足以為奇
　　　　例 It comes as no surprise that the film was a box-office hit.
　　　　　這部電影有好的票房並不令人意外。

(D) **surgeon** [ˈsɝdʒən] *n.* 外科醫生
比較
physician [fəˈzɪʃən] *n.*（尤指內科）醫生
例 David acquired the skills needed to become a surgeon.
大衛習得了當外科醫生必備的技術。

b. It comes as no surprise that... 為固定句構，故 (C) 項應為正選。

D **3.** 理由

a. (A) **so** [so] *conj.* 所以
例 Today is Friday, so I feel very happy.
今天是星期五，所以我感到特別開心。

(B) **once** [wʌns] *conj.* 一旦
例 The manager said he will retire once he reaches 60.
經理說他滿六十歲就要退休。

(C) **until** [ʌnˈtɪl] *conj.* 直到
例 Ed was on duty until three in the morning.
艾德一直值班到凌晨三點。

(D) **although** [ɔlˈðo] *conj.* 雖然，儘管
例 Although John is handsome, he isn't friendly.
雖然約翰長得很帥，但他並不友善。

b. 根據語意，(D) 項應為正選。

B **4.** 理由

a. (A) **costume techniques** 服裝技術
例 Hannah took a course to learn traditional costume techniques for cosplay.
漢娜選修了一門課程來學習傳統的服裝技術以製作角色扮演服飾。

(B) **photo opportunities** 拍照機會
例 The event organizers set up special photo opportunities for guests.
活動主辦方為來賓安排了特別的拍照機會。

(C) **shopping discounts** 購物折扣
例 Members can receive exclusive shopping discounts at participating stores.
會員可在合作商店獲得專屬的購物折扣。

(D) **processing workshops** （食品）加工研討會
　　workshop [ˈwɜk͵ʃɑp] *n.* 研討會；廠房，車間
　　例 The students attended food processing workshops to learn preservation techniques.
　　學生們參加食品加工研討會來學習保存技術。
b. 根據語意，可知 (B) 項應為正選。

A **5.** 理由
a. (A) **in attendance** 出席
　　例 The concert attracted over 3,000 people in attendance.
　　這場演唱會吸引了超過三千人到場觀賞。
(B) **in a rush** 急忙，慌忙
= in a hurry
　　例 Jenny was in a rush to catch her train.
　　珍妮匆匆忙忙地去趕火車。
(C) **in chaos** [ˈkeɑs] 混亂
　　例 My sister's room is always in chaos.
　　我妹妹的房間總是一團亂。
(D) **in vain** 徒勞無功；白費工夫
　　例 I tried very hard to persuade Gary to quit smoking, but in vain.
　　我努力勸蓋瑞戒菸，但卻徒勞無功。
b. 根據語意，(A) 項應為正選。

重要單字與片語

1. **gathering** [ˈɡæðərɪŋ] *n.* 集會
2. **identical** [aɪˈdɛntɪkl̩] *a.* 相同的
   identical twins　同卵雙胞胎
3. **fraternal** [frəˈtɝnl̩] *a.* 異卵的；如兄弟般的；兄弟的
   fraternal twins　異卵雙胞胎
4. **triplets** [ˈtrɪplɪts] *n.* 三胞胎
5. **quadruplets** [kwɑˈdruplɪts] *n.* 四胞胎
6. **register** [ˈrɛdʒɪstɚ] *vi. & vt.* 登記，註冊
   register for...　註冊……
= sign up for...
　　例 I'm going to register for a course on English literature this semester.
　　這學期我準備選修一門英國文學課程。

7. **in advance** 預先
　　例 If you want to eat out tonight, you should make a reservation in advance.
　　你今晚若想出去吃飯，應該要事先訂位。
8. **unwritten** [ʌnˈrɪtn̩] *a.* 不成文的
   an unwritten rule　潛規則，不成文規定
9. **guarantee** [͵ɡærənˈti] *vt.* 保證，擔保 & *n.* 保證
　　例 I guarantee that everything will be fine. Just wait and see.
　　我保證一切將會沒事。等著看吧。

二 文意選填

　　看一下四周，你會發現這句話真實存在於每一處：人類天生善於溝通。所有年齡層的人都喜愛與他人交談，甚至連小嬰兒在有能力說一種語言之前早就在努力發出某些聲音。他們試圖透過一般所稱的「寶寶語」來溝通。雖然聽障人士在溝通上會面臨一些困難，但他們使用一種非口語的溝通方式，也就是所謂的手語，來補償他們聽不見的事實。

　　在不熟悉手語的人當中常產生一些誤解，其中兩種誤解是手語的形式只有一種以及這種溝通方式是沒有文法的。事實上，並沒有通用的手語，反而是有一百多種的變化形存在，也就是說，某一個國家的人不太可能理解另一個國家的人使用的手語。舉例來說，英國人通常不熟悉美國手語，而墨西哥的聽障人士在與西班牙人溝通時會感到困惑，儘管上述兩組國家的人都分別說英語及西班牙語。而關於文法，手語確實有文法規範，這或許會讓聽覺正常的人感到驚訝。但是手語的文法跟一般口語的文法不盡相同。譬如，在美國手語中並沒有表示 be 動詞的手勢。但是它的型態通常都遵循了主詞—動詞—受詞的模式。因此，要說手語確實是一種「語言」是恰當的，它不只是一系列具意義、按某種隨意組合所使用的手勢，而是被世界上聽覺受損的人用來有效表達自己，並了解快樂、悲傷及各種情緒的訊息。

__I__ 6. **理由**
　　a. 空格前有主詞 babies（小嬰兒），且空格後有不定詞 to make，得知空格應置不及物動詞 struggle（努力），以形成下列固定用法：
　　struggle to V　　努力從事……
　　例 There are many families struggling to survive on low incomes.
　　　　有許多家庭靠著微薄的收入努力過活。
　　b. 根據上述，(I) 項應為正選。

__E__ 7. **理由**
　　a. 空格前有本句動詞 attempt（嘗試）及引導不定詞的 to，空格後有介詞詞組 through what is commonly called "baby talk"（透過一般所稱的「寶寶語」），得知空格應置原形不及物動詞。
　　b. 剩餘選項中可作不及物動詞的有 (B) compensate（彌補）、(E) communicate（溝通）及 (G) follow（遵循），惟根據語意，(E) 項應為正選。
　　c. **communicate** [kəˋmjunəˏket] *vi.* 溝通
　　例 The deaf communicate through sign language.
　　　　聽障人士透過手語溝通。

Unit 10

__B__ 8. 理由

a. 本句句構分析如下：

...they use a non-verbal type of communication referred to as sign language
　　　　S　V　　　　　　　　　　　　　　　O
to V...

由上述句構及空格後之介詞 for，得知空格應置原形不及物動詞。

b. 剩餘選項中可作不及物動詞的有 (B) compensate（彌補）及 (G) follow（遵循），惟根據語意，(B) 項應為正選。

c. **compensate** [ˋkɑmpənˌset] *vi.* & *vt.* 補償，彌補
compensate for...　　　　彌補……
compensate sb for sth　　補償某人某物

例 Diligence compensates for one's deficiencies.
勤能補拙。

d. 本句中的 ...a non-verbal type of communication referred to as sign language... 實為：

...a non-verbal type of communication which / that is referred to as sign language...

上列句構可省略關係代名詞 which / that，並將 be 動詞 is 改為 being 後省略，形成分詞詞組 referred to as sign language。

__D__ 9. 理由

a. 空格前有數量形容詞 a few（一些），用以修飾複數可數名詞，得知空格應置複數可數名詞。

b. 剩餘選項中 (D) misconceptions（誤解）及 (J) gestures（手勢）為複數可數名詞，惟根據語意，(D) 項應為正選。

c. **misconception** [ˌmɪskənˋsɛpʃən] *n.* 誤解，錯誤的觀念

__F__ 10. 理由

a. 空格位於作 means 受詞之 that 名詞子句中，而本句省略了 that，空格前有名詞子句的主詞 it 及 be 動詞 is，得知空格應置單數名詞或形容詞作主詞補語。

b. 剩餘選項中僅剩 (A) normal（正常的）、(C) identical（相同的）、(F) unlikely（不可能的）及 (H) confused（困惑的）為形容詞，惟根據語意，(F) 項應為正選。

c. unlikely 置入空格後形成下列固定句型：

It is unlikely (that)...　　……是不太可能的

例 It is unlikely we walk from Taipei to Hsinchu on foot!
我們不太可能從臺北走到新竹！

__H__ **11. 理由**

a. 空格前有主詞 deaf Mexicans（墨西哥的聽障人士）及原形 be 動詞，得知空格應置名詞或形容詞作主詞補語。

b. 剩餘選項中為名詞或形容詞的有 (A) normal（正常的）、(C) identical（相同的）及 (H) confused（困惑的）及 (J) gestures（手勢），惟根據語意，(H) 項應為正選。

c. **confused** [kənˋfjuzd] *a*. 感到困惑的

__A__ **12. 理由**

a. 空格前有介詞 with，空格後有名詞 hearing（聽力），得知空格應置形容詞，以與該名詞形成名詞詞組，作 with 的受詞。

b. 剩餘選項中為形容詞的有 (A) normal（正常的）及 (C) identical（相同的），惟根據語意，(A) 項應為正選。

c. **normal** [ˋnɔrml̩] *a*. 正常的

__C__ **13. 理由**

a. 空格前有主詞 They 及 be 動詞 are not，空格後有接受詞 the ones 的介詞 to，得知空格應置形容詞 identical（相同的），以與 to 形成下列固定用法：

be identical [aɪˋdɛntɪkl̩] **to...**　　與……相同的

例 I have a hat which is identical to yours.
　　我有一頂帽子，跟你的一模一樣。

b. 根據上述，(C) 項應為正選。

__G__ **14. 理由**

a. 空格前有本句主詞 the pattern（這個模式）及表強調語氣的助動詞 does，空格後有名詞詞組 the subject-verb-object pattern（主詞─動詞─受詞的模式），得知空格應置原形及物動詞。

b. 剩餘選項中 (G) follow（遵循）為原形及物動詞，且置入空格後符合語意，故為正選。

c. **follow** [ˋfalo] *vt*. 遵從；跟隨

例 Please follow these instructions to install the software.
　　請依照說明書的指示安裝軟體。

__J__ **15. 理由**

a. 空格前有介詞 of，空格後有介詞詞組 with meaning（具意義的），得知空格應置名詞，以被該介詞詞組修飾。

b. 剩餘選項 (J) gestures（手勢）為名詞，且置入空格後符合語意，故為正選。

c. **gesture** [ˋdʒɛstʃɚ] *n*. 手勢

Unit 10

重要單字與片語

1. **statement** [ˈstetmənt] *n.* 陳述；聲明
2. **naturally** [ˈnætʃ(ə)rəlɪ] *adv.* 天然地；天生地
3. **communicative** [kəˈmjunəˌketɪv] *a.* 健談的，善溝通的
4. **be referred to as...** 被稱作……
    = be called...
    例 Hollywood is often referred to as the capital of the film industry.
    好萊塢常被稱為電影業的中心。
5. **sign language** 手語
6. **universal** [ˌjunəˈvɝsḷ] *a.* 共同的，全世界的；普遍的
7. **variety** [vəˈraɪətɪ] *n.* 種類；變化
8. **be familiar with...** 熟悉……
    例 Susan is familiar with this type of music.
    蘇珊對這種音樂類型很熟悉。
9. **despite the fact (that)...** 儘管……
    例 We didn't win the basketball game despite the fact that we had tried our best.
    儘管我們盡了最大的努力，還是無法贏得這場籃球比賽。
10. **respectively** [rɪˈspɛktɪvlɪ] *adv.* 分別地
11. **regarding** [rɪˈgɑrdɪŋ] *prep.* 關於
12. **grammatical** [grəˈmætɪkḷ] *a.* 文法上的
13. **random** [ˈrændəm] *a.* 任意的，隨機的
14. **employ** [ɪmˈplɔɪ] *vt.* 運用；僱用
    例 I will employ the new technique I learned to fix this TV.
    我將會用我學到的新技術修理這臺電視機。
15. **hearing-impaired** [ˈhɪrɪŋɪmˌpɛrd] *a.* 聽力受損的

篇章結構

你若想將一場枯燥乏味的兒童派對變為刺激、喧騰又瘋狂的慶祝活動，那就來玩皮納塔吧。皮納塔是一種容器，通常以鮮豔裝飾的混凝紙漿或是布料製作而成，但有時皮納塔是用陶器做成。皮納塔裡面會裝滿玩具、糖果或其他點心，然後會有一根繩索讓它從天花板垂掛著。孩子們用棍子敲打皮納塔，試著釋出裡面各式各樣的好東西。隨著每一次揮擊，期待感不斷累積，使其成為派對中最令人興奮的精彩部分。最後皮納塔會被打破，在場的人爭先恐後地能抓多少好料就抓多少。

皮納塔的歷史尚不完全清楚。許多年以來，大家普遍相信皮納塔源於西班牙。這很可能發生在十四世紀初期。十六世紀末，西班牙人將它引進墨西哥，在當地成了一項備受喜愛的傳統。不過近年來，這項起源的說法引起熱議。諸多當代學者認為是中國人製作出第一種皮納塔。原因是有些證據顯示，曾生活在中國的義大利人馬可‧波羅，在十三世紀時將皮納塔帶回了歐洲。根據研究，對於當時的中國人來說，農曆新年期間的一項有趣活動，是用彩色

的木棍敲擊一個類似像皮納塔的容器 —— 該容器的形狀像公牛或母牛，並裝有各式各樣的種子 —— 以釋出容器內的東西。

　　總而言之，這些傳統的相似處是千真萬確的。一些歷史學家甚至推測，類似的風俗可能曾經出現在其他古老文化中，讓皮納塔的真正起源更加撲朔迷離。但不論是誰先想到這個點子，皮納塔一直都是小孩派對中很受歡迎的遊戲。如今，皮納塔的造型與主題更加多樣化且饒富創意，為孩子們帶來更多驚喜與樂趣。

D 16. 理由

a. 第一段第二至三句描述何謂皮納塔：皮納塔是一種 container（容器），用混凝紙漿或布料等做成，且裡頭會裝滿玩具或糖果等，然後會有一根繩索讓它從天花板垂掛著，又空格後兩句提到隨著每一次揮擊，期待感不斷累積，最後皮納塔 bursts open（會被打破），因此空格應填玩皮納塔的步驟之一，即如選項 (D) 所述「孩子們用棍子敲打皮納塔，試著釋出裡面各式各樣的好東西。」

b. 根據上述，(D) 項應為正選。

C 17. 理由

a. 第二段第二至四句提到許多年來，大家普遍相信皮納塔源於十四世紀初的西班牙，然後西班牙人於十六世紀末時將皮納塔引進墨西哥，成了一項備受喜愛的傳統，但空格後句卻提到很多當代學者認為是中國人製作出第一種皮納塔，因此空格前後語意相反，應使用含有轉折語氣的句子，即如選項 (C) 所述「不過近年來，這項起源的說法引起熱議。」

b. 根據上述，(C) 項應為正選。

B 18. 理由

a. 空格前句提到諸多當代學者認為是中國人製作出第一種皮納塔，又空格後句提到 according to research（根據研究），對於當時的中國人來說，農曆新年期間他們也會玩類似皮納塔的有趣遊戲，因此空格應是填學者抱持著這樣看法的理由，此正如選項 (B) 所述「原因是有些證據顯示，曾生活在中國的義大利人馬可·波羅，在十三世紀時將皮納塔帶回了歐洲。」

b. 根據上述，(B) 項應為正選。

A 19. 理由

a. 第一段提及皮納塔的玩法，第二段提到有人認為皮納塔源於西班牙，有人則認為是源於中國，並敘述皮納塔在中國的玩法，而不論是西方的皮納塔或中國的皮納塔，兩者玩法相似，因此空格應為結論句，即如選項 (A) 所述「總而言之，這些傳統的相似處是千真萬確的。」

b. 根據上述，(A) 項應為正選。

(E) 選項翻譯　皮納塔爆裂開來，弄傷了生日派對中的幾個孩子。

Unit 10

重要單字與片語

1. **turn A into B** 將 A 變成 B
   = change A into B
   = transform A into B
   = convert A into B
   例 The evil witch turned the handsome prince into a frog.
   壞心眼的巫婆將帥氣的王子變成一隻青蛙。

2. **dull** [dʌl] *a.* 枯燥乏味的

3. **container** [kənˈtenɚ] *n.* 容器

4. **be filled with...** 充滿……
   = be full of...
   例 My heart was filled with joy when I saw her again.
   再次見到她時,我的內心充滿喜悅。

5. **suspend** [səˈspɛnd] *vt.* 垂掛
   例 In one scary scene in this movie, there is a hand suspended from the ceiling.
   在這部電影的一個恐怖場景中,一隻手從天花板垂掛下來。

6. **release** [rɪˈlis] *vt.* 釋放

7. **goody** [ˈɡʊdɪ] *n.* 吸引人的東西;(常指)好吃的東西

8. **anticipation** [ænˌtɪsəˈpeʃən] *n.* 期待,預期

9. **highlight** [ˈhaɪˌlaɪt] *n.* 最精彩的部分 & *vt.* 突顯,強調

10. **burst** [bɝst] *vi.* & *vt.* (使)爆破,(使)爆炸(三態同形)

11. **scramble** [ˈskræmbl̩] *vt.* 爭搶
    scramble to + V 爭搶做……
    例 Waking up late, Peter got up and scrambled to put his clothes on.
    彼得睡過頭了,於是趕緊起床手忙腳亂地把衣服穿上。

12. **originate** [əˈrɪdʒəˌnet] *vi.* 源自
    originate in + 地方 源自某地
    originate from sth 源自某物
    例 Many Christmas traditions are thought to have originated in Germany.
    許多聖誕節的傳統被認為是起源於德國。

13. **dispute** [dɪˈspjut] *vt.* 爭執

14. **contemporary** [kənˈtɛmpəˌrɛrɪ] *a.* 當代的;現代的

15. **content** [ˈkɑntɛnt] *n.* (皮包、箱子裡的)所含之物;容納的東西;內容(恆用複數)
    注意 若表書、演講、電影的內容,則為不可數名詞。

16. **similarity** [ˌsɪməˈlærətɪ] *n.* 相似之處(可數);相似(不可數)

17. **undeniable** [ˌʌndɪˈnaɪəbl̩] *a.* 不可否認的

18. **hit** [hɪt] *n.* 受歡迎的人 / 事物;非常成功的人 / 事物

四 閱讀測驗

　　唐寧是世界上最著名的茗茶品牌之一，其歷史可追溯到超過三個世紀之前。該公司由湯瑪士·唐寧於 1706 年創立，他在東印度公司工作時學到關於茶的知識。當時茶在英國正開始變得時髦，但尚未普及。湯瑪士收購了湯姆咖啡館，開始改變這種情況。起初他的店販賣茶及多種其他飲料，但到了 1734 年，它擴大了三倍，改名為金獅，並且只賣茶。

　　不過湯瑪士的孫子理查·唐寧才可說是對該公司的發達以及英國的茶葉消費量做出最大貢獻的人。他於 1783 年接管公司。當時茶被課以重稅，為了逃避稅收，大量茶葉被走私進口。走私茶葉的品質大多很差，有些甚至摻雜了致命物質。作為倫敦茶商協會主席，理查深信所有人都應該享用優質茶。因此他去找當時的首相小威廉·彼得，建議將茶稅從 119% 大幅降低到 12.5%。彼得聽取理查的論點：透過增加合法的茶葉貿易，實際上政府收入是會增加的。首相的回應是在 1784 年通過《折抵法案》。結果證明理查是對的：合法茶葉銷量大幅增加，政府收到更多稅，而唐寧公司也蓬勃發展。

　　理查另一個顯著的成就是他找人在唐寧的倫敦店大門上方製作了一個新的招牌組合，包括顯眼的唐寧商標和金獅雕像，以紀念湯瑪士·唐寧茶館的店名。這個招牌組合變得非常有名，至今仍然存在。

D　20. 下列關於湯瑪士·唐寧的敘述何者正確？
　　(A) 他於 18 世紀初創立東印度公司。
　　(B) 他開湯姆咖啡館時只賣茶。
　　(C) 他於 1734 年生病後去世。
　　(D) 他的公司在他孫子的管理下獲致更大的成功。

理由
根據第二段第一句，可知 (D) 項應為正選。

D　21. 為什麼理查·唐寧被認為對公司和國家做出了重大貢獻？
　　(A) 他將公司併入倫敦茶商協會。
　　(B) 他在公司的熱門茶產品中添加了新成分。
　　(C) 他幫助英國居民克服對茶的厭惡。
　　(D) 他說服了政治領袖通過一項重要的法案。

理由
根據本文第二段倒數第一、二句，可知 (D) 項應為正選。

Unit 10

__C__ 22. 第二段中的 slashing 最有可能是什麼意思？
   (A) 使用刀片切割某物。
   (B) 強烈批評某事物。
   (C) 大幅減少數量。
   (D) 鞭打某物。

   理由
   根據本文第二段倒數第三句 "..., and suggested slashing the tax on tea from 119% to 12.5%."（……，建議將茶稅從 119% 大幅降低到 12.5%。）可知，(C) 項應為正選。

__C__ 23. 關於唐寧的店門，我們並未得知什麼？
   (A) 正式提出這項要求的是誰。
   (B) 它上頭到底有什麼。
   (C) 它建造的確切時間點。
   (D) 它位於何處。

   理由
   根據第三段第一、二句可知，唯有 (C) 項未提及，故為正選。

重要單字與片語

1. **stretch** [strɛtʃ] vi. 延續
   stretch back years / centuries
   追溯到多年／世紀前
   例 The debate stretches back over many years.
   該爭論可追溯到許多年前。

2. **found** [faʊnd] vt. 建立，創辦
   例 The United Nations was founded in 1945.
   聯合國創立於西元 1945 年。

3. **venue** [ˈvɛnju] n. （舉辦）場所，地點

4. **triple** [ˈtrɪpl̩] vt. & vi.（使）成為三倍 & a. 三倍的
   例 Ashley decided to stay on when the boss tripled her monthly salary.
   老闆將艾希莉的月薪加到三倍時，她就決定繼續待在公司了。

5. **take over (sth)** 接管／替（某事物）
   例 IBM will take over that company.
   IBM 將接管那家公司。

6. **taxed** [tækst] a. 徵稅的

7. **smuggle** [ˈsmʌgl̩] vt. 走私
   smuggle sth into + 地方　把某物走私到某地方
   例 The man was arrested for smuggling drugs into Malaysia.
   這名男子因走私毒品到馬來西亞而遭逮捕。

8. **get around** 逃避

9. **slash** [slæʃ] *vt.* 削減
   - 例 Although prices had already been slashed significantly for the sale, many prospective buyers still thought the items were too expensive.
   雖然這次拍賣的價格已大幅調降，但很多潛在買家仍覺得這些東西太貴了。

10. **revenue** [ˋrɛvənju] *n.* （政府）稅收；（公司）收入

11. **act** [ækt] *n.* 法案

12. **rake in...** 賺（大錢）

13. **blossom** [ˋblɑsəm] *vi. & n.* （果樹的花）開花；生長茂盛；興旺
   - 例 The apple trees in the garden are blossoming.
   花園內的蘋果樹開滿了花朵。

14. **commission** [kəˋmɪʃən] *vt.* 委任 & *n.* 佣金；委任
   - 例 The museum commissioned the artist to make a sculpture in remembrance of the curator.
   博物館委任這名藝術家製作一座雕像紀念該名館長。

15. **pass away** 過世
   - 例 The sorrowful old man missed his wife, who recently passed away.
   那位悲傷的老先生很思念他最近過世的老伴。

16. **merge** [mɝdʒ] *vt. & vi.* （使）合併
   merge with... 與……合併
   - 例 Small businesses were forced to merge with larger ones.
   小型企業被迫與較大型的企業合併。

17. **overcome** [͵ovɚˋkʌm] *vt.* 克服
   （三態為：overcome, overcame [͵ovɚˋkem], overcome）
   - 例 We have to overcome many hurdles in order to be successful.
   為了成功，我們必須克服許多障礙。

18. **convince** [kənˋvɪns] *vt.* 說服；使確信
   convince sb to + V 說服某人做……
   - 例 It seems that I can do nothing to convince my husband to quit smoking.
   我似乎拿不出辦法說服我老公戒菸。

五 混合題

中階掠食者既非頂級掠食者也非純獵物，而是介於其中間的掠食者：吃比牠們小的動物，同時要抵擋比牠們大的動物的攻擊。在珊瑚礁生態系統中，中階掠食魚類扮演著重要角色，確保其所處環境能維持在均衡狀態。牠們應對威脅的方式因而影響到自身的生存還有珊瑚礁的健康狀態。在發表於《科學報告》期刊的論文「中階掠食性珊瑚礁魚類面對鯊魚和人類威脅時的行為」中，主要作者 A. 阿松索洛－里維拉詳述她和其團隊針對這些海洋動物如何應對潛在的致命威脅所做的一項研究。

研究人員聚焦在澳洲大堡礁的鯛魚、石斑魚、龍占魚和鱸魚類。他們使用遙控水下攝影機監測這些魚類對兩種主要掠食者的反應：已知會在這類環境中叉魚的浮潛人類；以及黑鰭

Unit 10

礁鯊，他們是前述魚類的「潛在掠食者和／或致命競爭者」。[1] 為了確保有最準確的結果，研究者使用了會移動且看起來非常逼真的活動鯊魚模型。用作對照組的是無威脅性的活動假海龜和兩樣靜態物品。[2] 該研究測量的是「逃跑觸發距離（FID）」，根據作者的定義是「獵物開始逃離潛在威脅逼近的距離」。[3] 阿松索洛－里維拉與其團隊預期，當面臨威脅時，大一點的中階掠食者會比小一點的展現更佳的 FID 和更快的游泳速度。

　　他們觀察到，90% 的中階掠食性珊瑚礁魚類看到鯊魚時會逃跑，而在看到浮潛者時，則有 96% 的魚類會逃跑。相較之下，只有大約一半的魚會對海龜或其他物體做出相同反應。[4] 研究團隊也確實發現較大的魚面對威脅時比較小的魚展現較佳的 FID 和更快的游泳速度，而面對非威脅物則不然。他們推斷這可能會使珊瑚礁魚類「（放棄）與附近同種或他種個體進行覓食、互動或競爭的機會」，並可能「最終對珊瑚礁魚類的數量造成危機效應」。[5] 不過他們也提到所使用的對照組 —— 海龜和其他物體 —— 比活動鯊魚模型或浮潛者的體型來得小。因此，掠食者體型這個部分未來可做進一步的研究。

24. 中階掠食性珊瑚礁魚類應對海洋危險的方式可以決定牠們是否能夠<u>存活</u>以及珊瑚礁環境的健康狀態。

▎理由
空格前為助動詞 will，可得知空格應置原形動詞。根據本文第一段第四句 "The way they deal with the threats they face can therefore have an effect on their own survival and the health of the coral reef."（牠們應對威脅的方式因而影響到自身的生存還有珊瑚礁的健康狀態。）得知，空格應置與 survival 相關的動詞 survive。

25. FID 測量一種動物容許另一種<u>威脅</u>牠的動物靠多近才會逃跑的距離。

▎理由
空格前為關係代名詞 that，空格後為受詞 it，可得知空格應置動詞。根據本文第二段倒數第二句 "..., which the authors define as 'the distance prey allow a potential threat to approach before fleeing.' "（……，根據作者的定義是「獵物開始逃離潛在威脅逼近的距離」。）得知，空格應置與 threat 相關的動詞 threatens。

26. 本文中哪個字表示「會移動或看似移動，好像是活的」？

　　<u>animated</u>（可活動的；栩栩如生的）

▎理由
根據本文第二段第三句 "Animated models of the sharks, which moved and appeared to be very real, ..."（……會移動且看起來非常逼真的活動鯊魚模型。）可推測 animated（可活動的；栩栩如生的）應為正解。

27. 本文中哪些編號句子表達了研究的一項預測、一樁科學發現以及某個潛在缺點？
請在下方寫下對應的句子編號。

預測：[3]
發現：[4]
缺點：[5]

理由

根據編號 [3] 的句子提到阿松索洛一里維拉與其團隊預期，當面臨威脅時，大一點的中階掠食者會比小一點的展現更佳的 FID 和更快的游泳速度。得知此為預測。編號 [4] 的句子提到研究團隊也確實發現較大的魚面對威脅時比較小的魚展現較佳的 FID 和更快的游泳速度，而面對非威脅物則不然。得知此為科學發現。編號 [5] 的句子提到他們所使用的對照組比鯊魚模型或浮潛者要小。得知此為缺點。

重要單字與片語

1. **apex** [ˈɛpɛks] *n.* 頂點
2. **predator** [ˈprɛdətɚ] *n.* 掠食者，捕食者
3. **prey** [pre] *n.* 獵物
4. **simultaneously** [ˌsaɪmlˈtenɪəslɪ] *adv.* 同時地
5. **fend off...**　　抵擋，擊退……
   例 The old man fended off the attackers with his umbrella.
   那位老翁用雨傘擋開攻擊他的人。
6. **detail** [ˈditel] *vt.* 詳細描述／討論 & *n.* 細節
   例 The manager wanted a report detailing the pros and cons of our products.
   經理要一份詳細說明我們產品優缺點的報告。
7. **lethal** [ˈliθəl] *a.* 致命的
8. **snorkeler** [ˈsnɔrklɚ] *n.* 浮潛者

9. **animated** [ˈænəˌmetɪd] *a.* （模型）能活動的；栩栩如生的；動畫的
10. **flight** [flaɪt] *n.* 逃跑；躲避
    take flight　　逃走
11. **flee** [fli] *vt. & vi.* 逃避，逃離（三態為：flee, fled [flɛd], fled）
    例 The criminal managed to flee the country.
    該罪犯成功潛逃出境。
12. **confront** [kənˈfrʌnt] *vt.* 使面對
    be confronted with...　　面對……
    例 What would you do if you were confronted with such a problem?
    若你面對這樣一個難題，你會怎麼做？
13. **forage** [ˈfɔrɪdʒ] *vi.* 覓食；搜尋
    例 While camping, we saw a bear foraging for food in the woods.
    露營時我們看到一隻熊在樹林中覓食。

Unit 11

一、綜合測驗

　　吉祥物是身穿卡通人物服裝的表演者,在運動場合中可看到它們到處跳舞來娛樂觀眾。這些看似幽默的角色可以凝聚團隊精神與炒熱氣氛,據說它們也會帶來好運。吉祥物有時會試圖威嚇或取笑敵隊。從高中層級到奧運的隊伍都會使用吉祥物。它們也常出現在企業界中。吉祥物曾經只是大家歡笑的來源,現今則是一大商機。企業經常利用它們來建立強大且易識別的品牌形象。

　　mascot(吉祥物)一詞源自於法文的 *mascotte*,意思是幸運符。在六〇年代之前是用活生生的動物作為吉祥物。穿著服裝的吉祥物開始流行是因為《布偶歷險記》裡真人大小的知名電視明星布偶風靡兒童娛樂圈。這無疑讓吉祥物產業廣為發展。隨著媒體對吉祥物的關注不斷增加,這些角色在現今文化中依然佔有一席之地。在體壇中,每個隊伍都有屬於自己的吉祥物。以棒球來說,底特律老虎隊有胖虎。它身穿老虎的服裝。而費城費城人隊有費納寶 —— 一隻長相怪異、毛茸茸的綠色怪物,它大概是棒球界裡最受喜愛的吉祥物之一。

C　1. 理由

　　a. (A) **let go of sb/sth**　　釋放某人/某事
　　　　= release sb/sth
　　　　例 Let go of my hand, or I'll call the police.
　　　　　放開我的手,否則我要報警了。

　　　(B) **take care of sb/sth**　　照顧某人/某事
　　　　例 It is our duty to take care of our parents when they are old.
　　　　　當我們的父母年紀大時我們有責任照顧他們。

　　　(C) **make fun of sb/sth**　　取笑某人/某事
　　　　例 Making fun of one's appearance is very impolite.
　　　　　嘲笑一個人的外表是十分無禮的。

　　　(D) **make use of...**　　利用……
　　　　= take advantage of...
　　　　例 You may make good use of this summer vacation to broaden your horizons.
　　　　　你可以善用這個暑假來拓展你的視野。

　　b. 根據語意,(C) 項應為正選。

<u>D</u> **2.** 理由

 a. (A) **cause of frustration** 挫折的原因

   例 Danny's repeated mistakes were the main cause of frustration for the team.
   丹尼經常失誤是團隊感覺挫敗的主要原因。

  (B) **reason for competition** 競爭的原因

   例 A large prize pool is often a key reason for competition in esports.
   高額獎金通常是電子競技中競爭的主要原因。

  (C) **basis for criticism** 批評的依據

   例 The unfair policy provided a strong basis for criticism from employees.
   不公平的政策成為員工批評強而有力的依據。

  (D) **source of laughs** 笑聲的來源

   例 My brother's funny expressions were always a source of laughs at parties.
   我哥哥的搞笑表情總是派對上的笑聲來源。

 b. 根據語意，可知 (D) 項應為正選。

Unit 11

<u>A</u> **3.** 理由

 a. (A) **derive** [dɪˋraɪv] **from...** 源自……（此處 derive 為 vi.）
  = **be derived from...**（此處 derived 為過去分詞作形容詞）

   例 The story derives from an old legend.
   = The story is derived from an old legend.
   這個故事源自一則古老傳說。

  (B) **result from...** 起因於……
   = **arise from...**

   比較

   result in... 導致……

   例 The accident resulted from the driver's carelessness.
   這起意外起因於駕駛員的粗心。
   The driver's carelessness resulted in the accident.
   駕駛員的粗心導致了這起意外。

  (C) **expel sb from...** 將某人從……驅逐

   例 Wendy was expelled from school for cheating on exams.
   溫蒂因為考試作弊而被學校開除。

  (D) **withdraw from...** 從……退出

   例 The athlete's sore arm forced him to withdraw from the competition.
   這位運動員的手臂疼痛，迫使他退出比賽。

 b. 根據語意，(A) 項應為正選。

__B__ **4.** 理由

    a. (A) **experiment** [ɪkˋspɛrəmənt] *n.* 實驗

        例 The group opposed any experiments on living animals.
該團體反對用動物活體做任何的實驗。

      (B) **industry** [ˋɪndəstrɪ] *n.* 產業；工業

        例 In recent years, more and more graduates choose to get into the fashion industry.
近年來，越來越多的大學畢業生選擇進入時裝業。

      (C) **environment** [ɪnˋvaɪrənmənt] *n.*（生態）環境（常用單數）

        例 No plants can possibly grow in such a hostile environment.
不可能有植物能在如此惡劣的環境中生長。

      (D) **imagination** [ɪ͵mædʒəˋneʃən] *n.* 想像力

        例 A creative advertisement requires intelligence and imagination.
有創意的廣告需要智力與想像力。

    b. 根據語意，(B) 項應為正選。

__A__ **5.** 理由

    a. (A) **individual** [͵ɪndəˋvɪdʒʊəl] *a.* 個別的；個人的

        例 The department store cares about the needs of each individual customer.
該百貨公司在乎每一位顧客的需求。

      (B) **industrial** [͵ɪnˋdʌstrɪəl] *a.* 工業的

        例 That area of the country is industrial rather than agricultural.
該國的那個地區是工業區而非農業區。

      (C) **internal** [ɪnˋtɝnl̩] *a.* 內部的

        例 The accident victim had severe internal injuries.
這起事故的受害者受了嚴重的內傷。

      (D) **innocent** [ˋɪnəsn̩t] *a.* 清白的，無罪的
be innocent of...　　無……的罪

        例 Blair believes that her husband is innocent of the robbery.
布萊兒相信她的丈夫沒有犯下這起搶案。

    b. 根據語意，(A) 項應為正選。

重要單字與片語

1. **dress in...**　　穿著……
 = be dressed in...
 = dress oneself in...

例 Peter (was) dressed in a fashionable T-shirt yesterday.
 = Peter dressed himself in a fashionable T-shirt yesterday.
彼得昨天穿著一件時髦的 T 恤。

2. **cartoonish** [kɑrˋtunɪʃ] *a.* 卡通的
3. **spectator** [ˋspɛk͵tetɚ] *n.* 觀眾（可數）
4. **intimidate** [ɪnˋtɪmə͵det] *vt.* 威嚇，脅迫
   intimidate sb into + N/V-ing　脅迫某人做某事
   例 The bully intimidated his classmate into doing his homework for him.
   那個惡霸脅迫同學替他做作業。
5. **corporate** [ˋkɔrpərɪt] *a.* 企業的
6. **a lucky charm**　幸運符
7. **catch on**　流行
   = become popular

例 I believe that the dress you designed last year will catch on soon.
我相信妳去年設計的那套洋裝很快就會變流行。

8. **sweep** [swip] *vt.* 席捲，風靡；掃
（三態為：sweep, swept [swɛpt], swept）

例 A wave of racism has been sweeping the country since the civil war broke out.
自從內戰爆發以來，一波種族主義已席捲全國。

Unit 11

二 文意選填

　　你聽過新方舟（Ark Nova）嗎？它是全球第一個充氣式音樂廳。這個名字是賜給一個以希望及愛為構想的企畫。據說音樂有治療的力量。新方舟設計背後的創意團隊有一個想法，就是音樂或許可以撫慰幾千位因 2011 年日本極具毀滅性的地震和海嘯而遭受難以想像的損失的受災者。這場浩劫奪走了一萬八千多條人命。2013 年，新方舟這個模樣奇怪的建築物首次在當時受災最嚴重的地區搭建。

　　英國雕刻家安尼西・卡普爾以及日本建築師磯崎新想到一項創新的方法，解決了音樂會主辦人及其他想要策劃活動的人常會面臨到的問題。那就是表演場地匱乏。同時，他們的解決方法提供了更多的東西。這個綽號為紫色雷根糖的充氣式移動劇院能舒適地容納五百人。這使得這個令人驚嘆的場地成了許多小型音樂會、專題演講會及當代各種類型表演的絕佳選擇。新方舟不只是能充氣及任意移動而已，它奇特的雷根糖形狀和外部散發微弱紫光的牆也明顯展現了一種希望與歡樂的象徵。新方舟的內部是引人注目的球形，還有色調柔和的粉紅光優美地灑落在觀眾坐的長椅上。新方舟在兩個小時內即可完成充氣，而拆卸時可以更快，相當方便。

　　日本在歷史上面臨過許多問題。然而，日本人透過他們的創意和面對災難後的韌性而揚名。新方舟正是這些特質的出色例證。

C　6. 理由
　　a. 空格前有名詞 a project（一項企畫），空格後有介詞詞組 in hope and love（以希望及愛），得知空格應置分詞，以與介詞詞組形成分詞詞組修飾前面的名詞。

Unit 11

  b. 選項中 (A) erected（搭建）、(C) conceived（構想）、(F) claimed（奪取）、(G) distinguished（使揚名）及 (I) nicknamed（取綽號）均可作過去分詞，惟根據語意，(C) 項應為正選。

  c. 原句實為：
It is also the name which / that is given to a project which / that was conceived in hope and love.
  (1) 第一個形容詞子句可省略關係代名詞 which / that，並將 is 改為 being 後予以省略，形成分詞詞組 given to a project 修飾 the name。
  (2) 第二個形容詞子句可省略關係代名詞 which / that，並將 was 改為 being 後予以省略，形成分詞詞組 conceived in hope and love 修飾 a project。

  d. **conceive** [kənˋsiv] *vt.* 構思，設想
   例 John conceived a plan that we all supported.
    約翰構思了一個計畫，我們全都支持這個計畫。

J **7.** 理由

  a. 空格前有 that 名詞子句的主詞 music（音樂）及動詞 has，空格後有名詞 powers（力量），得知空格應置形容詞或名詞以與該名詞形成名詞詞組作 has 的受詞。

  b. 選項中為形容詞或名詞的有 (B) interior（內部（的））、(D) symbol（象徵）、(E) innovative（創新的）、(H) option（選擇）及 (J) healing（治療的），惟根據語意，(J) 項應為正選。

  c. **healing** [ˋhilɪŋ] *a.* 有治療功效的

F **8.** 理由

  a. 空格前有關係代名詞 which，指涉先行詞 the devastating earthquake and tsunami that struck Japan in 2011（2011 年日本極具毀滅性的地震和海嘯），空格後有名詞詞組 over 18,000 lives（一萬八千多條人命），得知空格應置及物動詞，以接該名詞詞組作受詞，且因本句描述過去的事，故應使用過去式。

  b. 剩餘選項中為過去式及物動詞的有 (A) erected（搭建）、(F) claimed（奪取）、(G) distinguished（使揚名）及 (I) nicknamed（取綽號），惟根據語意，(F) 項應為正選。

  c. **claim** [klem] *vt.* 奪取（生命）
   例 The flood claimed twenty lives.
   = The flood killed twenty people.
    這場洪水奪走了二十條人命。

A **9.** 理由

  a. 空格前有主詞 this odd-looking structure（這個模樣奇怪的建築物）、主詞的同位語 the Ark Nova（新方舟）及 be 動詞 was，得知空格可置名詞作主詞補語，或置及物動詞的過去分詞以與 was 形成被動語態。

  b. 剩餘選項中為名詞或及物動詞的過去分詞的有 (A) erected（搭建）、(B) interior（內部）、(D) symbol（象徵）、(G) distinguished（使揚名）、(H) option（選擇）及 (I) nicknamed（取綽號），惟根據語意，(A) 項應為正選。

c. **erect** [ɪˋrɛkt] *vt.* 建造，建立
   例 The city government erected a statue in the park in honor of the hero.
   市政府在公園內豎立了一座雕像以紀念這位英雄。

__E__ 10. 理由
   a. 空格前有片語動詞 came up with（想出）及不定冠詞 an，空格後有名詞 solution（解決辦法），得知空格應置以母音起首的形容詞，以形成名詞詞組作該片語動詞的受詞。
   b. 剩餘選項中以母音起首的形容詞有 (B) interior（內部的）及 (E) innovative（創新的），惟根據語意，(E) 項應為正選。
   c. **innovative** [ˋɪnəˏvetɪv] *a.* 新穎的，創新的

__I__ 11. 理由
   a. 空格前有名詞 theater（劇院）及一逗點，空格後為名詞詞組 the purple jelly bean（紫色雷根糖）及一逗點，得知逗點間的部分用以修飾 theater，最有可能為分詞詞組，因此空格內應置動詞的現在分詞或過去分詞。
   b. 剩餘選項中可作分詞的動詞有 (G) distinguished（使揚名）及 (I) nicknamed（取綽號），惟根據語意，(I) 項應為正選。
   c. 原句實為：
   The inflatable, portable theater, <u>which is</u> nicknamed the purple jelly bean, seats 500 people comfortably.
   上句可省略關係代名詞 which，並將 is 改為 being 後予以省略，形成分詞詞組 nicknamed the purple jelly bean 修飾主詞 The inflatable, portable theater。
   d. **nickname** [ˋnɪkˏnem] *vt.* 為……取綽號 & *n.* 綽號
   例 Because woodpeckers peck into tree trunks to find food, they are nicknamed tree doctors.
   啄木鳥因為啄食樹幹覓食的習性而有樹醫生的封號。

__H__ 12. 理由
   a. 空格前有不定冠詞 a 及形容詞 great（好的），得知空格應置單數名詞。
   b. 剩餘選項中 (B) interior（內部）、(D) symbol（象徵）及 (H) option（選擇）為單數名詞，惟根據語意，(H) 項應為正選。
   c. **option** [ˋɑpʃən] *n.* 選擇

__D__ 13. 理由
   a. 空格前有不定冠詞 a 及形容詞 striking（顯著的），空格後有介詞組 of hope and joy（希望與快樂的），得知空格應置單數名詞，以被介詞組修飾。
   b. 剩餘選項中 (B) interior（內部）及 (D) symbol（象徵）為單數名詞，惟根據語意，(D) 項應為正選。
   c. **symbol** [ˋsɪmbl̩] *n.* 象徵

Unit 11

__B__ **14.** 理由
    a. 空格前有定冠詞 The，空格後有介詞 of 引導的介詞詞組，得知空格應置名詞，以被後方的介詞詞組修飾。
    b. 剩餘選項中僅 (B) interior（內部）可作名詞，且置入空格後符合語意，故為正選。
    c. **interior** [ɪnˋtɪrɪɚ] *n.* 內部 & *a.* 內部的
        比較
        exterior [ɪkˋstɪrɪɚ] *n.* 外部 & *a.* 外部的

__G__ **15.** 理由
    a. 空格前有本句主詞 the Japanese（日本人）及現在完成式助動詞 have，空格後有反身代名詞 themselves（他們自己），得知空格應置及物動詞的過去分詞，以與 have 形成完成式，並接 themselves 作受詞。
    b. 剩餘選項中 (G) distinguished（使揚名）為及物動詞的過去分詞，且置入空格後符合語意及用法，故為正選。
    c. **distinguish** [dɪˋstɪŋgwɪʃ] *vt.* 使揚名；分辨，區別
        distinguish oneself   使自己揚名
        distinguish A from B   區別 A 與 B 的不同

重要單字與片語

1. **inflatable** [ɪnˋfletəbl] *a.* 可充氣的
2. **comfort** [ˋkʌmfɚt] *vt.* 撫慰，安慰
3. **in the wake of...** 繼……之後（尤指不好的事情）
    例 The airport was closed in the wake of the explosion.
    繼爆炸事件之後，機場就關閉了。
4. **devastating** [ˋdɛvəsˌtetɪŋ] *a.* 毀滅性的
5. **strike** [straɪk] *vt.*（災難）突然發生（三態為：strike, struck [strʌk], struck）
    例 Several natural disasters struck that country last month.
    上個月該國發生多起天然災害。
6. **stage** [stedʒ] *vt.* 策劃 & *n.* 舞臺；階段
7. **a shortage** [ˋʃɔrtɪdʒ] **of** + 可數／不可數名詞　短缺……
8. **portable** [ˋpɔrtəbl] *a.* 可攜式的，手提的
9. **seat** [sit] *vt.*（某場地）可容納……；使就座
    注意
    當 seat 表上述兩義時，其後要接「人」作受詞。
    例 This arena can seat 3,500 people.
    這座運動場可以容納三千五百人。
    比較
    sit [sɪt] *vi.* 坐（只有主動用法）
    例 Eva sat on the comfy sofa and fell asleep.
    伊娃坐在舒服的沙發上睡著了。
10. **mobile** [ˋmobl̩] *a.* 可移動的，流動的
11. **luminescent** [ˌluməˋnɛsn̩t] *a.* 發冷光的
12. **striking** [ˋstraɪkɪŋ] *a.* 明顯的，顯著的
13. **inflate** [ɪnˋflet] *vi.* & *vt.*（使）充氣
14. **deflate** [dɪˋflet] *vi.* & *vt.*（使）放氣
15. **throughout** [θruˋaʊt] *prep.* 在……期間；遍及……

16. **resiliency** [rɪˋzɪlɪənsɪ] *n.* （面對困境後的）復原力（不可數）（也作：resilience [rɪˋzɪlɪəns]）

17. **in the face of...**　面對（困難、危險、困境等）
   例 Gary was admired for his courage in the face of adversity.
   蓋瑞因他面對逆境時的勇氣而受到讚賞。

Unit 11

篇章結構

　　任何一場高爾夫錦標賽的最後一天，老虎伍茲都身穿最愛的紅色運動衫。多年來，伍茲了解紅色代表力量、掌控和熱情。不管是有意還是無意，伍茲利用這點作為利器，因為當他穿著紅色衣服時，幾乎無人能敵。許多粉絲也將他的紅色球衣與勝利聯想在一起，使其成為他競賽精神的象徵。

　　如今科學家跟上老虎伍茲的思考模式，更仔細研究顏色之間的關聯。科學家從先前的研究得知紅色能激起人們對食物和性方面的興趣。但現在他們相信，人們在從事需要注重細節或表現取向的工作時，紅色能激發他們的表現。有些人會對紅色敬而遠之，因為會聯想到救護車、停車標誌和危險。另一方面，藍色一直以來都被視為撫平人心的顏色。最近的研究則發現，藍色能讓人更具冒險精神和創造力。這是因為大多數人一想到藍色就會聯想到海洋、天空或是其他寬廣的空間。

　　多名教授測試了六百位民眾，看看受測者的表現是否會隨著看見紅色、藍色或白色而有所不同。測試的項目會有不同的顏色背景，受測者便在這種情況下進行文字或圖像測試。紅色背景組在記憶及有關拼字校正和標點符號方面有較佳的表現。而藍色背景組在使用積木的創意和利用各種形狀製作玩具上的表現比紅組來得優異。白色背景組則無明顯的差異。這些研究結果顯示，顏色可以成為影響人類行為與生產力的強大工具。

　　看來其他人似乎早就知道科學家現在所發現的測試結果。舉例來說，《紐約時報》編輯部有許多面牆壁被漆成如番茄罐頭般的紅色。再者，有創意的人一直都知道家裡一定要有一間漆成藍色的房間以刺激腦力。人們顯然一直在利用顏色來塑造環境並提升自身的能力。

　<u>E</u>　**16.** 理由
　　　a. 空格前句敘述多年來，伍茲了解紅色代表力量、掌控和熱情，呼應選項 (E) 所述 when Woods is wearing red, he is nearly impossible to beat（當伍茲穿著紅色衣服時，幾乎無人能敵）。
　　　b. 根據上述，(E) 項應為正選。

Unit 11

D **17.** 理由

　　a. 空格前句敘述科學家從先前的研究得知紅色能激起人們對食物和性方面的興趣，選項 (D) 語氣轉折說明他們（指科學家）現在相信當人們從事某些工作時若受到紅色激發（they are prompted by the color red），便能表現得更好，語意承接空格前句並形成對照。

　　b. 根據上述，(D) 項應為正選。

C **18.** 理由

　　a. 空格前句提及測試是為了觀察受測者的表現是否會受不同顏色所影響，選項 (C) 延伸說明測試的項目，即受測者在不同的顏色背景中進行文字或圖像測試，空格前句提到的三個顏色 red, blue, or white 呼應該選項中的 colored backgrounds（顏色背景）。

　　b. 根據上述，(C) 項應為正選。

B **19.** 理由

　　a. 空格前句提及有些人似乎早就知道科學家現在所發現的測試結果，而空格後句為此結果的其中一個例證，可知空格亦應提出該測試結果的例證，選項 (B) 即以 For example（舉例來說）起首並舉出 *The New York Times*' editorial department（《紐約時報》編輯部）牆面顏色的事例。

　　b. 根據上述，(B) 項應為正選。

(A) 選項翻譯　這就是為什麼餐廳和咖啡館很少用紅色或類似顏色來粉刷的原因。

重要單字與片語

1. **tournament** [ˈtɝnəmənt] *n*. 錦標賽，比賽
2. **be involved in...**　參與……；牽涉……
   例 Linda has been involved in three car accidents in the last two months.
   過去兩個月來，琳達涉入了三起車禍。
3. **signify** [ˈsɪɡnəfaɪ] *vt*. 表示；有……的意思
   例 This ring signifies my love for you.
   這只戒指代表我對你的愛。
4. **dominance** [ˈdɑmənəns] *n*. 優勢；支配（地位）
5. **enthusiasm** [ɪnˈθjuzɪˌæzəm] *n*. 熱情
6. **catch up with...**　迎頭趕上……
   例 If you don't study harder, you'll never catch up with us.
   要是你不用功點，就永遠趕不上我們。
7. **provoke** [prəˈvok] *vt*. 激起；誘導
   例 Don't provoke that dog. It will bite you.
   別惹那條狗。牠會咬你。
8. **be associated with...**　與……有關聯；使人聯想到……
   例 The English countryside is associated with magnificent gardens.
   英國鄉間會使人聯想到廣大的莊園。

9. **ambulance** [ˈæmbjələns] *n.* 救護車
10. **on the other hand** 另一方面
    例 Casey is a good singer, but on the other hand, she does not dance well.
    凱西歌唱得很好，但另一方面舞卻跳得不怎麼樣。
11. **calming** [ˈkɑmɪŋ] *a.* 令人平靜的
12. **explorative** [ɪkˈsplɔrətɪv] *a.* 探險的
13. **figure out...** 想出／理解……
    例 Ron spent a lot of time trying to figure out the answer to that complex question.
    榮恩花了很多時間設法想出那個複雜問題的答案。
14. **vary** [ˈvɛrɪ] *vi.* 變化，改變
    vary from... to... 從……到……有所不同
    例 My collection of books varies from historical novels to science fiction.
    我的藏書從歷史小說到科幻小說都有。
15. **with regard to...** 有關……
    例 With regard to Bobby's suggestions, we will discuss them fully.
    關於巴比的建議，我們會仔細討論。

16. **spellcheck** [ˈspɛlˌtʃɛk] *vt.* 檢查……拼字（本文為 V-ing 做動名詞使用）
17. **punctuation** [ˌpʌŋktʃʊˈeʃən] *n.* 標點符號（不可數）
18. **exceed** [ɪkˈsid] *vt.* 勝過；超過
    例 John's success in business exceeds his father's.
    約翰在事業上的成就超越他的父親。
19. **brick** [brɪk] *n.* 積木；磚塊
20. **noticeable** [ˈnotɪsəbḷ] *a.* 顯著的
21. **productivity** [ˌprodʌkˈtɪvətɪ] *n.* 生產力
22. **stimulate** [ˈstɪmjəlet] *vt.* 刺激，激勵
    例 The company tried to stimulate sales of their new product by advertising on the radio.
    這家公司設法藉由在廣播電臺打廣告來刺激新產品的銷售量。
23. **enhance** [ɪnˈhæns] *vt.* 增強
    例 Using high-quality materials can enhance the durability of your product.
    使用高品質的材料可以增強產品的耐用性。

Unit 11

四 閱讀測驗

絲路是一條長達六千五百公里的貿易路網，存在的時間介於西元前 130 年至西元 1453 年之間。它的多條路線連接了東西方，促進包括香料、寶石、皮革製品，當然還有絲綢等商品的交流。不過人們不間斷地來來往往，也加速了疾病的傳播。

十四世紀中葉，一種叫做黑死病的鼠疫沿著絲路傳播，最終造成全球數千萬甚至數億人死亡。歷史學家和研究人員爭論該疾病是源於中國西北部、西南部還是中亞地區。證據顯示十三世紀初的元朝鼠疫爆發，從河北省蔓延到湖南省。無論這是否是黑死病的首次出現，一般相信該疾病是透過寄生在老鼠身上的跳蚤傳染給人類的。老鼠這種小型齧齒動物在絲路沿

線的驛站中很常見。驛站不僅是疲憊的旅人和商人的休息站，也是黑死病理想的傳播地點。這場瘟疫逐漸擴散到中亞，消滅了現在吉爾吉斯和烏茲別克等國的地區多達 70% 的人口。

　　一直到最近，傳染病沿絲路傳播的說法都還缺乏真憑實據。然而一項發表在《考古學期刊：報告》的研究檢驗了兩千年前在中國西北部小型廁所裡的個人用廁籌，情況因而改觀。研究發現棒子上的糞便中有種叫做中華肝吸蟲的寄生蟲卵。這發現之所以重要，是因為中華肝吸蟲只會來自數百公里以外的中國東部和南部。研究結果顯示商人在絲路上跋涉了極遠的距離。正如該研究作者之一皮爾斯・米切爾在《對話》中所寫：「……我們現在確定絲路是古時散播傳染病的途徑。」

__B__ 20. 根據本文，下列關於黑死病的敘述何者正確？
(A) 它在烏茲別克和吉爾吉斯的老鼠上發病。
(B) 還不太清楚它實際從哪裡開始。
(C) 河北和湖南省的死亡人數較少。
(D) 可以幾乎確定它最初源自西方。

理由
根據第二段第二至第四句，可知 (B) 項應為正選。

__A__ 21. caravanserai（驛站）是什麼？
(A) 古代旅客住宿的一種型態。
(B) 一個可以治療受感染的商人的地方。
(C) 一種在絲路上行駛的交通工具。
(D) 一個買賣小動物的場所。

理由
根據本文第二段倒數第二句，可知 (A) 項應為正選。

__C__ 22. 《考古學期刊：報告》的研究如何得出結論？
(A) 藉由在一個地區的水中尋找肝吸蟲。
(B) 藉由檢驗公共廁所的空氣。
(C) 藉由找到旅客移動的確切證據。
(D) 藉由檢查皮蛋裡的寄生蟲。

理由
根據本文第三段倒數第二至三句，可知 (C) 項應為正選。

B 23. 作者為何在文末引用皮爾斯・米切爾的話？
(A) 用來對最新的絲路理論提出質疑。
(B) 用來強調一項研究的確定性。
(C) 用來說明證據難以取得。
(D) 用來強調需要進一步研究的必要。

理由
根據最後一段最後一句，可知 (B) 項應為正選。

重要單字與片語

1. **route** [rut / raʊt] *n.* 路線 & *vt.* 運送
2. **facilitate** [fəˋsɪlə͵tet] *vt.* 促進，幫助
   例 The new policies are expected to facilitate economic growth.
   這些新的政策預期會帶動經濟成長。
3. **commodity** [kəˋmɑdətɪ] *n.* 商品
4. **plague** [pleɡ] *n.* 瘟疫
5. **outbreak** [ˋaʊt͵brek] *n.* 爆發
6. **province** [ˋprɑvɪns] *n.* 省
7. **infest** [ɪnˋfɛst] *vt.* 寄生於
   例 Maggots infested the body of the dead rat that was rotting in the alley.
   巷子裡那隻腐爛的死老鼠身上長滿了蛆。
8. **rodent** [ˋrodn̩t] *n.* 齧齒類動物
9. **weary** [ˋwɪrɪ] *a.* 疲勞的
10. **parasite** [ˋpærə͵saɪt] *n.* 寄生蟲
11. **feces** [ˋfisiz] *n.* 糞便；排泄物（恆為複數）
12. **communal** [ˋkɑmjən̩l / kəˋmjunl̩] *a.* 公共的

五 混合題

世界上許多國家都擁有高鐵系統。然而最富有、強大的國家之一美國卻沒有。我們訪問了三個人對這個主題的看法。

查德
美國沒有高鐵系統的原因可以用一個字總結：自由度。高鐵列車也許很快速，但使用它們時仍要照時刻表和諸多限制來走。我們美國人更喜歡只有汽車才能提供的那種自由。幾十年來，汽車是我們生活方式不可或缺的一部分，讓我們能在自己選擇的時間從 A 點走到 B 點。難怪歷屆政府大力投資建設道路而不是高鐵線。鋪設鐵軌、建造新車站和購買最先進的列車的龐大成本完全不值得。

Unit 11

> **喬許**
> 在白宮工作多年的我，知道為重大交通工程籌措資金的困難度。就算我們真的有錢大力投資高鐵系統，由於州政府和地方政府必須參與，此類計畫在協調上的複雜度將大幅提升。例如對路線劃定的歧見、地方居民的反彈，以及應付許多不同層級的官僚作業等等。這很可惜，因為高鐵系統可以帶來許多好處：它可以創造許多工作機會、縮短大城市之間的交通時間，並有助於減少汙染。

> **倫子**
> 在日本，我們有非常優秀的高鐵系統，高效、準時又安全。我第一次到美國的時候，無法理解為何他們沒有高鐵系統。但我逐漸了解，這個國家的廣大土地是建設與運行高鐵系統的巨大障礙。某些城市之間的距離真的太遠，地形變化太大而使得高鐵行不通。而且美國人習慣在國內搭飛機往返，也已經有經濟實惠又便捷的航線網路供民眾利用。此外更有強大的航空公司聯合會來遊說政府偏袒他們的產業。這些團體會影響政治人物所作關於美國國內運輸的決策。

24. 查德認為美國沒有高鐵系統的原因是其人民偏好駕駛自己的私人車輛。

理由
空格前為不定冠詞 a，空格後為介詞 for，可得知空格應置單數可數名詞。根據查德看法的第三句 "We Americans prefer the freedom that only a car can provide."（我們美國人更喜歡只有汽車才能提供的那種自由。）得知，空格應置與 prefer 相關的單數可數名詞 preference。

25. 喬許指出在美國籌劃和建設高鐵系統會有許多的複雜問題／困難度，例如應付反對該計畫的地方居民。

理由
空格前為形容詞 many，可得知空格應置可數複數名詞。根據喬許看法的第一句 "..., I understand how difficult it is to secure funding for major transportation projects."（……，知道為重大交通工程籌措資金的困難度。）及第二句 "..., the necessary involvement of state governments and local authorities would massively complicate the coordination of such a project."（……，由於州政府和地方政府必須參與，此類計畫在協調上的複雜度將大幅提升。）得知，空格應置與 complicate 相關的可數複數名詞 complications 以及與 difficult 相關的可數複數名詞 difficulties。

26. 倫子理解美國沒有建設高鐵系統的原因是因為城市間距離遙遠。

理由

空格前為 be 動詞 are，空格後為介詞 from，可得知空格應置形容詞。根據倫子看法的第四句 "The distances between some cities are simply too vast, ..."（某些城市之間的距離真的太遠，……）得知，空格應置與 distances 相關的形容詞 distant。

27. 倫子回應中的哪個字表示「試圖說服民選官員修訂法律或採取特定行動」？

　　lobby（遊說）

理由

根據倫子看法的倒數第二句 "There are also powerful airline associations that lobby the government to favor their industry."（此外更有強大的航空公司聯合會來遊說政府偏袒他們的產業。）可推測 lobby（遊說）應為正解。

__C__ **28.** 下列哪方面的主題，每一位回應者皆有提到？
　　　　(A) 現存鐵路的情況。
　　　　(B) 替代交通工具選項。
　　　　(C) 政治領袖所做的選擇。
　　　　(D) 對擬定的鐵路路線的爭論。

　　　　理由

　　　　根據查德看法的倒數第二句、喬許看法的第二句及倫子看法的最後一句得知，(C) 項應為正選。

重要單字與片語

1. **sum up**　總結
2. **integral** [ˋɪntəgrəl] *a.* 不可或缺的
3. **successive** [səkˋsɛsɪv] *a.* 接替的，後繼的；連續的
4. **immense** [ɪˋmɛns] *a.* 巨大的
5. **authorities** [əˋθɔrətɪz] *n.* 有關當局（恆用複數）
6. **coordination** [koˏɔrdəˋneʃən] *n.* 協調（不可數）
7. **bureaucracy** [bjuˋrɑkrəsɪ] *n.* 官僚制度
8. **punctual** [ˋpʌŋktʃʊəl] *a.* 準時的
9. **implementation** [ˏɪmpləmɛnˋteʃən] *n.* 執行，實施（不可數）
10. **feasible** [ˋfizəbļ] *a.* 可行的
11. **lobby** [ˋlɑbɪ] *vt. & vi.* 遊說（國會議員）& *n.* 大廳
　　例 Those people were lobbying some congressmen to support their proposal.
　　那些人正在遊說若干國會議員支持他們的提案。

Unit 12

一 綜合測驗

　　侯格威村是一個與眾不同、具開創性的療養院，該院因為對於年老失智症病患的照顧方式特殊而獲得全球關注。侯格威村位於荷蘭阿姆斯特丹市郊，為村內的一百五十二名客戶提供不分日夜的特殊照護服務。他們的平均年齡是八十三歲且都被診斷出患有重度失智症。通常想到老人安養院就會想到令人沮喪的畫面 —— 老人家不開心地度過餘生 —— 但住在這間荷蘭療養院裡的老人卻更充滿活力也更快樂，他們整體上需要的藥物量比起住在大多數傳統療養院裡的老人來得少。

　　這是因為侯格威村的病患受到更妥善的照護，他們居住在一個安全、熟悉又人道的環境中，這些因素幫助減緩失智症患者所感受到的焦慮、困惑以及憤怒。除此之外，村內有二十五個活動社團讓老人們選擇參加，包括繪畫、騎單車、賓果遊戲以及烘焙。生活在侯格威村的老人雖然受失智症所苦，但能得到這麼好的照顧確實很幸運。

A 1. 理由
　　a. 本題測驗分詞構句的用法，原句實為：
　　　Hogewey is located just outside Amsterdam in the Netherlands, Hogewey offers special around-the-clock care for its 152 clients.
　　　上述兩個子句皆為完整的句構，但兩句無連接詞連接，故不合乎文法。因兩句的主詞相同，皆為 Hogewey（侯格威村），故可省略第一句的主詞，再把 be 動詞 is 改為現在分詞 being 後予以省略，保留過去分詞 located，形成分詞構句。
　　b. 根據上述，(A) 項應為正選。
　　c. **locate** [ˈloket / loˈket] vt. 使位於（常用於被動語態）
　　　be located in / on / at... 　位於……
　　　例 Our company is located in Zhongzheng District, Taipei City.
　　　　我們的公司位於臺北市中正區。

A 2. 理由
　　a. (A) **diagnose** [ˈdaɪəɡˌnoz] vt. 診斷
　　　　be diagnosed with + 疾病　　被診斷患有某疾病
　　　　例 Charles was diagnosed with terminal lung cancer.
　　　　　查爾斯經診斷發現罹患了肺癌末期。
　　　(B) **deal** [dil] vi. 處理（三態為：deal, dealt [dɛlt], dealt）
　　　　deal with...　　處理……
　　　　例 Rita doesn't know how to deal with naughty kids.
　　　　　麗塔不知道該如何應付調皮的小孩。

(C) **occupy** [ˈɑkjə͵paɪ] vt. 使忙碌
　　be occupied with + N/V-ing　　忙於……
　= be busy + V-ing
　　例 Those workers were occupied with building a new road.
　= Those workers were busy building a new road.
　　那些工人正忙著建造一條新路。

(D) **charge** [tʃɑrdʒ] vt. 控告，指控
　　charge sb with sth　　指控某人某罪行
　　例 Michael was charged with several counts.
　　麥可被控多項罪行。
　　＊count [kaʊnt] n. 罪狀

b. 根據語意，(A) 項應為正選。

D **3.** 理由

a. (A) **abstract idea**　　抽象的想法
　　例 Explaining an abstract idea to children requires simple examples and stories.
　　向孩童解釋抽象的想法需要簡單的例子和故事。

(B) **standard process**　　標準流程
　　例 The factory follows a strict standard process to ensure product quality.
　　這家工廠遵循嚴格的標準流程來確保產品品質。

(C) **unrelated concept**　　無關的概念
　　例 Some people believe that luck and success are completely unrelated concepts.
　　有些人認為運氣和成功是完全無關的概念。

(D) **typical image**　　典型的形象
　　例 The movie presents the typical image of a brave hero saving the world.
　　這部電影呈現了一個勇敢英雄拯救世界的經典形象。

b. 根據語意，可知 (D) 項應為正選。

C **4.** 理由

a. (A) **confidence** [ˈkɑnfədəns] n. 信心（不可數）
　　have confidence in...　　對……有信心
　　lose confidence in...　　對……失去信心
　　例 Kevin has confidence in his culinary skills.
　　凱文對自己的廚藝有信心。
　　＊culinary [ˈkʌlə͵nɛrɪ] a. 烹飪的

Unit 12

169

Unit 12

(B) **abortion** [əˋbɔrʃən] *n.* 墮胎
  例 Abortion is a highly controversial issue.
  墮胎是個有高度爭議的議題。

(C) **anxiety** [æŋˋzaɪətɪ] *n.* 焦慮（不可數）
  例 Rosie's anxiety about unemployment is understandable.
  蘿西對失業感到憂心忡忡，這點是可以理解的。

(D) **comfort** [ˋkʌmfɚt] *n.* 安慰；舒適
  例 I find comfort in listening to music whenever I feel troubled.
  每當我心煩時聽音樂就能找到慰藉。

b. 根據語意，(C) 項應為正選。

D 5. 理由

a. (A) **to some extent / degree**　就某種程度來說
  例 To some extent, the manager was responsible for the delay of the project.
  就某種程度而言，經理造成這次專案的延宕。

(B) **in short**　簡言之
 = in brief
  例 Andy often lies to us. In short, he is not trustworthy at all.
  安迪常常對我們說謊。簡而言之，他一點都不值得信賴。

(C) **to be honest**　老實說
 = frankly speaking
  例 To be honest, I don't think this is the best solution to the problem.
  老實說，我並不認為這是解決這個問題最好的辦法。

(D) **in addition**　此外
  例 Frank is a good father. In addition, he is also a considerate husband.
  法蘭克是位好爸爸。此外，他也是位貼心的丈夫。

b. 根據語意，(D) 項應為正選。

重要單字與片語

1. **pioneering** [ˏpaɪəˋnɪrɪŋ] *a.* 先驅的；開創的

2. **look after...**　照顧……
 = take care of...
  例 Helen will look after the baby while we are at the movies.
  我們去看電影時，海倫會照顧寶寶。

3. **elderly** [ˋɛldɚlɪ] *a.* 年長的
  the elderly　老年人

4. **dementia** [dɪˋmɛnʃə] *n.* 失智症（不可數）

5. **around-the-clock** [əˏraʊndðəˋklɑk] *a.* 不分日夜的，全天候的

6. **severe** [səˋvɪr] *a.* 嚴重的
7. **a nursing home** 療養院，安養院
8. **depressing** [dɪˋprɛsɪŋ] *a.* 令人沮喪的
9. **resident** [ˋrɛzədənt] *n.* 居民；住戶
10. **on the whole** 一般而言，整體上
    = in general
    = by and large
    = generally speaking
    例 On the whole, I agree with you.
    大致上我同意你。
11. **occupant** [ˋɑkjəpənt] *n.* 住戶
12. **fortunate** [ˋfɔrtʃənɪt] *a.* 幸運的

二 文意選填

　　乾淨的飲用水是世界上許多人都視為理所當然的事。然而，印度是全球人口第二稠密的國家，有大約十二億的人口，卻有相當大比例的居民生活條件很差。他們沒有穩定供給的乾淨水源。由於這個緣故，印度人所罹患的疾病中有四分之三源自於當地低品質的飲用水，這點或許不讓人意外。

　　印度大部分的飲用水及烹飪用水來自於小販，他們將水裝瓶後以高價出售。水價昂貴是其中一個讓人民一直處於貧窮的因素，然而這些高價瓶裝水的品質卻參差不齊。一位受過美式教育的印度人阿南德・夏提出一個可能可解決此一問題的辦法。他開了一間名為薩伐札爾的公司，這個梵文古字意思是「所有人的水」。

　　雖然夏選擇一個古字作為公司的名稱，但他利用的可是二十一世紀的科技。面對印度的水質問題，他的解決方法叫做「自動販水機」，這是一種高科技、電腦化的販水機，在供電量很少或無供電的村落，使用太陽能來處理水的過濾及紫外線照射。機器的操作方式很簡單，使用者只需要刷預先儲值的智慧卡。付以極低的兩元臺幣費用就可以取得四公升的安全用水，供飲用或是作其它用途。夏所使用的商業模式，在某些方面來說與零售商如統一超商相似：將設計精密的販水機的經銷權出售給當地的管理者。薩伐札爾目前提供服務給印度二十個邦裡的五百萬名消費者，在不久的將來這些數字一定會成長。

H　6. 理由
　　a. 空格前有介詞 with，空格後有名詞詞組 1.2 billion people（十二億人口），得知空格應置副詞以修飾該名詞詞組中的數量形容詞 1.2 billion。
　　b. 選項中 (C) incredibly（極為）與 (H) approximately（大約）為副詞，惟 (C) incredibly（極為）通常用於修飾一般形容詞，(H) approximately（大約）則通常修飾數字，故 (H) 項應為正選。
　　c. **approximately** [əˋprɑksəmɪtlɪ] *adv.* 大約（之後接數字）

B　**7. 理由**

　　a. 空格前有不定冠詞 a，空格後有名詞 supply（供給），得知空格應置形容詞，以修飾該名詞。

　　b. 選項中 (B) steady（穩定的）、(D) similar（類似的）及 (F) potential（可能的）均為形容詞，惟根據語意，(B) 項應為正選。

　　c. **steady** [ˈstɛdɪ] *a.* 穩定的

E　**8. 理由**

　　a. 空格位於 that 引導的名詞子句，主詞為複數名詞詞組 three quarters of the diseases（四分之三的疾病），空格後有介詞詞組 from the poor quality of drinking water there（來自當地低品質的飲用水），得知空格應置複數不及物動詞 stem（起因），以與其後的介詞 from 形成片語動詞 stem from（起因於……）。

　　　例 The riot that took place over the weekend stemmed from some immigration controversies.
　　　　週末發生的暴動起因於某些有爭議性的移民問題。

　　b. 根據上述，(E) 項應為正選。

　　c. 本句中 suffered by Indians 為形容詞子句 which / that are suffered by Indians（印度人罹患的）省略關係代名詞 which / that 及 are 而成的分詞詞組。

G　**9. 理由**

　　a. 空格前有介詞 in，得知空格應置名詞，以與介詞 in 形成介詞詞組作形容詞，修飾名詞 people（人民）。

　　b. 剩餘選項中 (A) process（過程）、(F) potential（可能性）、(G) poverty（貧窮）及 (J) technology（科技）為名詞，惟根據語意，(G) 項應為正選。

　　c. **poverty** [ˈpɑvɚtɪ] *n.* 貧窮

F　**10. 理由**

　　a. 空格前有數量詞 One，空格後有名詞 solution（解決辦法），得知空格應置形容詞，以修飾該名詞。

　　b. 剩餘選項中 (D) similar（類似的）及 (F) potential（可能的）為形容詞，惟根據語意，(F) 項應為正選。

　　c. **potential** [pəˈtɛnʃəl] *a.* 可能的，潛在的 & *n.* 潛力，潛能

J　**11. 理由**

　　a. 空格前有本句主詞 Shah 和及物動詞 utilizes（利用），得知空格應置名詞作該動詞的受詞，且被後面 that 引導的形容詞子句修飾。

　　b. 剩餘選項中 (A) process（過程）及 (J) technology（科技）為名詞，惟根據語意，(J) 項應為正選。

　　c. **technology** [tɛkˈnɑlədʒɪ] *n.* 科技

A 12. 理由
　　a. 空格位於關係代名詞 that 引導的形容詞子句中，空格前有形容詞子句的動詞 uses（使用）、受詞 solar power（太陽能）及 to，空格後有名詞 water（水），得知空格應置原形及物動詞，以與 to 形成不定詞，並接 water 作受詞。
　　b. 剩餘選項中 (A) process（處理）及 (I) operate（操作）為原形及物動詞，惟根據語意，(A) 項應為正選。
　　c. **process** [ˋprɑsɛs] *vt.* 處理 & *n.* 過程
　　　例 The computer processed all the data and came up with the results in no time.
　　　　 電腦一會兒就處理完所有資料並把結果顯示出來。

I 13. 理由
　　a. 空格前有主詞 The machines（這些機器）、be 動詞 are、作主詞補語的形容詞 simple（簡單的）及 to，得知空格應置原形動詞，以與 to 形成不定詞修飾主詞。
　　b. 剩餘選項中僅剩 (I) operate（操作）為原形動詞，且置入空格後符合語意，故為正選。
　　c. **operate** [ˋɑpəˏret] *vt.* 操作 & *vi.* 運轉
　　　例 The machine is quite complicated, so not everyone knows how to operate it.
　　　　 那臺機器相當精密複雜，所以並非每個人都知道如何操作它。

C 14. 理由
　　a. 空格前有不定冠詞 an，空格後有形容詞 low（低的），得知空格應置母音起首的副詞，用以修飾後方的形容詞。
　　b. 剩餘選項中 (C) incredibly（極為）為母音起首的副詞，且置入後符合語意並可修飾形容詞 low（低的），故為正選。
　　c. **incredibly** [ɪnˋkrɛdəblɪ] *adv.* 極為；難以置信地

D 15. 理由
　　a. 空格位於關係代名詞 that 引導的形容詞子句中，空格前有形容詞子句的動詞 is，空格後有介詞 to 及其受詞 retailers（零售商），剩餘選項 (D) similar（類似的）置入後，形成下列固定用法：
　　　A be similar to B　　A 與 B 類似
　　　例 Your taste in clothes is similar to mine.
　　　　 你對衣服的品味和我的類似。
　　b. 根據上述，(D) 項應為正選。

重要單字與片語

1. **take... for granted** 將……視為理所當然
　　例 We should appreciate our parents' dedication to the family instead of taking it for granted.
　　　 我們應當感激父母對家庭的奉獻，而不是將它視為理所當然。

Unit 12

2. **populous** [ˈpɑpjələs] *a.* 人口稠密的
3. **proportion** [prəˈpɔrʃən] *n.* 比例
4. **given** [ˈgɪvən] *prep.* 考慮到
   given the fact (that)... 因為……；考慮到……
   = given that...
   例 Given the fact Judy is experienced, we chose her to be our team leader.
   因為茱蒂經驗豐富，我們選她當組長。
5. **vendor** [ˈvɛndɚ] *n.* 小販
6. **utilize** [ˈjutəˌlaɪz] *vt.* 利用
   例 Scientists utilize waterfalls to generate electricity.
   科學家利用瀑布發電。
7. **computerize** [kəmˈpjutəˌraɪz] *vt.* 使電腦化
8. **dispenser** [dɪˈspɛnsɚ] *n.* 自動販賣機
9. **filtration** [fɪlˈtreʃən] *n.* 過濾（不可數）
10. **swipe** [swaɪp] *vt.* 刷（卡）
    例 Paul asked the clerk whether he could swipe his credit card to pay the bill or not.
    保羅詢問店員他是否能刷信用卡付帳。
11. **liter** [ˈlitɚ] *n.* 公升
12. **a business model** 商業模式
13. **franchise** [ˈfræntʃaɪz] *vt.* 出售（某物的）經銷權

篇章結構

　　每個文化都有迷信。在中國，人們不能用手指著月亮，孕婦不能使用剪刀，而數字四則被視為不吉利。在歐洲，打破鏡子會招來厄運，看見黑貓也會倒楣。這些來自世界各地有趣的傳聞並沒有科學根據，卻流傳著有趣的故事。許多迷信都深植於文化傳統中，往往反映了一個社會的價值觀或恐懼。

　　最耐人尋味的迷信之一就是十三號星期五。星期五在北歐的維京人眼裡曾是幸運日，也是一週中大家最喜歡舉行結婚典禮的日子。但歐洲其他地區的人想法則恰好相反。傳統上，歐洲船隻都會避免在星期五航行，如果當天又是十三號的話更是如此。但是，第一個發現新大陸的西方人克里斯多福‧哥倫布卻是在星期五啟航，而且同樣在星期五發現新大陸。

　　羅馬人視十三為不祥的數字，認為這個數字和死亡與毀滅有關。在古挪威人的傳說中，十三個人一起圍坐在桌邊尤其不吉利。基督徒也沿用這個迷信，因為耶穌被釘上十字架前的最後一頓晚餐就是和十二位門徒同坐。此外在中古時代，一般認為巫婆會召集十三個成員進行聚會。而在現代，有些飯店和醫院沒有第十三樓層，而包括瑞安航空和漢莎航空在內的某些航空公司也會省略飛機上的第 13 排座位。

　　綜觀這些傳說，不難發現為何有那麼多西方人提防十三號星期五。這或許就印證了大家說的「積習難改」。每年都有一、兩個十三號星期五，在這天，大家通常都會特別小心周遭事物。或許是因為人們意識到了十三號星期五這個迷信，因而現在在這個日子裡大家都比較平安了。像這樣的迷信顯示出，即使在現代社會，文化信仰仍然深深影響著人們的行為。

__A__ **16.** 理由
  a. 空格前句敘述最耐人尋味的迷信之一是十三號星期五，而選項 (A) 以 Friday（星期五）起首進一步說明這個日子，語意承接空格前句。
  b. 空格後句表示歐洲其他地區的人不同的想法，並進一步說明船隻避免在十三號星期五航行，而選項 (A) 提及維京人正面看待星期五這一天，與空格後句語意相對。
  c. 根據上述，(A) 項應為正選。

__D__ **17.** 理由
  a. 空格前句敘述傳統上歐洲船隻會避免在星期五航行，而選項 (D) 以轉折詞 However（然而）起首描述哥倫布卻是在星期五 set sail（啟航）及 spotted land（發現新大陸），兩句形成對照。
  b. 根據上述，(D) 項應為正選。

__E__ **18.** 理由
  a. 本段敘述十三被視為不吉利的數字，空格前兩句分別提及古挪威人的傳說及耶穌最後一頓晚餐的例子，而選項 (E) 以 In addition（此外）起首進一步舉中古時代 witches... convene their meetings with 13 members（巫婆會召集十三個成員進行聚會）為例說明。
  b. 根據上述，(E) 項應為正選。

__B__ **19.** 理由
  a. 前兩段分別提到星期五及數字十三在不同文化中被視為不吉利的象徵，呼應選項 (B) 中的 these are all combined（綜觀這些傳說）。
  b. 空格後三句敘述因為積習難改，因此人們在每年的十三號星期五這天會特別小心周遭事物，呼應選項 (B) 中所述 so many Westerners hold Friday the 13th as a day to be wary of（那麼多西方人提防十三號星期五）。
  c. 根據上述，(B) 項應為正選。

(C) 選項翻譯 這是歐洲人和美國人認為不吉利的許多日期之一。

重要單字與片語

1. **superstition** [ˌsupɚˈstɪʃən] *n.* 迷信
2. **point at...** 指著……
   例 It's not polite to point at people.
   用手指著別人很不禮貌。
3. **pregnant** [ˈprɛgnənt] *a.* 懷孕的
4. **scissors** [ˈsɪzɚz] *n.* 剪刀（由兩把刀合成，故恆用複數）
   a pair of scissors 一把剪刀
5. **basis** [ˈbesɪs] *n.* 基礎，根本，根據
6. **opposite** [ˈɑpəzɪt] *n.* 相反，對立
7. **be regarded as...** 被視為……
   例 The doctor is regarded as a leader in the field of cancer treatment.
   這位醫生被視為癌症治療領域的權威。

8. **connect A with B** 把 A 與 B 聯想在一起
   - 例 People often connect bullfighting with Spain.
     人們經常會把鬥牛和西班牙聯想在一起。

9. **convene** [kən'vin] *vt.* 召集（會議）& *vi.* 集會

10. **die hard** （觀念、信仰、習慣等）難以改變
    - 例 Old habits die hard.
      積習難改。

11. **pay attention to...** 注意……
    - 例 Parents should always pay attention to their children's emotional development.
      父母應該要時時注意孩子的情緒變化。

12. **surroundings** [sə'raʊndɪŋz] *n.* 環境（恆用複數）

13. **be aware of...** 注意 / 意識到……
    be unaware of... 沒注意 / 沒意識到……
    - 例 I wasn't aware of my spelling mistakes until Carl pointed them out to me.
      我沒注意到我拼錯字，直到卡爾幫我指出來。

四 閱讀測驗

對時常搭飛機的人而言，登機就好像搭車一樣，沒什麼好擔心的。不過，搭飛機會緊張的人則時常擔心自身的安全。近期，乘客在飛機上的安全又再度受到關注。

研究顯示，你可以做以下若干事情來保障你在飛行時的安全。第一點就是要多補充水分。也就是說在機場與飛行期間要避免酒精、咖啡因以及過鹹的食物，這有助你保持機警。當然，你應該注意聽起飛前的安全簡報，在搭機期間，也建議你全程應該緊緊或至少鬆鬆地扣著你的安全帶。

即使在飛行時最糟糕的事情真的發生了，有些方法或許可以讓你保持安全。由《時代》雜誌所做的研究就檢視了十五年間的飛機事故。該研究表示，機艙前段座位的致死率達 38%，而飛機中段座位的致死率甚至更高，達 39%。相對之下，機艙後段座位的致死率最低，只有 32%，而後段中間的一排座位特別安全。當然，有很多因素可以影響這種結果。舉例來說，如果在墜機期間，飛機的後段先著地的話，什麼事情都有可能發生。

然而，別讓這篇有關墜機的談論使你擔心太多，目前來說，搭飛機仍是最安全的交通方式。你在車禍中死亡的機率，還比在墜機中喪生的機率大上一百倍。儘管如此，如果上述的建議，能讓搭飛機會緊張的人感到內心平靜的話，他們可能會發現那些建議很值得遵守。

B 20. 本文的主旨是什麼？
   (A) 車禍與墜機之間的比較
   (B) 在飛機上保持安全的建議
   (C) 美國的某墜機事件
   (D) 坐在飛機前段的好處

   理由
   本文首段提及飛機的乘客安全受到關注，接下來並提出數項保持安全的建議，可知 (B) 項應為正選。

B 21. 本文未曾提及哪一項在機上保持安全的方法？
   (A) 搭機期間多補充水分
   (B) 喝酒或咖啡來幫助你放鬆
   (C) 聆聽安全簡報
   (D) 保持安全帶緊繫

   理由
   根據本文第二段第三句，可知 (B) 項應為正選。

C 22. 根據本文表示，飛機上坐哪個地方最安全？
   (A) A
   (B) B
   (C) C
   (D) D

   理由
   根據本文第三段第四句，可知 (C) 項應為正選。

D 23. 根據本文表示，你為什麼不應該太擔心搭飛機？
   (A) 墜機變得較不常見。
   (B) 民眾比較可能會搭車。
   (C) 飛機保險會理賠一切。
   (D) 搭飛機是最安全的旅行方式。

   理由
   根據本文第四段第一至二句，可知 (D) 項應為正選。

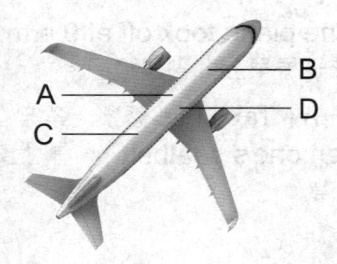

Unit 12

Unit 12

重要單字與片語

1. **board** [bɔrd] *vt.* & *vi.* 登（船、火車、飛機、公車等）
   例 The passengers lined up in an orderly fashion to board the plane.
   乘客們井然有序地排好隊準備登機。
   ＊in an orderly fashion　井然有序地

2. **hydrate** [ˋhaɪdret] *vt.* & *vi.* 補充水分
   hydrated [ˋhaɪdretɪd] *a.* 保水的，多水的
   例 Make sure you hydrate before exercising.
   運動前切記要多補充水分。

3. **caffeine** [ˋkæfiɪn] *n.* 咖啡因（不可數）

4. **take-off** [ˋtek͵ɑf] *n.* 起飛
   take off　　飛機起飛
   比較
   landing [ˋlændɪŋ] *n.* 著地
   land [lænd] *vt.* & *vi.* （使）著地
   例 The plane took off at 9 a.m.
   該飛機早上九點起飛了。

5. **fasten** [ˋfæsn̩] *vt.* 繫緊；紮牢
   fasten one's seatbelt　繫上某人的安全帶

   例 The flight attendants instructed the passengers to fasten their seatbelts.
   空服員指示乘客繫好安全帶。

6. **cabin** [ˋkæbɪn] *n.* 座艙；船艙
   cabin crew　客機艙組員（集合名詞，不可數）

7. **fatality** [fəˋtælətɪ] *n.* 死亡，（意外事故的）死亡人數

8. **perish** [ˋpɛrɪʃ] *vi.* 死亡
   例 The police still don't know how many people perished in the bombing.
   警方還不知道這場爆炸中的確切死亡人數。

9. **cover** [ˋkʌvɚ] *vt.* 理賠；給……保險，承保
   cover... against / for...　　為……保險……
   例 The policy covers fire damage.
   該政策理賠火災損失。
   Are you fully covered against theft?
   你有為自己保偷竊全險嗎？

五 混合題

長久以來，每週五天共四十小時的工作時間一直是許多公司的標準型態。然而近年來情況開始改變：彈性工時與遠端工作也逐漸成為常態。我們訪問了八位民眾，請他們分享對這個議題的看法與相關經驗。

(A) 阿方索
我覺得自己是具備前瞻思維的老闆，因此這幾年來，我都有提供員工彈性工作的選項。我覺得他們應該有權選擇比較能專注工作的地點。如果那個地方是舒適的家裡，那就在家工作好了。

(B) 貝弗莉

新冠疫情期間我不得不在家工作，但現在我已經恢復一週五天都在辦公室。家裡的干擾太多了 —— 小孩啦、狗狗啦、還有電視等等 —— 所以都待在辦公室對我比較好。

(C) 克里斯多夫

我是個自由撰稿人，所以可以任意選擇在哪裡工作，並且想換地點時就可以換。上禮拜我在東京，下禮拜我就要去臺北了。這可算是遠端工作模式的頂點了。在不同環境工作絕對是我的菜。

(D) 黛麗拉

我的公司有彈性工作制度，我大概有 60% 的時間會在辦公室。這樣的安排很平衡：週一和週五在家工作很好，但進辦公室和同事交流也很不錯。

(E) 恩里克

我不准員工在家工作。他們在家的效率不如辦公室、很難專注，而且還會跟團隊脫節。我是以身作則的：通常我一週有六天都在辦公室。

(F) 芙蕾雅

我不能在家工作，但我們公司正在試行一項很讚的新規定。我們一週只要工作四天，卻仍然領五天的薪水！公司的理論是：有充分休息、工作和生活間更平衡的員工更有動力在較短時間內完成工作。

(G) 傑洛德

在家工作有它的優勢，但我一般來說還是比較喜歡辦公室。我喜歡上班日的工作節奏，那種環境也能讓我保持專注。不過我實在討厭通勤的過程就是了。

(H) 海蓮娜

朝九晚五的工作制在現代社會已經過時，這種僵化的思維應該留在上個世紀。幸運的是，我的工作時間相當有彈性，我可以根據每天的工作量調整自己的時間。

24. 受訪者中有四位明確提及每週待在辦公室的天數。請按天數最多到最少的順序填入名字。

Enrique（恩里克）＞ Beverley（貝弗莉）＞ Freya（芙蕾雅）＞ Delilah（黛麗拉）

Unit 12

理由

根據 (B) Beverley（貝弗莉）的回應第一句 "... now I'm back in the office five days a week."（……現在我已經恢復一週五天都在辦公室。），得知她每週到辦公室工作的天數為五天。根據 (D) Delilah（黛麗拉）的回應 "... I go to the office sixty percent of the time... I enjoy working from home on Mondays and Fridays..."（……我大概有 60% 的時間會在辦公室……週一和週五在家工作很好……），得知她每週到辦公室工作的天數為三天。根據 (E) Enrique（恩里克）的回應最後一句 "... I'm regularly in the office six days a week."（……通常我一週有六天都在辦公室。），得知他每週到辦公室工作的天數為六天。根據 (F) Freya（芙蕾雅）的回應第一至二句 "I can't WFH... We get to do a four-day workweek..."（我不能在家工作……我們一週只要工作四天……），得知她每週到辦公室工作的天數為四天。故這四位受訪者每週待在辦公室的天數從最多到最少的排列順序為：Enrique（恩里克）（六天）＞ Beverley（貝弗莉）（五天）＞ Freya（芙蕾雅）（四天）＞ Delilah（黛麗拉）（三天）。

25. 下面這句話最有可能出現在誰的回答裡？
「海邊是我最喜歡的工作地點。」

Christof（克里斯多夫）

理由

根據 (C) Christof（克里斯多夫）的回應最後一句 "It's the ultimate remote-working arrangement, and I love being in different environments."（這可算是遠端工作模式的頂點了。在不同環境工作絕對是我的菜。），可推知克里斯多夫喜歡在不同的環境中工作，包括在海灘上，故 Christof（克里斯多夫）應為正解。

26. 誰在回應中暗示自己在公司擔任管理職位？

Alfonso（阿方索），Enrique（恩里克）

理由

根據 (A) Alfonso（阿方索）的回應第二句 "I like to think of myself as a forward-thinking boss, so I've been offering my staff flexible working arrangements for several years now."（我覺得自己是具備前瞻思維的老闆，因此這幾年來，我都有提供員工彈性工作的選項。），及 (E) Enrique（恩里克）的回應第一句 "I don't allow my employees to work from home."（我不准員工在家工作。），可推知兩位應為僱主，故 Alfonso（阿方索）、Enrique（恩里克）應為正解。

27. 有兩則回應中都用了一個字，意思是「對某特定事物賦予許多注意力」。這個字是什麼？

focused（專注的）

理由

根據 (A) Alfonso（阿方索）的回應第二句 "I think they should be allowed to work wherever they feel more focused."（我覺得他們應該有權選擇比較能專注工作的地點。）及 (G) Gerald（傑洛德）的回應第二句 "... the environment allows me to stay focused on my job."（……那種環境也能讓我保持專注。），可推知 focused（專注的）應為正解。

Unit 12

重要單字與片語

1. **flexible** [ˈflɛksəbl̩] *a.* 有彈性的，可變通的；可彎曲的
2. **forward-thinking** [ˈfɔrwədˌθɪŋkɪŋ] *a.* 高瞻遠矚的，有前瞻性思維的
3. **so be it** 就這樣吧
4. **freelance** [ˈfriˌlæns] *a.* 從事自由職業的
5. **catch up** 敘舊；趕上
   例 Let's grab some coffee and catch up on each other's lives this weekend.
   我們週末去喝個咖啡，敘敘舊。
   I missed the class yesterday and need to catch up on my homework.
   我昨天沒去上課，得趕上作業進度。
6. **disconnected** [ˌdɪskəˈnɛktɪd] *a.* 不連貫的，斷斷續續的
7. **motivated** [ˈmotɪˌvetɪd] *a.* 有動機的，積極的
8. **commute** [kəˈmjut] *vi.* & *n.* 通勤
   commute from A to B　從 A 通勤到 B
   commute between A and B
   在 A 與 B 之間來回通勤
   例 I used to commute from the suburbs to downtown by train.
   我以前搭火車從郊區通勤到市中心。
9. **alter** [ˈɔltə] *vt.* & *vi.* 改變 & *vt.* 修改（衣服）
   例 Daisy altered the design of the room to suit her personal style.
   黛西改變了房間的設計以符合她的個人風格。
10. **workload** [ˈwɜkˌlod] *n.* 工作量
11. **explicitly** [ɪkˈsplɪsɪtlɪ] *adv.* 明確地
12. **managerial** [ˌmænəˈdʒɪrɪəl] *a.* 管理的

Unit 13

一 綜合測驗

　　非洲是一個地雷數量遠超常規的地區，在這裡，老鼠跟這些致命的裝置有什麼關係呢？託一位名叫巴特・維京斯的男子的福 —— 他以前豢養老鼠作為寵物，答案是「關係很密切。」維京斯後來開始研究非洲大陸的地雷問題時偶然發現了一些研究，這些研究檢視沙鼠如何使用牠們的嗅覺來偵測地雷。這啟發他研究是否其他小型齧齒類動物也能執行類似的任務。維京斯回想起他的寵物鼠的智商及可訓練性，決定成立一個叫做 APOPO 的機構，訓練大囊鼠嗅出地雷的位置。這些老鼠通常被稱為「英雄鼠」，牠們體重輕，不會觸發爆炸，卻能偵測到埋藏的地雷。

　　APOPO 於 2003 年開始運作，從那時候起，該機構大大幫助了非洲國家莫三比克成為無地雷區。儘管 APOPO 所做的工作很出色，地雷仍對許多人民構成巨大的威脅。估計仍有數百萬枚地雷存在於六十多個國家裡。APOPO 以及它英勇的老鼠可望在往後的許多年繼續對抗這個致命的問題。

B　1. **理由**

　　a. (A) **in addition to...**　　除了……之外
　　　　　= on top of...
　　　　　= besides...
　　　　例 In addition to English, John speaks German and Italian.
　　　　　除了英語外，約翰還會說德語和義大利語。

　　(B) **thanks to...**　　由於 / 幸虧……
　　　　= due to...
　　　　= owing to...
　　　　= because of...
　　　　例 Thanks to your help, I was able to finish the work on time.
　　　　　幸虧有你的幫忙，我才能準時完成工作。

　　(C) **in terms of...**　　就……而言
　　　　例 In terms of money, John is rich, but in terms of knowledge, he is poor.
　　　　　就錢而言，約翰很富有，但就知識而言，他卻很貧乏。

　　(D) **apart from...**　　（在肯定句中）除……之外尚……（= in addition to...）；
　　　　　　　　　　　　（在否定句中）除……之外則無……（= except...）
　　　　例 Tom has a car apart from a house.
　　　　　湯姆除了一棟房子之外，還有一輛車子。
　　　　　Tom had nothing apart from a house.
　　　　　湯姆除了一棟房子之外，什麼都沒有。

　　b. 根據語意，(B) 項應為正選。

__D__ 2. 理由

    a. (A) **depress** [dɪˋprɛs] *vt.* 使沮喪
            depressed [dɪˋprɛst] *a.* 感到沮喪的
            depressing [dɪˋprɛsɪŋ] *a.* 令人沮喪的
        例 The thought of having to start all over again depressed Mary.
           想到必須從頭開始就讓瑪麗很沮喪。
      (B) **endure** [ɪnˋdʊr] *vt.* 忍耐
        例 The patient could not endure the pain and died.
           那位病患承受不了病痛而死亡。
      (C) **interpret** [ɪnˋtɝprɪt] *vt.* 解釋，闡釋；口譯
           interpret A as B   將 A 解釋為 B
        例 Do you think we should interpret Joseph's silence as approval?
           你認為我們應該把約瑟夫的沉默解釋為同意嗎？
      (D) **detect** [dɪˋtɛkt] *vt.* 偵測
        例 The dog detected drugs in the man's luggage.
           這隻狗在該名男子的行李中嗅出毒品。
    b. 根據語意，(D) 項應為正選。

__A__ 3. 理由

    a. (A) **(be) free of landmines**   沒有地雷
            landmine [ˋlændˏmaɪn] *n.* 地雷
        例 Soldiers carefully checked the area to ensure it was free of landmines.
           那些士兵仔細檢查該區域，以確保那裡沒有地雷。
      (B) **(be) full of explosives**   充滿爆炸物
        例 The abandoned warehouse was found to be full of explosives and highly dangerous.
           那間廢棄倉庫被發現裡面滿是爆炸物，非常危險。
      (C) **(be) rid of protection**   失去保護
        例 In the crowded airport, the celebrity was rid of protection, making him feel vulnerable.
           在擁擠的機場裡，那位名人失去了保護，讓他感到隨時可能會受到攻擊。
      (D) **(be) clear of controversies**   沒有爭議
           controversy [ˋkɑntrəˏvɝsɪ] *n.* 爭議
        例 The scientist wanted her research to be clear of controversies and based on facts.
           這位科學家希望她的研究沒有爭議，完全基於事實。
    b. 根據語意，可知 (A) 項應為正選。

Unit 13

D **4.** 理由

a. 原句實為：
Despite the good work <u>which</u> <u>is</u> <u>being</u> done by APOPO, landmines still pose a major threat to many people.
上句中的形容詞子句 which is being done 表正在進行的被動語態，修飾先行詞 the good work，其中 which is 可省略，形成分詞詞組 being done by APOPO。

b. 根據上述，(D) 項應為正選。

c. 本句中的 Despite 為介詞，之後接名詞詞組 the good work（出色的工作）作受詞。

C **5.** 理由

a. (A) **puzzle** [ˈpʌzl̩] *vt.* 使迷惑
   例 This question puzzles me a lot.
   這問題讓我很困惑。

(B) **persist** [pəˈsɪst] *vi.* 堅持
   persist in + V-ing　　執著從事……
   比較
   insist on + V-ing　　堅持要……
   例 Mike persists in learning English and never gives up.
   麥克學英文很執著，從不放棄。
   It was getting dark, but the boy insisted on staying outside.
   天色漸漸暗了，但那個男孩堅持要待在外頭。

(C) **estimate** [ˈɛstəˌmet] *vt.* 估計
   It is estimated + that 子句　　據估計……
   例 It is estimated that five hundred people were killed in the air crash.
   = An estimated five hundred people were killed in the air crash.
   據估計有五百人在這場空難中喪生。

(D) **raise** [rez] *vt.* 飼養（= keep）；舉起；引發（問題）；籌（款）
   例 I once raised / kept a cat as a pet.
   我曾養過一隻貓當寵物。

b. 根據語意，(C) 項應為正選。

重要單字與片語

1. **deadly** [ˈdɛdlɪ] *a.* 致命的

2. **research** [rɪˈsɝtʃ] *vt.* 研究 & [ˈrisɝtʃ] *n.* 研究（不可數，與介詞 on 並用）
   例 Mary researched her family's history, tracing it back to the 1600s.
   瑪麗研究她的家族史，並追溯到十七世紀。
   I did extensive research on computers before buying one.
   在買電腦前，我先對電腦做了廣泛的研究。

3. **continent** [ˈkɑntənənt] *n.* 大陸

4. **come across...** 與……不期而遇；偶然發現
   - 例 Paul came across Peter on his way home.
   保羅回家途中與彼得不期而遇。
5. **rodent** [ˈrodənt] *n.* 齧齒類動物
6. **recall** [rɪˈkɔl] *vt.* 回想，記得
7. **sniff out...** 嗅出……的味道
   - 例 All police dogs have been trained to sniff out drugs and explosives.
   所有警犬都已接受訓練，能嗅出哪裡有毒品或爆裂物。
8. **lightweight** [ˈlaɪtˌwet] *a.* 重量較輕的 & *n.* 一知半解的人；輕量級運動員
9. **trigger** [ˈtrɪɡɚ] *vt.* 引發 & *n.* 扳機；引發物
   - 例 Loud noises can easily trigger Carl's anxiety and make him feel uncomfortable.
   大聲的噪音很容易引發卡爾的焦慮，讓他感到不適。
10. **operate** [ˈɑpəˌret] *vi.* 運作 & *vt.* 操作
11. **pose a threat to...** 對……構成威脅
    - 例 Pollution poses a threat to marine life.
    汙染對海洋生物造成威脅。
12. **heroic** [hɪˈroɪk] *a.* 英勇的

Unit **13**

二 文意選填

大家經常把著色本和兒童聯想在一起；然而，曼陀羅著色本在成人之間已蔚為風潮。據說曼陀羅是宇宙的圖樣，以各式各樣的環形幾何圖案為特色，且根據許多印度的宗教，曼陀羅被視為靈性的覺醒。一般相信曼陀羅能幫助人們面對日常生活中跟情緒有關的問題，並透過著色揭露他們的心理狀態。

對於在處理壓力方面需要協助或是想了解自身情緒的人來說，曼陀羅著色本被證實極為有用。舉例來說，藉由讓人們在各種黑白圖像上嘗試運用不同的顏色，曼陀羅著色本有助於讓人感到放鬆。還有一件有趣的事值得注意，藉由審視一個人所選擇的顏色，你可以大幅了解一個人當下的感覺是如何。據說暗色表達負面的情緒，而亮色則表示一個人感受到較正面的情緒。例如，鮮紅色可能表示一個人感到自信。相對地，暗紅色顯示一個人感到害怕。

有些人相信曼陀羅有助於人們集中精神，而這些圖像已成為現代心理學的一部分。其中一位就是著名的心理分析學家卡爾・榮格，他生於 1875 年，卒於 1961 年。在他個人成長的時期，他注意到自己會畫曼陀羅。他將曼陀羅跟他的心智獲得新的理解及達於平靜聯繫在一起。如你所見，這些對稱的設計，可不是眼見的那麼簡單！

G 6. 理由
   a. 空格前有主詞 mandalas（曼陀羅），空格後有名詞詞組 a variety of encircled geometric patterns（各式各樣的環形幾何圖案），得知空格應置及物動詞，以接該名詞詞組作受詞，且因本句敘述事實，故應使用現在式。

Unit 13

　　b. 選項中為現在式及物動詞的有 (D) manage（處理）、(G) feature（以……為特色）、(I) indicate（顯示）及 (J) focus（集中），惟根據語意，(G) 項應為正選。

　　c. **feature** [ˈfitʃɚ] *vt.* 以……為特色

　　　例 The new Marvel film features many superheroes.
　　　那部新的漫威電影主打多位超級英雄。

A 7. 理由

　　a. 空格前有動詞 assist（協助）及其受詞 people（人們），由 assist 的用法 assist sb to V，得知空格應置原形動詞，而由空格後之介詞 with 得知此動詞應為不及物動詞。

　　b. 剩餘選項中可作不及物動詞且為原形的有 (A) cope（應付）、(D) manage（處理）、(I) indicate（顯示）及 (J) focus（集中），惟根據語意，(A) 項應為正選。

　　c. **cope** [kop] *vi.* 對抗，應付（與介詞 with 並用）

　　　例 I am convinced that he is able to cope with the problem.
　　　我相信他有處理這個問題的能力。

D 8. 理由

　　a. 空格前有關係代名詞 who 引導的形容詞子句之動詞 need（需要）、其受詞 help（幫助）及 to，得知空格應置原形動詞，以與 to 形成不定詞。

　　b. 剩餘選項中為原形動詞的有 (D) manage（處理）、(I) indicate（顯示）及 (J) focus（集中），惟根據語意，(D) 項應為正選。

　　c. **manage** [ˈmænɪdʒ] *vt.* 處理；管理

　　　例 Dad manages the household, while Mom works outside the home.
　　　爸爸掌管家務事，而媽媽則在外面工作。

H 9. 理由

　　a. 空格前有感官動詞 feel（覺得），得知空格應置形容詞。

　　b. 剩餘選項中 (C) positive（正面的）及 (H) relaxed（放鬆的）為形容詞，惟根據語意，(H) 項應為正選。

　　c. **relaxed** [rɪˈlækst] *a.* 放鬆的

B 10. 理由

　　a. 空格前有介詞 by（藉由），空格後有名詞 the colors（顏色），得知空格應置及物動詞之動名詞，以接該名詞作受詞。

　　b. 剩餘選項中 (B) examining（審視）及 (E) achieving（達到）為及物動詞之動名詞，惟根據語意，(B) 項應為正選。

　　c. **examine** [ɪgˈzæmɪn] *vt.* 審視

　　　例 The mechanic examined the car for problems.
　　　這位技工檢查這輛車的問題。

C **11.** 理由
a. 空格前有及物動詞的現在進行式 is experiencing（正在體驗），空格後有名詞 emotions（情緒），得知空格應置形容詞以修飾該名詞。
b. 剩餘選項中僅 (C) positive（正面的）為形容詞，且置入空格後符合語意，故為正選。
c. **positive** [ˈpɑzətɪv] *a.* 正面的

I **12.** 理由
a. 空格前有主詞 a bright red（鮮紅色）及助動詞 might，空格後有 that 引導的名詞子句 that the person is feeling confident（一個人感到自信），得知空格應置原形及物動詞，以接名詞子句作受詞。
b. 剩餘選項中可作原形及物動詞的有 (I) indicate（顯示）及 (J) focus（集中），惟根據語意，(I) 項應為正選。
c. **indicate** [ˈɪndɪˌket] *vt.* 顯示；指出
　例 Research indicates that sixty percent of schoolchildren are overweight.
　　研究顯示 60% 的學童過胖。

J **13.** 理由
a. 空格前有動詞 help（幫助）及其受詞 people，由 help 的用法 help sb (to) V 及空格後的名詞詞組 their minds（他們的心智），得知空格應置原形及物動詞。
b. 剩餘選項中僅 (J) focus（集中）為原形及物動詞，且置入空格後符合語意及用法，故為正選。
c. **focus** [ˈfokəs] *vt.* 集中；使專注
　例 Stop daydreaming. Focus your attention on your studies.
　　別再做白日夢了。專心在你的學業上吧。

F **14.** 理由
a. 本句為以代名詞 it 強調介詞片語的用法，句構如下：
It is / was + 介詞片語 + that 子句
空格位於此句構之 that 子句中，空格前有主詞 Jung，空格後有名詞子句 that he drew mandalas（他會畫曼陀羅），得知空格應置及物動詞，以接該名詞子句作受詞，且由 was 得知此動詞須用過去式。
b. 剩餘選項中僅 (F) noticed（注意）為過去式及物動詞，且置入空格後符合語意，故為正選。
c. **notice** [ˈnotɪs] *vt.* 注意
　例 I noticed (that) there was a difference in John's attitude toward me.
　　我發現約翰對我的態度變得不一樣了。

E **15.** 理由
a. 空格前有現在分詞詞組 gaining new understanding（獲得新的理解）及對等連接詞 as well as（以及），得知空格應置現在分詞，以與 gaining 對等。
b. 剩餘選項 (E) achieving（達到）為現在分詞，且置入後符合語意及用法，故為正選。

Unit 13

Unit 13

c. 原句實為：
He associated mandalas with his mind which / that gains new understanding as well as achieves peace.
上句可省略關係代名詞 which / that，並將動詞 gains 及 achieves 改為現在分詞 gaining 及 achieving，形成分詞詞組 gaining new understanding 及 achieving peace。

d. achieve [əˋtʃiv] vt. 達到，實現
例 If you work hard enough, you will achieve your goals.
如果你夠努力，就會達成目標。

重要單字與片語

1. **associate** [əˋsoʃɪˌet / əˋsosɪˌet] vt. 使……有關連
   associate A with B　將 A 與 B 聯想在一起
   例 Most people associate roses with love.
   大多數人把玫瑰與愛情聯想在一起。

2. **supposedly** [səˋpozɪdlɪ] adv. 據稱
   例 The house was supposedly built by a single person.
   這棟房子據說是憑一人之力蓋好的。

3. **variety** [vəˋraɪətɪ] n. 多樣性
   a variety of...　各式各樣的……
   例 Vending machines offer a variety of things, ranging from drinks to cigarettes.
   販賣機販售各式各樣的東西，從飲料到香菸一應俱全。

4. **geometric** [ˌdʒiəˋmɛtrɪk] a. 幾何的

5. **experiment** [ɪkˋspɛrəmənt] vi. 實驗（與介詞 with 或 on 並用）
   例 We experimented with several different chemicals.
   我們用不同的化學物質做實驗。
   Scientists often experiment on white mice in their laboratories.
   科學家在實驗室裡常拿白老鼠做實驗。

6. **There is more to sth than meets the eye.**　某事物不是眼見的那麼簡單。
   例 To tell you the truth, there is more to singing than meets the eye.
   老實跟你說，唱歌不是如你表面上看到的那麼簡單。

7. **symmetrical** [sɪˋmɛtrɪkḷ] a. 對稱的

篇章結構

　　你喜歡保留東西嗎？大多數人喜歡把那些平常用不太到的東西擺在家中，像是兒時玩具、紀念品、工具或是某天可能會派上用場的物品，但有些人就是不喜歡把任何東西丟掉。這些人被稱為囤積狂，在極端的案例中，囤積可是種嚴重的心理疾病。

　　精神科醫師辨識出幾種不同的囤積行為。最常見的就是單純囤積物品。囤積物品者會收集並保存那些會被大多數人丟掉的東西。舉例來說，囤積物品者會保留壞掉的東西或是已經過期很久的食物。這些垃圾不斷累積，通常會占掉家中許多空間，並逐漸對囤積物品者的健

康造成威脅。即使如此，囤積物品者對於任何丟掉自己收藏物品的意圖會強烈反抗。由於他們對這些物品產生強烈的情感依附，即使明知道它們已經沒有任何實際用途，仍然難以割捨。

其他的囤積行為還包括藏書癖和收藏動物。藏書狂會瘋狂收集書本。然而，他們到頭來常會因為藏書太多而根本沒辦法真正讀完。動物收藏者則收集寵物，而由於飼養的寵物數量過大，以致於他們沒辦法妥善照顧這些動物。但就像其他囤積者一樣，他們酷愛自己的收藏。這些動物收藏者根本很難了解這些行為正對自己及寵物造成傷害。在這兩種情況下，囤積者可能都沒有察覺到自己的行為對自身或他人健康產生的負面影響。

心理學家相信囤積行為其實是一種自然反應，因為許多動物也會囤積食物。人類只是把這種行為延伸到生活周遭的工具和其他物品上。不過，當這種反應失控時，就會對患者造成困擾。幸好囤積行為是少見的情形，而在櫥櫃裡藏一些舊東西以防緊急情況發生絕對是正常的行為。

Unit 13

__E__ **16. 理由**
a. 空格前句敘述囤積物品者囤積的垃圾逐漸占掉家中的空間並威脅囤積人的健康，而選項 (E) 以 Even so（即使如此）起首，語氣轉折說明囤積物品者會 fiercely resist any attempts to dispose of their collections（對於任何丟掉自己收藏物品的意圖會強烈反抗），their collections 即指空格前句的 This garbage。
b. 根據上述，(E) 項應為正選。

__C__ **17. 理由**
a. 空格前句敘述藏書狂會瘋狂收集書本，選項 (C) 接續說明藏書狂常會因為收藏量 too big for them to ever actually read（太多而根本沒辦法真正讀完），語意承接空格前句。
b. 根據上述，(C) 項應為正選。

__A__ **18. 理由**
a. 空格前兩句描述 animal hoarders（動物收藏者）的特性，而選項 (A) 提及動物收藏者很難了解 they are doing themselves and their pets harm（他們正對自己及寵物造成傷害），與空格前兩句同為關於動物收藏者的敘述。
b. 根據上述，(A) 項應為正選。

__D__ **19. 理由**
a. 空格前句提及囤積行為其實是一種自然反應，因為許多動物也會囤積食物，而選項 (D) 進一步說明人類只是 extend this behavior to the tools and objects that are part of everyday life（把這種行為延伸到生活周遭的工具和其他物品上），前後語意連貫。
b. 根據上述，(D) 項應為正選。

(B) 選項翻譯 治療師已經發現了幾種或許可以治療囤積症患者的方法。

Unit 13

重要單字與片語

1. **souvenir** [ˌsuvəˈnɪr] *n.* 紀念品
2. **come in handy** 派上用場，隨時用得到
   - 例 You'd better carry an umbrella with you; it will come in handy if it rains.
   你最好隨身帶把傘，萬一下雨的話會用得到。
3. **hoarding** [ˈhɔrdɪŋ] *n.* 貯藏，囤積（不可數）
   hoard [hɔrd] *vt.* 貯藏，囤積
4. **recognize** [ˈrɛkəɡˌnaɪz] *vt.* 識別；認出
   - 例 I can hardly recognize Lucy since she has lost so much weight.
   我幾乎認不出露西來，因為她瘦了好多。
5. **psychiatrist** [saɪˈkaɪətrɪst] *n.* 精神科醫師
6. **expiration** [ˌɛkspəˈreʃən] *n.* 到期，期滿
   the expiration date 有效日期；保存期限
7. **accumulate** [əˈkjumjəlet] *vi.* 累積，堆積
   - 例 William never lets his workload accumulate.
   威廉從不累積工作。
8. **take up...** 占用／占據……（時間或空間）
   - 例 The project took up most of Bill's time.
   那個專案占去比爾大部分的時間。
9. **bibliomania** [ˌbɪblɪəˈmenɪə] *n.* 藏書癖
   bibliomaniac [ˌbɪblɪəˈmenɪˌæk] *n.* 有藏書癖的人
10. **obsessively** [əbˈsɛsɪvlɪ] *adv.* 過度地；著魔地
11. **look after...** 照顧／照料……
    - 例 Can you look after my dog while I'm gone?
    我不在的時候可以請你照顧我的狗嗎？
12. **properly** [ˈprɑpɚlɪ] *adv.* 恰當地
13. **passionately** [ˈpæʃənɪtlɪ] *adv.* 熱情地
14. **be attached to sb/sth** 喜愛某人／某物
    - 例 Jimmy is attached to his new puppy.
    吉米很喜歡他剛養的小狗。
15. **be unaware of...** 不知道……；未察覺到……
    - 例 Many people are unaware of the effects of poor sleep.
    許多人沒有意識到睡眠不足的影響。
16. **well-being** [ˌwɛlˈbiɪŋ] *n.* 福祉，幸福（不可數）
17. **response** [rɪˈspɑns] *n.* 反應（與介詞 to 並用）
18. **get out of control** 失控
    - 例 My car got out of control and crashed into a tree this morning.
    今天早上我的車子失控撞上一棵樹。
19. **cupboard** [ˈkʌbɚd] *n.* 櫥櫃
20. **in case of...** 萬一／倘若……
    - 例 You should make sure that your car has a spare tire in case of a flat tire.
    你應該確保你的車子裡有個備胎以防萬一爆胎。
21. **emergency** [ɪˈmɝdʒənsɪ] *n.* 緊急情況
22. **perfectly** [ˈpɝfɪktlɪ] *adv.* 完全地；絕對地
23. **therapist** [ˈθɛrəpɪst] *n.* 治療師

四 閱讀測驗

　　一個世紀前，動物經常被用於科學實驗，而且當時對於使用牠們的規範遠比現在少得多。但值得一提的是，動物在許多醫學的重大進展中扮演了重要的角色。其中之一便是胰島素──一種可以幫助控制血糖含量的人體內激素──的發現。加拿大外科醫師弗雷德里克‧班廷用狗做實驗時發現了這種物質。班廷認為如果移除狗的胰臟，牠們就會罹患糖尿病，即身體無法控制血糖值的疾病。他也猜測如果能分離出胰臟中的某特定物質，那麼這種物質將可用來幫助調節狗的血糖值並治療這種疾病。

　　當然，他需要測試這些理論。為此，多倫多大學給了他一間實驗室、醫學生助手查爾斯‧貝斯特，並提供了一些狗。班廷和貝斯特接著在這些狗身上分離出後來稱為胰島素的物質，並將其注射到其他已切除胰臟的狗身上。*ScienceDirect* 指出，「在這過程中有好幾隻狗死亡」，迫使二人得常向有問題的供應商購買流浪狗。不管怎麼樣，到了 1921 年 7 月底，班廷和貝斯特終於成功使用胰島素注射將一隻狗的血糖值降低了將近一半。當明白無法從狗身上取得足夠的胰臟萃取物時，他們轉而向當地屠宰場購買小牛胎兒。

　　隔年年初，二人在生化學家詹姆斯‧B‧科利普的協助下，在一名十四歲男孩身上測試了他們的療程，結果他的血糖值有顯著地下降。平心而論，此團隊若沒有那些可供依賴的狗兒，是無法走到這個階段的。這些動物為糖尿病的治療革命做出了貢獻，將這種疾病從如同死刑轉變為可控的狀態。

__B__ 20. 根據本文，弗雷德里克‧班廷相信什麼事？
(A) 狗比人類更可能罹患糖尿病。
(B) 他可以在狗身上做實驗以找到治療某種疾病的方法。
(C) 他可以摘除胰臟而不會對健康造成傷害。
(D) 血糖值與胰臟幾乎無關。

理由
根據第一段倒數第一、二句，可知 (B) 項應為正選。

__C__ 21. 為何本文提及多倫多大學？
(A) 它反對在醫學實驗中使用狗。
(B) 它目前以創新的糖尿病研究而聞名。
(C) 它提供班廷進行實驗的工具。
(D) 它的研究人員在班廷之前幾個月就分離出胰島素。

理由
根據本文第二段第二句，可知 (C) 項應為正選。

Unit 13

D **22.** 班廷和貝斯特為何在他們的實驗中改使用小牛胎兒？
(A) 狗身上有太多其他疾病。
(B) 小牛胎兒和人類更相似。
(C) 他們對於死亡的流浪狗數量感到內疚。
(D) 他們無法從狗身上取得足夠的某種物質。

🔷 理由
根據本文第二段最後一句，可知 (D) 項應為正選。

C **23.** 關於胰島素的人體試驗，我們並未得知什麼？
(A) 人體試驗者的年齡。
(B) 實驗的結果。
(C) 人體試驗者的姓名。
(D) 實驗發生的時間。

🔷 理由
根據第三段第一句，可知僅有 (C) 項並未提及，故為正選。

🔖 重要單字與片語

1. **govern** [ˈgʌvɚn] vt. 統治，治理；管理，控制
   例 Many people think we should change the laws that govern charities.
   很多人認為我們應該改變管理慈善機構的法律。

2. **breakthrough** [ˈbrekˌθru] n. 突破

3. **insulin** [ˈɪnsəlɪn] n. 胰島素（不可數）

4. **hormone** [ˈhɔrmon] n. 荷爾蒙，激素

5. **pancreas** [ˈpæŋkrɪəs] n. 胰臟，胰腺

6. **isolate** [ˈaɪsəˌlet] vt. 隔離；孤立；分離
   例 After his wife died, John isolated himself from everyone.
   妻子死後，約翰便過著與世隔絕的生活。

7. **regulate** [ˈrɛgjəˌlet] vt. 規範；調節，調整
   例 Your health will be ruined if you do not regulate your life.
   你生活再不規律點，健康都要給毀了。

8. **grant** [grænt] vt. 授予，給予；承認，同意
   grant sb sth 給予某人某物
   例 The bank finally granted me a $4,000 loan.
   那家銀行終於同意給我那筆四千美元的貸款。

9. **extract** [ˈɛkstrækt] n. 萃取物

10. **calf** [kæf] n. 小牛（複數為 calves [kævs]）

11. **fetus** [ˈfitəs] n. 胎兒

12. **procure** [proˈkjʊr] vt. 取得，購買
    例 Mr. Lai procured many antiques during his travels in Europe.
    賴先生在歐洲旅遊期間買了不少的古董。

13. **canine** [ˈkenaɪn] n. 狗

14. **sentence** [ˈsɛntns] n. 句子；判刑 & vt. 判刑

15. **guilty** [ˈgɪltɪ] a. 有罪的；內疚的

五 混合題

　　大潭藻礁位於桃園。臺灣民眾參與一項是否同意在此處持續建設液化天然氣（LNG）接收站的公投。以下是四個人對於此事的意見。

李女士
大潭藻礁是充滿了魚類、鰻魚、螃蟹，甚至是海龜的天然奇觀。所以我強烈支持停止建設液化天然氣接收站。這是蓄意破壞環境的行為，將毀掉一處有七千五百年歷史的奇景。有人提出持續使用煤炭對國家是有害的。我理解我們需要減少對煤的依賴，但我個人看法是摧毀藻礁更糟糕。

王先生
我在大潭計畫上與政府合作多年。我明白這是一個大家意見兩極化的棘手議題，但我可以很誠實地說，我們已盡力限制液化天然氣接收站對藻礁可能造成的影響。藉由將接收站建在離岸 1.2 公里處，我們將可保護 90% 的藻礁環境免受任何影響。我們需要強化保障能源的充分供應是事實，而這就是該做的事。

白女士
多年來我都同情那些想要拯救藻礁奇觀的人以及住在藻礁裡的美麗生物。但我漸漸了解全球暖化是人類所面臨最大的威脅。因此現在我知道解決能源危機更為重要。我們亟需減少臺灣對煤炭的依賴以減少碳排放，而液化天然氣是達成此目標的最佳途徑。簡言之，建造液化天然氣接收站是兩害取其輕的做法。

陳先生
我曾強烈反對政府要在大潭藻礁建造液化天然氣接收站的初步計畫。我認為藻礁的生物多樣性遠比發電的需求重要。不過由於接收站計畫修訂將移至離海岸更遠處，我想該是放棄抗爭的時候了。這是個一舉兩得的合理折衷辦法：讓我們能保護大多數藻礁生物，同時強化臺灣能源供應的保障。

24. 王先生和陳先生都認同將液化天然氣接收站建在離海岸更遠的地方，可確保大部分藻礁會得到<u>保護</u>。

理由
空格前為定冠詞 the，空格後為介詞 of，可得知空格應置名詞。根據王先生意見的倒數第二句 "By building the terminal 1.2 kilometers out to sea, we will protect 90% of the reef

Unit 13

environment..."（藉由將接收站建在離岸 1.2 公里處，我們將可保護 90% 的藻礁環境……）及陳先生意見的最後一句 "...it allows us to protect the majority of the creatures in the reef..."（……讓我們能保護大多數藻礁生物……）得知，空格應置與 protect 相關的名詞 protection。

25. 雖然李女士和白女士皆提及臺灣需要<u>減少</u>使用煤炭，不過後者認為這是更迫切的事情。

理由

空格前為不定冠詞 a，空格後為介詞 in，可得知空格應置單數可數名詞。根據李女士意見的最後一句 "I understand that we need to reduce our dependence on it, ..."（我理解我們需要減少對煤的依賴，……）及白女士意見的倒數第二句 "We urgently need to reduce this island's reliance on coal so that we can cut carbon emissions, ..."（我們亟需減少臺灣對煤炭的依賴以減少碳排放，……）得知，空格應置與 reduce 相關的名詞 reduction。

26. 這些意見中的哪個片語表示「一個難以處理且造成許多分歧的問題」？

hot potato（棘手的事情，燙手山芋）

理由

根據王先生意見的第二句 "I realize the issue is a hot potato that many people disagree about, ..."（我明白這是一個大家意見兩極化的棘手議題，……）可推測 hot potato（棘手的事情，燙手山芋）應為正解。

CD **27.** 哪幾個人改變了他們對於在大潭藻礁建造液化天然氣接收站的看法？
  (A) 李女士
  (B) 王先生
  (C) 白女士
  (D) 陳先生

理由

根據白女士意見的第一至三句、陳先生意見的第一句及倒數第一至二句得知，(C)、(D) 應為正選。

重要單字與片語

1. **algal** [ˈælgəl] *a.* 海藻的
2. **referendum** [ˌrɛfəˈrɛndəm] *n.* 公投
3. **terminal** [ˈtɝmənl] *n.* 總站；航廈
4. **campaign** [kæmˈpen] *vi.* 從事運動 & *n.* （社會、宣傳）運動
    campaign against... 發起活動反對……

例 These groups campaigned against child abuse.
這些團體展開反虐童的活動。

5. **deliberate** [dɪˈlɪbərɪt] *a.* 故意的；謹慎的

6. **wreck** [rɛk] *vt.* 毀壞
   例 I wrecked my car this morning, but luckily no one was injured.
   今天早上我把車撞毀了，所幸無人受傷。

7. **a hot potato**　棘手的事情，燙手山芋

8. **sympathize** [ˈsɪmpəˌθaɪz] *vi.* 認同；同情（與介詞 with 並用）
   例 My father did not sympathize with my ideas.
   我父親並不認同我的想法。

9. **reliance** [rɪˈlaɪəns] *n.* 依賴（與介詞 on 並用）

10. **emission** [ɪˈmɪʃən] *n.*（氣體、光線等）排放
    carbon emissions　碳排放

11. **the lesser of two evils**　兩害中較輕微的一個

12. **initial** [ɪˈnɪʃəl] *a.* 初期的

13. **biodiversity** [ˌbaɪoˌdaɪˈvɝsətɪ] *n.* 生物多樣性（不可數）

14. **concede** [kənˈsid] *vt.*（不情願地）承認，（不情願地）讓與 & *vi.* & *vt.* 認輸
    concede that...　承認……
    例 I concede that we should have spent more time planning before we started the project.
    我承認我們本應在計畫開始前花更多時間來規劃。

15. **compromise** [ˈkɑmprəˌmaɪz] *n.* & *vi.* 妥協

Unit 13

Unit 14

一 綜合測驗

　　紐西蘭以友善的人民和天然美景聞名。然而，較鮮為人知的是這個國家或許是世界上按人口平均計算幫派數目最高的地區。紐西蘭的街頭幫派和機車黨以他們的暴力犯罪而聲名狼藉，包括傷害、搶劫和謀殺。這些犯罪活動使得幫派暴力成為執法機關面臨的嚴重問題。儘管如此，Tribal Huk —— 一個由少數族群所組成、位於北島外卡多地區的幫派 —— 卻以慈善的舉動獲得美名：為飢餓的學童供餐。

　　Tribal Huk 人稱「三明治幫」，其成員一天做五百個三明治，一週做五天，之後分送給當地的學生。該幫派每週花費紐幣 2,150 元，相當於新臺幣四萬元。對許多當地兒童來說，這些三明治是他們在學校期間獲得營養的主要來源。若是知道他們是自行籌措資金，這項糧食計畫便顯得更驚人。Tribal Huk 經營自己的農場，飼養動物以取得糧食計畫所使用的肉品。他們的努力獲得了教育工作者和社區成員的讚揚，因為這對當地學生產生了正面的影響。對這北島的幫派而言，能夠餵飽飢餓的學童無疑是妥善利用了時間與金錢的表現。

__A__ 1. 理由
   a. (A) **notorious** [noˋtɔrɪəs] *a.* 惡名昭彰的（= infamous [ˋɪnfəməs]）
      be notorious for...　　因……而聲名狼藉
      例 John is notorious for breaking his word.
      　　約翰因食言而聲名狼藉。
   (B) **indignant** [ɪnˋdɪgnənt] *a.* 憤慨的
      be indignant about / at...　　對……感到憤怒
      例 Mary was indignant about the discrimination she suffered in the office.
      　　瑪麗對於在辦公室受到歧視大感憤慨。
   (C) **ambiguous** [æmˋbɪgjuəs] *a.* 模稜兩可的
      例 The wording of this contract is highly ambiguous, isn't it?
      　　這合約的措辭很模稜兩可，不是嗎？
   (D) **mischievous** [ˋmɪstʃɪvəs] *a.* 頑皮的（= naughty）
      例 The student looked at the teacher with a mischievous smile.
      　　那名學生看著老師，露出頑皮的微笑。
   b. 空格後有介詞 for，根據語意及用法，可知 (A) 項應為正選。

__D__ 2. 理由
   a. (A) **receive criticism**　　遭受批評
      例 The company received criticism over its poor customer service.
      　　這家公司因糟糕的客戶服務而受到批評。

(B) **obtain a degree**　　獲得學位
　　例 My sister obtained a degree in biology from a famous university.
　　　我姊姊從一所知名大學獲得了生物學學位。
(C) **undergo punishment**　　遭受懲罰
　　undergo [ˌʌndɚˋgo] vt. 經歷；接受（治療、訓練）
　　（三態為：undergo, underwent [ˌʌndɚˋwɛnt], undergone [ˌʌndɚˋgɔn]）
　　例 The student underwent punishment for breaking school rules.
　　　這名學生因違反校規而受到懲罰。
(D) **gain a reputation**　　獲得好名聲
　　例 Renée gained a reputation as a hardworking and kind leader.
　　　芮妮獲得認真又體貼的領導者的好名聲。
b. 根據語意，可知 (D) 項應為正選。

C　**3.** 理由
　a. (A) **suspend** [səˋspɛnd] vt. 暫時停止
　　　例 Construction of the road was suspended for a few days during the typhoon.
　　　　颱風期間道路工程中斷了幾天。
　　(B) **vibrate** [ˋvaɪbret] vt. 震動
　　　例 Gina dug into her bag in search of her cell phone when it started to vibrate.
　　　　當她的手機開始震動時，吉娜便往包包裡頭找。
　　(C) **distribute** [dɪˋstrɪbjut] vt. 分配；分送，分發
　　　例 Volunteers helped to distribute supplies to the flood victims.
　　　　志工幫忙將補給品分送給水災災民。
　　(D) **certify** [ˋsɝtəˌfaɪ] vt. 認證
　　　例 This diploma certifies that you have finished high school.
　　　　這份文憑證明你已完成高中學業。
　b. 根據語意，可知 (C) 項應為正選。

C　**4.** 理由
　a. (A) **struggle** [ˋstrʌgl̩] n. & vi. 奮鬥；掙扎
　　　例 These people's struggle for independence bore fruit two years ago.
　　　　這些人爭取獨立的努力在兩年前有了成果。
　　(B) **tuition** [t(j)uˋɪʃən] n.（個人或小組的）教導；學費（不可數）
　　　例 Phoebe receives private tuition in English.
　　　　菲碧上私人的英文家教課。

Unit 14

Unit 14

(C) **equivalent** [ɪˋkwɪvələnt] *n.* 相等的事物

例 The word has no exact equivalent in Chinese.
這個字在中文裡沒有完全對應的說法。

(D) **harvest** [ˋhɑrvɪst] *n. & vt.* 收穫

例 Because of so much rain this year, we had a good harvest.
因為今年雨量充足，因此我們的農作物豐收。

b. 根據語意，可知 (C) 項應為正選。

A 5. 理由

a. 原句實為：
Tribal Huk operates its own farm <u>and raises</u> animals for meat to be used for their food program.
對等連接詞 and 連接兩個主詞相同的子句時，可省略 and 再將第二個子句的動詞 raises 改為現在分詞 raising，形成分詞構句。

b. 根據上述，可知 (A) 項應為正選。

重要單字與片語

1. **lesser known** 較鮮為人知的
2. **gang** [gæŋ] *n.* 幫派
3. **per capita** 按人計算的（地），人均的（地）

    例 What is the average per capita income in Taiwan?
    臺灣每個人的平均收入是多少？

4. **assault** [əˋsɔlt] *n. & vt.* 襲擊
5. **nonetheless** [ˏnʌnðəˋlɛs] *adv.* 儘管如此
6. **region** [ˋridʒən] *n.* 地區；範圍（= area）
7. **charitable** [ˋtʃærətəbl] *a.* 慈善的
8. **dub** [dʌb] *vt.* 把……稱作……；給……取綽號為……

    例 The actress was dubbed America's sweetheart.
    這名女演員被稱為美國甜心。

9. **nutrition** [n(j)uˋtrɪʃən] *n.* 營養（不可數）
10. **considering** [kənˋsɪdərɪŋ] *prep.* 考慮到……（= in view of... = in (the) light of...）；就……而論

    例 Considering how far you've traveled, you must be tired.
    想想你走了那麼遠的路，一定累了。
    John did quite well considering his age.
    就約翰的年紀而言，他做得相當不錯了。

二 文意選填

有數百萬人生活在瀕臨餓死的邊緣，尤其在非洲和亞洲，這不是什麼祕密了。同時，有一件令人羞愧的事就是，在西方世界約有 40% 的食物最後進了垃圾桶。單是在美國，一般家庭每年每戶丟棄的食物平均超過一千磅。這驚人的浪費量每年總計約達一千六百五十億美元。解決全球的飢餓問題不是一件簡單的工作，但杜絕浪費食物的問題是我們都可以也應該處理的事。

在歐洲，一項簡單卻有效、科技門檻低並能節省食物的措施最近越來越流行。這項措施稱作「共用冰箱」運動。同在一間辦公室工作或是同住一間宿舍的人不只可以共用冰箱，連裡面的東西也可以共享。和同事或室友共享一瓶牛奶或是一盒肉品已被證實能大量減少浪費的食物量。遵循一些簡單的規則並懷有做出改變的意願就能讓這項措施奏效。每樣食物都得標上製造或購買日期。將食物保存在防漏以及防止氣味散出的容器裡也很重要，還要適時地補充冰箱裡的東西。這項「共用冰箱」活動也在西班牙的巴斯克省進行更大規模的測試，在那裡的名稱叫作「團結冰箱」。在當地，食物就放置在市區街道上的公共冰箱裡。

除了處理浪費食物這個重要議題的預期目的之外，這種作法也有其他正面的效果。參與這場活動的人似乎變得沒那麼自私，而且更樂於與人合作。參與者說參與活動甚至喚醒了他們潛在的美德，就是同情和寬大。

H **6.** 理由
    a. 空格前有不定冠詞 a，空格後有名詞 fact（事實），得知空格應置形容詞以修飾該名詞。
    b. 選項中可做形容詞的有 (A) cooperative（樂於合作的）、(E) initiative（創始的）、(G) intended（預期的）及 (H) shameful（令人羞愧的），惟根據語意，(H) 項應為正選。
    c. 本句中 a shameful fact 作主詞補語，形成下列固定句型：
       It is a / an (+ adj.) + N + that 子句
       例 It is a pity that you can't join in the picnic.
          真可惜你不能去野餐。
    d. **shameful** [ˈʃemfəl] *a.* 令人羞愧的
       比較
       ashamed [əˈʃemd] *a.* 感到羞恥的
       例 John's behavior is shameful. I am ashamed of him.
          約翰的行為令人可恥。我為他感到可恥。

I **7.** 理由
    a. 空格前有單數主詞 an average family（一般的家庭），空格後有名詞詞組 over 1,000 pounds of food（超過一千磅的食物），得知空格內應置現在式第三人稱單數及物動詞，以接該名詞詞組作受詞。
    b. 剩餘選項中為現在式第三人稱單數及物動詞的僅有 (I) discards（丟棄），且置入空格後符合語意，故為正選。

Unit 14

c. **discard** [dɪsˋkɑrd] *vt.* 丟棄
   例 Remove the rotten food from the refrigerator and discard it.
   將冰箱裡餿掉的食物拿出來丟掉。

D **8.** 理由
   a. 空格前有主詞 This staggering waste（這驚人的浪費量），空格後有介詞 to，得知空格應置不及物動詞 amounts，以與 to 形成下列固定用法：
   amount to + 數字　　共計……
   例 The total cost of repairing our front door amounted to NT$30,000.
   我們前門的修繕費用總共是新臺幣三萬塊。
   b. 根據上述，(D) 項應為正選。

F **9.** 理由
   a. 空格前有助動詞 can and should（可以也應該），得知空格應置原形動詞。
   b. 剩餘選項中 (B) reduce（減少）及 (F) address（處理）為原形動詞，惟根據語意，(F) 項應為正選。
   c. **address** [əˋdrɛs] *vt.* 解決；對……發表演說 & [ˋædrɛs / əˋdrɛs] *n.* 地址；演說
   例 The issue of funding has yet to be addressed.
   資金問題尚未得到解決。

E **10.** 理由
   a. 空格前有不定冠詞 a 及形容詞詞組 simple yet effective low-tech food-saving（簡單卻有效、科技門檻低並能節省食物的），得知空格應置單數可數名詞，以被該形容詞詞組修飾。
   b. 剩餘選項中可作單數可數名詞的有 (C) scale（規模）及 (E) initiative（措施），惟根據語意，(E) 項應為正選。
   c. **initiative** [ɪˋnɪʃətɪv] *n.* 方案，措施

B **11.** 理由
   a. 空格前有 to 及副詞 drastically（大大地），空格後有名詞詞組 the amount of food（食物量），得知空格應置原形及物動詞，以與 to 形成不定詞，並被前面的副詞修飾，且接名詞詞組作受詞。
   b. 剩餘選項中僅 (B) reduce（減少）為原形及物動詞，且置入空格後符合語意，故為正選。
   c. 原句句構分析如下：
   Sharing a bottle of milk or a package of meat with coworkers or roommates
   　　　　　　　　　　　　　　(1)
   has already been shown to drastically reduce the amount of food that is wasted.
   　　(2)　　　　　　　　　　(3)　　　　　　　　　　　　(4)

(1) 動名詞詞組作主詞
(2) 現在完成被動式動詞
(3) 不定詞片語，修飾動詞 shown
(4) 關係代名詞 that 引導的形容詞子句，修飾先行詞 food

d. **reduce** [rɪˋd(j)us] *vt.* 減少；降低

例 The plane reduced its speed when it was about to land.
飛機要降落之前減慢了速度。

J 12. 理由

a. 空格前有助動詞 must 及 be 動詞原形 be，空格後有介詞 with，得知空格應置動詞的過去分詞 labeled（標明），以形成固定用法：
be labeled with sth　　標示著某物

例 The bottle was labeled with the name of the medicine inside.
這個瓶子上標示了內容物的藥名。

b. 根據上述，(J) 項應為正選。

C 13. 理由

a. 空格前有介詞 on、不定冠詞 a 和比較級形容詞 larger，得知空格應置單數可數名詞，以被 larger 修飾。

b. 剩餘選項中僅 (B) scale（規模）為單數可數名詞，置入空格後形成以下固定用法：
on a large scale　　大規模地

例 Pollution has caused changes to weather patterns on a large scale.
汙染已經大幅造成天氣型態的改變。

c. 根據上述，(C) 項應為正選。

G 14. 理由

a. 空格前有介詞 Besides（除了……之外）及代名詞所有格 its，空格後有名詞 purpose（目的），得知空格應置形容詞，以修飾該名詞。

b. 剩餘選項中 (A) cooperative（樂於合作的）及 (G) intended（預期的）為形容詞，惟根據語意，(G) 項應為正選。

c. **intended** [ɪnˋtɛndɪd] *a.* 預期的

A 15. 理由

a. 空格前有比較級形容詞 less selfish（較不自私的）、對等連接詞 and（以及）及 more（比較……），得知空格應置形容詞，以與 more 形成另一個比較級形容詞。

b. 剩餘選項 (A) cooperative（樂於合作的）為形容詞，且置入空格後符合語意，故為正選。

c. **cooperative** [koˋɑpərətɪv] *a.* 樂於合作的

Unit 14

Unit 14

重要單字與片語

1. **brink** [brɪŋk] *n.* 邊緣
   on the brink of...　　瀕臨……
   = on the verge of...
   例 Many animals are on the brink of extinction.
   許多動物正瀕臨絕種。

2. **staggering** [ˈstæɡərɪŋ] *a.* 驚人的

3. **approximately** [əˈprɑksɪmɪtlɪ] *adv.* 大約

4. **eliminate** [ɪˈlɪməˌnet] *vt.* 消除
   例 This air freshener eliminates smoke from your room.
   這臺空氣清淨機可消除你房裡的菸味。

5. **low-tech** [ˌloˈtɛk] *a.* 低技術的

6. **dormitory** [ˈdɔrməˌtɔrɪ] *n.* 宿舍

7. **drastically** [ˈdræstɪklɪ] *adv.* 大幅度地

8. **-proof** [pruf] *a.* 防……的
   waterproof [ˈwɑtɚˌpruf] *a.* 防水的
   bulletproof [ˈbʊlɪtˌpruf] *a.* 防彈的

9. **replenish** [rɪˈplɛnɪʃ] *vt.* 補充
   例 For the numerous fans, the record store replenished their stock right away.
   為了無數的樂迷們，唱片行立刻補貨。

10. **campaign** [kæmˈpen] *n.*（為某目的而發起的政治或社會）運動

11. **solidarity** [ˌsɑləˈdærətɪ] *n.* 團結（不可數）

12. **tackle** [ˈtækḷ] *vt.* 處理
    例 The government took extreme measures to tackle the problem of unemployment.
    政府採取激烈的手段處理失業問題。

13. **participant** [pɑrˈtɪsəpənt] *n.* 參與者

14. **awaken sth in sb**　　喚起某人的某物

15. **dormant** [ˈdɔrmənt] *a.* 潛藏的；休眠的

16. **virtue** [ˈvɝtʃu] *n.* 美德

17. **compassion** [kəmˈpæʃən] *n.* 同情（不可數）

18. **generosity** [ˌdʒɛnəˈrɑsətɪ] *n.* 慷慨，大方（不可數）

篇章結構

　　據估計，每天有八百名婦女死於與懷孕和生產相關的問題。其中包括致命的併發症，像是嚴重出血、難產和感染。雖然這些問題大多數都可治療，但通常會因為缺乏訓練和經驗而惡化。在衣索比亞，85% 的分娩在家中進行，由沒有什麼醫療經驗或根本沒有醫療經驗的家人和朋友協助。結果就是該國的產婦死亡率為全世界最高的國家之一，每十萬人就有四百二十起生產的死亡案例。可以拿這個數據和其他開發中國家的二百三十九起左右和已開發國家的十二起做個比較。為了因應衣索比亞這個令人擔憂的狀況，一個丹麥的非政府組織 —— 產婦基金會 —— 開發了一款旨在降低這個東非國家孕婦死亡率的手機應用程式。這項創新的做法目標是使醫學知識更好取得，並能立即被醫療資源有限地區的助產人員所使用。

　　這款名為「安全分娩」的應用程式設計的目的是教導協助生產的人如何處理接生的問題。這款應用程式利用容易理解的動畫教學影片，只要碰觸按鍵，就會提供可在危及生命的緊急狀況下使用的關鍵指示。2014 年開始進行試用，將七十八支配有該款應用程式的手機提供給衣索比亞的小鎮金比鎮上的助產士。她們使用該款應用程式十二個月後，處理產後出血的能力已有大幅進步。<u>在提供新生兒急救方面也觀察到同樣的結果。</u>由於這些樂觀的結果以及比爾與梅琳達・蓋茲基金會的財務援助，目前這款應用程式已運用在其他許多孕婦和新生兒死亡率高的國家。該應用程式的成功顯示數位工具在改善醫療資源不足地區的關鍵作用，在減少可預防的死亡案例上提供了新希望。這項技術也證明了即使在資源有限的情況下，生命仍可被拯救。

B **16.** 理由

    a. 空格前句提及與懷孕和生產相關的問題，與選項 (B) 敘述的 severe bleeding, prolonged labor, and infections（像是嚴重出血、難產和感染）形成關聯。

    b. 空格後句提及 most of these problems（這些問題大多數），呼應選項 (B) 中的 Among these issues are fatal complications（其中包括致命的併發症）。

    c. 根據上述，(B) 項應為正選。

E **17.** 理由

    a. 空格前句提及衣索比亞大部分的分娩由經驗不足的人士協助的問題，選項 (E) 的主詞 The result（其結果）即指涉該問題造成的結果。

    b. 空格後句提及開發中和已開發國家的死亡率，與選項 (E) 中提到的死亡率數字形成關聯。

    c. 根據上述，選項 (E) 填入後語意承先啟後，故為正選。

D **18.** 理由

    a. 上段末兩句提及一款旨在降低衣索比亞孕婦死亡率的手機應用程式，能立即被醫療資源有限地區的助產人員所使用，空格後句提及這款應用程式提供可在危及生命的緊急狀況下使用的關鍵指示，皆呼應選項 (D) 中的 The Safe Delivery App（「安全分娩」應用程式）及其設計的目的 teach birth attendants how to manage deliveries（教導協助生產的人如何處理接生的問題）。

    b. 根據上述，(D) 項應為正選。

C **19.** 理由

    a. 空格後句提及 Thanks to those promising results（由於這些樂觀的結果），暗示前面敘述至少兩種結果，空格前句提及助產士處理產後出血的能力大幅進步，為使用該款應用程式的成果，而選項 (C) 敘述在提供新生兒急救方面也觀察到同樣的結果，為使用該應用程式的另一種結果。

    b. 根據上述，(C) 項應為正選。

(A) 選項翻譯 這些在家分娩的作法對母親和嬰兒都會帶來多重危險。

重要單字與片語

1. **pregnancy** [ˈprɛɡnənsɪ] *n.* 懷孕，妊娠
2. **childbirth** [ˈtʃaɪldˌbɝθ] *n.* 分娩（不可數）

Unit 14

Unit 14

3. **complication** [ˌkamplə'keʃən] *n.* 併發症
4. **prolonged** [prə'lɔŋd] *a.* 延長的
5. **labor** ['lebɚ] *n.* 分娩；勞力
6. **infection** [ɪn'fɛkʃən] *n.* 感染
7. **treatable** ['tritəbḷ] *a.* 可治療的
8. **worsen** ['wɝsṇ] *vt. & vi.*（使）惡化
   例 The air pollution worsened Jim's cough.
   空氣汙染使吉姆愈咳愈厲害。
9. **medical** ['mɛdɪkḷ] *a.* 醫療的；醫學的
10. **maternal** [mə'tɝnḷ] *a.* 產婦的；母親的
11. **mortality** [mɔr'tælətɪ] *n.* 死亡率（不可數）
12. **compare** [kəm'pɛr] *vt.* 比較
    compare A with / to B　把 A 與 B 相比
    例 It doesn't do you any good to compare yourself with others.
    拿自己跟他人比較對你沒好處。
13. **alarming** [ə'lɑrmɪŋ] *a.* 驚人的，嚇人的；令人擔憂的
14. **innovative** ['ɪnə,vetɪv] *a.* 創新的
15. **accessible** [æk'sɛsəbḷ] *a.* 易取得的；可到達的；易理解的
16. **a birth attendant**　助產士

17. **delivery** [dɪ'lɪvərɪ] *n.* 分娩；遞送
18. **animated** ['ænə,metɪd] *a.* 動畫的
19. **instructional** [ɪn'strʌkʃənḷ] *a.* 提供指導的
20. **crucial** ['kruʃəl] *a.* 關鍵的
21. **instruction** [ɪn'strʌkʃən] *n.* 指示（多用複數）；教導（不可數）；（機器）使用說明（多用複數）
22. **emergency** [ɪ'mɝdʒənsɪ] *n.* 緊急事件
    the emergency room　急診室（常縮寫成 ER）
    in an emergency　在緊急狀態中
23. **at the touch / push of a button**
    非常容易地
24. **midwife** ['mɪd,waɪf] *n.* 助產士；接生婆
25. **postnatal** [ˌpost'netḷ] *a.* 產後的
26. **first aid**　急救（集合名詞，不可數）
27. **promising** ['prɑməsɪŋ] *a.* 有前途的，前景看好的
28. **deploy** [dɪ'plɔɪ] *vt.* 運用；部署
    例 An armored troop was deployed to crack down on the rebellion.
    一支裝甲部隊被派去平亂。
29. **plague** [pleg] *vt.* 荼毒，戕害 & *n.* 瘟疫
    be plagued with...　飽受……的折磨
    例 Africa is plagued with AIDS.
    非洲飽受愛滋病的折磨。

四 閱讀測驗

　　1923 年，美國自然歷史博物館（AMNH）的一組研究團隊在位於蒙古南部的戈壁沙漠發現一些恐龍蛋。他們推斷這些蛋是由一種稱為原角龍的有角恐龍所產下。然而在某個巢穴的蛋上方，該團隊發現一個不同恐龍的頭骨。美國化石專家亨利‧費爾費爾德‧奧斯本認為這隻無牙恐龍的強壯下顎應該是非常適合咬破恐龍蛋的，因此他推測這隻恐龍是在試圖偷蛋時被殺。他因而將其命名為偷蛋龍，拉丁文的意思是「偷蛋盜賊」。

七十年後，另一組研究團隊在戈壁沙漠的不同地區發現了類似的恐龍蛋巢。其中一顆蛋不僅形狀和 AMNH 發現的原角龍蛋相同，而且裡面還有一個小小恐龍骨架，好像是偷蛋龍。這發現推導到一個結論，就是七十年前發現的蛋其實就是偷蛋龍的蛋。所以偷蛋龍並沒有偷其他動物的蛋；牠是在照顧自己的蛋。而那強壯的下顎可能是為了咬碎甲殼類動物的硬殼。此外還發現偷蛋龍的骨架是在巢穴上方採孵蛋坐姿 —— 也就是坐在蛋上助其孵化，這支持偷蛋龍是在照顧蛋而非偷蛋的理論，這些恐龍的前肢有羽毛，且會做出一種顯示牠們保護與關愛天性的特定姿勢，更進一步支持了這個理論。

　　蒙大拿州立大學的研究人員大衛・瓦里奇奧認為，這些後期的發現也顯示偷蛋龍孵蛋主要是雄性的責任而非雌性。這是有道理的，因為證據顯示最早期的鳥類物種是由雄性扮演照顧的角色，如非洲的鴕鳥。鴕鳥和偷蛋龍之間的這種相似性，進一步支持了被廣為接受的理論，也就是鳥類是從像偷蛋龍這樣的雙足恐龍演化而來的。

A **20.** 為何亨利・費爾費爾德・奧斯本將這隻恐龍命名為偷蛋龍？
　　(A) 這個名字顯示牠的明顯行為。
　　(B) 這個名字基於牠的生理特徵。
　　(C) 這個名字來源是牠在蒙古的地點。
　　(D) 這個名字是完全隨機選擇的。

　　理由
　　根據第一段倒數第一至二句，可知 (A) 項應為正選。

D **21.** 1990 年代的研究人員證明了什麼？
　　(A) 1923 年的團隊展現出卓越的遠見。
　　(B) 偷蛋龍和原角龍其實是一樣的。
　　(C) 偷蛋龍比以前想像的更兇惡。
　　(D) 關於偷蛋龍的先前假設是錯誤的。

　　理由
　　根據本文第二段第三至四句，可知 (D) 項應為正選。

C **22.** 關於偷蛋龍的進食習慣，我們得知什麼？
　　(A) 牠巨大的牙齒能夠輕鬆撕裂肉。
　　(B) 牠主要以水果和蔬菜維生。
　　(C) 牠強壯的下顎能幫牠咬破食物。
　　(D) 牠發現吃小動物很困難。

　　理由
　　根據本文第二段第五句，可知 (C) 項應為正選。

Unit **14**

Unit 14

__C__ 23. 為何本文提及鴕鳥？
(A) 因為牠們也被指控偷蛋。
(B) 因為牠們也被美國自然歷史博物館研究。
(C) 因為此物種也是雄性負責照顧蛋。
(D) 因為這種鳥類來自於和偷蛋龍相同的地方。

理由
根據本文第三段倒數第二句，可知 (C) 項應為正選。

重要單字與片語

1. **lay** [le] *vt.* 放置；產（卵）（三態為：lay, laid [led], laid）
   例 The hen just laid an egg.
   那隻母雞剛剛下蛋了。

2. **skull** [skʌl] *n.* 頭骨

3. **crunch** [krʌntʃ] *vt.* 清脆的咬嚼
   例 Jane was crunching noisily on an apple before lunch.
   珍午餐前嘎吱嘎吱地啃著一顆蘋果。

4. **attempt** [əˋtɛmpt] *vt. & n.* 企圖，嘗試
   attempt to V　企圖／試著做……
   例 I attempted to warn Peter of the dangers of the task, but he just wouldn't listen.
   我想警告彼得那工作的危險性，但他根本聽不進去。

5. **clutch** [klʌtʃ] *n.* （尤指鳥巢裡的）一窩蛋

6. **skeleton** [ˋskɛlətən] *n.* （整具的）骨骼

7. **crack** [kræk] *vt. & vi.* （使）破裂
   例 Jack cracked open the eggs.
   傑克把蛋敲開。
   Most of the eggs Erin bought cracked when she dropped her basket.
   大部分艾琳買的蛋在她的籃子掉到地上時破掉了。

8. **brood** [brud] *vt.* 孵（蛋）（本文為現在分詞作形容詞用）
   例 After their mother brooded for two weeks, the young birds finally broke out of the eggs.
   經過兩個禮拜的孵蛋，小鳥終於破蛋而出了。

9. **indicative** [ɪnˋdɪkətɪv] *a.* 表明的；標示的
   be indicative of...　顯示……，透露……

10. **incubate** [ˋɪnkjuˏbet] *vt. & vi.* 孵（卵），孵化

11. **ostrich** [ˋɑstrɪtʃ] *n.* 鴕鳥

12. **accuse** [əˋkjuz] *vt.* 指控
    be accused of...　被指控……
    例 The man was accused of constantly harassing his neighbor.
    此男子被指控經常騷擾鄰居。

五 混合題

你或許在近幾年曾聽過「超級食物」這個詞。這個詞是拿來形容被視為對我們健康特別有益的食物。從藍莓到酪梨，某些營養師讚賞這些食物富含天然的維他命與礦物質。然而，超級食物真的值得讚揚，以及真的值得宣稱有益健康嗎？讓我們來看看其中兩種，一探究竟。

巴西莓（讀音為 ah-sigh-ee）是生長在中南美洲熱帶區的深紫色莓果。巴西莓在亞馬遜地區是一種主要的食物，但是在美國，你比較可能找到的是果汁，或是與燕麥及其他水果混成巴西莓果碗的形式。巴西莓的愛好者會說巴西莓富含抗氧化素，據說可以在體內中和造成癌症的自由基。然而，其效果在人體健康上的實際研究卻不足。再者，巴西莓的架上保存期限很短，所以巴西莓以果汁在販賣時，通常會含有添加的糖分。	**藜麥**（讀音為 keen-wah）也來自南美洲，尤其是在安地斯山區。它是一種全穀物，可以作為米飯的替代品，也可以是小菜，或入菜至其他食譜裡。藜麥的其中一項賣點就是富含完全蛋白質，這提供了我們身體所需的所有必要胺基酸。所以對素食者或吃全素的人而言，藜麥是很理想的蛋白質來源。然而，一份藜麥含有的熱量比一份糙米或義大利麵還高，這表示吃太多可能導致體重增加。

那麼，我們是否只要有機會，就一直吃巴西莓、藜麥以及其他超級食物呢？超級食物確實很健康，所以你該盡可能把它們納入飲食中。你若不這麼做，將會錯過取得一些維他命與礦物質。但更重要的是，飲食均衡總是比任何特別的超級食物來得更有益處，也就是吃許多不同的蔬果、含澱粉的碳水化合物，以及適量的蛋白質與奶製品。

24-25 根據本文完成下表。

超級食物	物質	效益
巴西莓	抗氧化素	**24.** 在體內中和造成癌症的自由基
藜麥	**25.** 完全蛋白質	提供了我們身體所需的所有必要胺基酸

理由

根據表格左欄第三句表示，巴西莓的愛好者會說巴西莓富含抗氧化素，據說可以在體內中和造成癌症的自由基（neutralize cancer-causing free radicals in the body），以及表格右欄第三句表示，藜麥的其中一項賣點就是富含完全蛋白質（complete proteins），這提供了我們身體所需的所有必要胺基酸，可知填入後應為正解。

Unit 14

26. 關於藜麥的句子編號為一至五號。請問哪一句最能指出藜麥的壞處？請寫下該句子的編號。

<u>　5　</u>

理由

根據本文描述藜麥編號五號的句子 "However, a serving of quinoa contains more calories than brown rice or pasta, meaning that consuming too much of it could lead to weight gain."（然而，一份藜麥含有的熱量比一份糙米或義大利麵還高，這表示吃太多可能導致體重增加），可知 ❺ 應為正選。

27. 作者在結論中說 If you don't（如果你不）指的是什麼？

他的意思是，「如果你不<u>把超級食物／它們納入飲食中</u>，將會錯過取得一些維他命與礦物質。」

理由

此處的 If you don't 實指若不從事前一句中的「把超級食物／它們納入飲食中」（include superfoods / them in your diet），可知填入後應為正解。

<u>　B　</u>　**28.** 下列哪一項最能表達作者對超級食物的看法？

　　(A) 健康但昂貴
　　(B) 有益但非必要
　　(C) 高糖且脂肪含量太高
　　(D) 不健康但有趣

理由

縱觀全文，在舉出的兩個超級食物的例子中，雖然提及有益的地方，但也指出壞處。另外，根據結尾段落第二至四句表示，我們可以盡可能把超級食物納入飲食中，才能取得一些維他命和礦物質，但飲食的均衡才更重要。可知 (B) 項應為正選。

重要單字與片語

1. **avocado** [ˌævəˈkado] *n.* 酪梨

2. **hail** [hel] *vt.* 歡呼，稱頌 & *vi.* 來自
   hail A as B　　將 A 譽為／稱頌為 B
   hail from...　　來自……
   例 The statue was hailed as a masterpiece in its day.
   該雕像被譽為當時的經典之作。
   John hails from a small town in Kansas.
   約翰來自堪薩斯州的一個小鎮。

3. **content** [ˈkɑntɛnt] *n.* 含量（常為單數或不可數）
   have a high / low fat content　脂肪含量很高／低

4. **claim** [klem] *n.* 主張，聲稱
   例 I make no claim to be an expert.
   我沒說我是個專家。

5. **staple** [ˈstepl̩] *a.* 主要的

6. **be rich / high in...** 富含……
   例 Orange juice is rich in vitamin C.
   柳橙汁富含維他命 C。

7. **antioxidant** [ˌæntaɪˈɑksədənt] *n.* 抗氧化劑

8. **neutralize** [ˈnjutrəˌlaɪz] *vt.* 使中和；使緩和
   例 We were able to neutralize the situation by talking to both of the arguing parties.
   我們藉由和爭執雙方對話來緩和形勢。

9. **shelf life** 貨架期，保存期限

10. **incorporate** [ɪnˈkɔrpəˌret] *vt.* 納入，併入
    incorporate A into B　　把 A 納入 B
    例 Benson was glad that his ideas had been incorporated into the project.
    班森很高興自己的構想被納入這項企劃案中。

11. **protein** [ˈprotin] *n.* 蛋白質

12. **serving** [ˈsɝvɪŋ] *n.* 一份，一客

13. **the bottom line** 底線，最重要的事實
    例 The bottom line for this job is that you must be enthusiastic about writing.
    這份工作的基本要求就是，你必須對寫作有熱忱。

14. **carbohydrate** [ˈkɑrbəˌhaɪdret] *n.* 碳水化合物

15. **modest** [ˈmɑdɪst] *a.* 不大的，適度的
    例 Prices on groceries tend to rise year by year, but at a modest rate.
    物價年年上漲，但幅度並不大。

Unit 14

Unit 15

一、綜合測驗

　　丹麥的 INDEX 設計獎於 2005 年設立，該獎項鼓勵人們為這個世界面臨的基本挑戰尋找解決方法，每兩年提供的獎金總額超過新臺幣一千七百萬元。任何人只要有與競賽的五個類別 —— 身體、家庭、工作、娛樂和學習以及社群 —— 相關的不錯想法，就會有獲獎的機會。就拿其中一個例子來說，2013 年的 INDEX 設計獎收到了一千多件來自七十多個國家的參賽作品。

　　其中最吸引人、在娛樂和學習類別獲獎的作品是一件名為「樹莓派」的設計。那是一款小型的廉價電腦，由劍橋大學的艾本．阿普頓和他的同事所研發。樹莓派的成本不到新臺幣一千元，設計目標是幫助兒童學習程式編碼，並儘可能將電腦提供給世界各地的人們。對於那些希望使世界更美好的人來說，INDEX 設計獎無疑提供了極大的誘因。如果你能透過你的想法造福世界，何不也用這些想法造福自己的荷包呢？

D **1. 理由**

a. (A) **imitate** [ˈɪməˌtet] *vt.* 模仿
例 Children often imitate their parents' behavior.
兒童通常會模仿父母的行為。

(B) **elevate** [ˈɛləˌvet] *vt.* 提高；提升
例 The activity was designed to elevate the mind of students.
該活動設計的目的是為了提升學生的心智能力。

(C) **relate** [rɪˈlet] *vt.* 使有關聯
be related to + N/V-ing　　和……有關；和……有親戚關係
例 This evidence is related to the murder.
這項證據與該起謀殺案有關。

(D) **stand** [stænd] *vt.* 有可能（用於下列詞組中）& *vi.* 站
stand a good chance of...　　很有可能……
例 You'll stand a good chance of passing the test if you study hard.
你如果用功唸書，就很有可能會通過考試。

b. 根據語意及用法，可知 (D) 項應為正選。

A **2. 理由**

a. (A) **example** [ɪgˈzæmpl̩] *n.* 範例
For example, ...　　舉例來說，……
= For instance, ...
例 I have a lot of work to do. For example, I have to clean my room.
我有很多工作要做。比方說，我必須打掃我的房間。

(B) **couple** [ˈkʌpl̩] *n.* 一對
 a couple of + 複數名詞 一對……；幾個……
 例 I've seen this girl a couple of times before.
  這女孩我之前見過幾次。

(C) **principle** [ˈprɪnsəpl̩] *n.* 原則
 in principle 原則上；基本上
 例 That idea is good in principle, but it won't work.
  那個點子基本上很好，但卻行不通。

(D) **disciple** [dɪˈsaɪpl̩] *n.* 門徒，弟子
 例 This theory is fundamental to the work of Noam Chomsky and his disciples.
  這個理論是諾姆‧喬姆斯基和其弟子的著作的基礎。

b. 根據語意，可知 (A) 項應為正選。

D 3. 理由

a. (A) **disappointing** [ˌdɪsəˈpɔɪntɪŋ] *a.* 令人失望的
 例 Last month's sales figures were very disappointing.
  上個月的銷售數字真令人失望。

(B) **forthcoming** [ˌfɔrθˈkʌmɪŋ] *a.* 即將到來的（= approaching）
 例 What are your plans for the forthcoming holidays?
  對於即將到來的假期你有什麼計畫？

(C) **exhausting** [ɪgˈzɔstɪŋ] *a.* 令人筋疲力盡的
 例 John prefers to watch TV after an exhausting day at work.
  約翰比較喜歡在勞累工作了一天後看看電視。

(D) **fascinating** [ˈfæsəˌnetɪŋ] *a.* 吸引人的
 例 From what I've heard, this movie is fascinating and well worth seeing.
  據我所知，這部電影非常棒，很值得一看。

b. 根據語意，可知 (D) 項應為正選。

B 4. 理由

a. 原句實為：
It is a small, inexpensive computer <u>which</u> <u>was</u> developed by Eben Upton and his colleagues at the University of Cambridge.
上句中的限定形容詞子句 which was developed by Eben Upton and his colleagues at the University of Cambridge 可簡化為分詞詞組，即刪除作主詞的關係代名詞 which，再將過去式 be 動詞 was 改為現在分詞 being 後予以省略。

b. 根據上述，可知 (B) 項應為正選。

Unit **15**

Unit 15

B 5. 理由

a. (A) **strong restriction**　嚴格的限制

例 The new law placed a strong restriction on smoking in public areas.
新法律對於在公共場所吸菸設下了嚴格的限制。

(B) **great incentive**　極大的誘因／鼓勵
incentive [ɪnˋsɛntɪv] n. 誘因；動機，原動力

例 The company offers a great incentive for employees who perform well.
這家公司為表現優異的員工提供豐厚獎勵。

(C) **major obstacle**　主要障礙

例 Lack of funds is a major obstacle to completing the project.
資金短缺是完成這個專案的一大障礙。

(D) **huge achievement**　巨大的成就

例 Winning the championship was a huge achievement for the team.
贏得冠軍對這支隊伍來說是一項巨大的成就。

b. 根據語意，可知 (B) 項應為正選。

重要單字與片語

1. **encourage** [ɪnˋkɝdʒ] vt. 鼓勵，激勵
   encourage sb to V　鼓勵某人從事……

   例 My teacher encouraged me to study abroad.
   我的老師鼓勵我出國留學。

2. **solution** [səˋluʃən] n. 解決辦法（與介詞 to 並用）

   例 There are no simple solutions to the problem of global warming.
   全球暖化這個問題沒有簡單的解決辦法。

3. **a cash award**　獎金

4. **worth** [wɝθ] prep. 值得
   worth + N/V-ing　值得……

   例 This award-winning novel is worth reading.
   這本得獎的小說值得一讀。

5. **category** [ˋkætəˏgorɪ] n. 範疇，類別

6. **contest** [ˋkɑntɛst] n. 競賽

7. **entry** [ˋɛntrɪ] n. 參賽作品
   the winning entry　獲獎的作品

8. **colleague** [ˋkɑlig] n. 同事

9. **coding** [ˋkodɪŋ] n. 編碼

10. **without (a) doubt**　毫無疑問地

    例 Nick is without doubt the best student I've ever taught.
    尼克無疑是我教過最棒的學生。

11. **benefit** [ˋbɛnəfɪt] vt. 有益於

    例 Exercise and a balanced diet benefit your health.
    運動和均衡飲食對你的健康有益。

二 文意選填

　　生活中沒有最珍貴的感官能力 —— 視覺 —— 必定是一項考驗，而這項考驗讓許多事情對盲人而言困難重重。漢斯‧約恩‧維貝格知道，如果有個看得見的人協助他們，視障人士面臨的許多問題便可迎刃而解，他因此想出了一個好點子，設計出一款應用程式。2012 年，維貝格與丹麥盲人協會合作，並與稱作機械貓的丹麥軟體工作室組成團隊，開發了一款取名為「你是我的眼」的革命性新應用程式。

　　「你是我的眼」背後的概念簡單卻有力。這款應用程式利用視訊讓使用者能夠與視力正常的人對話，並用智慧型手機的鏡頭指向任何東西，讓志工協助視障者處理他們的日常生活問題。「你是我的眼」這款程式已招募了超過十二萬名視障者和兩百萬名志工。當有人請求協助時，後者會收到通知並可以隨時決定是否要回應。多數情況下，志工與求助者之間的通訊可能只持續一、兩分鐘。如此短暫的時間卻能大大改善盲胞的生活。使用這款應用程式的十二萬名包括全盲或有其它視力受損問題的人再也不需要麻煩他們的鄰居了。舉例來說，現在他們也可以判斷冰箱裡的牛奶有沒有過期這樣的問題了。他們可以充滿自信，因為他們知道報名參加這項計畫的志工已準備就緒、有意願也有能力協助他們處理因為身體缺陷而面臨的考驗。

__F__ 6. **理由**

a. 空格前有 if 子句的主詞 a sighted person（看得見的人）和假設語氣 be 動詞 were，空格後有不定詞詞組 to help them（協助他們），得知空格應置形容詞作主詞補語，形成下列固定用法：
主詞 + be 動詞 + adj. + to V

b. 選項中為形容詞的有 (F) available（可利用的）及 (J) effective（有效的），惟根據語意，(F) 項應為正選。

c. 原句實為：
Hans Jorgen Wiberg knew that many of the problems faced by the visually impaired could be solved easily if a sighted person were available to help them, Hans Jorgen Wiberg came up with a great idea for an app.

上句包含兩個句構完整的子句，但兩個子句之間並無連接詞連接，不合乎文法。惟兩句有相同主詞 Hans Jorgen Wiberg，因此可將第一句的主詞省略，再將動詞 knew 改為現在分詞 knowing 形成分詞構句。

第一個子句中，作 Knowing 之受詞的 that 子句其主詞原為 many of the problems which / that are faced by the visually impaired，此處省略關係代名詞 which / that 與 are，形成分詞詞組修飾先行詞 problems。

d. **available** [əˋveləb̩l] *a.* 可利用的；（人）有空的；可提供或買得到的

Unit 15 ▶▶▶

B **7.** 理由
    a. 空格前有不定冠詞 a、形容詞 Danish（丹麥的）和不可數名詞 software（軟體），空格後有 by the name of...（稱作……），得知空格應置單數可數名詞，以形成名詞詞組。
    b. 選項中 (B) studio（工作室）、(C) point（要點）、(D) difference（差異）及 (I) communication（通訊）為單數可數名詞，惟根據語意，(B) 項應為正選。
    c. **studio** [ˋstudɪ͵o] *n.* 工作室；錄音室
        a dance studio   舞蹈教室

J **8.** 理由
    a. 空格前有主詞 The concept behind "Be My Eye"（「你是我的眼」背後的概念）、be 動詞 is、形容詞 simple（簡單的）和對等連接詞 but（但是），得知空格應置另一形容詞，以與 simple 形成對等，共同作主詞補語。
    b. 選項中僅剩 (J) effective（有效的）為形容詞，且置入空格後符合語意，故為正選。
    c. **effective** [ɪˋfɛktɪv] *a.* 有效的

C **9.** 理由
    a. 空格前有主詞 the app（這個應用程式）、動詞詞組 lets users talk with normal-sighted people（讓使用者與視力正常的人對話）及對等連接詞 and，空格後有名詞詞組 the smartphone camera（智慧型手機的鏡頭），得知空格應置另一個原形及物動詞，以與 talk 形成對等。
    b. 選項中 (C) point（指向）及 (G) bother（麻煩）為原形及物動詞，惟根據語意，(C) 項應為正選。
    c. **point** [pɔɪnt] *vt.* 將……指向
       例 The man drew a knife and pointed it at me.
          那名男子抽出了刀子指著我。

A **10.** 理由
    a. 空格前有主詞 The "Be My Eyes" program（「你是我的眼」這款程式）和現在完成式助動詞 has，空格後有名詞詞組 more than 120,000 blind people and two million volunteers（超過十二萬名視障者和兩百萬名志工），得知空格應置及物動詞的過去分詞，以與 has 形成現在完成式，並接名詞詞組作受詞。
    b. 剩餘選項中可作及物動詞的過去分詞有 (A) recruited（招募）及 (H) requested（請求），惟根據語意，(A) 項應為正選。
    c. **recruit** [rɪˋkrut] *vt.* 招募（新成員、新兵）
       例 Our club has recruited thirty new members this year.
          我們的俱樂部今年已招募了三十名新會員。

__H__ **11. 理由**

a. 空格位於副詞連接詞 when 引導的副詞子句中，空格前有主詞 help（協助）和 be 動詞 is，得知空格可置名詞、形容詞或被動語態的過去分詞作主詞補語。

b. 剩餘選項中為名詞、形容詞或過去分詞的有 (D) difference（差異）、(E) expired（過期）、(G) bother（麻煩）、(H) requested（請求）、(I) communication（通訊），惟根據語意，(H) 項應為正選。

c. **request** [rɪˋkwɛst] *vt.* 請求
request sb to V　　請求某人從事……
例 We were requested to assemble in the lobby.
　　我們被要求到大廳集合。

__I__ **12. 理由**

a. 空格前有定冠詞 the，空格後有關係代名詞 that（= which）引導的形容詞子句 that takes place between the volunteers and those who require their help（發生在志工與求助者之間的）和本句動詞 lasts（持續），得知空格應置單數可數或不可數名詞作本句的主詞。

b. 剩餘選項中為單數可數或不可數名詞的有 (D) difference（差異）、(G) bother（麻煩）及 (I) communication（通訊），惟根據語意，(I) 項應為正選。

c. **communication** [kəˌmjunəˋkeʃən] *n.* 通訊；溝通

__D__ **13. 理由**

a. 空格前有不定冠詞 a 及形容詞 huge（巨大的），得知空格應置名詞，以被該形容詞修飾。

b. 剩餘選項中 (D) difference（差異）及 (G) bother（麻煩）為名詞，惟根據語意，(D) 項應為正選。

c. **difference** [ˋdɪfərəns] *n.* 差異；差別
make a difference　　有所不同；改變
例 Your support will certainly make a big difference to the future of our company.
　　您的支持肯定會大大改變本公司的未來。

__G__ **14. 理由**

a. 空格前有動詞詞組 have to（必須），空格後有名詞詞組 their neighbors（他們的鄰居），得知空格應置原形及物動詞，以接名詞詞組作受詞。

b. 剩餘選項中僅剩 (G) bother（麻煩）為原形及物動詞，且置入空格後符合語意，故為正選。

c. **bother** [ˋbɑðɚ] *vt.* 麻煩；打擾
例 Jason's severe toothache has bothered him all day.
　　傑森嚴重的牙痛困擾了他一整天。

Unit 15

E 15. 理由

a. 空格位於 whether or not 引導的名詞子句中，空格前有名詞詞組 the milk in their refrigerator（他們冰箱裡的牛奶）作主詞及現在完成式助動詞 has，空格後有句點，得知空格應置不及物動詞的過去分詞，以與 has 形成現在完成式。

b. 剩餘選項 (E) expired（過期）為不及物動詞的過去分詞，且置入空格後符合語意及用法，故為正選。

c. **expire** [ɪkˈspaɪr] *vi.* 過期，期滿；（任期）屆滿
　例 When does your passport expire?
　　 你的護照何時會過期？

重要單字與片語

1. **valuable** [ˈvæljuəbl] *a.* 貴重的；寶貴的
2. **sense** [sɛns] *n.* 知覺；感覺；意義
3. **sight** [saɪt] *n.* 視力（= eyesight）（不可數）；景象
4. **the blind**　　盲人
 = blind people
 注意
 "the + adj." 可表具該形容詞特性之全體人 / 事 / 物，如：
 the physically challenged　身障人士
 = physically challenged people
5. **visually** [ˈvɪʒʊəlɪ] *adv.* 視覺上地
6. **impaired** [ɪmˈpɛrd] *a.* 受損的
 visually impaired　　視障的
 hearing impaired　　聽障的
 the visually impaired　視障人士
 （集合名詞，恆為複數）
 = visually impaired people
 the hearing impaired　聽障人士
 （集合名詞，恆為複數）
 = hearing impaired people
7. **sighted** [ˈsaɪtɪd] *a.* 看得見的
8. **revolutionary** [ˌrɛvəˈluʃənˌɛrɪ] *a.* 革命性的
9. **concept** [ˈkɑnsɛpt] *n.* 概念，想法
10. **volunteer** [ˌvɑlənˈtɪr] *n.* 志工
11. **notify** [ˈnotəˌfaɪ] *vt.* 通知
 notify sb of sth　　通知某人某事
 例 Bill notified the police of the date of the gathering.
 比爾通知警方該集會的日期。
12. **determine** [dɪˈtɜmɪn] *vt.* 判定；查明
 例 We set out to determine exactly what had happened that night.
 我們著手查明那天晚上確實發生的事情。
13. **refrigerator** [rɪˈfrɪdʒəˌretɚ] *n.* 冰箱
14. **be confident / safe / secure in the knowledge + that 子句**　知道……而放心
 例 John left home, safe in the knowledge that everyone was asleep.
 約翰知道大家都睡著了才放心離家。
15. **sign up for...**　報名（課程等）
 = register for...
 例 I'm going to sign up for Physics 101 this semester.
 這學期我準備選修基礎物理學。

篇章結構

　　如果你希望在斯德哥爾摩旅遊時有獨特的體驗，或你只是需要在這個瑞典首都待上一晚，巨無霸飯店可能就是你在尋找的地方。<u>如果你喜愛飛機的話尤其如此</u>。與其說巨無霸飯店是間真正的飯店，不如說是間旅舍，它是由波音 747 改建而成，有三十三間不同大小的房間，一共有八十張床鋪。儘管它的結構特殊，這間由飛機改建的旅舍在某些地方與其他旅舍雷同。舉例來說，因為空間有限，多數客房裡的旅客得共用公共衛浴。<u>相較之下，被改建成豪華套房的駕駛艙擁有面朝機場的絕佳視野和獨立浴室</u>。除此之外，這座奇特的旅舍主打一間設有機艙座椅、供旅客放鬆的休息室。飛機的一側機翼上還有一座瞭望臺，可讓任何人安穩地站在上面。這樣的環境讓旅客可以體驗在真正的飛機內過夜的難忘經歷，特別適合航空迷。這架飛機的設計與歷史更增添了其魅力，讓住客享受與傳統飯店截然不同的住宿體驗。

　　巨無霸飯店於 2008 年開幕，是由一位名叫奧斯卡‧迪奧斯的商人所打造，他當時想在機場附近開設一家飯店。<u>2006 年，正當迪奧斯思索著如何實現夢想時，他發現了一架曾經服務於泛美航空的老舊飛機</u>。他花了大約兩百萬歐元將這架飛機改造成獨一無二的旅舍，由起落架上的鋼鐵支架固定著。<u>迪奧斯把握買下這架波音 747 的機會並投入大筆資金裝修，提供人們一個難忘的特別經驗</u>。如果你是位飛機愛好者又恰好在瑞典，你絕對會愛上這裡。對於尋求刺激與新奇體驗的旅客而言，巨無霸飯店完美結合了舒適與創意，吸引來自世界各地的訪客。

Unit 15

__B__ **16.** 理由
- a. 空格後句提及該飯店是由 Boeing 747（波音 747）改建而成，呼應選項 (B) 中提到的 planes（飛機）。若不認識 Boeing 747，第一段倒數第四及第三句中的 airline seats（機艙座椅）和 the plane's wings（機翼）也提示了該飯店與飛機有關。
- b. 根據上述，(B) 項應為正選。

__D__ **17.** 理由
- a. 空格前句提及這間旅舍多數客房得共用公共衛浴，沒有獨立的衛浴，而選項 (D) 以 In contrast（相較之下）開頭，並敘述套房 has its own bathroom（有獨立浴室），與空格前句形成對比，語意連貫。
- b. 根據上述，(D) 項應為正選。

__A__ **18.** 理由
- a. 空格前句敘述巨無霸飯店的創始人迪奧斯想在機場附近開設一家飯店，呼應選項 (A) 中的 he was thinking about how to make his hopes a reality（他當時正在思索如何實現夢想）。

Unit 15

　　b. 空格後句敘述迪奧斯花了大約兩百萬歐元將這架飛機改建成旅舍，與選項 (A) 中的 came across an old aircraft（發現了一架老舊飛機）形成關聯。

　　c. 根據上述，(A) 項應為正選。

C 19. 理由

　　a. 空格前句提及他花了大約兩百萬歐元將這架飛機改建成旅舍，呼應選項 (C) 中的 seizing the opportunity to buy the 747 and pouring a lot of money into its refurbishment（把握買下這架波音 747 的機會並投入大筆資金裝修）。

　　b. 空格後句提及 you will definitely love this place（你絕對會愛上這裡），語意承接選項 (C) 中的 Diös is offering people a unique experience they won't soon forget.（迪奧斯提供人們一個難忘的特別經驗）。

　　c. 根據上述，(C) 項應為正選。

(E) 選項翻譯　缺乏公共空間是這間旅館顯著的特點。

重要單字與片語

1. **overnight** [ˋovɚˌnaɪt] a. 一夜之間的 & [ˌovɚˋnaɪt] adv. 一夜之間
2. **capital** [ˋkæpət!] n. 首都
3. **hostel** [ˋhɑst!] n.（免費或廉價的）旅舍（尤指青年旅舍）
4. **convert** [kənˋvɝt] vt. 轉變，變化（本文為過去分詞作形容詞）
   convert A into B　將 A 改造為 B
   例 Henry converted the garage into a workshop.
   亨利將車庫改造為工作間。
5. **communal** [kəˋmjun! / ˋkɑmjun!] a. 共用的
6. **cockpit** [ˋkɑkˌpɪt] n. 駕駛艙
7. **transform** [trænsˋfɔrm] vt. 使蛻變；轉變
   transform A into B　把 A 轉變成 B
   例 I transformed the kitchen into a study.
   我把廚房改造成書房。
8. **luxury** [ˋlʌkʃərɪ] n. 奢侈，豪華（不可數）；奢侈品（可數）
   lead a life of luxury　過奢侈的生活
9. **lounge** [laʊndʒ] n. 休息室
10. **aviation** [ˌevɪˋeʃən] n. 航空業
11. **enthusiast** [ɪnˋθjuzɪˌæst] n. 熱衷者
12. **aircraft** [ˋɛrˌkræft] n. 飛機，飛行器（單複數同形）
13. **hold sth in place**　將某物固定住
    例 I held the poster in place while my sister taped it to the wall.
    我壓住海報，而我妹妹用膠帶把它固定在牆上。
14. **refurbishment** [rɪˋfɝbɪʃmənt] n. 裝修
15. **adventurous** [ədˋvɛntʃərəs] a. 充滿刺激和危險的；大膽的
16. **novelty** [ˋnɑvltɪ] n. 新奇（不可數）；新奇的事物（可數）
17. **communal** [ˋkɑmjun!] a. 公共的，公有的

四 閱讀測驗

龐氏騙局是一種違法的投資計畫。它承諾以高報酬低風險來説服人們投入資金，但它卻是用新加入投資人的錢而非實際盈利來支付這些報酬。這種架構在仍有大量新人被引誘加入時還可以撐住。但它可能會因為以下三個主要原因的其中一個而土崩瓦解：主事者捲款潛逃、新投資人來源乾涸，或經濟的突然變化促使投資者想領回所有資金。

哪些投資機會實際上可能是龐氏騙局，有幾點警訊可供觀察。其一是投資在一定時間內會提供可觀的報酬。這之所以可疑是因為高報酬總伴隨較高的風險。另一項警訊是不論市況如何，投資都能提供穩定報酬。實際上，報酬本來應該會上下波動才對。還有另一項警訊是投資策略被形容成複雜到無法向客戶解釋。對此就應該有所警覺，因為所有投資訊息都應該無障礙取得才合理。

雖然證據顯示十九世紀就有類似騙局，但「龐氏騙局」一詞源於 1920 年代某名男子的作為：查爾斯・龐茲。幾個月內，這個義大利移民就以僅四十五天即可獲益 50% 的承諾，説服數萬美國投資人跟自己的錢説拜拜。就連《波士頓郵報》也刊登正面的報導，有效地鼓勵了讀者將他們的錢投資給這個人。然而報社編輯很快就對龐茲的快速崛起感覺可疑，並找人對他的商業交易進行調查，隨後發表了一系列的報導，不僅鉅細靡遺地揭露龐茲當下的騙局，還提及他十年前在加拿大的犯罪過往。經過調查，這場騙局崩塌，已經坑殺投資者一千五百萬美元的龐茲被判五年監禁。

__D__ 20. 下列哪一個字最有可能是第一段 enticed 的同義字？
(A) 嚇阻
(B) 使吃驚
(C) 背叛
(D) 引誘

理由
根據本文第一段第二句及第三句 "...there are still plenty of new investors who can be enticed to join."（……仍然有大量新人被引誘加入……。）可知 (D) 項最接近 enticed（引誘）的意思，故為正選。

__C__ 21. 下列哪種情況最有可能涉及龐氏騙局？
(A) 史蒂芬被鼓勵投資一萬美元到他朋友的新公司，最終給他些微報酬。
(B) 瑞秋被告知她的投資帶有一些風險，但閱讀合約的詳細內容讓她安心。
(C) 傑克被承諾就算經濟情勢不好，他的投資每個月都能得到新臺幣十萬元的報酬。
(D) 塔瑪拉被説服購買一間公司的股票和股份，該公司財務報告是可自由取得的。

理由
根據本文第二段第四至五句，可知 (C) 項應為正選。

Unit 15

<u>A</u> **22.** 根據本文，關於龐氏騙局，下列何者正確？
    (A) 當營運者捲款潛逃時就會崩潰。
    (B) 以十九世紀在義大利的一個複雜的計畫來命名。
    (C) 由於缺乏推廣，所以很難進行投資。
    (D) 通常是由公司而非個人經營。

理由
根據本文第一段最後一句，可知 (A) 項應為正選。

<u>D</u> **23.** 關於《波士頓郵報》進行的調查，我們得知什麼？
    (A) 最初對龐茲持懷疑態度，但逐漸變得更加正面。
    (B) 僅聚焦在查爾斯．龐茲 1920 年代在美國的犯行。
    (C) 從某編輯個人投資龐茲後開始。
    (D) 揭露了龐茲在另一個國家的非法活動細節。

理由
根據本文第三段倒數第二句，可知 (D) 項應為正選。

重要單字與片語

1. **scheme** [skim] *n.* 詭計，陰謀 & *vt.* & *vi.* 策劃，密謀

2. **persuade** [pɚˋswed] *vt.* 說服
   persuade sb to + V　說服某人做……
   例 Try to persuade Jerry to apologize to the teacher.
   試著說服傑瑞去向老師道歉。

3. **return** [rɪˋtɝn] *n.* 報酬；收益

4. **entice** [ɪnˋtaɪs] *vt.* 引誘；誘惑
   例 The salesman did everything he could to entice people to buy his products.
   這個業務員使出渾身解數引誘大家來買他的產品。

5. **withdraw** [wɪðˋdrɔ] *vt.* 提（款）（三態為：withdraw, withdrew [wɪðˋdru], withdrawn [wɪðˋdrɔn]）
   例 I used up all my spare money, so I'm going to withdraw some money from the bank this afternoon.
   我已經把身上所有的餘錢花完了，所以今天下午我要去銀行提錢。

6. **substantial** [səbˋstænʃəl] *a.* 大量的

7. **suspicious** [səˋspɪʃəs] *a.* 可疑的；多疑的，猜疑的

8. **consistent** [kənˋsɪstənt] *a.* 前後一致的；一貫的

9. **derive** [dɪˋraɪv] *vi.* 源自 & *vt.* 取得
   derive from...　源自……
   例 The story derives from an old legend.
   這篇故事源自一則古老傳說。

10. **convince** [kənˈvɪns] *vt.* 使確信；說服
    convince sb to + V　　說服某人做……
    例 It seems I can do nothing to convince my husband to quit smoking.
    我似乎拿不出辦法說服我老公戒菸。

11. **part with sth**　　捨棄某物，割愛某物
    例 Josh was unwilling to part with his old car.
    喬許不願意丟棄他的舊車。

12. **sentence** [ˈsɛntn̩s] *vt.* 判刑
    be sentenced to + 數字 + years in prison / jail　　被判若干年有期徒刑
    例 The robber was sentenced to ten years in prison.
    該搶匪被判十年有期徒刑。

13. **lure** [lʊr] *vt.* 引誘 & *n.* 誘惑
    例 Advertisements lure consumers into buying things they don't necessarily need.
    廣告會引誘消費者購買他們不見得需要的東西。

14. **yield** [jild] *vt.* 出產；讓出
    例 I believe this investment should yield a reasonable return.
    我相信這項投資可產生合理的報酬。

15. **skeptical** [ˈskɛptɪkl̩] *a.* 懷疑的
    例 Economists are highly skeptical about the government's economic reforms.
    經濟學家高度質疑政府的經濟改革。

16. **initiate** [ɪˈnɪʃɪˌet] *vt.* 開始
    例 Management decided to initiate a new marketing strategy.
    管理階層決定展開一套新的行銷策略。

Unit 15

五 混合題

　　幾乎每個人都知道鐵達尼號的故事：這艘「永不沉沒」的船在大西洋冰冷的海域沉沒，奪走了一千五百名乘客和船員的性命。很少人知道它是如何及為何被建造的。它的起源可追溯至 1907 年夏天兩位有權勢的人 ——「白星航運」董事總經理 J・布魯斯・伊斯梅和「哈蘭德與沃爾夫」造船廠董事長威廉・詹姆士・裴禮子爵 —— 的會面。面臨來自其他航運公司激烈競爭的伊斯梅，渴望建造前所未見最大、最豪華的海洋郵輪。根據《國家地理》雜誌報導，裴禮子爵馬上勾勒出符合這些標準的三艘船，並告訴伊斯梅他的公司會建造這些船。[1] 其中一艘就是鐵達尼號。

　　造船工程於 1909 年三月三十一日在愛爾蘭的貝爾法斯特架設龍骨（沿船底鋪設的長鋼條，形成船的基礎），正式開工。兩年當中約有三千名工匠、工程師和工人，在「哈蘭德與沃爾夫」造船廠的首席設計師湯瑪斯・安德魯斯的監督下建造鐵達尼號。[2] 等主結構建好後船隻下水。但內部裝潢工程又花了一年。鐵達尼號有九層樓高、四個街區長，有四臺電梯、一個泳池及一間豪華餐廳。[3] 說準確一點，在裝潢這艘世界最大汽輪上，是極盡奢華之能事。

　　但不幸且悲哀的是，船隻在安全方面偷工減料。安德魯斯堅持放上大量救生艇，但伊斯梅不理會他的擔憂，告訴安德魯斯說：「我不允許那麼多（救生艇）堆滿我的甲板，那會

讓乘客產生害怕的感覺。」此外，船的主體被分為十六個可密閉的隔艙。**[4]** 這是為了確保萬一船體破損，淹水將在可控範圍，船東聲稱就算有四個隔艙遭到淹沒，船還是可以保持浮力。然而由於削減成本，或說對安全性的忽視，這些隔艙頂部都沒有被密封。當鐵達尼號於 1912 年四月十日從南安普敦出發首航前往紐約時，據說有個水手對一名乘客說：「就連上帝來都無法讓這艘船沉沒。」歷史證明正好相反。

24. J・布魯斯・伊斯梅急於與其他航運公司競爭，並開始<u>建造</u>三艘大型豪華的海洋郵輪。

理由

空格前為動詞 commence，空格後為介詞 on，可得知空格應置名詞。根據本文第一段倒數第三句 "..., Ismay was eager to construct the biggest and most luxurious ocean liners the world had ever seen."（……伊斯梅，渴望建造前所未見最大、最豪華的海洋郵輪。）得知，空格應置與 construct 相關的名詞 construction。

25. 建造鐵達尼號的主體花了約兩年時間，而內部裝潢工程又花了十二個月才<u>完工</u>。

理由

空格前為定冠詞 the，空格後為介詞 of，可得知空格應置名詞。根據本文第二段第四句 "However, it took a further year for the interior work to be completed."（但內部裝潢工程又花了一年。）得知，空格應置與 completed 相關的名詞 completion。

26. 下列哪一個標題最適合各段內容？請將字母寫在對應的段落旁邊。

(A) 導致悲劇的安全疏忽。
(B) 沉船事件中的罹難者。
(C) 外部與內部的工程作業展開。
(D) 重要人物之間的會面。

第一段：<u>(D)</u>
第二段：<u>(C)</u>
第三段：<u>(A)</u>

理由

(1) 第一段主要敘述兩位高層人士 J・布魯斯・伊斯梅和威廉・詹姆士・裴禮子爵會面並決定建造鐵達尼號，故 (D) 應為最適合第一段的標題。

(2) 第二段主要描述鐵達尼號從龍骨鋪設開始，到主體建造完成並下水，再到內部裝潢的建設過程，故 (C) 應為最適合第二段的標題。

(3) 第三段指出鐵達尼號的安全問題，包括偷工減料、救生艇數量不足以及隔艙頂部未密封等，終至釀成悲劇，故 (A) 應為最適合第三段的標題。

__C__ **27.** 下述句子最適合標號 [1]、[2]、[3] 及 [4] 的哪個位置？

「頭等艙與二等艙的房間很豪華，甚至三等艙的房間也相對舒適。」

(A) [1]
(B) [2]
(C) [3]
(D) [4]

理由

根據本文第二段倒數第二句 "As tall as a nine-story building and as long as four city blocks, the *Titanic* featured four elevators, a swimming pool, and an opulent dining room."（鐵達尼號有九層樓高、四個街區長，有四臺電梯、一個泳池及一間豪華餐廳。）描述鐵達尼號的內部構造，及最後一句 "... no expense was spared when fitting out the largest steamer on the planet."（……，在裝潢這艘世界最大汽輪上，是極盡奢華之能事。）而題目句也是在說明其內部的豪華構造，使上下句形成關聯，故 **(C)** 項應為正選。

重要單字與片語

1. **stiff** [stɪf] *a.* 激烈的；硬的
2. **liner** [ˋlaɪnɚ] *n.* 大型客輪
   ocean liner　郵輪
3. **sketch** [skɛtʃ] *vt. & vi.* 畫草圖；素描 & *vt.* 概略 & *n.* 素描；草圖
   例 The artist sketched the mountains many times before making a painting of them.
   藝術家將群山入畫前先素描過很多次。
4. **criterion** [kraɪˋtɪrɪən] *n.*（評斷、批評的）標準（複數為 criteria [kraɪˋtɪrɪə]）
5. **course** [kɔrs] *n.* 過程；課程；路線
6. **oversee** [͵ovɚˋsi] *vt.* 監督，監察（三態為：oversee, oversaw [͵ovɚˋsɔ], overseen [͵ovɚˋsin]）
   例 Gloria was promoted to manager and now oversees a total of 25 employees in the marketing department.
   葛洛莉雅被升為經理，現在管理行銷部門一共二十五位員工。
7. **erect** [ɪˋrɛkt] *vt.* 建立；使豎立
   例 We erected a monument to honor the martyrs.
   我們建立一座紀念碑，以紀念這些烈士。
8. **no expense is spared**　不惜重金；不惜代價
9. **fit... out**　為……裝備 / 配備
10. **cut corners**　圖省事；貪便宜
11. **dismiss** [dɪsˋmɪs] *vt.* 對……不予理會，摒棄；開除
    例 The Ministry of Foreign Affairs dismissed the news report as a rumor.
    外交部視該項新聞報導為謠言而不予理會。
12. **clutter** [ˋklʌtɚ] *vt.* 塞滿，亂堆
    例 The storage room is cluttered with junk from my childhood.
    這間儲藏室堆滿了我小時候一些雜七雜八的東西。

Unit 15

13. **compartment** [kəmˈpɑrtmənt] *n.* 艙；隔間，包廂
14. **contain** [kənˈten] *vt.* 控制，遏制
15. **breach** [britʃ] *n.* 破裂；缺口；破壞
16. **afloat** [əˈflot] *a.* 漂浮的
17. **embark** [ɪmˈbɑrk] *vi.* 登（船、飛機）
    embark on / upon... 著手做……
    例 When you embark on such a task, you should realize that there will be difficulties.
    開始進行這種任務時，你就該了解會面臨重重困難。
18. **lavish** [ˈlævɪʃ] *a.* 鋪張奢華的，（花費）揮霍的
19. **heading** [ˈhɛdɪŋ] *n.* 標題，書名
20. **shortcut** [ˈʃɔrtˌkʌt] *n.* 捷徑
21. **external** [ɪkˈstɚnḷ] *a.* 外部的 & *n.* 外觀，外形

Unit 16

一、綜合測驗

　　有別於世界上許多女性，荷蘭女性相較於金錢或事業上的成功，更看重空閒時間。超過九成的荷蘭女性並未從事全職工作。不過，她們大多數的確都有兼職的工作，在荷蘭，從事兼職工作的女性人數占成年女性人口的 75%。荷蘭的女性似乎不為這些數據煩惱，如調查結果顯示，她們也不希望看到任何鼓勵女性更投入職場的舉措。當她們被問到若是可行的話是否想增加工作量時，僅有 4% 的受訪者回答「願意」。

　　荷蘭的女性非常享受她們的空閒時間，甚至已採取行動來保護她們免於非自願超時工作的權利。2000 年荷蘭通過了一條法案，聲明女性不能被僱主強制增加工時。因此，荷蘭女性對於工作的滿足感似乎就是無須工作太多時數。

__A__ 1. 理由
    a. (A) **employment** [ɪmˋplɔɪmənt] *n.* 僱用，就業，工作（均不可數）
        例 It is hard for many college graduates to find employment this year.
          今年很多大學畢業生找工作很困難。
      (B) **balcony** [ˋbælkənɪ] *n.* 陽臺
        例 The balcony's railing prevents people from falling over the edge.
          陽臺上的欄杆是用來防止有人從邊緣摔落。
      (C) **circulation** [ˏsɝkjəˋleʃən] *n.* 循環
        例 Jogging can help improve our blood circulation.
          慢跑可以改善我們的血液循環。
      (D) **extension** [ɪkˋstɛnʃən] *n.* 延伸；延長（與介詞 on 並用）
        例 Henry requested an extension on his loan repayments.
          亨利要求延長他償還貸款的時間。
    b. 根據語意，可知 (A) 項應為正選。

__D__ 2. 理由
    a. (A) prevent active engagement　　　阻止積極參與
      (B) conduct further investigation　　進行進一步調查
      (C) limit professional growth　　　　限制職業成長
      (D) encourage more participation　　鼓勵更多參與
    b. 前面提及荷蘭女性較看重空閒時間，多數從事兼職工作，占成年女性人口的 75%，而本句前半句敘述這些數據並不會讓荷蘭女性煩惱，可推知她們不會支持鼓勵女性更投入職場的舉措，故 (D) 項應為正選。

<u>B</u> 3. 理由
   a. 原句實為：
      <u>When</u> <u>they</u> <u>were</u> asked if they would like to work more if they could, only four percent of the respondents responded "yes."
      上句中 when 引導的從屬子句之主詞 they 與主要子句的主詞 the respondents 相同，故從屬子句可簡化為分詞構句，即省略連接詞 when、主詞 they 與 be 動詞 were 後保留 asked（被問道），此處為由被動語態簡化而來，故含有被動之意。
   b. (A) 項、(C) 項為主動用法，分別表「（正在）問」及「已經問了」，(D) 項則有表目的之意，表「為了問」，故這三項語意及用法不合，皆不可選。
   c. 根據上述語意及用法，可知 (B) 項應為正選。

<u>B</u> 4. 理由
   a. (A) **provided that...**　　倘若……（= if...）
      例 I'll help you out, provided that you promise to work hard.
      你若答應會努力，我就幫你。
     (B) **so much that...**　　如此……以至於……
      例 We love our daughter so much that we'll do everything we can to help her.
      我們如此深愛我們的女兒，因此會竭盡所能幫她。
     (C) **for fear that...**　　以免……，唯恐……
      例 I parked my car in the garage for fear that someone might steal it.
      我把我的車停在車庫裡，以免被人偷走。
     (D) **in order that...**　　為了 / 以便……
     = so that...
      例 I wear glasses in order that I can see better.
      我戴眼鏡是為了要看得更清楚。
   b. 根據上述語意及用法，可知 (B) 項應為正選。

<u>D</u> 5. 理由
   a. (A) **deny** [dɪˋnaɪ] *vt.* 否認，否定
      例 Edward denied stealing anything from the shop.
      艾德華不承認他有從店裡偷任何東西。
     (B) **sustain** [səˋsten] *vt.* 維持；支撐
      例 The man on the desert island sustained himself by drinking rainwater.
      坐困荒島的男子靠喝雨水維持生命。
     (C) **whine** [waɪn] *vi.* 呻吟；哀嚎
      例 Our dog whines in fear when it hears loud noises.
      我們的狗聽到巨大噪音時會發出害怕的哀嚎。

Unit 16

(D) **state** [stet] *vt.*（正式地）說；聲明
　例 The president stated he would not raise taxes.
　　總統聲明他不會增稅。

b. 根據語意，可知 (D) 項應為正選。

重要單字與片語

1. **the Netherlands** [`nɛðɚ·ləndz] 荷蘭（由若干地塊形成，故與定冠詞 the 並用）
   類似用語如：the Bahamas　巴哈馬（由若干群島形成）
2. **place** [ples] *vt.* 放置；安置
   例 Don't place the potato chips on the bed.
   不要把洋芋片放在床上。
3. **career** [kə`rɪr] *n.* 職業；生涯
   a career woman　職業婦女
4. **Dutch** [dʌtʃ] *a.* 荷蘭的
   the Dutch　荷蘭人(= Dutch people)
5. **equal** [`ikwəl] *vt.* 等同於；匹敵
6. **population** [ˌpɑpjə`leʃən] *n.* 人口
7. **figure** [`fɪgjɚ] *n.*（官方公布的）數字，數據
8. **survey** [`sɝve] *n.* 調查
9. **respondent** [rɪ`spɑndənt] *n.* 受調查者；回答者
10. **respond** [rɪ`spɑnd] *vt. & vi.* 回應
    respond to...　　回應 / 回答⋯⋯
    例 Jenny didn't respond to my question, which made me confused.
    珍妮沒有回答我的問題，讓我很困惑。

二 文意選填

我們生活在數位時代，很有意思的是竟能找到像保羅・麥哲倫這位來自葡萄牙並熱愛手寫信件的男子。麥哲倫十分喜愛這種老式的私人訊息，這促使他架設一個網站，透過郵寄明信片的方式讓大家彼此連繫。該網站叫做「郵件交流」，名稱由「郵件」與「交流」這兩個字簡單組成，讓大家免費註冊並登記地址。

「郵件交流」背後的概念就是參與者務必寄出明信片，才能收到他人寄的明信片。一開始，會員可以同時寄出五張明信片給其他已在網站註冊的人。久而久之，隨著寄出的明信片越來越多，一個人一次可寄出多達一百封明信片。這些明信片的地址皆為隨機產生。兩位參與者之間僅互寄一次明信片，除非他們自己想進一步通信。「郵件交流」很成功，讓麥哲倫大感意外。一開始是嗜好，卻受到許多關注，吸引了來自兩百多個國家約七十萬人列名該網站的會員。

因「郵件交流」網站廣受歡迎促使麥哲倫努力向會員推廣環境永續的理念。他利用該網站向人們傳達減輕環境衝擊的訣竅。例如，人們可以使用再生紙、在白天不需要人工照明的時候書寫以及選擇騎單車或步行前往郵局而不要開車。這一切都顯示麥哲倫知道人們需要思索他們的嗜好和興趣會如何影響這個世界。

I 6. 理由
   a. 空格前有 that 引導的形容詞子句之動詞 allows（允許）、people（人們）及 to，根據 allow 的用法 allow sb to V 及空格後的介詞 with，得知空格應置原形不及物動詞。
   b. 選項中可作原形不及物動詞的有 (A) lessen（減少）及 (I) connect（聯繫），惟根據語意，(I) 項應為正選。
   c. **connect** [kəˋnɛkt] *vt.* & *vi.* 連結；關聯
      例 For better or worse, smartphones make it easier to connect with others.
      不論好壞與否，手機讓我們更容易和彼此連結。

H 7. 理由
   a. 空格前為不定冠詞 a 及形容詞 simple（簡單的），空格後有介詞 of，得知空格應置單數可數名詞。
   b. 選項中可作單數可數名詞的有 (C) correspondence（通信）、(D) surprise（驚喜）及 (H) combination（組合），惟根據語意，(H) 項應為正選。
   c. **combination** [ˌkɑmbəˋneʃən] *n.* 組合

J 8. 理由
   a. 空格位於 that 名詞子句中，空格前有定冠詞 the，空格後有助動詞 must 及動詞 send（寄出），得知空格應置名詞作 that 子句的主詞。
   b. 剩餘選項中為名詞的有 (C) correspondence（通信）、(D) surprise（驚喜）及 (J) participants（參與者），惟根據語意，(J) 項應為正選。
   c. **participant** [pɑrˋtɪsəpənt] *n.* 參與者

E 9. 理由
   a. 空格前有 others，空格後有介詞詞組 with the website（在這個網站），得知空格可置及物動詞的過去分詞，以與介詞詞組組成分詞詞組修飾 others。
   b. 剩餘選項中 (E) registered（註冊）及 (G) attracted（吸引）為及物動詞的過去分詞，惟根據語意，(E) 項應為正選。
   c. 上述分詞詞組為 who / that are registered with the website 省略關係代名詞 who / that 及 are 而來。
   d. **register** [ˋrɛdʒɪstɚ] *vt.* & *vi.* 登記，註冊
      例 You should register your invention with the patent office to protect your interests.
      你應該到專利機構註冊你的發明以保障你的利益。

B 10. 理由
   a. 空格前有不定冠詞 a，空格後有單數可數名詞 basis（基礎），得知空格應置形容詞，以修飾 basis。
   b. 剩餘選項中 (B) random（隨機的）及 (F) artificial（人造的）為形容詞，惟根據語意，(B) 項應為正選，若選 (F) 項，則其前不定冠詞應改為 an。

Unit 16

  c. **random** [ˈrændəm] *a.* 隨機的，任意的
  d. **on a... basis**　以……為基礎
   例 Our family gets together on a yearly basis.
    我們家族每年會團聚一次。

C 11. 理由

 a. 空格前有定冠詞 the，得知空格應置名詞。
 b. 剩餘選項中可作名詞的有 (C) correspondence（通信）及 (D) surprise（驚喜），惟根據語意，(C) 項應為正選。
 c. **correspondence** [ˌkɔrəˈspɑndəns] *n.* 通信聯繫；一致

D 12. 理由

 a. 空格前有 to 及所有格 Magalhães'（麥哲倫的），得知空格應置情緒名詞 (D) surprise（驚訝），形成下列固定用法：
  (much) to sb's surprise, ...　（頗）令某人驚訝的是，……
  例 To my surprise, Adam passed the exam.
   令我驚訝的是，亞當考試及格了。
 b. 根據上述，(D) 項應為正選。

G 13. 理由

 a. 空格前為複合關係代名詞 what 引導的名詞子句作主詞，之後有現在完成式助動詞 has，空格後為名詞詞組 so much attention（許多關注），得知空格應置及物動詞的過去分詞，以與 has 組成現在完成式，並接名詞詞組作受詞。
 b. 剩餘選項中僅剩 (G) attracted（吸引）為及物動詞的過去分詞，且置入空格後符合語意及用法，故為正選。
 c. **attract** [əˈtrækt] *vt.* 吸引
  例 New York and Paris have attracted writers and artists for decades.
   紐約和巴黎幾十年來吸引了作家和藝術家。

A 14. 理由

 a. 空格前有 how 引導的名詞子句，主詞為 people（人們），之後接助動詞 can，空格後有名詞詞組 their environmental impact（他們對環境的衝擊），得知空格應置原形及物動詞，以接該名詞詞組作受詞。
 b. 剩餘選項中僅剩 (A) lessen（減少）為原形及物動詞，且置入空格後符合語意，故為正選。
 c. **lessen** [ˈlɛsn̩] *vt.* 減少；減輕
  例 The medicine will lessen your pain.
   這種藥能減輕你的疼痛。

F 15. 理由
    a. 空格前有數量詞 no，空格後為不可數名詞 lighting（照明），得知空格應置形容詞，以修飾該名詞。
    b. 剩餘選項 (F) artificial（人造的）為形容詞，且置入空格後符合語意，故為正選。
    c. artificial [ˌɑrtəˈfɪʃəl] a. 人造的；人工的

重要單字與片語

1. **digital** [ˈdɪdʒətl̩] a. 數位的
2. **passionate** [ˈpæʃənət] a. 熱情的，熱切的
3. **fondness** [ˈfɑndnəs] n. 喜愛，鍾愛
   have a fondness for... 喜好……
4. **handwritten** [ˈhændˌrɪtn̩] a. 手寫的
5. **prompt** [prɑmpt] vt. 激起；促使
   例 What prompted you to buy these flowers for me?
   是什麼原因促使你買這些花給我？
6. **sign up** 報名，登記（= register）
   例 Those who are interested in this course should sign up by next week.
   對這門課有興趣的人應該在下星期前報名。
7. **initially** [ɪˈnɪʃəlɪ] adv. 最初，起初
8. **over time** 漸漸地；隨著時間
   例 The relationship between Mary and Ed became more stable over time.
   瑪麗和艾德的關係隨著時間漸趨穩定。
9. **generate** [ˈdʒɛnəˌret] vt. 產生，帶來
   例 Tourism generates income for local businesses.
   觀光業為當地商家帶來了收入。
10. **popularity** [ˌpɑpjəˈlærətɪ] n. 普及，流行（不可數）
11. **sustainability** [səˌstenəˈbɪlətɪ] n. 永續性（不可數）
12. **distribute** [dɪˈstrɪbjut] vt. 分發
    例 The volunteers distributed food and clothes to the victims of the flood.
    義工們分發食物和衣服給這次水災的受災戶。
13. **impact** [ˈɪmpækt] n. & [ɪmˈpækt] vt. & vi. 影響
    have an impact on... 對……有影響／衝擊
    = have an influence on...
    = have an effect on...
14. **mindful** [ˈmaɪndfəl] a. 留心的，注意的

篇章結構

    隨著老年人口的比例不斷成長，越來越多人受到阿茲海默症和其他形式的認知能力受損所影響。事實上，據估計，一直到 2050 年將有二十億人達六十歲以上；其中一億三千五百五十萬人將患有失智症。隨著患者人數不斷增加，如何改善他們的日常生活已成為當務之急。雖然現在沒有治療失智症的方法，所幸有越來越多人採取行動幫助患者，協助使他們的生活更舒適一些。<u>其中一個例子就是姚彥慈以及她開發 Eatwell 所投入的努力。</u>

Unit 16

　　Eatwell 是一套專為阿茲海默症患者設計的餐具組，讓他們在沒有旁人的協助下用餐。Eatwell 有一項特色就是強調顏色。因為當失智症患者的食物和餐盤的顏色相同時，會對他們造成混淆，所以姚彥慈製作了藍色內層的碗，讓他們更容易區分食物和容器。此外，Eatwell 餐具組不容易讓食物灑出來，因為杯子和碗都做成不容易弄翻的樣式。餐具也設計成更容易握持，有益於那些肌肉控制能力較弱的患者。老年人在用餐時賦予他們更多自主性會讓他們更容易維持尊嚴，並減少照護者的負擔。

　　Eatwell 已被認可為一項能協助老年人的傑出產品。它在史丹佛長壽中心於 2014 年開辦的第一屆設計競賽中獲勝，打敗了來自其他十五個國家的五十一支隊伍，並抱回了美金一萬元的獎金。然而，姚彥慈創作 Eatwell 的主要目的並非是要贏得史丹佛的獎項。她說是她對已過世的奶奶 —— 她生前患有阿茲海默症 —— 的回憶激勵了她去幫助其他有類似問題的人。她希望透過 Eatwell，讓社會更關注為特殊需求人士設計用品的重要性。

E　16. 理由
　　a. 空格前句提及有越來越多人採取行動幫忙失智症患者，而空格後句，即第二段第一句，提及專為阿茲海默患者設計的餐具 Eatwell，皆呼應選項 (E) 中所述姚彥慈研發了 Eatwell。
　　b. 根據上述，(E) 項應為正選。

C　17. 理由
　　a. 空格後句敘述姚彥慈製作了藍色內層的碗，好讓失智症患者更容易區分食物和容器，呼應選項 (C) 所描述 Eatwell 的特色為 the focus on color（強調顏色）。
　　b. 根據上述，(C) 項應為正選。

A　18. 理由
　　a. 第二段主要描述 Eatwell 的產品特色，空格前句提及其顏色上的特色對失智症患者的助益，空格後兩句補充說明餐具也設計成更容易握持，並總結老年人在用餐時具自主性的好處，得知空格應舉出 Eatwell 的某項特色，選項 (A) 提及 Eatwell 餐具組讓食物不容易灑出來，即該產品的另一項特色。
　　b. 根據上述，(A) 項應為正選。

D　19. 理由
　　a. 空格前句提到姚彥慈的 Eatwell 餐具在設計競賽中獲獎，空格後句則敘述她對已過世奶奶的回憶激勵了她去幫助他人，選項 (D) 描述姚彥慈創作 Eatwell 的主要目的並非是要贏得史丹佛的獎項，可作為空格前句的轉折並承接空格後句的說明。
　　b. 根據上述，(D) 項應為正選。

(B) 選項翻譯　對於患有失智症的人來說，食用正確的營養補充品非常重要。

重要單字與片語

1. **proportion** [prəˋporʃən] *n.* 比例
2. **Alzheimer's disease** 阿茲海默症，老年癡呆症
3. **cognitive** [ˋkɑɡnətɪv] *a.* 認知的
4. **impairment** [ɪmˋpɛrmənt] *n.* 損害；損傷；缺陷
5. **cure** [kjʊr] *n.* & *vt.* 治療
6. **deterioration** [dɪˌtɪrɪəˋreʃən] *n.* 惡化；衰退（不可數）
7. **sufferer** [ˋsʌfərɚ] *n.* 患者
8. **tableware** [ˋtebl̩ˌwɛr] *n.* 餐具（集合名詞，不可數）
9. **feature** [ˋfitʃɚ] *n.* 特徵
10. **thereby** [ˋðɛrˌbaɪ / ðɛrˋbaɪ] *adv.* 藉此，由此
11. **What's more, ...** 此外，……
    例 Michelle is very beautiful. What's more, she is smart and humorous.
    蜜雪兒非常漂亮。而且她既聰明又幽默。
12. **spill** [spɪl] *n.* & *vt.* & *vi.* 灑落，潑出
13. **utensil** [juˋtɛnsl̩] *n.* 餐具；器具；用具
14. **grip** [ɡrɪp] *vt.* 緊握；吸引（注意力）
    （三態為：grip, gripped [ɡrɪpt], gripped）& *n.* 緊握；理解
    例 Selena gripped the steering wheel firmly while driving on the highway.
    賽琳娜在高速公路上開車時緊握方向盤。
15. **motor** [ˋmotɚ] *a.* 肌肉運動的
16. **maintain** [menˋten] *vt.* 維持
    例 That Italian restaurant tries to maintain a high level of service.
    那家義大利餐廳盡力維持高水準的服務品質。
17. **dignity** [ˋdɪɡnətɪ] *n.* 尊嚴（不可數）
18. **burden** [ˋbɝdn̩] *n.* 負擔
19. **caregiver** [ˋkɛrˌɡɪvɚ] *n.* 照護者；看護
20. **recognize** [ˋrɛkəɡˌnaɪz] *vt.* 認可
    例 The movie star was recognized as a great actor.
    這位影星被認為是一位很棒的演員。
21. **outstanding** [aʊtˋstændɪŋ] *a.* 傑出的
22. **establish** [ɪˋstæblɪʃ] *vt.* 設立，成立
    例 This hospital was established in 1942.
    這家醫院於 1942 年設立。
23. **longevity** [lɑnˋdʒɛvətɪ] *n.* 長壽（不可數）
24. **supplement** [ˋsʌpləmənt] *n.* 補充物；（雜誌／報紙的）副刊（皆為可數）& [ˋsʌpləˌmɛnt] *vt.* 補充

四 閱讀測驗

舞蹈瘟疫是某種詭異、持續三個月之久的奇特現象的名稱，於 1518 年夏天發生在現今的法國史特拉斯堡地區。在那年七月的一個大熱天，一個姓特羅菲亞的女子走出家門開始在街上不由自主地不停跳舞。在幾週內就有數百餘人加入她並瘋狂起舞。這些人幾乎連暫停下來喘口氣都沒有，更別說是休息飲食了。城裡的官員越來越擔心，決定唯一的解決之道就是鼓勵跳舞，希望這些患者會把自己累癱。為此，他們規劃了場館給這些人在裡面跳舞，並且

Unit 16

還配了樂手伴奏。然而這麼做只讓問題更嚴重。當時的報導說，某些跳舞的人跳到昏倒，並且死於心臟病、中風、熱衰竭等。這波瘋狂跳舞潮直到九月才開始逐漸消退。歷史學家把事件的平息歸功於官員把剩下跳舞的人送進深山向舞者的守護神聖維特請求寬恕。

多年來，關於這種舞蹈瘟疫的成因有好幾種理論。當時的在地醫生相信患者是苦於血液溫度過高，其他人則傳言他們是被惡魔附身。二十世紀的研究學者認為，這些跳舞的人可能是吃到會讓人產生幻覺與突然亂動的有毒黴菌汙染的麵包而食物中毒。不過食物中毒似乎不太可能導致患者跳舞跳這麼久的時間。最多人認同的當代理論是由對舞蹈瘟疫著墨甚多的歷史學家約翰・沃勒所提出。他認為這些跳舞的人是得到壓力引起的集體歇斯底里症。在十六世紀初，史特拉斯堡人民面臨農作物歉收、飢荒、梅毒與天花等疾病的散布。他們也深信聖維特可以詛咒他們，逼他們跳舞。壓力大的情況伴隨這樣的信仰，可能導致了突發而極端的行為，並像傳染病一樣擴散。這種行為的擴散會愈演愈烈，也是因為官員最初的決定是鼓勵跳舞而不是制止它。然而五個世紀之後的我們，似乎可以肯定永遠無法確切知道是什麼造成了舞蹈瘟疫。

D　**20.** 官員起初如何回應跳舞的現象？
(A) 他們禁止樂手與跳舞的人一起表演。
(B) 他們鼓勵跳舞的人飲食並放鬆。
(C) 他們帶跳舞的人進入深山。
(D) 他們讓民眾更方便跳舞。
理由
根據本文第一段第五、六句，可知 (D) 項應為正選。

C　**21.** 有關舞蹈瘟疫，我們從本文中得知什麼？
(A) 帶頭跳舞的女子在中風後昏倒。
(B) 許多參與的民眾得了天花。
(C) 它被限制在現今被稱做法國的單一城市區域。
(D) 聖維特拒絕原諒那些參與的民眾。
理由
根據本文第一段第一句，可知 (C) 項應為正選。

B　**22.** 關於造成舞蹈瘟疫原因的理論，本文沒有提及下列哪一項？
(A) 跳舞的人吃過布滿黴菌的麵包。
(B) 某宗教團體影響了跳舞的人。
(C) 跳舞的人血液溫度過高。
(D) 高壓事件導致極端的情緒。
理由
根據本文未提及宗教團體，可知 (B) 項應為正選。

__C__ 23. 第二段的 They 指的是誰？
(A) 死去的跳舞民眾。
(B) 歷史學者。
(C) 史特拉斯堡的市民。
(D) 市區的在地醫生。

理由
根據本文第二段第六、七句，可知 (C) 項應為正選。

重要單字與片語

1. **plague** [pleg] *n.* 瘟疫
   the Plague / plague　　鼠疫，黑死病
2. **bizarre** [bɪˋzɑr] *a.* 古怪的，奇異的
   例 James likes to collect various bizarre costumes.
   詹姆士喜歡收集各式各樣的奇裝異服。
3. **spectacle** [ˋspɛktəkḷ] *n.* 奇觀
4. **unfold** [ʌnˋfold] *vi.* 呈現，展開
   例 As the news unfolded, Steve couldn't help but stare at the TV in amazement.
   這則新聞被報導出來時，史提夫不禁驚訝地盯著電視看。
5. **authority** [əˋθɔrətɪ] *n.* 有關當局（恆用複數）；權威（不可數）
6. **afflict** [əˋflɪkt] *vt.* 使痛苦，折磨（本文為過去分詞作形容詞）
   例 Molly has been afflicted with deafness from birth.
   莫莉從出生就飽受失聰之苦。
7. **end** [ɛnd] *n.* 目的；末端
   to this end　　為此
   例 To this end, we must work together to achieve our common goals.
   為此，我們必須合作以達成我們共同的目標。

8. **intensify** [ɪnˋtɛnsəˏfaɪ] *vt.* 使變激烈；加強 & *vi.* 加劇，增強
   例 The police are intensifying their search for the missing boy.
   警方加強尋找那名失蹤的男孩。
9. **collapse** [kəˋlæps] *vi.* 昏倒；倒塌
   例 Jully collapsed from exhaustion after completing her first marathon race in scorching heat.
   朱莉在大熱天跑完她首次的馬拉松賽後累倒了。
10. **die down**　　逐漸變小，逐漸變弱
11. **allege** [əˋlɛdʒ] *vt.*（無證據的）宣稱
    allege that...　　宣稱……
    例 An anonymous caller alleged that a bomb had been planted on the aircraft.
    某匿名者打電話宣稱飛機上有炸彈。
12. **contract** [kənˋtrækt] *vt.* 感染
    例 Nearly half of the adult population there has contracted malaria.
    那裡有近半數的成年人感染了瘧疾。
13. **hallucination** [həˏlusṇˋeʃən] *n.* 幻覺
14. **-induced** [ɪnˋdjust] *a.* 由……所引起的
    stress-induced illness　　壓力引起的疾病

Unit 16

15. **hysteria** [hɪsˋtɪrɪə] *n.* 歇斯底里（不可數）
    hysterical [hɪsˋtɛrɪkl̩] *a.* 歇斯底里的
16. **syphilis** [ˋsɪfələs] *n.* 梅毒（不可數）
17. **smallpox** [ˋsmɔl͵pɑks] *n.* 天花（不可數）
18. **epidemic** [͵ɛpəˋdɛmɪk] *n.* 傳染病
19. **facilitate** [fəˋsɪlə͵tet] *vt.* 促進，幫助
    例 The new policies are expected to facilitate economic growth.
    這些新的政策預期會帶動經濟成長。

五 混合題

　　日本有意要將輻射汙水排放至太平洋。這些廢水曾受到 2011 年福島第一核電廠災難的汙染。以下是四位民眾對此決定的意見。

海斗
我能夠理解民眾對遭汙染廢水將排放進入海中的事感到憂心，但身為科學家，我看的是證據。事實上，被排放的廢水量與龐大的海水量相比，簡直是微乎其微，這意味任何既有的輻射將會被大幅稀釋。此外，那些廢水已經用最先進的科技方法處理過，以期將輻射物質的濃度降到比可接受水準還要低很多的地步。所以我完全可以接受這個決定。

隆
我當漁民超過四十年，不得不說將廢水排放至海洋的計畫讓我感到非常不安。官員堅稱那很安全，但我覺得可能會對環境造成嚴重的後果。如果小型的海洋動植物受到汙染，隨後被較大的動物吃掉，輻射物質就會在魚類身體裡累積，最終進了人類的肚子。這個過程可能會用上許多年，所以我擔心排放廢水的長期影響是極度不確定的事情。

尤娜
幾個韓國朋友來日本找我，他們聽說了輻射廢水要排放至太平洋的計畫。他們擔心那些廢水會流到他們的國家，對人民健康及漁業造成負面影響。老實說，我不覺得這種事真的會發生，但大眾的觀感是應該列入考慮的重點。如果民眾開始擔心核廢料處理的問題，他們可能會開始對核電普遍失去信心。

櫻
身為核電廠的資深工作人員，我知道不把廢水排放至海洋才更加危險。將廢水儲存在陸地上的儲存槽具有極大的風險，因為儲存槽可能會在另一起地震或意外中破損，可能會汙染土壤。此外，我知道排放含輻射物質氚的廢水是常見的做法，不僅是這裡，全世界都在這麼做。只是因為福島事故上了頭條，所以民眾才會更加關注。

24. 海斗了解有些人對於海洋可能會被輻射廢水汙染感到憂慮，但是他對該計畫並無異議。

理由

空格前有定冠詞 the 以及形容詞 potential，空格後有介詞 of，得知空格應置名詞。根據海斗意見的第一句 "I can understand people's worries about the release of contaminated water into the ocean, ..."（我能夠理解民眾對遭汙染廢水將排放進入海中的事感到憂心，……）得知，空格應置與 contaminated 相關的名詞 contamination。

25. 尤娜有些外國朋友表達擔心廢水的排放，因為他們擔心廢水會流往他們的國家。

理由

空格前有現在完成式 have expressed，空格後有介詞 about，得知空格應置名詞。根據尤娜意見的第二句 "They are concerned that the water could flow to their country..."（他們擔心那些廢水會流到他們的國家，……）得知，空格應置與 concerned 相關的名詞 concern 或 concerns。

<u>D</u> **26.** 櫻表示「常見的做法」這片語時，她在暗示什麼？
(A) 大眾普遍認為排放汙染廢水很危險。
(B) 許多人相信他們在報紙上讀到有關核能的事。
(C) 地震發生頻繁而且輕易就會損壞核電廠。
(D) 許多核電廠讓輻射廢水流入海洋。

理由

根據櫻意見的最後兩句 "Also, I'm aware that the release of water contaminated with tritium—one of the radioactive elements—is common practice, not just here but around the world. It is only because the Fukushima disaster made headlines that people have taken more notice."（此外，我知道排放含輻射物質氚的廢水是常見的做法，不僅是這裡，全世界都在這麼做。只是因為福島事故上了頭條，所以民眾才會更加關注。）得知，(D) 項應為正選。

<u>ADE</u> **27.** 有關受訪者的意見，下列哪些陳述是正確的？
(A) 隆跟櫻的職業影響了他們對事情的意見。
(B) 海斗跟櫻都同樣擔心儲存在陸地上的輻射廢水。
(C) 尤娜與海斗都以科學背景的角度對廢水的事情表達意見。
(D) 隆比其他人更擔心對海洋環境的影響。
(E) 尤娜與櫻都談到該計畫對民眾意見的影響。
(F) 隆與海斗都懷疑官方對廢水排放的說法。

理由

根據隆意見的第一句以及櫻意見的第一句；根據隆意見的第二、三句；根據尤娜意見的倒數兩句以及櫻意見的最後一句，得知 (A)、(D)、(E) 應為正選。

Unit 16

重要單字與片語

1. **radioactive** [ˌredɪoˈæktɪv] *a.* 有輻射的，放射性的
   radiation [ˌredɪˈeʃən] *n.* （核）輻射；放射，散發（不可數）

2. **wastewater** [ˌwestˈwɔtɚ] *n.* 廢水（不可數）

3. **contaminate** [kənˈtæməˌnet] *vt.* 汙染（本文為過去分詞當形容詞用）
   contamination [kənˌtæməˈneʃən] *n.* 汙染（不可數）
   例 Toxic waste from the factory contaminated the groundwater.
   那間工廠排出的有毒廢棄物汙染了地下水。

4. **volume** [ˈvɑljəm] *n.* 量，容量；音量
   a large volume of + 不可數名詞
   大量的……
   = a large amount of + 不可數名詞
   例 We need a large volume of money and manpower for this project.
   我們需要大量的財力及人力才能推動這個計畫。

5. **present** [ˈprɛzənt] *a.* 存在的，出現的

6. **dilute** [daɪˈlut] *vt.* 稀釋，沖淡
   例 Dilute this medicine powder in water and drink it three times a day.
   把藥粉溶於水中，一天喝三次。

7. **concentration** [ˌkɑnsənˈtreʃən] *n.* 濃度

8. **insist** [ɪnˈsɪst] *vt.* 堅稱；堅決認為，堅持要求
   insist that + S + (should) + 原形動詞
   堅持要求……
   例 John insists that these problems are not his fault.
   約翰堅稱這些問題不是他的錯。
   My dad insists that I (should) study in Milan.
   我老爸堅持要求我在米蘭唸書。

9. **accumulate** [əˈkjumjəˌlet] *vi. & vt.* 累積，堆積
   例 The snow accumulated during the night, and the city looked all white the next morning.
   雪累積了一整晚，隔天早上整個城市看起來一片雪白。
   Edward accumulated a large fortune investing in the stock market.
   艾德華投資股市累積了一大筆財富。

10. **perception** [pɚˈsɛpʃən] *n.* 看法；感知

11. **disposal** [dɪˈspozl̩] *n.* 處理，清除

12. **faith** [feθ] *n.* 信心；信仰
    have faith in... 對……有信心
    例 You should have faith in me and know that I won't let you down.
    你應該對我有信心，知道我是不會讓你失望的。

13. **soil** [sɔɪl] *n.* 土壤

14. **headline** [ˈhɛdˌlaɪns] *n.* （報紙）頭條新聞

15. **approach** [əˈprotʃ] *vt.* 著手處理

16. **skeptical** [ˈskɛptɪkl̩] *a.* 懷疑的
    be skeptical about / of... 對……表示質疑
    例 Economists are highly skeptical about the government's economic reforms.
    經濟學家高度質疑政府的經濟改革。

Unit 17

一 綜合測驗

　　當你想到棺材,心裡會浮現什麼?大多數人會將棺材和簡易的長方形箱子的形象聯想在一起。在非洲國家迦納,有些人被埋葬在更別具創意的箱子裡,這些箱子就叫做夢幻棺材。這些精美的創作有各式各樣的形狀和大小,製作目的是為了反映死者生活的某方面。舉例來說,如果死者生前是飛行員,他可能被埋葬在形狀像飛機或噴射機的棺材裡,若生前是水手,則可能被安置在看起來像戰艦的棺材裡。有些農民甚至被埋葬在形狀如同巨型玉米或可可莢的棺材中,象徵他們對農業的奉獻精神。擁有一具手工打造的夢幻棺材並在裡頭度過永生,被認為是一項殊榮和受尊敬的象徵,因為只有獲得某些成就的一家之主才能埋葬在夢幻棺材裡。至於那些打造夢幻棺材、才華洋溢的工匠,他們在迦納和全世界都被認為是出類拔萃的藝術家。他們的作品曾在國際藝術展覽中展出,展現這一傳統的藝術價值。

B 1. 理由

　　a. (A) **compensate** [ˈkɑmpənˌset] *vi.* & *vt.* 補償(與介詞 for 並用)
　　　　　compensate for...　　彌補……
　　　= make up for...
　　　　　例 Hard work compensates for one's slowness.
　　　　　　 勤能補拙。

　　　(B) **associate** [əˈsoʃɪˌet / əˈsosɪˌet] *vt.* 使……有關連
　　　　　associate A with B　　將 A 與 B 聯想在一起
　　　　　例 Most people associate the color pink with girls.
　　　　　　 大部分的人把粉紅色與女生聯想在一起。

　　　(C) **terminate** [ˈtɝməˌnet] *vt.* 終結;終止
　　　　　例 The boss didn't terminate my contract after all. Instead, he gave me a raise.
　　　　　　 老闆到頭來並沒有終止我的契約,他反而幫我加薪。

　　　(D) **prevail** [prɪˈvel] *vi.* 盛行;獲勝
　　　　　例 The disease prevails in this region.
　　　　　　 這種疾病在這個地區流行。

　　b. 根據語意及用法,可知 (B) 項應為正選。

D 2. 理由
　　a. 原句實為：
　　　In the African country of Ghana, some people are buried in much more creative containers <u>which are</u> called fantasy coffins.
　　　上句中的形容詞子句 which are called fantasy coffins（被稱作夢幻棺材）可簡化為分詞片語，即刪除作主詞的關係代名詞 which，再將 be 動詞 are 改為現在分詞 being 後予以省略，保留過去分詞 called（被稱作）。
　　b. 根據上述，可知 (D) 項應為正選。

B 3. 理由
　　a. (A) **condemned** [kənˋdɛmd] *a.* 被判死刑的
　　　　condemn [kənˋdɛm] *vt.* 譴責；宣判（刑罰）
　　　　condemn sb to...　　判某人……罪
　　　　例 The judge condemned the man to death.
　　　　　法官判那名男子死刑。
　　　(B) **deceased** [dɪˋsist] *a.* 過世的，死去的
　　　　例 Whenever I think of my deceased grandpa, I feel sad.
　　　　　每當想起我過世的祖父，我就悲從中來。
　　　(C) **insured** [ɪnˋʃʊrd] *a.* 有保險的
　　　　例 Our house is sufficiently insured against fire.
　　　　　我們的房子保了足夠的火險。
　　　(D) **learned** [ˋlɝnɪd] *a.* 有學問的，博學的
　　　　例 Mr. Wang is such a learned and amiable teacher that all his students like him.
　　　　　王老師是個如此博學又和藹可親的老師，因此所有學生都喜歡他。
　　b. "the + adj." 表複數名詞，指具該形容詞特質的全體，本題選項中的形容詞均可作此用法：the condemned（被定罪的人）、the deceased（死者）、the insured（被保險人）、the learned（有學問的人）。
　　c. 根據語意及用法，可知 (B) 項應為正選。

A 4. 理由
　　a. (A) **resemble** [rɪˋzɛmbḷ] *vt.* 和……相像
　　　　= look like...
　　　　例 Many people say I resemble John Kennedy.
　　　　　很多人說我長得很像約翰・甘迺迪。
　　　(B) **flourish** [ˋflɝɪʃ] *vi.* 興盛，繁榮
　　　　例 The plants flourished in my backyard.
　　　　　植物在我的後院生長得欣欣向榮。

Unit 17

241

Unit 17

(C) **devour** [dɪˈvaʊr] *vt.* 狼吞虎嚥地吃

例 Mike devoured an entire chocolate cake.
麥克吃掉了整塊巧克力蛋糕。

(D) **groan** [gron] *vi.* 呻吟

例 Henry was groaning in pain.
亨利痛苦地呻吟著。

b. 根據語意，可知 (A) 項應為正選。

D **5.** 理由

a. (A) **endure inconvenience** 忍受不便

例 Travelers must endure inconvenience when flights are delayed due to bad weather.
旅客在航班因惡劣天氣而延誤時，必須忍受不便。

(B) **overcome obstacles** 克服障礙

例 Athletes train daily to overcome obstacles in competitions.
運動員每天訓練以克服比賽中的障礙。

(C) **expect afterlife** 期待來生
afterlife [ˈæftɚˌlaɪf] *n.* 來生

例 Many religions teach their believers to expect afterlife.
許多宗教教導信徒要期待來生。

(D) **spend eternity** 度過永生
eternity [ɪˈtɝnətɪ] *n.* 永生

例 Some believe they will spend eternity in paradise after death.
有些人相信他們死後會在天堂度過永生。

b. 根據語意，可知 (D) 項應為正選。

重要單字與片語

1. **coffin** [ˈkɔfɪn / ˈkɑfɪn] *n.* 棺材
2. **sth comes to mind** 心裡想到某事
   注意 come to mind 不加所有格，故不說 sth comes to my mind，但可說 sth comes into my mind。
3. **rectangular** [rɛkˈtæŋgjəlɚ] *a.* 長方形的
4. **bury** [ˈbɛrɪ] *vt.* 埋葬；使投入，使埋首
   be buried in... 埋首於 / 專心……
   = bury oneself in...

   例 Whenever you see him, Tom is buried in his studies.
   不論你何時看到湯姆，他都埋首於課業中。

5. **fantasy** [ˈfæntəsɪ] *n.* 幻想
6. **elaborate** [ɪˈlæbərət] *a.* 精緻的；詳盡的
7. **reflect** [rɪˈflɛkt] *vt.* 反映

   例 This song reflects my feelings about you.
   這首歌反映了我對你的感覺。

8. **battleship** [ˈbætl̩ˌʃɪp] *n.* 戰艦
9. **pod** [pɑd] *n.* 豆莢
10. **symbolize** [ˈsɪmbl̩ˌaɪz] *vt.* 象徵，代表
    例 White doves symbolize peace and hope in many different cultures worldwide.
    白鴿在許多不同文化中象徵著和平與希望。
11. **dedication** [ˌdɛdəˈkeʃən] *n.* 奉獻（不可數）（與介詞 to 並用）
12. **handcrafted** [ˈhændˌkræftɪd] *a.* 手工的
13. **craftsman** [ˈkræftsmən] *n.* 工匠
14. **elite** [ɪˈlit / eˈlit] *a.* 菁英的；出類拔萃的 & *n.*（社會）菁英分子（集合名詞，不可數，之前置 the）

二 文意選填

　　聖卡安是墨西哥加勒比海岸線的一塊大區域，由聯邦政府保護，育有各種動植物。該地區是聯合國教科文組織的世界文化遺產，內有二十處哥倫布發現新大陸之前的考古遺址以及全球第二大的海岸堡礁。這塊先前未開發的區域原本應該是世界的瑰寶。然而，由於一場巨大的人為浩劫，這個地區已經變成像是世界的垃圾倉庫。每年有那麼多垃圾被丟進海洋，造成大部分的海洋物種受到負面影響，無數的垃圾被沖上聖卡安的海岸已屢見不鮮，這個問題引起了藝術家亞歷山卓．杜蘭的關切。

　　杜蘭定期收集隨著海浪堆積於聖卡安的垃圾。接著他讓這些醜陋的物品蛻變為色彩豐富而美妙的雕刻作品。杜蘭熱衷於引起大眾關注海洋汙染這個嚴重的問題，對他而言，聖卡安就是他的工作室。他拼湊出來的藝術作品是一項計畫的一部分，他稱該計畫為「沖上岸」。他運用想像力為他的雕刻作品創作出有趣又獨特的藝術感，把垃圾變得像自然界的物體一樣，例如魚、水果和海藻。他取用這些令人反感的垃圾，然後把垃圾變得很漂亮。他目前蒐集了來自六大洲共五十個不同國家的垃圾。他的藝術作品強調的訊息就是無論我們的自然環境目前看起來有多麼原始，它其實正不斷受到威脅。因此，我們的自然環境絕對無法免於全球消費主義的衝擊和隨之而來的汙染。

Unit 17

J　**6.** 理由
　　a. 空格前有定冠詞 the，空格後有第三人稱單數動詞 contains（包含），得知空格應置單數可數名詞或不可數名詞作本句主詞。而句首另有 A UNESCO World Heritage Site（聯合國教科文組織的世界文化遺產）及一逗點，可知 A UNESCO World Heritage Site 應為主詞的同位語。
　　b. 選項中為單數可數名詞或不可數名詞的有 (B) catastrophe（浩劫）、(D) project（計畫）、(F) imagination（想像力）、(H) passion（熱情）及 (J) region（地區），惟 (J) 項與主詞之同位語語意相關，故為正選。
　　c. **region** [ˈridʒən] *n.* 區域

Unit 17

E 7. 理由

a. 空格前有 be 動詞 is，空格後有不定詞 to be，得知空格應置 supposed（認為應該），以形成下列固定用法：

 be supposed to V 被認為應該……

 例 Tom was supposed to bring food to the party, but he forgot.
  湯姆應該要帶食物去派對，但他忘了。

b. 根據上述，(E) 項應為正選。

B 8. 理由

a. 空格前有不定冠詞 an 和形容詞 enormous（巨大的）及 man-made（人為的），得知空格應置單數可數名詞，以形成名詞詞組作介詞 due to 的受詞。

b. 剩餘選項中為單數可數名詞的有 (B) catastrophe（浩劫）、(D) project（計畫）、(F) imagination（想像力）及 (H) passion（熱情），惟根據語意，(B) 項應為正選。

c. **catastrophe** [kəˋtæstrəfɪ] *n.* 浩劫

 例 The earthquake in Japan was a real catastrophe.
  日本的那場地震真是一場大災難。

A 9. 理由

a. 空格前有 that 引導的形容詞子句之主詞 the waves（海浪）及現在完成式助動詞 have，得知空格應置動詞的過去分詞。此處關係代名詞 that 指涉先行詞 garbage（垃圾），且在形容詞子句中作空格中動詞的受詞，故此動詞應為及物動詞。

b. 剩餘選項中僅剩 (A) deposited（使沉積）為及物動詞的過去分詞，且置入空格後符合語意及用法，故為正選。

c. **deposit** [dɪˋpɑzɪt] *vt.* 使沉積

 例 The river deposited a layer of sand over the area.
  這條河在該地區淤積了一層沙。

G 10. 理由

a. 空格前有主詞 he，空格後有名詞詞組 ugly items（醜陋的物品），得知空格應置及物動詞，以接該名詞詞組作受詞。

b. 剩餘選項中為及物動詞的有 (C) stresses（強調）及 (G) transforms（轉變），惟根據語意，(G) 項應為正選。

c. **transform** [trænsˋfɔrm] *vt.* 轉變；變化

 transform A into B 將 A 轉變為 B
= convert A into B
= change A into B
= turn A into B

 例 Keran transformed the kitchen into a study.
  凱倫把廚房改造成書房。

__H__ **11. 理由**

    a. 空格前有不定冠詞 a，空格後有介詞 for，得知空格應置單數可數名詞。

    b. 剩餘選項中為單數可數名詞的有 (D) project（計畫）、(F) imagination（想像力）及 (H) passion（熱情），惟根據語意，(H) 項應為正選。

    c. **passion** [ˈpæʃən] *n.* 熱情，熱愛
       have a passion for... 熱愛……

__D__ **12. 理由**

    a. 空格前有不定冠詞 a，得知空格內應置單數可數名詞。

    b. 剩餘選項中為單數可數名詞的有 (D) project（計畫）及 (F) imagination（想像力），惟根據語意，(D) 項應為正選。

    c. **project** [ˈprɑdʒɛkt] *n.* 計畫

__F__ **13. 理由**

    a. 空格前有代名詞所有格 his，得知空格應置名詞。

    b. 剩餘選項中僅剩 (F) imagination（想像力）為名詞，且置入空格後符合語意，故為正選。

    c. **imagination** [ɪˌmædʒəˈneʃən] *n.* 想像力

    d. 原句實為：
       For his sculptures, he uses his imagination to come up with interesting, unique art, and converts garbage into likenesses of natural objects such as fish, fruit, and algae.
       上句中對等連接詞 and 連接兩個主詞相同的子句，故可省略 and 再將第二個子句的動詞 converts 改為現在分詞 converting，形成分詞構句。

__I__ **14. 理由**

    a. 空格前有使役動詞 makes 及受詞 them，空格後有形容詞 beautiful，得知空格應置不及物動詞作 makes 的補語。

    b. 剩餘選項中僅剩 (I) appear（看起來）為不及物動詞，且置入空格後符合語意，故為正選。

    c. **appear** [əˈpɪr] *vi.* 看起來

__C__ **15. 理由**

    a. 空格前有單數主詞 His art（他的藝術作品），空格後有名詞詞組 the message（訊息）作受詞，得知空格應置第三人稱單數及物動詞，以接該名詞詞組作受詞。

    b. 剩餘選項 (C) stresses（強調）為第三人稱單數及物動詞，且置入空格後符合語意，故為正選。

    c. **stress** [strɛs] *vt.* 強調
       例 Mr. Johnson stresses the importance of punctuality.
       強森先生很強調守時的重要性。

Unit 17

Unit 17

重要單字與片語

1. **federally** [ˈfɛdərəlɪ] *adv.* 由聯邦政府
2. **coastline** [ˈkostˌlaɪn] *n.* 海岸線
3. **flora and fauna** [ˌflɔrə ənd ˈfɔnə] （一個地區的）植物和動物
   注意
   此為固定搭配詞組，兩個名詞均為不可數。
4. **UNESCO** [juˈnɛsko] *n.* 聯合國教科文組織
   = the United Nations Educational, Scientific, and Cultural Organization
5. **heritage** [ˈhɛrətɪdʒ] *n.* 遺產（集合名詞，不可數）
6. **archaeological** [ˌɑrkɪəˈlɑdʒɪkl̩] *a.* 考古的
7. **coastal** [ˈkostl̩] *a.* 海岸的
8. **a barrier reef** 堡礁
9. **pristine** [ˈprɪstin] *a.* 完好的，原始的
10. **enormous** [ɪˈnɔrməs] *a.* 巨大的
11. **man-made** [ˌmænˈmed] *a.* 人為的；人造的
12. **junk** [dʒʌŋk] *n.* 垃圾（集合名詞，不可數）
    junk food　垃圾食物
13. **dump** [dʌmp] *vt.* 丟棄
    本句句首為介詞 With 所引導表附帶狀態的情狀介詞詞組，用法如下：
    with + 受詞 + 現在分詞（表主動）或過去分詞（表被動）
    > David was standing there with his legs shivering.
    （shivering 是現在分詞，表主動）
    大衛站在那兒兩腳發抖。
    John was standing there with his eyes shut.
    （shut 是過去分詞，表被動）
    約翰閉著眼睛站在那兒。
14. **species** [ˈspiʃiz] *n.* 物種（單複數同形）
    a species of bird　一種鳥
    two species of birds　兩種鳥
15. **marine** [məˈrin] *a.* 海洋的
16. **countless** [ˈkaʊntləs] *a.* 無數的
17. **sculpture** [ˈskʌlptʃɚ] *n.* 雕刻
18. **convert** [kənˈvɜt] *vt.* 轉變
    > The land owner converted the old house into a hotel.
    地主將這棟舊屋改成一家旅館。

篇章結構

　　盜版，又稱非法重製，長久以來持續傷害著音樂產業。現在盜版問題已滲透到出版業了。越來越多人認為使用電子書和電子閱讀器很方便。那種普及程度伴隨而來的就是更可能會有人將出版品放在非法的分享網站上。當這種事發生時，出版商會虧損很多錢，因為會有數百萬人非法下載免費的書籍，而不是去書店購買或付費後合法下載。出版業因為這些非法活動到底損失了多少難以估計。然而，如果音樂產業是某種指標，那確實是一大筆錢。而作者也會受到直接影響，因為他們的書籍若被盜版，會使得他們應得的版稅大幅縮水。

出版業可以採取什麼措施來對抗這個如此普遍又日益嚴重的問題呢？<u>有個方法就是大幅降低在網路上販售的電子書售價，以鼓勵消費者購買合法下載的資料</u>。這大概能說服某些人，特別是那些對於從檔案分享網站上下載資料已感到一陣內疚的人。此外，提供類似音樂串流服務那樣具吸引力的訂閱模式，也能讓讀者更願意選擇合法方式。然而，對於那些把違反智慧財產權視為無可厚非的人，這個方法不太可能改變他們的看法。畢竟，不用付錢仍比獲得優惠的折扣還要吸引人。

　　另一個選擇是出版商密切監控非法下載，找出那些竊取網路出版品的人，並將他們告上法庭。<u>不過，鑑於這個問題的規模龐大，這個選項似乎不太可行</u>。針對個別侵權者採取法律行動不僅成本高昂還十分耗時，這使得版權法更難有效執行。因此，出版業看來注定要遭受和音樂產業相同的命運，那就是每年的收入由於盜版和科技的進步而不斷下滑。若無法開發出新的解決方案，數位出版的未來將持續面臨重大挑戰。

C　**16.** 理由
  a. 空格前句敘述越來越多人認為使用電子書和電子閱讀器很方便，呼應選項 (C) 中的 that popularity（那種普及程度）。
  b. 空格後句敘述當這種事發生時，會有數百萬人非法下載免費的書籍，與選項 (C) 中的 someone will place publications on illegal file-sharing websites（會有人將出版品放在非法的分享網站上）形成關聯。
  c. 根據上述，(C) 項應為正選。

E　**17.** 理由
  a. 空格前句提及非法下載免費的書籍，呼應選項 (E) 中的 all this illegal activity（這些非法活動）。
  b. 空格前句敘述非法下載書籍的行為會讓出版商虧損很多錢，空格後句提及 it is a large sum（那是一大筆錢），而選項 (E) 敘述出版業的損失難以估計，均與商業收入相關。
  c. 根據上述，(E) 項應為正選。

A　**18.** 理由
  a. 空格前句提問出版業可以採取什麼措施來對抗盜版問題，而選項 (A) 以 One way would be...（有個方法就是……）提出方法，即 significantly lower the price of e-books sold online to encourage shoppers to purchase legal downloads（大幅降低在網路上販售的電子書售價，以鼓勵消費者購買合法下載的資料），回應了空格前句的提問。
  b. 根據上述，(A) 項應為正選。

Unit 17

B 19. 理由

a. 空格前句敘述出版商可以用打擊盜版的手段，即監控非法下載，找出竊取網路出版品的人並將他們告上法庭，空格後敘述針對個別侵權者採取法律行動成本高且極耗時，使得版權法難有效執行，並提出悲觀的預測，暗示了空格前提到的方法可能效果不彰，呼應選項 (B) 所述 this option hardly seems feasible.（這個選項似乎不太可行）。

b. 根據上述，(B) 項應為正選。

(D) 選項翻譯 幸運的是，出版業的受創程度並不像音樂產業那樣嚴重。

重要單字與片語

1. **piracy** [ˈpaɪrəsɪ] *n.* 盜版（不可數）
   pirate [ˈpaɪrət] *vt.* 盜版 & *n.* 海盜
   例 The man was caught trying to pirate software and sell it online.
   那名男子因試圖盜版軟體並在網路上販售而被逮捕。

2. **illegal** [ɪˈlig!̩] *a.* 非法的
   比較
   legal [ˈlig!̩] *n.* 合法的

3. **find one's way into...** 進入……
   例 Amanda found her way into the music business by taking part in a singing contest.
   艾曼達以參加歌唱比賽的方式進入音樂圈。

4. **likelihood** [ˈlaɪklɪhʊd] *n.* 可能性（不可數或常為單數）
   in all likelihood 十之八九，很可能

5. **publication** [ˌpʌblɪˈkeʃən] *n.* 出版品；出版
   publish [ˈpʌblɪʃ] *vt.* 出版
   publishing [ˈpʌblɪʃɪŋ] *n.* 出版業

6. **download** [ˌdaʊnˈlod] *vt.* 下載 & [ˈdaʊnˌlod] *n.* 下載的資料
   比較
   upload [ʌpˈlod] *vt.* 上傳 & [ˈʌpˌlod] *n.* 上傳的資料

7. **indication** [ˌɪndəˈkeʃən] *n.* 顯示，表示

8. **royalty** [ˈrɔɪəltɪ] *n.* 版稅（常用複數）；皇室（集合名詞，不可數）

9. **measure** [ˈmɛʒɚ] *n.* 措施
   take measures 採取措施

10. **battle** [ˈbæt!̩] *vt. & vi.* 打擊；與……作戰 / 搏鬥 & *n.* 戰役
    例 Lisa battled bravely against lung cancer.
    麗莎勇敢地對抗肺癌。

11. **widespread** [ˈwaɪdˌsprɛd] *a.* 普遍的

12. **persuade** [pɚˈswed] *vt.* 說服
    persuade sb to V 說服某人做……
    = **convince sb to V**
    例 Tony persuaded me to join the French Club.
    湯尼說服我加入法文社。

13. **twinge** [twɪndʒ] *n.* 刺痛
    a twinge of guilt 一陣內疚

14. **subscription** [səbˈskrɪpʃən] *n.* 訂閱

15. **streaming** [ˈstrimɪŋ] *n.* 串流

16. **intellectual** [ˌɪntəˈlɛktʃʊəl] *a.* 智力的；聰明的；知性的
    intellectual property rights 智慧財產權

17. **discount** [ˈdɪskaʊnt] *n.* 折扣
    give / offer a 30% discount on sth 給予某物七折折扣

18. **monitor** [ˈmɑnətɚ] *vt.* 監視 & *n.* 監視器
    例 During Saddam Hussein's reign, Iraqi people were monitored by secret police.
    在海珊掌權期間，伊拉克人民都受到祕密警察的監視。
19. **offender** [əˈfɛndɚ] *n.* 犯法的人，罪犯
20. **time-consuming** [ˈtaɪmˌkənˌs(j)umɪŋ] *a.* 耗時的
21. **copyright** [ˈkɑpɪˌraɪt] *n.* 版權；著作權
22. **destine** [ˈdɛstɪn] *vt.* 使命中注定（常用被動語態）
    be destined to V　注定要做……
    = be bound to V

    例 Julie is destined to become a famous artist.
    茱莉注定會成為知名的藝術家。
23. **decline** [dɪˈklaɪn] *n.* 沒落，下跌 & *vi.* 下降
    be on the decline　不斷下降
    = be on the decrease
    比較
    be on the rise　不斷上漲
    = be on the increase
24. **revenue** [ˈrɛvənju] *n.* 收入

四 閱讀測驗

　　2022 年，南亞國家巴基斯坦遭受嚴重洪災，該國總理形容為「開國以來最嚴重的洪災」。這場洪災淹沒巴基斯坦三分之一的國土，影響三千三百萬人，導致超過一千七百人喪生。數十萬頭家畜被沖走，數百萬英畝農作物毀損。

　　洪災的主要原因之一是雨季降雨量遠大於常態。雖然雨季在灌溉農作物和填補湖泊和水壩的水位上非常重要，但 2022 年的降雨規模對該國來說大到超過該國的負荷能力。例如信德省六到八月間的降雨量超過三十年平均值的四倍。衛星雲圖顯示，位於該省的印度河已經變成一座寬一百公里的湖泊。

　　另一項造成影響的因素是，除了北極和南極之外，巴基斯坦擁有世界上最多的冰川。這些在喜馬拉雅山脈中的大冰塊通常在冬季積聚，然後在春季慢慢融化。然而 2022 年春季，巴基斯坦經歷一場打破氣溫紀錄的嚴重熱浪，導致冰川加速融化。平常會吸收這些融冰水的湖泊無法容納，導致大量水突然溢出，再加上雨季的雨，形成嚴重水災。

　　毫無疑問，氣候變遷是雨季更強降雨以及熱浪更容易發生的主要原因。然而也該承認巴基斯坦政府未能從該國上一次在 2010 年發生的大洪災中吸取教訓並投資改善基礎建設，也是重要原因。根據英國廣播公司報導，在那次震驚世界的事件後「政府未能相應做出變革」，造成十二年後「規模嚴重的災情。」

　　此外，森林砍伐也是巴基斯坦的大問題。樹木不斷被砍伐，做為城市發展和農地使用的空間。在喜馬拉雅山脈較低的區域，這種做法很可能增加地表徑流和土壤侵蝕，因此加劇洪災。

Unit 17

__B__ 20. 第一段的 engulfed 最有可能是什麼意思？
(A) 完全守衛並保護某物。
(B) 完全包圍並覆蓋某物。
(C) 徹底拒絕並抵抗某事物。
(D) 大力推廣並鼓勵某事物。

理由

根據第一段第二句 "The floods engulfed a third of Pakistan's land area, ..."（這場洪災淹沒巴基斯坦三分之一的國土，……）可知 (B) 項應為正選。

__D__ 21. 關於 2022 年巴基斯坦洪災，我們可推斷什麼？
(A) 沒有 2010 年洪災那麼嚴重。
(B) 只有影響信德省。
(C) 是冬季期間的大問題。
(D) 嚴重影響農業。

理由

根據本文第一段最後一句，可知 (D) 項應為正選。

__C__ 22. 第二至第四段中討論哪幾項巴基斯坦洪災的原因？
(A) 缺乏資金；水壩無用；政府忽視
(B) 強降雨；砍伐樹木；城市區域擴大
(C) 強降雨；氣溫升高；政府忽視
(D) 砍伐樹木；火山爆發；氣溫升高

理由

根據本文第二段提及 2022 年的降雨規模大到難以負荷，第三段提及巴基斯坦經歷打破氣溫紀錄的嚴重熱浪，導致冰川加速融化，讓湖泊無法容納，第四段則提及政府未能吸取 2010 年大洪災的教訓來做出變革。可知 (C) 項應為正選。

__B__ 23. 作者如何總結本文？
(A) 藉由進一步詳細探討氣候變遷的影響。
(B) 藉由提供另一項洪災的可能原因。
(C) 藉由概述巴基斯坦如何改善其防洪措施。
(D) 藉由預測巴基斯坦的洪災可能會變得更加嚴重。

理由

根據本文最後一段提出森林砍伐也是一個主要的問題，可知 (B) 項應為正選。

重要單字與片語

1. **engulf** [ɪnˈgʌlf] *vt.* 淹沒；包圍
   例 The tsunami engulfed several houses along the seashore.
   海嘯吞噬了好幾間沿岸的房屋。

2. **livestock** [ˈlaɪvˌstɑk] *n.*（統指馴養的牛、羊、馬等）牲口（恆為複數，該字即為複數）

3. **monsoon** [mɑnˈsun] *n.* 季風季節；雨季

4. **sheer** [ʃɪr] *a.* 完全的，純然的

5. **at play**　　有影響

6. **glacier** [ˈgleʃɚ] *n.* 冰川，冰河

7. **accelerate** [əkˈsɛləˌret] *vt. & vi.*（使）加速

   例 The candidate proposed measures to accelerate the rate of economic growth.
   候選人提出加速經濟發展的辦法。

8. **acknowledge** [əkˈnɑlɪdʒ] *vt.* 承認
   例 David acknowledged that his mistake had led to the failure of the mission.
   大衛承認他的疏失導致這次任務的失敗。

9. **erosion** [ɪˈroʒən] *n.* 侵蝕（不可數）
   soil erosion　　土壤侵蝕

10. **predict** [prɪˈdɪkt] *vt.* 預測
    例 Dad predicted that I would win the contest, and he was right.
    老爸預測我會贏得這次的比賽，結果他是對的。

五 混合題

超加工食品（UPFs）是指透過工業程序製作而成的食品。它們含有大量在家庭烹飪中通常不會使用的成分。請在這個討論區分享你對超加工食品的看法。

(A) 安雅
超加工食品顯然對健康無益，但真的很好吃，不是嗎？看電影時不來個一大袋洋芋片怎麼行呢？我最喜歡起司的多力多滋了。

(B) 畢夫
我認為政府該給超加工食品貼上大大一張健康警示標籤，來保護大眾的健康。含糖汽水、泡麵、雞塊 —— 它們受到的待遇應該比照香菸。

(C) 克莉絲朵
我不會說這些食品是健康的，但我偶爾會吃，就當是放縱一下自己。如果我要辦生日派對或其他慶祝活動，一定會準備蛋糕、甜甜圈和大包裝洋芋片。

Unit 17

Unit 17

(D) 多明尼克
我是醫療專業人士，知道許多研究都已證實：超加工食品比例很高的飲食習慣，常與肥胖、糖尿病、高血壓和心臟疾病有關，因為這些食品常含有大量鹽分、添加糖分和反式脂肪。

(E) 愛瑪
一部分的我會因為在家裡弄超加工食品而感到內疚，但最終我還是覺得它們方便而且便宜。例如烤箱即食披薩和微波爐料理，我覺得它們是低收入族群的福音。

(F) 法拉德
我想到油膩膩的漢堡、炸雞、熱狗和魚柳條時，說真的會有點噁。我覺得這類食品對社會大眾有害，應該被禁掉才對。

(G) 喬琪娜
我們不應該把某些食物妖魔化，這樣會導致人們產生飲食失調問題。把超加工食品當作均衡飲食的一部分是可以的，當零食偶爾吃吃沒問題，我自己就是這樣。

(H) 休
這些食品很難躲得掉，不是嗎？從大量生產的白麵包、早餐穀類，一直到鹹的洋芋片，每個禮拜在超市購物時很難不買這些東西，也很難不把它們納入日常飲食。

(I) 艾歐娜
超加工食品含有氫化脂肪、人工甜味劑、填充劑和高果糖玉米糖漿，還有許多其他成分。這些食品只提供沒營養的熱量，而不是提供身體所需營養的維生素、礦物質和纖維素。

(J) 朱利亞斯
我大多數時候都靠著意志力保持健康的飲食習慣，但是人偶爾也該犒賞自己一下嘛！速食店的漢堡、薯條和汽水，就是對我其他時候都那麼乖的獎勵。

24. 在上述討論區的討論 (A) 到 (J) 中，哪些人的回應主要是基於事實而非個人意見？請在下方寫出對應的字母。

<u>(D), (I)</u>

理由

(D) Dominic（多明尼克）的回應 "... numerous studies have linked a diet high in UPFs to obesity, diabetes, high blood pressure, and heart disease because they're often high in salt, added sugars, and trans fats."（……許多研究都已證實：超加工食品比例很高的飲食習慣，常與肥胖、糖尿病、高血壓和心臟疾病有關，因為這些食品常含有大量鹽分、添加糖分和反式脂肪。）以及 (I) Iona（艾歐娜）的回應 "UPFs contain hydrogenated fats, artificial sweeteners, bulking agents, and high fructose corn syrup, among many other ingredients. They provide empty calories rather than the vitamins, minerals, and fiber that our bodies require for adequate nutrition."（超加工食品含有氫化脂肪、人工甜味劑、填充劑和高果糖玉米糖漿，還有許多其他成分。這些食品只提供沒營養的熱量，而不是提供身體所需營養的維生素、礦物質和纖維素。），都是客觀的事實陳述而非個人意見，故 (D)、(I) 應為正解。

25. 以下的句子跟哪些人有關係？在下方寫出對應的名字。
「他或她只會偶爾吃超加工食品。」

Crystal（克莉絲朵），Georgina（喬琪娜），Julius（朱利亞斯）

理由

根據 (C) Crystal（克莉絲朵）的回應第一句 "... I eat them every so often as an indulgent treat."（……我偶爾會吃，就當是放縱一下自己。）、(G) Georgina（喬琪娜）的回應最後一句 "... they can be enjoyed as treats from time to time—just as I do."（……當零食偶爾吃吃沒問題，我自己就是這樣。）及 (J) Julius（朱利亞斯）的回應第一句 "A burger, fries, and soda from a fast-food restaurant is my reward for being good the rest of the time."（速食店的漢堡、薯條和汽水，就是對我其他時候都那麼乖的獎勵。），可推知 Crystal（克莉絲朵）、Georgina（喬琪娜）、Julius（朱利亞斯）應為正解。

26. 在討論區的討論中，哪一個字的意思是「可能會造成危害的事物」？

menace（危險，構成威脅的事物）

理由

根據 (F) Farad（法拉德）的回應第二句 "I consider these types of food to be a menace to society..."（我覺得這類食品對社會大眾有害……），可推知 menace 一字表示「可能會造成危害的事物」，故 menace（危險，構成威脅的事物）應為正解。

_C_ 27. 在討論區中，哪一種超加工食品被提及的次數最多？

理由

Farad（法拉德）和 (J) Julius（朱利亞斯）提到漢堡（二次），(B) Biff（畢夫）和 (J) Julius（朱利亞斯）提到汽水（二次），(A) Anya（安雅）、(C) Crystal（克莉絲朵）、(H) Hugh（休）都提到洋芋片（三次），泡麵僅 (B) Biff（畢夫）提到（一次），可知洋芋片被提到的次數最多，故 (C) 項應為正選。

Unit 17

重要單字與片語

1. **big fat** 徹底的；極度的（加強語氣用語）
2. **nugget** [ˈnʌgɪt] n. 小塊
   a chicken nugget 雞塊
3. **every so often** 偶爾，有時
   = from time to time
   = every now and then
   = on occasion
   = at times
   = sometimes / occasionally
   例 Jeff goes hiking in the mountains every so often to enjoy the fresh air.
   傑夫偶爾會去山上健行，享受新鮮空氣。
4. **indulgent** [ɪnˈdʌldʒənt] a. 縱容的，寬容的
5. **diabetes** [ˌdaɪəˈbitiz] n. 糖尿病（不可數）
6. **trans fat** 反式脂肪
7. **greasy** [ˈgrisɪ] a. 油膩的
8. **menace** [ˈmɛnəs] n. 危害，威脅
9. **demonize** [ˈdimənˌaɪz] vt. 將……妖魔化
   例 Some people demonize technology instead of learning to use it wisely.
   有些人把科技妖魔化，而不是學習如何明智地使用它。
10. **hydrogenated** [haɪˈdrɑdʒənˌetɪd] a. 氫化的（在食物的脂肪中加入氫）
    hydrogenated fat 氫化脂肪
11. **sweetener** [ˈswitn̩ɚ] n. 甜味劑
12. **a bulking agent** 填充劑
13. **fructose** [ˈfrʌkˌtos] n. 果糖
14. **syrup** [ˈsɪrəp] n. 糖漿
15. **adequate** [ˈædɪkwət] a. 足夠的，適當的
16. **nutrition** [n(j)uˈtrɪʃən] n. 營養（不可數）
17. **willpower** [ˈwɪlˌpaʊɚ] n. 意志力
18. **deserve** [dɪˈzɝv] vt. 應得
    deserve + N 應/值得……
    = deserve to + V
    例 After working hard all year, you deserve (to have) a nice vacation by the beach.
    你辛苦工作了一整年，應該去享受一次美好的海濱假期了。

Unit 18

一 綜合測驗

　　生態膠囊屋是由一間斯洛伐克的公司所研發的蛋形居住空間，是永續生活的極致典範。這種袖珍、可移動的住家重量約一千五百公斤，透過海運、拖吊、空運，甚或是由馱畜拉動，幾乎可搬運到任何地方。它的流動性使它成為需要在偏遠地區臨時住宿的人的理想選擇。附著於屋頂上的風力渦輪機和太陽能板有助於電池發電並使生態膠囊屋對生態環境無害。這些可再生能源使居民能夠在不依賴傳統電力網的情況下舒適生活。

　　此外，膠囊屋的設計有助於蒐集雨水和露水以供作水源。這一切表示有了生態膠囊屋，沒有水電公共設施的生活也是可能的。這種居住空間甚至提供了許多正常生活的便利，像是洗熱水澡、自來水、沖水馬桶和熱騰騰的飯菜。膠囊屋的特色包括了小廚房、折疊床、儲藏室、方便的工作區域和大型的窗戶。雖然內部大小只有十一平方公尺（約四坪大小），但兩個人一同居住綽綽有餘。

__A__ 1. 理由
  a. 原句實為：
     The compact, portable home, which weighs roughly 1,500 kilograms, can be transported almost anywhere through shipping, towing, airlifting, or even by being pulled by pack animal.
  b. 上句中的非限定形容詞子句 which weighs roughly 1,500 kilograms 可簡化為分詞詞組，即省略作主詞的關係代名詞 which，再將現在式第三人稱單數動詞 weighs 改為現在分詞 weighing。
  c. 根據上述，可知 (A) 項應為正選。

__C__ 2. 理由
  a. (A) **consume energy**　消耗能源
     例 Modern appliances consume energy even when they are turned off.
     現代化的電器即使關閉電源時仍然會消耗能源。
     (B) **produce competition**　引發競爭
     例 Lower prices often produce competition among businesses.
     低價通常會引發企業之間的競爭。
     (C) **generate electricity**　產生電力
     generate [ˈdʒɛnəˌret] vt. 產生（光、電、熱）；造成，引起
     例 Solar panels efficiently generate electricity from sunlight.
     太陽能板能有效利用陽光來產生電力。

(D) **supply opportunities** 提供機會

例 The new project will supply opportunities for young entrepreneurs.
這個新計畫將為年輕企業家提供機會。

b. 根據語意，可知 (C) 項應為正選。

C 3. 理由

a. (A) **In other words, ...** 換句話說，……

例 There is hardly anything Daisy cannot do. In other words, she is a genius.
幾乎沒什麼事是黛西做不來的。換言之，她是個天才。

(B) **After all, ...** 畢竟，……

例 Don't blame the whole thing on Frank; after all, he is only a child.
別把整件事都怪罪在法蘭克身上；畢竟，他只是個孩子。

(C) **In addition, ...** 此外，……

例 Sandra is helpful. In addition, she always wears a smile.
桑德拉很樂於助人。此外，她總是面帶笑容。

(D) **On the one hand, ...** 一方面，……

本詞組常與下列詞組搭配使用：
On the other (hand), ... 另一方面，……

例 On the one hand, Tim supports feminists' demands; on the other, he wants a traditional wife.
一方面，提姆支持女性主義者的訴求；另一方面，他卻希望有一個很傳統的太太。

b. 根據語意，可知 (C) 項應為正選。

B 4. 理由

a. (A) **splendid** [ˈsplɛndɪd] *a.* 極好的；華麗的

例 There are many splendid villas in Bali.
峇里島上有許多華麗的別墅。

(B) **regular** [ˈrɛɡjələ] *a.* 正常的；規律的

例 A regular bowling alley is sixty feet long.
正規的保齡球球道長六十呎。

(C) **controversial** [ˌkɑntrəˈvɝʃəl] *a.* 有爭議性的

例 The origin of the human race has been a controversial subject.
人類的起源一直是個具爭議性的話題。

(D) **fragile** [ˈfrædʒəl] *a.* 脆弱的；易碎的

例 This box is full of fragile items, so please handle it with care.
這箱子裝滿了易碎物品，所以請小心處理。

b. 根據語意，可知 (B) 項應為正選。

Unit 18

__A__ 5. 理由

a. (A) **include** [ɪnˋklud] vt. 包括，包含

例 A ten percent service charge is included in the bill.
帳單內含百分之十的服務費。

(B) **resolve** [rɪˋzɑlv] vt. 解決

例 It seems that the problem of drug trafficking in the Philippines is too serious to be resolved.
菲律賓的販毒問題似乎太嚴重而無法解決。
＊trafficking [ˋtræfɪkɪŋ] n. 非法交易

(C) **consult** [kənˋsʌlt] vt. 查閱；諮詢

例 For more information, please consult our manual.
欲知更多資訊，請查閱我們的說明書。

(D) **devote** [dɪˋvot] vt. 奉獻
devote / dedicate / apply oneself to + N/V-ing　致力於……

例 Henry has begun to devote himself to his studies.
亨利已開始專心向學。

b. 根據語意，可知 (A) 項應為正選。

重要單字與片語

1. **shaped** [ʃept] a. 具有特定形狀的（常與名詞並用，構成複合形容詞）
heart-shaped [ˋhɑrt͵ʃept] a. 心形的
egg-shaped [ˋɛg͵ʃept] a. 蛋形的

2. **ultimate** [ˋʌltəmɪt] n. 極致典範 & a. 極致的，終極的；最後的

3. **sustainable** [səˋstenəb!] a. 可維持的，可持續的；不破壞生態平衡的
an environmentally sustainable society
一個保持生態環境平衡的社會

4. **compact** [kəmˋpækt] a. 袖珍的，體積小卻很精實的

5. **portable** [ˋpɔrtəb!] a. 可移動的；可攜帶的

6. **transport** [trænˋsport] vt.（用交通工具）運送

例 Each week, the farmers transport their produce to the markets in the city.
農夫們每星期將農產品運送到城裡的市場。

7. **tow** [to] vt. 拖吊

例 Mandy had to have her car towed after it broke down.
曼蒂的車拋錨了，只好請人把車拖走。

8. **airlift** [ˋɛrlɪft] vt. 空運（人員或物資）

例 Medical supplies have been airlifted to the disaster area.
醫療物資已空運至災區。

9. **mobility** [moˋbɪlətɪ] n. 流動性

10. **turbine** [ˋtɝbaɪn] n. 渦輪

11. **panel** [ˋpæn!] n. 面板

12. **attach** [əˋtætʃ] *vt.* 繫上，貼上，裝上
    attach A to B　　將 A 繫或附在 B 上面
    例 Attach four batteries to a loudspeaker.
    　　在擴音器上裝入四顆電池。

13. **grid** [grɪd] *n.* 電力網；網格
    power grid　　　電力網路
    off the grid　　不依賴公共電力系統

14. **facilitate** [fəˋsɪləˌtet] *vt.* 有助於
    例 Mike's explanation facilitated my understanding of the situation.
    　　麥克的解釋有助於我對情況的了解。

二 文意選填

　　你大概從未把霧視作一種天然資源。然而，採集霧的過程就可以證明，霧的確可作為一種天然資源。採集霧的方式是利用許多帶有細網的面板，將水滴收集到儲存槽裡，之後作飲用水或其他用途。這種低科技門檻的節能運動運用起來既獨特又巧妙，非洲國家摩洛哥的西迪伊夫尼地區就在做這種事。當霧通過四十塊置於一千兩百二十五米高的山頂上的面板時，一種所謂凝結的過程會在細網上形成水滴，向下滴入容器裡。收集到的水會透過管線網路運送至五個村落，那裡住了約四百人。居民生平第一次可以從水龍頭取得乾淨的水。

　　住在西迪伊夫尼那五個村落的居民運用採集霧這項綠能科技，大幅改變了他們的生活。以往為了從離家很遙遠的水井取得足夠的水，村落的婦女得走上耗費四小時的疲憊行程。此外，在乾旱期間，村落裡的人必須運載額外的用水到村子裡，這可是一項龐大的開支。相形之下，採集霧相當便宜，無須耗費精力，也不會造成汙染。由於優點多多，採集霧可望能擴展到摩洛哥其他迫切需要乾淨飲用水的地區。

C **6.** 理由
　a. 空格前有第三人稱單數主詞 the process of fog harvesting（採霧的過程），空格後有 that 引導的名詞子句，得知空格應置第三人稱單數動詞。
　b. 選項中為第三人稱單數動詞的有 (C) proves（證明）及 (I) requires（需要），惟根據語意，(C) 項應為正選。
　c. **prove** [pruv] *vt.* 證明
　　例 I can't prove that Henry is right.
　　　我不能證明亨利是對的。

D **7.** 理由
　a. 空格前有形容詞 other（其他的），得知空格應置複數可數名詞。
　b. 選項中為複數可數名詞的有 (D) purposes（目的）、(F) trips（行程）及 (G) advantages（優點），惟根據語意，(D) 項應為正選。
　c. **purpose** [ˋpɝpəs] *n.* 目的
　　for the purpose of + V-ing　　為了……目的
　　on purpose　　故意（= purposely）

Unit **18**

Unit 18

E 8. 理由
- a. 空格前有主要子句的主詞 a process（一個過程），空格後有介詞 as 及名詞 condensation（凝結），得知空格可置不及物動詞的過去分詞，以與後面介詞及名詞組成分詞詞組修飾 process。
- b. 剩餘選項中僅 (E) known（為人所知）為不及物動詞的過去分詞，且置入空格後符合語意，故為正選。
- c. 上述分詞詞組為 which / that is known as condensation 省略關係代名詞 which / that 及 is 而來。
- d. **be known as...** 以……的身分而聞名
  = be famous as...
  = be renowned as...
  > 例 Bruce Lee was known as a martial arts master and a famous movie star.
  > 李小龍以身為武術大師與知名影星著稱。

A 9. 理由
- a. 空格前有主詞 the collected water（收集到的水）及 be 動詞 is，得知空格可置形容詞作主詞補語，或置及物動詞的過去分詞，以與 is 形成被動語態。
- b. 剩餘選項中為形容詞或及物動詞的過去分詞僅剩 (A) transported（被運送），置入空格後形成 is transported to...（被運送到……），符合語意及用法，故為正選。
- c. **transport** [trænˋspɔrt] *vt.* 運送
  > 例 The ship transported the new trucks to Europe.
  > 這艘船將那些新卡車載往歐洲。

B 10. 理由
- a. 空格前有及物動詞 have（有），空格後有 to 及名詞詞組 clean water（乾淨的水），得知空格應置 access（使用的權利），形成下列固定用法：
  have access to... 接觸到……；有權進入 / 使用……
  > 例 These students have access to the laboratory.
  > 這些學生可使用這間實驗室。
- b. 根據上述，(B) 項應為正選。

H 11. 理由
- a. 空格前有指示形容詞 this 及形容詞 green（綠能的），得知空格應置單數名詞，以與 green 形成名詞詞組作動詞 using（使用）的受詞。
- b. 剩餘選項中為單數名詞的有 (H) technology（科技）及 (J) drought（乾旱），惟根據語意，(H) 項應為正選。
- c. **technology** [tɛkˋnɑlədʒɪ] *n.* 科技

__F__ 12. 理由

    a. 空格前有及物動詞 make（做）和形容詞 exhausting（令人疲憊的），得知空格應置名詞以與 exhausting 形成名詞詞組作 make 的受詞。

    b. 剩餘選項中 (F) trips（行程）、(G) advantages（優點）及 (J) drought（乾旱）為名詞，惟根據語意，(F) 項應為正選。

    c. **trip** [trɪp] *n.* 行程；旅行
       make a trip to + 地方　　到某地旅行
    = take a trip to + 地方
    = go on a trip to + 地方

__J__ 13. 理由

    a. 空格前有介詞 during（在……期間）、名詞 times（時期）及介詞 of，得知空格應置名詞作介詞 of 的受詞。

    b. 剩餘選項中 (G) advantages（優點）及 (J) drought（乾旱）為名詞，惟根據語意，(J) 項應為正選。

    c. **drought** [draʊt] *n.* 乾旱

__I__ 14. 理由

    a. 本句前有 be 動詞 is，後有對等連接詞 and 連接另一動詞 create，得知空格應置另一動詞，以與 is 及 does not create 形成對等。

    b. 剩餘選項中僅 (I) requires（需要）為動詞，且置入空格後符合語意，故為正選。

    c. **require** [rɪˋkwaɪr] *vt.* 要求；需要
       例 This lamp requires a 120-watt light bulb.
       這座檯燈須用一百二十瓦的燈泡。

__G__ 15. 理由

    a. 空格前有數量形容詞 many（許多的），得知空格應置複數可數名詞。

    b. 剩餘選項 (G) advantages（優點）為複數可數名詞，且置入空格後符合語意，故為正選。

    c. **advantage** [ədˋvæntɪdʒ] *n.* 優勢；優點；益處，便利

重要單字與片語

1. **fog** [fɑg] *n.* 霧
2. **resource** [ˋrisɔrs] *n.* 資源
3. **harvest** [ˋhɑrvɪst] *vt.* 收穫
    例 The farmers had to harvest the rice before the typhoon came.
    農人必須在颱風來臨之前收割稻穀。
4. **droplet** [ˋdrɑplɪt] *n.* 小水滴
5. **storage** [ˋstɔrɪdʒ] *n.* 儲藏（不可數）
6. **unique** [juˋnik] *a.* 與眾不同的；獨有的
7. **peak** [pik] *n.* 頂峰；巔峰
8. **condensation** [ˌkɑndənˋseʃən] *n.* 凝結（不可數）

Unit 18

Unit 18

9. **trickle** [ˈtrɪkl̩] *vi.* 涓涓地流
10. **reside** [rɪˈzaɪd] *vi.* 居住
11. **expense** [ɪkˈspɛns] *n.* 開銷
    at sb's expense 用某人的經費
    例 Mary studied abroad at her parents' expense.
    瑪麗的父母出錢供她留學。

12. **in contrast** 相較之下
    例 Sarah is usually quiet. In contrast, her brother is always noisy.
    莎拉通常很安靜。相較之下，她的弟弟一向很吵。
13. **urgently** [ˈɝdʒəntlɪ] *adv.* 緊急地，急迫地

篇章結構

　　正如同世界上許多地區一般，印度性別不平等的問題很嚴重。該國在文化上偏愛兒子甚於女兒，這造成了一種情況，即男女的比例僅為 1000 比 933。這個人口問題對女性造成了若干阻礙，包括歧視。近年來，印度政府和各種組織不斷努力提高大眾對性別不平等問題的意識，並推升女性權利。其中北印度哈里亞納邦畢畢普爾村的村委會的努力尤其值得關注。

　　那裡男女比例失衡的情形比印度的平均狀況還嚴重，男女的比例是 1000 比 877，為了對抗印度人對於女性的負面態度，畢畢普爾村的村委會成員想出一個新奇的點子：設計一場自拍比賽，讓父母展現對女兒的驕傲。要參加的民眾只要拍下自己和女兒的照片，並透過通訊軟體提交照片即可。這個簡單卻極具影響力的活動鼓勵家庭公開慶祝女兒的存在，此舉有助於挑戰根深蒂固的文化規範。

　　該活動的迴響和整體的效果超出了籌辦者的預期。有將近八百位民眾從哈里亞納邦各地和印度其他一些地方寄來照片。由於寄來的照片數量龐大，得獎人數從一位增加至三位，還增設了十五個安慰獎。除了獲得獎盃和證書，每位得獎者還獲頒兩千一百盧比的獎金（約美金二十五元）。

　　這場比賽甚至引起了印度總理納倫德拉·莫迪的關注，他還在他的廣播節目上宣傳這項活動。總理的支持使該活動得到全國民眾的認可，吸引了更多人參與。另一種讓全國和其他國家都認識該活動的方式就是透過社交媒體。許多人在網路上分享他們的自拍照，引發關於性別平等的討論，並促使其他地區採取類似的舉措。畢畢普爾村的比賽可望鼓舞更多人努力協助解決印度性別不平等的問題。

<u>C</u> **16. 理由**

a. 空格前句敘述近年來，印度政府和各種組織不斷努力提高大眾對性別不平等問題的意識，並推升女性權利，而選項 (C) 提及 Efforts by the council of a village called Bibipur in the northern Indian state of Haryana（北印度哈里亞納邦畢畢普爾村的村委會的努力），且第二段第一句敘述畢畢普爾村想要對抗印度人對於女性的負面觀感而舉辦自拍比賽，與此選項形成關聯。

b. 根據上述，(C) 項應為正選。

D **17.** 理由

    a. 空格前句提及畢畢普爾村設計了一場自拍比賽，而選項 (D) 敘述參加（比賽）的方法為 take photos of themselves with their daughters and submit the pictures through a messaging app（拍下自己和女兒的照片，並透過通訊軟體提交照片），語意承接空格前句作進一步說明。

    b. 根據上述，(D) 項應為正選。

A **18.** 理由

    a. 空格前句敘述將近八百位民眾寄照片來參賽，而選項 (A) 提及 Due to the volume of submissions（由於寄來的照片數量龐大），得獎人數增加並增設安慰獎，呼應參賽者眾多，語意與空格前句相關。

    b. 根據上述，(A) 項應為正選。

B **19.** 理由

    a. 空格後句提及 His endorsement gave the campaign nationwide recognition（他的支持使該活動得到全國民眾的認可），而選項 (B) 敘述 Indian Prime Minister Narendra Modi... promoted it on his radio program（印度總理納倫德拉‧莫迪……在他的廣播節目上宣傳這項活動），His 即指印度總理，兩句相互呼應。

    b. 根據上述，(B) 項應為正選。

(E) 選項翻譯　性別不平等並不是印度農村唯一面臨的嚴重問題。

重要單字與片語

1. **gender** [ˈdʒɛndɚ] n. 性別
2. **inequality** [ˌɪnɪˈkwɑlətɪ] n. 不平等
　比較
　equality [ɪˈkwɑlətɪ] n. 平等
3. **cultural** [ˈkʌltʃərəl] a. 文化的
4. **lead to...** 造成……
　= cause...
　= give rise to...
　例 Stress can lead to mental and physical problems.
　　壓力會造成身心問題。
5. **obstacle** [ˈɑbstəkl] n. 阻礙，障礙
6. **discrimination** [dɪˌskrɪməˈneʃən] n. 歧視
　racial discrimination　種族歧視
　sex discrimination　性別歧視
7. **ratio** [ˈreʃo] n. 比例
8. **come up with...**　想出（點子、方法）
　例 How did you come up with such a great idea?
　　你怎麼想出這麼棒的點子？
9. **selfie** [ˈsɛlfɪ] n. 自拍照
10. **participate** [pɑrˈtɪsəˌpet] vi. 參與
　　participate in...　參與……
　= take part in...
11. **submit** [səbˈmɪt] vt. 交付；呈遞
　例 Submit your outline to the teacher before writing your research paper.
　　寫研究報告前先把你的大綱交給老師看。
12. **deep-rooted** [ˈdipˈrutɪd] a. 根深蒂固的

13. **exceed** [ɪkˋsid] *vt.* 超過；超越
14. **volume** [ˋvaljum] *n.* 數量；容量；體積
15. **consolation** [ˌkɑnsəˋleʃən] *n.* 安慰
16. **endorsement** [ɪnˋdɔrsmənt] *n.* 支持，認可；簽署；代言，業配
17. **spark** [spɑrk] *vt.* 激發，引發 & *vi.* 冒火花 & *n.* 小火花

例 The movie sparked my interest in space exploration.
這部電影激發了我對太空探索的興趣。

18. **prompt** [prɑmpt] *vt.* 促使 & *a.* 立刻的
    prompt sb to + V　促使某人決定做……

例 Bobby's illness prompted him to adopt a healthier lifestyle.
巴比的疾病促使他採取更健康的生活方式。

四　閱讀測驗

　　製藥公司對處方藥品的命名是漫長又複雜的過程，在藥物上市前好幾年就已經啟動。第一階段通常會聘請創意公司建議幾個可能的名稱。創意公司會基於它對製藥公司和藥物用途的了解，提出吸引人又盡可能獨特的名稱。由於藥物往往會在全球範圍銷售，它會盡量避免在其他語言不好發音的名稱及字母如 H、J 和 W 等。第二階段是由製藥公司的法律和商轉團隊負責，他們要一起從創意公司提供的決選名單中挑出他們最青睞的選項。最終階段是由監管機構來核准名稱，在美國的話就是食品藥物管理局（FDA）。主管機關必須確認該名稱沒有暗示新藥優於現有藥物，也沒有對新藥的療效作任何保證。它還得確認該名稱的口語或書寫形式都不會和現有藥物的名稱太像。這是為了減少在開藥、配藥或服用新藥時出現藥名混淆的機會，因為那會有致命的後果。

　　已核准的藥物名稱可以大致分為兩類。第一類名稱是提示藥物的所屬類別。例如阿莫西林（Amoxicillin）是一種抗生素，用於治療細菌感染，其名稱中包含字尾「cillin」，因為它是一種盤尼辛林（penicillin）：一種來自青黴菌的抗生素。因此你會發現這一類抗生素族群中的其他藥物名稱也以「cillin」結尾。第二類名稱的設計是用來引發使用者的情緒感受。例如魯尼斯塔（Lunesta）用於治療失眠，其中包含字首「lune」，因為這是法語「月亮」的意思。因此這個名稱暗示夜晚，藉以引發睡眠的感覺。

C　20. 關於製藥命名的過程，我們得知什麼？
　　(A) 它通常仰賴需要藥物的家庭的情緒反應。
　　(B) 它試圖納入製藥公司的名稱。
　　(C) 它在藥物公開販售的幾年之前就已經開始。
　　(D) 它需要特定的創意公司來選擇最終的藥物名稱。

理由
根據本文第一段第一句，可知 (C) 項應為正選。

___C___ **21.** 根據本文，關於新藥的名稱下列哪一項不需要 FDA 確認？
(A) 和其他藥物有適當的區別。
(B) 不對其藥效做出承諾。
(C) 藥品外包裝上這個名稱可以放得剛剛好。
(D) 它未聲稱優於其他藥物。

> 理由
> 根據第一段倒數第二至三句，可知 (C) 項應為正選。

___B___ **22.** 下列哪一項最有可能是第一段中 administered 的意思？
(A) 由一個國家或地區管理。
(B) 調劑藥物給某人。
(C) 以懲罰形式分配。
(D) 負使用某條法律的責任。

> 理由
> 根據第一段最後一句 "...when the new drug is prescribed, administered, or taken, ..."（……在開藥、配藥或服用新藥時……）可知，(B) 項應為正選。

___D___ **23.** 一家製藥公司製造了一種新型的抗生素。根據本文，下列哪一項最適合做它的名稱？
(A) Cillinesta.
(B) Howjocillin.
(C) Antiluner.
(D) Adrocillin.

> 理由
> 根據第二段第四句提及抗生素類的藥物會以「cillin」結尾以及第一段第四句提及會避免使用 H、J 和 W 等字母。可知 (D) 項應為正選。

重要單字與片語

1. **prescription** [prɪˋskrɪpʃən] *n*. 處方，藥方
   prescribe [prɪˋskraɪb] *vt*. 開立（藥方）；規定
   例 The doctor prescribed some medicine for my bad cough.
   醫生為我嚴重的咳嗽開了一些藥。

2. **pharmaceutical** [ˏfɑrməˋsutɪkl̩] *a*. 製藥的

3. **hit the market** 上市
4. **commercial** [kəˋmɝʃəl] *a*. 商業的
5. **body** [ˋbɑdɪ] *n*. 機構
6. **administer** [ədˋmɪnəstɚ] *vt*. 管理；執行/實施（法律等）；給予（藥物、治療等）
   例 The doctor administered the vaccine to the villagers.
   那位醫師為村民注射疫苗。

Unit 18

7. **lethal** [ˈliθəl] *a.* 致命的
8. **antibiotic** [ˌæntɪbaɪˈɑtɪk] *n.* 抗生素 & *a.* 抗生素的
9. **suffix** [ˈsʌfɪks] *n.* 後綴，字尾
10. **prefix** [ˈprifɪks] *n.* 前綴，字首
11. **commence** [kəˈmɛns] *vi.* & *vt.* 開始；著手
    例 The ceremony will commence in half an hour.
    典禮將在半小時後開始。

五 混合題

朝觀是一年一度前往沙烏地阿拉伯伊斯蘭聖城麥加的宗教之旅。所有成年的穆斯林理應一生得去一次。以下是兩名完成朝觀之旅的人的故事。

阿布杜拉住在杜拜，是極為虔誠的穆斯林。他年輕力壯，經常參與極限運動。所以雖然他付得起去麥加的機票錢，但他選擇徒步兩千公里以到達聖地的朝觀之旅。許多同儕提醒他這將會是極為艱困的旅程，而他們說得有道理：阿布杜拉必須面對高溫以及崎嶇多變的地形，而且還沒有遮蔭處。不過他細心地規劃路程並鍛鍊體魄以因應體力的耗損，而途中他也得到許多善心陌生人的幫助。他也將此視為對他宗教虔誠的完美考驗。兩個月後他終於抵達麥加，要說他已經精疲力盡是一點也不誇張，但他感受到熱情的歡迎以及大家的團結一心，這給了他力量進行必要的儀式來履行他的宗教義務。重要元素之一就是要在兩座丘陵之間來回走七遍。在阿布杜拉艱苦的旅程後，相比之下這個實在太輕鬆了！

法蒂瑪和她父母住在蘇格蘭。他們不是富裕人家：她父親開一間僅賺點蠅頭小利的小服裝店。但法蒂瑪的雙親多年來一直夢想參與朝觀之旅，於是法蒂瑪決心讓此夢想成真。她存下每一分閒錢長達二十年，直到夠買三張從愛丁堡到吉達的機票為止。此時她的父母已變得相當孱弱，沒有什麼體力。所以法蒂瑪必須在搭機和前往麥加的車程中全程照顧他們。但一到了那裡，她父母就像重獲新生一般。受到世界最大聚會活動之一的凝聚力所鼓舞，法蒂瑪和雙親加入其他朝聖者一起在薩法山與馬爾瓦山之間徒步往返。他們還向三根柱子丟石頭，象徵他們拒絕誘惑。法蒂瑪的父母非常感謝這個女兒，因為她讓他們實現了終身的夢想。

24. 許多阿布杜拉的朋友都提醒他，從杜拜到麥加的朝觀之旅會有許多**挑戰**。

理由

空格前為形容詞 numerous，可得知空格應置複數可數名詞。根據阿布杜拉故事的第四句 "Many of his peers warned him that it would be a supremely challenging journey, ..."（許多同儕提醒他這將會是極為艱困的旅程，……）得知，空格應置與 challenging 相關的複數可數名詞 challenges。

25. 法蒂瑪的**決心**對幫助她父母實現參加朝觀的夢想來說非常重要。

理由

空格前為人名 + 所有格 Fatima's，空格後為過去式 be 動詞 was，可得知空格應置名詞。根據法蒂瑪故事的第三句 "..., and Fatima was determined to turn that dream into reality."（……，於是法蒂瑪決心讓此夢想成真。）得知，空格應置與 determined 相關的名詞 determination。

26. 法蒂瑪這段文章中，their 指的是什麼？

Fatima's and her parents'（法蒂瑪的和她的父母的）

理由

前句提及法蒂瑪和她的父母加入了其他朝聖者在兩座山之間徒步往返的活動，本句前半句敘述他們（法蒂瑪和她的父母）向三根柱子丟石頭，可推知 their 指涉法蒂瑪和她的父母，他們以丟石頭的動作象徵拒絕誘惑的涵義，故 Fatima's and her parents' 應為正解。

BD 27. 下列關於阿布杜拉和法蒂瑪的敘述何者正確？

(A) 他們因金錢的考量來選擇交通工具。
(B) 他們在朝聖者群體中感受到團結與和諧。
(C) 他們的旅程均有超過二十年的精心規劃。
(D) 他們在兩座山丘間步行往返多次。
(E) 他們的參與受到麥加極度高溫的影響。
(F) 他們被扔石頭，作為宗教儀式的一部分。

理由

根據阿布杜拉故事的倒數第二至三句及法蒂瑪故事的倒數第三句得知，(B)、(D) 應為正選。

Unit 18

重要單字與片語

1. **religious** [rɪˋlɪdʒəs] *a.* 宗教的；虔誠的
2. **Islamic** [ɪsˋlæmɪk] *a.* 伊斯蘭的；伊斯蘭教徒的
3. **undertake** [ˌʌndɚˋtek] *vt.* 進行，承接；承諾，保證（三態為：undertake, undertook [ˌʌndɚˋtʊk], undertaken [ˌʌndɚˋtekən]）
   - 例 If you plan to undertake this task, you'd better be prepared for some difficulties.
   如果你要從事這項工作，最好有面臨困難的準備。
4. **pilgrimage** [ˋpɪlgrəmɪdʒ] *n.* 朝覲，朝聖
   pilgrim [ˋpɪlgrɪm] *n.* 朝聖者
5. **devout** [dɪˋvaʊt] *a.* 虔誠的
6. **peer** [pɪr] *n.* 同輩，同儕
7. **exertion** [ɪgˋzɝʃən] *n.* 費力；盡力
8. **exaggeration** [ɪgˌzædʒəˋreʃən] *n.* 誇大
   It is no exaggeration to say (that)...
   說……一點也不誇張
   - 例 It's no exaggeration to say Patrick is a real giant. He is 200 centimeters tall.
   要說派屈克真是個巨人，一點也不誇張。他身高有兩百公分。
9. **ritual** [ˋrɪtʃʊəl] *n.* 儀式；例行公事 & *a.* 儀式的
10. **by no means**　絕非，絕不
    - 例 Mary is by no means a clever girl.
    瑪麗絕不是一個聰明的女孩。
11. **frail** [frel] *a.* 虛弱的；脆弱的
12. **a new lease on life**　重獲新生；更有活力
13. **collective** [kəˋlɛktɪv] *a.* 集體的，共同的
14. **harmony** [ˋhɑrmənɪ] *n.* 和諧

Unit 19

一 綜合測驗

　　眾所皆知，一般來說吃水果有益健康。特別是一種長在外表奇特的猴麵包樹上的果實，似乎對人類和環境極其有益。這種超級水果含有大量的鎂、鈣、鐵、維生素 C 和鉀。關於後兩項元素，這種猴麵包樹果實的維生素 C 含量是柳橙的六倍，鉀含量則是香蕉的四倍。對於鉀含量偏低的人或需要額外補充維生素 C 以增強免疫力的人來說，這種水果特別有幫助。

　　此外，其鈣含量是牛奶的兩倍，而鎂含量比菠菜還高，並富含抗氧化物，後者若分量適中有助於保護細胞並讓細胞維持健康的時間更長久。另外，猴麵包樹果實中的抗氧化物在減少發炎上舉足輕重，對整體健康至關重要。猴麵包樹也藉由幫助支撐農場幾個世代來造福人類，因為這種巨大的樹木通常可存活好幾百年。猴麵包樹與其果實除了為人類帶來這一切好處外，也是許多種動物重要的食物來源和棲身之處。

D 1. 理由
- a. (A) **barren** [ˋbærən] *a.* （土地）貧瘠的
  - 例 The land is barren; in other words, nothing can grow on it.
    這塊地很貧瘠；換言之，上面長不出任何東西來。
  - (B) **complex** [kəmˋplɛks] *a.* 複雜的
    - 例 The professor spent three hours explaining the complex theory.
      教授花了三個小時解釋那個複雜的理論。
  - (C) **manageable** [ˋmænɪdʒəb!] *a.* 可應付的；可管理的
    - 例 Frustration is inevitable but manageable.
      挫折無法避免，但可以處理。
  - (D) **beneficial** [͵bɛnəˋfɪʃəl] *a.* 有益的
    - be beneficial to...　　對……有益
    - 例 Exercise is beneficial to your health.
      運動對健康有益。
- b. 根據語意，可知 (D) 項應為正選。

A 2. 理由
- a. (A) **contain** [kənˋten] *vt.* 包含，包括
  - 例 This drink doesn't contain any alcohol.
    這杯飲料不含任何酒精成分。
  - (B) **provoke** [prəˋvok] *vt.* 激怒；煽動
    - 例 Don't provoke that dog. It might bite you.
      不要激怒那隻狗。牠可能會咬你。

(C) **reverse** [rɪˋvɝs] *vt.* 顛倒，翻轉
例 No matter how hard Oedipus tried, he couldn't reverse his destiny in the end.
不論伊底帕斯如何努力嘗試，他最終仍是無法扭轉他的命運。

(D) **shriek** [ʃrik] *vi.* 尖叫 & *n.* 尖叫聲
例 Karen shrieked out loud when she saw a mouse in her kitchen.
凱倫在廚房裡看見一隻老鼠時放聲尖叫。

b. 根據語意，可知 (A) 項應為正選。

B 3. 理由
a. (A) **for the sake of...** 為了⋯⋯的緣故
例 John and Mary stayed together for the sake of their children.
約翰和瑪麗為了孩子的緣故還在一起。

(B) **with respect to...** 有關⋯⋯
= with / in regard to...
= regarding / concerning...
例 What did the bank manager say with respect to your request for a loan?
有關你申請貸款一事，銀行經理怎麼說？

(C) **by means of...** 藉由⋯⋯
例 Al solved his drinking problem by means of group therapy.
艾爾藉由團體治療解決了他的酗酒問題。

(D) **prior to...** 在⋯⋯之前
例 Prior to the accident, George was in perfect health. Now, he has trouble walking.
事故發生前喬治非常健康。現在他卻不良於行。

b. 根據語意，可知 (B) 項應為正選。

D 4. 理由
a. (A) **rare levels** 含量稀少
例 The scientist found rare levels of radiation in the area.
那位科學家在該地區發現了少量的輻射。

(B) **equal portions** 相等的份量
例 The host carefully divided the cake into equal portions for the guests.
主人仔細地將蛋糕分成相等的份量給賓客。

(C) **insufficient quantities** 數量不足
例 Insufficient quantities of vitamins can lead to serious health issues.
維生素攝取量不足可能導致嚴重的健康問題。

Unit 19

(D) **moderate amounts** 適當的數量

例 Drinking moderate amounts of coffee can boost concentration and alertness.
適量飲用咖啡可以提高專注力和警覺性。

b. 根據語意，可知 (D) 項應為正選。

B 5. 理由

a. (A) **fraction** [ˈfrækʃən] *n.* 小部分；微量
a fraction of... 一小部分的……

例 Vicky spends only a small fraction of her earnings on clothes.
維琪只花一小部分她賺的錢買衣服。

(B) **generation** [ˌdʒɛnəˈreʃən] *n.* 世代

例 Our generation gets married at a later age.
我們這一代較為晚婚。

(C) **banquet** [ˈbæŋkwɪt] *n.* 宴會，宴席

例 Are you going to the awards banquet on Saturday night?
你會去參加星期六晚上的頒獎宴會嗎？

(D) **adolescent** [ˌædəˈlɛsnt] *n.* 青春期的男女

例 I was quite rebellious when I was an adolescent.
我青少年時期相當叛逆。

b. 根據語意，可知 (B) 項應為正選。

重要單字與片語

1. **particular** [pəˈtɪkjələ] *a.* 特定的
   in particular 尤其；特定的（常置名詞後）

   例 Are you looking for anything in particular, sir?
   先生，您在找特定的東西嗎？

2. **amount** [əˈmaʊnt] *n.* 數量（與不可數名詞並用）
   a large amount of + 不可數單數名詞 大量的……
   a large number of + 可數複數名詞 眾多的……

   例 Paul has made a large amount of money.
   保羅賺了不少錢。

   Mike has collected a large number of foreign stamps.
   麥克收集了為數不少的外國郵票。

3. **magnesium** [mæɡˈnizɪəm] *n.* 鎂（不可數）

4. **calcium** [ˈkælsɪəm] *n.* 鈣（不可數）

5. **potassium** [pəˈtæsɪəm] *n.* 鉀（不可數）

6. **element** [ˈɛləmənt] *n.* 元素

7. **immunity** [ɪˈmjunətɪ] *n.* 免疫；豁免

8. **possess** [pəˈzɛs] *vt.* 擁有

   例 Sally possesses many qualities that would make her an excellent teacher.
   莎莉擁有許多特質，會使她成為一位很棒的老師。

9. **spinach** [ˈspɪnɪtʃ] n. 菠菜（不可數）
10. **considerable** [kənˈsɪdərəbl] a. 大量的；比較
    considerate [kənˈsɪdərɪt] a. 體貼的
11. **antioxidant** [ˌæntɪˈɑksɪdənt] n. 抗氧化物
12. **inflammation** [ˌɪnfləˈmeʃən] n. 炎（症）
13. **habitat** [ˈhæbəˌtæt] n. 動物棲息地

二、文意選填

　　赤腳學院是一間設立於印度的非政府組織。該學院在四十年前由一群人數不多、但受過良好教育的大學畢業生所創立。他們想要找到替代方法來解決在該國農村地區普遍的貧窮問題。這個機構的其中一門主要課程與太陽能相關，其目標是讓低度開發的農村社會變得更能自給自足。另一項目標是讓弱勢族群自主，尤其是未受過教育的婦女。

　　若想更領會赤腳學院的課程帶來的影響，首先需要了解印度最貧困地區的居民所面對的問題。在許多社區，電力不是短缺就是根本不存在，所以常常使用木柴來取暖、做飯，甚至照明。沒有木柴的時候，常用煤油代替。然而，那種油對居民來說不但昂貴，對環境也有害。

　　赤腳學院的太陽能課程傳授太陽能工程技術，為期六個月，對象是三十五歲以上不識字的婦女。這些剛受訓完的婦女一回到她們的社區便能使用接上電池的太陽能燈具組和面板。此外，該課程的費用全部由赤腳學院支付，參與課程的社區當地也成立了電子器材維修工作室。赤腳學院透過一項五萬美元的投資購買太陽能設備，此舉有助於提供足夠一百二十個家庭使用的能源，因此減少了他們對於木柴和煤油的依賴。赤腳學院藉由這種方式訓練婦女為自己的社區能源供應盡一份力，達成了一個值得尊敬的目標，就是在極需正面改變的地方改變民眾的生活。

I　6. 理由
　　a. 空格前有主詞 It 及 be 動詞 was，空格後有介詞 by 引導的介詞詞組，得知空格應置及物動詞的過去分詞，以與 was 及 by 形成被動語態。
　　b. 選項中為及物動詞的過去分詞的有 (B) accomplished（達成）及 (I) established（設立），惟根據語意，(I) 項應為正選。
　　c. **establish** [ɪˈstæblɪʃ] vt. 建立，創立（= set up）
　　　例 The school board of directors decided to establish a fund to help poor students.
　　　　學校董事會決定成立一項基金來資助清寒的學生。

Unit 19

Unit 19

C 7. 理由
   a. 空格前有形容詞 alternative（替代的），得知空格應置名詞以被該形容詞修飾。
   b. 選項中為名詞的有 (C) methods（方法）及 (H) expenses（花費），惟根據語意，(C) 項應為正選。
   c. **method** [ˈmɛθəd] *n.* 方法

J 8. 理由
   a. 空格前為一完整句子，得知後面應置 problems 的修飾詞，而空格後有代名詞 those 及關係代名詞 who 引導的形容詞子句 who live in India's poorest districts（居住在印度最貧困地區的），故空格置及物動詞的分詞以接 those 作受詞。
   b. 選項中為及物動詞的分詞的有 (B) accomplished（達成）、(D) reducing（減少）、(F) returning（返回）及 (J) facing（面對），惟根據語意，(J) 項應為正選。
   c. 此處 facing 為形容詞子句 which / that faces 省略關係代名詞 which / that 並將動詞 faces 改為現在分詞 facing 而來。
   d. **face** [fes] *vt.* 面對；朝向
      例 Even though there are so many challenges (which are) facing her, Anna still persists in what she is doing.
      儘管安娜要面對那麼多的挑戰，她仍然堅持她的所為。

A 9. 理由
   a. 空格前有 be 動詞 is 和 either，空格後有對等連接詞 or 及形容詞 nonexistent（不存在的），得知空格應置另一形容詞，以與 or 形成對等，即下列固定用法：
      either A or B　　不是 A 就是 B
      例 John is either sick or tired.
      約翰不是病了就是累了。
   b. 剩餘選項中為形容詞的有 (A) scarce（短缺的）、(B) accomplished（有才藝的）、(E) available（可取得的）及 (G) harmful（有害的），惟根據語意，(A) 項應為正選。
   c. **scarce** [skɛrs] *a.* 短缺的；稀少的

E 10. 理由
   a. 空格位於 When 引導的副詞子句中，空格前有子句的主詞 it（指前句中的 firewood（木柴））、be 動詞 is 和否定副詞 not，得知空格應置形容詞或分詞作主詞補語。
   b. 剩餘選項中為形容詞或分詞的有 (B) accomplished（達成）、(D) reducing（減少）、(E) available（可取得的）、(F) returning（返回）及 (G) harmful（有害的），惟根據語意，(E) 項應為正選。
   c. **available** [əˈveləbl̩] *a.* 可取得的；可用的

__G__ **11.** 理由

    a. 空格前有動詞 has，空格後有名詞 effects（影響），得知空格應置形容詞修飾該名詞。

    b. 剩餘選項中為形容詞的有 (B) accomplished（有才藝的）及 (G) harmful（有害的），惟根據語意，(G) 項應為正選。

    c. **harmful** [ˋhɑrmfəl] *a.* 有害的
       be harmful to sb/sth　　對某人或某物有害

__F__ **12.** 理由

    a. 空格前有介詞 Upon（一……），得知空格應置名詞或動名詞作其受詞。

    b. 剩餘選項中為名詞或動名詞的有 (D) reducing（減少）、(F) returning（返回）及 (H) expenses（花費），惟根據語意，(F) 項應為正選。

    c. **return** [rɪˋtɜn] *vi.* 返回 & *vt.* 還給
       例 The moment George returned to his hometown, the neighbors welcomed him.
       喬治一回到家鄉，就受到鄰居們的歡迎。

    d. **upon** [əˋpɑn] *prep.* 一……（就……）
       Upon + V-ing, 主要子句
   = As soon as 引導的副詞子句, 主要子句
   = The moment 引導的副詞子句, 主要子句
       例 Upon seeing Mary, I cried.
       = As soon as I saw Mary, I cried.
       = The moment I saw Mary, I cried.
       我一見到瑪麗就哭了。

__H__ **13.** 理由

    a. 空格前有及物動詞 pays（支付）和數量形容詞 all（全部的），得知空格應置名詞。

    b. 剩餘選項中僅剩 (H) expenses（費用）為名詞，置入空格後符合語意及用法，故為正選。

    c. **expense** [ɪkˋspɛns] *n.* 花費，支出

__D__ **14.** 理由

    a. 空格前為一完整句子及一逗點，空格後有名詞詞組 their reliance on firewood and kerosene（他們對於木柴和煤油的依賴），得知空格應置剩餘選項中的 (D) reducing（減少），以接該名詞詞組作受詞。此處 reducing 原為形容詞子句 which reduces their... 省略關係代名詞 which 並將動詞 reduces 改為現在分詞 reducing 而來。

    b. 根據上述，(D) 項應為正解。

    c. **reduce** [rɪˋdjus] *vt.* 減少；降低
       例 The new law was enacted to reduce crime.
       制訂這條新法是為了減少犯罪。

Unit 19

Unit 19

B 15. 理由

a. 空格前有現在完成式助動詞 has，空格後有名詞詞組 a worthy objective（一個值得尊敬的目標），得知空格應置及物動詞的過去分詞，以與 has 組成現在完成式。

b. 剩餘選項 (B) accomplished（達成）為及物動詞之過去分詞，置入空格後符合語意及用法，故為正選。

c. **accomplish** [əˈkɑmplɪʃ] *vt.* 達到（目標）；完成（任務）

例 How on earth did you accomplish this difficult task in such a short time?
你究竟是如何在這麼短的時間內完成這項艱難的任務？

重要單字與片語

1. **decade** [ˈdɛked] *n.* 十年
2. **well-educated** [ˌwɛlˈɛdʒəˌketɪd] *a.* 受過良好教育的
3. **alternative** [ɔlˈtɝnətɪv] *a.* 替代的；另類的
4. **poverty** [ˈpɑvɚtɪ] *n.* 貧窮（不可數）
5. **rural** [ˈrʊrəl] *a.* 鄉村的
   比較
   urban [ˈɝbən] *a.* 城市的
6. **institution** [ˌɪnstəˈtuʃən] *n.* 機構
7. **program** [ˈprogræm] *n.* 課程；學程
8. **underdeveloped** [ˌʌndɚdɪˈvɛləpt] *a.* 低度開發的
9. **self-sufficient** [ˌsɛlfsəˈfɪʃənt] *a.* 自給自足的
10. **empower** [ɪmˈpaʊɚ] *vt.* 使自主；賦予權力

例 The new law empowered the police to search private houses.
新的法律讓警察有權力搜索民宅。

11. **appreciate** [əˈpriʃɪˌet] *vt.* 了解；欣賞；感激

例 Do you fully appreciate the risk you are taking?
你完全了解你所冒的風險嗎？

12. **nonexistent** [ˌnɑnɪgˈzɪstənt] *a.* 不存在的
13. **numerous** [ˈn(j)umərəs] *a.* 眾多的，許多的
14. **illiterate** [ɪˈlɪtərət] *a.* 不識字的
    比較
    literate [ˈlɪtərət] *a.* 識字的
15. **investment** [ɪnˈvɛstmənt] *n.* 投資
16. **thereby** [ˈðɛrˌbaɪ / ðɛrˈbaɪ] *adv.* 因此
17. **worthy** [ˈwɝðɪ] *a.* 值得的；值得尊敬的
    worthy of + N/Ving   值得……
18. **objective** [əbˈdʒɛktɪv] *n.* 目標

篇章結構

常言道：「狗是人類最好的朋友。」擁有一隻菲多或來福為伴可能很有趣，但重要的是飼主得確保給他們的寵物充分的機會進行戶外運動。不過，由於市區裡針對狗的所有限制，這麼做會是一項挑戰。這包括了市中心的公園和其他受歡迎的遊樂場所的禁令。此外，許多城市的大眾運輸工具禁止攜帶動物。

對於沒有車子或搭不起計程車的人來說，在他們試圖帶著他們的狗離開城市的時候，這會造成問題。因此許多狗主人努力尋找可以讓他們的愛狗自由奔跑以及與其他狗狗交流的合適場所。對香港的寵物飼主來說，還好有兩位民眾厭倦了這個情況，終於決定對此採取行動。他們開創了一項對寵物友善的公車服務，稱作狗狗巴士。

從 2012 年起，香港的狗主人們開始利用狗狗巴士。這項公車服務在週末和公定假日提供了香港各地和周邊地區的許多路線，並在若干遊憩區設有站牌。這讓飼主可以輕鬆帶著愛犬前往海灘、登山步道及開放式公園，不再需要擔憂受到交通限制。這些年來狗狗巴士已定期新增站牌，發展成一條半永久式的路線，並相當受到香港愛狗人士的喜愛。

狗主人對於能夠更容易和他們的狗狗一起旅遊感到興奮，所以對於狗狗巴士這項活動一向感到興致勃勃。舉個例子說明熱烈的程度，狗狗巴士的臉書社群已擁有大量按讚數，並有許多狗狗在公園和海灘的歡樂照片。一些飼主甚至透過該服務規劃團體出遊活動，使這成為狗狗和飼主得以外出社交的大好機會。狗狗巴士的成功也激發了關於香港公共交通是否應更具寵物友善性的討論。狗狗巴士很顯然是一項香港狗主人極為重視的服務。

D **16. 理由**

    a. 空格後句提及公園和其他受歡迎的遊樂場所的禁令，呼應選項 (D) 中提及的 the restrictions related to dogs in urban areas（市區裡針對狗的限制）。選項 (D) 置入空格後，後句的主詞 These 即指該選項中的 restrictions，而 Doing so（這麼做）則指空格前句中的 give their pets sufficient opportunities for outdoor exercise（給他們的寵物充分的機會進行戶外運動），語意承先啟後。

    b. 根據上述，(D) 項應為正選。

A **17. 理由**

    a. 空格前兩句敘述對狗運動的限制及交通問題對狗主人帶來困擾，許多狗主人因而努力尋找可以讓愛狗奔跑及與其他狗狗交流的合適場所，選項 (A) 中的 were fed up with the situation（厭倦了這個情況）指涉所述的不便。

    b. 空格後句提及一項新服務 a pet-friendly bus service（對寵物友善的公車服務），而選項 (A) 中的 decided to do something about it（決定對此採取行動）所指的行動即此項新交通服務。

    c. 根據上述，(A) 項應為正選。

C **18. 理由**

    a. 空格前句，即第二段末句提及一項新公車服務 99 Bus（狗狗巴士），而選項 (C) 敘述狗狗巴士於 2012 年啟用，承接前句並進一步說明。

    b. 空格後句提及公車服務的內容，句中主詞 The bus service（這項公車服務）承接選項 (C) 作進一步說明。

    c. 根據上述，(C) 項應為正選。

Unit 19

B 19. 理由
  a. 第三段最後一句提及狗狗巴士相當受到香港愛狗人士的喜愛，空格後句則舉例說明這項服務如何受到歡迎，而選項 (B) 敘述愛狗人士對於此項服務感到 thrilled（興奮的）以及 enthusiastic（興致勃勃），皆為顯示狗狗巴士服務受到正面的評價。
  b. 根據上述，(B) 項應為正選。

(E) 選項翻譯 如果沒有適當的運動，狗狗會出現許多同樣困擾主人的健康問題。

重要單字與片語

1. **companion** [kəmˋpænjən] *n.* 同伴
2. **enjoyable** [ɪnˋdʒɔɪəbḷ] *a.* 有趣的；愉快的
3. **challenging** [ˋtʃæləndʒɪŋ] *a.* 有挑戰性的
4. **restriction** [rɪˋstrɪkʃən] *n.* 限制
5. **ban** [bæn] *n.* 禁令
   impose a ban on...　　對⋯⋯施以禁令
   lift the ban on...　　解除對⋯⋯的禁令
6. **prohibit** [prəˋhɪbɪt] *vt.* 禁止
   prohibit sb from + V-ing　禁止某人做⋯⋯
   = forbid sb to V
   例 The government prohibits stores from selling alcohol to minors.
   政府禁止商家販賣酒類給未成年人。
7. **socialize** [ˋsoʃəˌlaɪz] *vi.* 與人交際
   socialize with sb　與某人交際
   例 David enjoys socializing with new people at business conferences.
   大衛喜歡在商務會議上與新朋友交流。
8. **be fed up with...**　受夠⋯⋯
   例 Cindy is fed up with her neighbor's noises.
   辛蒂已經受夠了她鄰居所製造的噪音。
9. **outskirts** [ˋaʊtˌskɝts] *n.* 郊區（恆用複數）
   on the outskirts of...　在⋯⋯的周遭，在⋯⋯的郊區
10. **barrier** [ˋbærɪr] *n.* 障礙（物）
11. **thrilled** [θrɪld] *a.* 興奮的
12. **enthusiastic** [ɪnˌθ(j)uzɪˋæstɪk] *a.* 熱忱的
    be enthusiastic about + N/V-ing
    對⋯⋯充滿熱忱
13. **outing** [ˋaʊtɪŋ] *n.* （團體的）遠足，短途旅行
14. **valued** [ˋvæljud] *a.* 重要的；有用的；有價值的
15. **plague** [pleg] *vt.* 使難受，受煎熬 & *n.* 瘟疫
    例 Health problems have plagued Kenny for years, affecting his daily life.
    健康問題困擾了肯尼多年，影響了他的日常生活。

四 閱讀測驗

　　西元前五世紀初，希臘是由一群相互征戰的城邦組成。然而在西元前 480 年時，許多城邦團結起來對抗一個共同的敵人：決心將希臘納入波斯帝國的薛西斯國王麾下的波斯軍隊。薛西斯和他的三十萬大軍推進通過幾個希臘地區，不戰即成功將它們占領之後，來到一個叫做溫泉關的狹窄山隘。在那裡等待著他們的是斯巴達城邦國王列奧尼達、他的七千名士兵，和一隊三百名訓練精良的死士。

　　薛西斯期待斯巴達人會了解到他們寡不敵眾而立刻投降。不過列奧尼達認為山隘地形對斯巴達人有利，因為敵軍的移動會受限，無法部署足夠的兵力。結果列奧尼達大體上賭對了：當波斯人攻擊時，很明顯他們並不適合在那種環境作戰，而斯巴達人則有更優良的訓練和武器。當越來越多的波斯士兵被殺死，他的軍隊被迫撤退，薛西斯極為憤怒。

　　他很幸運，有一名當地的牧羊人決定背叛斯巴達人，告訴薛西斯一條避開山隘的替代路線。這條路線讓薛西斯在山隘另一側擺上一萬名士兵，因而將斯巴達人包圍。雖然對情勢感到震驚，列奧尼達卻拒絕投降，誓言要和他的三百名戰士留下來奮戰至死。斯巴達人英勇奮戰，先用槍矛和劍，後來赤手空拳，但最終還是被擊敗。列奧尼達陣亡，他的三百名戰士也大多喪生。然而他們並沒有無妄犧牲。他們勇敢抵抗的故事激勵了其他希臘城邦繼續對抗波斯人，希臘人在後來的戰役中取得了決定性的勝利。

B 　20. 根據本文，在溫泉關戰役前發生何事？
　　　　(A) 波斯帝國已經被嚴重削弱。
　　　　(B) 波斯軍隊已征服希臘許多地區
　　　　(C) 希臘統治者已被另一個國王取代。
　　　　(D) 希臘人已與波斯人簽署和平協議。

　　　　理由
　　　　根據本文第一段第三句，可知 (B) 項應為正選。

B 　21. 為什麼薛西斯認為斯巴達人會馬上向攻擊者投降？
　　　　(A) 斯巴達人不熟悉山隘。
　　　　(B) 波斯士兵比斯巴達人多很多。
　　　　(C) 波斯人俘虜了斯巴達軍隊的領袖。
　　　　(D) 斯巴達人之中有紀律問題。

　　　　理由
　　　　根據本文第二段第一句，可知 (B) 項應為正選。

D **22.** 波斯人如何取得對斯巴達人的優勢？
   (A) 藉由獲得更好的武器。
   (B) 藉由增派數千名士兵。
   (C) 藉由騙得列奧尼達投降。
   (D) 藉由聽從一名背叛之人的建議。

   理由
   根據第三段第一、二句，可知 (D) 項應為正選。

C **23.** 哪一組字是列奧尼達和他的三百名戰士在溫泉關戰役中的情緒變化之最佳描述？
   (A) 震驚的 → 幸運的 → 無望的
   (B) 安心的 → 恐懼的 → 樂觀的
   (C) 自信的 → 驚訝的 → 無懼的
   (D) 受騙的 → 有望的 → 成功的

   理由
   根據本文第二段提及列奧尼達認為山隘地形對斯巴達人有利，但第三段則提及他對於薛西斯在山隘另一側駐紮士兵，包圍他們感到震驚，但他們誓言奮戰至死，可知 (C) 項應為正選。

重要單字與片語

1. **band together** 團結；聯合
2. **squad** [skwɑd] *n.* 小隊，小組
3. **outnumber** [aʊtˋnʌmbɚ] *vt.*（數量上）勝過（本文為過去分詞作形容詞用）
   例 New Zealand is a country where the sheep population outnumbers the human population.
   紐西蘭是個羊口多於人口的國家。
4. **surrender** [səˋrɛndɚ] *vi.* & *vt.*（使）投降 & *n.* 投降
   例 After days of battle, the enemy troops finally surrendered.
   經過連日交戰，敵軍終於投降。
5. **terrain** [ˋtɛrən] *n.* 地形；地勢（不可數）
6. **deploy** [dɪˋplɔɪ] *vt.* 調動，部署（部隊等）

   例 The Minister of National Defense agreed to deploy another five hundred troops to guard this region.
   國防部長同意再派遣五百名軍隊來保衛這個地區。
7. **retreat** [rɪˋtrit] *vi.* & *n.* 撤退
   例 The troops retreated when they knew they couldn't win the battle.
   當部隊發覺打不贏這一仗後便撤退了。
8. **betray** [bɪˋtre] *vt.* 背叛；（無意中）暴露
   例 That man betrayed his wife to the secret police.
   那個男子將老婆出賣給祕密警察。

9. **perish** [ˈpɛrɪʃ] *vi.* 慘死，猝死
   例 Hundreds of passengers perished in the plane crash.
   有好幾百名乘客在此空難中喪生。

10. **resistance** [rɪˈzɪstəns] *n.* 抗拒；（身體的）抵抗力

11. **decisive** [dɪˈsaɪsɪv] *a.* 決定性的；果決的；確定的

五 混合題

給學生家庭作業的好處與壞處是什麼？我們詢問了四個人的意見。

傑克
我是用功的學生，一向準時完成並繳交家庭作業。不過你若知道我並不喜歡做作業而且覺得有些作業沒有意義時，應該不會感到太意外。家庭作業理應幫助我們更理解上課所教的科目，但實質上我覺得幾乎沒用。許多時候感覺像是老師只是為了該寫作業而交代作業。還有就是我們得用寶貴的空閒時間來做作業。這影響到我們參加課外活動與從事有成就感的嗜好的能力，是種負面的影響。

班
我給學生的每項家庭作業，在加強課堂上剛教過的概念與科目上都扮演著關鍵的角色。它是特別設計來幫助學生增進他們的理解。當然，家庭作業得因材施教，意思是隨著學生的年紀增長，給他們的作業量與難度也會提升。家庭作業也幫助即將畢業的學生學習時間管理技能。能夠在期限內做完工作，在當今的職場中是很基礎的技能。

媞娜
沒有人喜歡做家庭作業，我們的作業多到爆炸，還要準時完成，讓我們學生備感壓力。但客觀一點說，我知道家庭作業是校園生活的必要部分。它幫我們鞏固講過課程中的知識，並幫我們對還沒講的課程有所準備。如果沒有家庭作業，我們無法在課堂討論中提出精彩的發言。家庭作業也給予我們用自己的節奏讀書的較大彈性，譬如說如果我們覺得某科特別難，我們就能多花點時間在那科上。

蜜雪兒
我理所當然會給所有的學生交代家庭作業。不過有時候我實在很難體會家庭作業的益處，而且覺得我們給太多作業了。它們加重學生的壓力，而他們已經對考試及其他的投

Unit 19

入事項感到焦慮了。我了解並非所有學生都擁有可安心寫作業的家庭環境，而我擔心他們的福祉。家庭作業也大幅增加我的工作量，因為我得要準備作業、批改，還要盯著那些沒寫完作業的學生。

24. 傑克表示老師給他的家庭作業分量影響了他對課外休閒活動的<u>參與</u>。

理由

空格前有代名詞所有格 his，空格後有介詞 in，得知空格應置名詞。根據傑克意見的最後一句 "This has a negative impact on our ability to participate in extracurricular activities and rewarding hobbies."（這影響到我們參加課外活動與從事有成就感的嗜好的能力，是種負面的影響。）得知，空格應置與 participate 相關的名詞 participation。

25. 班在幫家庭作業辯護時提到年齡，表示年齡較大的學生能夠對付較<u>困難的</u>作業。

理由

空格前有副詞 more，空格後有名詞 tasks，得知空格應置形容詞。根據班意見的第四句 "This means that as the age of the students increases, so does the amount and difficulty of the homework I give them."（意思是隨著學生的年紀增長，給他們的作業量與難度也會提升。）得知，空格應置與 difficulty 相關的形容詞 difficult。

請根據意見填入正確的名字。

26. 媞娜指出太多家庭作業會讓學生感到憂慮，<u>蜜雪兒</u>也同樣提及這項論述。

理由

根據蜜雪兒意見的第三句 "Homework increases the pressure on the students, who are already feeling anxious about exams and other commitments."（它們加重學生的壓力，而他們已經對考試及其他的投入事項感到焦慮了。）得知，空格應置 Michelle。

27. 班與媞娜認可家庭作業有助加強課堂所教的概念，但<u>傑克強烈懷疑這項論述</u>。

理由

根據傑克意見的第三句 "It's supposed to help us understand the topics from class better, but I think this rarely happens in practice."（家庭作業理應幫助我們更理解上課所教的科目，但實質上我覺得幾乎沒用。）得知，空格應置 Jake。

28. 在意見中的哪個片語表示「聯絡或找到某人以取得某物」？

chase up（催促）

理由

根據蜜雪兒意見的最後一句 "Homework also massively increases my workload, as I have to prepare the assignments, grade them, and chase up the students who haven't completed them."（家庭作業也大幅增加我的工作量，因為我得要準備作業、批改，還要盯著那些沒寫完作業的學生。），可推知 chase up 應為正解。

重要單字與片語

1. **diligent** [ˈdɪlədʒənt] *a.* 勤勉的
2. **in practice** 實際上
   例 Well, that sounds good in theory, but I don't know if it will work in practice.
   嗯，理論上那聽起來不錯，但我不知道它實際上是否可行。
3. **sake** [sek] *n.* 理由，緣故
   for the sake of... 為了……的緣故
   例 For the sake of your health, you should break the habit of smoking immediately.
   為了你的健康著想，你應立刻戒掉抽菸的習慣。
4. **extracurricular** [ˌɛkstrəkəˈrɪkjələ] *a.* 課外的
5. **reinforce** [ˌriɪnˈfɔrs] *vt.* 增強，強化
   例 Keeping a diary helps to reinforce your writing skills.
   寫日記可幫助強化你的寫作技巧。

6. **pitch** [pɪtʃ] *vt.* 調整至某水準
7. **objectively** [əbˈdʒɛktɪvlɪ] *adv.* 客觀地
   例 Objectively speaking, Duke can't possibly succeed if he doesn't work harder.
   客觀地說，若杜克不更加努力，他絕無成功的可能。
8. **solidify** [səˈlɪdəˌfaɪ] *vt.* 強化，鞏固
9. **chase sb up** 催促某人
   例 I need to chase my colleague up about the project deadline tomorrow.
   我得催促我同事有關專案明天到期的事。
10. **reference** [ˈrɛfərəns] *vt.* 談及，提及
    例 I will reference this book to support my argument in the research paper.
    我會談及這本書來支持我研究報告中的論述。

Unit 19

Unit 20

一 綜合測驗

澳門以賭博聞名，但那裡也是一些精彩娛樂活動的大本營，其中包括一個非看不可的景點，就是新濠天地的水舞間。八十五分鐘的表演在座位可容納兩千人的圓形劇場中舉行，主打令人驚奇的道具、精湛的跳水特技、令人嘆為觀止的體操表演和水舞。劇場裡還有一座巨大的水池，內含將近四百萬加侖的水量，足以填滿五座奧運規格的游泳池。

表演開場時是一名漁夫在一艘小船上的平靜景象，但隨著一艘海盜船的船桅從水池深處升起以及漁夫消失在漩渦裡，很快就變成一片混亂。之後，表演者從船桅的索具一盪而下，接著潛入下方水池十公尺深處。表演沒有隨著海盜船沒入水中而當場結束。相反地，海盜船被一座厚實的舞臺取代，表演者在臺上繼續為觀眾帶來震撼。最棒的是，置於舞臺各處的兩百四十多根水柱搭配著音樂，以「水舞」的形式朝空中噴水，高度超過十八公尺。這絕對是非看不可的景象！

C 1. 理由

a. 原句實為：
The 85-minute show features amazing props, great diving stunts, breathtaking gymnastics, and dancing water, the 85-minute show takes place in a circular theater that holds 2,000 seats.
上句包含兩個句構完整的子句，但兩個子句之間並無連接詞連接，不合乎文法。惟兩句有相同主詞 the 85-minute show（八十五分鐘的表演），因此可將第一句的主詞省略，再將動詞 features 改為現在分詞 featuring 形成分詞構句。

b. 根據上述用法，(C) 項應為正選。

A 2. 理由

a. (A) **massive** [ˈmæsɪv] *a.* 巨大的；大而重的
   例 A massive sign just fell off the building.
   一個巨大的招牌剛從那棟建築上掉落。

(B) **slight** [slaɪt] *a.* 輕微的；微小的
   例 The rain sent a slight chill down my back.
   雨水從我的背上流下，使我感到些微寒意。

(C) **prosperous** [ˈprɑspərəs] *a.* 繁榮的，興隆的
   例 Although the city is prosperous, the standard of living is on the decline.
   雖然這城市很繁榮，但是它的生活水準正在下降。

(D) **parallel** [ˈpærəlɛl] *a.* 平行的
   例 The gymnast swung on the parallel bars.
   那位體操員在雙槓上搖擺。
b. 根據語意，可知 (A) 項應為正選。

B 3. 理由
   a. (A) **hint at failures**　暗示失敗
      hint at...　暗示……
      例 The movie's ending hints at a sequel next year.
      這部電影的結局暗示了明年會有續集。
   (B) **turn into chaos**　變成混亂
      turn into...　變成……
      chaos [ˈkeɑs] *n.* 混亂（不可數）
      be in chaos　處於混亂的狀態
      例 Over the course of several years, Terence's small business turned into a global company.
      經過數年時間，泰倫斯的小型企業變成了一家全球性公司。
      I spent the whole afternoon tidying up my room because it was in chaos.
      我花了一整個下午整理房間，因為裡面亂七八糟。
   (C) **stir up memories**　喚起回憶
      stir up + N　喚起……
      例 The writer's new book stirred up strong emotions in the younger generation.
      那位作家的新書喚起了年輕一代強烈的情緒。
   (D) **contribute to progress**　促使進步
      contribute to + N/V-ing　促進……
      例 Reading books contributes to the expansion of one's knowledge and the development of critical thinking skills.
      閱讀書籍有助於拓展知識並培養批判性思維能力。
   b. 根據語意，可知 (B) 項應為正選。

D 4. 理由
   a. (A) **procedure** [prəˈsidʒɚ] *n.* 程序
      例 Let me acquaint you with our company's standard operating procedure.
      讓我來帶你熟悉一下我們公司的標準作業程序。

Unit 20

  (B) **maintenance** [ˈmentənəns] *n.* 維持；維修（不可數）

   例 With the car in the maintenance shop, Martha had to take the bus to work.
   因為車子進廠保養，所以瑪莎不得不搭公車上班。

  (C) **superstition** [ˌsupɚˈstɪʃən] *n.* 迷信

   例 Many superstitions actually have scientific explanations behind them.
   許多迷信背後其實都有科學上的解釋。

  (D) **entertainment** [ˌɛntɚˈtenmənt] *n.* 娛樂，樂趣（不可數）；娛樂節目（可數）

   例 There wasn't much entertainment in the tiny village.
   這個小村莊裡沒有太多娛樂活動。

 b. 根據語意，可知 (D) 項應為正選。

B 5. 理由

 a. (A) **suppress** [səˈprɛs] *vt.* 鎮壓

   例 The dictator took measures to suppress opposition.
   那名獨裁者採取措施來鎮壓反對勢力。

  (B) **coordinate** [koˈɔrdn̩ˌet] *vt.* 協調；相配

   例 The manager coordinated the arrangements for the company trip.
   經理協調安排員工旅遊事宜。

  (C) **nominate** [ˈnɑməˌnet] *vt.* 提名
   nominate sb as...　　提名某人擔任……

   例 Victor nominated Carol as the head of the committee.
   維克特提名卡蘿為委員會的主席。

  (D) **strengthen** [ˈstrɛŋθən] *vt.* 鞏固，加強

   例 Doing push-ups is a great way to strengthen your chest.
   做伏地挺身是強化胸肌絕佳的方法。

 b. 根據語意，可知 (B) 項應為正選。

重要單字與片語

1. **be known for...**　以……聞名
= be famous for...
 例 That restaurant is known for its fried chicken.
 那間餐廳以炸雞出名。

2. **gambling** [ˈgæmblɪŋ] *n.* 賭博（不可數）
 gamble [ˈgæmbl̩] *vi.* 賭博

 例 James loves to gamble by buying lottery tickets each week.
 詹姆斯喜歡每個禮拜買彩券來賭一賭。

3. **fantastic** [fænˈtæstɪk] *a.* 極好的

4. **must-see** [ˈmʌstˌsi] *a.* 必看的 & *n.* 必看的事物

5. **attraction** [ə`trækʃən] *n.* 吸引人的事物
6. **amazing** [ə`mezɪŋ] *a.* 令人驚奇的
7. **gymnastics** [dʒɪm`næstɪks] *n.* 體操（不可數）
8. **circular** [`sɝkjəlɚ] *a.* 圓形的
9. **pirate** [`paɪrət] *n.* 海盜
10. **whirlpool** [`wɝl͵pul] *n.* 漩渦
11. **thrill** [θrɪl] *vt.* 令人興奮或激動 & *n.* 興奮；激動
    It thrills sb to V　從事……令某人興奮激動
    > It thrills me to hear that you are doing so well, Chris.
    > 克里斯，聽到你表現這麼好，真令我興奮。

二、文意選填

棒球在臺灣流行到不可思議的地步，它是那麼流行以至於被視為島上的代表運動。該運動如此受歡迎的一個理由就是距今超過八十五年前，有一支來自嘉義、暱稱為 Kano（編按：嘉農，指日據時代的「嘉義農林學校」）的傳奇隊伍取得成功。Kano 成軍於 1928 年，當時臺灣被日本帝國統治，Kano 的隊員包括了日本人、漢人及原住民。是島上唯一一支有非日籍運動員的隊伍。

Kano 是一支優秀的球隊，事實上，他們非常優秀以至於獲得了代表臺灣參加日本的全國高等學校棒球錦標賽的參賽權。這項比賽簡稱為「甲子園」，在日本備受尊崇，還是該國歷史最悠久的錦標賽。儘管 Kano 在六百三十支從日本帝國各地前來參與這場盛事的其他球隊中不被看好，隊員們藉由超出眾人期望的表現證明了自己。Kano 在首三場賽事中輕易地擊敗了對手，替自己取得了甲子園決賽的一席資格。這被認為是一項幾乎像奇蹟般的成就。然而，Kano 如童話故事般贏得冠軍的結局並沒有發生；最後，一支更強勁的日本隊伍以四比零的成績完勝 Kano，讓這支來自臺灣的隊伍名列第二。Kano 在比賽中優異的表現贏得了日本隊伍的尊敬。此外，在臺灣人之間掀起了一股對棒球的濃厚興趣，這成為了一股熱潮，推動這項運動取得了持續至今的地位。

__B__ 6. 理由
a. 空格前有不定冠詞 a，空格後有單數可數名詞 team（隊伍），得知空格應置形容詞，以修飾該名詞。
b. 選項中可作形容詞的有 (B) legendary（傳奇的）、(F) miraculous（奇蹟般的）、(G) defeated（被擊敗的）及 (J) aboriginal（原住民的），惟根據語意，(B) 項應為正選。
c. **legendary** [`lɛdʒəndɛrɪ] *a.* 傳說中的；非常有名的

Unit 20

__J__ **7.** 理由

    a. 空格前有 be 動詞 were、兩個形容詞 Japanese, Han Chinese（日本人、漢人），及對等連接詞 and，得知空格應置另一個形容詞，以與前面兩個形容詞形成對等。

    b. 剩餘選項中可作形容詞的有 (F) miraculous（奇蹟般的）、(G) defeated（被擊敗的）及 (J) aboriginal（原住民的），惟 (J) 項與空格前的兩個形容詞語意相關，故應為正選。

    c. **aboriginal** [ˌæbəˈrɪdʒənḷ] *a.* 原住民的

__H__ **8.** 理由

    a. 空格前有過去式及物動詞 had（有）、副詞 any（任何）和形容詞 non-Japanese（非日籍的），得知空格應置名詞以被該形容詞修飾，並組成名詞詞組作 had 的受詞。

    b. 剩餘選項中為名詞的有 (A) counterparts（對應的人或物）、(E) expectations（期望）及 (H) athletes（運動員），惟根據語意，(H) 項應為正選。

    c. **athlete** [ˈæθlit] *n.* 運動員

__D__ **9.** 理由

    a. 空格位於 that 子句中，空格前有子句的主詞 they，空格後有名詞詞組 the right（權利），得知空格應置及物動詞，以接該名詞詞組作受詞。

    b. 剩餘選項中為及物動詞的有 (C) esteemed（尊敬）、(D) earned（贏得）、(G) defeated（擊敗）及 (I) propelled（推動），惟根據語意，(D) 項應為正選。

    c. **earn** [ɝn] *vt.* 贏得；賺得

      例 Henry earned decent pay at his new job.
      亨利的新工作薪水還不錯。

__C__ **10.** 理由

    a. 空格前有 be 動詞 is 及副詞 highly（高度地），得知空格應置及物動詞的過去分詞，以被該副詞修飾，並與 is 組成被動語態。

    b. 剩餘選項中為及物動詞的過去分詞的有 (C) esteemed（尊敬）、(G) defeated（擊敗）及 (I) propelled（推動），惟根據語意，(C) 項應為正選。

    c. **esteem** [ɪˈstim] *vt.* 尊敬（= look up to）

      例 Bill is highly esteemed for his medical research.
      比爾因為他的醫學研究而備受尊崇。

__E__ **11.** 理由

    a. 空格前有介詞 beyond（超出），得知空格應置名詞，作 beyond 的受詞。

    b. 剩餘選項中為名詞的有 (A) counterparts（對應的人或物）及 (E) expectations（期望），惟根據語意，(E) 項應為正選。

c. **expectation** [ˌɛkspɛkˈteʃən] *n.* 期望（多用複數）
   meet sb's expectations　達成某人的期望
   = live up to sb's expectations

G **12.** 理由

a. 空格前有主詞 Kano 和副詞 easily（輕易地），空格後有名詞詞組 their opponents（他們的對手），得知空格內應置及物動詞，以接該名詞詞組作受詞。

b. 剩餘選項中 (G) defeated（擊敗）及 (I) propelled（推動）為及物動詞，惟根據語意，(G) 項應為正選。

c. **defeat** [dɪˈfit] *vt.* 擊敗，打敗 & *n.* 失敗，挫敗
   例 The powerful army defeated its enemy easily.
   這支強大的軍隊輕而易舉地擊潰了敵人。

F **13.** 理由

a. 空格前有不定冠詞 a 及副詞 nearly（幾乎），空格後有名詞 achievement（成就），得知空格應置形容詞以修飾該名詞，並被 nearly 修飾。

b. 剩餘選項中僅 (F) miraculous（奇蹟般的）為形容詞，且置入空格後符合語意，故為正選。

c. **miraculous** [məˈrækjələs] *a.* 奇蹟般的；不可思議的

A **14.** 理由

a. 空格前有代名詞所有格 their 和形容詞 Japanese（日本的），得知空格應置名詞，以被 Japanese 修飾。

b. 剩餘選項中僅 (A) counterparts（對應的人或物）為名詞，且置入空格後符合語意，故為正選。

c. **counterpart** [ˈkaʊntɚˌpɑrt] *n.* 對應的人或物
   例 The company sent two salespeople to negotiate with their counterparts.
   公司派了兩位業務員與對方的業務員協商。

I **15.** 理由

a. 空格位於關係代名詞 that 引導的形容詞子句中，that 指涉前面的先行詞 passion（熱情；熱潮），作形容詞子句的主詞，且空格後有名詞詞組 the sport（這項運動），得知空格應置及物動詞，以接該名詞詞組作受詞。

b. 剩餘選項 (I) propelled（推動）為及物動詞，且置入空格後符合語意，故為正選。

c. **propel** [prəˈpɛl] *vt.* 推動，推進
   例 The force of the wind propelled the garbage can across the lawn.
   強風把垃圾筒從草坪的一邊吹到另一邊。

Unit **20**

Unit 20

重要單字與片語

1. **incredibly** [ɪnˋkrɛdəblɪ] *adv.* 不可思議地

2. **so much so that...** 到如此程度以至於……
   此處 much so 代替之前的形容詞或副詞
   例 The restaurant was noisy, so much so (= noisy) that I couldn't put up with it and had to leave.
   餐廳非常吵鬧，吵到我無法忍受只得離開。
   注意
   本文中 Baseball in Taiwan is incredibly popular, so much so that...
   = Baseball in Taiwan is incredibly popular, so popular that...

3. **signature** [ˋsɪgnətʃɚ] *a.* 有代表特色，體現個體特徵的
   a signature dish　　招牌菜

4. **nickname** [ˋnɪk͵nem] *vt.* 給……取綽號 & *n.* 綽號
   例 Mary nicknamed John "Piggy."
   瑪麗給約翰取了個綽號叫「小豬」。

5. **form** [fɔrm] *vt. & vi.* 形成；組成
   例 We formed a circle and danced around the campfire.
   我們圍成一個圓圈並繞著營火跳舞。

6. **imperial** [ɪmˋpɪrɪəl] *a.* 帝國的
   an imperial family　　皇室

7. **represent** [͵rɛprɪˋzɛnt] *vt.* 代表
   例 Mr. Johnson was chosen to represent the company at the meeting.
   強森先生被選派代表公司出席該會議。

8. **championship** [ˋtʃæmpɪən͵ʃɪp] *n.* 冠軍賽；冠軍身分

9. **tournament** [ˋtɝnəmənt] *n.* 錦標賽

10. **underdog** [ˋʌndɚ͵dɔg] *n.* 處於劣勢的人或隊伍

11. **opponent** [əˋponənt] *n.* 對手

12. **achievement** [əˋtʃivmənt] *n.* 成就

13. **a fairy tale** 童話故事

14. **superb** [suˋpɝb] *a.* 優秀的

篇章結構

　　魯比克方塊是有史以來最成功的益智玩具。它挑戰了數百萬人的心智，並成為智力與解決問題能力的象徵。然而這種玩具很不容易玩，許多人試了幾次後就無可奈何地雙手一攤、發誓不再嘗試然後放棄。<u>魯比克方塊由身兼建築師和教授的匈牙利人爾諾・魯比克於 1974 年發明，一開始叫做魔術方塊。</u>魯比克於一九七〇年代後期將魔術方塊授權給美國的理想玩具公司後，這種由白色、紅色、藍色、綠色、黃色和橘色多個正方形組成的玩意兒便改以發明者的名字來命名。

　　魯比克發明魔術方塊後不久，他讓他的學生試玩他的這項發明，結果他們非常喜歡。<u>這讓這位教授得出一個結論：他這個具創意的方塊可能會有廣大的吸引力。</u>結果證明魯比克的推論是正確的。在理想玩具公司的行銷推廣下，魯比克方塊幾乎是一炮而紅，成為一九八〇年代的指標性玩具。魯比克方塊的吸引力相當大，很快就確立了它在流行文化中的地位。這

個方塊出現於電影、電視節目以及音樂影片中。一些名人甚至公開展示自己解魔方的技巧，進一步提高了它的吸引力。不過，就像許多曾經大受歡迎的玩具一樣，後來大眾對魯比克方塊的興趣減退。

<u>然而，隨著網際網路的問世，這個玩具再度捲土重來。</u>世界方塊協會（WCA）於 2004 年成立，目標是在全世界推廣公平的競賽。<u>該協會舉辦許多活動，像是使用不同大小方塊的活動、單手和只用腳操作的競賽，以及參賽者蒙上眼睛的活動。</u>這些競賽催生了一群「速解方塊玩家」新世代，他們花費數小時練習以精進技巧。魯比克方塊的吸引力依舊，而它的歷久不衰造就了上億個方塊的銷量，成為世界上最暢銷的玩具之一。

__D__ **16.** 理由

a. 空格後句提及人名 Rubik（魯比克），可知空格應出現此一人名，選項 (D) 即介紹魯比克方塊的發明人為 Ernö Rubik（爾諾・魯比克）。

b. 空格後句提及魯比克方塊後來改以其發明者的名字命名，語意對應選項 (D) 所述 it was first called the Magic Cube（一開始叫做魔術方塊）。

c. 根據上述，(D) 項應為正選；置入空格後，後句中的 it 即指 (D) 項中的 it，即魯比克方塊。

__A__ **17.** 理由

a. 空格前句中的 his students（他的學生）與選項 (A) 中的 the professor（這位教授）語意相關，his 即指涉 the professor。

b. 空格前句提及魯比克的學生喜歡他的發明，選項 (A) 敘述某事讓魯比克推測 his innovative cube might have broad appeal（他這個具創意的方塊可能會有廣大的吸引力），某事指涉空格前句。而空格後句敘述魯比克（的推論）是正確的，延續說明了選項 (A) 中的推論。

c. 根據上述，(A) 項應為正選。

__E__ **18.** 理由

a. 第二段最後一句敘述魯比克方塊原本大受歡迎，但後來大眾對它的興趣減退，而選項 (E) 以轉折語氣詞 However（然而）起首並提到 the toy made a comeback（這個玩具再度捲土重來），the toy 即指涉魯比克方塊，兩句語意相關且連貫。

b. 根據上述，(E) 項應為正選。

__C__ **19.** 理由

a. 空格前句提及世界方塊協會於 2004 年成立並訴求推廣公平的競賽，選項 (C) 提及 holds numerous events（舉辦許多活動）並列舉活動項目，進一步說明空格前句，句中主詞 It 即指涉世界方塊協會，而 events（活動）和 contests（競賽）則呼應空格前句的 competitions（競賽）。

b. 根據上述，(C) 項應為正選。

(B) 選項翻譯　這些學生對魔方的信心比魯比克本人還要強。

Unit 20

重要單字與片語

1. **puzzle** [ˈpʌzl] *n.* 謎題;拼圖
2. **vow** [vaʊ] *vt.* & *n.* 誓言;發誓
   例 All of Pat's friends vowed to support him in the election.
   派特所有的朋友發誓在這次選舉中支持他。
3. **architect** [ˈɑrkəˌtɛkt] *n.* 建築師
4. **license** [ˈlaɪsəns] *vt.* 授權,批准 & *n.* 執照
   例 This company is licensed to produce Disney toys.
   這間公司獲得授權,得以生產迪士尼的玩具。
5. **multiple** [ˈmʌltəpl] *a.* 多重的
6. **conclusion** [kənˈkluʒən] *n.* 結論
   lead sb to a conclusion　讓某人得出一個結論
   come to a conclusion　做出結論
   = reach a conclusion
7. **appeal** [əˈpil] *n.* 吸引力(不可數)
8. **instant** [ˈɪnstənt] *a.* 立即的 & *n.* 頃刻
9. **iconic** [aɪˈkɑnɪk] *a.* 具指標性的;圖像的
10. **celebrity** [səˈlɛbrətɪ] *n.* 名人(可數);名聲,名氣(不可數)
11. **showcase** [ˈʃoˌkes] *vt.* 展示(優點)
    例 The chef showcased his cooking skills in a live demonstration.
    這位廚師在現場示範中展示了他的烹飪技巧
12. **boost** [bust] *vt.* 增加,提升 & *n.* 促進,推動
    例 The government launched a campaign to boost tourism.
    政府發起了一項促進觀光的活動。
13. **decline** [dɪˈklaɪn] *vi.* 衰退;下跌 & *n.* 下跌
    例 Car sales declined greatly as a result of the economic crisis many years ago.
    多年前,由於受到金融危機影響,汽車的銷售量大幅下滑。
14. **make a comeback**　東山再起,捲土重來;復出
    例 Five years after retiring, the basketball player decided to try to make a comeback.
    退休五年之後,那名籃球選手決定復出。
15. **promote** [prəˈmot] *vt.* 提倡,倡導;推廣
    例 Our company promotes education by offering scholarships to the poor.
    本公司提供獎學金給窮困的人,以推廣教育。
16. **blindfold** [ˈblaɪndˌfold] *vt.* 蒙住……的眼睛
17. **dedicate** [ˈdɛdəˌket] *vt.* 奉獻;(音樂作品、書等)獻給
    dedicate A to B　將 A 奉獻給 B
    例 The doctor dedicated years to researching cancer treatments.
    這位醫生花費多年研究治療癌症的方法。
18. **longevity** [lɑnˈdʒɛvətɪ] *n.* 長壽(不可數)
19. **best-selling** [ˌbɛstˈsɛlɪŋ] *a.* 暢銷的

四 閱讀測驗

電鰻是利用身體裡某種細胞（稱為放電細胞）來發電的一種魚類。被電鰻的神經系統啟動時，它們會產生電擊來對抗掠食者、電昏獵物，以及在電鰻居住的南美洲黑暗又汙濁的水域中導航。電鰻的發電能力啟發了科學家尋求製造可用於人體內的替代電源。

耶魯大學和國家標準暨技術研究院的研究團隊建立了一個電腦模型，來判斷人造細胞在發電方面是否優於電鰻的天然細胞。該團隊發現，與電鰻體內數千個製造能量的放電細胞相比，只需要幾十個人造細胞就能產生足夠的能量，安全地為人體內的小型醫療植入物供電。雖然該團隊的人造細胞尚未製造出來，但他們已經創造了一幅重要的藍圖，其潛能讓人拭目以待。

來自弗立堡大學和密西根大學的另一個研究團隊使用一種特殊印表機來製造由含鹽或純水的細胞組成的透明薄片。這是模仿電鰻含鈉或鉀的放電細胞。當薄片以特定方式折疊時，這些物質會結合在一起產生電力。這也是模仿電鰻的放電細胞作用，因為它們有正負極，類似微型電池。當電鰻想要產生電擊時，其神經系統會向放電細胞傳遞訊息，要它們合作產生電流。該團隊希望他們的薄片所產生的穩定低電流能夠為心律調整器、植入式藥量釋放裝置和健康監測器供電。他們目前正在努力提高此發明的效率。雖然在實際用於人體之前還有很長的路要走，但該團隊對其成功寄予厚望。

D 20. 關於電鰻，我們並未得知什麼？
   (A) 電擊的用途為何。
   (B) 牠們的特殊細胞含有什麼。
   (C) 牠們如何產生電擊。
   (D) 牠們典型的食物為何。

   理由
   根據本文第一段第二句提及電擊的用途，第三段第二句提及電鰻的細胞含有什麼，第三段第四至五句提及牠們如何產生電擊。唯 (D) 項並未在本文中提及，故為正選。

C 21. 耶魯大學團隊發現何事？
   (A) 沒辦法將他們的構想做成可行的版本。
   (B) 他們的裝置可能會釋放有害毒素到人體。
   (C) 他們建構的細胞比電鰻的細胞效率更高。
   (D) 電鰻用相當少的細胞發電。

   理由
   根據本文第二段第二句，可知 (C) 項應為正選。

Unit 20

<u>C</u> **22.** 關於這兩個研究團隊，下列敘述何者正確？

(A) 他們都希望改善電鰻的生活條件。

(B) 他們是由兩個相同機構的研究員所組成。

(C) 他們都希望將他們的發現用於醫療用途。

(D) 他們正等待批准才能繼續他們的工作。

理由

根據本文第二段倒數第二句及第三段倒數第三句，可知 (C) 項應為正選。

<u>B</u> **23.** 從本文可推斷何事？

(A) 電鰻的能力無法在實驗室裡複製。

(B) 這些團隊所研究的裝置尚未付諸實行。

(C) 實驗中使用電鰻引發道德上的關切。

(D) 這些實驗改變了我們對電鰻的了解。

理由

根據本文第二段最後一句及第三段最後一句，可知 (B) 項應為正選。

重要單字與片語

1. **eel** [il] *n.* 鰻
   electric eel   電鰻
2. **activate** [ˈæktəˌvet] *vt.* 啟動
   例 If you punch in the code, the alarm will be activated.
   如果你輸入密碼，警報器就會啟動。
3. **outperform** [ˌaʊtpɚˈfɔrm] *vt.* 勝過，超過
   例 Shirley is very competitive; she always tries to outperform the other workers.
   雪莉很好強；她總是努力要在工作表現上勝過其他員工。
4. **implant** [ɪmˈplænt] *n.* 植入物 & *vt.* 植入，移植
   implantable [ɪmˈplæntəbl̩] *a.* 可植入的
5. **intriguing** [ɪnˈtrigɪŋ] *a.* 非常有趣的
6. **transparent** [trænsˈpɛrənt] *a.* 透明的
7. **mimic** [ˈmɪmɪk] *vt.* 模仿（三態為：mimic, mimicked [ˈmɪmɪkt], mimicked）
   例 We all roared with laughter when Tom mimicked Prof. Usher giving a lecture.
   看見湯姆模仿厄許教授講課，我們哄堂大笑。
8. **current** [ˈkɝənt] *n.* 電流
9. **dispenser** [dɪˈspɛnsɚ] *n.* 分配器，分發裝置
10. **a long way to go**   很長的路要走，很多工作要做
11. **put... into practice**   將……付諸實行
    例 I want to put my idea into practice as soon as possible.
    我想將我的理念儘早付諸實行。
12. **ethical** [ˈɛθɪkl̩] *a.* 道德的

五 混合題

除了傳統的經濟評估方式（如國內生產毛額和消費者物價指數）之外，還有一些非傳統的方式。以下是其中兩種。

大麥克指數是《經濟學人》雜誌於 1986 年所發明。它用麥當勞那一款知名漢堡的價格作為一個國家貨幣強弱的指標。它以購買力平價的經濟理論為基礎，該理論認為各國匯率的長期走向，應是趨向讓某些特別選定商品（所謂「一籃子商品」）的價格變成相等。用大麥克作為這個「商品籃子」的代表，是用一種輕鬆的方式讓一般人更容易理解此理論。該雜誌彙整了世界各地大麥克的價格，將它們換算成共同貨幣美元，然後比較這些轉換後的美元價格。例如在 2023 年，一個大麥克在美國售價為 5.36 美元，在挪威的價格相當於 6.59 美元，在墨西哥相當於 4.19 美元。這意味挪威克朗相對美元被高估了，而墨西哥披索則被低估。因此前者貨幣可能傾向貶值，而後者傾向升值。

Freddo 指數是使經濟學更易於讓一般人理解的另一種方式，但這個指數僅專用於某特定國家：英國。它用吉百利品牌的 Freddo 巧克力棒來評估通貨膨脹的程度，並衡量英國的生活成本。因此這套方法比大麥克指數還要單純。2006 年，一根 Freddo 巧克力棒的價格是 10 便士。如果我們依通貨膨脹率調整，意味在 2023 年一根 Freddo 巧克力棒應該賣 16 便士左右。然而其價格在 2010 年就已經超過這個金額，賣到了 17 便士，到了 2023 年，一根巧克力棒實際上已經賣到 26 便士。儘管這十七年來巧克力棒的重量幾乎都沒變。根據目前趨勢，到 2030 年其價格大約會是 35 便士。這些數字顯示 Freddo 巧克力棒價格增加的速度遠超過通膨率，這也對英國的生活成本危機投下了一道小小的陰影。

24.《經濟學人》雜誌收集世界各地的大麥克價格資料，並將其**轉換**為美元。

理由

空格前為不定冠詞 a，空格後為介詞 of，可得知空格應置單數可數名詞。根據大麥克指數的第五句 "..., converts them into the common currency of the US dollar, ..."（……，將它們換算成共同貨幣美元，……）得知，空格應置與 converts 相關的單數可數名詞 conversion。

Unit **20**

Unit 20

25. Freddo 指數於 2006 年開始計算時，一根 Freddo 巧克力棒的價格是十便士。如果我們依通貨膨脹率調整，十七年後一根巧克力棒的價格應該是十六便士。

理由

空格前為不定冠詞 an，空格後為過去分詞 based，可得知空格應置單數可數名詞。根據 Freddo 指數第五句 "If we adjust for inflation, ..."（如果我們依通貨膨脹率調整，……）得知，空格應置與 adjust 相關的單數可數名詞 adjustment。

26. 本文中哪個片語表示「讓人們花特定金額的錢」？

set people back（讓人們花一筆錢）

理由

根據 Freddo 指數倒數第四句 "..., a bar actually set people back 26 pence."（……，一根巧克力棒實際上已經賣到 26 便士。）可推測 set people back（讓人們花一筆錢）應為正解。

AE 27. 根據本文，關於大麥克指數和／或 Freddo 指數，下列哪些敘述是正確的？
　　(A) 它們皆以常見的日常產品為基礎。
　　(B) Freddo 指數比大麥克指數複雜。
　　(C) 它們聚焦於同一國家的生活成本。
　　(D) 大麥克指數是在 Freddo 指數之後所創立的。
　　(E) 它們皆設計供普羅大眾來應用。
　　(F) Freddo 指數幫助人們減少在零嘴上的花費。

理由

根據大麥克指數的第二、四句及 Freddo 指數的第一、二句得知，(A)、(E) 應為正選。

重要單字與片語

1. **assess** [əˋsɛs] vt. 評估；對……估價
   例 More clinical trials are needed before pharmacologists can assess the effectiveness of this new drug.
   藥理學家需要更多的臨床實驗才能評估這個新藥物的效用。

2. **currency** [ˋkɝənsɪ] n. 貨幣

3. **equalize** [ˋikwəˏlaɪz] vt. 使平等
   例 The new rules passed by the government were meant to equalize the employment situation in the country.
   政府通過的新規定旨在使該國的就業狀況均衡化。

4. **lighthearted** [ˋlaɪtˏhɑrtɪd] a. 輕鬆愉快的；隨便的

5. **accessible** [əkˋsɛsəbl̩] *a.* 易理解的；可到達的；易取得的

6. **compile** [kəmˋpaɪl] *vt.* 彙編（成冊）
   例 Seventeen linguists spent nearly seven years compiling this dictionary.
   十七位語言學家花了近七年彙編這本字典。

7. **convert** [kənˋvɝt] *vt.* & *vi.* 轉變
   convert A into B　　將 A 變成 B
   例 I'd like to convert some dollars into pounds, please.
   我想要把一些美元換成英鎊，麻煩你。

8. **equivalent** [ɪˋkwɪvələnt] *n.* 相等物 & *a.* 相等的
   the equivalent of sth　　某物的相等物

9. **depreciate** [dɪˋpriʃɪˏet] *vi.* & *vt.* （使）貶值
   例 This model of car has depreciated in value very quickly.
   這款車的價值下跌甚快。

10. **appreciate** [əˋpriʃɪˏet] *vi.* （貨幣）升值 & *vt.* 感激；欣賞
    例 The US dollar keeps depreciating, while the Euro keeps appreciating.
    美元持續貶值，而歐元則持續升值。

11. **inflation** [ɪnˋfleʃən] *n.* 通貨膨脹，物價上漲（不可數）

12. **exceed** [ɪkˋsid] *vt.* 超過
    例 Don't exceed the speed limit when driving.
    開車時不要超速。

13. **set sb back**　　花去某人一筆錢

14. **substantially** [səbˋstænʃəlɪ] *adv.* 在很大程度上；相當多地

國家圖書館出版品預行編目（CIP）資料

學測英文五大關鍵題型：綜合測驗、文意選填、篇章結構、閱讀測驗、混合題－詳解本 / 賴世雄作. -- 再版.
-- 臺北市：常春藤數位出版股份有限公司, 2025.06
面；　公分. --（常春藤 108 課綱核心素養・升大學系列；A104N-2）
ISBN 978-626-7225-92-9（平裝）
1. CST：英語教學　2. CST：讀本
3. CST：中等教育
524.38　　　　　　　　　　　　　114006135

填讀者問卷
送熊贈點

常春藤 108 課綱核心素養・升大學系列【A104N-2】
學測英文五大關鍵題型：綜合測驗、文意選填、篇章結構、閱讀測驗、混合題－詳解本【增修版】

總 編 審	賴世雄
終　　審	梁民康
執行編輯	許嘉華
編輯小組	畢安安・施盈如・Nick Roden・Brian Foden
設計組長	王玥琦
封面設計	王穎緁
排版設計	王穎緁・林桂旭
法律顧問	北辰著作權事務所蕭雄淋律師
出 版 者	常春藤數位出版股份有限公司
地　　址	臺北市忠孝西路一段 33 號 5 樓
電　　話	(02) 2331-7600
傳　　真	(02) 2381-0918
網　　址	www.ivy.com.tw
電子信箱	service@ivy.com.tw
郵政劃撥	50463568
戶　　名	常春藤數位出版股份有限公司
定　　價	380 元（2 書）
出版日期	2025 年 6 月　再版

©常春藤數位出版股份有限公司 (2025) All rights reserved.　　Y000061-3588
本書之封面、內文、編排等之著作財產權歸常春藤數位出版股份有限公司所有。未經本公司書面同意，請勿翻印、轉載或為一切著作權法上利用行為，否則依法追究。

如有缺頁、裝訂錯誤或破損，請寄回本公司更換。　　【版權所有　翻印必究】

征服 108 新課綱

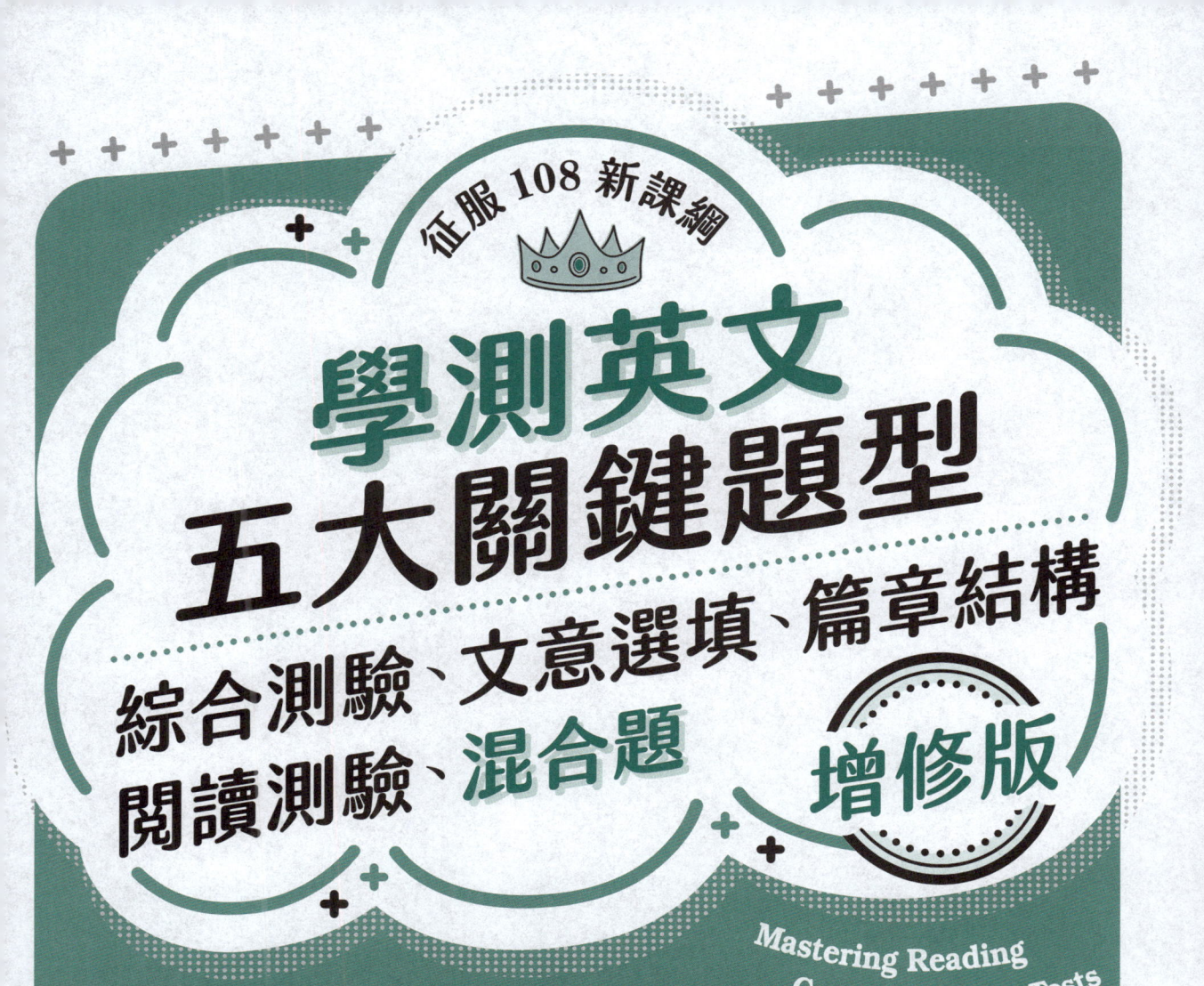

學測英文
五大關鍵題型

綜合測驗、文意選填、篇章結構
閱讀測驗、混合題

增修版

Mastering Reading
Comprehension Tests

試題本

Preface 序

在科技與網路的帶動下,我們的世界已成為一個緊密不可分的地球村,英語不但成為溝通的重要橋梁,更是個人與世界接軌不可缺的基本能力。為迎合世界潮流,提升學生的英語能力,學科能力測驗英文考科已朝向多元化的方向命題,旨在測驗考生如何統整資訊、邏輯推理與獨立思考的能力,以因應未來所需。

綜觀而言,新實施的英語文課綱著重培養學生的「核心素養」,期望學生能透過英語能力獲取新知。

為此,本人召集常春藤中外編輯團隊,研討 108 課綱大學學測考題命題重點方向,特編撰《學測英文五大關鍵題型:綜合測驗、文意選填、篇章結構、閱讀測驗、混合題》一書。全書共 20 回,每回均涵蓋五大題型,文章選材豐富多元,以素養導向跨越各個領域;題型設計參考教育部所公布的準則與大學學測考題,緊扣趨勢,翻譯通順,解析詳盡,期盼對莘莘學子有所助益。各位若能熟讀本書並反覆練習,未來參加英文學科能力測驗,必能勇奪高分!

CONTENTS 目錄

Unit 01
綜合測驗 ………………………………… 2
文意選填 ………………………………… 3
篇章結構 ………………………………… 4
閱讀測驗 ………………………………… 6
混合題 …………………………………… 8

Unit 02
綜合測驗 ………………………………… 12
文意選填 ………………………………… 13
篇章結構 ………………………………… 14
閱讀測驗 ………………………………… 16
混合題 …………………………………… 18

Unit 03
綜合測驗 ………………………………… 20
文意選填 ………………………………… 21
篇章結構 ………………………………… 22
閱讀測驗 ………………………………… 24
混合題 …………………………………… 26

Unit 04
綜合測驗 ………………………………… 28
文意選填 ………………………………… 29
篇章結構 ………………………………… 30
閱讀測驗 ………………………………… 32
混合題 …………………………………… 34

Unit 05
綜合測驗 ………………………………… 38
文意選填 ………………………………… 39
篇章結構 ………………………………… 40
閱讀測驗 ………………………………… 42
混合題 …………………………………… 44

Unit 06
綜合測驗 ………………………………… 46
文意選填 ………………………………… 47
篇章結構 ………………………………… 48
閱讀測驗 ………………………………… 50
混合題 …………………………………… 52

Unit 07
綜合測驗 ………………………………… 54
文意選填 ………………………………… 55
篇章結構 ………………………………… 56
閱讀測驗 ………………………………… 58
混合題 …………………………………… 60

Unit 08
綜合測驗 ………………………………… 62
文意選填 ………………………………… 63
篇章結構 ………………………………… 64
閱讀測驗 ………………………………… 66
混合題 …………………………………… 68

Unit 09
綜合測驗 ………………………………… 70
文意選填 ………………………………… 71
篇章結構 ………………………………… 72
閱讀測驗 ………………………………… 74
混合題 …………………………………… 76

Unit 10
綜合測驗 ………………………………… 78
文意選填 ………………………………… 79
篇章結構 ………………………………… 80
閱讀測驗 ………………………………… 82
混合題 …………………………………… 84

Unit 11
綜合測驗	86
文意選填	87
篇章結構	88
閱讀測驗	90
混合題	92

Unit 12
綜合測驗	94
文意選填	95
篇章結構	96
閱讀測驗	98
混合題	100

Unit 13
綜合測驗	102
文意選填	103
篇章結構	104
閱讀測驗	106
混合題	108

Unit 14
綜合測驗	110
文意選填	111
篇章結構	112
閱讀測驗	114
混合題	116

Unit 15
綜合測驗	118
文意選填	119
篇章結構	120
閱讀測驗	122
混合題	124

Unit 16
綜合測驗	126
文意選填	127
篇章結構	128
閱讀測驗	130
混合題	132

Unit 17
綜合測驗	134
文意選填	135
篇章結構	136
閱讀測驗	138
混合題	140

Unit 18
綜合測驗	144
文意選填	145
篇章結構	146
閱讀測驗	148
混合題	150

Unit 19
綜合測驗	152
文意選填	153
篇章結構	154
閱讀測驗	156
混合題	158

Unit 20
綜合測驗	160
文意選填	161
篇章結構	162
閱讀測驗	164
混合題	166

Unit 01

一、綜合測驗　說明：本題型的題幹為段落式短文，選文中含數個空格，每題一個空格，請依文意選出最適當的一個選項。

　　In 1974, Betty and Jock Leslie-Melville bought an old mansion twenty miles from the Kenyan capital, Nairobi. The couple then spent several months and a considerable amount of money __(1)__ the property.

　　As the founder of the African Fund for Endangered Wildlife, Betty was aware of the __(2)__ faced by the Rothschild giraffe, which, with only a few hundred living in the wild, was facing extinction. Consequently, when the couple moved into their dream home, they also moved a pair of Rothschild giraffes to the 120 acres of __(3)__ forest surrounding their property. This action required saving not only the giraffes __(4)__ the land that was going to be used for houses and factories. In 1984, Jock Leslie-Melville died, and Betty decided to use her ten-room home as a hotel. She called the hotel the Giraffe Manor.

　　Each morning, several of the property's Rothschild giraffes make their way to the hotel to have breakfast with the hotel's guests. The giraffes gently place their heads through the hotel's windows, allowing guests the opportunity to hand-feed them. This unique, up-close-and-personal contact provides travelers with a(n) __(5)__. Also, it funds a sanctuary for one of Mother Nature's most appealing animals.

1. (A) repeating　　(B) relying　　(C) repairing　　(D) receiving
2. (A) mansion　　(B) prison　　(C) silence　　(D) challenge
3. (A) memorial　　(B) natural　　(C) loyal　　(D) mineral
4. (A) but　　(B) or　　(C) and　　(D) so
5. (A) state-of-the-art technology　　(B) run-of-the-mill trip
　 (C) once-in-a-lifetime experience　　(D) out-of-the-question plan

1. _____　2. _____　3. _____　4. _____　5. _____

二 文意選填

說明：本題型的題幹為段落式短文，以一篇含十個空格的選文搭配十個選項，每題一個空格，請依文意在文章後所提供的選項中分別選出最適當者。

Unit 01

Depression is one of the most common medical conditions. In fact, ten percent of all people will experience depression at least once. Those who __(6)__ from depression experience feelings of intense sadness, anxiety, and negative emotions. Life experiences, such as the death of a loved one, may cause depression. However, it may also occur for no __(7)__ reason.

Many people with depression will visit their doctor and receive treatment. Unfortunately, others feel so much guilt and shame that they won't even discuss their problems with their family, let alone a doctor. This can be extremely __(8)__ because severe depression may eventually lead to suicide.

In 2003, an 18-year-old girl's father __(9)__ suicide because of untreated depression. Losing her father caused her to also experience depression and she began to abuse alcohol to __(10)__ her pain. Fortunately, she received treatment from a doctor and __(11)__.

She then established Project Semicolon, an __(12)__ that provides hope for those who have depression. Project Semicolon draws __(13)__ to depression by asking people to get a tattoo of a semicolon. A semicolon is used to __(14)__ making a sentence that could otherwise be ended. Those who don't want a permanent tattoo can draw a __(15)__ semicolon somewhere on their body with a pen.

- **A** temporary
- **B** committed
- **C** remove
- **D** apparent
- **E** attention
- **F** dangerous
- **G** organization
- **H** continue
- **I** recovered
- **J** suffer

6. _____ 7. _____ 8. _____ 9. _____ 10. _____

11. _____ 12. _____ 13. _____ 14. _____ 15. _____

Unit 01

篇章結構

說明：本題型的題幹為段落式短文，以一篇含四個空格的選文搭配四個選項，每題一個空格，請依文意在文章後所提供的選項中分別選出最適當者，填入空格中，使篇章結構清晰有條理。

　　You enter a crowded classroom. People seem to be staring at you. You hear laughter from a group of students in the corner. Are they laughing at you? Instantly, your heart starts to pound, and you desperately want to hide. Your palms start sweating, and your body feels tense.

　　If this experience is familiar to you, you may have social anxiety disorder. __(16)__ For those who experience these feelings, it can be almost impossible to enjoy talking to others, being with friends, or even simply going out in public. Even routine tasks like ordering food or making a phone call can feel overwhelming.

　　Social phobia has many forms, from fear of speaking in public to feeling uncomfortable in groups. It can cause unpleasant physical symptoms like sweating, blushing, difficulty breathing, and feeling sick. There are several explanations as to why people have social phobia. It can be passed down genetically from parents to children. __(17)__ The experience might have left the victim with a terrible fear of ending up in a similar situation again. Negative past experiences such as bullying or criticism can also contribute to this fear.

　　Luckily for those who have social phobia, the condition is treatable. __(18)__ Meditation and relaxation exercises can also help. Most importantly, there are techniques that can help to cure it altogether. One of the most common methods is experiencing the uncomfortable social situations a little bit at a time with the help of a psychologist. __(19)__ Over time, small successes can build confidence and make social interactions easier.

　　For some, social phobia stands in the way of a lot of enjoyment that most people take for granted. However, with the right treatment, social situations can be fun and enjoyable for everyone.

A Also known as social phobia, social anxiety disorder is a condition that causes individuals to become anxious when they have to interact with other people.

B This method has been proven to help those with social anxiety disorder to confront and understand their fear.

C Social phobia can also develop if the victim has been badly embarrassed in front of others.

D For one thing, there are drugs that help control the symptoms.

E You realize that the students were actually laughing at a video one of them had uploaded to YouTube.

Unit
01

16. _____   17. _____   18. _____   19. _____

四 閱讀測驗
說明：每題請根據本篇文章之文意選出最適當的一個選項。

Until the mid-20th century, most mothers had little option when it came to dealing with their babies' and toddlers' toiletry needs. They had to use cloth diapers, which were awkward to fasten and time-consuming to wash, and they tended to leak. Marion Donovan was one mother who had to deal with this on a daily basis. Donovan had been brought up by her father, an engineer, who cultivated in her an inquiring mind and a desire for invention. She was therefore perfectly placed to come up with a solution to the diaper problem.

At first, Donovan took a shower curtain and cut it into pieces to create diaper covers that were waterproof. Then, she began using breathable parachute cloth for the covers instead. These covers could be washed and reused. She also introduced snap fasteners that meant the size of the diaper could be adjusted. Finally, she added an insert for an absorbent diaper panel that could be stuffed with tissue paper and then thrown away once used. Believing her invention resembled a boat, Donovan named it "the Boater."

However, the men who dominated the manufacturing industry of the 1940s were initially less than impressed. "They said, 'We don't want it. No woman has asked us for that,'" she later recalled. Opting to manufacture the diapers herself, Donovan found a distributor in a department store chain in 1949. Two years later, she received a patent for her diaper cover, which she sold to the Keko Corporation for what would be US$10 million today. It would be another decade before Pampers began mass-producing their own version of fully disposable diapers, but Marion Donovan's position in history had already been assured.

20. What do we learn about Marion Donovan?
    (A) She was a single mother with two children.
    (B) She trained hard to be an engineer.
    (C) She also invented a large sailing vessel.
    (D) She was heavily influenced by a parent.

21. What is the main purpose of the second paragraph?
    (A) To outline the problems with disposable diapers.
    (B) To detail the different stages of Donovan's design.
    (C) To address complaints about traditional cloth diapers.
    (D) To probe deeper into Donovan's life before the invention.

22. Which of the following is true about Marion Donovan's invention?
    (A) Its patent was sold to Pampers for several millions of dollars.
    (B) It had several restrictions on its shape, size, and comfort level.
    (C) Its inner and outer layers were made primarily of thick tissue paper.
    (D) It had parts that could be used again and others that were disposable.

23. Why is the quote "We don't want it. No woman has asked us for that" included in the passage?
    (A) To prove that females are the primary caregivers for children and babies.
    (B) To show that fully disposable diapers were less popular than expected.
    (C) To illustrate the obstacles that Donovan had to overcome.
    (D) To explain why Donovan abandoned her first design.

20. _____   21. _____   22. _____   23. _____

Unit 01

五 混合題 說明：請根據文章之文意選出或寫出一個最適當的答案。

Artificial intelligence (AI) is a hot-button issue, and many people have strong views about whether it is having a positive or negative effect on society. We asked a range of people for their opinions.

(A) Albert
Training and running AI systems requires huge amounts of energy, inevitably leading to increased carbon emissions. I worry that this will hasten environmental damage. That's why I spend a great deal of time campaigning against this technology and the enormous data centers that house AI systems.

(B) Brigit
AI is a relatively new technology, but it's already transforming the way I work. From analyzing patient records to providing assistance in diagnosing diseases, AI systems have revolutionized my job. I use them on a daily basis and can't wait to see how they develop in the future.

(C) Cedric
I've been writing about artificial intelligence for years. Most of my books have centered around an imagined future where AI has spiraled out of control and taken over the world, leading to the downfall of humanity. I hope that won't happen in real life, but I fear it might.

(D) Dalia
It's quite simple: AI is a threat to job security. My role is to look after the rights of the workers in my industry, but this is getting harder and harder to do as managers replace them with AI systems. Stable employment will soon be a thing of the past.

(E) Elias
I'm excited by the power and possibilities of AI. I've read that it's already improving efficiency, automating tedious tasks, and advancing research. With strong international safeguards in place, I firmly believe it will help solve global challenges such as hunger and climate change.

(F) Fatima
The potential economic benefits of artificial intelligence are huge! Instead of getting distracted by job losses in some industries, we should be focusing on AI's ability to boost productivity, drive innovation, and create new jobs in industries we've barely even conceived of.

(G) Gustav
I spent months writing the music and lyrics to my most well-known songs; apparently, AI can produce songs in seconds. Leave aside the question of whether the tunes are actually any good. A far more pressing concern is what this means for artistic integrity and the future of human creativity.

(H) Hilda
I admit that I often use ChatGPT to help me write papers, but my joy at this assistance is far outweighed by my fears about the misuse of AI. For example, it can create deepfake videos which manipulate people into believing things that aren't true.

24. Which of the people best match the following descriptions? Write the LETTERS of the people below.（配合）

    (1) Labor union leader: _____
    (2) Science fiction author: _____
    (3) Environmental activist: _____
    (4) Famous musician: _____

25. Who indicates in their response that they have personal experience of using AI systems?（簡答）

    _____

26. Which word in the responses most likely means "a recording that replaces someone's face or voice with that of someone else in a way that appears real"?（簡答）

    _____

27. Based on the responses, which of the following statements is accurate?（單選）

(A) Neither Fatima nor Hilda is troubled by the scare stories about AI.
(B) Cedric is fearful about the future of AI, and Elias is likewise worried.
(C) Albert and Brigit share concerns about the impact of AI technology.
(D) Both Elias and Fatima are enthusiastic about the possible benefits of AI.

24. (1) _____ (2) _____ (3) _____ (4) _____

25. _____

26. _____

27. _____

Unit 02

一 綜合測驗

說明：本題型的題幹為段落式短文，選文中含數個空格，每題一個空格，請依文意選出最適當的一個選項。

When Jim Thompson graduated from college with an architecture degree, he was prepared for a quiet, ordinary life. That was until war   (1) . He then volunteered to serve in the US Army in World War II. As a soldier and a spy, he fought in Italy and France before being stationed in Bangkok, Thailand. While he was in the Thai capital, the war ended.

Thompson fell in love with Thailand and the Thai culture, especially the traditional silk-making. He realized that modern   (2)   were destroying the small silk industry. To rescue the industry, he decided to use his business skills to   (3)   the Thai Silk Company. His company's silk soon became famous around the world. Remarkably, the company employed thousands of Thai women to work from home   (4)   in a factory. This arrangement meant they could still look after their children while making a living.

In 1967, while vacationing in Malaysia, Thompson went for a walk in the jungle and mysteriously disappeared without a   (5) . His body has never been found.

1. (A) broke up (B) broke out (C) broke off (D) broke down
2. (A) organic foods (B) natural resources
   (C) medical supplies (D) synthetic fabrics
3. (A) establish (B) threaten (C) endure (D) isolate
4. (A) less than (B) more than (C) rather than (D) other than
5. (A) trap (B) concept (C) breeze (D) trace

1. _____ 2. _____ 3. _____ 4. _____ 5. _____

二 文意選填

說明：本題型的題幹為段落式短文，以一篇含十個空格的選文搭配十個選項，每題一個空格，請依文意在文章後所提供的選項中分別選出最適當者。

Between 1975 and 1979, Pol Pot, a murderous dictator, ruled Cambodia. His (6) political party, called the Khmer Rouge, closed schools, hospitals, and factories. Entire cities were relocated to the country where people were (7) to labor on farms with primitive tools.

An estimated three million Cambodians died after Pol Pot instructed the Khmer Rouge to murder anybody (8) his government's policies, educated intellectuals, or those with ethnic genes. Pol Pot lost power after neighboring Vietnam, with help from Russia, (9) and took control of the country in 1980.

With the country in (10) , the new government searched for ways to bring the country's culture back to life. One such idea was the National Circus School of Cambodia—an innovative program to teach students the skills for performing Cambodian circus art, which has been (11) in Cambodia for over 1,000 years.

Most of the students that (12) enrolled at the school were orphans. Many of these children survived by (13) recyclable trash from the streets. They were earning (14) enough money for one small daily subsistence meal. The school has given these students a much better life than they would have otherwise had.

The school's first teachers were Vietnamese and Russian. They taught acrobatics, and ten star pupils received further training from experts in Russia. Eventually, the school trained students in China, Vietnam, and France. These days, the National Circus School of Cambodia performs daily and is one of Cambodia's most successful (15) .

- **A** invaded
- **B** brutal
- **C** ruins
- **D** opposing
- **E** initially
- **F** undertakings
- **G** forced
- **H** barely
- **I** popular
- **J** gathering

6. _____   7. _____   8. _____   9. _____   10. _____

11. _____   12. _____   13. _____   14. _____   15. _____

Unit 02

篇章結構

說明：本題型的題幹為段落式短文，以一篇含四個空格的選文搭配四個選項，每題一個空格，請依文意在文章後所提供的選項中分別選出最適當者，填入空格中，使篇章結構清晰有條理。

　　Giving birth is one of the most life-changing events a woman can experience. The first few months of a baby's life can be extremely challenging for a mother. __(16)__ There is the fatigue caused by irregular sleep patterns, breastfeeding, and a mountain of bills to pay. Many new mothers also struggle with emotional changes, such as postpartum depression and anxiety. The first few weeks of life are critical, and with this in mind, many countries provide assistance to parents and their newborn babies. One such considerate government is Finland.

　　Finland is a large, wealthy Scandinavian country. __(17)__ The Finnish government provides paid parental leave of up to 320 working days. __(18)__ The Finnish Baby Box program, which was established over eighty years ago, provides diapers, bibs, food, clothes, toys, a mattress, and blankets for parents. These supplies ensure that babies have a safe and comfortable start in life. The items in the baby box are currently valued at €140. The program has been credited as one of the reasons Finland boasts the world's lowest infant mortality rate. Additionally, it encourages parents to seek medical checkups, as they must register for healthcare services to receive the box.

　　When Danielle Selassie, a resident of the USA, heard about the Finnish program, she decided to establish a similar program in her home state in the US. Called "Babies Need Boxes," it provides essential items just like the Finnish Baby Box. However, this program doesn't have sufficient funds. __(19)__ Despite this limitation, the program has already helped hundreds of struggling mothers. The phenomenal success of Ms. Selassie's not-for-profit organization is likely to see it expand into other states. With increased funding, the program could benefit even more families in need.

Ⓐ This is especially true if the baby is the mother's first.
Ⓑ Ms. Selassie credits the Finnish Baby Box program with saving her baby daughter's life.
Ⓒ Hence, it has adequate financial support to develop its social welfare programs.
Ⓓ Therefore, only poor single mothers, rather than all mothers, receive the box.
Ⓔ Also, parents receive what is known as the Finnish Baby Box.

16. _____   17. _____   18. _____   19. _____

Unit 02

四 閱讀測驗 說明：每題請根據本篇文章之文意選出最適當的一個選項。

Back in 1997, Mike Coots was like most teenagers living in Hawaii. The energetic 17-year-old would head to the coast for a few hours of surfing whenever he had the chance. Little did he know, however, that his favorite leisure activity would one day change the course of his life.

One morning, Coots and a friend decided to catch a few waves at their favorite beach when tragedy struck. The pair were only a few hundred meters from shore when they noticed a large tiger shark approaching rapidly. They both frantically began to paddle as fast as they could to escape the dangerous predator. Unfortunately, for one of them, **this** was not enough. The killer fish sank its razor-sharp teeth into Coots' right leg. Coots continuously punched the man-eater as hard as he could until the shark finally released its grip and swam off. In extreme pain and suffering from shock, he made it back to dry land with the help of his friend.

Coots had lost a dangerous amount of blood and was falling in and out of consciousness, so bystanders placed him on the back of an old truck and rushed him to the nearest hospital. Doctors saved his life, but the heartbreaking decision to amputate his leg at the calf was unavoidable. When he regained consciousness after the operation, Coots expressed his gratitude to everybody that had saved his life and bravely and graciously accepted his fate.

When Coots had completed several months of painful rehabilitation and had learned to walk using a prosthetic leg, he returned to surf at the same beach where he had lost his right leg to the sea creature. He also began to lobby Hawaiian politicians for the protection of sharks, which at the time were hunted by fishermen for their fins. Mike Coots' campaign was ultimately successful when the Hawaiian government banned the sale and possession of shark fins. Mike Coots had turned his personal tragedy into a public triumph.

20. What is this passage mainly about?
    (A) How a teenager gracefully handled a personal tragedy.
    (B) Why protecting tiger sharks is vitally important.
    (C) Why the problems faced by surfers in Hawaii are increasing.
    (D) How people working together can save somebody's life.

21. What does the word "**this**" in the second paragraph refer to?
    (A) The desire to catch a wave.
    (B) The effort to get away from the shark.
    (C) The right time to call for help.
    (D) The struggle to stop bleeding.

22. Which words are used in the passage to describe the shark that attacked Mike Coots?
    (A) tragedy, killer fish, triumph
    (B) dangerous predator, man-eater, fate
    (C) dangerous predator, killer fish, sea creature
    (D) man-eater, fate, jaws

23. Based on the passage, which statement is true about Mike Coots?
    (A) He suffered psychological trauma after the tragedy.
    (B) He campaigned to make Hawaiian beaches safer.
    (C) He lost a limb after a vicious attack in the ocean.
    (D) He has yet to finish his physical rehabilitation sessions.

20. _____   21. _____   22. _____   23. _____

Unit 02

五 混合題
說明：請根據文章之文意選出或寫出一個最適當的答案。

We asked four people for their opinions on zoos. Here are their responses.

Manon
I know from personal experience that, when managed effectively, zoos can be very educational places. Through our guided tours and informative displays, we have helped to raise awareness about a huge range of animals from all over the world. Seeing remarkable creatures like tigers, pandas, and giraffes up close is an awesome experience. If visitors to our wonderful animal park are introduced to these animals from an early age, they grow up with respect for them and a desire to protect them.

Camille
I'll get straight to the point: zoos are cruel. No matter how many improvements have been made over the years, zoos still keep animals in environments that are far from natural. As a member of an animal rights group, I'm trying to alert the world to the fact that zoo animals suffer from both physical and psychological problems. I urge people who see unhappy animals locked in cages and forced to stay in captivity to take pictures and post them on social media. This will raise awareness of our vital cause.

Gabriel
Zoos make great contributions to animal welfare, both within their walls and in the wider world. The zoo I have a financial interest in, for instance, is involved in breeding programs that aim to conserve endangered species, such as gorillas, giant pandas, cheetahs, and wild horses. Once the zoo has safely bred these animals in captivity, they release some of them into the wild. It is important that we all provide financial assistance to help zoos improve and expand these programs. From my work, I also know zoos undertake important research in areas from animal behavior to disease prevention, adding immeasurably to the sum of human knowledge of the animal world.

Lucas
People always claim that zoos help kids to learn about animals, but to my mind, this is a false argument. The poor animals are not living in their natural environment, so they are not exhibiting their normal behavior. Thus, kids are not getting a true

picture of the animals when they visit zoos. That's why I show them documentaries that were actually filmed in the wild instead of taking the children on field trips to zoos. I want the young people of today, including my own, to be properly educated about all the wonderful creatures on this planet, but quite frankly, they can't get that from a zoo.

24-25 請從文章中找出最適當的單詞（word）填入下列句子空格中，並視語法需要做適當的字形變化。每格限填一個單詞（word）。（填充）

Gabriel is positive in his assessment of zoos, stating that they ___24.___ to animal welfare through breeding programs and vital research.

In contrast to Manon, Lucas believes that zoos are not a good way for children to receive an ___25.___ about the huge variety of animals in our world.

26. Which word in Camille's and Gabriel's responses means "the situation in which an animal or a person is kept somewhere and not allowed to leave"?（簡答）

27. Which of the following roles best suit the respondents? Choose TWO roles for each respondent. Each role can only be used once.（配合）

| (A) zoo owner | (B) citizen | (C) investor | (D) protester |
| (E) zoo keeper | (F) teacher | (G) researcher | (H) parent |

Manon: ___、___
Camille: ___、___
Gabriel: ___、___
Lucas: ___、___

24. _____ 25. _____

26. _____

27. Manon: ___、___   Camille: ___、___
    Gabriel: ___、___   Lucas: ___、___

Unit 03

一 綜合測驗 説明：本題型的題幹為段落式短文，選文中含數個空格，每題一個空格，請依文意選出最適當的一個選項。

    Izakaya restaurants have been around for a long time. They __(1)__ Japan, sometime during the Edo period between the 1600s and 1800s. There is some uncertainty about their city of origin; some say it was Tokyo, while others believe izakayas started in Osaka. These humble establishments are readily identified by the red paper lanterns hanging outside of them. Originally, izakayas were frequented by __(2)__, mostly men, who wanted to drink sake after work. Simple food was eventually added to keep customers happy and drinking. Over time, izakayas became more than just places for drinking; they turned into community hubs where people could relax and bond over food.

    Nowadays, both __(3)__ enjoy meeting and socializing at izakaya restaurants, and they have become a staple of modern Japanese cuisine. Patrons usually start with a beer while __(4)__ on the food. Yakitori (grilled chicken on skewers), karaage (bite-sized pieces of fried chicken), and a variety of tofu preparations are all __(5)__ choices. Dishes are served on small plates and shared by all. Izakaya restaurants have recently become popular abroad, especially in the United States. As a result, many izakayas abroad have adjusted their menus to include local flavors while still maintaining their traditional charm.

1. (A) adapted to   (B) concentrated on   (C) originated in   (D) cooperated with
2. (A) salaried workers   (B) dismissed employees
   (C) adopted children   (D) retired teachers
3. (A) reminders   (B) genders   (C) disorders   (D) borders
4. (A) decided   (B) deciding   (C) decide   (D) decides
5. (A) historical   (B) critical   (C) vertical   (D) typical

1. _____ 2. _____ 3. _____ 4. _____ 5. _____

二 文意選填

說明：本題型的題幹為段落式短文，以一篇含十個空格的選文搭配十個選項，每題一個空格，請依文意在文章後所提供的選項中分別選出最適當者。

Coffee, believed to have originated in Africa, was first enjoyed black without anything added. A few hundred years ago, Europeans began __(6)__ milk to their coffee. The practice __(7)__ and eventually became the most common way to consume the beverage. However, it was not until the mid 1980s that the latte art craze began to take hold. The term latte art __(8)__ to those beautiful, artistic designs floating on top of coffee drinks served in coffee shops. A New York barista named David Schomer is __(9)__ with starting this trend. His articles have appeared in coffee magazines, and he wrote the first book on the subject of latte art. At the same time in Italy, barista Luigi Lupi was also creating latte art.

Latte art creation is not simple. It is a meticulous, exacting process that takes __(10)__ to master. In addition, it requires a special kind of milk called microfoam. To make microfoam, steam is added to regular milk, which is rapidly __(11)__. The next step, pouring the hot milk into the espresso, is the hardest part. The microfoam must be poured in such a way that the milk gets in first. Finally, the barista pours the foam on top, __(12)__ those exquisite patterns.

Coffee-drinking has come into __(13)__ for many years in Taiwan. Coffee drinkers are everywhere, and Taiwan even __(14)__ its own coffees. Taiwan coffees do well at the World Barista Championship (WBC), the premier international coffee competition, and are gaining international respect. Each year the WBC showcases baristas from over fifty countries. Their coffees are prepared to exacting standards, presented as performance, and __(15)__ in the categories of taste, creativity, technical skill, and presentation. Attending the WBC would be a great way to check out cutting-edge latte art.

Ⓐ heated　　**Ⓑ** credited　　**Ⓒ** perseverance　　**Ⓓ** creating
Ⓔ produces　　**Ⓕ** refers　　**Ⓖ** adding　　**Ⓗ** spread
Ⓘ favor　　**Ⓙ** judged

6. _____　　7. _____　　8. _____　　9. _____　　10. _____

11. _____　　12. _____　　13. _____　　14. _____　　15. _____

Unit 03

Unit 03

篇章結構 說明：本題型的題幹為段落式短文，以一篇含四個空格的選文搭配四個選項，每題一個空格，請依文意在文章後所提供的選項中分別選出最適當者，填入空格中，使篇章結構清晰有條理。

No one would ever want to be lost or stranded in the wild. While for most people the chances of being stuck on the side of a mountain or getting lost in the woods are very low, it never hurts to know what to do to survive in such a situation. It could make the difference between life and death.

If you are lost in the wild, the first step is to find shelter which will provide protection from the elements. __(16)__ In cold climates, staying dry is extremely important. A layer of wet clothes combined with a chill in the air could prove deadly in the wild. Wet extremities such as fingers and toes can become frostbitten in a matter of minutes. In hotter climates, another danger exists. __(17)__

Since humans can live without food longer than they can live without water, it is essential to find drinkable water as soon as possible. If you are near a river or lake, dig a small hole several feet away. This helps filter the water before you drink it. __(18)__ In the morning, the dew that has collected can be drunk.

Should your time in the wild be longer than expected, finding food will be necessary. Foraging for nuts and berries is sometimes the best option. However, it is important to eat only what is familiar. Trying unknown varieties of berries or other plants isn't a good idea because they may be poisonous.

Of course, the best way to survive in the wild is to be prepared beforehand. If there's any chance you will get lost, make sure your friends or family know your plans. __(19)__

A From direct exposure to the sun, a person may suffer from heatstroke or dehydration.

B By telling others where you're going and what you're planning to do, you could be avoiding a potential disaster.

C Lighting a fire in this way will attract the attention of any mountain rescue teams.

D A cave, a hollowed-out tree, or even large rocks can give temporary shelter from the wind.

E Another method for acquiring water is to lay a piece of plastic on the ground overnight.

16. _____   17. _____   18. _____   19. _____

Unit
03

四 閱讀測驗

說明：每題請根據本篇文章之文意選出最適當的一個選項。

Montesquieu was a French lawyer, philosopher, and writer who lived between 1689 and 1755. His most famous work is *The Spirit of the Laws*, which was published in 1748. Over the course of one thousand pages, Montesquieu examines human laws, social institutions, and types of governments, categorizing the latter as republics, monarchies, or despotisms. This categorization became very well-known at the time as it differed from the typical way of classifying forms of government. Montesquieu argues that certain types of government are more suitable for certain types of societies and that climate and geography can have an impact on this.

Having traveled extensively in Europe and found the English political system particularly impressive, Montesquieu also argues passionately in *The Spirit of the Laws* in favor of the separation of powers. This is the division of political authority into three distinct branches: legislative, judicial, and executive. He states that this separation helps to encourage liberty and prevents people from abusing their power. Montesquieu's argument in this area was so persuasive and forceful that it later inspired the Constitution of the United States of America. *The Spirit of the Laws* was thus highly regarded and influential—yet also controversial—in Montesquieu's lifetime and beyond.

Another of his celebrated works is *Persian Letters*. Although published anonymously in 1721, the book's true author was an open secret and gave Montesquieu his first taste of fame. The book is comprised of a series of letters written by two fictional travelers from Persia—modern-day Iran—who comment on French culture and society. This device allows Montesquieu to express his own views and criticize everything from religion to the monarchy to the class system in a humorous way. It received very favorable reviews at the time for being both entertaining and challenging, and it helped to position Montesquieu as one of the key philosophers of the Age of Enlightenment.

20. How is the article arranged?
    (A) By chronological date.
    (B) By Montesquieu's travels.
    (C) By publishing location.
    (D) By Montesquieu's achievements.

21. Which of the following statements is true about *The Spirit of the Laws*?
    (A) It contains quotes from the Constitution of the United States of America.
    (B) It divides types of governments in a way that was not usual at the time.
    (C) It discusses the serious flaws with the political system in England.
    (D) It argues that the separation of powers is an outdated concept.

22. What do we learn about *Persian Letters*?
    (A) It represents Montesquieu's own thoughts and opinions.
    (B) It is extremely critical of the culture and society in Persia.
    (C) Montesquieu's reputation declined after it was published.
    (D) Montesquieu's contemporaries did not know that he wrote it.

23. Which set of words is used in the article to describe Montesquieu's writing?
    (A) famous, passionately, influential, favorable
    (B) typical, forceful, humorous, challenging
    (C) well-known, persuasive, controversial, entertaining
    (D) famous, impressive, highly regarded, anonymously

20. _____   21. _____   22. _____   23. _____

五 混合題

說明：請根據文章之文意選出或寫出一個最適當的答案。

Illegal logging occurs across the world, from Africa and Asia to Europe and South America. We spoke to two people to get their views on this unlawful activity.

Luiz
I'm not going to sugarcoat the truth: I am an illegal logger. For me, though, it's not an issue of legality; it's a matter of life and death. The income I receive from chopping down trees and selling the wood to the highest bidder is vital for my family and me to survive. Where I live, on the edge of the Amazon Rainforest, there are virtually no employment opportunities, so I have to create my own. To my mind, the far bigger criminals are those who buy and sell the wood: the people looking to make a huge profit by peddling it to rich westerners who want fine furniture made from rare and precious trees. Yet I'm the one who takes all the risks. I have to locate the desired trees, chop them down, transport them across dangerous terrain, and deal with the unsavory characters who buy them. Perhaps if the government were more interested in improving the education system around here or providing job training for people like me, I wouldn't have to do these things. But, to put it bluntly, they don't care.

Juliana
Illegal logging has serious environmental consequences. The uncontrolled chopping down of trees leads to the destruction of essential habitats for countless creatures, potentially causing the extinction of many animal and plant species. It also makes a significant, negative contribution to climate change, as deforestation releases huge amounts of carbon dioxide into the atmosphere. Illegal loggers claim that they have no alternative but to engage in criminal activities. However, the existence of legal loggers—those who have taken the time and effort to get the proper permits—disproves this myth and exposes the real truth. To discourage illegal loggers, we need to focus relentlessly on sustainable logging and make this the only acceptable practice. We also need to raise awareness among consumers about the true origins of the wood, paper, or furniture they are purchasing. If people know certain products are produced through illegal logging and are taught about the devastation this practice can cause, they will be less likely to buy those products. If there is no demand, there will be no supply, and illegal logging will become a thing of the past.

24-25 請從各意見中找出最適當的單詞（word）填入下列句子空格中，並視語法需要做適當的字形變化。每格限填一個單詞（word）。（填充）

Luiz claims that if people like him were ____24.____ properly, they would not have to engage in illegal logging.

Juliana believes that we should concentrate on sustainable logging and ensure that this is the sole type of logging that people will ____25.____ .

26. Which word in Juliana's response means "a commonly believed but false idea"?
（簡答）
_____

27. Which opinions about illegal logging are NOT expressed in either of the responses?
（多選）
(A) Illegally chopping down trees affects both people and animals.
(B) Teaching people about illegal logging will lead to its end.
(C) Retrieving driftwood after storms should be illegal everywhere.
(D) Taking part in illegal logging helps some people to survive.
(E) The penalties for illegal logging are not severe enough.
(F) Those who distribute the wood are guiltier than the loggers.

24. _____   25. _____

26. _____

27. _____

Unit 03

Unit 04

一 綜合測驗

說明：本題型的題幹為段落式短文，選文中含數個空格，每題一個空格，請依文意選出最適當的一個選項。

Kite flying first appeared in Asia over 3,000 years ago and has long been a part of many global cultures. Its variants, kite fighting and kite running, are __(1)__ activities on the Indian subcontinent and also in the Middle East and South America. The Wright brothers' invention of the first airplane was aided by their __(2)__ of kites in flight. Kites have many __(3)__ uses, such as in rescue missions, scientific experiments, and wind energy generation. Today, kite flying continues to be a popular pastime, enjoyed by people of all ages worldwide, with festivals held to celebrate its rich history.

Ranier Hoffman is one of the world's top kite makers, having designed over 300 soaring, spectacular kites while winning several German kite-making championships along the way. One of his aerodynamic works was __(4)__ in the German Museum of Technology. This gifted artist and craftsman __(5)__ of making exquisite kites, sharing his passion at the Berlin University of Applied Sciences. Hoffman designs only one kite per year, but to the delight of kite-flying enthusiasts, twenty of his eye-catching creations are mass-produced by German toy companies. His work continues to inspire future generations of kite enthusiasts, keeping the tradition of kite making alive.

1. (A) good-liked   (B) well-liked   (C) good-looking   (D) well-liking
2. (A) prevention   (B) accusation   (C) observation   (D) corruption
3. (A) practical   (B) medical   (C) physical   (D) tropical
4. (A) disdained   (B) displayed   (C) dismissed   (D) disassembled
5. (A) clarifies the point   (B) expresses the opinions
   (C) discovers the techniques   (D) teaches the art

1. _____ 2. _____ 3. _____ 4. _____ 5. _____

二、文意選填

說明：本題型的題幹為段落式短文，以一篇含十個空格的選文搭配十個選項，每題一個空格，請依文意在文章後所提供的選項中分別選出最適當者。

We live in the age of information. Information, or knowledge, is now considered as precious as gold. Laws known as intellectual property laws exist to protect the rights of those who discover, create, or otherwise come up with the kinds of information we value, __(6)__ the information holder takes the time to register his or her copyright. Books, songs, movies, software, art, and inventions and technologies of every kind are included. Virtually nothing is exempt. Copyright is the word used to describe someone's __(7)__ right to sell or produce such a product. Copyrights are __(8)__ for a specified period of time. Once a copyright expires, the product may become part of the public domain. This means that anyone can then legally use it. During the time a music copyright is in effect, singers or musicians who perform that music publicly are __(9)__ to pay a certain fee to the copyright holder.

"Happy Birthday to You" is easily the __(10)__ song in the English language. Composed by Mildred and Patty Hill over 130 years ago, this simple, catchy tune has been sung by billions all over the world, conquering continents and language barriers at the same time. The Hill sisters sold their song, which was re-sold several times before it ended up in the hands of __(11)__ giant Warner Music Group. There is some __(12)__ about when the copyright expired. Some sources state 1921, while others claim the copyright __(13)__ valid until 1963. In any case, Warner Music Group claimed they should be paid every time "Happy Birthday to You" is played on TV, radio, or in films. Reasoning such uses are public performances, Warner took the matter to __(14)__. To the __(15)__ of many, the judge ruled the company's copyright claim was not on legal grounds, and dismissed the case. Now we can all sing "Happy Birthday to You" without worrying.

Unit 04

- **A** provided
- **B** best-known
- **C** remained
- **D** valid
- **E** relief
- **F** entertainment
- **G** exclusive
- **H** required
- **I** uncertainty
- **J** court

6. _____   7. _____   8. _____   9. _____   10. _____

11. _____ 12. _____ 13. _____ 14. _____ 15. _____

Unit 04

篇章結構

說明：本題型的題幹為段落式短文，以一篇含四個空格的選文搭配四個選項，每題一個空格，請依文意在文章後所提供的選項中分別選出最適當者，填入空格中，使篇章結構清晰有條理。

　　Although seen as punishment for a crime committed, a prison term rarely rehabilitates a criminal to become a productive member of society. __(16)__ That is why the Bard Prison Initiative was created by the State of New York: to reverse this trend. This challenging and selective program provides an opportunity for inmates enrolled in it to earn a college degree. The idea behind the initiative is that an educated ex-convict has a much greater chance to break free of the criminal life. Not all who apply are accepted, and with good reason. Enrollment into the program is a test of perseverance and determination. The 300 prison inmates currently enrolled are not allowed access to the internet. __(17)__ In spite of these challenges, this innovative program has been highly successful. Only 3% of Bard Prison Initiative graduates return to prison. __(18)__

　　Recently in a public debate, the Bard Prison Initiative's debate team faced off against three students from the Harvard College Debating Union—and won. The prison team had to argue that children who are not US citizens should not be permitted to attend school—an idea that was contrary to their genuine beliefs. Even though they were debating against their will, thorough preparation and a unique argument enabled the Bard Prison Initiative's debate team to soundly defeat their better-funded, less restricted, and better-educated Harvard competitors. __(19)__ The success of this initiative shows that people can overcome very difficult obstacles and turn over a new leaf as long as they are given the opportunity.

A Nor are they allowed the use of textbooks or even library books without the permission of the prison guards.

B This is in strong contrast to the state's general prison population, where 40% return to prison within three years.

C It is a sad fact that all too many criminals are released and put back in jail for committing another crime.

D Within two weeks, the inmate had committed a new crime and been sent back to prison.

E The victory was a glorious moment both for the prison team and for the program.

16. _____   17. _____   18. _____   19. _____

Unit 04

四 閱讀測驗

說明：每題請根據本篇文章之文意選出最適當的一個選項。

    Venus flytraps are fascinating plants that grow primarily in the American states of North and South Carolina. They are found in areas such as bogs and wetlands, which have soils that are high in acidity but low in nutrients. For this reason, the plants have evolved to acquire their nutrition in an unusual way; that is, through the consumption of insects and the meat of other small creatures.

    The physical characteristics of Venus flytraps enable them to accomplish this **carnivorous** task. For instance, they have curved leaves that are hinged in the middle, allowing the leaves to fold together and snap shut over unsuspecting prey in less than a second. Their leaves feature small trigger hairs on their surfaces that tell them to close when they are touched twice quickly. According to *Smithsonian* magazine, this means that the plants can cleverly distinguish "between the brush of a scrambling beetle and the plop of a raindrop." Once the leaves have closed, enzymes help the plant to digest the insect and absorb its nutrients over the course of an average of ten days. Each leaf—which also has spiny teeth along its edges and in many ways resembles an open clam—can perform this activity around three times before it falls off the plant. In addition, Venus flytraps have small white flowers that are pollinated by insects in the spring.

    Sadly, though, Venus flytraps are considered a vulnerable species. In South Carolina, housing developments are rapidly encroaching on the plant's natural habitat. In North Carolina, despite growing in protected areas, the plants are frequently targeted by poachers, who take advantage of the shallow roots and the fact that flytraps tend to grow together in clusters. There is also far too much demand for the plants globally, as people are captivated by their unique appearance and behavior. Conservation efforts are underway that will hopefully protect the Venus flytrap for future generations.

20. What do we discover about Venus flytraps?
    (A) They grow in areas that are not damp or acidic enough.
    (B) They have leaves that slam shut when touched two times.
    (C) They have many tiny hairs and teeth on their flowers.
    (D) They can't tell the difference between insects and raindrops.

21. What does "**carnivorous**" in the second paragraph most likely mean?
    (A) insect-spraying
    (B) leaf-growing
    (C) meat-eating
    (D) vegetable-planting

22. Which threat to Venus flytraps is NOT mentioned in the article?
    (A) Poachers ignoring the rules and stealing them.
    (B) Climate change affecting their ability to grow.
    (C) Too many people seeking them as they're unusual.
    (D) Houses being built where they typically grow.

23. Which image most likely shows a Venus flytrap?
    (A)   (B) 
    (C)    (D)

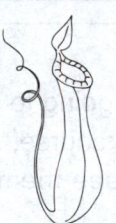

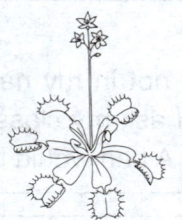

Unit 04

20. _____   21. _____   22. _____   23. _____

Unit 04

五 混合題 說明：請根據文章之文意選出或寫出一個最適當的答案。

Smartphones are essential to modern life, but there has been a raging debate as to whether students should be banned from using smartphones in schools. Please use this forum to contribute your opinions to that debate.

(A) Anna
I think it's better that we have access to our phones during school hours. That way, we can contact our parents if there's an emergency, or tell them we're staying late for a club or going out with friends.

(B) Boris
Rather than ban phones, we should focus on integrating them into the curriculum. I've noticed that my students are much more engaged when I incorporate technology into my lessons. Everyone has a phone, so we should let them use it!

(C) Chloe
My son was a victim of cyberbullying. It made him anxious about going to school, so I support any measure that reduces kids' access to phones. Of course, they'd still be able to use their phones after school, but at least they'd escape them for a few hours.

(D) Deepak
Generally speaking, banning things is not in my nature, but phones are a major distraction during lessons. Even when I ask my class not to use their phones, they sneak a look at them under their desks. A ban would be much easier to police.

(E) Elena
Banning phones would not stop us students being distracted during class. We'd just find other ways to occupy our time, like talking or passing notes. Anyway, I sometimes use my phone to look up information that can help me in my studies.

(F) Felix

Don't get me wrong: I love my phone. But if there were a ban, maybe we would talk to each other during breaks rather than just stare at our screens. Plus, some kids use their phones to bully other kids, so a ban would put a stop to that.

(G) Giselle

My friends who are teachers often complain about phone use in schools. As a trained psychologist, I know how dangerous phones can be. Excessive smartphone use is linked to behavioral problems, sleep disturbances, weak communication skills, and anxiety.

(H) Hiroshi

Technology is a part of life now; there's no point trying to change that. Instead, schools should encourage children to use their phones responsibly. Besides, I want my daughter to be able to contact me immediately if there's an emergency.

24. Put the names of the people into the table below to show whether they are more likely to be for or against a smartphone ban in schools.（填充）

For a ban	Against a ban

25. Which of the people are most likely teachers? Write the names below.（簡答）

_____

26. Which of the following sentences best summarizes Giselle's opinion?（單選）

(A) Teachers should act to prevent smartphone use instead of just complaining.
(B) Using phones too much is associated with a number of negative outcomes.
(C) Psychologists are seeing patients of all ages who are addicted to their phones.
(D) Using smartphones too much in the evening can make kids sleepy during class.

Unit 04

24.

For a ban	Against a ban
_____	_____
_____	_____
_____	_____

25. _____

26. _____

Unit 05

一 綜合測驗

說明：本題型的題幹為段落式短文，選文中含數個空格，每題一個空格，請依文意選出最適當的一個選項。

　　Fruit bats are one of the roughly 1,000 species of bats found around the world. They are different from most other bats in that, while most species feed on insects, their diet consists of, as their name clearly __(1)__, fruit. The bats also eat flowers, which means they help to pollinate many plant species. Another thing that distinguishes fruit bats from other species is that they __(2)__ instead of a kind of radar known as echolocation. This keen sense of smell helps them locate ripe fruit and fragrant flowers, guiding them to their next meal.

　　Unfortunately for fruit bats living in the rainforests of northern Australia, a tick that has been imported from South America is killing them off in large numbers. __(3)__ this crisis, the Tolga Bat Hospital in Australia has leapt into action. They have assembled a group of __(4)__ biologists and animal lovers who regularly check the rainforest to see if baby bats have fallen from trees. This might happen when their mothers have __(5)__ the tick disease. Back at the bat hospital, the staff helps nurse baby bats back to health by caring for them and feeding them milk. Having saved hundreds of bats this way, the Tolga Bat Hospital is truly a friend to the fruit bat.

1. (A) imposes　　　　(B) implies　　　　(C) imagines　　　　(D) imitates
2. (A) focus on sound　(B) adjust to light　(C) react to touch　　(D) rely on scent
3. (A) In contrast to　　(B) In favor of　　 (C) In response to　　(D) By means of
4. (A) frustrated　　　 (B) introverted　　 (C) dedicated　　　　(D) intimidated
5. (A) died of　　　　 (B) talked of　　　 (C) looked for　　　 (D) died for

1. _____　2. _____　3. _____　4. _____　5. _____

二 文意選填

說明：本題型的題幹為段落式短文，以一篇含十個空格的選文搭配十個選項，每題一個空格，請依文意在文章後所提供的選項中分別選出最適當者。

The white-headed capuchin monkey's natural habitat is in Central America and northern South America, where they travel in troops of roughly twenty members. Even if you've never been to those places, it's likely that you've seen the (6) with their long tails, mostly black-haired bodies, pink faces, and white hair on their necks and shoulders. Along with chimpanzees, they are the most commonly seen primates in movies. All three *Night at the Museum* movies (7) a white-headed capuchin named Crystal the Monkey. That monkey, which seems to have been born a natural comic actress, is also in *George of the Jungle* and the *American Pie* movies.

In addition to putting white-headed capuchin monkeys into movies, humans have also found another very meaningful use for these highly (8) animals. It has come to our attention that they have the potential to help people with mobility (9) . A non-profit organization called Helping Hands: Monkey Helpers for the Disabled was set up in 1979, (10) the capuchins and also teaching people how best to interact with the monkeys. The monkeys have several (11) over other creatures that are traditionally used as service animals, such as seeing-eye dogs or companion cats for the elderly. For one thing, they have hands with fingers that (12) them to perform a wide variety of common, useful tasks. People with (13) physical functions can thus be assisted. These tasks include turning the pages of books, pressing buttons on electronic devices, (14) straws into bottles, and picking up dropped objects. Also, since the white-headed capuchins have hair rather than fur, people are less likely to develop an allergy to their non-human helpers. One more benefit is that they often live more than thirty years, making them good, long-term (15) . Let's all make a toast, or at least eat a banana, in honor of the white-headed capuchin monkeys!

Unit 05

Ⓐ enable　　Ⓑ inserting　　Ⓒ intelligent　　Ⓓ disabilities
Ⓔ impaired　　Ⓕ training　　Ⓖ partners　　Ⓗ feature
Ⓘ creatures　　Ⓙ advantages

6. _____　　7. _____　　8. _____　　9. _____　　10. _____

11. _____　　12. _____　　13. _____　　14. _____　　15. _____

Unit 05

篇章結構 說明：本題型的題幹為段落式短文，以一篇含四個空格的選文搭配四個選項，每題一個空格，請依文意在文章後所提供的選項中分別選出最適當者，填入空格中，使篇章結構清晰有條理。

　　Aamir Khan, the son of a prominent film producer, was born in 1965. __(16)__ Over the years, he has built a reputation for choosing diverse and meaningful roles that challenge societal norms. After committing to a role, Khan focuses intently on becoming the character so as to be as convincing as possible. His work ethic toward his roles and other projects is so strong that he has acquired a nickname: Mr. Perfectionist. This dedication can be seen in his physical transformations and extensive research for each role. His hard work has helped him earn numerous awards during his career, which has spanned more than four decades so far.

　　However, Khan has another side. He is passionately interested in political, humanitarian, and environmental issues. __(17)__ UNICEF named him a Goodwill Ambassador for the South Asian region. Through this role, he has actively promoted children's rights, education, and health initiatives. In 2013, *Time* magazine included him in its list of the 100 Most Influential People in the World.

　　Khan has had a significant impact on Indian society through a talk show he created called *Satyamev Jayate*, or *Truth Alone Prevails*. __(18)__ The show has covered issues such as gender inequality, child labor, and corruption, sparking nationwide discussions. However, his views are sometimes considered to be controversial. His ideas, recommendations, and causes have not always been popular in India, a conservative country. __(19)__ Despite facing criticism, he remains committed to using his influence to advocate for meaningful change. He hopes that his efforts will keep raising the tough questions that many people in society prefer to ignore.

Ⓐ In this movie, Khan plays an amateur wrestler who trains his daughters in the sport.

Ⓑ Still, Khan continues to fight for social justice and try to change the world for the better.

Ⓒ He uses the program to tackle the social problems that are widespread in India.

Ⓓ These interests have given him an even greater influence outside the entertainment world.

Ⓔ He is one of the most famous and successful figures in the Indian film industry known as Bollywood.

16. _____   17. _____   18. _____   19. _____

Unit 05

Unit 05

四 閱讀測驗 説明：每題請根據本篇文章之文意選出最適當的一個選項。

　　Body armor has been used throughout human history to protect warriors, knights, and soldiers from enemy weapons. The materials used for the armor are reflective of both the technological developments of the time and the type of weapons the armor was required to repel. Primitive civilizations likely used some form of armor. There is evidence, for example, that warriors in China in the 11th century BC wore armor made of several layers of rhinoceros skin.

　　Many people nowadays, though, probably think of the Middle Ages when they hear the word "armor," and that 1,000-year-long period did indeed feature two major types of protective covering. The first was chain mail. Usually constructed from small interlocking iron rings, chain mail had actually been in use since the days of the Roman Empire, but its ability to offer reasonable protection from spears, swords, and arrows saw it become more commonplace in the Middle Ages. Plate armor, meanwhile, developed during the latter half of the period. Typically made of steel, plate armor grew in sophistication until it could allow the wearer an almost total range of movement. Tiny metal plates even covered individual finger joints. With its superior strength and ability to **deflect** lethal weapons so that they changed course, plate armor had largely replaced chain mail by the time the Middle Ages drew to a close.

　　Modern body armor is both strong and lightweight. One example is the synthetic material Kevlar, which was developed by a Polish-American chemist named Stephanie Kwolek in the 1960s and is commonly used in the manufacture of bulletproof vests. Soldiers often wear body armor that combines Kevlar with ceramic plates. These plates are inserted into pockets in the bulletproof vests, lending extra protection against rifle rounds that are fired at high speed.

20. In what order did the following types of body armor appear?
    a. plates of steel
    b. animal skins
    c. rings of iron
    d. artificial substances

    (A) d > a > b > c
    (B) a > d > c > b
    (C) c > b > d > a
    (D) b > c > a > d

21. Why is the Roman Empire mentioned in the article?
    (A) Because Romans wore armor that allowed them to move easily.
    (B) Because a specific type of body armor was used during that period.
    (C) Because Roman soldiers used the same materials as Chinese warriors.
    (D) Because armor from that long-ago era has yet to be bettered.

22. Which is the most likely meaning of "**deflect**" in the second paragraph?
    (A) To make something feel pain.
    (B) To allow something to easily enter.
    (C) To prevent something from being strong.
    (D) To cause something to change direction.

23. How does the author conclude the article?
    (A) By detailing the background of a famous chemist.
    (B) By mentioning similarities between old and new armor.
    (C) By providing contemporary examples of body armor.
    (D) By discussing the history of firearms and bullets.

20. _____   21. _____   22. _____   23. _____

Unit 05

Unit **05**

五 混合題 說明：請根據文章之文意選出或寫出一個最適當的答案。

Whether parents should give their children an allowance is a topic that arouses a variety of opinions. We asked two parents and two children for their take on the matter.

Paula
I used to give my daughter a weekly allowance. I thought it would teach her to be financially independent and responsible with money. I wanted her to learn that there are things that are essential to buy and things that are desirable to buy, and we can't always have both. But she didn't prioritize her spending at all. Her allowance also gave her a sense of entitlement: she took it for granted that she should get the money and even argued with me about the amount. So, I put my foot down and canceled her allowance.

Viola
Getting an allowance is great! Having more control over my own finances makes me feel like a responsible adult, and because my allowance is linked to how many chores I complete, I have been motivated to help out around the house more. I even volunteer to clean the toilet and unclog the drains, which are the worst chores in the world! Receiving that money at the end of the week, though, makes all the hard work seem worthwhile, and I feel that my efforts have been truly rewarded.

James
Without doubt, giving my son an allowance has helped him to become an independent young man. He now has much more confidence when dealing with money, and the allowance has helped him to learn the value of money. If he intends to buy something, he checks its price and calculates how long it will take him to have enough cash. Then, he sets money aside every week until he has the required amount. These are vital skills that will help him in his adult life. Based on our experience, I would encourage all parents to give their children an allowance.

Franklin
I love getting an allowance! Being able to go out with my friends and spend my own money is great. It's not just about having money to treat myself, though. I'm very interested in helping others and giving back to the community, so I've started

donating small amounts to local charities. I think it's very important that those who have the means help the less fortunate in society. I plan to always use part of my allowance for this purpose, and I hope I can inspire my friends to do the same.

24-25 請從文章中找出最適當的單詞（word）填入下列句子空格中，並視語法需要做適當的字形變化。每格限填一個單詞（word）。（填充）

The fact that Viola's allowance is connected to the number of chores she does has given her the ___24.___ to help out more at home.

James is convinced that providing his son with an allowance has made the boy more ___25.___ when dealing with financial matters.

26. Which word in the responses means "the belief that you deserve a certain privilege or a special kind of treatment"?（簡答）

_____

27. Which of the following financial concepts do the respondents focus on? Write the correct LETTER next to the correct name.（配合）
    (A) Differentiating needs from wants
    (B) Making socially responsible decisions
    (C) Understanding budgeting and saving
    (D) Appreciating the rewards of labor

    Paula: _____
    Viola: _____
    James: _____
    Franklin: _____

24. _____   25. _____

26. _____

27. Paula: _____   Viola: _____   James: _____   Franklin: _____

Unit 06

一 綜合測驗　說明：本題型的題幹為段落式短文，選文中含數個空格，每題一個空格，請依文意選出最適當的一個選項。

　　Restaurant dining is as much a social activity as it is a dining experience. Some people, therefore, believe that dining alone is reluctantly undertaken only by the lonely. Nothing could be further from the truth.　(1)　, many people prefer to dine alone, and there are numerous reasons why.

　　First, after a long day at work, indulging in some quality "me time" is an excellent way to　(2)　. This may involve reading a book or watching a favorite TV drama online while eating. These activities would be impossible if a companion insisted on making small talk or asking for advice on how to　(3)　their latest personal crisis. Dining alone also allows for quiet reflection, offering a rare chance to relax without distractions.

　　Another godsend is being able to eat exactly what you want. For example, dining with a vegan dramatically reduces the dining options　(4)　. Without such constraints, solo diners have the freedom to enjoy their favorite foods without compromise. Finally, dining alone allows one to fully enjoy the　(5)　without being distracted by others. In the absence of conversation, a person can focus entirely on the flavors of the dish.

1. (A) As a result　　(B) In addition　　(C) As usual　　(D) In fact
2. (A) unwind　　(B) depart　　(C) unpack　　(D) delay
3. (A) coincide with　　(B) consult with　　(C) suffer from　　(D) deal with
4. (A) improbable　　(B) available　　(C) dependable　　(D) incapable
5. (A) color and shape of a dish　　(B) weight and texture of a plate
   (C) aroma and taste of a meal　　(D) sound and content of a chat

1. _____　2. _____　3. _____　4. _____　5. _____

二、文意選填

說明：本題型的題幹為段落式短文，以一篇含十個空格的選文搭配十個選項，每題一個空格，請依文意在文章後所提供的選項中分別選出最適當者。

　　Personal hygiene is essential for the health of individuals, and for the well-being of communities. Whether it is brushing our teeth after each meal or changing our clothes daily, hygiene is   (6) . This fact is particularly the case in community meeting places such as public transportation hubs   (7)   hundreds, if not thousands, of people are forced to share confined spaces. By merely touching the surface of an escalator handrail or ticket counter, billions of   (8)   dangerous germs are instantly transferred from person to person. These germs may   (9)   anything from a cold or flu virus to gastroenteritis or a deadly strain of hepatitis. The only practical way to prevent diseases such as these from spreading is for everybody to wash their hands   (10)   at least three or four times a day.

　　In Sri Lanka, where public transport is notoriously cramped and overcrowded, a health company called the Asiri Hospital Group joined forces with a large, successful advertising agency to not only raise   (11)   of hygiene on public transport but to also provide a practical solution—the Soap Bus Ticket. The Soap Bus Ticket is made from paper infused with a piece of pleasantly fragrant soap,   (12)   is also a powerful disinfectant. When a passenger arrives at his or her   (13) , instead of disposing of their ticket in the trash, they use it to wash their hands. In addition to the Soap Bus Ticket, posters are strategically placed in bus stops, and in public toilets—where soap is rarely if ever available—that promote the benefits of   (14)   hygiene. The environmentally friendly tickets also   (15)   the issue of disposing of millions of discarded tickets used throughout the country daily. There can be no doubt that this hands-on advertising campaign is just the ticket when it comes to preventing the spread of disease.

Unit 06

(A) include (B) thoroughly (C) proper (D) awareness
(E) crucial (F) destination (G) where (H) address
(I) which (J) potentially

6. _____   7. _____   8. _____   9. _____   10. _____

11. _____   12. _____   13. _____   14. _____   15. _____

Unit 06

> **篇章結構**　說明：本題型的題幹為段落式短文，以一篇含四個空格的選文搭配四個選項，每題一個空格，請依文意在文章後所提供的選項中分別選出最適當者，填入空格中，使篇章結構清晰有條理。

When Angie Tagalog gave birth to her son, Brian, it was not the moment of joy that she had anticipated: her son was born without arms. For the first year of Brian's life, Angie cried daily. ___(16)___ However, she felt that her sadness would have a negative effect on her son. Hence, Angie pulled herself together and started to encourage her son to try as many things as he could. She believed that fostering a positive mindset in Brian was the key to helping him build confidence and independence.

To Angie's delight, Brian—with her encouragement—overcame his disability. Incredibly, he learned to use his legs and feet as though they were arms and hands. As time went by, he learned to do almost everything other boys of his age could do, such as playing video games and driving a car. He also developed his skills as an artist. ___(17)___ His determination and perseverance moved those around him, proving that physical limitations do not define a person's potential.

Brian's interest in art inspired him to pursue a career as a tattoo artist, and several years ago, he was successfully trained to be a certified tattoo artist. ___(18)___ He applied for one job after another, but unfortunately, no established tattoo parlor was willing to hire him. Despite his undeniable talent, many employers hesitated, doubting whether he could meet customers' expectations.

After a few years of receiving rejection letters and not being called back, Brian decided to open his own tattoo parlor called Tattoos by Foot in Tucson, Arizona, where he was raised. ___(19)___ His incredible ability and unique story turned his shop into a must-visit destination for tattoo enthusiasts. This success has, in turn, generated huge amounts of interest from media outlets and online. Through social media and news features, his work has gained widespread recognition, inspiring countless people around the world.

A These accomplishments confirmed that Brian could do anything that he set his mind on.
B To his great surprise, his own business thrived, attracting local and international customers.
C However, gaining certification proved easy compared to finding employment.
D Seeing his amazing designs, the company immediately offered Brian employment.
E The thought of the immense challenges and difficult life that lay ahead of her disabled son upset her greatly.

16. _____   17. _____   18. _____   19. _____

Unit
06

四 閱讀測驗　說明：每題請根據本篇文章之文意選出最適當的一個選項。

　　Despite originating in India, curry is one of Japan's favorite dishes. In fact, curry is so prevalent in Japan that many people consider it to be the national dish.

　　The arrival of curry in Japan coincided with the spread of the British Empire throughout the 19th century. The British had developed their own version of curry, which was essentially a simplified version of the multitude of curries that they encountered in India. ❶ Although the British did not colonize Japan, they established Japan-based businesses during the Meiji era to capitalize on the trade of products with British colonies, such as India and what we now know as Pakistan and Bangladesh. Curry was one of many products introduced to Japan during this period. ❷ It is said that this introduction first occurred when British sailors, who were carrying curry powder, became shipwrecked and were rescued by a Japanese fishing boat. Although we don't know whether this is true or not, we do know that the Japanese instantly fell in love with the spicy flavor of this delicious dish.

　　Since curry was introduced into Japan, its taste has evolved to be less spicy and much sweeter. This is in sharp contrast to the Indian version. ❸ Broadly speaking, the Japanese have developed three distinct types of curry dishes: curry rice, curry noodles, and curry pastry. While Japanese curry commonly includes pork or chicken and vegetables, many of Japan's 47 prefectures have a curry dish that locals consider their own because it **reflects** the local ingredients. Hiroshima, for instance, is famous for its curries made with oysters. Compared to traditional Japanese cuisine, which tends to be quite elaborate, curry recipes are quick and easy to prepare. ❹ This is one of the reasons why schools and the Japanese armed forces regularly serve curry dishes and why curry is so popular among busy Japanese families.

20. Which of the following aspects about Japanese curry is NOT discussed in the passage?
    (A) What is usually in it.
    (B) Where it came from.
    (C) Who typically eats it.
    (D) How it is often made.

21. According to the passage, what did the British do to Indian curry?
    (A) Added Japanese flavors to it.
    (B) Made their own variety of it.
    (C) Asked for permission to sell it.
    (D) Increased the number of spices in it.

22. Which of the sentences marked with a number is an assumption rather than a fact?
    (A) ❶
    (B) ❷
    (C) ❸
    (D) ❹

23. Which of the following is the closest meaning to "**reflects**" in the third paragraph?
    (A) To throw back.
    (B) To think about.
    (C) To demonstrate.
    (D) To show an image.

Unit 06

20. _____   21. _____   22. _____   23. _____

Unit 06

五 混合題
說明：請根據文章之文意選出或寫出一個最適當的答案。

Orcas—also known as killer whales—are huge, black-and-white sea mammals. Found in oceans across the world, they are renowned for their high levels of intelligence and sophisticated communication skills. In the early 2020s, there were numerous reports of orcas seemingly attacking fishing boats off the coasts of Spain and Portugal. Typically, the creatures would target and ram the rudders of the small vessels, leaving them damaged and, in a tiny number of cases, even causing them to sink. Sailors and fishermen reported that the female leader of the pod would be the first to attack the boat, and then the younger orcas would imitate her behavior. Scientists and researchers came up with two main theories as to why this was happening.

The first theory was that a female orca had been through a traumatic experience, such as colliding with a boat or becoming entangled in unlawful fishing nets. This incident prompted her to start acting aggressively toward boats and knowingly or unknowingly teaching the younger members of her pod to act in the same way. The Portuguese biologist Alfredo López Fernandez believed that this was the most likely theory. He told the website *Live Science* that a "traumatized orca is the one that started this behavior of physical contact with [boats]." He noted, however, that most encounters between orcas and sailing vessels did not lead to harm for the boat or the crew, and that the behavior was quite risky for the orcas, who might have become injured themselves by ramming the rudders.

The second theory was that these were not attacks; they were playful incidents. This was based on the belief that, given the size and strength of orcas, if they had truly wanted to destroy a boat or harm the humans inside, they would very easily have been able to do so. While the true motivations were unknown, David Lusseau, a sustainability scientist based in Denmark, speculated to *Newsweek* that they could have included "play, social behavior, dexterity practice, fun," or a number of other reasons rather than revenge for having experienced trauma. Naturally inquisitive and playful, the orcas could simply have been seeking enjoyment. Regardless of their actual intentions, it is worth considering that the fishing boats were in the orcas' natural environment, not the other way around. As Nuria Riera, a Spanish volunteer conservationist, told the BBC: "We have to remember that the sea is their home—we're the intruders."

24-25 請從文章中找出最適當的單詞（word）填入下列句子空格中，並視語法需要做適當的字形變化。每格限填一個單詞（word）。（填充）

One theory about why orcas started ramming fishing boats was that a female orca had undergone a traumatic experience, such as being involved in a ___24.___ with a boat, and then began behaving aggressively toward other boats.

Another theory was that the orcas, who could cause immense harm to people or ___25.___ to boats if they wanted to, were enjoying themselves and having fun, not looking for vengeance.

26. Which word in the introductory paragraph shares the same meaning as the word in quotation marks in the following sentence?（簡答）

    When she goes to a KTV, Marianne always tries to "copy" the way her idol sings.

    _____

27. What do we NOT learn about the attacks?（單選）
    (A) The general location of the incidents.
    (B) The part of the boats the orcas focused on.
    (C) The total number of these occurrences.
    (D) The outcome of a minority of the events.

24. _____

25. _____

26. _____

27. _____

Unit 06

Unit 07

一、綜合測驗

說明：本題型的題幹為段落式短文，選文中含數個空格，每題一個空格，請依文意選出最適當的一個選項。

Lauren Singer is a New York University graduate who majored in environmental studies. She is __(1)__ convinced that she should live a near zero-waste life. She has __(2)__ all the trash she has been unable to avoid or recycle in a small 16oz jar. Included in the jar are the stickers that are stuck on fresh fruit and vegetables and the __(3)__ that attach price labels to the second-hand clothing that Singer suggests we buy. These small items highlight how difficult it is to eliminate waste completely, but Singer's commitment shows that reducing waste is possible with thoughtful choices.

Through her website, Trash is for Tossers, Singer provides helpful hints for others who would also like to lessen the amount of trash they generate. She shares practical strategies for reducing waste in daily life. __(4)__ obvious advice, such as taking reusable bags and containers when shopping, Singer explains how to make zero-packaging environmentally friendly toothpaste and delicious homemade salad dressing. These alternatives help minimize plastic waste. Visitors to Singer's website are also encouraged to __(5)__ healthy eating habits. To find out more about Lauren Singer, visit trashisfortossers.com.

1. (A) evenly   (B) namely   (C) firmly   (D) widely
2. (A) convicted   (B) collided   (C) conceded   (D) collected
3. (A) plastic tags (B) wooden pegs   (C) printed receipts (D) rubber bands
4. (A) On account of (B) As well as   (C) On behalf of   (D) As far as
5. (A) embrace   (B) displace   (C) preface   (D) replace

1. _____   2. _____   3. _____   4. _____   5. _____

二 文意選填

說明：本題型的題幹為段落式短文，以一篇含十個空格的選文搭配十個選項，每題一個空格，請依文意在文章後所提供的選項中分別選出最適當者。

Italy has provided some iconic foods and beverages that have taken the world by storm. Pizza, spaghetti, and expresso coffee are among the most famous. Tiramisu, the delicious layered cake, is quickly becoming just as well-known.

Tiramisu is made by combining a unique collection of __(6)__, which includes lady finger biscuits, cream cheese, egg yolks, coffee, sugar, and cocoa powder. The recipe also has numerous __(7)__ that include adding wine or brandy and custard. It is sometimes __(8)__ with whipped cream, fruit or berries in either a round glass that shows off the layers or as a square slice.

The __(9)__ of tiramisu are not certain; however, most culinary scholars agree that it was first concocted in the late 1960s in northern Italy. There is also a less reputable report claiming it was created to honor a duke that visited Tuscany in the 17th century. This is highly __(10)__, as there are no tiramisu recipes mentioned in recipe books before the late '60s. What's more, the word, tiramisu, didn't appear in dictionaries until the 1980s.

Roberto Linguanotto, the owner of a restaurant in Treviso, called Le Beccherie, and his apprentice, Francesca Valori, claim to have created the cake. Their claim is somewhat __(11)__ because Valori's maiden name is Tiramisu. However, a pastry chef in the same town also claims to have created the recipe. He says it took two years to perfect the recipe and insists that he __(12)__ Roberto Linguanotto's restaurant with the dessert.

There is also another __(13)__. It describes how the wife of an Italian World War II soldier made the dessert for her husband to take to the __(14)__ line. Food was __(15)__, so the woman scraped together some leftovers to create the dessert. No matter which story you believe, everyone agrees that tiramisu is delicious.

Ⓐ supplied   Ⓑ variations   Ⓒ convincing   Ⓓ origins
Ⓔ served   Ⓕ ingredients   Ⓖ myth   Ⓗ scarce
Ⓘ unlikely   Ⓙ front

6. _____   7. _____   8. _____   9. _____   10. _____

11. _____ 12. _____ 13. _____ 14. _____ 15. _____

Unit 07

Unit 07

三、篇章結構
說明：本題型的題幹為段落式短文，以一篇含四個空格的選文搭配四個選項，每題一個空格，請依文意在文章後所提供的選項中分別選出最適當者，填入空格中，使篇章結構清晰有條理。

    A man sits on stage with a large doll-like puppet on his lap. __(16)__ The audience knows that it's really the man speaking, not the dummy, but the ventriloquist amazes the crowd by not moving his lips at all—no one is able to see any sign that he is speaking. The audience is often left wondering how the ventriloquist can control his voice so skillfully. The man and the dummy have a conversation, and they make jokes and trade insults. It's a battle of wits that makes for some hilarious moments. This is a typical modern-day ventriloquist's show.

    Long before dummies and jokes, ventriloquists had spiritual roles. They would speak without moving their lips, which seemed like a strange kind of magic. The voices seemed to come right from their stomachs. Ancient cultures thought that these mysterious voices were supernatural messages. __(17)__

    As time passed, ventriloquists' stunts came to be seen as simple entertainment instead of spiritual messages. The art of ventriloquism changed at the end of the 19th century when a comedian named Fred Russell performed the first ventriloquist act with a dummy. __(18)__ Later, several ventriloquists and their dummies became household names. Buffalo Bob Smith and his dummy Howdy Doody were probably the most widely known in the US, becoming big stars of radio and television in the mid-1900s. __(19)__

    Today, all kinds of ventriloquist acts can be found, from the classic children's TV shows on YouTube to adult comedians with dirty jokes. Despite changing times, ventriloquism continues to entertain audiences. This strange and amusing talent has turned out to be a great way to entertain both young and old.

A Another famous puppet called Lamb Chop was a big hit with young children.

B When the man speaks to it, the puppet, or "dummy," responds to him in its own voice.

C Sadly, ventriloquist acts have fallen out of fashion in recent years.

D It was believed that the voices from ventriloquists' bellies were spirits, and people thought that these spirits predicted the future.

E These shows mostly involved Russell demonstrating his ability to "throw" his voice, or drink a glass of water while the dummy talked to the audience.

16. _____   17. _____   18. _____   19. _____

四 閱讀測驗　說明：每題請根據本篇文章之文意選出最適當的一個選項。

　　Being an astronaut takes its toll on the body due to the unique conditions and environment of space travel. The very weak gravity in a spacecraft, for example, leads to bone loss and muscle weakening. According to NASA, during a spaceflight, bones can lose up to 1.5 percent of their mineral density every month, while muscle mass is lost at a faster rate than on Earth. This is because the lack of significant gravity means astronauts' bones and muscles are essentially not being used to support and move their bodies. In an attempt to combat this, NASA encourages astronauts to perform specific exercises designed for spacecraft.

　　Space travel also impacts the immune system, stressing the body out and leaving astronauts vulnerable to catching colds and other viruses. Germs, meanwhile, spread easily in the closed environment of a spacecraft. According to *National Geographic*, astronauts on board the International Space Station (ISS) have developed breathing infections and skin rashes. Research reported in the magazine indicates that ISS crew members experience "a drop in immune function within days of arrival at the ISS." While studies into the reasons for this are ongoing, NASA is taking saliva and blood samples from astronauts to monitor changes in their immune systems.

　　The effects of space travel are not only physical; they can be psychological, too. Even though the crew go through intensive training before they head into orbit, being confined to a relatively small space station for months on end can be a shock to the system. The astronauts may feel disconnected from their families back on Earth, fatigued due to a disrupted day-night cycle, and bored because of their restricted environment. All of this can lead to mental health issues. To counteract this, NASA is researching whether virtual reality can be used to create calming environments for astronauts and boost their mood.

20. What do we learn about astronauts' muscles and bones?
    (A) They waste away completely due to the lack of exercise.
    (B) They are inevitably used more in the unique space environment.
    (C) They become less strong than they were when the astronauts were on Earth.
    (D) They are affected by the types of space suits the astronauts wear.

21. What does the research quoted in *National Geographic* show?
    (A) Breathing infections take hours, not days, to spread on the ISS.
    (B) Skin rashes are significantly less severe on the ISS than Earth.
    (C) Astronauts in space become less able to think clearly.
    (D) The immunity of ISS astronauts declines almost immediately.

22. Which potential psychological effect of space travel is NOT mentioned in the article?
    (A) Experiencing feelings of boredom.
    (B) Being tired due to sleeping difficulties.
    (C) Feeling separated from close relatives.
    (D) Being anxious due to the intense pressure.

23. Which of the following can be inferred from the article?
    (A) The ISS has increased the amount of training its astronauts complete.
    (B) Germs and viruses are more active on the ISS than other space stations.
    (C) NASA is constantly trying to reduce the problems astronauts face.
    (D) Medications are significantly less effective when taken in space.

20. _____ 21. _____ 22. _____ 23. _____

Unit 07

Unit 07

五 混合題
說明：請根據文章之文意選出或寫出一個最適當的答案。

    Wildfires brought death and destruction to the Hawaiian island of Maui in August 2023. Here are the stories of four people who lived through the disaster.

Malia
It all happened so suddenly. No sooner had I smelled smoke than the whole neighborhood was engulfed in flames. Luckily, my neighbor has a car, and he helped me and some others get to safety. I don't know for sure, but I fear my beautiful home has been completely destroyed. The strong winds and dry conditions of recent days combined to create the perfect storm for these wildfires. But I keep dwelling on this question: why did the siren that is supposed to warn us about emergencies not go off? Why did the system fail?

Kaimana
I knew that the weather conditions were not good. So, when we received calls from concerned members of the public telling us that downed power lines were causing fires, I feared the worst. I immediately ordered my officers to head to the most at-risk areas and help residents in any way they could. But the tragic fact is that, faced with such a powerful natural foe, there is only so much that we could do. I also had to think of the safety of the men under my command, who put their lives on the line.

Ariel
I love surfing and the warm, welcoming Hawaiian people, so I've been coming to Maui for many years. I always thought they had a robust emergency warning system in place, but I guess this time it failed. It was like the authorities were completely unprepared. Surely the bone-dry weather and powerful winds prior to the wildfires should've set some alarm bells ringing. I, along with other guests at my hotel, had to jump into the sea to escape the flames. It was utterly terrifying, and I thank God that we were saved.

Nalu

In the midst of such a tragedy, it is natural that people look to me—a senior civil servant, someone in a position of authority—for answers. Reporters and residents have confronted me about why the emergency siren did not go off, calling it a mistake that cost lives. But the siren is typically used to warn of tsunamis, which necessitate a completely different emergency response. Instead, I believe we need to look at why downed power lines were left on in such dangerous weather conditions. In the fullness of time, an official inquiry will discover the real causes of this disaster.

The content above has been adapted from real events.

24-25 請從文章中找出最適當的單詞（word）填入下列句子空格中，並視語法需要做適當的字形變化。每格限填一個單詞（word）。（填充）

The responses point to several possible causes of the wildfires on Maui and why they resulted in so much destruction: the apparent ___24.___ of the emergency warning system; the downed power lines; and the dry and ___25.___ conditions prior to the fires.

26. Which phrase in Malia's response means "a very bad situation caused by a combination of negative circumstances"?（簡答）

    _____

27. Who are the people that gave the responses? Write their names in the correct positions below.（配合）

    (A) Police chief: _____
    (B) Tourist: _____
    (C) Mayor: _____
    (D) Local: _____

24. _____   25. _____

26. _____

27. (A) _____   (B) _____   (C) _____   (D) _____

Unit 08

一 綜合測驗

說明：本題型的題幹為段落式短文，選文中含數個空格，每題一個空格，請依文意選出最適當的一個選項。

Alexander Hamilton was a talented politician, an influential lawyer, and a respected financier. As one of the USA's founding fathers, he also fought hard for America's __(1)__. His contributions played a crucial role in shaping the nation's early financial system.

In 2015, Hamilton's life story was immortalized in a Broadway musical called *Hamilton*. The play is based on Hamilton's biography, which was published in 2004, and has received __(2)__ from critics and audiences alike. The musical's innovative storytelling and diverse cast have helped it gain widespread popularity, leading to __(3)__ box office success.

The story of the protagonist's childhood and marriage unfolds before Hamilton's revolutionary activities __(4)__. His rise to power in the George Washington administration involves political struggles against hostile opponents. These conflicts highlight the __(5)__ that shaped early American politics. The performance reaches a climax when Hamilton meets an untimely death in a duel with Aaron Burr, an unsuccessful political candidate.

The show is radically different from other historical musicals because of its modern hip-hop music soundtrack, which is accompanied by rap-style dialogue and lyrics. This unique blend of history and contemporary music has made *Hamilton* an unforgettable theatrical experience.

1. (A) correspondence (B) independence (C) persistence (D) adolescence
2. (A) peril (B) pursuit (C) offense (D) acclaim
3. (A) unpredictable (B) unemployed (C) unconditional (D) unprecedented
4. (A) take place (B) take action (C) take turns (D) take sides
5. (A) close friendships (B) intense rivalries
   (C) peaceful alliances (D) economic strategies

1. _____ 2. _____ 3. _____ 4. _____ 5. _____

二 文意選填

說明：本題型的題幹為段落式短文，以一篇含十個空格的選文搭配十個選項，每題一個空格，請依文意在文章後所提供的選項中分別選出最適當者。

A recent American study undertaken by Professor Warren Booth from the University of Tulsa in Oklahoma has made a sensational discovery—a small percentage of female snakes living in the wild are capable of reproducing without males.

How did researchers make the (6) discovery? It was discovered after removing pregnant copperhead and cottonmouth snakes from their natural environments. Two of the snakes that gave birth had an identical genetic make-up to their (7). This DNA evidence confirmed that no males had been (8) in the reproduction process. The study concluded that between 2.5 and 5 percent of wild snake litters could potentially (9) from asexual reproduction.

Virgin births are common in invertebrates such as ants and bees. However, they are (10) in vertebrates. In fact, the only known cases have been in specimens that were held in captivity and separated from males. Previously, scientists thought hormones or a virus—as is the case with some wasps— (11) these virgin births in captivity. Another theory (12) that a redundant asexual reproductive process, which was necessary when males were not always available in prehistoric times, was reactivated by an environment without males. Virgin births would, therefore, function as a reproductive backup providing a greater (13) of a species' long-term survival. The discovery made by Professor Booth and his research team has brought these theories into (14), as their study involved snakes that got pregnant without the involvement of males, even though males were present. However, Peter Baumann of the University of Kansas Medical Center in the US suggests that if asexual reproduction is in fact a reproductive backup, the number of virgin births in the wild may (15) as individual species numbers dwindle.

(A) offspring (B) increase (C) rare (D) chance
(E) suggested (F) triggered (G) question (H) involved
(I) result (J) fascinating

6. _____   7. _____   8. _____   9. _____   10. _____

11. _____ 12. _____ 13. _____ 14. _____ 15. _____

Echolocation is a form of perception by means of sound waves and echoes. __(16)__ When bats hunt in the dark, they emit sonar signals with high frequencies and in very rapid bursts. The signals fly out from the bats, and when these signals hit an object, such as a tree, a bird, or preferably a tasty insect, they bounce back to the bats. __(17)__ That is, bats use the echoes from the sounds they produce to find what they're looking for; this is what we call echolocation.

Other animals use echolocation as well. Dolphins are one of the good examples. However, it might surprise you to learn of another creature that has been found to use echolocation: humans. Not all humans have this ability, but a few have developed it as a skill to compensate for their physical limitations. One such person is an American man named Ben Underwood. Ben is completely blind, and no trace of light reaches his brain. __(18)__ As he moves around, he makes "clicking" sounds to gain information about his surroundings. Scientists have studied Ben's ability and found that his brain processes the echoes of the clicking sounds in a way similar to how sighted people process visual information.

Interestingly, although people who have lost their sight can no longer gain visual knowledge from their surroundings because of their nonfunctional eyes, the section of the brain called the visual cortex does not become useless. __(19)__ As Ben puts it, "I can hear that wall behind you over there. I can hear right there—the radio, and the fan." His story has inspired many visually impaired individuals to explore echolocation as a tool for greater independence. Through echolocation, Ben and other visually impaired people can communicate with the world, and the world responds to the call.

Ⓐ Ben studied these flying creatures for years before putting his theory into practice.
Ⓑ Nevertheless, he has adapted to his blindness in an amazing way.
Ⓒ Bats are one of the most commonly known users of this ability.
Ⓓ For Ben, for instance, echolocation replaces the eyes and helps to form "visual" images in his brain.
Ⓔ Following the signals that bounce back to them, bats can determine where their prey is and snatch it in midair.

16. _____ 17. _____ 18. _____ 19. _____

Unit
08

Unit 08

四 閱讀測驗 說明：每題請根據本篇文章之文意選出最適當的一個選項。

On May 13, 1787, eleven ships under the command of Captain Arthur Phillip set sail from Portsmouth, England. These ships were known as the First Fleet, and their destination was Australia. On board the fleet were over 1,400 people, around half of whom were convicts sentenced to "transportation" to a faraway prison as punishment for their crimes. The other half was made up of sailors, navy soldiers, government officers, and early settlers who wanted to build a new life in a planned British colony in Botany Bay, Australia. It took the fleet around eight months to journey 24,000 kilometers—via supply stops in Brazil and South Africa—to their destination. Remarkably, given the weather conditions and spread of disease, the vast majority of travelers survived the trip.

Upon arrival at Botany Bay, though, Phillip and his crew were less than impressed. **The specific location had been chosen partly because of explorer Captain James Cook's earlier, favorable account of it.** However, in reality, the bay was too shallow, the soil too poor in quality, and the freshwater sources too scarce to support the establishment of a new colony. Thankfully, Phillip found a much more promising bay that was sheltered and fertile and located just to the north. He named it Sydney Cove after the prominent British politician Baron Sydney, and the fleet settled there on January 26, 1788.

The settlement of this first British colony had a profound impact on Australia. It laid the foundations for a population and economic boom as more settlers and immigrants from Britain and beyond landed on the shores of the continent. The introduction of the English legal system and the spread of the English language changed the society and culture forever. However, the arrival of the First Fleet also ultimately led to the forced removal of indigenous communities, and the inevitable introduction of diseases such as smallpox devastated these populations.

20. What do we discover about the First Fleet?
    (A) Its initial purpose was to be a floating prison for criminals.
    (B) Its captain was an explorer who was also a government official.
    (C) It was comprised entirely of people who had committed crimes.
    (D) It did not travel directly from England to Australia.

21. What does the sentence that begins "**The specific location...**" imply in the second paragraph?
    (A) Captain Cook had not been impressed by Botany Bay.
    (B) Botany Bay was not the first choice for the settlement.
    (C) James Cook had visited Australia before Arthur Phillip.
    (D) Early explorers produced inaccurate maps of Australia.

22. Why did Captain Phillip change the location of the first British settlement?
    (A) He was unable to find the original choice due to bad weather.
    (B) He discovered that Sydney Cove had more favorable conditions.
    (C) He failed to reach a deal with the locals concerning Botany Bay.
    (D) He was advised by a major British politician to change course.

23. What is the main idea of the last paragraph?
    (A) The conflict between the colonists and locals turned violent.
    (B) The population of Australia increased slowly after 1788.
    (C) The arrival of the settlers had positive and negative effects.
    (D) The English system of law is no longer used in Australia.

20. _____ 21. _____ 22. _____ 23. _____

Unit
08

五 混合題

說明：請根據文章之文意選出或寫出一個最適當的答案。

　　Everyone knows that getting a sufficient amount of sleep is essential for a healthy mind and body, but this is often easier said than done. We asked several people to comment on this topic, referring to their personal experiences.

(A) Arthur
I hold a senior management position in an advertising agency and often have to work late, so getting eight hours' sleep is a pipe dream. I usually get five or six hours. It's not enough, but at least it's usually uninterrupted.

(B) Bella
I used to have trouble sleeping, but ever since I started avoiding screens for two hours before bedtime, I've slept like a baby. Now, I wake up feeling refreshed. I'd advise everyone to put away their phones and tablets long before they go to bed.

(C) Cleetus
Well, I've got a busy social life and have to get up early for work, so I definitely don't get enough sleep during the week. I always sleep in on weekends, though, and if occasionally I have trouble sleeping, I take a melatonin supplement.

(D) Doris
My new baby wakes up several times during the night, so my sleep is constantly interrupted. I nap during the day when she's sleeping in a vain attempt to catch up, but I've resigned myself to living like this—at least for a few months.

(E) Ernie
I sleep like a log for around ten hours a night. I achieve this by keeping my bedroom cool and dark and sticking to a regular sleep schedule: I always go to bed at 10 p.m. and get up around 8 a.m.

(F) Fern
I try to get seven hours of sleep a night and usually achieve this. I have a fixed nighttime routine that involves drinking a cup of chamomile tea and taking a relaxing, hot shower. There's nothing like a good night's sleep!

(G) Gideon
The mattress in my bedroom is too soft, which impacts my sleep quality. I need to get a new one. I'm not sure how much sleep I get each night, but I know it's not optimal. Maybe I should get a smartwatch to monitor it.

(H) Heidi
When I was young, I didn't care about getting enough sleep and would sacrifice my sleep time for socializing. Now I'm a bit older, I know how essential it is and get eight hours a night. Reading a book helps me to drop off.

24. Are the following statements about the interviews TRUE or FALSE?（是非題）

(1) Doris credits her regular nighttime routine and daily nap with helping her sleep like a baby.	☐ True ☐ False
(2) Gideon uses wearable technology to ensure he has a consistently deep, restorative night's sleep.	☐ True ☐ False
(3) Bella's sleep has been transformed by a decision to stop using her electronic devices before bed.	☐ True ☐ False
(4) Cleetus relies on a medically prescribed sleeping tablet to make him fall asleep each night.	☐ True ☐ False

25. Which word in the responses means "most desirable, satisfactory, or suitable"?（簡答）

　_____

26. From the most sleep to the least sleep, which of these puts the people in the correct order?（單選）

　(A) Ernie > Arthur > Heidi > Fern
　(B) Arthur > Fern > Ernie > Heidi
　(C) Ernie > Heidi > Fern > Arthur
　(D) Heidi > Fern > Arthur > Ernie

24.

(1)	(2)	(3)	(4)
☐ True ☐ False	☐ True ☐ False	☐ True ☐ False	☐ True ☐ False

25. _____

26. _____

Unit 09

一 綜合測驗

說明：本題型的題幹為段落式短文，選文中含數個空格，每題一個空格，請依文意選出最適當的一個選項。

　　In 2006, Justin Kan attached a webcam to his head and began to broadcast his life live on the internet. Justin.tv was born. This idea quickly caught the public's attention, drawing curious viewers. After a year or so, Kan ceased streaming his life and instead turned Justin.tv into a website where anyone could __(1)__ and stream live to and from mobile devices and computers. Over time, this grew to include __(2)__ TV shows and tutorials, as well as gaming content. It became a versatile platform for content creators.

　　By 2011, the gaming __(3)__ of Justin.tv had grown to be so popular that it was given its own URL, Twitch.tv. Gamers then had a __(4)__ social media platform and all the tools they needed to stream their gameplay or watch other players stream theirs. The popularity of the site __(5)__, and it soon became the internet's fourth largest source of traffic behind Netflix, Google, and Apple. When Twitch was put up for sale, it was passed up by the technology giant Google. Then, in August of 2014, Amazon purchased Twitch for approximately US$1 billion. This acquisition solidified Twitch's success as a streaming platform.

1. (A) build a network　　　　　　　(B) launch a channel
   (C) purchase a server　　　　　　(D) gain some support
2. (A) not more than　(B) not a little　(C) a good many　(D) a far cry from
3. (A) province　(B) myth　(C) gender　(D) category
4. (A) sophisticated　(B) redundant　(C) sacred　(D) tedious
5. (A) plunged　(B) split　(C) skyrocketed　(D) froze

1. _____　2. _____　3. _____　4. _____　5. _____

二 文意選填

說明：本題型的題幹為段落式短文，以一篇含十個空格的選文搭配十個選項，每題一個空格，請依文意在文章後所提供的選項中分別選出最適當者。

On average, consumers spend a million dollars every single minute of every single day on beauty products. That makes the beauty industry __(6)__ for the generation of more than US$426 billion of economic growth annually.

Products sold by the cosmetic industry __(7)__ eye shadow, eyeliner, and mascara, which help to make eyes look big and bright; lipstick and lip gloss for creating sensational-looking lips; and foundation and blush, which will hide any blemishes and make skin look silky smooth. Also, there are thousands of color variations and hundreds of applicators used to __(8)__ cosmetics. What's more, knowing the correct application techniques and using just the right amount of makeup are __(9)__ if a person doesn't want to end up looking like a circus clown.

Beauty vlogger Michelle Phan has become a YouTube superstar. Ms. Phan __(10)__ in beauty products. She provides teenage girls and young women with entertaining and informative tutorials along with beauty __(11)__ and other handy hints. Also, she teaches the importance of intangible __(12)__, such as confidence and attitude, along with techniques for obtaining perfect posture.

Ms. Phan is from Boston and is the daughter of Vietnamese immigrants. She launched her YouTube channel in 2008 and now has over 300 videos and eight million __(13)__. Her channel, which has a staggering 1.3 billion views, provides Ms. Phan with an annual income that __(14)__ US$1 million. She has also used her massive following to __(15)__ a lucrative sponsorship deal with a French cosmetics company, Lancôme Paris, and create a thriving bricks-and-mortar business called Ipsy, which Forbes values at US$500 million.

A apply	**B** tips	**C** receive	**D** subscribers
E specializes	**F** essential	**G** include	**H** exceeds
I responsible	**J** qualities		

Unit 09

6. _____   7. _____   8. _____   9. _____   10. _____

11. _____   12. _____   13. _____   14. _____   15. _____

Unit 09

篇章結構

說明：本題型的題幹為段落式短文，以一篇含四個空格的選文搭配四個選項，每題一個空格，請依文意在文章後所提供的選項中分別選出最適當者，填入空格中，使篇章結構清晰有條理。

    Macarons are those light and delicious sweet treats from France that seem to have caught on everywhere. From the best Parisian bakeries to pastry shops in Germany and Japan to coffee shops in the US, these meringue-based treats are captivating many people around the world. __(16)__ When it comes to macarons, meringue always takes center stage.

    Royal pastry chefs of Italy's Medici family were thought to have brought macarons to France in 1533, for the wedding of Catherine de' Medici and Henry II of France. According to another source, macarons were created in 1791 in a French convent. __(17)__

    The early 20th century saw the arrival of the modern macaron: a tiny pastry sandwich consisting of two pieces and a middle filling of buttercream, jelly, or ganache—a sweet, creamy chocolate mixture. __(18)__ However, these delectable treats were hardly limited to Parisian pastry shops.

    The macaron's huge popularity can be seen online or in movies, TV shows, magazine articles, and books like *I Love Macarons*, written by a Japanese pastry chef. These now-ubiquitous treats are sold by a wide variety of stores and food retailers. Macaron consumption is higher than ever, and new variations show up all the time. In Amiens, France, macarons are made with almond paste, honey, and fruit. Japanese bakeries substitute peanut flour for almond flour. In Japan and South Korea, green tea powder or leaves are used to make an Asian style macaron. __(19)__

    In addition, March 20 is World Macaron Day. On that day, participating shops not only offer free macarons but also donate money to local charities. Don't miss this golden opportunity to eat a large number of macarons for free.

Ⓐ This newer creation was originally called the Gerbet or Paris macaron.

Ⓑ Just in case you didn't know, meringue is a mixture of egg whites and icing sugar, typically used as a topping for pies and cakes.

Ⓒ This macaron flavor is known to have been the personal favorite of Henry II and his new wife.

Ⓓ The Hongdae area of Seoul in South Korea even has shops selling macaron ice cream sandwiches.

Ⓔ Whatever the truth, the macaron has slowly gained more and more attention.

16. _____ 17. _____ 18. _____ 19. _____

Unit 09

四 閱讀測驗　說明：每題請根據本篇文章之文意選出最適當的一個選項。

When most people think of butterflies, they picture beautiful, delicate insects flying around in gardens or parks, not poisonous creatures that make long-distance journeys, remarkably finding their way back to their homes after spending the winter in warmer spots. The reason people don't routinely think of butterflies in this way is that there is only one species that fits this description: the monarch butterfly.

The fact that monarchs are poisonous helps to protect them from predators. The insects have this attribute because, when they are caterpillars before they transform into butterflies, they feed on the milkweed plant. This has led to them also being known as milkweed butterflies. The monarch's wings are also unusual, as they feature a distinctive vein-like pattern with spots all around the edges. Other butterflies, meanwhile, have plain edges or only a few spots, while some have markings that look like eyes. As for the migratory habits of the monarchs, it should be pointed out that not all monarchs behave in this way. Actually, only the last generation of monarch butterflies born each year follows a two-way migratory pattern. This is because the majority of monarchs born in the spring and summer live only up to five weeks and therefore have no need to journey to locations with moderate temperatures to survive the winter.

In North America, beginning in September and October, large populations of monarch butterflies travel from Canada and the United States to central Mexico, flying as far as 5,000 kilometers to reach their destinations. Then, starting in March, **they** begin the return journey northward, with females laying the eggs of the next generation along the way. Scientists have long been fascinated by the monarchs' ability to find their way home, a remarkable sense of direction believed to be related to the location of the sun and the magnetic pull of the Earth. These distinctive attributes make monarchs not your average butterflies.

20. According to the passage, what makes monarchs poisonous?
    (A) Their unusual mating habits.
    (B) A special substance on their wings.
    (C) Their diet when they are caterpillars.
    (D) A gene passed down through the generations.

21. Which of the following represents the monarch butterfly?
    (A)   (B)
    (C)   (D)

22. What does the word "**they**" in the third paragraph refer to?
    (A) The destinations
    (B) The next generations
    (C) The monarch butterflies
    (D) The scientists

23. Which of the following is NOT true about monarch butterflies?
    (A) Every generation of monarch butterflies travels south for the winter.
    (B) The migration of monarchs commences in North America in the fall.
    (C) Some monarch butterflies are alive for little more than one month.
    (D) The monarchs' abilities are connected to our planet's force of attraction.

20. _____   21. _____   22. _____   23. _____

Unit
09

五 混合題

說明：請根據文章之文意選出或寫出一個最適當的答案。

TikTok is a hugely popular social media platform that allows users to create and share short videos. Four people gave us their views on this app.

(A) Zoe
Every time I want to escape from exams and homework, I reach for TikTok. Watching some creative, hilarious videos really helps me to relax and feel less stressed. I try to restrict myself to watching them for only a few minutes, and I usually succeed. But sometimes I do get carried away. However, TikTok isn't solely a fun distraction; it's also an educational tool that can help me with my schoolwork. If I can track down some short, snappy, informative videos on TikTok about a particular topic, then I can understand and remember the details much better.

(B) Dale
My daughter uses TikTok all the time—in her bedroom, in the car, even at the dinner table—and she argues that it helps her to unwind and feel less stressed. However, I think she's just wasting her time. She sits there endlessly scrolling, pausing to watch pointless videos about animals or babies or people dancing. She claims that they're entertaining; I contend that they're dangerously mind-numbing. I also worry a lot about the inappropriate content that she might stumble across.

(C) Alicia
You might expect that I—a high school teacher—would be against TikTok. You might think that I would consider it a time-wasting diversion from more important tasks like work or study. But I've been pleasantly surprised by its ability to engage my students and get them interested in topics they would've previously dismissed as boring. I've even asked my students to use TikTok as part of a homework task. So, I think that, as long as it's only used occasionally and in the correct circumstances, the app can be a handy educational tool.

(D) Tyler

I used to be a regular user of TikTok. I would spend hours scrolling through the app, watching videos about food and sports. But I came to realize that I wasn't actually achieving anything. In fact, I was doing exactly the opposite: neglecting homework, forgetting about family events, and ignoring my friends. These days, I have banned myself from using it entirely. Whenever I see people mindlessly watching pointless videos on their phone, I laugh at them. They're wasting their lives looking at a screen while I'm out doing something actually productive.

24-25 請從文章中找出最適當的單詞（word）填入下列句子空格中，並視語法需要做適當的字形變化。每格限填一個單詞（word）。（填充）

The responses mainly revolve around TikTok being considered a ___24.___ of time, its use as a tool for education, and its ability to help users relieve ___25.___.

26. Which word in Alicia's response means "something that takes your attention away from something else"?（簡答）

27. From least addicted to TikTok to most addicted, put the responses in order based on the people or current circumstances they describe.（填充）

   1. _____ < (C) < 2. _____ < 3. _____

24. _____ 25. _____

26. _____

27. 1. _____ < (C) < 2. _____ < 3. _____

Unit 10

一 綜合測驗

說明：本題型的題幹為段落式短文，選文中含數個空格，每題一個空格，請依文意選出最適當的一個選項。

The city of Twinsburg in the US state of Ohio is quite appropriately named as it holds the world's largest gathering of twins: Twins Day. This special festival, which has taken place each summer since 1976, __(1)__ multiple births of identical twins, fraternal twins, triplets, quadruplets, and other sets of multiples, attracting people from various cities in North America, Europe, Africa, and Asia. However, since the annual event is held in the United States, it should come as no __(2)__ that the majority of attendees are American. The festival is free for multiples who register in advance and for the residents of Twinsburg, __(3)__ anyone—whether or not they have a twin—may join the fun for a small fee.

For those participating in Twins Day, there is a lot of fun to be had, including a wiener roast to welcome everyone, contests, and musical performances often performed by twins. One unwritten rule, which guarantees there are always great __(4)__ , is that all twins must dress alike. Whether those __(5)__ are twins or not, Twins Day is an unforgettable festival that offers a lot of laughs and enjoyable moments. You could even say that Twins Day is twice as much fun as other festivals.

1. (A) celebrates (B) celebrated (C) celebrate (D) celebrating
2. (A) surface (B) surgery (C) surprise (D) surgeon
3. (A) so (B) once (C) until (D) although
4. (A) costume techniques (B) photo opportunities
   (C) shopping discounts (D) processing workshops
5. (A) in attendance (B) in a rush (C) in chaos (D) in vain

1. _____ 2. _____ 3. _____ 4. _____ 5. _____

二、文意選填

說明：本題型的題幹為段落式短文，以一篇含十個空格的選文搭配十個選項，每題一個空格，請依文意在文章後所提供的選項中分別選出最適當者。

　　Look around and you'll see the truth of this statement everywhere: humans are naturally communicative beings. People of all ages love to talk to one another, and even babies   (6)   to make sounds long before they have the ability to speak a language. They attempt to   (7)   through what is commonly called "baby talk." Although those who are deaf face challenges when communicating, they use a non-verbal type of communication referred to as sign language to   (8)   for the fact they cannot hear.

　　Among those who are not familiar with signing, there are often a few   (9) , two of which are that there is only one type of sign language and that this type of communication has no grammar. In fact, there is no universal sign language; rather, more than 100 varieties exist, which means it is   (10)   a person from one country can understand the sign language used by a person of another nation. For example, people from England usually aren't familiar with American Sign Language, while deaf Mexicans will be   (11)   when communicating with Spaniards despite the fact people from those pairs of countries speak English and Spanish, respectively. Regarding grammar, it might surprise people with   (12)   hearing that sign language actually uses grammatical rules. However, they are not   (13)   to the ones used when speaking. For instance, there is no gesture for the "be" verb in American Sign Language. However, the pattern does generally   (14)   the subject-verb-object pattern. Thus, it is correct to call sign language a "real language," not just a system of   (15)   with meaning used in some kind of random order, employed by hearing-impaired people around the world to effectively express themselves and understand messages of joy, sadness, and a whole range of other emotions.

(A) normal　　　(B) compensate　　(C) identical　　(D) misconceptions
(E) communicate　(F) unlikely　　　(G) follow　　　(H) confused
(I) struggle　　　(J) gestures

6. _____　7. _____　8. _____　9. _____　10. _____

11. _____　12. _____　13. _____　14. _____　15. _____

Unit 10

篇章結構 說明：本題型的題幹為段落式短文，以一篇含四個空格的選文搭配四個選項，每題一個空格，請依文意在文章後所提供的選項中分別選出最適當者，填入空格中，使篇章結構清晰有條理。

  If you want to turn a dull children's party into an exciting, noisy, and wild celebration, then introduce a piñata. A piñata is a container that is usually made of brightly decorated papier-mâché or cloth, but sometimes it is made of pottery. A piñata is filled with toys, candy, or other treats, and a rope is used to suspend it from the ceiling. __(16)__ The anticipation builds with every swing, making it an exciting highlight of any party. Eventually, the piñata bursts open, and partygoers scramble to get as many goodies as they can.

  The history of the piñata is not entirely known. For many years, it was commonly believed that piñatas originated in Spain. This likely occurred in the early part of the 14th century. Piñatas were later introduced by the Spanish into Mexico in the late 16th century, and piñatas became a much-loved tradition there. __(17)__ Many contemporary scholars believe the Chinese were responsible for creating the first kind of piñata. __(18)__ According to research, for the Chinese people at that time, one of the fun activities during Chinese New Year was to hit a similar container—which was shaped like an ox or a cow and was filled with various types of seeds—with colored sticks to release the contents.

  __(19)__ Some historians even suggest that similar customs existed in other ancient cultures, adding to the mystery of the piñata's true origin. No matter who first came up with the idea, though, piñatas are always a big hit at any party for children. Today, they come in various creative shapes and themes, making them even more exciting for kids.

A All in all, the similarities between the traditions are undeniable.

B The reason is that some evidence suggests Marco Polo, an Italian who had been living in China, brought the piñata back to Europe in the 13th century.

C In recent years, however, this explanation of the origin has been hotly disputed.

D Children attempt to release the assorted goodies inside the piñata by hitting it with a stick.

E The piñata burst open, injuring several children at the birthday party.

16. _____   17. _____   18. _____   19. _____

四 閱讀測驗　說明：每題請根據本篇文章之文意選出最適當的一個選項。

　　Twinings is one of the most famous tea brands in the world, with a history stretching back over three centuries. The company was founded in 1706 by Thomas Twining, who had learned about tea while working for the East India Company. Back then, tea was becoming fashionable in the United Kingdom, but it was far from widely popular. Thomas began to change that when he purchased Tom's Coffee House. At first, his venue sold tea alongside many other beverages, but by 1734, it had tripled in size, been renamed The Golden Lyon, and was selling only tea.

　　However, it was Thomas's grandson, Richard Twining, who arguably made the greatest contribution to the company's success and the UK's level of tea consumption. He took over the business in 1783. At that time, tea was heavily taxed and was smuggled into the country in huge quantities in an attempt to get around that tax. Much of the smuggled tea was of poor quality, and some was even mixed with deadly substances. As Chairman of the London Tea Dealers association, Richard passionately believed that excellent-quality tea should be available to everyone. He therefore approached the Prime Minister, William Pitt the Younger, and suggested **slashing** the tax on tea from 119% to 12.5%. Pitt listened to Richard's argument that this would actually boost government revenues through increased legal tea trading, and he reacted by passing the Commutation Act of 1784. Richard was proved right: legal tea sales soared, the government raked in more tax, and the Twinings company blossomed.

　　Another of Richard's notable achievements came when he commissioned a new display above the entrance to the Twinings store in London. It featured the distinctive Twinings logo and a statue of a golden lion to honor the name of Thomas Twining's tea shop. The display became very famous, and it still exists today.

20. Which of the following statements about Thomas Twining is correct?
    (A) He founded the East India Company in the early 1700s.
    (B) He just sold tea when he opened Tom's Coffee House.
    (C) He passed away after an illness in the year 1734.
    (D) His company achieved greater success under his grandson.

21. Why is Richard Twining regarded as having made a major contribution to both the company and the country?
    (A) He merged the company with the London Tea Dealers.
    (B) He added new substances to the company's popular teas.
    (C) He helped UK residents to overcome their dislike of tea.
    (D) He convinced a political leader to pass an important law.

22. What does "**slashing**" most likely mean in the second paragraph?
    (A) To use a blade to cut something.
    (B) To criticize something strongly.
    (C) To reduce an amount greatly.
    (D) To whip something.

23. What do we NOT learn about the entrance to the Twinings store?
    (A) Who formally requested it.
    (B) What is actually featured on it.
    (C) When it was specifically erected.
    (D) Where it is located.

20. _____   21. _____   22. _____   23. _____

Unit 10

五 混合題 　說明：請根據文章之文意選出或寫出一個最適當的答案。

Mesopredators are neither apex predators, nor are they solely prey. Rather, they are mid-level predators that feed on smaller creatures while simultaneously fending off attacks by larger creatures. In coral reef ecosystems, mesopredatory fish play an essential role in ensuring that their environment remains balanced. The way they deal with the threats they face can therefore have an effect on their own survival and the health of the coral reef. In the article "Behaviour of mesopredatory coral reef fishes in response to threats from sharks and humans"—published in the journal *Scientific Reports*—lead author A. Asunsolo-Rivera details a study that she and her team undertook into how these sea creatures reacted to potentially lethal threats.

The researchers focused on snappers, groupers, emperors, and grunts in Australia's Great Barrier Reef. They used remote underwater cameras to monitor the response of the fish to two main predators: snorkelers, who are known to go spearfishing in these types of environments, and blacktip reef sharks, which are "a potential predator and/or a lethal competitor" of the previously mentioned fish. **[1]** Animated models of the sharks, which moved and appeared to be very real, were used to guarantee the most accurate results. Animated versions of non-threatening sea turtles and two inanimate objects were also used as controls. **[2]** The study measured Flight Initiation Distance (FID), which the authors define as "the distance prey allow a potential threat to approach before fleeing." **[3]** Asunsolo-Rivera and her team anticipated that larger mesopredators would exhibit a greater FID and faster swimming speeds than smaller mesopredators when confronted with the threats.

They observed that 90% of the mesopredatory reef fish took flight at the sight of the sharks, while 96% did so at the sight of the snorkelers. By contrast, only around half of the fish reacted in the same way to the sea turtles or other objects. **[4]** The team did indeed discover that larger mesopredatory reef fish displayed greater FIDs and faster swimming speeds than smaller mesopredatory reef fish when faced with the threats as opposed to the non-threats. They concluded that this may cause reef fish to "[forgo] the opportunity to forage, interact or compete with other individuals of the same or other species" that are near them, and that this may "ultimately create risk effects within reef fish populations." **[5]** They did, however, note that the controls that they used—the sea turtles and other objects—were smaller than the animated shark models or the snorkelers. Thus, size of predators is one aspect that could be studied further in the future.

24-25 請從文章中找出最適當的單詞（word）填入下列句子空格中，並視語法需要做適當的字形變化。每格限填一個單詞（word）。（填充）

The methods mesopredatory coral reef fish use to cope with dangers in the ocean can determine whether they will ___24.___ and how healthy the reef environment is.

Flight Initiation Distance measures how close an animal will allow another creature that ___25.___ it to get before it moves away.

26. Which word in the article means "moving or appearing to move as if alive"?（簡答）

27. Which of the numbered sentences in the article state a prediction, a scientific finding, and a potential drawback of the study? Write down the NUMBERS of the sentences below.（配合）

    Prediction: _____
    Finding: _____
    Drawback: _____

24. _____ 25. _____

26. _____

27. Prediction: _____ Finding: _____ Drawback: _____

Unit 11

一 綜合測驗

說明：本題型的題幹為段落式短文，選文中含數個空格，每題一個空格，請依文意選出最適當的一個選項。

　　Mascots are performers dressed in cartoonish suits, and they can be seen dancing around at sports events, entertaining the spectators. These humorous-looking characters are a focus for team spirit and excitement, and are also said to bring good luck. Sometimes mascots try to intimidate or __(1)__ the opposing team. Teams from the high school level to the Olympic Games use mascots. They are also common in the corporate world. Once merely a __(2)__, mascots are now big business. Companies often use them to build a strong, recognizable brand identity.

　　The word mascot is __(3)__ the French word mascotte, or lucky charm. Before the 1960s, live animals were used. Suited mascots caught on as those famous life-sized puppet TV stars, the Muppets, swept children's entertainment. This undoubtedly expanded the mascot __(4)__. The growing popularity of mascots in the media has contributed to their continued success and presence in today's culture. In the sports world, each team has its own __(5)__ mascot. In baseball, the Detroit Tigers have PAWS. He dresses in a tiger costume. The Philadelphia Phillies have Phillie Phanatic, a bizarre-looking, furry, green creature, which is probably one of baseball's most-loved mascots.

1. (A) let go of　　(B) take care of　　(C) make fun of　　(D) make use of
2. (A) cause of frustration　　　　(B) reason for competition
   (C) basis for criticism　　　　　(D) source of laughs
3. (A) derived from　(B) resulted from　(C) expelled from　(D) withdrawn from
4. (A) experiment　(B) industry　(C) environment　(D) imagination
5. (A) individual　(B) industrial　(C) internal　(D) innocent

1. _____　2. _____　3. _____　4. _____　5. _____

二 文意選填

說明：本題型的題幹為段落式短文，以一篇含十個空格的選文搭配十個選項，每題一個空格，請依文意在文章後所提供的選項中分別選出最適當者。

Unit 11

Have you ever heard of the Ark Nova? It is the world's first inflatable concert hall. It is also the name given to a project (6) in hope and love. It has been said that music has (7) powers. The creative team behind Ark Nova's design had the idea that music might be able to comfort the thousands of people who suffered unthinkable loss in the wake of the devastating earthquake and tsunami that struck Japan in 2011, which (8) over 18,000 lives. In 2013, this odd-looking structure, the Ark Nova, was (9) for the first time, in the same area that was most directly hit by the disaster.

British sculptor Anish Kapoor and Japanese architect Arata Isozaki together came up with an (10) solution to a problem often faced by concert promoters and others who might want to stage an event. This concerns a shortage of performance venues. At the same time, their solution offered something more. This inflatable, portable theater, (11) the purple jelly bean, seats 500 people comfortably. That makes the amazing venue a great (12) for any number of smaller concerts, workshops, and contemporary performance pieces of all genres. Not only is the Ark Nova inflatable and completely mobile, its unusual jelly-bean shape and exterior luminescent purple walls present a striking (13) of hope and joy. The (14) of the Ark Nova is noticeably sphere-shaped, and soothing shades of pink light shine down beautifully on its benches for the audience to sit on. Conveniently, the Ark Nova can inflate in just two hours and can deflate much faster.

Throughout its history, Japan has had its share of problems. However, the Japanese have (15) themselves through their creativity and their resiliency in the face of disaster. The Ark Nova is a shining example of these qualities.

- **A** erected
- **B** interior
- **C** conceived
- **D** symbol
- **E** innovative
- **F** claimed
- **G** distinguished
- **H** option
- **I** nicknamed
- **J** healing

6. _____   7. _____   8. _____   9. _____   10. _____

11. _____   12. _____   13. _____   14. _____   15. _____

Unit 11

篇章結構 説明：本題型的題幹為段落式短文，以一篇含四個空格的選文搭配五個選項，每題一個空格，請依文意在文章後所提供的選項中分別選出最適當者，填入空格中，使篇章結構清晰有條理。

On the final day of any golf tournament that he is involved in, Tiger Woods wears his favorite red shirt. Over the years, Woods has realized that red signifies power, dominance, and enthusiasm. __(16)__ Many of his fans have come to associate his red shirt with victory, making it a symbol of his competitive spirit.

Now, scientists are catching up with Tiger Woods' way of thinking and are looking more closely at color connections. Scientists knew from previous studies that red provoked an interest in food and sexual activity. __(17)__ Red is also associated with ambulances, stop signs, and danger, so some people want to avoid this color. On the other hand, blue has always been known as a calming color. Recently, it was found to help people be more explorative or creative. This is because most people associate blue with oceans, the sky, or other wide-open spaces.

Professors tested 600 people to figure out if their performances varied when they were shown the colors red, blue, or white. __(18)__ The red group could remember things better and performed at a higher level with regard to spellchecking and punctuation. The blue group exceeded the red group at making creative uses for a brick or creating toys from shapes. There wasn't a noticeable difference with the white group. These findings suggest that color can be a powerful tool in influencing human behavior and productivity.

It seems as though others have known for years what scientists are now just figuring out. __(19)__ Also, creative people have long known that one room in their house or apartment needs to be blue to stimulate their minds. It is clear that people continue to use colors to shape their environments and enhance their abilities.

Ⓐ That is why restaurants and cafés are rarely painted in red or similar colors.

Ⓑ For example, many of the walls in *The New York Times'* editorial department are painted tomato-can red.

Ⓒ Participants performed tasks with words or images displayed against colored backgrounds.

Ⓓ But now, they believe that people perform better on detail- or performance-oriented tasks if they are prompted by the color red.

Ⓔ Consciously or unconsciously, he uses this to his advantage because when Woods is wearing red, he is nearly impossible to beat.

16. _____   17. _____   18. _____   19. _____

四 閱讀測驗　說明：每題請根據本篇文章之文意選出最適當的一個選項。

　　The Silk Road was a 6,500-kilometer-long network of trade routes that existed between 130 BC and 1453 AD. Its numerous paths connected the East to the West and facilitated the exchange of commodities including spices, precious stones, leather goods, and, of course, silk. The constant movement of people, though, also enabled the faster spread of disease.

　　In the mid-14th century, a form of bubonic plague called the Black Death journeyed along the Silk Road and ultimately killed tens or even hundreds of millions of people across the world. Historians and researchers debate whether the disease had its origins in northwestern China, southwestern China, or Central Asia. There is evidence of an outbreak that stretched from Hebei to Hunan provinces in China during the Yuan dynasty in the early 1330s. Whether this was the first appearance of the Black Death or not, it is generally accepted that the disease was transmitted to humans via fleas that had infested rats. These small rodents were a common sight at caravanserais along the Silk Road. The caravanserais served not only as rest stops for weary travelers and traders but also as ideal transmission sites for the Black Death. Gradually, the plague made its way across Central Asia, wiping out up to 70 percent of the populations in countries we now know as Kyrgyzstan and Uzbekistan.

　　Until relatively recently, there was a lack of hard evidence of the spread of infectious diseases along the Silk Road. However, a study published in the *Journal of Archaeological Science: Reports* that examined 2,000-year-old personal hygiene sticks from small toilets at a caravanserai in northwest China changed all that. It found evidence of eggs from a parasite called the Chinese liver fluke in the feces on the sticks. This is significant because the Chinese liver fluke is only found hundreds of kilometers away in eastern and southern China. The findings suggest that traders traveled huge distances on the Silk Road. As one of the study's authors, Piers Mitchell, wrote in *The Conversation*: "... We now know for sure that the Silk Road was responsible for spreading infectious diseases in ancient times."

20. According to the article, which of the following statements about the Black Death is true?
    (A) It developed in rats in Uzbekistan and Kyrgyzstan.
    (B) It is somewhat unclear as to where it actually began.
    (C) It killed fewer people in Hebei and Hunan provinces.
    (D) It is almost certain that it first evolved in the West.

21. What is a caravanserai?
    (A) A form of ancient accommodations for travelers.
    (B) A place where infected traders could be treated.
    (C) A type of vehicle that traveled on the Silk Road.
    (D) A site at which to buy and sell small animals.

22. How did the study from the *Journal of Archaeological Science: Reports* come to its conclusions?
    (A) By looking for liver flukes in a region's water.
    (B) By examining the air at communal restrooms.
    (C) By finding solid proof of travelers' movements.
    (D) By checking for parasites in century eggs.

23. Why does the author quote Piers Mitchell at the end of the article?
    (A) To cast doubt on the latest Silk Road theories.
    (B) To emphasize the definitive nature of a study.
    (C) To show that evidence is difficult to obtain.
    (D) To highlight the need for more research.

20. _____   21. _____   22. _____   23. _____

Unit 11

五 混合題 說明:請根據文章之文意選出或寫出一個最適當的答案。

Many countries in the world have a high-speed rail system. However, one of the richest and most powerful nations, the United States of America, does not. We talked to three people about their views on this topic.

Chad
The reason why the US lacks a high-speed rail system can be summed up in one word: freedom. High-speed trains might be fast, but using them still necessitates timetables and restrictions. We Americans prefer the freedom that only a car can provide. The automobile is an integral part of our way of life and has been for decades, allowing us to get from point A to point B at a time of our own choosing. So, it's no wonder that successive governments have invested heavily in building roads rather than constructing high-speed rail lines. The immense costs associated with laying tracks, building new stations, and purchasing the most advanced trains would simply not be worth it.

Josh
As someone who has worked at the White House for a long time, I understand how difficult it is to secure funding for major transportation projects. Even if we did have the money to invest heavily in a high-speed rail system, the necessary involvement of state governments and local authorities would massively complicate the coordination of such a project. For instance, there would be disagreements over the route, opposition from local residents, and many different layers of bureaucracy to deal with. It's a shame because a high-speed rail system would bring numerous benefits: it would create lots of jobs, reduce journey times between big cities, and help to lower pollution.

Rinko
In Japan, we have an excellent high-speed rail system that is efficient, punctual, and safe. When I first came to the US, I could not understand why they didn't have one. However, I have come to realize that the enormous size of this country is a huge barrier to the construction and implementation of a high-speed rail system. The distances between some cities are simply too vast, and the terrain too diverse,

to make it feasible. Plus, Americans are used to flying across the country, and there is already a fantastic network of affordable and convenient air routes for people to use. There are also powerful airline associations that lobby the government to favor their industry. These groups influence politicians when they're making decisions about transportation in the United States.

Unit 11

24-26 請從文章中找出最適當的單詞（word）填入下列句子空格中，並視語法需要做適當的字形變化。每格限填一個單詞（word）。（填充）

Chad believes the reason the US does not have a high-speed rail system is that its citizens have a ___24.___ for driving their own personal vehicles.

Josh points out that the organization and construction of a high-speed rail system in the US would involve many ___25.___, such as dealing with local residents who object to the scheme.

Rinko appreciates that the reason a high-speed rail system has not been established in the US is because many cities are ___26.___ from each other.

27. Which word in Rinko's response means "to try to persuade an elected official to change a law or take a particular action"?（簡答）

    _____

28. Which of the following aspects of the topic is addressed by EACH of the respondents?（單選）
    (A) The state of existing railway lines.
    (B) Alternative transportation options.
    (C) The choices made by political leaders.
    (D) Arguments about proposed rail routes.

24. _____   25. _____   26. _____

27. _____

28. _____

Unit 12

一 綜合測驗

說明：本題型的題幹為段落式短文，選文中含數個空格，每題一個空格，請依文意選出最適當的一個選項。

Hogewey is a pioneering care facility with a difference, one that is attracting worldwide attention for the way it looks after elderly patients with dementia. __(1)__ just outside Amsterdam in the Netherlands, Hogewey offers special around-the-clock care for its 152 clients. Their average age is 83, and all of them have been __(2)__ severe dementia. While the __(3)__ of an old-age nursing home is a depressing one—the elderly joylessly living out the rest of their days—the residents of the Dutch facility are much more active and happier and require less medicine on the whole than the occupants of most traditional care centers.

The reason for this is linked to the better care that Hogewey's patients receive, with people living in a safe, familiar, and humane environment, all of which help to reduce the amount of __(4)__ , confusion, and anger that dementia sufferers feel. __(5)__ , they can choose from 25 activity clubs, including painting, cycling, bingo, and baking. The elderly at Hogewey, although they suffer from dementia, are fortunate indeed to be treated so well.

1. (A) Located (B) Locates (C) Locating (D) To be located
2. (A) diagnosed with (B) dealt with (C) occupied with (D) charged with
3. (A) abstract idea (B) standard process
   (C) unrelated concept (D) typical image
4. (A) confidence (B) abortion (C) anxiety (D) comfort
5. (A) To some extent (B) In short (C) To be honest (D) In addition

1. _____ 2. _____ 3. _____ 4. _____ 5. _____

二、文意選填

說明：本題型的題幹為段落式短文，以一篇含十個空格的選文搭配十個選項，每題一個空格，請依文意在文章後所提供的選項中分別選出最適當者。

Clean drinking water is something that many people around the world take for granted. However, in India, which is the second most populous country on the planet, with (6) 1.2 billion people, a sizeable proportion of its citizens live in miserable conditions. They don't have access to a (7) supply of clean water. Given this fact, it is perhaps not surprising that three quarters of the diseases suffered by Indians (8) from the poor quality of drinking water there.

Most of the water used for drinking and cooking in India comes from vendors who bottle it and sell it at expensive prices. However, despite the high cost, which is one factor that keeps people in (9) , the bottled water is not always of good quality. One (10) solution to this problem has been developed by an American-educated Indian named Anand Shah. He started a company called Sarvajal, an ancient Sanskrit word meaning "water for all."

Despite choosing an ancient word for his company's name, Shah utilizes (11) that is very much 21st century. His answer to India's water problem is called a "water ATM," which is a type of high-tech, computerized water dispenser that uses solar power to (12) water by both filtration and UV lighting in villages where electricity is in poor supply or unavailable. The machines are simple to (13) : users simply need to swipe a pre-paid smart card. For an (14) low NT$2 fee, they will receive four liters of safe water to use for drinking and other purposes. Shah uses a business model that is, in some ways, (15) to retailers like 7-Eleven stores: the sophisticated water dispensers are franchised to local management. Sarvajal currently serves five million consumers across twenty Indian states, and these figures are sure to grow in the near future.

Ⓐ process　　Ⓑ steady　　Ⓒ incredibly　　Ⓓ similar
Ⓔ stem　　Ⓕ potential　　Ⓖ poverty　　Ⓗ approximately
Ⓘ operate　　Ⓙ technology

6. _____　7. _____　8. _____　9. _____　10. _____

11. _____　12. _____　13. _____　14. _____　15. _____

Unit 12

篇章結構

說明：本題型的題幹為段落式短文，以一篇含四個空格的選文搭配五個選項，每題一個空格，請依文意在文章後所提供的選項中分別選出最適當者，填入空格中，使篇章結構清晰有條理。

  Every culture has superstitions. In China, one should not point at the moon, nor should a pregnant woman use scissors, and the number four is considered unlucky. In Europe, breaking a mirror is thought to bring about bad luck, as is the sight of a black cat. These colorful stories from around the world have no basis in scientific thought, but they provide amusing tales to tell. Many superstitions have deep cultural roots and often reflect the values or fears of a society.

  One of the most interesting superstitions is about Friday the 13th. __(16)__ Those in other parts of Europe felt the opposite. European ships have traditionally avoided sailing on a Friday, especially if it fell on the 13th. __(17)__

  The number 13 was regarded as unlucky by the Romans, who connected it with death and destruction. In Norse legend, 13 people sitting at a table was especially unlucky. Christians also adopted this belief because the Last Supper, Christ's final meal before his crucifixion, had the 12 apostles and Jesus seated together. __(18)__ Nowadays, some hotels and hospitals do not have a 13th floor, while some planes operated by airlines including Ryanair and Lufthansa omit the 13th row.

  __(19)__ It appears, as they say, that some old habits die hard. Each year has one or two Friday the 13ths. On these days, people often pay more attention to their surroundings. It may be that people are now safer on Friday the 13th because they are aware of this superstition. Superstitions like this one show how deeply cultural beliefs can shape our behaviors, even in today's world.

A Friday was once considered a lucky day for the Vikings of northern Europe and the favorite day of the week to hold a wedding.

B When these are all combined, it is easy to see why so many Westerners hold Friday the 13th as a day to be wary of.

C It is one of many dates that Europeans and Americans believe to be unlucky.

D However, Christopher Columbus, the first known Westerner to explore the New World, set sail on a Friday and spotted land on a Friday, too.

E In addition, in the Middle Ages, witches were thought to convene their meetings with 13 members.

Unit 12

16. _____ 17. _____ 18. _____ 19. _____

四 閱讀測驗

說明：每題請根據本篇文章之文意選出最適當的一個選項。

　　For frequent flyers, boarding an airplane is much like getting in a car: nothing to worry about. Nervous flyers, though, are often concerned about their safety. And, recently, there has been renewed interest in passenger safety on aircraft.

　　Research shows that there are several things you can do to help you stay safe while flying. Rule number one is to keep hydrated. This means avoiding alcohol, caffeine, and salty foods at the airport and during the flight, which helps you to stay alert. You should, of course, pay attention to the safety briefing before take-off, and it is also recommended that you keep your seatbelt fastened—at least loosely—for the duration of the flight.

　　There may be ways in which you can stay safe while flying even if the worst does happen. A study conducted by *Time* magazine looked at airplane accidents over a 15-year period. The study showed that seats at the front of the cabin had a 38% fatality rate, while the figure for seats in the middle of the plane was even higher at 39%. In contrast, seats at the back of the cabin had the lowest fatality rate—at 32%—with those in the middle of a row at the back being particularly safe. Of course, there are many factors that can affect this outcome. If the back of the plane were to hit the ground first during a crash, for example, anything could happen.

　　Don't let this talk of plane crashes worry you too much, though; flying is still by far the safest method of transport. Your chances of dying in a car crash are one hundred times greater than your chances of perishing in a plane crash. Nevertheless, nervous flyers may find the above advice worth following if it gives them peace of mind.

20. What is this passage mostly about?
    (A) A comparison between car crashes and plane crashes
    (B) Suggestions for staying safe on a plane
    (C) A plane crash in the US
    (D) The benefits of sitting at the front of an aircraft

21. What method of staying safe on an airplane is NOT mentioned in the passage?
    (A) Stay hydrated during the flight
    (B) Drink alcohol or coffee to help you relax
    (C) Listen to the safety briefing
    (D) Keep your seatbelt fastened

22. According to the passage, where is the safest place to sit on a plane?
    (A) A
    (B) B
    (C) C
    (D) D

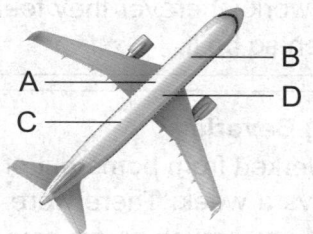

23. According to the passage, why should you not worry too much about flying?
    (A) Plane crashes are becoming less common.
    (B) People are more likely to travel by car.
    (C) The flight insurance covers everything.
    (D) Flying is the safest way to travel.

20. _____   21. _____   22. _____   23. _____

Unit 12

Unit 12

五 混合題
說明：請根據文章之文意選出或寫出一個最適當的答案。

For many years, the five-day, 40-hour workweek was the norm in many offices. However, in recent years, this has started to change, with flexible and remote working also becoming commonplace. We asked eight people for their opinions on this subject and their experiences related to it.

(A) Alfonso
I like to think of myself as a forward-thinking boss, so I've been offering my staff flexible working arrangements for several years now. I think they should be allowed to work wherever they feel more focused. If that's in the comfort of their own home, then so be it.

(B) Beverley
I worked from home out of necessity during Covid, but now I'm back in the office five days a week. There were far too many distractions at home—my kids, the dog, the TV—so I much prefer being in the office full-time.

(C) Christof
As a freelance writer, I'm able to choose where I work from and move to different locations when I please. Last week, I was in Tokyo; next week, I'm going to Taipei. It's the ultimate remote-working arrangement, and I love being in different environments.

(D) Delilah
My company has a flexible working policy, and I go to the office sixty percent of the time. It's a nice balance: I enjoy working from home on Mondays and Fridays, but it's also good to go back into the office so I can catch up with my colleagues.

(E) Enrique
I don't allow my employees to work from home. They wouldn't be as productive, they'd struggle to concentrate, and they'd get disconnected from the rest of the team. I lead by example: I'm regularly in the office six days a week.

(F) Freya
I can't WFH, but my company is testing an amazing new policy. We get to do a four-day workweek and still get paid for five days! The theory is that well-rested employees with a better work-life balance are more motivated to accomplish their tasks in less time.

(G) Gerald
Working from home has its benefits, but I usually prefer being in the office. I like the structure of an office workday, and the environment allows me to stay focused on my job. I really hate commuting to the office, though.

(H) Helena
Working nine to five is an outdated concept in the modern world; that kind of rigid thinking should have been left in the last century. Luckily, my job is very flexible, and I can alter my schedule on a daily basis depending on my workload.

Unit 12

24. FOUR of the people explicitly state how many days they spend in the office each week. From the most to the fewest days, put their names in order.（填充）

    Enrique > _____ > _____ > _____

25. Who would most likely include the following line in their response:
    "My favorite destinations are those where I can work from the beach."（簡答）

    _____

26. Who indicates in their response that they occupy a managerial position in a company?（簡答）

    _____

27. TWO of the responses use a word that means "giving a lot of attention to one particular thing." What is that word?（簡答）

    _____

24. Enrique > _____ > _____ > _____

25. _____

26. _____

27. _____

Unit 13

一 綜合測驗

說明：本題型的題幹為段落式短文，選文中含數個空格，每題一個空格，請依文意選出最適當的一個選項。

　　What do rats have to do with landmines in Africa, a place with more than its fair share of these deadly devices? (1) a man named Bart Weetjens, who used to keep rats as pets, the answer is "a lot." When Weetjens later began researching the problem of landmines on the African continent, he came across some research that examined how gerbils could use their sense of smell to (2) landmines. This inspired him to explore whether other small rodents could perform similar tasks. Recalling the intelligence and trainability of his pet rats, Weetjens decided to form an organization called APOPO, which trains giant pouched rats to sniff out landmines. These rats, often called "HeroRATs," are lightweight enough to avoid triggering explosions while detecting buried mines.

　　APOPO began operating in 2003, and since then, it has greatly helped the African country of Mozambique become (3) . Despite the good work (4) by APOPO, landmines still pose a major threat to many people. It has been (5) that millions of landmines still exist in more than sixty countries. Hopefully, APOPO and its heroic rats will continue to fight this deadly problem for many years to come.

1. (A) In addition to　　(B) Thanks to　　(C) In terms of　　(D) Apart from
2. (A) depress　　(B) endure　　(C) interpret　　(D) detect
3. (A) free of landmines　　(B) full of explosives
   (C) rid of protection　　(D) clear of controversies
4. (A) to do　　(B) doing　　(C) is done　　(D) being done
5. (A) puzzled　　(B) persisted　　(C) estimated　　(D) raised

1. _____　2. _____　3. _____　4. _____　5. _____

二 文意選填

說明：本題型的題幹為段落式短文，以一篇含十個空格的選文搭配十個選項，每題一個空格，請依文意在文章後所提供的選項中分別選出最適當者。

People usually associate coloring books with children; however, mandala coloring books have become popular among adults. Supposedly pictures of the universe, mandalas (6) a variety of encircled geometric patterns and, according to many Indian religions, are seen as a spiritual awakening. They are believed to assist people to (7) with the emotional issues of everyday life and, through the coloring of them, reveal their state of mind.

For people who need help to (8) stress or who want to find out about their feelings, mandala coloring books have proven to be useful. By letting people experiment with different colors within a range of black-and-white designs, for example, they help people feel (9) . It's also interesting to note that you can tell a lot about how a person is feeling by (10) the colors that he or she chooses. Dull colors are said to express negative emotions while bright colors suggest a person is experiencing more (11) emotions. For example, a bright red might (12) that the person is feeling confident. In contrast, a dull red suggests that he or she is experiencing fear.

Some believe that mandalas can help people (13) their minds, and these designs have become part of modern psychology. One of those people was the famous psychoanalyst Carl Jung, who lived from 1875 to 1961. It was during times of his own personal growth that Jung (14) that he drew mandalas. He associated mandalas with his mind gaining new understanding as well as (15) peace. As you can see, there is a lot more to these symmetrical designs than meets the eye!

Ⓐ cope **Ⓑ** examining **Ⓒ** positive **Ⓓ** manage
Ⓔ achieving **Ⓕ** noticed **Ⓖ** feature **Ⓗ** relaxed
Ⓘ indicate **Ⓙ** focus

6. _____   7. _____   8. _____   9. _____   10. _____

11. _____   12. _____   13. _____   14. _____   15. _____

Unit 13

篇章結構 說明：本題型的題幹為段落式短文，以一篇含四個空格的選文搭配五個選項，每題一個空格，請依文意在文章後所提供的選項中分別選出最適當者，填入空格中，使篇章結構清晰有條理。

    Do you like to hold on to things? Most people like to keep some things of limited use around the house—childhood toys, souvenirs, tools, or items that may come in handy one day—but some people hate to throw anything out. These people are called hoarders, and in extreme cases, hoarding can be a serious mental illness.

    There are several kinds of hoarding behavior recognized by psychiatrists. The most common is simple object hoarding. Object hoarders collect and keep things most people would simply throw away. For instance, they will keep things that are broken or food long past its expiration date. This garbage accumulates, usually taking up a lot of space and often increasing the health risks of living in the hoarder's home. (16) The emotional attachment to these objects can make it especially difficult for hoarders to part with anything, even when it is clear they no longer serve a purpose.

    Other kinds of hoarding include bibliomania (藏書癖) and animal hoarding. Bibliomaniacs obsessively collect books. (17) Animal hoarders collect pets and often have so many that they can't look after them properly. Yet, like other hoarders, they are passionately attached to their collection. (18) In both cases, the hoarders may be unaware of the negative effects their behavior has on their own well-being or the well-being of others.

    Psychologists believe that hoarding behavior is actually a natural response because many animals also hoard food. (19) Nevertheless, when this response gets out of control, it can become a real problem for the sufferer. Fortunately, hoarding is a rare condition, and storing some old junk in a cupboard just in case of an emergency is perfectly normal behavior.

A It is hard for these animal hoarders to see that they are doing themselves and their pets harm.

B Therapists have identified several potential treatments for those who hoard objects.

C However, they often end up having collections too big for them to ever actually read.

D Humans just extend this behavior to the tools and objects that are part of everyday life.

E Even so, hoarders will fiercely resist any attempts to dispose of their collections.

16. _____   17. _____   18. _____   19. _____

Unit 13

四 閱讀測驗　說明：每題請根據本篇文章之文意選出最適當的一個選項。

A century ago, animals were frequently used in scientific experiments, and there were far fewer regulations governing their use than there are today. However, it is important to note that animals played a crucial role in many medical breakthroughs. One of these was the discovery of insulin: a hormone in the body that can help to control the amount of sugar in the blood. The Canadian surgeon Frederick Banting used dogs in his experiments that led to the detection of this substance. Banting believed that if he removed the pancreases from dogs, those animals would develop diabetes: a disease in which the body cannot control its blood sugar level. He also suspected that if he could isolate a specific substance in the pancreas, then that substance could be used to help regulate the dogs' blood sugar levels and treat the disease.

Naturally, he needed to test these theories. To this end, the University of Toronto granted him a laboratory, the assistance of medical student Charles Best, and a supply of dogs. Banting and Best proceeded to use the dogs to isolate what would come to be known as insulin and inject it into other dogs that had had their pancreases removed. *ScienceDirect* notes that "quite a few dogs died during the procedures," forcing the two men to buy street dogs, often from suppliers that did not have a good reputation. Nevertheless, in late July, 1921, Banting and Best successfully used an injection of insulin to reduce a dog's blood sugar level by almost a half. Realizing that they could not obtain enough of the pancreatic extract from dogs, they switched to calf fetuses, which they procured from local slaughterhouses.

Early the following year, the two men, with the assistance of a biochemist named James B. Collip, tested their procedure on a 14-year-old boy, whose blood sugar level dropped dramatically. It is fair to say that the team could not have gotten to this stage without those dependable canines. The animals contributed to a revolution in the treatment of diabetes, turning the disease from a death sentence into a manageable condition.

20. According to the article, what did Frederick Banting believe?
    (A) That dogs were more likely than humans to develop diabetes.
    (B) That he could experiment on dogs to find a cure for a disease.
    (C) That he could remove pancreases without harming health.
    (D) That blood sugar levels had little to do with the pancreas.

21. Why is the University of Toronto mentioned in the article?
    (A) It objected to the use of canines in medical experiments.
    (B) It is currently known for its groundbreaking diabetes research.
    (C) It provided Banting with the means to conduct his experiments.
    (D) Its researchers isolated insulin several months before Banting did.

22. Why did Banting and Best switch to using calf fetuses in their experiments?
    (A) The dogs had too many additional illnesses.
    (B) The calf fetuses were more similar to humans.
    (C) They felt guilty about the number of dead street dogs.
    (D) They were unable to get enough of a substance from dogs.

23. What do we NOT learn about the human trial of insulin?
    (A) The age of the human subject.
    (B) The result of the experiment.
    (C) The name of the human subject.
    (D) The time of year it took place.

20. _____   21. _____   22. _____   23. _____

Unit 13

五 混合題
說明：請根據文章之文意選出或寫出一個最適當的答案。

The Datan algal reef is located in Taoyuan. Taiwanese citizens took part in a referendum on whether to allow the construction of a liquefied natural gas (LNG) terminal to continue at this location. Here are four people's opinions on the matter.

Ms. Li
The Datan algal reef is a fascinating natural wonder that is full of fish, eels, crabs, and even sea turtles. That's why I campaigned strongly against the construction of the LNG terminal. It's a deliberate act of environmental damage that will wreck a 7,500-year-old marvel. People argue that continuing to use coal will be bad for this country. I understand that we need to reduce our dependence on it, but in my opinion, destroying the reef would be far worse.

Mr. Wang
I have worked with the government on the Datan project for many years. I realize the issue is a hot potato that many people disagree about, but I can honestly say we have tried our best to limit the impact the LNG terminal will have on the algal reef. By building the terminal 1.2 kilometers out to sea, we will protect 90% of the reef environment from any effects at all. The simple fact is that we need to strengthen our energy security, and this is the way to do it.

Ms. Bai
For many years, I strongly sympathized with those who want to save the wonderful algal reef and all the beautiful creatures that call it home. However, I have come to realize that global warming is the biggest threat that mankind faces. Therefore, I now know that solving the energy crisis is more important. We urgently need to reduce this island's reliance on coal so that we can cut carbon emissions, and liquefied natural gas is the best way to achieve this goal. Quite simply, constructing the LNG terminal is the lesser of two evils.

Mr. Chen

I campaigned hard against the government's initial plans to build the LNG terminal at the Datan algal reef. I argued that the biodiversity of the reef was far more important than the need to produce electricity. However, given the revised plans to move the terminal further away from the coast, I concede that it is time to give up the fight. It's a reasonable compromise that kills two birds with one stone: it allows us to protect the majority of the creatures in the reef while boosting Taiwan's energy security.

24-25 請從文章中找出最適當的單詞（word）填入下列句子空格中，並視語法需要做適當的字形變化。每格限填一個單詞（word）。（填充）

Both Mr. Wang and Mr. Chen acknowledge that constructing the LNG terminal further out to sea will ensure the ___24.___ of most of the algal reef.

While both Ms. Li and Ms. Bai reference the need for a ___25.___ in Taiwan's use of coal, the latter believes that it is a more pressing concern.

26. Which phrase in the opinions means "a problem that is difficult to deal with and causes a lot of disagreement"?（簡答）

_____

27. Who have changed their minds about the siting of the LNG terminal at the Datan algal reef?（多選）
    (A) Ms. Li
    (B) Mr. Wang
    (C) Ms. Bai
    (D) Mr. Chen

24. _____ 25. _____

26. _____

27. _____

Unit 13

Unit 14

一、綜合測驗

說明：本題型的題幹為段落式短文，選文中含數個空格，每題一個空格，請依文意選出最適當的一個選項。

New Zealand is well known for its friendly people and untouched beauty. Lesser known, however, is the fact that the country is home to perhaps the world's highest number of gangs per capita. New Zealand's street gangs and motorcycle gangs are __(1)__ for their violent crimes, including assault, robbery, and murder. These criminal activities have made gang-related violence a serious issue for law enforcement. Nonetheless, Tribal Huk, an ethnic gang in the Waikato region of the North Island, has __(2)__ for some charitable behavior: feeding hungry school children.

Dubbed "the sandwich gang," Tribal Huk members make 500 sandwiches a day, five days a week, which are then __(3)__ to local students. This costs the gang NZ$2,150, the __(4)__ of NT$40,000, per week. Many children in the area rely on these sandwiches as their primary source of nutrition during the school day. The program is even more amazing considering that it is self-funded. Tribal Huk operates its own farm, __(5)__ animals for meat to be used for their food program. Their efforts have gained praise from educators and community members who recognize the positive impact on local students. Feeding hungry kids is certainly a worthwhile use of time and money for this North Island gang.

1. (A) notorious (B) indignant (C) ambiguous (D) mischievous
2. (A) received criticism (B) obtained a degree
   (C) undergone punishment (D) gained a reputation
3. (A) suspended (B) vibrated (C) distributed (D) certified
4. (A) struggle (B) tuition (C) equivalent (D) harvest
5. (A) raising (B) raised (C) raises (D) being raised

1. _____ 2. _____ 3. _____ 4. _____ 5. _____

二 文意選填

說明：本題型的題幹為段落式短文，以一篇含十個空格的選文搭配十個選項，每題一個空格，請依文意在文章後所提供的選項中分別選出最適當者。

It is no secret that millions of people, especially in Africa and Asia, live on the brink of death from hunger. At the same time, it is a __(6)__ fact that in the West roughly 40% of all food ends up in the garbage. In the US alone, an average family __(7)__ over 1,000 pounds of food per year. This staggering waste __(8)__ to approximately US$165 billion annually. Solving the problem of global hunger is no easy task, but eliminating food waste is something we all can and should __(9)__.

In Europe, a simple yet effective low-tech food-saving __(10)__ has recently been gaining in popularity. It's called the "sharing a refrigerator" movement. People who work together in an office or live in a dormitory can share not only a common refrigerator but also its contents. Sharing a bottle of milk or a package of meat with coworkers or roommates has already been shown to drastically __(11)__ the amount of food that is wasted. Following a few simple rules and the desire to make a difference are all it takes to make it work. Each food item must be __(12)__ with the date it was made or purchased. Keeping the food in leak- and smell-proof containers is also important, along with timely replenishing of the fridge's contents. The "sharing a fridge" campaign has also been tried on a larger __(13)__ in the Basque province of Spain, where it is called "Solidarity Fridge." Here food is offered in public refrigerators right on the city streets.

Besides its __(14)__ purpose of tackling the important issue of food waste, this practice has had some other positive effects. People involved in the campaign seem to become less selfish and more __(15)__. Participants say their involvement has even awakened the dormant virtues of compassion and generosity in them.

Unit 14

(A) cooperative   (B) reduce   (C) scale   (D) amounts
(E) initiative   (F) address   (G) intended   (H) shameful
(I) discards   (J) labeled

6. _____ 7. _____ 8. _____ 9. _____ 10. _____

11. _____ 12. _____ 13. _____ 14. _____ 15. _____

Unit 14

三、篇章結構

說明：本題型的題幹為段落式短文，以一篇含四個空格的選文搭配五個選項，每題一個空格，請依文意在文章後所提供的選項中分別選出最適當者，填入空格中，使篇章結構清晰有條理。

    It is estimated that 800 women die every single day from pregnancy- and childbirth-related issues. __(16)__ While most of these problems are treatable, they are typically worsened by lack of training and experience. In Ethiopia, 85% of births take place at home, assisted by family and friends with little or no medical experience. __(17)__ Compare this with a rate of 239 or so in other developing countries and 12 in developed countries. In response to this alarming situation in Ethiopia, the Maternity Foundation, a Danish non-governmental organization, developed a smartphone app intended to lower the maternal death rate in the East African nation. This innovative approach aimed to make medical knowledge more accessible and immediately usable for birth attendants in areas with limited healthcare resources.

    __(18)__ Using easy-to-understand animated instructional videos, this app gives crucial instructions to be used during life-threatening emergencies at the touch of a button. In 2014, testing began as 78 phones with the app were given to midwives in the small Ethiopian town of Gimbie. After 12 months of using the app, the midwives' ability to handle postnatal bleeding had greatly improved. __(19)__ Thanks to those promising results and financial support from the Bill and Melinda Gates Foundation, the app has now been deployed in many other countries that are plagued with high rates of maternal and infant mortality. The app's success shows the vital role that digital tools can play in transforming healthcare in underserved areas, offering new hope to reduce the number of preventable deaths. This technology is proving that even with limited resources, lives can be saved.

Ⓐ These home births pose multiple dangers to both mothers and babies.

Ⓑ Among these issues are fatal complications like severe bleeding, prolonged labor, and infections.

Ⓒ The same result was observed with the provision of first aid to infants.

Ⓓ The Safe Delivery App, as it is called, is designed to teach birth attendants how to manage deliveries.

Ⓔ The result is one of the highest maternal mortality rates in the world: 420 deaths per 100,000 births.

16. _____ **17.** _____ **18.** _____ **19.** _____

Unit 14

四 閱讀測驗　說明：每題請根據本篇文章之文意選出最適當的一個選項。

In 1923, a team of researchers from the American Museum of Natural History (AMNH) found some dinosaur eggs in the Gobi Desert, which is located in southern Mongolia. They concluded that the eggs had been laid by a horned dinosaur called *Protoceratops*. However, on top of the eggs in one nest, the team discovered the skull of a different dinosaur. Believing that this toothless dinosaur's strong jaw would have been ideal for crunching eggs, the American fossil expert Henry Fairfield Osborn assumed that the dinosaur had been killed while attempting to steal the eggs. He therefore named it *Oviraptor*, which means "egg robber" in Latin.

Seventy years later, a different team of researchers found similar clutches of eggs in a different area of the Gobi Desert. Not only did one of the eggs have an identical shape to the *Protoceratops* eggs that the AMNH had discovered, but it also contained a tiny skeleton of a dinosaur that seemed to be an *Oviraptor*. This led to the conclusion that the eggs found seven decades previously were actually *Oviraptor* eggs. Consequently, the *Oviraptor* hadn't been stealing another creature's eggs; it had been taking care of its own eggs. That strong jaw, meanwhile, was probably used to crack open the hard shells of shellfish. Additional discoveries of *Oviraptor* skeletons sitting on top of nests in brooding positions—that is, sitting on eggs so that they hatch—supported the theory that *Oviraptor* cared for rather than stole eggs. These dinosaurs had feathered front limbs and a certain posture that was indicative of a protective and caring nature, which further supported the theory.

David Varricchio, a researcher from Montana State University, believes that these later discoveries also show us that males rather than females were primarily responsible for incubating *Oviraptor* eggs. This makes sense, as there is evidence that the males in early bird species—such as an African bird called the ostrich—acted in a caretaking role. This similarity between ostriches and *Oviraptor* provides yet more support for the widely accepted theory that birds evolved from two-legged dinosaurs like *Oviraptor*.

20. Why did Henry Fairfield Osborn name the dinosaur *Oviraptor*?
    (A) The name was indicative of its apparent behavior.
    (B) The name was based on its physical features.
    (C) The name was derived from its Mongolian location.
    (D) The name was chosen completely at random.

21. What did the researchers in the 1990s prove?
    (A) That the 1923 team showed remarkable foresight.
    (B) That *Oviraptor* and *Protoceratops* were actually the same.
    (C) That *Oviraptor* was more vicious than previously thought.
    (D) That previous assumptions about *Oviraptor* were wrong.

22. What do we learn about the eating habits of *Oviraptor*?
    (A) Its huge teeth allowed it to tear meat easily.
    (B) It existed mainly on fruit and vegetables.
    (C) Its powerful jaw helped it to break open its food.
    (D) It found consuming small animals difficult.

23. Why are ostriches mentioned in the article?
    (A) Because they were also accused of stealing eggs.
    (B) Because they were also studied by the AMNH.
    (C) Because the males of that species also cared for eggs.
    (D) Because the birds came from the same place as *Oviraptor*.

20. _____   21. _____   22. _____   23. _____

五 混合題

說明：請根據文章之文意選出或寫出一個最適當的答案。

You've probably heard the term "superfoods" in recent years. It is used to describe foods that are considered particularly beneficial for our health. From blueberries to avocados, these foods are hailed by some nutritionists for their naturally high content of vitamins and minerals. But are superfoods truly worthy of the praise and the health claims? Let's take a look at two to find out.

Açaí (pronounced *ah-sigh-ee*) **berries** are deep purple berries that are grown in tropical Central and South America. They're a staple food in the Amazon region, but in the US, you'll more likely find them as a juice or in a blended form in an açaí bowl, along with oats and other fruits. Fans of açaí berries like to point out that they are rich in antioxidants, which are said to neutralize cancer-causing free radicals in the body. However, actual studies of the effects on human health are in short supply. Also, açaí berries have a short shelf life, so when they're sold as juices, they often contain added sugars.	❶ **Quinoa** (pronounced *keen-wah*) also hails from South America—specifically the Andes Mountains. ❷ It is a whole grain that can be used as an alternative to rice, as a side dish, or incorporated into other recipes. ❸ One of its main selling points is the fact that it is high in complete proteins, which provide all the essential amino acids our bodies need. ❹ This means that quinoa is an ideal source of protein for vegetarians and vegans. ❺ However, a serving of quinoa contains more calories than brown rice or pasta, meaning that consuming too much of it could lead to weight gain.

So, should we be eating açaí berries and quinoa—along with other superfoods—at every available opportunity? Superfoods are clearly healthy, so by all means include them in your diet. **If you don't**, you'll be missing out on some vitamins and minerals. But the bottom line is that a balanced diet—containing lots of different fruits and vegetables, starchy carbohydrates, and modest amounts of protein and dairy—will always be more beneficial than any specific superfood.

24-25 Using the information in the passage, complete the table below.（填充）

Superfood	Substance(s)	Beneficial Effect
Açaí berries	antioxidants	24. _____
Quinoa	25. _____	provide all the essential amino acids our bodies need

26. The sentences about quinoa are numbered ❶ to ❺. Which sentence best indicates a negative point about quinoa? Write down the NUMBER of the sentence below.（單選）

27. What does the author mean by saying, "If you don't" in the conclusion?（簡答）
He means, "If you don't _____, you'll be missing out on some vitamins and minerals."

28. Which of the following best describes the author's opinion of superfoods?（單選）
(A) Healthy but expensive
(B) Beneficial but not vital
(C) Sugary and too fatty
(D) Unhealthy but interesting

24. _____

25. _____

26. _____

27. _____

28. _____

Unit 15

一 綜合測驗

說明：本題型的題幹為段落式短文，選文中含數個空格，每題一個空格，請依文意選出最適當的一個選項。

　　Established by Denmark in 2005, the INDEX: Award encourages people to find solutions to the basic challenges that the world faces, offering cash awards worth more than NT$17 million in total every two years. Anyone with good ideas related to the five categories of the contest—body, home, work, play and learning, and community— (1)   a chance of winning. To give just one   (2) , during the 2013 INDEX: Award, over 1,000 entries were received from more than 70 countries.

　　One of the most   (3)   entries which earned a prize in the play and learning category was something called the Raspberry Pi. It is a small, inexpensive computer   (4)   by Eben Upton and his colleagues at the University of Cambridge. Costing under NT$1,000, the Raspberry Pi was designed with the goal of helping children learn coding and getting computers in the hands of as many people around the world as possible. Without doubt, for people wishing to make the world a better place to live, the INDEX: Award offers a   (5) . If you can benefit the world with your ideas, why not benefit your pocket with them as well?

1. (A) imitates　　(B) elevates　　(C) relates　　(D) stands
2. (A) example　　(B) couple　　(C) principle　　(D) disciple
3. (A) disappointing　(B) forthcoming　(C) exhausting　(D) fascinating
4. (A) to develop　(B) developed　　(C) developing　(D) develops
5. (A) strong restriction　　　(B) great incentive
　 (C) major obstacle　　　　(D) huge achievement

1. _____　2. _____　3. _____　4. _____　5. _____

二、文意選填

說明：本題型的題幹為段落式短文，以一篇含十個空格的選文搭配十個選項，每題一個空格，請依文意在文章後所提供的選項中分別選出最適當者。

Living without one's most valuable sense—sight—is certainly a challenge, one that makes many things difficult for the blind. Knowing that many of the problems faced by the visually impaired could be solved easily if a sighted person were __(6)__ to help them, Hans Jorgen Wiberg came up with a great idea for an app. Working with the Danish Blind Society and teaming up with a Danish software __(7)__ by the name of Robocat in 2012, Wiberg created a revolutionary new app that he called "Be My Eyes."

The concept behind "Be My Eyes" is simple but __(8)__. Through the use of a video link, the app lets users talk with normal-sighted people and __(9)__ the smartphone camera at anything to allow volunteers to help them with their daily problems. The "Be My Eyes" program has __(10)__ more than 120,000 blind people and two million volunteers. The latter are notified when help is __(11)__, and can decide whether to respond at any given time. In most cases, the __(12)__ that takes place between the volunteers and those who require their help lasts perhaps only a minute or two. Even such a small amount of time, however, can make a huge __(13)__ to blind people's lives. The 120,000 blind and otherwise visually impaired people using the app no longer have to __(14)__ their neighbors. They can now deal with the problem, for example, of determining whether or not the milk in their refrigerator has __(15)__. They can feel confident in the knowledge that the volunteers who have signed up for the program are ready, willing, and able to help with the challenges they face because of their disability.

(A) recruited (B) studio (C) point (D) difference
(E) expired (F) available (G) bother (H) requested
(I) communication (J) effective

6. _____ 7. _____ 8. _____ 9. _____ 10. _____

11. _____ 12. _____ 13. _____ 14. _____ 15. _____

Unit
15

篇章結構

說明：本題型的題幹為段落式短文，以一篇含四個空格的選文搭配五個選項，每題一個空格，請依文意在文章後所提供的選項中分別選出最適當者，填入空格中，使篇章結構清晰有條理。

　　If you want a unique experience while traveling in Stockholm or just need an overnight stay in the Swedish capital, the Jumbo Stay Hotel may be exactly what you're looking for. __(16)__ Actually a hostel rather than a true hotel, the Jumbo Stay Hotel is a converted Boeing 747 that has 33 rooms of various sizes with a total of eighty beds. Despite its special structure, this plane-converted hostel is similar in some ways to other hostels. For example, due to the limited space, guests in most of the rooms need to share communal bathrooms and showers. __(17)__ In addition, the unusual hostel features a lounge with airline seats to relax in. There is also an observation deck on one of the plane's wings on which anyone can stand safely. This setting offers an unforgettable opportunity to sleep in a real airplane, making it ideal for aviation enthusiasts. The plane's design and history only add to its charm, as guests enjoy an experience unlike any traditional hotel.

　　Opened in 2008, the Jumbo Stay Hotel was created by a businessman named Oscar Diös, who wanted to develop a hotel near the airport. __(18)__ He spent roughly two million euros to turn the plane into a one-of-a-kind hostel, which is held in place by steel cradles on the landing gear. __(19)__ If you are a fan of planes who happens to be in Sweden, you will definitely love this place. For those looking for an adventurous stay with a twist, Jumbo Stay offers the perfect combination of comfort and novelty, making it an attraction for visitors from all over the world.

A In 2006, while he was thinking about how to make his hopes a reality, Diös came across an old aircraft that had previously been in the service of Pan Am.

B This is particularly true if you love planes.

C By seizing the opportunity to buy the 747 and pouring a lot of money into its refurbishment, Diös is offering people a unique experience they won't soon forget.

D In contrast, the cockpit, which has been transformed into a luxury room with a good view of the airport, has its own bathroom.

E The lack of communal spaces is one noticeable aspect of the hostel.

16. _____   17. _____   18. _____   19. _____

Unit
15

四 閱讀測驗　說明：每題請根據本篇文章之文意選出最適當的一個選項。

　　A Ponzi scheme is an illegal investment scheme. It involves persuading people to make an investment with the promise of high returns and little risk, but it pays them those returns using the money from new investors rather than from actual profits. The scheme can sustain itself while there are still plenty of new investors who can be **enticed** to join. However, it can fall apart for one of three main reasons: the operator disappears with all of the money; the flow of new investors dries up; or a sudden change in the economy prompts investors to try to withdraw all of their money.

　　There are several warning signs that an investment opportunity might actually be a Ponzi scheme. One sign is that the investment offers a substantial profit by a certain time. This is suspicious because high returns always carry more risk. Another sign is that the investment offers consistent returns regardless of market conditions. In reality, returns should naturally go up and down. Yet another sign is that the investment strategies are described as too complex to explain to clients. This should set alarm bells ringing as all investment information should be freely available.

　　Although there is evidence of similar schemes from the 19th century, the term "Ponzi scheme" derives from the actions of one man in the 1920s: Charles Ponzi. Over the course of several months, this Italian immigrant convinced tens of thousands of investors in the US to part with their money by promising a 50 percent return after only 45 days. Even *The Boston Post* printed favorable reports that effectively encouraged readers to invest their money with the man. However, editors at the newspaper soon became suspicious of Ponzi's rapid rise and commissioned an investigation into his business dealings. A series of articles was published that revealed details of not only Ponzi's current scheme but also his criminal past in Canada a decade earlier. Following the investigation, the scheme collapsed, and Ponzi, having cheated investors out of US$15 million, was sentenced to five years in prison.

20. Which of the following is most likely a synonym of "**enticed**" in the first paragraph?
    (A) deterred
    (B) startled
    (C) betrayed
    (D) lured

21. Which of the following situations most likely involves a Ponzi scheme?
    (A) Steven was encouraged to invest US$10,000 in his friend's new business, which eventually yielded him a modest profit.
    (B) Rachel was told that her investment carried some risk, but reading the details in the contract put her mind at ease.
    (C) Jack was promised a NT$100,000 return on his investment every month even though the state of the economy was poor.
    (D) Tamara was persuaded to buy some stocks and shares in a company whose financial reports were freely accessible.

22. According to the passage, what is true of Ponzi schemes?
    (A) They can collapse when the person running them vanishes with the cash.
    (B) They are named after a complicated project in 19th-century Italy.
    (C) They can be very difficult to invest in due to a lack of promotion.
    (D) They are usually operated by companies rather than individuals.

23. What do we learn about the newspaper investigation conducted by *The Boston Post*?
    (A) It was initially skeptical of Ponzi but gradually became more positive.
    (B) It focused solely on Charles Ponzi's crimes in the 1920s in the US.
    (C) It was initiated after an editor personally invested money with Ponzi.
    (D) It revealed details of Ponzi's illegal activities in another country.

20. _____   21. _____   22. _____   23. _____

Unit 15

五 混合題 說明：請根據文章之文意選出或寫出一個最適當的答案。

Almost everyone knows the story of the *Titanic*: the "unsinkable" ship that sank in the icy waters of the Atlantic, claiming the lives of 1,500 passengers and crew. Fewer are aware of how and why it was constructed. Its origins can be traced back to the summer of 1907 and a meeting between two powerful men: J. Bruce Ismay, managing director of the shipping company White Star Line, and Lord William James Pirrie, chairman of the shipbuilding company Harland and Wolff. Facing stiff competition from other shipping companies, Ismay was eager to construct the biggest and most luxurious ocean liners the world had ever seen. According to *National Geographic*, Lord Pirrie immediately sketched three ships that matched these criteria and told Ismay that his company would build them. **[1]** One of these was the *Titanic*.

Building work began on March 31, 1909, in Belfast, Ireland, with the laying of the keel: the long piece of steel that runs along the bottom of a ship and forms its foundation. Over the course of two years, around 3,000 craftsmen, engineers, and laborers—overseen by Harland and Wolff's chief designer, Thomas Andrews—worked on the *Titanic*. **[2]** Once the main structure had been erected, the ship was launched. However, it took a further year for the interior work to be completed. As tall as a nine-story building and as long as four city blocks, the *Titanic* featured four elevators, a swimming pool, and an opulent dining room. **[3]** It is accurate to say that no expense was spared when fitting out the largest steamer on the planet.

Unfortunately—and tragically—some corners were cut in terms of safety. Andrews had pushed for the inclusion of a large number of lifeboats, but Ismay had dismissed his concerns, telling the designer, "I'll not have so many [lifeboats] cluttering up my decks and putting fear into my passengers." The main body of the ship, meanwhile, had been divided into sixteen closeable compartments. **[4]** This was to ensure that water could be contained in the event of a breach, and it was claimed that the ship would stay afloat even if four of them flooded. However, through cost-cutting or lack of concern for safety, the compartments had not been sealed at the top. When the *Titanic* embarked on its maiden voyage from Southampton to New York on April 10, 1912, a deckhand reportedly told a passenger, "God Himself could not sink this ship." History was to prove otherwise.

24-25 請從文章中找出最適當的單詞（word）填入下列句子空格中，並視語法需要做適當的字形變化。每格限填一個單詞（word）。（填充）

J. Bruce Ismay was anxious to compete with other companies in the shipping industry and commence ____24.____ on three huge, lavish ocean liners.

While the erection of the main body of the *Titanic* took around two years, the ____25.____ of the inner work took another twelve months.

26. Which of the following headings is the most suitable for each paragraph? Write down the letter next to the appropriate paragraph.（配合）

   (A) Safety shortcuts that led to tragedy.
   (B) The people who died in the sinking.
   (C) External and internal work takes place.
   (D) A meeting between influential figures.

   Paragraph 1: _____
   Paragraph 2: _____
   Paragraph 3: _____

27. In which of the positions marked [1], [2], [3], and [4] does the following sentence best belong?（單選）

   "The first- and second-class rooms were luxurious, and even the third-class accommodations were comparatively comfortable."

   (A) [1]
   (B) [2]
   (C) [3]
   (D) [4]

24. _____   25. _____

26. Paragraph 1: _____
    Paragraph 2: _____
    Paragraph 3: _____

27. _____

Unit 16

一 綜合測驗

說明：本題型的題幹為段落式短文，選文中含數個空格，每題一個空格，請依文意選出最適當的一個選項。

　　Unlike many women around the world, the females of the Netherlands place a higher value on free time than on money or career success. More than 90 percent of Dutch women do not work full-time. Most, though, do have part-time __(1)__, with the number of part-time female workers in Holland equaling 75 percent of the adult female population. Dutch women don't seem to be bothered by these figures, nor do they wish to see anything done to __(2)__ by women in the workplace, as can be seen in the results of a survey. __(3)__ if they would like to work more if they could, only four percent of the respondents said "yes."

　　Women in the Netherlands enjoy their free time __(4)__ they have even taken action to protect their right not to work more than they want to. In 2000, a law was passed in Holland that __(5)__ women can't be forced by an employer to work more hours. Thus, job satisfaction among Dutch women appears to be not having to work too many hours.

1. (A) employment (B) balcony (C) circulation (D) extension
2. (A) prevent active engagement (B) conduct further investigation
   (C) limit professional growth (D) encourage more participation
3. (A) Asking (B) Asked (C) Having asked (D) To ask
4. (A) provided that (B) so much that (C) for fear that (D) in order that
5. (A) denies (B) sustains (C) whines (D) states

1. _____ 2. _____ 3. _____ 4. _____ 5. _____

二、文意選填

說明：本題型的題幹為段落式短文，以一篇含十個空格的選文搭配十個選項，每題一個空格，請依文意在文章後所提供的選項中分別選出最適當者。

It's interesting, in this digital age we live in, to find a person like Paulo Magalhães, a man from Portugal, who has a passionate fondness for handwritten letters. Magalhães' love of this kind of old-fashioned personal message is so great that it prompted him to develop a website that allows people to __(6)__ with each other by mailing postcards. Called Postcrossing—a simple __(7)__ of the words "post" and "crossing"—the internet site lets people sign up for free and list their addresses.

The idea behind Postcrossing is that the __(8)__ must send postcards in order to receive them. Initially, members are allowed to send five postcards at the same time to others __(9)__ with the website. Over time, as an individual sends out more and more postcards, he or she can mail as many as 100 at a time. The addresses are all generated on a __(10)__ basis. Exchanges between postcrossers occur only once unless they wish to carry on the __(11)__ further on their own. Much to Magalhães' __(12)__, Postcrossing has become a big success. What started out as a hobby has __(13)__ so much attention that roughly 700,000 people from more than 200 nations are now listed as members of the website.

The popularity of Postcrossing has prompted Magalhães to make efforts to promote environmental sustainability to its members. He uses the website to distribute tips on how people can __(14)__ their environmental impact. For example, they could use recycled paper, write during the day, when no __(15)__ lighting is required, or choose to ride a bicycle or walk to the post office instead of driving a car there. All of this shows that Magalhães is mindful that people need to consider how their hobbies and interests may impact on the world.

Unit 16

(A) lessen　　(B) random　　(C) correspondence　　(D) surprise
(E) registered　(F) artificial　(G) attracted　　(H) combination
(I) connect　　(J) participants

6. _____　7. _____　8. _____　9. _____　10. _____

11. _____　12. _____　13. _____　14. _____　15. _____

Unit 16

篇章結構

說明：本題型的題幹為段落式短文，以一篇含四個空格的選文搭配五個選項，每題一個空格，請依文意在文章後所提供的選項中分別選出最適當者，填入空格中，使篇章結構清晰有條理。

　　As the proportion of elderly people continues to grow, more and more people are being affected by Alzheimer's disease and other forms of cognitive impairment. As a matter of fact, it is estimated that by 2050, two billion people will be sixty and older; 135.5 million of them will have dementia. With the increasing number of cases, finding ways to improve patients' daily lives has become a priority. Fortunately, although there is no cure for dementia, more and more is being done to assist sufferers and help make their lives somewhat better. ___(16)___

　　Eatwell is a tableware set designed especially for people with Alzheimer's disease so that they can eat without the help of others. ___(17)___ Since it can be confusing for people with dementia when their food and plates have the same colors, Yao made bowls that are blue on the inside, thereby making it easier for them to tell the difference between food and containers. ___(18)___ The utensils are also designed to be easier to grip, helping those with weak motor skills. Giving the elderly more independence when they are eating allows them to better maintain their dignity and reduces the burden on caregivers.

　　Eatwell has been recognized as an outstanding product that assists the elderly. It won the first annual design contest established in 2014 by the Stanford Center on Longevity, beating out 51 other teams from 15 countries and taking home US$10,000 in prize money. ___(19)___ She said it was memories of her late grandmother, who had Alzheimer's, that motivated her to help people with similar problems. Through Eatwell, she hopes to raise awareness about the importance of designing for people with special needs.

Ⓐ What's more, spills are less common with Eatwell because the cups and bowls are made to be difficult to knock over.

Ⓑ Taking the right food supplements is essential for those with dementia.

Ⓒ One feature of Eatwell is the focus on color.

Ⓓ However, Yao's primary purpose in creating Eatwell was not to win the Stanford prize.

Ⓔ One example of this is Sha Yao and the efforts she has put into developing Eatwell.

16. _____   17. _____   18. _____   19. _____

四 閱讀測驗 說明：每題請根據本篇文章之文意選出最適當的一個選項。

    The Dancing Plague is the name given to a bizarre, three-month-long spectacle that unfolded in the now-French city of Strasbourg in the summer of 1518. One hot day in July of that year, a woman surnamed Troffea left her home and began dancing uncontrollably and unstoppably in the streets. Within weeks, she had been joined by hundreds of other wild dancers. These people barely paused for breath, let alone to rest, eat, or drink. The authorities in the city became increasingly concerned and decided that the only solution was to encourage the dancing in the hope that the afflicted would tire themselves out. To this end, they organized halls for the people to dance in and musicians to accompany the dancers. However, this only intensified the problem. Reports from the time suggest that some of the dancers collapsed and died from heart attacks, strokes, or heat exhaustion. It was not until September that the crazed dancing began to die down. Historians generally attribute this to the fact that the authorities transported the remaining dancers into the mountains to pray to Saint Vitus—the patron saint of dancers—for forgiveness.

    Several theories about what caused the Dancing Plague have been suggested over the years. At the time, local doctors believed that the victims were suffering from overheated blood, while others alleged that they had become possessed by demons. In the 20th century, researchers thought that the dancers might have contracted food poisoning by eating bread contaminated with a toxic mold that can cause hallucinations and sudden movements. However, it seems unlikely that this would have resulted in the victims dancing for such a prolonged period. The most-favored current theory was suggested by the historian John Waller, who has written extensively on the Dancing Plague. He believes that the dancers were suffering from stress-induced mass hysteria. During the early 16th century, the citizens of Strasbourg were faced with harvest failures, periods of starvation, and the spread of diseases such as syphilis and smallpox. **They** also believed strongly that Saint Vitus could curse them by forcing them to dance. The stressful situations coupled with this belief could have prompted sudden, extreme behavior that then spread like an epidemic. The spread of this behavior would have been made worse by the authorities' initial decision to facilitate the dancing rather than stop it. Five centuries later, though, it seems certain that we will never know for sure what caused the Dancing Plague.

20. How did those in charge initially react to the dancing?
    (A) They banned musicians from performing with the dancers.
    (B) They encouraged the dancers to eat, drink, and relax.
    (C) They took the dancers up into the mountains.
    (D) They made it easier for people to dance.

21. What can we learn from the article about the Dancing Plague?
    (A) The woman who started it collapsed after suffering a stroke.
    (B) Many of the people who took part in it developed smallpox.
    (C) It was confined to one urban area in what we now call France.
    (D) Saint Vitus refused to forgive the people who took part in it.

22. Which theory about what caused the Dancing Plague is NOT mentioned in the article?
    (A) The dancers consumed bread that was moldy.
    (B) A religious group influenced the dancers.
    (C) The blood of the dancers became too hot.
    (D) Stressful events led to extreme emotions.

23. Who does "**They**" refer to in the second paragraph?
    (A) The dancers who passed away.
    (B) The historical researchers.
    (C) The citizens of Strasbourg.
    (D) The local doctors in the city.

Unit 16

20. _____   21. _____   22. _____   23. _____

Unit 16

五 混合題
說明：請根據文章之文意選出或寫出一個最適當的答案。

Japan intends to release radioactive wastewater into the Pacific Ocean. This wastewater was contaminated by the Fukushima Daiichi nuclear power plant disaster of 2011. Here are four people's opinions on this decision.

Kaito
I can understand people's worries about the release of contaminated water into the ocean, but as a scientist, I look at the evidence. The fact is that the amount of wastewater being released will be tiny in comparison to the vast volume of the ocean, which means that any radiation present will be massively diluted. Besides, the water has already been treated with the most advanced technological methods to lower the concentration of radioactive elements well below acceptable levels. That's why I'm completely comfortable with the decision.

Takashi
I have been a fisherman for over 40 years, and I have to say that the plan to release the wastewater into the sea makes me very uneasy. Officials insist that it's safe, but I think there could be severe environmental consequences. If small sea animals and plants become contaminated and are then eaten by larger ones, the radioactive elements could accumulate in fish and ultimately end up being consumed by humans. All of this could take years, so I fear that the long-term consequences of the wastewater release are too much of an unknown.

Yuna
Several friends from South Korea are visiting me in Japan at the moment, and they have heard about the plan to release the radioactive wastewater into the Pacific. They are concerned that the water could flow to their country and have a negative impact on citizens' health and the fishing industry. To be honest, I doubt this would actually happen, but public perception is an important factor that should be considered. If people begin to worry about the disposal of nuclear waste, they might begin to lose faith in nuclear power in general.

Sakura
As a senior official at the nuclear plant, I know that the greater danger lies in *not* releasing the wastewater into the ocean. Storing it in tanks on land poses a far bigger risk, as the tanks could be damaged in another earthquake or accident,

potentially contaminating the soil. Also, I'm aware that the release of water contaminated with tritium—one of the radioactive elements—is **common practice**, not just here but around the world. It is only because the Fukushima disaster made headlines that people have taken more notice.

24-25 請從文章中找出最適當的單詞（word）填入下列句子空格中，並視語法需要做適當的字形變化。每格限填一個單詞（word）。（填充）

Kaito knows that some people are anxious about the potential ___**24.**___ of the ocean by radioactive wastewater, but he is comfortable with the plan.

Yuna has a number of foreign friends who have expressed ___**25.**___ about the release of the wastewater, as they worry it will flow to their country.

26. What does Sakura imply when she uses the phrase "common practice"?（單選）
    (A) Releasing contaminated water is widely considered to be risky.
    (B) Many people believe what they read in newspapers about nuclear power.
    (C) Earthquakes happen often and can easily damage nuclear plants.
    (D) Many nuclear power plants let radioactive wastewater flow into the sea.

27. Which of the following are true statements about the people's views?（多選）
    (A) The careers of both Takashi and Sakura have influenced their opinions on this matter.
    (B) Kaito and Sakura share worries about the storage of radioactive wastewater on land.
    (C) Yuna and Kaito both approach the wastewater issue from a scientific background.
    (D) Takashi is more worried than the others about the effects on the marine environment.
    (E) Both Yuna and Sakura talk about how the plan has affected the opinions of the general public.
    (F) Takashi and Kaito are both skeptical about the official interpretation of the wastewater release.

24. _____   25. _____

26. _____

27. _____

Unit 16

Unit 17

一、綜合測驗

說明：本題型的題幹為段落式短文，選文中含數個空格，每題一個空格，請依文意選出最適當的一個選項。

　　When you think of coffins, what comes to mind? Most people would __(1)__ coffins with images of simple rectangular boxes. In the African country of Ghana, some people are buried in much more creative containers __(2)__ fantasy coffins. These are elaborate creations that come in a variety of shapes and sizes and are made to reflect the life of the __(3)__ in some way. If a person was a pilot, for example, he may be buried in a coffin __(4)__ a plane or a jet, while a person who was a sailor might be placed to rest in one that looks like a battleship. Some farmers have even been buried in coffins shaped like giant ears of corn or cocoa pods, symbolizing their dedication to agriculture. It is considered an honor and a sign of respect to have a handcrafted fantasy coffin in which to __(5)__ since only the heads of families who have achieved some level of success may be buried in one. As for the talented craftsmen who build the fantasy coffins, they are considered to be elite artists in Ghana and around the world. Their work has even been displayed in international art exhibitions, showcasing the artistic value of this tradition.

1. (A) compensate　　(B) associate　　(C) terminate　　(D) prevail
2. (A) calling　　(B) to call　　(C) having called　　(D) called
3. (A) condemned　　(B) deceased　　(C) insured　　(D) learned
4. (A) resembling　　(B) flourishing　　(C) devouring　　(D) groaning
5. (A) endure inconvenience　　(B) overcome obstacles
   (C) expect afterlife　　(D) spend eternity

1. _____　2. _____　3. _____　4. _____　5. _____

二 文意選填

說明：本題型的題幹為段落式短文，以一篇含十個空格的選文搭配十個選項，每題一個空格，請依文意在文章後所提供的選項中分別選出最適當者。

Sian Ka'an is a large, federally protected part of Mexico's Caribbean coastline, home to a variety of flora and fauna. A UNESCO World Heritage Site, the (6) contains twenty pre-Columbian archaeological sites and the world's second-largest coastal barrier reef. The formerly pristine area is (7) to be a global treasure. However, due to an enormous man-made (8) , it has become something of a storehouse for the world's trash. With so much junk dumped into the ocean each year that most species of marine life have been negatively affected, it is common for countless pieces of garbage to be washed up on the shores of Sian Ka'an, a problem that has attracted the attention of artist Alejandro Durán.

On a regular basis, Durán gathers up garbage that the waves have (9) at Sian Ka'an. Then he (10) ugly items into wonderful sculptures full of great colors. For Durán, who has a (11) for drawing the public's attention to the serious problem of the pollution of our oceans, Sian Ka'an is his studio. The artistic work he has put together is part of a (12) he has dubbed "Washed Up." For his sculptures, he uses his (13) to come up with interesting, unique art, converting garbage into likenesses of natural objects such as fish, fruit, and algae. He takes these disgusting pieces of trash and makes them (14) beautiful. So far, he has collected garbage from fifty different countries on six continents. His art (15) the message that no matter how undeveloped our natural environment may seem at the moment, it is under constant threat. It is therefore never truly safe from the impact of global consumerism and the pollution it brings.

A deposited　　**B** catastrophe　　**C** stresses　　**D** project
E supposed　　**F** imagination　　**G** transforms　　**H** passion
I appear　　**J** region

6. _____　7. _____　8. _____　9. _____　10. _____

11. _____　12. _____　13. _____　14. _____　15. _____

Unit
17

Unit 17

篇章結構

說明：本題型的題幹為段落式短文，以一篇含四個空格的選文搭配五個選項，每題一個空格，請依文意在文章後所提供的選項中分別選出最適當者，填入空格中，使篇章結構清晰有條理。

　　Piracy, or illegal copying, has been hurting the music industry for a long time. Now it has found its way into the book publishing world. More and more people find it convenient to use e-books and e-readers.　(16)　When that happens, publishers lose a lot of money because millions of people illegally download free copies of books rather than buy them at bookstores or pay for legal downloads.　(17)　However, if the music industry is any indication, it is a large sum indeed. Authors, too, are directly affected, as they lose well-earned royalties when their books are pirated.

　　What measures can the publishing industry take to battle this problem, one that is so widespread and growing?　(18)　This would likely persuade some people, especially those who already feel a twinge of guilt when they download from file-sharing sites. Additionally, offering attractive subscription models, similar to music streaming services, could make legal access more appealing. However, it is unlikely to change the minds of those who view violating intellectual property rights as an acceptable thing to do. After all, paying nothing is still more appealing than getting a great discount.

　　Another option would be for publishers to monitor illegal downloads closely, find those who steal their online publications, and take them to court.　(19)　Legal action against individual offenders is expensive and time-consuming, making it difficult to enforce copyright laws effectively. Thus, it looks as though book publishing is destined to suffer the same fate as the music industry: a continual decline in annual revenue due to piracy and advancements in technology. Unless new solutions are developed, the future of digital publishing will continue to face significant challenges.

A One way would be to significantly lower the price of e-books sold online to encourage shoppers to purchase legal downloads.

B Given the size of the problem, though, this option hardly seems feasible.

C With that popularity, there is a greater likelihood that someone will place publications on illegal file-sharing websites.

D Fortunately, the publishing industry has not been hit as hard as the music industry.

E It is difficult to estimate just how much the publishing industry is losing from all this illegal activity.

16. _____   17. _____   18. _____   19. _____

Unit
17

Unit 17

四 閱讀測驗 說明：每題請根據本篇文章之文意選出最適當的一個選項。

During 2022, the South Asian nation of Pakistan was hit by severe flooding that was described by its prime minister as "the worst in the country's history." The floods **engulfed** a third of Pakistan's land area, affecting 33 million people and leading to the loss of over 1,700 lives. Hundreds of thousands of livestock were swept away and millions of acres of crops were lost.

One of the main causes of the floods was a significantly heavier monsoon season than was typical. Although the monsoons are considered vital for their role in watering crops and refilling lakes and dams, the sheer scale of the 2022 rains proved too much for the country to cope with. The province of Sindh, for example, received over four times as much rain between June and August as the 30-year average. Satellite images showed that the Indus River, located in the province, had transformed into a lake that was 100 kilometers wide.

Another factor at play is that, aside from the Arctic and Antarctic, Pakistan is home to the most glaciers in the world. These large masses of ice in the Himalayas usually gain volume during the winter and then melt slowly during the spring. However, in the spring of 2022, Pakistan experienced a severe heat wave that broke temperature records and caused accelerated glacial melts. The lakes that would normally absorb these melts were unable to cope. This triggered sudden releases of water that, combined with the monsoon rains, led to the extreme flooding.

Climate change undoubtedly played a major role in making the monsoon rains heavier and heat waves more likely. Yet, it is important to also acknowledge the failure of the Pakistani government to learn lessons from the country's previous major flood in 2010 and invest in infrastructure improvements. According to the BBC, "government failures to make adaptive changes" following that shocking event "contributed to the scale of devastation" twelve years later.

In addition to this, deforestation is a major problem in Pakistan. Trees are regularly felled to clear space for both urban development and the use of land for agriculture. In lower lying areas of the Himalayas, this practice very likely increased surface runoff and soil erosion and therefore worsened the flooding.

20. What is most likely the meaning of "**engulfed**" in the first paragraph?
    (A) Defended and protected something fully.
    (B) Surrounded and covered something completely.
    (C) Refused and resisted something entirely.
    (D) Promoted and encouraged something strongly.

21. What can we infer about the 2022 floods in Pakistan?
    (A) They were not as bad as the 2010 floods.
    (B) They only affected the province of Sindh.
    (C) They were a huge problem during winter.
    (D) They badly affected the farming industry.

22. Which causes of the floods in Pakistan are discussed in paragraphs 2 to 4?
    (A) Lack of funding; failure of dams; government neglect
    (B) Intense rain; cutting down trees; increase in urban areas
    (C) Intense rain; increased temperatures; government neglect
    (D) Cutting down trees; volcanic eruptions; increased temperatures

23. How does the writer conclude the article?
    (A) By going into more detail on the impact of climate change.
    (B) By providing yet another potential cause of the floods.
    (C) By outlining how Pakistan could improve its flood defenses.
    (D) By predicting that floods in Pakistan are likely to get worse.

20. _____   21. _____   22. _____   23. _____

Unit 17

Unit 17

五、混合題
說明：請根據文章之文意選出或寫出一個最適當的答案。

Ultra-processed foods (UPFs) are those that have been prepared using industrial processes. They contain a large number of ingredients that wouldn't typically be used when people are preparing food at home. Please share your views on UPFs on this forum.

(A) Anya
Obviously, UPFs aren't great for your health, but they're delicious, aren't they? Who can say no to a big bag of chips when they're watching a movie? Nacho Cheese Doritos are my personal favorite.

(B) Biff
In my opinion, governments should put big fat warning labels on ultra-processed foods to protect public health. Sugary sodas, instant noodles, chicken nuggets—they should be treated the same as cigarettes.

(C) Crystal
I'm not going to claim they're healthy, but I eat them every so often as an indulgent treat. And if I host a birthday party or some other celebration, I always serve cakes, doughnuts, and sharing bags of chips.

(D) Dominic
As a medical professional, I know that numerous studies have linked a diet high in UPFs to obesity, diabetes, high blood pressure, and heart disease because they're often high in salt, added sugars, and trans fats.

(E) Emma
Part of me feels guilty for serving ultra-processed foods at home, but ultimately I find them convenient and affordable. Things like oven-ready pizzas and microwavable meals—I think they're great for those on low incomes.

(F) Farad
When I think of greasy burgers, fried chicken, hot dogs, and fish sticks, I honestly feel sick. I consider these types of food to be a menace to society and believe they should be banned.

(G) Georgina
We shouldn't demonize certain foods. Doing so causes people to develop eating disorders. Eating UPFs is fine as part of a balanced diet, and they can be enjoyed as treats from time to time—just as I do.

(H) Hugh
They're difficult to avoid, aren't they? From mass-produced white bread to breakfast cereals to bags of salted chips, it's hard not to buy them in your weekly supermarket shop and include them in your regular diet.

(I) Iona
UPFs contain hydrogenated fats, artificial sweeteners, bulking agents, and high fructose corn syrup, among many other ingredients. They provide empty calories rather than the vitamins, minerals, and fiber that our bodies require for adequate nutrition.

(J) Julius
I exercise my willpower and eat healthily most of the time, but everyone deserves a treat every now and then! A burger, fries, and soda from a fast-food restaurant is my reward for being good the rest of the time.

Unit 17

24. From (A) to (J) in the above forum discussion, which ONES deal primarily in facts and not opinions? Write the LETTERS below.（多選）

25. Which people does this sentence relate to?（簡答）
"He or she only consumes ultra-processed foods on occasion."

Unit 17

26. Which word on the forum discussion carries the meaning of "something that is likely to cause harm"?（簡答）
_____

27. Which of these UPFs is mentioned most frequently on the forum?（單選）

(A) [burger]   (B) [soda]   (C) [chips]   (D) [instant noodles]

24. _____

25. _____

26. _____

27. _____

Unit 18

一 綜合測驗

說明：本題型的題幹為段落式短文，選文中含數個空格，每題一個空格，請依文意選出最適當的一個選項。

    The Ecocapsule, an egg-shaped living space developed by a Slovakian company, is the ultimate in sustainable living. The compact, portable home, (1) roughly 1,500 kilograms, can be transported almost anywhere through shipping, towing, airlifting, or even being pulled by pack animal. Its mobility makes it ideal for people who need temporary housing in remote locations. A wind turbine and solar panels attached to the roof help its battery (2) and make the Ecocapsule environmentally friendly. These renewable energy sources allow residents to live comfortably without depending on traditional power grids.

     (3) , the design of the pod facilitates the collection of rainwater and dew for use as a water supply. All this means that living totally off the grid is possible with the Ecocapsule. The space can even offer many of the comforts of (4) living, such as hot showers, running water, a toilet that can be flushed, and hot meals. Features (5) a kitchenette, folding bed, storeroom, handy workspace, and large windows. Although the interior is just 11 square meters in size, the pod is able to house two people with ease.

1. (A) weighing (B) weighs (C) weighed (D) to be weighed
2. (A) consume energy (B) produce competition
   (C) generate electricity (D) supply opportunities
3. (A) In other words (B) After all (C) In addition (D) On the one hand
4. (A) splendid (B) regular (C) controversial (D) fragile
5. (A) include (B) resolve (C) consult (D) devote

1. ____ 2. ____ 3. ____ 4. ____ 5. ____

二 文意選填

說明：本題型的題幹為段落式短文，以一篇含十個空格的選文搭配十個選項，每題一個空格，請依文意在文章後所提供的選項中分別選出最適當者。

It is likely you have never thought of fog as a type of natural resource. However, the process of fog harvesting __(6)__ that it can indeed be one. Fog harvesting is the use of many panels with a fine mesh in order to collect tiny droplets of water in a storage tank, to be used later for drinking and other __(7)__. This clever use of a unique, low-tech type of green activity is happening in the Sidi Ifni region of the African country of Morocco. As fog passes through the forty panels placed atop a 1,225-meter mountain peak, a process __(8)__ as condensation causes water droplets to form on the mesh and trickle downwards into containers. Through a pipe network, the collected water is __(9)__ to five villages, in which about 400 people reside. People can have __(10)__ to clean water from taps for the first time in their lives.

Fog harvesting has transformed the lives of those living in the five villages of Sidi Ifni that are using this green __(11)__. In the past, in order to get enough water from wells that were a long distance from their homes, the women of the villages needed to make exhausting __(12)__ that took four hours. In addition, during times of __(13)__, people of the villages had to bring extra water in, which was a costly expense. In contrast, fog harvesting is quite cheap, __(14)__ no energy, and does not create any pollution. Because of all its many __(15)__, it is hoped that fog harvesting can be expanded to other parts of Morocco that urgently require clean drinking water.

A transported **B** access **C** proves **D** purposes
E known **F** trips **G** advantages **H** technology
I requires **J** drought

6. _____ 7. _____ 8. _____ 9. _____ 10. _____

11. _____ 12. _____ 13. _____ 14. _____ 15. _____

Unit 18

篇章結構

說明：本題型的題幹為段落式短文，以一篇含四個空格的選文搭配五個選項，每題一個空格，請依文意在文章後所提供的選項中分別選出最適當者，填入空格中，使篇章結構清晰有條理。

    As is the case in many parts of the world, India has a serious problem with gender inequality. The cultural preference in that country for sons over daughters has created a situation where there are only 933 women per 1,000 men. This population issue has led to various obstacles for females, including discrimination. In recent years, the Indian government and various organizations have been working to raise awareness about gender inequality and promote women's rights. __(16)__

    To combat negative attitudes among Indians towards females, village council members of Bibipur—a place where the ratio of females to males (877 girls for every 1,000 boys) is even worse than the average in India—came up with a novel idea: a selfie contest designed to show parents' pride in their daughters. __(17)__ This simple yet powerful campaign encouraged families to celebrate their daughters publicly, helping to challenge deep-rooted cultural norms.

    The response to the campaign and its overall impact exceeded the expectations of its organizers. Nearly 800 people sent in photos from all over Haryana and a few other parts of India. __(18)__ As well as receiving a trophy and a certificate, winners were each awarded 2,100 rupees (about US$25).

    __(19)__ His endorsement gave the campaign nationwide recognition and encouraged more people to participate. Another way awareness of the campaign spread throughout the country and to other nations was through social media. Many people shared their selfies online, sparking discussions about gender equality and prompting similar initiatives in other regions. Hopefully, Bibipur's contest will inspire even more efforts to help solve India's gender inequality problems.

A Due to the volume of submissions, the number of prize winners was raised from one to three, and 15 consolation prizes were also added.

B The contest even caught the attention of Indian Prime Minister Narendra Modi, who promoted it on his radio program.

C Efforts by the council of a village called Bibipur in the northern Indian state of Haryana are particularly noteworthy.

D To participate, people simply had to take photos of themselves with their daughters and submit the pictures through a messaging app.

E Gender inequality is not the only serious problem that rural India suffers from.

16. _____   17. _____   18. _____   19. _____

Unit 18

The naming of prescription drugs by pharmaceutical companies is a long and complicated process that begins several years before a drug hits the market. The first stage usually involves the hiring of a creative agency to suggest several possible names. This agency will use its knowledge of the pharmaceutical company and the purpose of the drug to propose names that are both appealing and as unique as possible. As drugs tend to be marketed worldwide, the agency will try to avoid names—as well as letters such as H, J, and W—that are difficult to pronounce in other languages. The second stage involves the pharmaceutical company's legal and commercial teams, which work together to select their favored option from the creative agency's shortlist. The final stage involves the approval of the name by a regulatory body, which in the US is the Food and Drug Administration (FDA). This body needs to ensure that the name does not imply that the new drug is superior to an existing drug nor make any guarantees about the new drug's effectiveness. It also must make sure that the name is not too similar to that of an existing drug in either the spoken or written format. This is to reduce the chances of medication errors when the new drug is prescribed, **administered**, or taken, which could potentially have lethal results.

Approved drug names can be broadly broken down into two categories. The first is names that include a reference to the class of drugs to which they belong. For instance, Amoxicillin, which is an antibiotic that is used to treat bacterial infections, includes the suffix "cillin" because it is a form of penicillin: a class of antibiotics that come from *Penicillium* molds. You will therefore find that other drugs in this family of antibiotics also end in "cillin." The second category is names that are designed to create an emotional feeling in the user. For instance, Lunesta, which is used to treat insomnia, includes the prefix "lune" because that is the French word for "moon." The name therefore implies nighttime and evokes a sense of sleep.

20. What do we learn about the process of naming pharmaceutical drugs?
    (A) It often relies on emotional responses from families that need the drugs.
    (B) It attempts to incorporate the name of the pharmaceutical company.
    (C) It commences several years prior to the drug being sold to the public.
    (D) It requires a specific creative agency to select the final drug name.

21. Based on the article, which of the following does the FDA NOT have to ensure about the name of a new drug?
    (A) That it is suitably different from other drugs.
    (B) That it does not make a promise to be effective.
    (C) That it is able to fit properly on the drug packaging.
    (D) That it does not claim to be better than other drugs.

22. Which is most likely the meaning of "**administered**" in the first paragraph?
    (A) Governed by a country or region.
    (B) Given as a remedy to someone.
    (C) Dealt out as a form of punishment.
    (D) Responsible for the use of a law.

23. A pharmaceutical company has created a new type of antibiotic. Based on the article, which of the following would be the most suitable name for it?
    (A) Cillinesta.
    (B) Howjocillin.
    (C) Antiluner.
    (D) Adrocillin.

20. _____ 21. _____ 22. _____ 23. _____

Unit 18

五 混合題

說明：請根據文章之文意選出或寫出一個最適當的答案。

The Hajj is an annual religious journey to the Islamic holy city of Mecca in Saudi Arabia. All adult Muslims are expected to undertake it once in their lifetime. Here are the stories of two people who completed the pilgrimage.

Abdullah lives in Dubai and is an extremely devout Muslim. He is also young and fit and regularly engages in extreme sports. So, while he could afford to travel to Mecca by plane, he chose to make the 2,000-kilometer pilgrimage to that holy destination on foot. Many of his peers warned him that it would be a supremely challenging journey, and they were right: Abdullah had to deal with high temperatures, harsh and varied terrain, and a lack of shelter. However, he had planned it carefully and trained his body for the physical exertion, and he was helped by many kind strangers on the way. He also viewed it as the perfect test of his religious devotion. When he finally arrived in Mecca after two months, it is no exaggeration to say that he was exhausted, but the warm welcome and sense of unity he experienced gave him the strength to perform the required rituals and fulfill his religious duty. One of the key elements is to walk seven times between two hills. After Abdullah's difficult journey, that was easy by comparison!

Fatima lives in Scotland with her mother and father. They are by no means a rich family: her father owns a small clothing store, which barely turns a profit. However, it had long been the dream of Fatima's parents to take part in the Hajj pilgrimage, and Fatima was determined to turn that dream into reality. She saved every spare penny she had for over two decades until she had enough for three airfares from Edinburgh to Jeddah. By this time, her parents were getting quite frail and didn't have much strength, so Fatima had to take care of them throughout the flight and the car journey to Mecca. Once there, though, it was like her mom and dad had a new lease on life. Inspired by the sense of togetherness at one of the largest gatherings of people in the world, Fatima and her parents joined the other pilgrims on the trip back and forth on foot between the hills of Safa and Marwah. They also threw stones at three pillars to represent **their** rejection of temptation. Fatima's parents were so grateful to their daughter for allowing them to fulfill their lifelong ambition.

24-25 請從各別的文章中找出最適當的單詞（word）填入下列句子空格中，並視語法需要做適當的字形變化。每格限填一個單詞（word）。（填充）

Lots of Abdullah's friends warned him that his pilgrimage from Dubai to Mecca would involve numerous ___24.___ .

Fatima's ___25.___ was vital in helping her mother and father achieve their ambition of participating in the Hajj.

26. What does "**their**" refer to in Fatima's passage?（簡答）

_____

27. Which of the following statements are correct about BOTH Abdullah and Fatima?
（多選）
(A) Their choice of transportation was influenced by money.
(B) They felt a sense of collective harmony among the pilgrims.
(C) Their journeys took more than twenty years to carefully plan.
(D) They walked multiple times between one hill and another.
(E) Their participation was affected by the extreme heat in Mecca.
(F) They had stones thrown at them as part of a religious ritual.

24. _____ 25. _____

26. _____

27. _____

Unit 19

一 綜合測驗

說明：本題型的題幹為段落式短文，選文中含數個空格，每題一個空格，請依文意選出最適當的一個選項。

It is well known that eating fruit in general is good for your health. One fruit in particular from the strange-looking baobab tree appears to be extremely __(1)__ to people and the environment. This superfruit __(2)__ high amounts of magnesium, calcium, iron, vitamin C, and potassium. __(3)__ those latter two elements, baobab fruit has six times the amount of vitamin C that an orange does and four times as much potassium as a banana. It is particularly good for people with low potassium levels or those who need extra vitamin C for immunity.

Moreover, it possesses twice the amount of calcium found in milk, more magnesium than spinach, and considerable levels of antioxidants, which in __(4)__ tend to protect cells and keep them healthy for longer periods of time. Additionally, the antioxidants in baobab fruit play a role in reducing inflammation, which is crucial for overall wellness. The baobab tree also assists people by helping to support farms for __(5)__ as the large trees usually live hundreds of years. On top of all the good baobab trees and their fruit do for humans, they are also an important food source and habitat for many species of animals.

1. (A) barren (B) complex (C) manageable (D) beneficial
2. (A) contains (B) provokes (C) reverses (D) shrieks
3. (A) For the sake of (B) With respect to (C) By means of (D) Prior to
4. (A) rare levels (B) equal portions
   (C) insufficient quantities (D) moderate amounts
5. (A) fractions (B) generations (C) banquets (D) adolescents

1. _____ 2. _____ 3. _____ 4. _____ 5. _____

二 文意選填

說明：本題型的題幹為段落式短文，以一篇含十個空格的選文搭配十個選項，每題一個空格，請依文意在文章後所提供的選項中分別選出最適當者。

　　Barefoot College is a non-governmental organization based in India. It was __(6)__ four decades ago by a small group of well-educated college graduates. They want to find alternative __(7)__ of addressing the poverty so common in the rural parts of their country. One of the institution's main programs involves solar power, and its goal is to allow underdeveloped rural communities to become more self-sufficient. Another goal is to empower the underprivileged, particularly uneducated women.

　　In order to better appreciate the impact of Barefoot College's program, it is first necessary to understand the problems __(8)__ those who live in India's poorest districts. Electricity is either __(9)__ or nonexistent in numerous communities, so for heating, cooking, and even lighting, firewood is commonly used. When it is not __(10)__, kerosene is often used instead. However, not only is that oil expensive for villagers, but it also has __(11)__ effects on the environment.

　　Barefoot College's solar program teaches solar engineering skills to illiterate women over the age of 35 for six months. Upon __(12)__ to their communities, these newly trained women are able to access solar lamp kits and panels linked to batteries. Also, under the program, for which Barefoot College pays all __(13)__, a local electronic workshop for repairs is established in the communities involved. Through an investment of US$50,000 in solar equipment, Barefoot College helps to provide sufficient power for 120 households, thereby __(14)__ their reliance on firewood and kerosene. By training women in this way to help provide energy to their communities, Barefoot College has __(15)__ a worthy objective, one that is changing lives in places where positive change is vitally required.

(A) scarce　　(B) accomplished　　(C) methods　　(D) reducing
(E) available　(F) returning　　　 (G) harmful　　(H) expenses
(I) established (J) facing

6. _____　7. _____　8. _____　9. _____　10. _____

11. _____　12. _____　13. _____　14. _____　15. _____

Unit 19

三、篇章結構 說明：本題型的題幹為段落式短文，以一篇含四個空格的選文搭配五個選項，每題一個空格，請依文意在文章後所提供的選項中分別選出最適當者，填入空格中，使篇章結構清晰有條理。

  As the saying goes, "A dog is man's best friend." Having a Fido or a Rover as a companion can be enjoyable, but it is important that owners make sure to give their pets sufficient opportunities for outdoor exercise. __(16)__ These include bans in parks and at other popular recreational areas in city centers. In addition, animals are prohibited on public transportation in many cities.

  For people who don't own their own cars or can't afford to take taxis, this presents a problem when they try to get out of town with their dogs. As a result, many dog owners struggle to find suitable places where their pets can run freely and socialize with other dogs. __(17)__ They created a pet-friendly bus service known as 99 Bus.

  __(18)__ The bus service provides plenty of routes around Hong Kong and its outskirts on weekends and public holidays, with stops at several recreational areas. This has made it much easier for pet owners to bring their dogs to beaches, hiking trails, and open parks without worrying about transportation barriers. Over the years, 99 Bus has added new stops regularly and has developed into a semi-permanent line that is much appreciated by the dog lovers of Hong Kong.

  __(19)__ To give an example of this enthusiasm, the 99 Bus Facebook group already has a great number of likes and contains numerous photos of happy dogs in parks and at beaches. Some owners even organize group outings through the service, making it a great way for both pets and humans to socialize. The success of 99 Bus has also inspired discussions about making public transportation in Hong Kong more pet-friendly. Clearly, it's a service that is highly valued among the dog owners of Hong Kong.

A Fortunately, for pet owners in Hong Kong, two people who were fed up with the situation finally decided to do something about it.

B Thrilled at being able to travel more easily with their dogs, dog owners have been very enthusiastic about the 99 Bus campaign.

C Since 2012, dog owners in Hong Kong have been able to take advantage of 99 Bus.

D Doing so, though, can be challenging due to all of the restrictions related to dogs in urban areas.

E Without proper exercise, dogs can develop many of the same health problems that plague their owners.

16. _____   17. _____   18. _____   19. _____

Unit 19

四 閱讀測驗　説明：每題請根據本篇文章之文意選出最適當的一個選項。

　　At the turn of the 5th century BC, Greece was a collection of city-states that were often at war with each other. However, in 480 BC, many of these city-states banded together to fight against a common foe: the Persian army under the command of King Xerxes, who was determined to incorporate Greece into the Persian Empire. Having advanced through several regions of Greece and occupied them without a fight, Xerxes and his 300,000-strong army headed for a narrow mountain pass called Thermopylae. Awaiting them was Leonidas, king of the city-state of Sparta, along with his army of 7,000 soldiers and a highly trained squad of 300 loyal warriors.

　　Xerxes anticipated that the Spartans would realize they were hugely outnumbered and surrender immediately. Leonidas, though, believed that the terrain of the mountain pass gave the Spartans an advantage, as the enemy's movements would be restricted and they would be unable to deploy sufficient numbers of their troops. Leonidas was largely proved right: when the Persians attacked, it became clear that they were not suited to fighting in that environment, while the Spartans had superior training and weapons. As more and more of his troops were killed and his army was forced to retreat, Xerxes became furious.

　　Luckily for him, a local shepherd decided to betray the Spartans and told Xerxes about an alternative route that avoided the mountain pass. This route allowed Xerxes to position 10,000 of his men on the other side of the pass and therefore surround the Spartans. Although shocked at what had happened, Leonidas refused to surrender; instead, he vowed that he and his 300 warriors would stay and fight to the death. The Spartans fought bravely and courageously, first with spears and swords and then with their hands, but were ultimately defeated. Leonidas was killed in battle, and most if not all of his 300 men perished, too. However, their sacrifice was not in vain. The story of their bravery and resistance inspired other Greek city-states to continue fighting against the Persians, and the Greeks won decisive victories over their enemy in later battles.

20. According to the article, what had happened prior to the battle at Thermopylae?
    (A) The Persian Empire had been severely weakened.
    (B) The Persian army had conquered many areas of Greece.
    (C) The Greek ruler had been replaced with a different king.
    (D) The Greeks had signed a peace agreement with the Persians.

21. Why did Xerxes think the Spartans would yield to the attackers right away?
    (A) The Spartans were not familiar with the mountain pass.
    (B) There were far more Persian soldiers than Spartans.
    (C) The Persians had captured the Spartan army's leader.
    (D) There were discipline problems among the Spartans.

22. How did the Persians gain the advantage over the Spartans?
    (A) By acquiring much better weapons.
    (B) By bringing in thousands more troops.
    (C) By fooling Leonidas into surrendering.
    (D) By following the advice of a disloyal man.

23. Which set of words best describes the progression of feelings of Leonidas and his 300 warriors during the battle of Thermopylae?
    (A) stunned → lucky → hopeless
    (B) secure → fearful → optimistic
    (C) confident → surprised → fearless
    (D) deceived → hopeful → successful

20. _____   21. _____   22. _____   23. _____

Unit 19

Unit 19

五 混合題 說明：請根據文章之文意選出或寫出一個最適當的答案。

What are the pros and cons of giving students homework? We asked four people for their opinions.

Jake
As a diligent student, I always complete my homework and hand it in on time. However, you won't be too shocked to learn that I dislike doing it and find some of it pointless. It's supposed to help us understand the topics from class better, but I think this rarely happens in practice. At times, it feels like the teacher is giving us the homework for the sake of it. Also, we have to use our precious free time to get it done. This has a negative impact on our ability to participate in extracurricular activities and rewarding hobbies.

Ben
Every piece of homework I give to my students plays a vital role in reinforcing the ideas and topics that I have just taught during class. It is specifically designed to help them improve their understanding. Of course, it needs to be pitched at the right level. This means that as the age of the students increases, so does the amount and difficulty of the homework I give them. Homework also helps students who are about to leave school to learn time-management skills. Being able to meet deadlines is an essential skill in today's work environment.

Tina
No one enjoys doing homework: we get far too much of it, and completing it on time makes us students feel stressed. But, speaking objectively, I know that it is a necessary part of school life. It helps us to solidify our knowledge from previous lessons and prepare for upcoming lessons. Without homework, we wouldn't be able to make good contributions in classroom discussions. Homework also gives us more flexibility to work at our own pace: if we find a topic particularly challenging, for instance, we can spend more time on it.

Michelle
Naturally, I give homework to all of my students. However, I sometimes struggle to see the benefits of it and feel we give too much of it. Homework increases the pressure on the students, who are already feeling anxious about exams and other commitments. I'm aware that not all students have a suitable home environment to work in, and I worry about their well-being. Homework also massively increases my workload, as I have to prepare the assignments, grade them, and chase up the students who haven't completed them.

24-25 請從文章中找出最適當的單詞（word）填入下列句子空格中，並視語法需要做適當的字形變化。每格限填一個單詞（word）。（填充）

Jake states that the amount of homework he gets affects his ____24.____ in leisure pursuits outside of school.

Ben references age when arguing in favor of homework, stating that older students can cope with more ____25.____ tasks.

26-27 Based on the opinions, fill in the blanks with the correct names.（填充）

Tina points out that too much homework can make students feel worried, and ____26.____ also mentions this argument.

While Ben and Tina recognize that homework helps to strengthen the ideas that are taught during lessons, ____27.____ has serious doubts about this argument.

28. Which phrase in the opinions means "to contact or find someone in order to get something"?（簡答）

_____

24. _____   25. _____

26. _____   27. _____

28. _____

Unit 20

一 綜合測驗

說明：本題型的題幹為段落式短文，選文中含數個空格，每題一個空格，請依文意選出最適當的一個選項。

    Macau is known for gambling, but it is also home to some fantastic entertainment, including a must-see attraction: the House of Dancing Water at the City of Dreams. __(1)__ amazing props, great diving stunts, breathtaking gymnastics, and dancing water, the 85-minute show takes place in a circular theater that holds 2,000 seats. It also includes a __(2)__ pool containing nearly four million gallons of water, which is enough to fill five Olympic-sized swimming pools.

    The show begins with a peaceful scene of a fisherman in a small boat, but it quickly __(3)__ as the masts of a pirate ship rise from the depths of the pool, and the fisherman vanishes in a whirlpool. After that, performers swing from the rigging on the masts and then dive ten meters into the pool below. The __(4)__ doesn't end there, as the pirate ship disappears under the water. Instead, it is replaced by a solid stage on which performers continue to thrill the audience. Best of all, more than 240 water jets placed in various sections of the stage are __(5)__ with music to shoot water over 18 meters high into the air in a form of "dancing water." It's definitely a sight to see!

1. (A) Featured   (B) To feature   (C) Featuring   (D) Being featured
2. (A) massive   (B) slight   (C) prosperous   (D) parallel
3. (A) hints at failures   (B) turns into chaos
   (C) stirs up memories   (D) contributes to progress
4. (A) procedure   (B) maintenance   (C) superstition   (D) entertainment
5. (A) suppressed   (B) coordinated   (C) nominated   (D) strengthened

1. _____   2. _____   3. _____   4. _____   5. _____

二 文意選填

說明：本題型的題幹為段落式短文，以一篇含十個空格的選文搭配十個選項，每題一個空格，請依文意在文章後所提供的選項中分別選出最適當者。

　　Baseball in Taiwan is incredibly popular, so much so that it is considered to be the island's signature sport. One of the reasons the sport enjoys such great popularity is the success of a __(6)__ team more than 85 years ago, one from Chiayi that was nicknamed Kano. Formed in 1928, a time when Taiwan was under Imperial Japan's rule, Kano included players who were Japanese, Han Chinese, and __(7)__. It was the only team on the island that had any non-Japanese __(8)__.

　　Kano was a good team, so good in fact that they __(9)__ the right to represent Taiwan at Japan's National High School Baseball Championship. Known simply as Koshien, it is a competition that is highly __(10)__ in Japan and is the longest-running tournament in that nation. Despite being the underdogs in a major contest that involved 630 other teams from throughout the Japanese empire, the players proved themselves by performing beyond __(11)__. In their first three games, Kano easily __(12)__ their opponents, securing themselves a spot in the Koshien finals. This was viewed as a nearly __(13)__ achievement. A fairy tale ending of Kano winning the championship, however, did not happen; in the end, a more powerful Japanese team soundly beat Kano by a score of 4-0, leaving the Taiwan-based team in second place. Kano's superb performance in the competition earned the team the respect of their Japanese __(14)__. Moreover, it sparked a huge interest in baseball among the Taiwanese, which turned into a passion that __(15)__ the sport to a status that continues to this day.

Ⓐ counterparts　Ⓑ legendary　Ⓒ esteemed　Ⓓ earned
Ⓔ expectations　Ⓕ miraculous　Ⓖ defeated　Ⓗ athletes
Ⓘ propelled　Ⓙ aboriginal

6. _____　7. _____　8. _____　9. _____　10. _____
11. _____　12. _____　13. _____　14. _____　15. _____

The Rubik's Cube is the most successful puzzle toy of all time. It has challenged the minds of millions and become a symbol of intelligence and problem-solving skills. It is so difficult, though, that many people simply give up after several tries, throwing their hands up in complete frustration and vowing never to attempt it again.   (16)   After Rubik licensed it in the late 1970s to the US Ideal Toy Company, the plaything with multiple squares colored white, red, blue, green, yellow, and orange was renamed after its inventor.

When Rubik let his students try out his invention shortly after its creation, they enjoyed playing with it so much.   (17)   As it turned out, Rubik was quite right. Under Ideal's marketing push, the Rubik's Cube was an almost instant success, turning into an iconic toy of the 1980s. Its attraction was so great that it quickly established itself as a part of pop culture. The cube appeared in movies, TV shows, and music videos. Some celebrities even showcased their cube-solving skills in public, further boosting its appeal. Like many toys that have enjoyed immense popularity, though, interest in the Rubik's Cube eventually declined.

  (18)   The World Cube Association (WCA) was created in 2004 with the goal of promoting fair competitions around the world.   (19)   These competitions have helped create a new generation of "speedcubers" who dedicate hours to mastering solving techniques. The attraction of the Rubik's Cube still continues, and its longevity has resulted in sales of hundreds of millions of cubes, making it one of the world's best-selling toys.

A This led the professor to the conclusion that his innovative cube might have broad appeal.

B These students had a lot more faith in the cube than Rubik himself.

C It holds numerous events, such as those involving various-sized cubes, one-handed and foot-only contests, as well as ones where contestants are blindfolded.

D Developed by a Hungarian architect and professor named Ernö Rubik in 1974, it was first called the Magic Cube.

E However, with the arrival of the internet, the toy made a comeback.

16. _____   17. _____   18. _____   19. _____

Unit 20

四 閱讀測驗

說明：每題請根據本篇文章之文意選出最適當的一個選項。

Electric eels are fish that use cells in their bodies called electrocytes to produce electricity. When activated by the eel's nervous system, they can generate electric shocks to defend themselves from predators, stun prey, and navigate through the dark, dirty waters of South America in which they reside. The ability of electric eels to produce power has served as inspiration for scientists seeking to create alternative electricity sources that could be used inside the human body.

A team of researchers from Yale University and the National Institute of Standards and Technology created a computer model to determine whether artificial cells could outperform an electric eel's natural cells in terms of energy production. The team discovered that, in contrast to the thousands of electrocytes that produce energy in an eel, only a few dozen artificial cells would be required to produce sufficient energy to safely power small medical implants in the human body. Although the team's artificial cells have yet to be produced, they have created an important blueprint, and the possibilities are intriguing.

Another team of researchers from the University of Fribourg and the University of Michigan used a specialized printer to produce transparent sheets made up of cells containing either salt or pure water. This mimics the eel's electrocytes, which contain either sodium or potassium. When the sheets are folded in a certain way, the substances combine together to produce electricity. This, too, mimics what happens in the eel's electrocytes, which have positive and negative poles, rather like tiny batteries. When the eel wants to produce an electric shock, its nervous system sends a message to the electrocytes to act together to produce an electric charge. The team hopes that the steady, low current produced by their sheets could power pacemakers as well as implantable medication dispensers and health monitors. They are currently in the process of improving the efficiency of their creation. Although there is a long way to go before it can actually be used in a human being, the team has high hopes for its success.

20. What do we NOT learn about electric eels?
    (A) What the functions of the shocks are.
    (B) What their special cells include.
    (C) How they deliver electric shocks.
    (D) What their typical diet is comprised of.

21. What did the Yale University team discover?
    (A) That it will be impossible to create a working version of their idea.
    (B) That their device might release harmful toxins into human bodies.
    (C) That the cells they modeled are more efficient than an eel's cells.
    (D) That electric eels generate electricity using remarkably few cells.

22. Which of the following statements about the two research teams is true?
    (A) They both hope to improve living conditions for electric eels.
    (B) They are made up of researchers from the same two institutions.
    (C) They both want to utilize their discoveries for medical purposes.
    (D) They are awaiting approval before they can continue their work.

23. What can be inferred from the article?
    (A) The abilities of electric eels cannot be recreated in laboratories.
    (B) The devices the teams worked on have not yet been put into practice.
    (C) The use of electric eels in experiments raises ethical concerns.
    (D) The experiments have altered what we know about electric eels.

20. _____   21. _____   22. _____   23. _____

Unit 20

Unit 20

五 混合題 說明：請根據文章之文意選出或寫出一個最適當的答案。

Aside from the conventional ways of assessing the economy, such as Gross Domestic Product and the Consumer Price Index, there are some unconventional ways. Here are two of them.

The Big Mac Index was created by *The Economist* magazine in 1986. It uses the cost of the famous McDonald's hamburger as an indicator of the strength or weakness of a country's currency. It is based on the economic theory of purchasing-power parity, which states that, over time, exchange rates should move toward a rate that equalizes the cost of a basket of goods. Using a Big Mac to represent this "basket of goods" is a lighthearted way to make the theory more understandable and accessible by the man on the street. The magazine compiles the prices of Big Macs from around the world, converts them into the common currency of the US dollar, and then compares these converted prices. In 2023, for instance, a Big Mac cost US$5.36 in the US, the equivalent of US$6.59 in Norway, and the equivalent of US$4.19 in Mexico. This suggested that the Norwegian krone was overvalued against the US dollar while the Mexican peso was undervalued. Thus, the former currency may have been inclined to depreciate, or lose value, while the latter currency may have been inclined to appreciate, or increase in value.

The Freddo Index is another means of making economics more understandable for the average person, but this index focuses on one specific country: the United Kingdom. It uses the Cadbury's Freddo chocolate bar to assess the level of inflation and measure the cost of living in the UK. As such, its methodology is less complicated than the Big Mac Index. In 2006, a Freddo cost 10 pence. If we adjust for inflation, this means that a Freddo should have cost around 16 pence in 2023. However, it had already exceeded that amount by 2010, when it was priced at 17 pence, and in 2023, a bar actually set people back 26 pence. This is despite the fact that the weight of the chocolate treat barely altered over the course of 17 years. On current trends, it will cost around 35 pence by 2030. This all shows that the price of a Freddo has increased substantially faster than the rate of inflation, and it paints a slightly worrying picture of the cost-of-living crisis in the United Kingdom.

24-25 請從文章中找出最適當的單詞（word）填入下列句子空格中，並視語法需要做適當的字形變化。每格限填一個單詞（word）。（填充）

The Economist magazine gathers together data on the prices of Big Macs from around the world and makes a ____24.____ of them into American dollars.

When the Freddo Index started in 2006, a Freddo bar cost ten pence. If we make an ____25.____ based on inflation, one bar should have cost sixteen pence seventeen years later.

26. Which phrase in the article means "to cost people a specific amount of money"?（簡答）

    _____

27. Based on the article, which of the following statements about the Big Mac Index and/or the Freddo Index are true?（多選）
    (A) They are both based around common, everyday products.
    (B) The Freddo Index is more complex than the Big Mac Index.
    (C) They are focused on the cost of living in the same country.
    (D) The Big Mac Index was created after the Freddo Index.
    (E) They are both designed to be used by ordinary people.
    (F) The Freddo Index helps people to spend less on treats.

    24. _____   25. _____

    26. _____

    27. _____

Unit **20**

常春藤 108 課綱核心素養．升大學系列【A104N-1】
學測英文五大關鍵題型：綜合測驗、文意選填、
篇章結構、閱讀測驗、混合題－試題本【增修版】

總 編 審	賴世雄
終　　審	梁民康
執行編輯	許嘉華
編輯小組	畢安安．施盈如．Nick Roden．Brian Foden
設計組長	王玥琦
封面設計	王穎緁
排版設計	王穎緁．林桂旭
法律顧問	北辰著作權事務所蕭雄淋律師
出 版 者	常春藤數位出版股份有限公司
地　　址	臺北市忠孝西路一段 33 號 5 樓
電　　話	(02) 2331-7600
傳　　真	(02) 2381-0918
網　　址	www.ivy.com.tw
電子信箱	service@ivy.com.tw
郵政劃撥	50463568
戶　　名	常春藤數位出版股份有限公司
定　　價	380 元（2 書）
出版日期	2025 年 6 月　再版

©常春藤數位出版股份有限公司 (2025) All rights reserved.　　Y000061-3588
本書之封面、內文、編排等之著作財產權歸常春藤數位出版股份有限公司所有。未經本公司
書面同意，請勿翻印、轉載或為一切著作權法上利用行為，否則依法追究。

如有缺頁、裝訂錯誤或破損，請寄回本公司更換。　　【版權所有　翻印必究】